SINATRA

ALSO BY J. RANDY TARABORRELLI

After Camelot: A Personal History of the Kennedy Family—1968 to the Present

Jackie, Ethel, Joan: Women of Camelot

Once Upon a Time: Behind the Fairy Tale of Princess Grace and Prince Rainier

Elizabeth

The Secret Life of Marilyn Monroe

Michael Jackson: The Magic, the Madness, the Whole Story, 1958–2009

The Hiltons: The True Story of an American Dynasty

Becoming Beyoncé: The Untold Story

SINATRA

Behind the Legend

J. RANDY TARABORRELLI

GRAND CENTRAL
PUBLISHING

NEW YORK   BOSTON

Copyright © 1997, 2015 by Rose Books, Inc.

Grand Central Publishing
Hachette Book Group
1290 Avenue of the Americas
New York, NY 10104

www.HachetteBookGroup.com

Printed in the United States of America

RRD-C

First Edition: August 2015
10 9 8 7 6 5 4 3 2 1

Grand Central Publishing is a division of Hachette Book Group, Inc.
The Grand Central Publishing name and logo is a trademark of Hachette Book Group, Inc.

The Hachette Speakers Bureau provides a wide range of authors for speaking events. To find out more, go to www.hachettespeakersbureau.com or call (866) 376-6591.

The publisher is not responsible for websites (or their content) that are not owned by the publisher.

LCCN: 2015942863
ISBN: 978-1-4555-3057-1

For Rose Marie Taraborrelli

CONTENTS

Author's Note to the 2015 Edition   xv
Preface   xix

Part One
BEGINNINGS

L'America   2
Marty and Dolly   5
Frank Is Born   7
Young Frank   9
Hoboken Days   17
Early Aspirations   20
Nancy   25
Early Singing Days   27
Midwife   32
"Let Frankie In"   35
Toni   38
Frank and Nancy Marry   40

Part Two
FIRST BLUSH OF SUCCESS

Harry James   44
Tommy Dorsey   48
Self-Invention   52
Marital Weakness   54

Dorothy   58
Dispute with Dorsey   59
"Sinatra-Mania"   63
Making Do   69
1943   71
Breaking the Dorsey Contract   73
Anchors Aweigh to Los Angeles   76

Part Three
BIG TIME

The Voice: 1945–46   84
The House He Lives In   86
Marilyn Maxwell   88
Lana Turner   91
Family Intervention   97
The Diamond Bracelet   99
Frank and the Mob   102
Nancy Makes a Decision   105
In Cuba with the Boys   106
Regret   109
The FBI and the Reporter   109

Part Four
THE AVA YEARS

Ava Gardner   116
1948–49   119
The Affair Begins   122
Lana's Warning to Ava   126
"Absolutely Not"   128
A Take-Charge Kind of Woman   129
Empty   132
Ava: "Nancy Will Thank Me One Day"   135
Frank at the Copa   139
Gunplay   142

Brink of Despair   145
Need   148
Nancy Files for Separation   149
1951   153
The Suicide Attempts   156
Ava Comes to Dinner   161
Frank and Ava Marry   163

Part Five
DOWNWARD SPIRAL

His Only Collateral Was a Dream   170
Mogambo   173
Ava's Pregnancies   175
Filming From Here to Eternity   180
Frank Signs with Capitol   183

Part Six
BACK ON TOP

Success   188
The Final Straw   190
Vegas Investment   192
Conflicted Christmas   193
Marilyn Monroe—Take One   196
After Frank?   198
1954: Academy Award   200
Sammy Davis's Accident   202
Golden   204
Pack Master   208
Lauren "Betty" Bacall   210
Which Is the Real Dad?   212
1957–58   215
Betty's Heartbreak   216

Part Seven
THE RAT PACK YEARS

The Rat Pack   224

JFK   227

Stark Duality   228

The Execution of Private Slovik   233

On the Way to the White House   235

The Kennedys Worry About Frank and Sammy   236

Part Eight
AND MARILYN MONROE

Reprise   242

Sinatra's Preinaugural Gala   244

Sinatra Makes a Deal with the Devil   246

The Return of Marilyn Monroe   248

Sinatra Betrays Giancana   250

The Problem with Marilyn   254

Publicity Stunt Engagement   256

JFK Snubs Sinatra   259

Elvis   263

Frank's Plan to Marry Marilyn   265

Memories of Marilyn   267

Swinging '63   270

Frank and Ava Redux   273

Sinatra Surrenders His Gaming License   276

Part Nine
THE KIDNAPPING OF FRANK SINATRA JR.

Planning a Kidnapping   284

Frank on Frank Jr.: "I Got a Good Kid Here"   285

Delusional Thinking   288

Kidnapping Frankie   291

"Kidnapping My Kid?"   296

Close Call 298

"Shoot Me and See What Happens" 299

The Ransom Demand 301

Frank: "You Know You're a Dead Man, Right?" 304

Frankie Is Released 305

Capturing the Kidnappers 307

The Trial 308

Kidnapping Postscript 312

Growing Up Sinatra 313

Prelude to the Best 315

Part Ten
THE MIA YEARS

Mia 320

First Blush of Romance 322

Mia and Frank in Palm Springs 323

Getting to Know You 325

Red Flag 327

Fish Out of Water 329

The Other Side of Frank 330

Confronting Sinatra 333

Nancy's Marriage Ends 333

Dolly on Mia: "This Is Trouble. Mark My Words." 335

The Walter Cronkite Interview 337

What to Do About Mia? 340

"No More Little Girl" 342

Boots and Strangers 344

Mia Meets the Family 346

Frank and Mia Marry 348

Mia Meets Ava 351

Unkind 353

"Somethin' Stupid" 355

Personality Disorder 356

Rosemary's Baby 359

Divorce—Sinatra Style 363

Frank Fires George Jacobs   364
Cycle of Pain   366
Coda   368

Part Eleven
TRANSITION

Changing Times   372
My Way   374
Marty Sinatra—Rest in Peace   376
A $22.5 Million Deal . . . at Dolly's House   378
More Mob Questions   380
Surprising Political Support   382
Another Vegas Showdown   384
Retirement?   385
Nixon-Agnew   388

Part Twelve
THE BARBARA YEARS

Barbara Marx   392
Barbara: Trying to Fit In   396
Cheshire Contretemps   398
Spiro, Barbara, and the Aussies   401
Finding Her Way   404
End of an Era   407
Jackie? Or Barbara?   407
Or Maybe Ava?   409
Frank and Barbara Get Engaged   411
Surprise Prenup?   414
Frank and Barbara Marry   417
Dolly Sinatra—Rest in Peace   420
"Who Died and Left Barbara Boss?"   423
Adopting a New Sinatra?   427
Frank's Secret Annulment   432
Sammy's Fall from Grace   439

Trilogy   441
Barbara Meets "the Boys"   443
"Who Took That Shot?"   445
Sinatra Sets the Record Straight—His Way   446
Frank and Nancy Tour Together   452
As If She Had a Choice   455

Part Thirteen
THAT'S LIFE

The Kitty Kelley Matter   462
Frank and Barbara Separate   465
Sick over the Kitty Kelley Book   469
Prudent?   471
The Sinatra Sisters Reach Out to Barbara   474
Rat Pack Redux?   477
The Trouble with Dean   481
The Sinatra Daughters' Revolt   485
Ava: "I Always Thought We Would Have More Time"   488
Sammy—Rest in Peace   489
Dinner with the Sinatras   491
Father-and-Son Detente   497
A Sad Ending for Jilly   500
Prodigal Daughters   502
Tina's Miniseries   503
Frank's Secret Daughter?   506
Duets   507
One More for the Road   509
Sinatra: Eighty Years—Her Way?   512

Part Fourteen
AND NOW THE END IS NEAR . . .

Eightieth Birthday Family Showdown   516
"Goodbye, Dag"   520
A Fourth Wedding Ceremony   522

Surrounded by Love 523

Fine 528

Afterword: A Final Consideration 531

Source Notes and Acknowledgments 539

Index 567

AUTHOR'S NOTE TO THE 2015 EDITION

I wrote the first draft of this book almost twenty years ago. It was November 1996 when I finished the manuscript. A year later, in November 1997, the first edition of *Sinatra: Behind the Legend* was published.

I had met Mr. Sinatra four times backstage at concerts in Los Angeles and Las Vegas in the 1980s. While those sorts of meet-and-greet moments after a performance are never fully satisfying, the four opportunities I had to shake the man's hand and tell him how much he meant to me and my Italian-American family were nevertheless thrilling. "Thank you for saying that," he told me after his show that opened the new Universal Amphitheatre in Los Angeles on July 30, 1982. The concert also starred his daughter Nancy. "I really appreciate it. Always a pleasure to meet another dago," he added with a chuckle. "Dad!" Nancy exclaimed. "How do you know this guy's not gonna write that you called him a dago?" She was kidding; Frank laughed at the joke. "'Cause the little dago knows better than to go dere," he said, winking at me. (I did know better, which is why I waited thirty-two years to share this anecdote!)

Immersing myself in his life and times for this book made me feel an even closer connection to Frank, but of course I wanted a full interview with the man himself. I tried in 1996 and again in 1997 while I was writing the book, but he was so ill during that time, it proved impossible. "It's just not going to happen," his first wife,

Nancy, told me. "I think maybe you're a few years too late." I understood, of course.

There's no telling where a biographer's quest for information will take him, and what sorts of characters will cross his path in the course of that adventure. Working on this book led me to interview a number of bizarre and colorful figures, including the man who kidnapped Frank Sinatra Jr.

I was about seven when I heard that Frank Sinatra's son had been kidnapped. Maybe because I'd also heard a little about Sinatra's alleged mob ties from my Italian-American grandparents, I recall thinking to myself, "What kind of *dope* would kidnap Frank Sinatra's kid?" As a youngster, I couldn't quite grasp the seriousness of the situation. But as a grown man, I was determined to better understand it. When I found Barry Keenan, he had never before told his story, other than in the form of testimony at his trial. It was a powerful experience for me to hear a blow-by-blow account of one of the most high-profile crimes of the 1960s from the kidnapper himself—all of which you will find in these pages.

In May 1998, about six months after *Sinatra: Behind the Legend* was published, I was still promoting it on television programs when Frank passed away. The book was reissued at that time, again in hardcover, as *Sinatra: A Complete Life*. After the publication of that reissue, many people contacted me to tell me that I'd "missed" them in my research. While the goal of any biographer is to interview as many sources as possible, it's impractical to locate *every* person who ever had contact with a subject. (As it was, my researchers and I found more than four hundred.)

Happy that so many new sources had reached out to me, in January 1999, I began working on a revised edition, interviewing individuals such as Frank's longtime valet, George Jacobs (with whom I conducted three interviews). Additionally, I went back to the tapes of interviews from years ago and extracted new material from them. However, before that edition (which would have been issued in paperback) had a chance to see the light of day, my publisher went out of business. Therefore, other than the hardcover edition from 1998, this book has not been available since that time. Now, eighteen years later, I am proud to finally bring forth a fully revised and updated edition of *Sinatra: Behind the Legend*, published to coincide with what would have been Frank Sinatra's centenary birthday.

J. Randy Taraborrelli
Summer 2015

PREFACE

I think I would like to be remembered as a man who brought an innovation to popular singing, a peculiar, unique fashion that I wish one of these days somebody would learn to do so it doesn't die where it is. I would like to be remembered as a man who had a wonderful time living his life and who had good friends, a fine family, and I don't think I could ask for anything more than that, actually. I think that would do it.

—Frank Sinatra to Walter Cronkite, November 16, 1965

Frank Sinatra was like a flawed diamond—brilliant on the surface, imperfect beneath. Of course, it was those flaws, those hidden complexities, that made him human, and in many ways defined his persona. If one really wants to understand Frank, though, one must travel from lower Manhattan across the Hudson River to Hoboken, New Jersey, where Sinatra is a hometown hero.

Everyone in Hoboken seems to know someone who knew someone *else* who once knew Frank or his family. Every Italian bartender, delicatessen owner, dry cleaner, pizzeria worker, and thrift store proprietor over the age of fifty seems to have a good Sinatra story, a juicy Sinatra rumor, or an inconsequential Sinatra anecdote about that time he or she ran into the man himself and rubbed shoulders with greatness. In Hoboken, the Sinatra tales flow freely.

Frank Sinatra was the most famous person who ever came from Hoboken. They still love him there and they're still proud of him. One can see it in their eyes when they speak of him, when they pull from their wallets a dog-eared photograph they took "at Frankie's brilliant concert at the Latin Casino in Cherry Hill, New Jersey," or when they play that special Sinatra tune on the bar's jukebox, the one they danced to at their wedding and that their own children and grandchildren will dance to at theirs...the one that still brings tears to their eyes.

When in Hoboken—a city whose Park Avenue library has a glass-encased second-floor shrine to Sinatra filled with an impressive trove of memorabilia—a Sinatra biographer has to sift through the legends to find the real facts of his life. There are endless stories that have been repeated so often—handed down from one generation to another—that today no one can even remember whence they originated, let alone whether or not they're accurate.

All of it—the truth, the legends—says something about the endurance of Frank Sinatra and the impact he had on not only the people of Hoboken but on our culture as a whole. One thing is certain: There is nobody as popular, as respected, and as adored as the man the people of Hoboken will forever lovingly refer to as "Frankie."

Part One

BEGINNINGS

L'America

In the late 1800s, Hoboken, New Jersey, a former resort area for the New York wealthy, was a run-down and destitute city. However, it was also a place of expectation and promise for many ambitious newcomers. With hope in their hearts, if not money in their pockets, they had come to the New World on crowded, rat-infested passenger liners and disease-ridden cargo ships. The Dutch, Swedes, Finns, English, Irish, and Scottish were all represented before 1700. The Germans and French Huguenots had arrived by 1750.

The Irish came in 1845 because of the great potato famine in Ireland; many of them went into the booming factories rather than return to the uncertainty of farming. The Germans arrived in 1848 after a revolution failed to produce a democracy. They were the most educated of the tide of immigrants and quickly became the aristocracy of the cities in which they settled.

By then, although there was still plenty of farmland left, New Jersey—sometimes called "the Foreign State" because it was home to so many immigrants—was rapidly becoming industrialized, a process that had started in 1830 when canals and railroads started to crisscross the state. Factories produced glass, iron, leather, oil, and munitions (Colt made his revolver in New Jersey until he went bankrupt and moved to Connecticut), clothes, hats, coaches, cabinetware, and chairs, among other day-to-day items. From New York City, just across the river, came a steady supply of immigrants to work in those factories.

Although manufacturing brought prosperity to the state, it also resulted in a lack of zoning. In 1861, one enterprising developer, Charles K. Landis, envisioned Vineland, a planned business and industrial area to be run by New Englanders. But he needed labor to clear the woods and later raise crops for the residents. Landis considered the Italians to be hardworking and industrious, so he sent printed notices to Italian cities extolling Vineland's wide streets, shady trees, and Mediterranean climate, none of which actually existed. So the Italians—the first group in New Jersey to actually be solicited for immigration—came with great eagerness to this new land of transformation, a country they called *l'America*. Among them were John and Rosa Sinatra, born and raised in Agrigento, Sicily. After the birth of their son, Anthony Martin (Frank's father, Marty), they migrated to the United States and settled in working-class Hoboken.

In this town, a person could reshape his life, embrace good fortune, and in the process make previously unimaginable sums of money.

At least that was the dream.

The reality was that with only so many available opportunities, life in America would be a constant struggle for many of its adoptive children; every day would pose a challenge to spirit and dignity as they attempted to find ways to earn a living. The work was hard; newcomers toiled in poorly equipped factories or in menial jobs as street cleaners and garbage collectors. Some of the lucky ones became barbers, a tradition of self-employment that would be passed down from generation to generation of Italian Americans. After arriving from Sicily, John Sinatra, who couldn't read or write English, supported his family by making pencils for the American Pencil Company. He earned eleven dollars a week.

Some immigrants would soon come to the conclusion that they might have been better off in their homeland. Defeated, many of them would return to their native lands; others would stay in the United States and lead sparse, desperate lives, cursing the day they had ever left the old country.

However, some would make it. Some, like the Sinatras, would see the realization of their dreams. They would be the lucky ones, as would their children.

In 1910, New Jersey had a higher percentage of immigrants than any other state. The census that year showed that less than two-fifths of the population had native-born parents, and Hoboken was no exception. In one five-block section of West Hoboken lived Armenians, English, French, Germans, Greeks, Italians, Spanish, Turks, Syrians, Romanians, Poles, Russians, Chinese, Japanese, Austrians, Swiss, Jews, Belgians, and Dutch.

As each new group arrived, they were looked down upon by those who had already established themselves; often even their own assimilated countrymen treated them with scorn. In Hoboken, since the Germans were the social elite, they could boast of several German-language newspapers, *Biergärten*, and brass bands. Their reign in Hoboken would last until the beginning of World War I, in 1914, when their pro-German sympathies led several to be arrested as spies and many more to be kept under constant surveillance until the end of the war. During that time, the Irish would ascend to the ruling class.

Although most of the Irish were poor and had a reputation for being rowdy, they banded together and elected their own, controlling politics and police and governmental jobs and contracts.

The Italians were considered third on the rung of the social ladder. While the Germans and Irish lived in well-appointed homes, the Italians resided in broken-down tenements. Snubbed and ridiculed, they were looked upon as intellectually inferior. The downtown neighborhood in which they lived, Little Italy, was considered a ghetto by outsiders. But, like all races and ethnic groups, these Italian immigrants were proud people, working to attain a better life for themselves and their families. Their heritage defined who they were and informed them with certain principles. They maintained their self-respect in spite of the class structure and in turn reared their children in Little Italy so that their personalities too were imbued with self-esteem and dignity.

Generally, the children were well behaved in Little Italy. Any parent could discipline any child; if a youngster misbehaved, he could easily get whacked on the side of the head by a neighbor or even a stranger. It was completely acceptable. Some books about Sinatra have given readers the impression that Hoboken was a living hell. However, to its residents it was home, and no matter how bad it may have been, it was a better place than the old country, because it was a place where children could have dreams. They didn't have money, but they had more: They had liberty; they had hope.

While Italian-American youngsters were taught to respect themselves and their elders, they were also fighters. It was in their blood. Their tenacity came naturally.

A confident, assertive, and sometimes even combative nature seemed to be ingrained in just about every kid whose parents or grandparents had ever immigrated to Hoboken. And as in many impoverished areas, there were warring street gangs.

"It was a tough neighborhood," said Tina Donato, whose grandparents lived in Hoboken. "You had to have your wits about you. You had to walk around with eyes in the back of your head. But it had heart. So yes, appropriately enough, Frank Sinatra would be born into a place with great heart, a place of passion."

Marty and Dolly

$\mathcal{F}$rank Sinatra's parents, Marty and Dolly, were raised in a town of dissimilar personalities and cultures, so it is no surprise that they too were a study in contrasts.

As a young man, blue-eyed, ruddy, and tattooed Marty Sinatra—born Antonino Martino Sinatra on May 4, 1892, in Lercara Friddi, province of Palermo, Sicily—suffered from asthma and other breathing problems stemming from his work at the American Pencil Company. "Inhaling the dust wrecked his lungs," Frank once explained. "He couldn't do any better because he had nobody to teach him English." Marty ended up distinguishing himself as a prizefighter, boxing under the name Marty O'Brien. He and his parents believed that his life in Hoboken, dominated and controlled largely by the Irish and by Irish politicians, would be easier if he adopted an Irish name for professional bouts. O'Brien was the name of his manager. Later, when he quit boxing in 1926 after breaking his wrist, Sinatra would work as a boilermaker in a shipyard.

"He was a very quiet man," Frank would recall of his mild-mannered father. "A lonely man. And shy. You could hear him wheezing. If he had an attack, a coughing spell, he'd disappear—find a hole in the wall somewhere and be outside before you knew it. I adored him."

Marty fell in love with the blonde, blue-eyed Natalie Catherine "Dolly" Garavente, daughter of Italian immigrants from Genoa. Dolly, born on December 26, 1896, accompanied her parents to America when she was two years old. She was a fair-skinned woman who was often mistaken for Irish (and who as an adult would not be above using her non-Italian appearance to her advantage when doing business in the neighborhood or when "being Irish" suited her purposes).

Their romance blossomed quickly, despite their dissimilarity. Whereas he was quiet, reflective, and brooding, she tended to be loud, impulsive, and fiery. A strong-minded and spirited woman, Dolly usually prevailed in any heated discussion between them. Marty was ambitious—if he weren't, he would not have been in her life, because she detested lazy men—but he was clearly much more easygoing than Dolly.

There were other differences as well. Marty's family were grape growers in the old country, while Dolly's were educated lithographers. Whereas Marty was illiterate, Dolly had an elementary education. Marty's parents were less than enthusiastic about the relationship. They didn't like Genoans, felt that they were elitists. Their wish was for Marty to marry a Sicilian girl, someone "of your own kind." Of course, Dolly's parents were also not pleased about the romance. They, in turn, believed that Sicilians were of a lower class than Genoans. Surely, they insisted, Dolly could find a more suitable mate.

The disapproval of the Sinatras and Garaventes shadowed the relationship between Marty and Dolly in its early days, and it seemed that they would have no future together at all if they listened to their parents. Why should they suppress their affection for one another? Why should they focus on their differences when they had so much in common? They were young, they had fun...they were in love. They also shared a core belief that life was what you make it, and they both wanted better lives.

Still, Marty was uncertain about how to proceed with Dolly. He wanted to wait, see if his parents could perhaps be swayed, give it some time. However, Dolly vehemently disagreed. "Now is the time," she said. "Why wait? Life is short. I want to get married *now*."

Dolly was the type of person who became more determined to accomplish something when she was told she couldn't or shouldn't do it. For instance, in 1919 she would chain herself to city hall as a protest on behalf of woman suffrage; that's the kind of independent-thinking woman she was. The mere fact that her parents disapproved of the relationship was an added incentive for her. In her mind, it made her attraction to Marty all the more exciting and romantic. Therefore she convinced Marty that the two of them should elope.

For Marty—a good son who wanted to please his parents, not defy them—eloping was asking a lot. Dolly felt the same way about her own parents. However, she was more determined not to allow others to impose their prejudices on her, and if she couldn't please her family she would just proceed with her life and hope they'd one day see things her way.

Dolly and Marty eloped on February 14, Valentine's Day, in 1913. They were married at city hall in Jersey City.

To the senior Garaventes' and Sinatras' credit, though extremely put out after hearing of the elopement, they soon changed their views. A year later, by the time Dolly was pregnant with Frank, both families had come to terms with the marriage and had pulled together. Rather than torment her own parents, who felt strongly that she was "living in sin," especially after she was pregnant, Dolly agreed to a church ceremony that would be performed before family members.

After their wedding, Marty and Dolly moved into a dilapidated four-story building in the heart of Little Italy, at 415 Monroe Street in Hoboken, that was shared by eight other families.

Frank Is Born

*O*n December 1, 1915, the forty-seventh annual convention of the Woman Suffrage Association of New York State met at the Astor Hotel in the hope that 1916 would be the year when women would finally get the vote. (It would not happen until 1920.) Meanwhile, *The Magic Flute* was playing at the Metropolitan Opera House in New York, and Ethel Barrymore was starring in *Our Mrs. McChesney* at the Lyceum. *The Birth of a Nation*, D. W. Griffith's epic film, was advertised as the "Most Stupendous Dramatic Spectacle the Brain of Man Has Yet Visioned and Revealed." Also, for five dollars down and a promised payment of five dollars a month, a person could take home a Victrola and a stack of records, just in time for Christmas.

On December 12, 1915, in the middle of an East Coast snowstorm, Frank Sinatra was born to Dolly Sinatra in her bedroom on Monroe Street.

The building where Frank was born was torn down many years ago. Today, a brick arch and gold-and-blue star on the sidewalk mark a hallowed spot in an otherwise battered and neglected part of town. Engraved within the star are the words "Francis Albert Sinatra. The Voice. Born here at 415 Monroe Street. December 12, 1915."

It was a difficult breech birth; the doctors used forceps to deliver the thirteen-and-a-half-pound baby from the ninety-two-pound woman. The infant nearly died during the delivery; in fact, the panicked doctor was taken aback by the child's survival. The baby was scarred on his ear, neck, and cheek, and his eardrum pierced, all by the clumsy use of forceps. Unfortunately, because of the troublesome birth and the damage it caused her own body, Dolly would never be able to bear another child.

In order to assist the infant in breathing, Dolly's mother, who was a capable midwife, held him under cold running water until his tiny, fragile lungs began to draw air. Kicking and screaming its way into the world, the baby would live. "They had set me aside in order to save my mother's life," Frank once explained. "And my grandmother had more sense than anyone in the room, as far as I was concerned. I have blessed that moment in her honor ever since because otherwise I wouldn't be here."

Dolly was just nineteen when Frank was born, Marty twenty-three. They named the child Francis Sinatra. (Though his middle name is Albert, it does not appear on the official birth certificate.) Frank was baptized on April 2, 1916, at St. Francis Holy Roman Catholic Church. According to an account from the historical records at the Hoboken library, he was given his name by accident. Apparently Dolly and Marty had selected Frank Garrick, who worked for the *Jersey Observer*, to be the baby's godfather and Anna Gatto as godmother. Before the baptism, the story goes, the priest asked Garrick his name. He answered, "Frank." When the child was baptized, the priest absentmindedly christened the baby Francis instead of Martin, the name he was supposed to be given.

Dolly was not present at the christening; she was still home recovering from the birth, so she couldn't do anything about the error. Marty didn't bother to correct the priest. Thus the boy ended up being named Francis Sinatra. In the end, Dolly didn't object because she felt that her son's name would be a good link to his Irish—and potentially powerful—godfather.

It's a good story and has long been the accepted account. However, it doesn't appear to be true, because on the birth certificate that was filled out five days after Frank's birth (months prior to the baptism), it clearly says "Francis Senestro." In fact, the name Francis is practically the only thing the apparently non-Italian clerk who filled out the form got right. He misspelled "Sinatra" as well as "Garavente" and listed Frank's father's country of birth as the United States rather than Italy.

Marty and Dolly unofficially gave their son the middle name Albert. Therefore, on a corrected birth certificate filed twenty-three years after the original, Frank's name was recorded as "Francis A. Sinastre." Again, it was wrong.

Young Frank

The United States officially entered World War I on April 6, 1917. Shortly thereafter, American troops began arriving in Hoboken to board ships bound for France. Along with Newport News, Virginia, Hoboken was the center of shipping for the duration of the conflict. The city would be under full military control until the armistice. Soldiers guarded the piers and patrolled the streets looking for German sympathizers.

Meanwhile, President Woodrow Wilson shut down the city's 237 waterfront bars and introduced federal Prohibition to Hoboken, making it the first city in the country to experience it. However, it was difficult for the government to enforce Prohibition laws; local authorities simply wouldn't cooperate. People wanted to drink alcohol, and a great deal of money was generated by selling mixed drinks and beer. Thus northern New Jersey became a virtual haven for anti-Prohibition activity. Soon, *uomini rispettati* (men of respect) began infiltrating the neighborhood, manufacturing and distributing alcoholic beverages while officials, many of whom received hefty kickbacks in the form of cash or favors, looked the other way. These so-called men of respect were actually powerful gangsters who thought of themselves as above the law and had the connections and persuasive power to get away with all sorts of criminal activity, not only in Hoboken but up and down the eastern seaboard.

An enterprising couple, Marty and Dolly Sinatra took full advantage of this laissez-faire climate and opened their own saloon at Fourth and Jefferson Streets in Hoboken, "Marty O'Brien's." (The bar was registered in Dolly's name because Marty was now a fireman working for the Hoboken Fire Department and was not permitted to own such establishments.) At around this time, as Frank once remembered, his father was known to occasionally aid bootleggers. "He was one of the tough guys," Sinatra said in a lecture at Yale Law School in the spring of 1986. "His job was to follow trucks with booze so that they weren't hijacked. I was only three or four, but I remember in the middle of the night I heard sounds, crying and wailing. I think my old man was a little slow, and he got hit on the head. Somebody opened up his head, and he came home and was bleeding all over the kitchen floor. My mother was hysterical. After that, he got out of that kind of business. That's when they opened a saloon."

"Anytime we saw a drunk in the streets, we'd say that he was part of the MOB, meaning Marty O'Brien's pub," said Tony Macagnano, another boyhood friend of Frank's. "Us kids didn't go around there a lot. We were a little afraid of Marty. He was a grouchy kind of guy with a mad kisser on him. But he never said anything to hurt us. Dolly would have knocked him dead if he did. She was great, always laughing and joking and hollering, but Marty never said much. Just grunted a lot."

Because she owned a bar, Dolly befriended a number of *uomini rispettati*, including Sicilian-born Waxey Gordon, a prominent underworld figure in the neighborhood. "They had a lot of shady friends because of the bar they ran," said one close friend of the Sinatras. "Face it. They owned a bar during Prohibition. If you think they didn't have friends in the right places, you're kidding yourself. Dolly could talk shit with the best of them. She was a real character; nobody intimidated her."

As the establishment's barmaid, Dolly was the wisecracking, tough mother figure whom many people in the neighborhood came to for honest advice. Also, if a person needed a job, he would appeal to Dolly. She was the one with connections. She knew everyone in town and could solve pretty much anyone's problem by calling in favors.

Helen Fiore Monteforte, who lived at 414 Monroe Street, across the street from the Sinatras, recalled Dolly: "She was a vivacious, beautiful, blue-eyed woman with light skin and strawberry blonde hair. A real go-getter, she was constantly pushing to get her family ahead. She was a hell-raiser who would sing gaily and dance joyously right on the table at the famous Clam Broth House in Hoboken. She loved life, had tremendous charm, did a great deal of public service work for the community without being paid a dime. One thing that was always true of her, she could light the fire under anyone when she needed something accomplished."

Enterprising, ambitious, and politically conscious, Dolly would in years to come become a Democratic committeewoman. Using her gregarious, self-assured personality to her best advantage, she soon developed considerable political influence in Hoboken. For instance, she was often called upon by Irish politicians who needed Italian votes in Little Italy; she could be counted on to deliver at least six hundred votes from her neighborhood, which gave her the kind of influence most people in the neighborhood simply did not possess. She had power, everyone knew it—and she basked in it.

Well-spoken in the English language as well as in many Italian dialects, Dolly was an unusual woman, given the time and circumstances of her world. However, she was not easy to get along with; she could be extremely judgmental, was known to have deep-seated prejudices against the other "classes," and held firm to her beliefs. When she considered running for mayor, Marty was opposed to it; he felt that the position would make her more intolerable, that she would wield too much power and he wasn't sure how she would handle it. (Ultimately, she did not throw her hat into the ring.)

Steve Capiello of Hoboken, who knew Dolly well, recalled, "She was ahead of her time. Unlike some women of today, who speak of women's rights but do nothing about them, she was a woman of action. She supported me during the onset of my political career, and ultimately I was elected mayor of Hoboken. She could speak with a longshoreman's vocabulary if necessary, or be eloquent if she had to impress the political hierarchy in order to make a point."

Hoboken was a tough place, and the women who immigrated there from Italy were equal to the challenge. Indeed, a woman had to have a toughness about her as well as a sense of enterprise and imagination to embark on the journey to a new life in America. Women who were dainty by nature would remain behind in Italy and enjoy safe, limited lives. Tough, ambitious women like Dolly's mother, Rosa Garavente, and Dolly herself hungered for more. They felt they *deserved* more. In turn, they usually attracted men who were equally ambitious.

"Dolly had the bluest language of any female I'd ever known," Doris Corrado, a former Hoboken librarian, said. "One time she walked into a party from pouring-down rain and the first thing she said when she got in the door was, 'Holy Jesus! It's raining sweet peas and horseshit out there.' Her mouth dripped with honey one minute, and the next it was 'Fuck this' and 'Fuck that.'"

Certainly Italian-American women like Dolly could seem crude to the outside world as they hollered at their kids while trying to get "them little bastards" into the kitchen to eat homemade manicotti and meatballs before the sauce (which Dolly called "gravy") got cold. But that was just the way they were, the way they expressed affection, the way they lived their lives—tough, bold, maybe even sometimes profane, but still capable of great love. Dolly Sinatra didn't have time to be cordial; she had things to do. Her friends and family loved her, and she loved them in return, which was enough for her. She was a formidable woman in every way, and by far the greatest influence on Frank Sinatra's life. She certainly dominated everyone around her, just as Frank would when he became her age. An Italian-American son couldn't help but be influenced by such a mother.

So devoted was Dolly to her many pursuits outside the home that from the ages of six to twelve, Frank was often in the care of his maternal grandmother, and his aunts. He has also said that he spent a great deal of time with "a kindly old Jewish woman," who has only been identified by the name of Mrs. Golden, a woman he continued to visit until her death in the early 1950s.

Recalled his cousin John Tredy, "[Dolly and Marty] didn't have too much time for Frankie when he was young. I think they felt he was always underfoot. Frank was left to his own devices; he rarely did homework, for instance. He was rambunctious as a student; I think he skipped one entire year without his parents being any the wiser."

Other accounts of Frank's childhood have painted him as soft-spoken and extremely sensitive, a quiet child. It was said that his personality as a youngster more resembled his father's than his mother's. John Tredy has said, "He was a soft kind of boy. Like his father, Marty. Frankie was the quietest little boy."

His childhood friend Helen Fiore Monteforte described young Sinatra as "impeccably dressed, never disheveled. A fedora on. As a young boy, a fedora on. Even in the summertime."

Thoughtful and sensitive, he was sometimes taunted by other youngsters in the neighborhood. "Prejudice is nothing new to me," Frank once said. "When I was a kid, I lived in a tough neighborhood. When somebody called me 'a dirty little guinea,' there was only one thing to do—break his head."

Not only was he sometimes ridiculed because of his ancestry, but Frank was also singled out because of his appearance. They called him "Scarface," referring to the scars that had been left from his difficult birth. They often beat and bullied him. In some respects, Frank seemed like a misfit to the other boys by the time he enrolled at David E. Rue Junior High in 1928, and his mother only made matters worse by dressing him in Little Lord Fauntleroy suits, handmade by her own mother. He had such a wide array of "outfits," so many pants, in fact, that some people in the neighborhood called him "Slacksey O'Brien."

"We were walking down the street," one of his friends remembered, "and someone said, 'Hey, you little wop,' to Frank as he passed by. I said, 'Frank, just keep on walkin'.' And Frank said, 'I'm gonna walk all over his *face*, that's where I'm gonna walk.' And that was that, the fight was on. Frank got beat real bad. He wasn't much of a fighter, but not for lack of trying. Afterward, I said to him, 'Frankie, was it worth it? C'mon!' And he said, 'Hell yeah, it was worth it. He'll never call me a wop again.' Two days later, same thing, same guy. 'Hey, you little wop.' And the fight was on again…and Frank got beat up again."

"I'll never forget how it hurt when the kids called me a dago when I was a boy," he later said. "It's a scar that lasted a long time and which I have never quite forgotten. It isn't the kids' fault," he noted. "It's their parents. They would never learn to make racial and religious discriminations if they didn't hear that junk at home." Likely because of what he saw during his childhood, Frank would always be outspoken when he or his friends—no matter their race, ethnic background, or appearance—were slurred or insulted in any way. He would go on to often speak out publicly for racial tolerance, especially at times when it was unpopular to do so.

It was Frank's father, Marty, who contributed to the often unexpected side of his son's character: his brooding pensiveness, his kindness, and his loyalty to his friends. But his near obsession with cleanliness, his unyielding stubbornness, and his legendary temper can clearly be traced to his mother. Sometimes young Frank would become so angry that he lost control of himself. For instance, he became so unhappy about the scars of his birth that he managed to track down the doctor who had delivered him. Angry eleven-year-old Sinatra went to the doctor's home, determined to beat him up for having disfigured him. Luckily, the doctor wasn't in.

"Hell, he was as scrappy as they come," said Joey D'Orazio, two years younger than Frank, who once lived in what he proudly called "Dolly's neighborhood."

"What's with this 'poor little Frankie' crap I read about all the time? He was tough as nails. He was a wisecracking kid who talked back to his mother but had the greatest respect for her, as we all did for our mothers. She popped him upside his head and called him terrible names—'you little son of a bitch' was her favorite phrase—but you didn't get offended by anything, not if you lived in Hoboken, that's for sure.

"Yeah, he got beat up by some of the kids. I beat him up myself once, over what I don't even remember," said D'Orazio with a chuckle.

"I just remember hitting him and knocking him to the ground, out cold. But he beat other kids up in return, the kids he could take on. They called him names, he called *other* kids names.

"He was a little dago—and I say that with love because I'm an old dago myself now—and like all the other little dagos in the neighborhood, he had a terrible temper. You could be shootin' marbles with him and he'd go off on you if he lost and take all your damn marbles from you anyway. 'I never lose,' he would say. 'That day I lose, that's gonna be some day, 'cause it ain't ever gonna happen.'"

Frank grew up in a competitive culture. Not only was each ethnic group battling for territorial control, but in a manufacturing town like Hoboken, whenever there was a dip in the economy, everyone was affected. There was always competition for work; whom one knew was extremely important, especially for lucrative jobs controlled by politicians. A rivalry among most of the young men in Hoboken started with a competition for girls: who got the most prized ones and who got them fastest. Frank took this particular competition quite seriously.

"He had a fight with my dad over a girl once, and he yelled at my old man—scared the hell out of him, I was told—used words my old man had never even heard before, and he lived in the same neighborhood!" exclaimed Tom Gianetti, the son of another childhood friend of Sinatra's, Rocky Gianetti.

Gianetti said that his father told him that when Frank was about thirteen, he would take girls "into the back alley" and have sex with them. A sweet-talker, he could have pretty much any girl he wanted. If he had his way with her, though, she was his forever—at least as far as he was concerned. Indeed, Sinatra always seemed to have a confidence that he could have any girl he wanted, especially as he grew older. In many ways, as we shall see, he certainly had his share of deep insecurities. However, he rarely questioned his power over the opposite sex and his ability to sweep a woman off her feet. Especially as a famous adult, he would take full advantage of it. He would also be extremely territorial of the women with whom he became involved. Certainly his true friends would know better than to go anywhere near any woman considered a conquest by Frank Sinatra, no matter how many years had passed.

From an early age—long before he was famous—Frank also had a petulant, self-entitled bent that dictated that if he didn't get his way, he not only did not want to be in the game, he didn't even want to know the other players. He was an only child in an Italian-American culture and at a time when most people had large families. Children who have siblings usually learn about cooperation and sharing, about having to be reasonable. Not Frank. As an adult, he would always want—and usually manage to get—everything his way. If that wasn't possible, if he was crossed, he would simply disappear from the offender's life.

"My old man [Rocky Gianetti] made the mistake of dating one of Frankie's girls about two years after [Sinatra] had sex with her, and that's when they had the fight," said Tom Gianetti. "Frank said, 'You broke my one rule. Don't go after any girl I had sex with.' He said terrible, terrible things to my father. What a mouth, what a temper. My old man said he was scared. Frankie was in his face like he was going to kill him, and he hadn't even seen this girl in two years. 'Think you're better than I am?' he was screaming at my old man. 'Think she liked it better? Well, think again. Think again!' After that, it was never the same between them.

"My old man would see Frankie walking down the street, and he'd say, 'Frankie boy, whatcha doing?' and Frankie would just stare straight ahead like he wasn't even there. Like he didn't even exist. My father would always say, 'Oh, c'mon, Frank, don't be an idiot. It was just a broad.' Nothing. Just silence. He got that [kind of behavior] from Dolly," said Gianetti. "Dolly could write you off like you didn't exist if you pissed her off. I saw it happen plenty of times. She would walk down the street, someone would say hello, and she would just walk by as if she hadn't heard or seen a thing." Indeed, Frank never spoke to Rocky Gianetti again.

With the passing of the years, as we shall see, Frank would customarily cut from his life people he believe had slighted him. While it may be easy to blame some of this callous behavior on his celebrity and the entitlement that often comes with being famous, the truth is that Frank never had what most people would consider a normal sense of proportion about what constituted an insult worth banishing someone from his life. Like Dolly, he seemed always able to turn off all affection for a friend and completely break all communication with him if he felt in any way betrayed. "My son is just like me," Dolly Sinatra once said. "You cross me, I never forget. You cross him, he never forgets."

Hoboken Days

The desire to sing professionally came upon Frank Sinatra as a teenager. By 1930, when he enrolled in A. J. Demarest High School at Fourth and Garden, he had become addicted to the radio, which, as the primary source of American entertainment since 1922, introduced America to big-band music and to vocalists like Bing Crosby and Russ Columbo. The fifteen-year-old liked the way he sounded when he sang along with the popular singers during their live broadcasts. Young Frankie thought that perhaps he might want to sing for a living too—unless something better presented itself. To that end, he joined the school glee club. He sang at parties, for his friends, in school talent shows, and at other functions; in doing so, he received a warm response from his fellow students, which he enjoyed.

"He was singing here and there," said one relative. "But it wasn't like he had a burning desire. He was really just exploring his options. 'You wanna hear me sing?' he'd ask. And we'd say, 'Hell, no, Frankie. Let's play ball.' He'd say, 'Fine,' and that was that."

By 1930, the family had moved to a bigger, three-bedroom apartment in a much better neighborhood, at 703 Park Avenue in Hoboken. The new home was less than a half mile away from the Sinatras' former residence on Monroe and Garden, but in Hoboken at that time, a few yards could make a big difference in how one lived. The house was—and still is today—the biggest on the block. Whereas all the other row houses have three floors, this one, which sits near the end of the block, has five. Thirty-six glass panes, in two vertical columns of bow windows), face the street. It seems to tower over everything, impressive even today; back in 1930 it must have been a real showplace.

"They were always moving up," said Steve Capiello. "These weren't your regular Hoboken folk. They were doing exciting things, making money, looking good, having a good life. When Frankie became a star, his press agent was always trying to give the impression that he was a slum kid. I remember thinking to myself, 'Hey, if he was a slum kid, then what the hell was I?' My family had no money at all and we had twelve kids under one roof, in three rooms. We were having it hard, but not the Sinatras."

Another childhood friend, Joe Lissa, remembered, "Being an only kid made all the difference in the world. Frank had more because he didn't have to share with brothers and sisters. He even had his own bedroom. None of the rest of us had *half* of what he had. I don't think I knew one other kid that was an only child, not one other one! He always wore brand-new black-and-whites [shoes] that his mother bought him. He even had his own charge account at Geismer's department store! Come on!"

The Sinatras and their neighbors always had good times in Hoboken. There were block parties during hot summer evenings when Dolly would show off her braciola. Young Frank liked to play the popular ball games of the day with his pals—chink ball and penny ball—and no one could shoot marbles or flip baseball cards like Frankie. If things became dull, he and his pals would take a train into "Filluff-e-ah" (Philadelphia) and eat hoagies, even though they could just as easily be bought in Hoboken. "Gimmeya hoagie, hold da onions," Frank would say, always concerned about how his breath would affect his influence on the girls. Headed back home on the train, Frank and his buddies would stuff themselves full of Tastykakes, cupcakes that were at the time only made and sold in Philadelphia.

Sometimes Frank and his buddies would borrow his dad's bright red Chrysler—when he was a teenager, he was the only one among his friends who had access to a car—and drive "down da shore" (the resort area of the eastern coastline) to "walk da boards" (the boardwalk) of "Lanic Cidy" (Atlantic City).

While some accounts of Frank's life have painted these years as sad and lonely, that really wasn't the case. It is true that Frank was not happy in high school; a poor and distracted student, he often found himself in trouble. It's been reported that he quit after just forty-seven days in high school, though that seems unlikely. Frank said he lasted a little longer than that, but records at the school are unclear. (Nancy

Sinatra says that her father quit in his senior year.) At any rate, he did in fact leave high school one day, never to return. His parents were inconsolable about his decision, but he was as resolved about his life as they were about theirs. "My father was called into the principal's office for about the seven hundredth time," Frank used to joke. "And he said, 'Here's the diploma, now get him the hell out of this school.'"

Frank took a few business classes at the Drake Business School for one semester and mulled over the idea of enrolling in the Stevens Institute of Technology, the oldest college of mechanical engineering in the country, which happened to be in Hoboken. However, the urge to sing professionally was beginning to take hold. When his mother found pictures of Bing Crosby on his bedroom walls and questioned him about them, she learned that her only son was considering becoming an entertainer, not an engineer.

Dolly must have remembered that as a much younger child he had sung in the bar that she and Marty owned. But that was all in fun, to amuse the patrons—an extension of Dolly's humor. She never imagined that her son would be serious about singing, even though she had heard about, but never attended, some of his glee club performances. When she realized that Frank was really mulling over the possibility of singing for a living, she did what any other Italian-American mother in Hoboken would when informed that her dreams of a college education, or at least a steady job, for her son would probably not materialize: She threw a shoe at him.

"You ain't gonna be no singer," Dolly told Frank, according to his memory.

"But, Ma! Maybe it's what I do best," Frank protested.

"How do you know what you do best? You little son of a bitch," she shot back, raising her voice. "I'll tell you what you do best. You get a job, big shot. *That's* what you do best. I don't wanna hear another word about it, either."

Marty Sinatra proved to be just as challenging an opponent to Frank's ambitions. Frank's father was a hardworking immigrant who held fast to *la terra promessa*—the Promised Land—and to the upward mobility, the good life, that the American dream had to offer. As a fireman for the Hoboken Fire Department, he didn't make a fortune, but he was satisfied. In fact, it was the Sicilian way—as his own father had once explained—to have just a taste of the good life and then to build from there. *Fari vagnari u puzzi*—wet their beaks—is what Sicilians called it. Certainly they could do just that in this free country.

In 1932, because of the success of Dolly's bar and her determination to put aside for a rainy day any extra money it had been able to generate over the years, she and Marty were able to again raise their standard of living by purchasing a three-story (plus cellar), four-bedroom house at 841 Garden Street in Hoboken for $13,400—quite a sum for the times. (Back then, these structures were called "Father, Son, Holy Ghost" homes, to denote the three floors.) It was one of the most expensive properties in the county. All of the homes on the street were pretty much the same: seven to ten cement steps leading from the sidewalk to the front door, another entrance, at street level, to what is known as the cellar, where wine was often kept and where a second kitchen usually existed, and a "coal bin." Across the street is the Joseph F. Brandt Middle School.

Early Aspirations

Jeet yet?" Frank would ask any visitor to the Sinatra home. Translation: "Did you eat yet?"

The answer coming back from anyone who knew his mother's reputation as a cook would be, "*No, jue?*" "No, did you?"

"Ma will make you something. Whaddya want?"

Dolly Sinatra almost always had food cooking on the stove or baking in the oven of her new kitchen, though no one could quite understand when she had the time to prepare it.

"You'd walk in the door and sitting on the kitchen table would be a huge antipasto," remembered one relative, "with pepperoncini, olives, giardiniera, anchovies, and prosciutto. Or she would have hot escarole soup [chicken broth with escarole greens, vegetables, eggs, and small meatballs], which was something you never made except maybe on holidays, or for holidays. You'd say, 'Dolly, when the hell did you have time to do all this?' and she'd always say, 'Whaddya talkin' about? Time? You *make* the time. Now eat.'"

Dolly and Marty had made a good life for themselves and their son despite their limited educations. Both were filled with pride and happiness knowing that they could probably afford to send Frank to college. Though it would be tight, they'd been planning it for years. Since Marty was illiterate, the idea of a son of his going to college was vitally important to him. So when Frank dropped out of high school and then announced that he had no intention of pursuing a higher education, Marty couldn't believe his audacity and what he viewed as his sheer stupidity. Indeed, during these desperate times, when millions of unemployed Americans could only dream of a college education for their children, for young Frank to decline such an opportunity was, at least as far as Marty was concerned, unconscionable. He didn't want his son to turn out the way he had; at least that's what he said.

In truth, there was nothing wrong with the way Marty Sinatra had turned out. He couldn't read or write English—and Frank said once that he would never embarrass his father by reminding him of it—but he was a hardworking, loving man. Like many parents, though, he wanted more for his kid than what he had achieved in his own life. Though one Sicilian proverb said, "Do not make your child better than you are," Marty didn't subscribe to that kind of thinking at all, believing it to be old-fashioned. "A son's life should *always* make his father's life look bad," he would say.

Outraged at the prospect of his son turning out to be a "freeloader," Marty called young Frank a "quitter."

"I ain't no quitter, Pop," Frank would say in his defense, according to his memory.

"You ain't goin' to school, you don't wanna work, you're a quitter," Marty would insist. "I don't even want to talk about it no more, quitter!"

For years afterward, whenever Frank would change direction in his life, his old man would shout that demoralizing name out at him: "quitter." Perhaps Marty hoped that the derisive term would somehow spur his son on to a greater sense of responsibility. However, it hurt Frank deeply; he would never forget it.

"I ain't no quitter," Frank would scream at Marty.

"Don't raise your voice to your father," Dolly would shout before smacking Frank hard on the back of the head with the palm of her hand.

"But he called me a quitter."

"He's your *father*," Dolly would remind her son. "He can call you anything he wants to call you. Now, get outta here, you little son of a bitch quitter."

Still, Marty's use of the term likely had the desired effect: It motivated Frank. "I think it gave him incentive," said one relative, "to prove his old man wrong. Not an unusual story, but Frank's just the same."

In early 1932, to placate his father, sixteen-year-old Frank got a job in the Tietjen and Lang shipyards. Then he worked for Lyons and Carnahan in New York City, unloading crates of books. ("Do you know what a thrill it is to get a hernia for $62.50 a week lifting six-hundred-pound crates with another little guy and a hand truck?" Frank used to joke.) Bored there, he took another job for the United Fruit Lines, working in the refrigeration units of cargo ships. When he quit that job, saying that he'd had it with manual labor, his father became disgusted again with the "quitter."

"You don't want to work," he told him one morning over breakfast, "then get the hell out. You want to be a bum, go somewhere else and be a bum." Marty told his son that his grandparents hadn't immigrated all the way to the United States "from It-lee [Italy]" just so that Frank could be a freeloader.

"I was shocked," Frank recalled. "I remember the moment. My father said to me, 'Why don't you get out of the house and go out on your own?' What he really said was, 'Get out.' And I think the egg was stuck in there [in my throat] for about twenty minutes, and I couldn't swallow it. My mother, of course, was nearly in tears, but we 'agreed' that it might be a good thing. So I packed up a small case I had and went to New York."

Frank took a room in New York City, but his timing must have been wrong. He couldn't get work as a singer, or as anything else. He returned to Hoboken.

"So, you ready to go to work *now*, Mr. Smarty Pants?" Dolly wanted to know. "Mr. Big-Shot Singer." Then, after a beat, she would grin at him, smack him on the head, and ask, "So, you a star yet, or what?" Though they were opposed to their son's aspirations to be a singer, deep down Dolly and Marty, like most devoted parents of their time and place, couldn't resist encouraging him, at least a little. In fact, by the time Frank got back from New York, Dolly wanted him to sing almost as much as he did. She figured that if he was willing to leave home and go to New York, maybe he did have a goal, or at least some kind of idea of what he wanted to do with his life. However, this was Hoboken, not Hollywood. She didn't know how to assist him.

"I had heard that it was on her mind, though," said Doris Sevanto, who was raised in Hoboken and was a friend of the Sinatras. "My mother told me that Dolly started asking guys with clubs to maybe give her kid a job, and Frankie worked in one club in Hoboken for a while. But that fell through when he had a fight with the proprietor. Dolly would say, 'You know, that little son of a bitch son of mine, he wants to sing. And he ain't half bad. I think he might make it. But don't tell *him* that. He's already too big for his britches.'"

"The way most immigrant Italian parents were in Hoboken and in other cities at the time was that they supported their kids' goals in life, even when their kids were doing something they didn't like," said singer Tony Martin. "Sure, you tried to talk the kid out of it, you hit him, you tried to knock reason into him, but then if he didn't listen and you did your best, you finally said, 'All right, fine. Now, what can I do to help?'"

Marty and Dolly were parents who well understood and could relate to the notion of rebellion. After all, it was that same sense of defiance that had spurred their own parents to immigrate to the United States.

"So how could they not support their kid's dreams?" observed Tina Donato, who spent summers in Little Italy with her grandparents and knew the Sinatras well. "Anyone who says they didn't, that's a person who didn't understand one of the most important things about the Italian-American way of life. You don't knock your kid down, you build your kid up. Or, at the very least, you make them think you're knocking him down when you're actually building him up. That was the case with all the Italian parents in my family, and I know it was the case with Frankie's too. Marty, yeah, well, he wanted something else for Frankie. But after he knew Frankie wanted to be a singer, he was in his corner too, even if only secretly."

Dolly and Marty lent Frank the sixty-five dollars he needed to buy a portable public-address system and sheet-music arrangements so that he could work in local nightclubs. If he was going to do this "goddamned thing," as Dolly called it—be a performer—then he would have a distinct edge over the other young men in the neighborhood who were attempting to do the same thing. Most of them didn't have their own sound system and arrangements, did they? The Sinatra parents made certain their kid did, though.

"I started collecting orchestrations," Frank once explained. "Bands needed them. I had them. If the local orchestras wanted to use my arrangements, and they always did because I had a large and up-to-the-minute collection, they had to take singer Sinatra too. Nobody was cheated. The bands needed what they rented from me, and I got what I wanted too. While I wasn't the best singer in the world, they weren't the best bands either."

With his sound system and music, Frank—who was about seventeen by this time—started singing with small bands in clubs on weekends and evenings. His mother even helped him get bookings at Democratic Party meetings. He also performed at school dances. The more his parents and friends began to approve of his growing ambition, the more concrete Frank's plans became, until finally the idea of becoming a successful entertainer was a goal he now admitted that he hoped to realize.

He continually listened to Bing Crosby and tried to emulate that crooner's voice in the shower. However, he quickly decided that he wanted his own style, not Bing's. Too many other young men at the time were attempting to mimic Crosby's vocal stylings, or as Frank has said, "Boo-boo-booing like Bing," on such hits as "Just One More Chance" and "I Found a Million-Dollar Baby (in a Five-and-Ten-Cent Store)."

Sinatra, whose voice was in a higher register than Bing's anyway, said later that he was determined to be "a different kind of singer." He would remember, "Bing was on top, and a bunch of us—Dick Todd, Bob Eberly, Perry Como, Dean Martin—we were trying to break in. It occurred to me that maybe the world didn't need another Crosby.

I decided to experiment a little and come up with something different. What I finally hit on was more the bel canto Italian school of singing. It was more difficult than Crosby's style, much more difficult."

With Frank's enthusiasm for singing contagious, Dolly and Marty began to marvel at his talent. "When he would sing around the house, he was good, and we were, I don't know, *surprised*," Dolly once admitted. They were relieved and heartened to see him finally focus on a goal.

Certainly many Italian-American young men from cities across the country had the same goal as Frank. The names are now legendary: Dean Martin, Perry Como, Frankie Laine, Tony Bennett, Vic Damone, and many others—all good Italian-American boys whose foulmouthed but loving mothers probably threw shoes at them or smacked them on the backs of their heads upon first learning of their improbable aspirations. None, however, would ever be as famous or as successful—or as wealthy—as *the* Italian American: Frank Sinatra.

Nancy

*I*t was the summer of 1934 when eighteen-year-old Frank Sinatra met seventeen-year-old Nancy Carol Barbato, daughter of Mike Barbato, a plasterer from Jersey City. (Nancy has also been identified as Nancy Rose Barbato; however, her daughter Nancy says that her middle name is Carol.)

"My mother came from a poor family in Jersey City, New Jersey," Frank Sinatra Jr. recalled. "When I once asked her, 'Mom, how did you make it with eight sisters at home?' she answered, 'Frankie, sometimes we ate, sometimes we didn't.' They had no money. 'So, you didn't have the things you wanted as you were growing up?' I asked. 'No, I didn't,' my mother said. 'I learned at an early age that if you want to get something—you want to go out and buy yourself a tape recorder or a bicycle? You have to go out and get a job. Go out and make some money and buy it, then it's really yours. No one ever gave us anything, ever.' My mother always worked at one thing or another. It was the only way. It's how she raised me, too."

During his youth, Frank would often spend his summers with a favorite aunt, Mrs. Josephine Garavente Monaco—Aunt Josie—who owned a beach house in Long Branch, on the Jersey shore. Josephine, Dolly's sister, recalled, "He used to drive us crazy, playing the ukulele on the porch all the time. He would sit there and play, kind of lonesome. Then, one day, I noticed him talking to a pretty little dark-haired girl who was living across the street for the summer. She was Nancy."

Nancy was doing her nails on the front porch of the home in which she was living for the summer with her father, Mike, and her aunt and uncle and their families, when Frank approached her, ukulele in hand. "Yo. What about me?" he said with a wink. "I could use a manicure too."

Frank couldn't help himself; he was immediately attracted to this beautiful girl. "We had a wonderful summer together. When it was over, I figured, 'Well, that's it, it's over.'" She was pretty, funny, had a great little figure, and thought he was handsome. What else did an eighteen-year-old need from a girl?

When the season ended, Frank and Nancy went back to their respective homes, he to Hoboken and she to Jersey City, just one town away. However, the romance would continue for the next four years. Frank would take the bus to visit and date her; Nancy would give him the fare if he didn't have it. Once, when he was broke, Nancy sent him one of her gloves with a dollar bill stuffed in each finger.

These would actually be the most romantic years of their long, sometimes tortured relationship. He would write poetry for her, and they would spend long hours listening to opera on the Victrola. They would go to the beach, walk the boards, and eat Creamsicles until they were both sick to their stomachs. He would try to teach her how to play canasta, a complicated card game that involves melding sets of seven or more cards. But he wasn't very good at it himself, so they would spend more time laughing than playing.

Of this time, Frank remembered, "I was singing for two dollars a night at club meetings. I sang at social clubs and at roadhouses, sometimes for nothing or for a sandwich or cigarettes—all night for three packs. But I worked on one basic theory," he recalled. "Stay alive. Get as much practice as you can. Nancy was there for all that. She was right there at my side."

Frank sensed that Nancy would be the kind of mate who would allow him to explore life as an entertainer. After discussing with her the reality that such a life offers few guarantees, he sensed that she understood. There was something about her that made him believe she would be loyal to him, no matter what. "I'm goin' straight to the top," he warned her. "And I don't want no dame draggin' on my neck."

"I won't get in your way," she promised.

"I'm serious 'bout this, Nancy," he said. "You *wit* me?

"I'm wit you, Frankie," she responded. "I'll always be wit you."

Early Singing Days

On September 8, 1935, nineteen-year-old Frank Sinatra got his first big break when he auditioned to appear on the popular *Major Bowes and His Original Amateur Hour.* Bowes's NBC radio show was broadcast live from the Capitol Theatre in New York. (It was launched on New York radio in 1934 and went national a year later.) Frank once recalled, laughing, "Bowes used to come on the air, and he used to say, 'The wheel of fortune spins, 'round and 'round she goes, where she stops, nobody knows.' That was the dullest opening I ever heard on any radio show."

"He was a pompous bum with a bulbous nose," Sinatra said of Major Bowes years after the fact, in 1966, as part of his nightclub act. "He useta drink Green River [liquor]. He was a drunk, this guy. I don't know if you ever heard of Green River, but it takes the paint off your deck if you got a boat. Fifty-nine cents a gallon, baby."

At the time of Frank's tryout, another act auditioned, a group calling themselves the Three Flashes—Fred "Tamby" Tamburro, Pat "Patty Prince" Principe, and James "Skelly" Petrozelli. It was either Bowes's idea to team Frank with this other act from Hoboken and call them the Hoboken Four or it was Dolly's, depending on which of the two accounts one wishes to believe. At any rate, when the quartet performed the Bing Crosby–Mills Brothers hit "Shine" on Bowes's show, they were a success.

On what was the *American Idol* of its day, a host encouraged listeners to telephone a special number and vote for their favorites among the acts. The Hoboken Four generated a huge number of telephone votes with their performance. In retrospect, the most astonishing thing about Frank's first appearance on the *Amateur Hour* is that his voice was already in place. He didn't have the intelligence or feeling that would come later, but the voice was most definitely there. The group, with Frank on lead, would make several more appearances.

Frank had his first opportunity to tour as a singer at about sixty-five dollars a week when Bowes asked him and the Hoboken Four to tour with one of Bowes's many amateur companies. This was a great opportunity for the young Sinatra, performing with sixteen other acts—tap dancers, jugglers, mouth organists, and more—in front of enthusiastic audiences in different cities, honing his talent as a singer as well as his ability as a performer.

Sinatra worked with the Hoboken Four for about three months, until the end of 1935, when the other three members began resenting all the attention he received from audiences. It was difficult for Frank to hold himself back and try to blend in with a group. He couldn't help flirting with the women in the audience, winking at them, showing a lot more personality than the other fellows during performances. It caused a great deal of dissension.

With so much infighting taking place within the group—some of it actually physical—Frank, who had never intended to be in a group in the first place, decided to leave the act. "I had been thinking solo, solo, *solo*," he remembered. It had been a good experience, but he knew it was time to end it and move on. Besides, he missed his parents terribly (he'd been sending his mother letters and photographs from the road), as well as Nancy.

Upon his return, though, Frank was greeted by Marty's strong disapproval of the decision he'd made to leave the Hoboken Four. As far as Marty was concerned, his son had just "quit" another job.

A loud argument ensued. Marty's routine was the usual: His son would never amount to anything; he was a "quitter." For his part, Frank sang the same refrain: His father didn't understand his ambitions. Why couldn't he be more supportive? Actually, Frank was more angry now than hurt by Marty's attitude. In fact, he grew even more determined to prove his "old man" wrong.

Dolly just wanted a little peace and quiet. She was tired of the constant arguing between her husband and son. "*The two of you are driving me nuts,*" she would scream at them. "Frankie wants to sing, Marty. Jesus Christ Almighty, just let him sing, will ya?"

Dolly's personal power had long ago influenced her private life with Marty. In a culture and at a time when the man was the head of the family, she always played that role in the Sinatra household, and everyone who knew the Sinatras understood as much. She and Marty never pretended that he was boss. "Fine, whatever you say, Dolly," Marty would tell her. He would back down every time. "I don't listen, and I don't talk," he would say with a soft smile.

Back in Hoboken, Frank continued his career as a solo singer at the Rustic Cabin, a roadhouse in nearby Englewood Cliffs, two miles north of the George Washington Bridge.

It was at about this time that Frank met an aggressive song promoter named Hank Sanicola. It wasn't long before they became pals and Hank took on the unofficial job of "managing" Frank. Sanicola, also of Sicilian heritage, would be one of Sinatra's right-hand men for years to come; later, he would even sometimes play piano for him.

"I was always the strong arm," Sanicola, a former amateur boxer, once said. "I knew how to fight. I used to step in and hit for Frank when they started ganging up on him in bars."

"Yeah, he's a great dag," Frank would say of Hank. (Frank used to call his buddies of Italian-American heritage the nickname "dag," a shortened version of "dago," a racial slur, but which to Frank meant *paisano*.)

Sanicola booked him a regular job at the Rustic Cabin, where he would make between fifteen and thirty dollars a week waiting tables and singing with the Harold Arden house band on WNEW in New York, broadcast throughout the Tri-State Area. "We had a blind piano player," Frank once recalled. "Completely blind, with a shiny, bald head. Between dance sets, I would push his little half-piano around. We'd go from table to table, and he'd play and I'd sing. There was a dish out on the piano. People would put coins in the dish."

Frank almost didn't get the job, since, as it happened, Harold Arden didn't much like him. Frank really wanted it, "but the bandleader doesn't like me," he complained to Dolly. His mother told him that that was just fine. She didn't like the idea of his singing in a club all night anyway.

"Frank just looked at me," she would recall in an interview many years later. "He took his dog, Girlie, in his arms and went up to his room. Then I heard him sobbing. I stood it for a couple of hours," she remembered, "and I suppose I realized then, maybe for the first time, what singing really meant to Frankie. So I got on the phone, and I called Harry Steeper, who was mayor of North Bergen, president of the New Jersey musicians' union, and an assistant to James 'Little Caesar' Petrillo, president of the American Federation of Musicians. As fellow politicians, we used to do favors for one another. I said, 'What can we do? Frankie wants to sing at the Rustic Cabin, and the bandleader doesn't like him.' I told him what happened, and I asked him to see to it that Frankie got another tryout, and this time I said, 'See to it that he gets the job.'"

Harry told Dolly that it was as good as a done deal. Frank got the job.

Helen Fiore Monteforte recalled that Dolly was so anxious that her son make a good impression at the Rustic Cabin, she "papered" the place with friends. She invited Helen's entire family and paid for everyone's tickets. "She was very generous, but also knew that the people present would benefit Frank at his shows."

"I guess that's when it started for Frankie," said Joey D'Orazio, Sinatra's friend from Hoboken. "He knew he was gonna be a star then. We all went to the Cabin to see him. I mean, he was good, you know? He was no *Sinatra*, though. Not yet. I told him, 'Hey, Frankie, you ain't bad, but you could use some work.' And he was insulted. 'Screw you and your whole family,' he said. 'If you can't pay a guy a decent compliment, don't be comin' 'round here. Whatcha think, I *need* to hear you tearin' me down?' Either you were with him or you were against him; that was Frankie."

Frank once remembered the night Cole Porter showed up in the audience at the Rustic Cabin. "I had been so infatuated with his music, I couldn't believe he was sitting out there. I dedicated the next song, 'Night and Day,' to Mr. Porter. However, I proceeded to forget all the words. I kept singing 'Night and Day' for fifteen bars. Many, many years later, I got to know Mr. Porter quite well. We were doing a film [*High Society*], and he called me aside and said, 'I don't know if you remember meeting me at some nightclub you were working.' I said, 'Oh yeah.' And he said, 'So do I. That was about the worst performance I ever heard.'"

As well as working at the Rustic Cabin, Frank would commute back and forth to New York just to keep his finger on the pulse of what was going on in that city's nightlife. He would sneak into nightclubs to watch other popular entertainers perform, and learn all he could from their acts. He would get himself booked on every radio show whose producers would let him sing—anything he could think of to possibly get ahead in show business. He was so determined to make it, he actually spent some of his hard-earned money on a voice-and-diction coach whose job it was to help him lose his thick New Jersey accent.

Throughout this time, Frank continued dating Nancy Barbato, who was supportive and understanding of his goals. She continually encouraged him and spent many hours bolstering his self-confidence. "I know you can make it," she told him, according to her own recollection.

"How do you know that?" Frank asked, holding her in his arms.

"Because you're the most talented, most handsome man I've ever met," she said, flattering him, and meaning it too.

"And just how many talented, handsome men have you met?" he asked with mock suspicion.

"Just one," she demurred.

In early 1937, his cousin Ray helped Frank get a job on a fifteen-minute NBC radio program—which would turn out to be a regular spot for the young singer—for seventy cents a week. "He'd do anything he could," said another cousin. "It didn't matter where, when, or for how much. If he could sing, he'd sing. And you know what? By the time he was twenty-one, he was getting to be good. Damn good. In fact, I told him, 'Frankie, man, you can sing.' And he said, 'No kiddin', you idiot. That's what I been tryin' to tell ya.'"

For a while, Frank actually toyed with the idea of changing his name to Frankie Trent, in honor of his cousin John Tredy, who died of tuberculosis at twenty-eight. (Tredy was the first professional entertainer in the family; he played the banjo in a group and sang.) He thought it might be a good idea to lose the ethnicity attached to the name Sinatra, and had a few fliers printed up with the new name. (Imagine what they might be worth today!) However, Dolly warned him that Marty would "kick his ass" if he ever changed his name. Later, Frank said, "Changing my name, man, that was the best thing I ever *didn't* do."

Midwife

Throughout Frank's youth, Dolly Sinatra had worked as a midwife, just another of the many duties she took upon herself to perform in Hoboken. This wasn't unusual. At this time, most babies in the United States were delivered by women who were not licensed doctors but were trained to assist in childbirth. As a midwife, Dolly was also often asked to terminate pregnancies. Always the pragmatist, she simply felt she was doing a service to the community. If an unmarried Italian Catholic woman became pregnant, her life could be ruined due to social and religious conventions. Some families in the neighborhood had as many as seven mouths to feed. An addition to a family that large—even if it was a daughter having the child—was usually unwanted. Dolly would take care of it. Like everything else in her world, it could be handled.

It is true that Dolly, a Catholic, was breaking what was considered by most Italian Catholics to be "God's law" by performing these sorts of surgeries. However, the Sinatras were not very religious; they rarely attended church. "I got my own religion," Dolly used to say. "I know what I'm doing. God knows what I'm doing. And God wouldn't have given me the idea to do it if he didn't want me doin' it." (It should also be noted that Dolly assisted many more births than she did abortions.)

"There are things about organized religion which I resent," Frank would say years later. "Christ has been revered as the Prince of Peace, but more blood has been shed in his name than any other figure in history. You show me one step forward in the name of religion and I'll show you a hundred retrogressions."

"My mother was thirteen and pregnant," remembered Debra Stradella, whose mom lived in Hoboken at the time. "She told me that she didn't know what to do; she was scared that she would be ostracized. My grandmother called Dolly to say that her daughter needed help, but that they could not afford to pay. I think it was twenty-five dollars. Dolly said they could pay three dollars a month until it was taken care of.

"My grandmother took my mother to Dolly's home on Garden Street. She had a table set up in her cellar. She came downstairs with a little black bag, and she did the surgery herself. My mother told me the whole thing took maybe fifteen minutes. She used to tell us this story, and we would just cringe.

"But Dolly was kind to my mother," Debra Stradella added. "She checked on her every week for a month, coming to her home and administering different medicines. She was like a savior, even though what she was doing was—well, I guess it was wrong."

It's safe to say that some in Hoboken didn't approve of Dolly's activities, which were quite illegal. "She was a criminal" is how one Hoboken resident puts it today. "Plain and simple. She performed abortions. You can't glorify her."

In 1937, Dolly found herself in trouble. There had been complications to a surgery she'd performed in her cellar. The patient had to be rushed to the hospital, was in critical condition when she arrived, and nearly died. Dolly was promptly arrested and charged with a felony. Eventually she was convicted and put on probation for five years. Undaunted, she continued performing her work, even while on probation. In fact, she was arrested several more times after that incident, but was never jailed, probably because of her political connections.*

---

* Today, in the Hudson County courthouse, there are no official records of Dolly Sinatra's arrest in Hoboken in the summer of 1937. It is whispered among certain residents that she was able to use her influence to have those records "misplaced." There is, however, a record documenting an arrest, on February 27, 1939, when Dolly was arraigned in Hudson Special Sessions Court for performing another illegal surgery. She pleaded no contest before Judge Lewis B. Eastmead.

"I know that Dolly was ashamed when she was arrested, but angry as hell," said the daughter of a friend of hers still living in Hoboken. "She honestly didn't think she was doing anything wrong. She told my aunt, 'Jesus Christ, what is wrong with this town? What's the big deal? What's the problem?' I know that she and Frankie had a row about this. I heard she slapped him hard. She was angry with him. She became passionate when talking about these operations. She thought she was doing the right thing, that there were too many hungry, unwanted kids in Hoboken as it was."

That Dolly Sinatra was able to avoid jail after her arrest and still perform surgeries to terminate unwanted pregnancies in spite of her probation spoke of the power she wielded in her community. Today, Hoboken residents who remember her—and the offspring of those who are no longer around—speak of her with a sort of awed fascination. Not only was she able to successfully defy legal, religious, and social conventions by running a bar that sold liquor during Prohibition, but she also scoffed at the law by performing illegal abortions. She was nothing if not unique.

With her political clout, she was a force to be reckoned with in the neighborhood. By flouting legal and religious standards, she demonstrated to any of the seventy thousand Hobokenites who took notice that she was one of the most powerful women, indeed one of the most influential Italians, in the city. Just as her son would become years later, she was practically a *padrone*.

"People became scared to death of her," said another former Hoboken resident. "How did she do it? they wondered. She began to change from a woman who was beloved in the neighborhood to one who was greatly feared. They would point at her and whisper. And to her, well, that was just fine. To her, that just meant they were paying attention, they were respecting her. 'They think I'm a hero,' she would say proudly. 'Well, maybe I am. Maybe I am.' It never occurred to her that some of them may have been pointing because they thought she was a criminal. It was astonishing, really, what she got away with. However, Frank sometimes suffered as a result."

When one of Frank's girlfriends at the time, Marion Brush Schreiber, tried to get him a job at a Friday night dance at Our Lady of Grace School, she remembered, "the Irish Catholics wouldn't let him in because of the scandals involving his mother. They would have nothing to do with him. When he found this out, he went into one of his terrible moods," Schreiber recalled. "He'd get real sullen and sour, and you couldn't get a word out of him. There were no tantrums. Just an ugly silence that could sometimes last for hours." Said the former Hoboken resident, "It was hard on Frankie, but he loved his mother, and that was the end of it. She could do no wrong in his eyes, no matter what she did.

"Once, a guy came up to him in a bar and made a crack about his mom. He was drunk, or he never would have said it. Few people ever actually spoke ill of Dolly in public," she recalled, "just secretly amongst themselves in whispers. Frankie was all over that guy, punching and kicking him. They had to pull Frankie off him.

"There was blood all over the floor. 'I don't give a shit what you say about me,' he said as they were throwing him out of the place, 'but don't eva, *eva* talk about my ma like that. *Eva!*"

"Let Frankie In"

*I*n 1938, twenty-two-year-old Frank Sinatra was young, handsome, charming, and, as a result of his bravado, able to have sex with virtually any young woman he set his sights on. He had a girlfriend, but what he did on the side had nothing to do with Nancy, as far as he was concerned. He would always be good at compartmentalizing his life in that regard. Most of his dalliances were with women she'd never become aware of anyway, at least not at this stage of their relationship.

"He had more broads around than you ever saw," said saxophonist Harry Schuchman, who helped Frank get his audition at the Rustic Cabin. "I used to sit there and watch the gals with Frank and think, 'What do they see in him? He's such a skinny little guy.'"

With a laugh, Joey D'Orazio added, "The older he got, he didn't get any more good-looking, I'll say that much for him. He was a skinny guy, ordinary-looking, gawky, his Adam's apple protruded, and his ears stuck out. But he had more charisma and magnetism than anyone around. The broads—they swarmed all over him whenever he got offstage after a performance. He'd actually tie them to the bed and make love to them, man! They let him do that! No one did that kind of stuff in the thirties in Hoboken, no one I ever knew, anyway."

"All I know is that he could get all the tail he wanted," Fred Tamburro of the Hoboken Four once said. "Part of it had to do with him being a singer. The girls, they liked that. This guy had an appetite for sex like no one I ever knew. He would screw a snake if he could hold it still long enough."

"Yes, you could say he had sex on the brain," said Nancy Venturi, one woman who dated Frank at this time. "He would make love to any girl who came along, as I remember it. There was something intense about his lovemaking, at least it was with me. He was extremely erotic, sexy, an intense kisser. I'm an old woman now, but yes, I remember it, all of it."

"Jesus, Frankie, you sure like having sex, don't you?" Nancy recalled having asked him on their first date, just after he had finished pawing at her on her parents' couch.

Frank was taken aback. "Sex is something I can do myself, baby," he told her. "In fact, I do it every day, all by myself, you know, *that* kind of sex. But what I want is to make love to you in a way you'll never forget. So c'mon, let Frankie in," he said as he unzipped her dress. "Let me love you, baby. Let big Frankie in."

"Well, that just took my breath away," Nancy Venturi recalled. "Oh, my God, he had me. This was 1938; guys in our neighborhood didn't talk like that. They didn't know how to sweet-talk a girl, but Frankie did. He wasn't a love-'em, leave-'em type, either. He'd stay the night, or at least slip out early in the morning, before my parents awakened. I felt loved. But I was thirteen, even though I looked maybe eighteen. So what the hell did I know about love?

"One night, when we had sex, just as he reached *that moment*, he whispered in my ear, 'I love you, Nancy.' I was thrilled. My heart was beating out of my little chest.

"The next day I told one of my girlfriends about it. She said, 'You fool. His girlfriend's name is also Nancy!' I suddenly knew he meant *her*, not me. So I called him and said we could never see each other again. I was getting so hooked on him, I was afraid I would get hurt."

Frank's reaction to Nancy's telephone call? "Okay, baby. If that's the way you want it. See ya 'round," he said. "Think of me the next time you have *that* kind of sex."

Three months later, Nancy Venturi thought she was pregnant. "I was upset," she said. "I was just a kid, thirteen! Frankie was the only boy I'd ever let touch me. So I called him in tears and said, 'Oh my God, Frankie, I think I'm pregnant.' He said, 'Oh no. That ain't good.'"

"What are we gonna do?" Nancy asked, bewildered.

"I dunno. What do you want to do?" Frank asked.

"Pray, I guess," she suggested. "Will you go to church with me?"

"Sure, if that's what you want," Frank agreed. "But I'm thinkin' we should maybe think of something better." Then, as a second thought, he added, "Okay, maybe you're right. Maybe we should pray that Dolly doesn't beat the crap outta me."

Years later, Nancy recalled, "There was a church on Seventh and Jefferson. Frankie and I went there, and we knelt in front of the altar. He closed his eyes, bowed his head, and said, 'God, you know what? If this girl here is pregnant, I'm in big trouble with Ma, and I don't need no aggravation right now. So c'mon, God, gimme a break, will ya? Make her not be pregnant. Okay? So, uh…thanks a lot, God, and…uh. That's it. So…uh…amen, all right?'

"I turned to him and said, 'Frankie, what the heck kind of prayer is that?'

"And he got mad. He said, 'What the hell you want outta me, Nancy? Jesus Christ! That's the best prayer I can come up with on such short notice. You're the one who dragged me down here, and now you expect me to be a *priest*? If you wanna add somethin', go 'head.' Then Frank motioned to the crucifix. 'I'm sure he's still listenin'. Go *'head!*'

"I thought a lightning bolt was going to strike us both down before we even got out of that church, the way he talked. I said, 'Oh my God! Let's just get outta here. Quick.'"

While Frank's prayer may not have been the most eloquent, it appeared to have done the trick, because the next morning Nancy Venturi had what she called her "monthly."

"I called Frankie and said, 'It worked! I ain't pregnant,'" she remembered. "And he said, 'Well, there you go, Nancy. Next time, don't be questioning my prayers.' We were about to hang up when he said, 'If you need me to perform any other miracles, just call me.'"

Toni

In 1938, Frank turned twenty-three and Nancy twenty-one. They were engaged and enjoying what Nancy thought was a committed relationship. He was keeping his flings well hidden, but then he met an attractive older brunette named Toni Francke (Antoinette Della Penta Francke), from Lodi, New Jersey. Like the others, it was supposed to just be physical, but Toni got swept away by it. She felt more strongly about Frank than he did about her, and she made sure he knew it. "I love you, Frankie. I think we should get married," she told him one day.

"Whad'ya, crazy?" Frank asked. "That ain't part of the deal at all!"

Frank went a little further with Toni than he had his other girls, bringing his parents to Lodi for a macaroni dinner with her family. This was new. From the outset, Dolly didn't like Toni, mostly because she lived in Lodi, where, as far as Dolly was concerned, only the lowly resided. After the Sinatras got back to Hoboken, Dolly called Toni "cheap trash." However, Frank was never one to make distinctions about social class, and it was a subject about which he and Dolly constantly argued. "But this girl is trouble, mark my words," Dolly told him. "Something's not right about her. She's got a crazy look in her eye. She's too serious about you, too. What are you gonna do about Nancy?"

"Nothin'," Frank said. "This don't got nothin' to do with her."

Dolly couldn't even finish the conversation, she was so appalled. She stormed from the room. Frank was somewhat influenced by his mother's concern, because soon after, he stopped calling Toni. Though she pestered him for weeks, even telling him that she was pregnant, he was finished with her. Duly rejected, Toni took the "scorned woman" routine to new and novel heights: She actually had Frank arrested! The cops came and cuffed him after his midnight performance at the Rustic Cabin on December 22, 1938. The curious charge: "breach of promise."

In her complaint, Toni claimed that Frank, "being then and there a single man over the age of eighteen years, under the promise of marriage, did then and there have sexual intercourse with the said complainant [on November 2 and 9] who was then and there a single female of good repute of chastity whereby she became pregnant."

Most of what Francke charged in her complaint was either suspect or fabricated. For instance, she claimed that Frank gave her a diamond ring, which was unlikely, given the state of his finances at the time. Toni also insisted that she and Nancy Barbato had a brawl at the Rustic Cabin over Frank, yet she and Nancy had never met. Furthermore, she claimed that Frank told her he had to marry Nancy "or her father will kill me because she's pregnant." Nancy was not pregnant; she did not give birth to their first child until 1940. Of course, it's always possible that Frank might have told Toni that Nancy was expecting.

The problem, though, was that Toni Francke *was* pregnant, and this time Frank wasn't able to perform one of his little "miracles." He wasn't sure it was his baby, claiming that Francke had been with many other men. But he still had to spend sixteen hours in the Bergen County jail; the mug shot survives.

"He was plenty pissed off," said Joey D'Orazio. "He called me up the next day and said, 'That broad is crazy. We went out for pasta fagioli, had a good time, went back to her place, and hit the sheets. So what? Next thing I know, this dame is tellin' me she's pregnant and I'm in the slammer. Like I'm the only guy she ever did it with. I didn't even have a good time with her!'"

The charges against Sinatra were dropped when it was learned that Francke was actually married at the time of her rendezvous with Frank. Undaunted, Francke then filed a new complaint on December 22 charging Frank with having committed adultery. "She's got some nerve, that one," Frank said. "She was the one committing adultery! I didn't even know she was married!" That complaint also was eventually dismissed.

"It was a big mess, Frank and this girl, Toni," said Salvatore Donato, an acquaintance of the Sinatra family's at the time. "She ended up having a miscarriage in her third month. There was a lot of screaming and hollering in the Sinatra household over that nut job, believe you me."

Shortly after the complaint was dismissed, Toni went to the Sinatra home and got into a dispute with Dolly when Dolly refused to apologize for Frank's behavior. Dolly tricked Toni into going down to the cellar with her—"We can talk about this down there so Marty don't hear"—then quickly ran back up the stairs and locked the door. "*Call the police*," she told Marty. "I just locked that crazy broad in the cellar!" When the authorities arrived, they arrested Toni and charged her with disorderly conduct. She was eventually given a suspended sentence.

For twenty-three-year-old Frank, the local publicity he received was unwelcome. "Songbird Held in Morals Charge" read the headline in the *Hudson Dispatch* on December 23, 1938. This would be his first introduction to the intrusion of the media into his private life, and he didn't much like it. Joey D'Orazio recalled, "He called up someone at the newspaper and said, 'I'm comin' down there and I'm gonna beat your brains out, you hear me? I'm gonna kill you and anyone else who had anything to do with that article. And by the way, I ain't no songbird, you idiot. A dame, *that's* a songbird.'"

Frank and Nancy Marry

Of course, Toni Francke wasn't the only woman with whom the young Frank Sinatra was cavorting in 1938—she just happened to come forward. It worried Nancy. "I don't know that he can be true to me," she told Dolly at the time. Dolly liked Nancy and wanted to encourage her relationship with Frank because she thought marriage might tame him. She told her to be patient with her son and assured her that when she was his wife she wouldn't have to worry about this kind of behavior. "She told my mother, 'Frankie found a girl I like,'" said the daughter of a friend of Dolly's. "'She's no whore, at least. So that's a good thing. Frankie's had too many whores. But this girl, Nancy, she'd better watch him. My little son of a bitch son is gonna give her trouble.'"

Dolly and Nancy knew in their hearts he would never be faithful.

Most of the married Italian men they had known believed that what they did on their own time was their own business. It's not known if Marty had ever been unfaithful to Dolly, but it probably wouldn't have surprised her if he had. For Nancy's part, she knew her father cheated on her mother—for women in their world, that was just the way things were.

Nancy had no idea Frank was being unfaithful to her until the night he was arrested. By this time they'd been intimate, and for Nancy, a Catholic, it was a major step in a relationship. She assumed that their lovemaking meant that she belonged to Frank and vice versa. That's why she agreed to marry him. However, his actions with Toni suggested otherwise.

Having so completely trusted him, when Nancy learned of the affair with Toni she was not only deeply hurt but disillusioned. Her mother had looked the other way, but Nancy was determined that this kind of behavior would not mar her own marriage. She and Frank had a number of emotional scenes regarding Toni, until finally she made him "swear to God" that he would never be unfaithful to her again.

"Was she the first woman you've been with since we've been together?" Nancy finally asked Frank through her tears.

"No," Frank said. "But she's the last."

Frank didn't want to lose Nancy. She was someone on whom he could depend completely; she was very supportive of his aspirations even when it looked as though he would never make money as a singer and even when his parents had lost patience with his choice of career. While he felt bad about the Toni Francke incident, he still convinced himself it had nothing to do with Nancy. But he assured her that such a thing would never again occur.

Frank was so sweet and gentle with her, and he seemed so genuinely contrite about what had happened with Toni, that she agreed to go through with the wedding plans.

Frank and Nancy were married on February 4, 1939, at Our Lady of Sorrow Church in Jersey City. Monsignor Monteleon performed the ceremony. Twenty-one-year-old Nancy wore a simple, full-length white taffeta gown with a deep neckline and short train. On her head she placed a coronet of white fabric trimmed with pearls, with a three-quarter-length veil. She wore white satin open-toed shoes. Twenty-three-year-old Frank appeared in a cutaway tuxedo with black-and-gray pinstriped pants and a matching silk tie. He wore a white flower in his lapel.

Nancy once remarked, "Frank gave me his own sentimental wedding present—a bag of jelly beans with a diamond watch inside. When the big day finally came, there were maybe fifty members of the family on each side of the aisle. They had all given us furniture for our new apartment. I was wearing my sister's wedding dress, and the ring—a gold band with a cluster of diamonds—had been his mother's. I don't think I'd ever seen Frank so happy in his whole life."

"Yous have a long life," Dolly said in a wine toast later at her home during a small reception for a few friends and family members. For a first course, Dolly served pasta fagioli, the same meal Frank said got him into trouble with Toni Francke. He decided not to have any of it. Instead, he sat and waited for the homemade gnocchi. "Nobody makes gnocchi like Ma," he boasted. "I just hope she gives Nancy the recipe." There was also a reception at Nancy's family's home on Arlington Avenue in Jersey City; wine and sandwiches were served.

Because the newlyweds couldn't afford a honeymoon, they immediately moved into a small apartment in Jersey City, which they rented for forty-two dollars a month. It would be completely furnished with wedding presents from relatives. Frank then resumed his fledgling career, and Nancy went to work as a secretary at American Type Founders in Elizabeth, New Jersey.

Part Two

FIRST BLUSH OF SUCCESS

Harry James

Without Nancy's support, it would have been difficult for Frank to continue in the entertainment business. If he got lucky, he might have made it without her—he was talented and determined—but with a supportive wife at his side, he had the kind of morale booster he needed to face the rejection and disappointment that often come before success.

Frank felt certain that if he could get a job with Harry James's band as a vocalist, his struggles would be over. (He had spent a short time with the Bob Chester band in early 1939, but not even his closest followers can remember for how long, so it must not have made much of an impression on anyone. It was probably just a few performances at the New Yorker Hotel.) Nancy took a fifteen-dollar advance on her salary so that Frank could have publicity photos taken in order to give them to trumpeter James, who had recently left the Benny Goodman band to front his own ensemble.

At this time, the big-band sound was an art form completely unique to America. Lasting roughly from the end of the Great Depression until the end of World War II, this exciting era in popular music generated some of the most memorable music in the country's history. Fronting such a band was every struggling vocalist's great ambition.

Frank had a friend give the new photos to Harry James, and soon after, James went to the Rustic Cabin to see him perform. As he later defined it, Harry was impressed with "Frank's way of talking a lyric."

As it happened, James was auditioning vocalists at the Lincoln Hotel in New York. While all of the other singers were weighed down with stacks of arrangements, Frank showed up with nothing but a cocky grin on his face. He sauntered over to the piano player, told him what he wanted to sing and in what key...and then he sang. "They were auditioning a lot of people that day," said musician Arthur "Skeets" Herfurt, "but the musicians said that when they heard Sinatra, that was it. There was no doubt about it."

On June 30, 1939, Frank made his debut with the Harry James Band (also billed as Harry James and His Music Makers)—which itself was just three months old—at the Hippodrome Theatre in Baltimore performing "Wishing" and "My Love for You." For the rest of the summer and into the fall, the band toured to enthusiastic audiences. Frank would remember those days fondly.

"The kid's name is Sinatra," Harry James told one inquiring reporter. (Harry reportedly wanted to change Frank's name to Frankie Satin. Sinatra refused.) "He considers himself the greatest vocalist in the business. Get that! No one's ever heard of him. He's never had a hit record. He looks like a wet rag. But he says he is the greatest. If he hears you compliment him," James said, perhaps only half joking, "he'll demand a raise tonight."

Arranger Billy May, who would go on to work on many of Frank's most memorable songs, met him at this time. He said, "I thought he was a good singer. But the musicians in Harry's band had the opinion that he was a smart-ass Italian kid."

"I was young and full of zip, zap, and zing," Frank remembered in 1965, "and I was also full of myself."

Night after night on the road—on trains, by automobile caravan, via buses—performing in small, dingy clubs or large halls with terrible acoustics, Frank, with his hair in a floppy pompadour, was never happier—he was singing and being paid for it. Nancy went along on this early tour and the two were together around the clock, blissful in their new marriage. Nancy would one day reflect on those years as being the happiest in their relationship. As her husband performed his love songs onstage in his dapper suit, she would watch dreamily from the wings, almost as if she were falling more in love with him with each performance. "He's so wonderful," she would say. "How did I get so lucky?"

Young women would wait for Frank after the show, hoping he would pay attention to them. "I'm married," he would say. "My wife'll kill me if I even look at yous."

There was little money. Sometimes nightclub owners didn't pay the full amount that had been promised. Band and crew ate fried onion sandwiches much of the time. Nancy would prepare an entire meal of hamburger, spinach, and mashed potatoes for four people (herself, Frank, and the band's arranger and drummer) with a dollar. If they could find some capicola at a local butcher shop for "sangwiches," their day was made. They redeemed soda bottles for the return of cash deposits. It was a difficult time in many respects, but Frank and Nancy were happy just the same. When they learned that Nancy was pregnant, they were elated.

That same year, Frank recorded his earliest songs with the Harry James Band. The very first was on July 13 in New York, where they were appearing at the time at the Roseland Ballroom. The 78 rpm record, "From the Bottom of My Heart," backed by "Melancholy Mood," was issued on the Brunswick label. Then, on August 31, the James band recorded "All or Nothing at All," with a vocal refrain by Frank Sinatra. Sinatra would go on to record the song three more times over the years, but the original version is the most effective rendition. After recording a few more memorable songs with Harry James, on November 8, Frank recorded his last two: "Ciribiribin," which was James's theme song, and "Every Day of My Life."

Artistically, Frank's association with the Harry James Band was an unqualified success. He benefited tremendously from James's example of showmanship and artistry, but commercially he wanted more. Business at the box office was sluggish. During one gig at Victor Hugo's in Beverly Hills, the band was interrupted by the owner, who stopped the show in the middle of one of Frank's numbers. He was frustrated because so few people had shown up in the audience. The performers didn't even get paid for that particular engagement.

Frank was ready to move on.

While playing the Hotel Sherman in Chicago, the James band appeared in a benefit show for the musicians' union with other popular groups at the time, including the Tommy Dorsey Orchestra, one of the most popular in the country. Dorsey, known at the time as "the Sentimental Gentleman of Swing," had his eye on Frank and wanted to hire him to replace his vocalist, Jack Leonard. It would pay about seventy-five dollars a weekend and it would be a long-term contract.

Frank was thunderstruck, mostly because he had once auditioned for Dorsey with disastrous results. He had been so awed by Dorsey's presence at that tryout, he couldn't even sing. "I could only mouth air," he remembered. "Not a sound came out. It was terrible."

But that was then. Now Sinatra was more polished and experienced. He had proved himself with Harry James and he wanted the job. And with Nancy pregnant and the James band not doing very well commercially, Frank knew he had to leave Harry.

Luckily for Frank, Harry James was understanding, telling him that if he truly believed that the Dorsey band provided a better opportunity for him, then he should take advantage of it. Technically, he didn't have to let Frank go; he still had seventeen months on his contract. James later told radio interviewer Fred Hall, "Nancy was pregnant and we weren't even making enough money to pay Frank the seventy-five dollars he was supposed to get. So he wanted to go with Tommy Dorsey, and I said, 'Well, if we don't do any better in the next six months or so, try to get me a job too!'"

Harry James always believed that Frank Sinatra would be a star; there was never any question in his mind about it. He was gracious enough to let Frank go without a fuss, and for that Frank would always be grateful. (Frank was replaced in James's band by Dick Haymes.)

Still, it was difficult for the loyalist in Frank to leave the man who had given him his first big break. He felt a strong allegiance to James, who had become like a brother to him. He once recalled the final night with James's band, after their show at the Shea Theatre in Buffalo in January 1940: "The bus pulled out with the rest of the boys [on their way to the next tour stop, Hartford, Connecticut] at about half past midnight. I'd said goodbye to them all, and it was snowing, I remember. There was nobody around, and I stood alone with my suitcase in the snow and watched the taillights disappear. Then the tears started, and I tried to run after the bus. I figured to myself, I ain't never gonna make it . . . There was such spirit and enthusiasm in that band. I hated leaving it."

Frank and Harry would again collaborate on July 19, 1951, at Columbia Records for three songs: "Castle Rock," "Deep Night," and "Farewell, Farewell to Love." They would also sometimes appear in concerts together in the years to come, most notably at Caesars Palace in 1968 and 1979. They also appeared together on a John Denver special in 1976 and performed an excellent rendition of their song "All or Nothing at All."

Harry James died in July 1983 of lymphatic cancer. He worked up until a week before his death.

Tommy Dorsey

When Tommy Dorsey finally explained the preposterous terms of Frank Sinatra's contract, Frank was stunned. The deal Dorsey thought was equitable would mean that Frank would give up a third of his earnings *for life*, plus 10 percent for Tommy Dorsey's agent. A total of 43 percent of every dime Frank was to make for the rest of his career would go to Tommy Dorsey (after the original two-year term of their contract had expired, for which Frank would make seventy-five dollars a week, though that sum would soon be doubled). Maybe Frank put it best when he said, "Dorsey was a crook. Plain and simple."

Frank decided to accept Tommy's terms, though he realized that the deal was terribly unfair. He wasn't thinking of any future ramifications it might have; he just wanted to sing and be famous. He also knew that Dorsey had auditioned baritone Allan DeWitt for the position. Even though DeWitt didn't work out, the competition served to remind Frank that there were other men in the business willing to accept such a dreadful contract just for the opportunity to work with Tommy Dorsey. (Indeed, many young singers throughout the history of entertainment have signed deals as bad, but probably none worse.)

The onerous terms of his deal aside, the future looked bright for twenty-four-year-old Frank Sinatra as he took his place on the bandstand in front of Tommy Dorsey's orchestra in January 1940. The band was in the midst of a tour and the group's manager sent Frank a ticket to join them. At this time, the Dorsey organization boasted a memorable lineup of musicians that included Buddy Rich,

Bunny Berrigan, Joe Bushkin, and Ziggy Elman; arrangers such as Axel Stordahl, Paul Weston, and Sy Oliver; and singers Jo Stafford and the Pied Pipers—and now Frank Sinatra. Because it was so long ago, there is some discrepancy as to exactly where Frank actually joined the Dorsey orchestra. Dorsey's press agent, Jack Egan, and Sinatra's daughter Nancy insist it was in Indianapolis (at the Lyric Theatre on February 2). But Dorsey's clarinetist, Johnny Mince, believes it was in Sheboygan, Wisconsin. Others, like Jo Stafford, say it was either Minneapolis or Milwaukee. Frank himself said it was Baltimore, memorable to him because it occurred after he played twenty-seven innings of softball with his bandmates.

"It was like going from one school to another," Frank remembered. "I was really kind of frightened. I was nervous, but I faked a couple of tunes, and I knew the lyrics of some songs, so we did all right with the audience."

It wasn't an easy transition for Frank—or even for the other musicians—when he took over as the male singer with the band. Because he was so cocky, the band disliked him immediately. Some of them mocked him by calling him "Lady Macbeth" due to his obsession with cleanliness. Still, no matter what they said about him, they couldn't help but be awed by his sheer talent.

Of Frank's early performances with the band, singer Jo Stafford, who joined about a month before Frank, said, "[Sinatra] was very young [with a] slim figure and more hair than he needed. We were all sitting back, like, 'Oh, yeah? Who are you?' Then he began to sing. Wow, I thought, this is an absolutely new, unique sound. Nobody had ever sounded like that. In those days, most male singers' biggest thing was to try and sound as much like Bing Crosby as possible. Well, he didn't sound anything like Bing. He didn't sound like anybody else that I had ever heard. I was mightily impressed."

The show would usually start with the band playing Dorsey's theme song, "I'm Getting Sentimental Over You," followed by the hit "Marie." Then Dorsey would introduce Connie Haines for a number or two, followed by Jo Stafford and the Pied Pipers. After that, Ziggy Elman would do a trumpet solo, and then drummer Buddy Rich would, as they say, "take it home." Finally, Frank would sing a big number, maybe "South of the Border." He would also do perky duets with Connie Haines, such as "Let's Get Away from It All" and "Oh, Look at Me Now." Of course, the show would vary over the years, and as Frank became more popular, he would be featured much more frequently.

The band traveled by bus, as most bands did at the time. They were difficult days, but rewarding. "What can I say?" Frank reminisced. "For six months, the band gave me the cold shoulder—they loved Jack Leonard—until I proved myself. Finally, I did, and we became a unit. We worked damn hard, city after city. Just trying to get along, you know, learning about each other, learning about the road, trying to be entertaining. It was a good time. I missed my family, though. Missed Nancy. She was pregnant, so it was tough."

On February 1, 1940, Frank recorded his first two songs with Tommy Dorsey's band, "The Sky Fell Down" and "Too Romantic." Then it was back on the road, to Indiana, Michigan, New Jersey, and New York City. In New York the band appeared at the Paramount Theatre from mid-March into mid-April. Then, on May 23, 1940, Frank, the Pied Pipers, and Tommy Dorsey and his orchestra recorded "I'll Never Smile Again."

With the war raging in Europe and threatening to involve the United States, "I'll Never Smile Again" seemed to typify the kind of rueful resignation that would soon envelop the world. The record, with a plaintive delivery by Sinatra and elegant harmony by the Pied Pipers, would become his first big hit, and would hold the number one position on Billboard's charts for twelve consecutive weeks. Frank would go on to perform this classic song for the next forty years, on television and in concert.* "I got ten dollars for recording it," said Connie Haines. "Frank got twenty-five."

Frank's career would never be the same after "I'll Never Smile Again." That record catapulted him to stardom and gave him top

---

* Frank would also record this wonderful song for Capitol Records on May 14, 1959 (for the No One Cares album), and for Reprise on October 11, 1965 (available on A Man and His Music). There is also a recording of the song from April 23, 1940. However, it is not known whether or not that version of the song was actually issued. Sinatra historians insist it was not.

billing in the band, much to the chagrin of drummer Buddy Rich. In fact, a rivalry between the two erupted into physical altercations on more than one occasion. Because his ego was rising as fast as the record rose on the charts, Frank's relationship with the other band vocalist, Connie Haines, began to deteriorate as well. He refused to share a mike with her—though he was forced to do so at times— calling her a "cornball." Ultimately, he found himself suspended for two weeks as a result of disagreements with her. Clearly, Frank—a man not given to compromise and cooperation—didn't belong in a group environment. He never cared for either Rich or Haines and told his friends that he despised "the both of 'em." (In October 1944, though, after Frank Sinatra became famous, Buddy Rich went to visit him backstage at the Paramount Theatre and mentioned that he wanted to start his own band. Frank wrote a check for $40,000 and handed it to the startled drummer. "Good luck. This'll get you started," Frank said with a slap to Rich's back.)

Harry James's road manager, George A. "Bullets" Durgom, noted at the time, "This boy's going to be very big if Tommy doesn't kill him first. Tommy doesn't like Frankie stealing the show, and he doesn't like people who are temperamental, like himself."

Broadway columnist and noted Sinatra biographer Earl Wilson went to see Frank perform around this time at the Meadowbrook Ballroom in Meadowbrook, New Jersey. Afterward, Wilson interviewed the singer. Of the experience, he remarked, "He spoke of his dreams and ambitions and said he was going to be the biggest star in the country. 'You'll see,' he said. Physically, he was less than impressive. The Sinatra frame was not only slender but fragile looking. The cheeks were hollow. He wore a bow tie, a thin wool sweater, and a dark suit. He seemed still a boy, and that added a charm to his cockiness. He had a lot of hair that straggled down the upper part of his right cheek, about to the bottom of his ear. He also had a spit curl. His hair, when he came offstage, was tousled looking. 'Sexy,' the girls said later."

Self-Invention

On June 8, 1940, Nancy Sinatra gave birth to the couple's first child, Nancy Jr., at Margaret Hague Maternity Hospital in Jersey City. Her husband of eighteen months wasn't at her side. "I was working the Hotel Astor in New York, I believe," Frank said later. "I hated missing that. I did. It was just a taste of things to come, man. When I think of all the family affairs and events I would miss over the years because I was on the road. But this was really the first one." Tommy Dorsey had been such a mentor to Sinatra that Frank chose him to be godfather of his firstborn.

Later that month, NBC hired the band to take over for Bob Hope on a summer-replacement variety show, Frank's first national radio exposure. Because the ratings were strong, the network began airing a Dorsey series, *Summer Pastime*, on Tuesday nights. It ran for three and a half months and further exposed Frank to a large listening audience.

In an article he wrote for *Life* in 1965, Frank remembered that these days with the Dorsey band were some of the most influential on his singing style. Tommy didn't work much with him, he remembered, because most of his attention was on the band members. Left to his own devices, Frank absorbed everything around him—including the way Dorsey played trombone—and tried to integrate it into his artistry.

As it happened, Tommy Dorsey could play a musical phrase as long as sixteen bars all the way through, it seemed, without taking a single breath. "How the hell does he do that?" Frank had wondered even before he joined the band. He knew that if he could sustain a note as long, he would be able to sing with much more dramatic impact. (He also believed that many singers ruined their songs by taking breaths in the wrong places, thereby interfering with the melody as well as the lyric's message.)

Sinatra would sit behind Dorsey on the bandstand and watch him closely, trying to see if he would sneak in a breath. Finally, after many dates, Frank realized that Dorsey had what he called "a sneak pinhole in the corner of his mouth." It wasn't an actual pinhole, of course, but rather a tiny place where Dorsey was sucking in air. It was Frank's idea to make his voice work in the same way, not sounding like a specific instrument but "playing" the voice as if it *were* an instrument.

He realized that in order to do this—to sustain those notes in a seamless fashion—he would need extraordinary breath control. To that end, he began an intense swimming regimen in public pools, which he would find in cities on tour. As he held his breath and took laps underwater, he would sing song lyrics in his head and approximate the time he would need to sustain certain notes.

When he was back in Hoboken, Frank would continue his training by running on the track at the Stevens Institute of Technology. He would run one lap and trot the next, singing to himself, holding notes, practicing.

"But that still wasn't the whole answer," he remembered. "I still had to learn to sneak a breath without being too obvious."

Indeed, it was easier for Tommy Dorsey to camouflage his breathing technique through his "pinhole" while he was playing the trombone because the mouthpiece covered his mouth. For Frank, this would mean more work, more training. Eventually it paid off. Because his breath control had become so powerful, he was able to sing six bars—sometimes eight—without taking in air. Other singers were lucky to be able to sing two or four. Frank had learned to sneak in air from the sides of his mouth, making it appear that he could sing forever without taking a breath. When he did decide to take that breath, he would do it in as dramatic a fashion as possible, effecting a gasp of anguish when he needed it, when it suited the lyric of the torch song being performed.

All of this training was a closely held trade secret at the time; Frank never explained any of it until years later when he felt other singers could benefit from his experience. In the 1940s, though, he well understood that part of the magic of his art was to make it appear effortless. That it all looked so simple was just part of the illusion. "It was easy," he said later. "It just wasn't simple."

Just as he intended, his breathing technique proved as crucial in the telling of his stories as it was in the delivery of his songs. His uncanny ability as a vocalist did not go unnoticed by those in his profession. They knew he could do astonishing things with his voice;

they just didn't know how he did them. "I'd never heard a popular singer with such fluidity and style," songwriter Sammy Cahn once noted. "Or one with his incredible breath control. Frank could hold a phrase until it took him into a sort of paroxysm. He actually gasped, and his whole being seemed to explode, to release itself. I'd never seen or heard anything like it."

Frank even used a microphone and mike stand—standard equipment for amplification—in a way that was unique for the times. Most singers just stood woodenly in front of the mike and hoped that their voices would be carried to the rafters. Not Sinatra. "They never understood that a microphone is their instrument," he would say of some of his colleagues. "It's like they're part of an orchestra, but instead of playing a saxophone, they're playing a microphone."

Frank would tenderly hold the microphone stand like a considerate lover during romantic ballads or jerk it roughly if he felt he needed that kind of impact on a brassier number. He would back away from the mike when a dramatic note needed to soar to the heavens and echo, or step into it if he wanted the crowd to hear just the slightest sigh or breath. The girls would swoon in the audience when Frank was onstage, as much for his voice as for the unusual way he performed. The way he romanced a mike and mike stand was somehow erotic and became an important part of his appeal. He was just five feet ten and a half (maybe just five feet nine, depending on which family member is asked), 138 pounds, and with a twenty-nine-inch waist, but onstage he seemed like a passionate dynamo, especially when he quivered that lower lip. Paradoxically, he also seemed vulnerable, needy. The total package was irresistible.

In every way, Frank Sinatra invented the way he wanted to be, the way he saw himself, the way he wanted others to see him.

Marital Weakness

After baby Nancy was born and her mother could no longer travel with Frank, the marriage began to show some weaknesses. Frank was busy with his career, filming his first movie, *Las Vegas Nights*, in October 1940, for which he was paid a measly fifteen dollars a day to sing "I'll Never Smile Again" on camera. He played another engagement at the Paramount in New York in January 1941, and the first of twenty-nine single releases with Dorsey, "Without a Song," was recorded on January 20, 1941.

Naturally, there were other women on the road. In Frank's mind, what Nancy didn't know wouldn't hurt her.

But Nancy knew.

Patti Demarest was a friend of Nancy Sinatra's at this time; they lived in the same apartment complex on Bergen Avenue in Jersey City. She recalled, "Nancy came to my door one day in tears, the baby in her arms. I said, 'My goodness, what's the matter?' and she said, 'That son of a bitch is cheating on me again.' 'Again?' I asked, since this was the first I had heard of this. And she said, 'He's been cheating on me from the very beginning.'"

Many of Frank's friends knew his marriage was in trouble early on. "It must have been sometime in 1940," Sammy Cahn once said. "He was a restless soul even then. He told me how unhappy he was being a married man."

Joey D'Orazio, Frank's Hoboken friend, recalled, "We were sitting at a bar in Hoboken. Frank had just gotten off the road, he was visiting his ma, and he was a big shot now. I wanted to know what it was like for him, you know? He said, 'Joey boy, a chump like you will *never* know what it's like for me, that's how on top of the world I am.' I had to laugh. That was so typically Frank. Then he said, 'I can have any dame I want. That's the best part. They can't get enough of me. I snap my finger when I get off that stage, and they're at my feet, like puppies, man, lapping me up.'"

D'Orazio told Frank, "You're a married man now. You can't be doing that."

Frank threw back a scotch and water and said, "Well, I can't help myself. What can I say?"

"Bullshit," Joey said. "You *can* help yourself."

Frank slammed his glass on the bar and looked Joey straight in the eyes. "No," he said firmly. "I can't. Got that? I don't want to. And I'm not going to. So keep your mouth shut about it," he said, his tone threatening, "because I don't want to hurt Nancy. This has nothing to do with her. It's no big deal."

"Frank, it *is* a big deal," Joey insisted.

"All right, I know it's a big deal. What d'ya think, I'm stupid?" Frank said as he threw some money on the bar. "How can you understand what it's like for me? You and I, we live in different worlds now."

Then he got up and stormed angrily out of the bar. This certainly wasn't the first time Sinatra would justify his bad behavior by blaming it on the pressure of his celebrity, and it wouldn't be the last.

Nancy still loved Frank. It wasn't easy, though, because he had become so self-centered, wanting what he wanted without any thought given to the hurt it might cause her. She attempted time and time again to overlook his faults, believing that if she was just more patient and understanding he would come around. However, what actually happened was that he began to resent her for her tolerance.

"If you want to cheat on me, go right ahead, see if I care," she told him one night at a nightclub in New York. They were with friends, enjoying a night on the town in Manhattan. Frank had been flirting intensely with a cocktail waitress. He seemed somewhat taken aback by Nancy's offer.

"Who says something like that to her husband?" he asked. "That's ridiculous. Don't say that, Nancy. What's wrong with you?"

"Well what do you *want* me to say, Frank?" she said, looking him straight in the eye. "You're not gonna stop, and we both know it."

"You're not supposed to *like* it, though," he said angrily.

"I *don't* like it," she shot back. "But what am I supposed to do about it?"

"You're *supposed* to not mention it at all," Frank said as he peeled some money off a wad and threw it down at the table. "Now you've gone and made me feel bad in front of our friends. That ain't right, Nancy. That just ain't right." Once again, he stormed off.

Nancy was rattled. "Excuse me," she told her friends as she ran off to the ladies' room.

It wasn't that Frank didn't love her. He did. However, he was bored. He wanted something—someone—else. New and different excited him, not the same old Nancy. Unfortunately, as we shall see, this would prove to be a perpetual problem for him. "Simply put, he was a man who was never fully satisfied," his daughter Tina would note many years later. "He was someone who could not fully commit.

Maybe he was too self-involved to commit, I don't know. I think it's safe to say that few men of his generation were very introspective. He just was who he was; Frank, for better or worse. Take him or leave him. If you were in a relationship with him, you had to either go along with his inability to commit or jump ship. Because he was Sinatra, most people in his life were more than happy to go along with it just to be a part of his world. For a time there, my mother certainly did just that. She would readily admit as much."

Though Nancy did "go along with it," she still longed for Frank to accept the typical domestic role of husband and father and help raise a family. She well knew, though, that when he wasn't at home in New Jersey with her and the baby, he led a fast-paced, glamorous life. When he was on tour, he actually *could* have anyone he wanted.

* * *

The hysteria Frank Sinatra and the band caused on the road was surprising even to them. In fact, something unusual had occurred: Sinatra had become a sensation.

"I think that my appeal was due to the fact that there hadn't been a troubadour around for ten or twenty years, from the time that Bing had broken in and went on to radio and movies," Frank said later. "And he, strangely enough, had appealed primarily to older people, middle-aged people. When I came on the scene and people began noticing me, I think the kids were looking for someone to cheer for. I began to realize that there must be something to all this commotion. I didn't know exactly what it was, but I figured I had something that must be important."

Tommy Dorsey was astounded by the reaction of the female audience members to Frank. He knew for certain he had struck gold when he signed this singer to that ridiculous contract. He once recalled, "I used to stand there on the bandstand so amazed I'd almost forget to take my solos. You could almost feel the excitement coming up out of the crowds when that kid stood up to sing. Remember, he was no matinee idol. He was a skinny kid with big ears. And yet what he did to women was something awful."

"Maybe if I'm *more* of a woman," Nancy told Patti Demarest one night when Frank was on the road and didn't call after the show.

"Maybe I can keep him at home. Maybe if I pray to God more. That could be it. Maybe I'm not praying to God enough."

"Oh, he'll come back," Patti told her. "But you *do* have to try to be better. Make him know that you're all he needs. Lose some weight, Nancy. Buy some new clothes. Get your hair done."

Dorothy

*B*ack in October 1940—about four months after Nancy was born— while Frank was in Los Angeles with the band to perform at the Palladium and to appear in *Las Vegas Nights*, he met a striking blonde actress, mostly an extra, named Alora Gooding. Her real name was Dorothy Bonucelli; Frank knew her as Dorothy. As well as being an extra, she worked in the casinos in Nevada as a cocktail waitress and a hat check girl. She also told Frank that she knew the mobster Benjamin "Bugsy" Siegel, which intrigued him. As Frank sang "I'll Never Smile Again" in *Las Vegas Nights*, it was Dorothy who posed in front of him as the girl to whom he was singing. Her day job at the time was at the Garden of Allah hotel, as a daytime greeter. While the two flirted, she mentioned her other job, and, sure enough, the next day Frank showed up at the hotel and booked a night there. Before long, they were having an affair.

Frank became convinced that he wanted to be with Dorothy. Within a week, she had moved into his suite at the Hollywood Plaza, where the band stayed when on the West Coast.

"He was crazy about her, really in love with her," said his friend Nick Sevano. "She was his first brush with glamour, and he was mad for her."

Finally, Frank confessed to Nancy that he had fallen for another woman. Of course, she was crushed, but she was also angry. He then said he wanted out of the marriage; he wanted to be with Dorothy. Nancy wouldn't hear of it. She knew her husband. This was just another of his silly flings, she quickly decided; he'd get over it. Meanwhile, she would just have to ride this latest affair out. Frank's cheating had nothing to do with her, anyway—or at least that's what she would tell some people at the time. He had his life, she would say, and she had hers. As long as he was there for her when she needed him, all was well.

Frank was making almost $15,000 a year—decent money for the times. He was a good provider, Nancy told friends. He didn't abuse her, at least not physically. He loved his daughter, and, she felt, in his own way he also loved her. She was reaching, of course—trying to pinpoint whatever positive aspects of their relationship she could find to not only cope with his behavior but maintain her dignity in the face of it. However, those in her tight-knit circle knew the truth: Deep down, Nancy had come to believe that she simply wasn't enough for Frank. Doris Sevanto said, "Sometimes, she would say, 'It'll pass. It'll pass. I know what I'll do. I'll diet. I'll lose ten more pounds. He'll love me then.'"

Eventually, Frank told Nancy he would stop seeing Dorothy Bonucelli.

Many years later, however, the Sinatra family would learn that Frank hadn't really stopped seeing Dorothy at all. In fact, forty-four years from this time, they would learn that Dorothy had become pregnant by Frank and that she gave birth to his child—a girl she named Julie.

Dispute with Dorsey

In January 1942, *Billboard* named Frank Sinatra top band vocalist, replacing Bing Crosby. He had also moved Crosby out of the top of the *Down Beat* popularity poll, which Crosby had occupied for six years.

On January 19, Frank cut his first records without the Tommy Dorsey band for RCA's Bluebird label. Tommy wasn't very happy about the prospect of Frank working alone in the studio—and with Dorsey's arranger, Axel Stordahl—but he knew that he needed to keep the young singer happy, and Frank was eager to do some recording work on his own. Therefore, at this time, with a small, mellow band—no brass—Frank recorded "The Night We Called It a Day";

his first version of "Night and Day";* "The Song Is You"; and "The Lamplighter's Serenade."

By this time, Frank was clearly Dorsey's star attraction. The audience's reaction to him was so strong that he wanted to do more as a performer and not have to work within the confines of a band. He wanted to go solo.

"I'm gonna be the biggest singer in the business, as big as they come," he told Joey D'Orazio one day. It was a familiar refrain. He said the same thing to Sammy Cahn, among others. When Cahn agreed, telling him, "There is no way anything can get in your way," Frank was filled with a sense of empowerment. "You *do* believe, then, don't you?" he said to Cahn, excitedly grabbing his arm. Certainly Frank believed in his own potential. But he became even more excited when he was able to convince others, and with his prodigious talent that wasn't difficult to do.

"Frank was making secret plans to strike out on his own," Hank Sanicola once said. "He wanted to be bigger, better. He didn't want to be Dorsey's boy any longer. Columbia Records was interested in him. People were talking about him. But none of this was anything Tommy wanted to hear. He wanted his band members to just stay with him for life."

Frank had learned a lot from Tommy Dorsey, just as he had from Harry James. From Dorsey, Sinatra began to fully understand that a vocalist doesn't necessarily have to sing a song the same way every time he performs it, though that was what most singers did at the time. Dorsey taught Sinatra to personalize a melody so that it was unique to the moment, yet still familiar to fans. Dorsey's tip to inter-

---

* It's noteworthy that Sinatra would return again and again over his recording career to the early numbers he'd sung, and each new version presented new insights, reappraisals, and artistic growth. Much of his later Capitol repertoire repeated that of Columbia, sometimes in similar arrangements, but the Capitol versions achieved a depth of artistry and feeling that those of Columbia only foreshadowed. Though much of Sinatra's recording repertoire consisted of remakes, in fact he was never known as a remake artist. He could literally fashion new songs out of old ones, as he did with "Night and Day," which he recorded seven times between 1942 and 1977.

pret a lyric as the mood struck—to improvise and not stick solely to the written melody—went a long way toward making each of Frank's performances interesting not only to his audience, but also to himself. Indeed, Tommy Dorsey's influence would definitely inform the final creation of Frank Sinatra as a unique artist.

Frank had also made some fine records with Tommy, including "Pale Moon," "Oh, Look at Me Now," and "Blue Skies." However, it was time for him to move on.

In early 1942, while the two were in a dressing room in Washington, twenty-six-year-old Frank told Tommy he was leaving the band. "I'm ready to go. I want to leave the orchestra," Frank recalled telling him. Dorsey, always the taskmaster, looked at him with the indifference of a schoolteacher who had heard it all before from his students. "What for?" he said. "You know you're doing great with the band, and we've got a lot of arrangements for you."

"I know that, Tommy," Frank said. "But it's time for me to go out on my own. I want to give you a full year's notice. I think that's fair."

"Well, I don't think so," Dorsey said dismissively, looking down at his sheet music. "I don't think so at all."

Frank was not dissuaded. "Well, I'm leaving," he said. "I just thought you should know. I think you might want to consider Dick Haymes. He's a helluva singer."

"Listen, you've got a contract," Tommy said, becoming angry.

"Well, I had one with Harry too," Frank said naively. "And he took it and tore it up."

"I'm not Harry," Tommy shot back.

"Again, I'm giving you a year's notice," Frank said before leaving. "This time next year, I'm leaving."

From that time on, Tommy only spoke to Frank when absolutely necessary. Frank wasn't the least bit concerned about Dorsey's attitude, though; he was busy planning his new career, contacting promoters, booking agents, and others in the entertainment industry who he knew would be able to assist him when the time was right. He was also taking diction classes with instructor John Quinlan in New York in an ultimately futile attempt to lose his New Jersey accent.

However, he would learn to enunciate perfectly when performing. Frank was driven and would do whatever he felt he had to in order to make it in the competitive record business.

Through Tommy Dorsey's road manager, George A. "Bullets" Durgom, Frank would meet and befriend Emmanuel "Manie" Sacks, a recording executive from Columbia. Sacks, the head of Columbia's artists and repertoire (A&R) division, believed he could make additional contacts for Frank in the industry and possibly even sign him to Columbia. (At the time, Frank was still under contract to RCA because of his arrangement with Dorsey.) Manie, a charming man who would make a big imprint on the music industry, would go on to become one of Frank's dearest friends.

Frustrated by Frank's determination to leave the band despite his opposition, Tommy finally agreed to let him go. However, he told him that the contract—which by now Frank referred to as "a ratty piece of paper"—would remain in effect. He fully expected a third of Sinatra's income for the rest of Frank's life, plus 10 percent for his agent. He didn't care that people who heard about this arrangement thought he was a crook.

Frank decided he would deal with Tommy on the matter of the contract later. The first order of business would be to leave the band before Dorsey changed his mind.

Frank performed his last concert with Tommy Dorsey at the Circle Theater in Indianapolis on September 3, 1942. Sinatra introduced his replacement that evening, Dick Haymes, who would stay with Dorsey for only six months before embarking on his own solo career.

Many band singers, such as Ginny Simms, Ray Eberle, and Jack Leonard, failed to make the transition from dance band to center stage. That didn't worry Frank. After all, he realized that they were just vocalists who stood stiffly in front of bandstands. Frank had spent years trying to excel at his craft, constantly honing his skill at breath control, lyrical phrasing, and microphone technique. Now all that time and effort was starting to pay off.

"Sinatra-Mania"

On Frank Sinatra's twenty-seventh birthday, December 12, 1942, he was onstage at the Mosque Theatre in Newark. As fate would have it, Bob Weitman, manager of the Paramount Theatre, saw Sinatra perform that night. He was impressed. He then asked Benny Goodman, the so-called King of Swing, if he minded having Frank on a bill with him and his band at the Paramount, near Times Square, at the end of December. Goodman's response: *"Who the hell is Frank Sinatra?"* Not many people would be asking that question, though, after Frank's dates at the Paramount.

During the war, the film industry flourished. Americans began to find distraction from the troubles of war in enormous movie theaters being built across the country. The urban movie theaters, in particular, were huge, with big, ornate lobbies decorated with mirrors and fancy chandeliers, plush padded seats, balconies, and uniformed ushers with flashlights to show patrons to their seats. Many theaters opened as early as eight-thirty in the morning; because so many people worked swing and graveyard shifts during wartime, schedules were turned upside down and there was always an audience available to fill the seats.

The program was often a double feature of movies plus shorts, like the Movietone News, which included a war report. Theaters often also featured a live show, especially in the larger cities. In New York, for instance, Radio City Music Hall featured the Rockettes, a precision tap-dancing chorus line. Big bands were often part of the show, as at the Paramount, where Frank would do six, sometimes seven shows a day during his first engagement there.

"I went to rehearsal at seven-thirty in the morning," Frank said of opening day—New Year's Eve—"and looked at the [Paramount Theatre] marquee, and it said, 'Extra Added Attraction: Frank Sinatra,' and I said, 'Wow!'"

Ironically, the film playing at the Paramount that night was Bing Crosby's *Star-Spangled Rhythm*, which received top billing.

This would turn out to be an extraordinary debut for him. The moment he was introduced on opening night by Jack Benny, the young girls in the audience went berserk. They immediately started crying out, "*Frankeeeeee, Frankeeeee.*" It was so sudden, this adulation, that everyone was taken by surprise.

"What the hell was that?" Benny Goodman wondered.

"Five thousand kids, stamping, yelling, screaming, applauding," Frank remembered. "I thought the roof would come off."

"I thought the goddamned building was going to cave in," Jack Benny said.

The audience—mostly comprised of teenage girls, who were known as "bobby-soxers" because of the white socks they wore*—simply wouldn't leave after the show; they would attempt to stay through several performances, and the only way to get rid of them was for the theater's manager to screen the dullest films he could find, along with *Star-Spangled Rhythm*, between shows.

Frank had become an overnight sensation. Word about him had spread as a result of his recordings and radio appearances, creating a fan base of youngsters who were growing more and more interested in him, until it suddenly exploded into a cultural phenomenon at the Paramount. With the show a record-breaking success—primarily because of Sinatra's contribution—the original two-week engagement was extended for two more months.

Frank was so grateful to his new fans for their support, he had his assistant road manager, Richie Lisella, buy dozens of turkey sandwiches at Walgreens for the girls who stayed in their seats all day long rather than risk losing them to newcomers. He never pandered to this audience, either, by compromising his vision simply for acceptance and applause. In other words, he didn't restrict his show to songs the audience knew and loved. Instead, he sang intelligent, poignant love songs chosen for their lyrical content, regardless of their recognition factor—though in fact they were rarely heard over the din of the audience's response.

---

* The uniform of the day often was a sweater over a pleated knee-length skirt, white socks, and saddle shoes or penny loafers. After school and on weekends, skirts and sweaters were exchanged for dungarees (today known as jeans), rolled up to just over the ankles, along with a man's cotton or wool buffalo-checked shirt.

Although "Sinatra-mania," as it was immediately dubbed by the press, did affect some older women, and men of all ages, thirteen- to fifteen-year-old girls became his biggest fans. What accounted for this sudden phenomenon? One theory was that his new audience was too young to have boyfriends and Frank provided a stand-in love object. Even though they knew he was married and a father—on Nancy's birthday there were enough gifts sent by fans to fill an orphanage— he was "safe" because he was unattainable. On the other hand, even though he was older, he was so thin and boyish-looking he could have been one of them.

"Psychologists have tried to go into the reasons why, with all sorts of theories," Frank said of the pandemonium he had caused. "It was the war years, and there was a great loneliness. I was the boy in every corner drugstore, the boy who'd gone off to war."

His more ardent fans went to great lengths to secure a piece of him. In the winter, girls were known to dig up snowprints of his feet and take them home to their freezers. Ashes from his cigarettes became prized mementos. Hotel maids were bribed to let his fans lie between his sheets before they made the bed in which he had slept. He very quickly ended up with two thousand fan clubs.

Because of his success at the Paramount, Frank hired a new press agent, forty-one-year-old George Evans, who had been introduced to him by their mutual friend Nick Sevano. Evans, an enthusiastic PR man, represented a host of show-business icons, including Lena Horne, Duke Ellington, and Dean Martin and Jerry Lewis. "Make me the biggest star there is," Frank told him. "Whatever it takes. I got the talent, now you do what you gotta do."

The first idea George Evans had was to have one of his assistants hire a gaggle of girls to scream like mad whenever Frank sang one of his romantic ballads in any theater anywhere. Each youngster was paid five dollars for her services. It was hardly necessary, though. The audience was already so enthusiastic, they practically drowned out Evans's employees. To make Sinatra's performance even more inter-esting, though, Evans decided that some of the girls should actually faint during one of Frank's numbers. (Of course, only members of Sinatra's camp knew that these youngsters had been planted through-out the theater.) Much to Evans's amazement, thirty girls fainted one night. But only twelve had been hired. Then the girls started throwing their little brassieres onto the stage.

"Jesus Christ, can you believe this?" Frank asked his pals backstage after one show. He remembered those days in an interview years later. "I was feeling everything," he said. "Happy? I don't know. I wasn't unhappy, let's put it that way. I never had it so good. Sometimes I wonder whether anybody had it like I had it, before or since. It was the damnedest thing, wasn't it? But I was too busy ever to know whether I was happy or even to ask myself. I can't remember for a long time even taking time out to think."

"Frank was flying high, and we were proud of him," said his longtime friend Joey D'Orazio. "After all, he'd worked hard to get where he was. We still had a lot of laughs. He was the same ol' Frankie. I don't think he changed a bit. He was cocky, but hell, he was always cocky. But one thing was for sure: We liked him more when he was happy, and he was pretty happy during this time.

"He was spending money like crazy, I remember. He bought all of his pals from Hoboken watches and sweaters. 'Anything you need, you come to me,' he said. 'And if your mother or father need something, you tell 'em to call me too.' I mean, he wasn't the kind of guy who ever forgot his buddies from the old neighborhood, you know?" (Frank's wardrobe had also become quite impressive: fifty suits, two dozen sports coats, over a hundred pairs of dress pants, sixty pairs of shoes. His floppy bow ties, which became a trademark, were handmade by his wife, Nancy.)

To make sure Frank stayed a sensation, George Evans gave away free tickets to other youngsters, just to be sure the house was always packed, no matter the time of day, no matter the city. He also contacted the press and made certain that photographers were present to document Sinatra's effect on young people. Soon all of the country was reading and talking about the singer in the floppy bow tie, the one now being referred to by some of the media as "the Voice."*

---

* Though George Evans's friends credit him with nicknaming Sinatra "the Voice," it has also been reported that the appellation actually came from Sinatra's agent, Harry Kilby, who dubbed Sinatra "the voice that thrills millions."

Evans also arranged press interviews, photo sessions, autograph parties, radio-station visits—whatever it took to spread the word that young Sinatra had arrived. In press releases Evans actually rewrote Frank's history, lopping two years off his age, having him "graduate" from high school, making him athletic and his parents native-born. Dolly was even transformed into a Red Cross nurse! Eagerly, she played along with the hype. In fact, when Frank was rejected for military service because of a hearing problem—likely the result of the forceps used during his difficult birth—Dolly lamented to a reporter, "Oh, dear, Frankie wanted to get in so badly because he wanted to have our pictures taken together in uniform." (Though he rarely if ever complained about it, Sinatra would always suffer some degree of hearing loss, which makes his success in the music business all the more amazing.)

Evans also passed the word that Frank was a slum kid, born into an impoverished family that had struggled with financial woes in a gang-infested neighborhood. Frank played along. It was just public relations, he figured, and all a part of the game. Indeed, Evans's successful campaign was largely responsible for the wide scope of Sinatra's early fame. That Frank had been working for years to invent himself as a vocalist and entertainer helped significantly, but Evans certainly made the most of Frank's talent.

"Dolly was calling everyone she knew in Hoboken and bragging about her kid," Joey D'Orazio remembered. "To hear her talk, he was the biggest thing since Moses.

"A bunch of us drove Dolly and Marty and some other family members to one show, and Frank asked me to bring Marty backstage afterwards. Frankie was extremely nervous. 'My old man never wanted me to sing,' he told me. 'What do you think he's gonna say now? You think he'll be proud, Joey boy?' I said, 'Jesus Christ, Frank, you're the hottest thing in show business. Of course he's proud.' Frank looked sad and said, 'I'm not so sure. You don't know my old man. This isn't his thing, this whole singing jazz. If it was up to him, I'd be workin' on the docks.'

"I got the feeling that a lot depended on Marty's reaction," D'Orazio continued. "Even though Frank was a star, I felt that if Marty didn't have the proper response, it would have ruined everything."

When Marty remained a bit quiet during the show, D'Orazio was concerned. "I can't hear a goddamned thing over the noise in this joint," the senior Sinatra complained during one ballad. "Is he any good or not? I can't hear him."

After Frank's final bows, Joey escorted Marty to the backstage door.

"It was madness there," D'Orazio said. "We couldn't get in. I remember that there was some kind of mix-up on the guest list. Frank's *paisano* Hank [Sanicola] forgot to put our name on it, and I was about to take Marty away rather than have him be embarrassed. Suddenly, Marty says to this big guy at the door, 'Hey, pal, that was my kid up there on that stage. I'm his ol' man, and if you don't let me back there, I'm gonna knock you out. You got that?' I was amazed. Marty was usually pretty quiet, but he really wanted to get backstage to see his kid. The guard was convinced, and he let us through."

Backstage, Frank's small dressing room was crammed with excited well-wishers. When Marty walked into the room, all eyes turned to him. It was as if everyone somehow knew that a significant moment was about to occur. "Hey, Pop," Frank greeted his father as he cut through the crowd and headed toward him.

"Well, what'd ya think, Pop," he asked with a cautious smile.

"Who could hear?" Marty responded. "Nobody could hear anything. How do *you* hear what you're doing?"

Frank had to laugh. "So, I'm still a quitter? Or what?"

Marty's eyes teared up. "My son ain't no quitter," he said as he embraced Frank. "My son's a big shot."*

---

* Every Monday for years, Marty Sinatra received a one-hundred-dollar check from "Sinatra Enterprises," mailed to the Hoboken Fire Department where he worked—a secret gift from Frank to his father, "for him to do with whatever he wants, without Ma knowing," Frank explained to one friend with a wink.

Making Do

*F*rank's hotheaded personality would often get the better of him and he was often disagreeable and unreasonable. "A real prick," George would say when describing Frank to intimates. "The worst kind there is, because not only does he have to prove you wrong, he has to make you agree that he just proved it."

Plagued by insomnia his entire life, Frank—always an erudite, socially conscious man—would read into the early hours of the morning. He would devour a wide variety of books, his particular interest having to do with racial tolerance. His favorites included *An American Dilemma* by Gunnar Myrdal; *History of Bigotry in the United States* by Gustavus Myers, and the novel *Freedom Road* by Howard Fast. It would take him hours to fall asleep; he rarely got enough.

In the morning, he was tired and irritable, and by the afternoon he was giving everyone hell, in part because he was so sleep-deprived. Evans, however, could somehow always deal with the irascible side of Sinatra's personality. He thought of it as a combination of artistic temperament and Italian stubbornness. The one problem he and Sinatra could not reconcile, though, was a more serious one: Frank's philandering.

"George had a meeting with Frank one afternoon in his office at 1775 Broadway—the first of many on the subject—and it turned into a screaming match," recalled Ted Hechtman, who was a New York friend and business associate of George Evans's. (The two would become partners when Evans opened his West Coast office.) "He told him flat out, 'You have to stop with the dames.' And Frank was adamant. 'That's got nothin' to do with nothin.' That's my own private business, George. So keep your nose out of it.'

"'But it *does* have to do with your career, Frankie,' George told him. 'If word gets out you're cheating on your wife, how do you think those kids who idolize you are gonna feel? I'm telling you, you could be ruined.'

"'It's *your* job to make sure it doesn't get out,' Frank insisted. 'That's what I'm paying you for. And not only that, if it does get out, you're fired, hear? So keep it out of the press, simple as that.'

"'I can't guarantee that,' Evans said angrily. 'Keep your trousers zipped, Frank. That's all I ask.'

"Frank yelled at him, 'Listen, pallie, do what you gotta do to keep it out of the papers, and I'll do what I gotta do to keep myself happy. Because if I'm happy, I sing good. If I sing good, we *all* make money,' he stated. 'I don't have to explain this to my own wife. Why am I talkin' to *you* about it? Now get out of here.'

"'Hey, this is *my* office, Frankie,' George reminded him. '*You* get out.'"

Frank stormed off.

In the spring of 1943, Nancy Sinatra became pregnant again; this news was the subject of a press release that George was thrilled to disseminate to the media. George's worries were over—for about a week.

Ted Hechtman recalled, "Then Nancy called George—which would be the first of many calls like this one—and said that she couldn't find Frank and she needed him because little Nancy was sick with some baby illness.

"George made some calls and tracked Frank down at a seedy hotel outside Jersey City. Upset, he went down there and pounded on the door. When there was no answer, he just let himself in; the door was unlocked. No one was in the room, but George heard something going on in the bathroom. He walked in, and there was Frankie and this stripper whose name was—I'll never forget it as long as I live—'Lips Luango.'

"'Frankie,' George blurted out, 'What about Nancy? You ever give her even a second thought? Jesus, look at you, with Lips Luango of all people!'

"And, as George told me, the dame burst out into tears and whined, 'But I thought you said you and her was gettin' a *divorce*, Frankie. And that you and me, we was gettin' *married*. How could you lie to me after all we've meant to each other?'

"And while Frank was scrambling around looking for a towel, he shouted, '*Shaddup!* Like I'm gonna marry a broad named Lips?'"

George Evans was appalled by his client's immature behavior. But in fact, Frank couldn't have cared less about George's opinion. He was just angry with him for breaking in on him and his paramour.

Once again, when he and Frank discussed "Lips" over a drink, he said, "Keep your nose out of my business." Then he threw a half-filled glass of Dubonnet at him. "Your job is just to keep me in the papers. Nancy's fine with what's going on."

But she wasn't fine with it.

"By the end of 1942, the only reason Frank and Nancy would ever be intimate was to possibly procreate," said Patti Demarest. "I think she wanted children because she wanted to be loved and needed by *somebody*, since she was not getting that from Frank. In fact, she began to resent him, not even want him anymore. He had changed her, made her bitter, made her sometimes even hate herself for the choices he was forcing her to make. She had gotten tougher, angrier. She wasn't the same naïve girl he had married, that's for sure."

Frank was not up to the task of being a good father. He loved Nancy Jr., but always had something else on his mind, and as much as he wanted to be with the baby, he was too preoccupied to really be present in the moment. Nancy began to understand that if she was going to continue having children, she would have to accept Frank's limitations as a father. But she would, as she put it at the time, "make do." After all, without Frank, Nancy was an unmarried mother with no prospect of a well-paying job. With him, she was the wealthy wife of a major star. At the time, the choice seemed clear, if not easy.

1943

The year began on a high note for twenty-seven-year-old Frank Sinatra. With his career now taken off, he was featured on the cover of practically every show-business-related magazine on the newsstands.

In January he was back at the Paramount, this time with Johnny Long's band, in another successful monthlong engagement there. In February, he became a regular (along with Beryl Davis and Eileen Barton) on the radio show *Your Hit Parade*. Also that month, Columbia Pictures released his first film without the Tommy Dorsey band, *Reveille with Beverly* (in which Frank just had a cameo role singing "Night and Day"), starring future MGM costar, tap dancer Ann Miller.

Early in the year, Frank and Nancy bought a seven-room home on Lawrence Avenue in Hasbrouck Heights, New Jersey, for about $25,000. Because there was no fence around the property, the home became a favorite stalking site for Frank's eager fans. Indeed, the Sinatras soon grew used to having little privacy.

George Evans, Hank Sanicola, and others in his management/ booking team realized that Frank's longevity depended on his appeal to a wider audience than just the youngsters who had been causing such a sensation. They wanted him to play the Copacabana at 10 East 60th Street in Manhattan, a new club that featured major adult-oriented performers like Jimmy Durante and Sophie Tucker. The Copa manager, Jules Podell, decided not to hire him, though, fearing he wouldn't draw an adult crowd. Instead, in late March 1943, Frank was booked into the Riobamba, on East 57th Street, another venue that catered to adults. Frank was unhappy, however, when he learned that he was billed as an "Extra Added Attraction" in a nightclub that was about to go out of business. Still, the engagement at the Riobamba was a major success, and was standing room only. Sammy Cahn was present on opening night, and he recalled that "the audience was not [a bunch of] bobby-soxers. This was an adult, mature, sophisticated, two-o'clock-in-the-morning Manhattan audience."

Earl Wilson reported, "Frank was in a dinner jacket, and he was wearing a wedding band. He had a small curl that fell almost over his right eye. With trembling lips—I don't know how he made them tremble, but I saw it—he sang 'She's Funny That Way' and 'Night and Day' and succeeded in bringing down the house. It was a wondrous night for all of us who felt we had a share in Frankie. The New York Post's pop-music critic, Danny Richman, leaned over to me and said, 'He sends me.'"

After the engagement at the Riobamba, it seemed that Frank could do no wrong. For his next engagement back at the Paramount, he was paid $2,500 a week; his initial gig there, with Benny Goodman, earned him $150 a week.

In June, Frank recorded his first sides at the Columbia studios, with the Bobby Tucker Singers. (Because of a long-running musicians' strike, he was forced to record nine songs a cappella, including

"You'll Never Know," "People Will Say We're in Love," and, most notably, "The Music Stopped.") Later in the year, "All or Nothing at All" (which Frank had recorded in 1939) would be reissued by Columbia during the musicians' strike. It would become a major hit for him. (Frank would go on to record this song three more times, in 1961, 1966, and 1977.)

On August 12, 1943, Frank and his entourage—including Hank Sanicola and arranger Axel Stordahl—arrived in Pasadena, California. Frank was scheduled to appear as himself in *Higher and Higher*, his first acting role in a movie, and also at the Hollywood Bowl in a series of concerts. Hysterical fans nearly caused a riot when he got off the train in Pasadena.

Breaking the Dorsey Contract

*W*hile in Los Angeles, Frank finally decided to confront Tommy Dorsey about the contract he had signed when he first began to sing for his band. Thirty-three and a third percent of his gross earnings to Dorsey? Forever? And another 10 percent for Dorsey's agent? "That's the most fucked-up thing I ever heard of," Frank told Hank Sanicola, who was now officially managing him. Frank was supposed to have been paying Tommy from all engagements, including those at the Copa, Riobamba, and Paramount, but he was way behind in his payments, much to Dorsey's indignation.

Bing Crosby suggested that he had better find a way out of the situation soon, before he started making millions. Frank agreed, and he actively pursued a strategy of trying to get out of the contract. He began giving press interviews claiming that Dorsey was cheating him out of money. Immediately, Frank's fans started a letter-writing campaign against Dorsey. Then George Evans organized a campaign of Sinatra fans to picket Dorsey's opening at the Earle Theatre in Philadelphia.

Soon, Sinatra and Dorsey filed lawsuits against each other. Dorsey was unwilling to budge. He didn't care that the deal was grossly unfair—Frank had agreed to it when he was desperate for a job, and now Dorsey was going to hold him to it.

In August 1943, attorneys for Sinatra and Dorsey attempted to work out a settlement whereby that contract would be canceled. Manie Sacks—Frank's new friend from Columbia Records—found an attorney for Sinatra named Henry Jaffe, who also represented the American Federation of Radio Artists. Jaffe was able to use his connection with AFRA to convince Dorsey that if he continued to stand in Sinatra's way, he might have "just a little trouble" continuing his lucrative NBC radio broadcasts. Frank had been represented at this time by the Rockwell-O'Keefe agency, but he wanted to be with the bigger, more established MCA, which was interested in him. Finally it was agreed that MCA would put up the money to get Frank out of his Dorsey deal. Dorsey was paid $60,000—$25,000 of which came from Frank, who borrowed it from Manie Sacks. (That's more than $825,000 in today's market.) For its investment, MCA got the services of Frank Sinatra and agreed that it would split its commission on Sinatra with Rockwell-O'Keefe until 1948.

Years later, rumors began to surface that Frank had actually used certain underworld connections to convince Tommy Dorsey that he should release him from the overbearing contract. The story was that New Jersey mobster Willie Moretti intervened on Frank's behalf, putting a gun to Dorsey's head and forcing him to release Sinatra from his contract. Moretti continually bragged that he had done this favor for Sinatra, until he was murdered gangland-style in 1951. Frank insisted that the story was untrue and that he relied entirely on his legal team to extricate himself from the unfair Dorsey contract.

"The truth is that Hank Sanicola had a couple buddies—not real underworld characters but just some frightening fellows that he and Sinatra both knew—threaten Dorsey that if he didn't let Frankie out of the contract, there'd be trouble," Joey D'Orazio recalled. "I know this because Hank called me up and asked me to fly to Los Angeles and go with this motley crew to Dorsey's office. I refused to do it. I had a wife and kid, and I didn't want to end up in some Los Angeles jail if things got out of hand.

"I know these hoodlums who went out there, because some of us hung out together, and when they got back, that's all they wanted to talk about. They told me that Sanicola didn't want Sinatra to know any of the details. 'Just take care of it,' he said. He didn't know for sure if it was necessary; they were close to ending it with Dorsey anyway. 'He just needs a little nudge,' he told me.

"He always wanted Sinatra to be able to claim that he didn't know *nuttin'* about *nuttin'* if it all blew up. He was always protecting Sinatra, Sanicola was.

"In the end, these characters told Dorsey that they'd break his arms, that he'd never play again if he didn't sign some papers that would let Frankie out of that contract. What a joke, threatening Tommy Dorsey, who was a tough guy himself. He laughed in their faces and mocked them, saying, 'Oh yeah, look at how scared I am. Tell Frank I'm scared to death. Then tell him I said, "Go to hell," for sending his goons to beat me up.'

"The guys were stunned. Then Tommy said, 'All right, fine. Forget it. I'll sign the papers, that's how sick I am of Frank Sinatra, the no-good bum. The hell with him.'"

According to D'Orazio, it wasn't much of an intimidation. In fact, one of the guys was so excited about meeting Dorsey, he had to be talked out of going back and asking for his autograph after they left his office.

Betty Wilken—daughter of Bea Wilken, a Los Angeles friend of Tommy Dorsey's wife, Pat Dane—recalled, "My mother often told me that Tommy was as difficult as they come, a temperamental, argumentative person that you didn't want to cross. She also told me that Pat and Tommy hated Frankie for years because they felt he had sent his fellows to hurt Tommy. It was always said that Frank was lucky Tommy hadn't killed all of his pals right there on the spot. He was that angry."

Tommy Dorsey was never happy about the way it ended with Sinatra; he felt that he had a gold mine in Frank's talent, and on top of that, he didn't like losing. He later gave credence to Joey D'Orazio's version of how Sinatra extricated himself from the contract when he told *American Mercury* magazine in 1951 that during a breakdown in negotiations with Sinatra's attorneys, he was visited by three businesslike men who talked out of the sides of their mouths and ordered him to "sign or else."

"Well, I just hope you fall on your ass," Tommy Dorsey told Frank Sinatra in parting. Frank was too busy to care about Dorsey's bitterness; as soon as the contract with Dorsey was settled, he signed a seven-year deal with RKO to make movies, the first of which would be *Higher and Higher* with Jack Haley and Michèle Morgan. This film would mark his acting debut, even though it consisted of portraying himself singing five songs, including "I Couldn't Sleep a Wink Last Night" (which was nominated for an Academy Award).

Tommy Dorsey died suddenly in his sleep in 1956. Though Sinatra and Dorsey were never really close friends, they did see each other from time to time in later years and even worked together on a few occasions. Just months prior to his death, Dorsey and Sinatra appeared together at the Paramount Theatre in New York. Sinatra also recorded an album in the 1960s, *I Remember Tommy*, for Reprise, which paid tribute to Dorsey. Sinatra never tired of talking about the Tommy Dorsey days, both the good and the bad; he always had special memories of those years, despite the bitterness of the breakup.

Anchors Aweigh to Los Angeles

On January 10, 1944, Nancy Sinatra gave birth to a son at the Margaret Hague Maternity Hospital in Jersey City. Again, Frank could not be present for the birth; he was in Los Angeles filming *Step Lively*, his second movie for RKO. At the moment Nancy gave birth, he was actually on the air in the middle of a radio broadcast.

The Sinatras had decided in advance that if it were a boy, the child would be named Franklin (after Franklin Delano Roosevelt) Wayne Emmanuel (after Frank's very close friend Manie Sacks) Sinatra. But in the end they settled on Francis Wayne Sinatra, which eventually became Frank Sinatra Jr.

In retrospect, the very popular photographs of Nancy in her hospital bed seem almost surreal. Surrounded by press photographers, she cradled the infant in her arms with a framed publicity photograph of her husband on her lap. It was as if Frank was more a symbol in her life that an actual husband; at least that's how cynics in the media viewed it.

Frank was proud to have a son, and he wanted to be a good father, but there was always something in his career or personal life that kept him from completely committing to parenthood. Nancy, meanwhile, suppressed her anger and disappointment and focused on raising her two babies. She tried to find solace in the fact that she and the children never wanted for anything—except Frank.

Shortly after the birth of his son, Frank met Louis B. Mayer, the head of MGM, at a benefit for the Jewish Home for the Aged. Mayer was so impressed with Frank's performance of "Ol' Man River" that he decided to put him under contract to MGM, where, according to its slogan, there were "More Stars Than There Are in the Heavens." Frank would be in excellent company; some of the other contract players were Gene Kelly, Fred Astaire, Clark Gable, and Esther Williams. He would soon sign a $1.5 million, five-year contract with the studio, which, after some negotiation, preempted the RKO contract.

A few months later, Frank told Nancy he felt it was time to move from New Jersey to the West Coast. He went on to purchase Mary Astor's large Mediterranean-style estate at 10051 Valley Spring Lane in Toluca Lake, a Los Angeles suburb.

Nancy was reluctant. At least on the East Coast she had friends she could rely on when she couldn't depend on her husband, or when he was away, which was most of the time. To whom would she be able to confide in California? On the other hand, Frank was making over a million dollars a year now. He belonged in Los Angeles—MGM was there—and if Nancy wanted to continue to be supportive, she had to go along with the plan and keep her discontent to herself. She agreed to the move and eventually her parents and six siblings would also move to the West Coast; if Frank wasn't going to be around, at least she had the rest of her family near her for support.

The Sinatras traveled by train on the 20th Century Limited and the Super Chief from New York to Pasadena to begin their West Coast experience. There, Frank would continue to try to balance his career with his family life. While he loved his son, his daughter really lit up his life. He doted on her, taking her on canoe rides on the lake that abutted the family home, where he taught her to swim. They also had breakfast together every morning. In these early days, he loved being a father and actually had the time to devote to it. This time together set the stage for a close relationship between Frank and

Nancy Jr. They always seemed to understand each other, and, more important, she always knew when to push and when to hold back. They were on the same wavelength, so to speak, and it would be that way until the day he died.

On June 15, 1944, Frank began work on his first MGM film under the new contract, in *Anchors Aweigh*, with Gene Kelly. The plot was simple: Kelly and Sinatra are sailors who get into mischief while on leave. The movie was considered harmless fun when it was released, and it would prove to be a big success at the box office.

During production of *Anchors Aweigh*, Sinatra made waves with the studio's PR department by speaking out against the production. He had become annoyed with the shooting schedule and told a reporter he was actually thinking of quitting films because "most pictures stink, and the people in them, too." Jack Keller—who worked on the West Coast for Frank's publicist, George Evans—did his best to put out the flames caused by Sinatra's statement by writing an apology for Frank and then getting it published by a national wire service.

As was his usual custom with moviemaking, Frank wanted to have his way with *Anchors Aweigh*, which meant he wanted Sammy Cahn to work with Jule Styne on the film. However, the film's producer, Joe Pasternak, and the studio didn't want Cahn. After a war of words with Pasternak, Sinatra won. In the end, a grateful Cahn got the job and did extraordinary work on it, making Sinatra proud—and making him right, again.

Frank then clashed with producer Pasternak over the viewing of dailies. A "daily" is the industry's term for film shot on a particular day, which is often viewed by the director, cameramen, makeup artists, and other crew members to determine how the movie is progressing. MGM had a strict policy that actors were not to see dailies. It was Pasternak's experience that no actor ever liked what he saw in a daily and that such dissatisfaction only caused trouble on the set. However, when Sinatra was told by Pasternak that he would not be viewing his footage, he became upset; there were many arguments about the matter. Finally, Pasternak relented and promised Frank he would show him some of the more recent dailies in what he called "a private viewing." However, when Sinatra showed up for the viewing with six pals,

Pasternak became upset and refused to allow the group to see the footage. Frank quit the film. But then he returned a few days later. This type of mercurial behavior when reported by the media—and these stories were somehow *always* leaked to reporters—only served to make Sinatra appear to his public to be what, it could be argued, he really was: quite difficult.

Meanwhile, behind the scenes of *Anchors Aweigh*, Gene Kelly took the clumsy, inexperienced Frank Sinatra under his wing and worked diligently to transform him into a credible dancer. Sinatra did the best he could; however, as it turned out, it would be his eyes that betrayed him, not his feet. Those Sinatra baby blues registered clear uncertainty and with each step seemed to ask, *What's next?* In fact, Gene Kelly joked to Frank that he "set dancing back twenty years."

The movie was hard work for Sinatra, emotionally as well as physically. In fact, he lost four pounds during the first week of rigorous rehearsal, which he couldn't afford to lose because he weighed only about 125 pounds. He wanted to make a good impression, and it frightened him that he was in a film that was perhaps beyond him. Thus he was impatient with Kelly and wanted to cut many of the dance sequences. However, Kelly sensed that Sinatra could get through it if he persevered; in fact, Gene Kelly was so devoid of ego, he actually tailored the routines so that Sinatra looked good, even if that meant he, Kelly, couldn't show off as much as he might have wanted to. "He's one of the reasons I became a star," Sinatra would later say of his friend Gene Kelly.

* * *

On October 11, 1944, Frank Sinatra opened a three-week engagement at the Paramount Theatre. Youngsters started lining up for tickets at 4:30 a.m. By the time the thirty-six-hundred-seat theater opened at 8:30 (the first of Frank's five shows a day would begin at noon) it was filled to capacity. The problem arose when audience members refused to leave the theater; they stayed through performance after performance. Outside, there were ten thousand people in line, six abreast. Another twenty thousand milled around Times Square, stopping traffic, trying to figure out what the commotion was about. Two hundred policemen were called from guard duty at the Columbus Day Parade, a few blocks away on Fifth Avenue. Those fans trying to get into the theater became boisterous and rowdy when the line didn't move. A riot broke out. "The worst mob scene in New York since nylons went on sale," joked one New York police officer.

By the time the melee was over, 421 police reserves, 70 patrolmen, 50 traffic cops, and 200 detectives had become involved. The ticket booth was destroyed, and nearby shop windows were broken. The press dubbed it "the Columbus Day Riot."

"Most of his fans are plain, lonely girls from lower-middle-class homes," noted E. J. Jahn Jr. of the *New Yorker*. "They are dazzled by the life Sinatra leads and wish they could share it. They insist that they love him, but they do not use the verb in its ordinary sense. As they apply it to him, it is synonymous with 'worship.'"

Frank was getting fairly accustomed to this kind of circus developing whenever he made an appearance. Nothing surprised him anymore. He couldn't go out without bodyguards, he could no longer enjoy a meal in a restaurant with friends, and when he went back to Hoboken to visit his parents, it was a major news event. "I think this is the way it's going to be from now on," he cautioned Nancy. "We'd better get used to it."

However, George Evans was concerned that the success could be fleeting and that his core audience might grow out of their Sinatramania. He wanted Frank to focus on broadening his adult fan base. But it was incomprehensible to Frank that the teenagers who were presently lavishing such love and attention on him could ever lose interest.

After a recording session on December 19, 1944, in Hollywood, George Evans and his West Coast partner, Jack Keller, had a brief conversation about the future. Evans took off his spectacles and, while cleaning them, shook his head and said, "The kid won't listen."

"I think he's about to get his heart broke," Keller added.

"Yeah. This isn't going to last forever," Evans said. "Look at what's happening to Rudy Vallée. He was as big as Frank a couple years ago, and now people are moving on from him already. [In fact, Vallée's last hit song was 1943's 'As Time Goes By.'] This isn't going to last for Frank. It's just the way the business works."

"Try telling him that," Keller said.

"He doesn't want to hear it," Evans agreed.

There was one person close to Frank who did pay heed to George Evans's concerns, and that was Nancy. In recent months, she and Frank had begun to argue vociferously about the money he was spending. Never one to be prudent when it came to finances even back when he didn't have the money, the always generous Frank had begun buying clothing, household furnishings, and extravagant gifts for friends and family members. He also took the most lavish of vacations, sometimes with Nancy, sometimes without. Moreover, he made risky investments that promised unreasonably lucrative payoffs with no concern for the future when these ventures didn't pan out.

It fell upon Nancy to be responsible for budgeting the household and professional finances. While she was amazed at how much money Frank was bringing in, she was even more astonished at how much was being spent—which was most of it. "You're always worrying about the future," Frank told her. "Live for today. Live for now. Not tomorrow."

"There's not gonna be a tomorrow," Nancy warned her husband, "if we don't start saving up for it."

Part Three

BIG TIME

The Voice: 1945–46

In 1945 and 1946, in addition to making films at MGM, Frank Sinatra would record some of his most memorable songs. Much of the material recorded during this period would go on to be considered Sinatra classics, including "I Should Care," "Put Your Dreams Away," and "I Have But One Heart." There is a very strong body of work from this time, but for many fans, the Oscar Hammerstein–Richard Rodgers song "If I Loved You" (from *Carousel*) is at the top of the list. On this one, Frank is at his vibrant, yearning best. He'd become known as a performer who made women swoon, and it was easy to forget what a talented singer he had evolved into until one listened to this stellar performance. All told, there would be twelve recording sessions in 1945 and fifteen in 1946, producing a total of ninety songs, some of which would be compiled and released on a number of successful albums, like *The Voice* (his first 78 rpm album).

The Voice is considered by some popular-music historians to be the first "concept album." No singer before Sinatra—not even Bing Crosby—seemed to comprehend the potential of an album as something more than just a collection of unrelated songs. Frank realized that the tunes could connect to one another and be sequenced in a way that would tell a complete emotional story, as the songs on *The Voice* did. He would actually sit down and plan an album song by song before recording it. It was important to him that no one else—neither producer nor arranger—have final say over the choice of songs that would be recorded. Sometimes songwriters such as Jimmy Van Heusen and Sammy Cahn would offer suggestions, of course, but Frank had veto power.

Once in the studio, Frank always took his recording sessions seriously. Unlike many vocal artists, he was involved in some way in nearly every aspect of the session, from choosing the musicians to fine-tuning the arrangements. He had great appreciation for most music—jazz, classical, as well as pop—and understood it thoroughly, even if he couldn't read it. It often comes as a surprise that Sinatra never learned to read music. In fact, the skill of reading sheet music eluded many successful composers and musicians. Irving Berlin, for instance, couldn't read, and neither can Paul McCartney. Elton John was able to read music in his youth, but says he has long since forgotten. Luciano Pavarotti is another singer who couldn't read. Obviously, it's not always necessary. In Frank's case, he was guided by his instincts. If the music didn't sound right to him, it didn't matter if it was technically correct. "I'm not the kind of guy who does a lot of brain work about why or how," he once said. It had to *feel* right. Or as he would say, it had to "swing."

Frank always told his producers to make sure they got his first performance on tape, as it would probably be the best. Anything after—and there would usually be many more takes—he felt suffered because he had expended so much commitment, energy, and concentration on that first take.

Through the years, Frank worked only with orchestrators or arrangers who could interpret the music his way: Axel Stordahl, Nelson Riddle (who was an unknown in the business when he started with Sinatra but would go on to do more than half of his albums), and other giants in the field whose names would become synonymous with Sinatra's success: Billy May, Gordon Jenkins, Johnny Mandel, Neal Hefti, George Siravo, Robert Farnon, and Don Costa. Because Frank knew which orchestrator worked best on which kind of song, he always selected songs with the orchestrator in mind, and vice versa.

No orchestrator ever really challenged Frank, though they all gave input, which he welcomed. Gordon Jenkins once said that he would never question Frank's ideas because "I've never seen him wrong. Every suggestion that he's ever made to me has been an improvement." However, Frank was never a dictator in the recording studio. He knew that no singer could expect cooperation on future projects if he alienated the best orchestrators in the business. Besides that, he was eager for their involvement because, technically at least, they all knew far more than he did. He welcomed examples of their artistry and creativity as much as they delighted in his.

Another key to Frank's success was that he understood his audience and what was expected of him. Though he was well-read, he never flaunted his knowledge or acted in a way that would make him appear to be superior to his fans. In truth, he *was* one of them: an unpretentious guy from Hoboken who just happened to make it big. His wealth, his women, and his growing power never put distance between himself and his audience, for his fans *wanted* him to be successful, and they too relished his success. As long as Frank Sinatra's music reflected a common human experience—pain, joy, heartbreak, or redemption—his fans were happy.

The House He Lives In

*I*n May 1945, Frank embarked on his first USO tour. He, Phil Silvers, and company successfully toured abroad, singing for the troops for seven weeks. Unfortunately, when the contingent returned to the States on July 6, 1945, Frank made a few disparaging comments about the USO ("Shoemakers in uniform run the entertainment division. Most of them had no experience in show business."), thereby causing another controversy. Defenders of the USO, such as writer Lee Mortimer, a protégé of Walter Winchell's who would become Frank's greatest nemesis in the media, harshly rebuked him. Unfortunately, Frank's comments generated more negative attention than any goodwill he might have been able to spread on his tour. From this imbroglio, George Evans learned that one never knew what Frank was going to say or how the media would react to it.

Not fazed by any negative response to the USO tour, Sinatra then went on the record expressing a social concern for the youth of America—and this before it was fashionable for entertainers to do so. He felt that if he had the attention of America's youth, he should do something positive with it. To that end, he spoke in high school auditoriums and at youth centers across the country. He also wrote articles about juvenile delinquency, which George Evans distributed to schools nationwide. Moreover, he spoke to high school editors of newspapers about race relations, encouraging students to be as tolerant as possible "if you want a better world for yourselves." He wanted to do his fair share.

At this time, Frank also made an excellent, critically acclaimed ten-minute-long film called *The House I Live In*, about religious and racial tolerance, in which he played himself. It was directed by Mervyn LeRoy, produced by Frank Ross, and written by Albert Maltz; all profits from this, his final RKO film, went to anti–juvenile delinquency programs and organizations.

In the film, Sinatra walks out of a studio after a recording session to have a smoke. He comes across a gang of kids hurling epithets at a Jewish boy. "Look, fellas," Frank tells the boys, "religions make no difference except to a Nazi or somebody as stupid." He says that he would be "a first-class fathead" if he were the type of person who would hate a man because of his ethnicity or religion. Then he sings the title song, a ballad written by Lewis Allan and Earl Robinson, which would go on to become one of his signature songs. A reporter from *Cue* magazine wrote, "The picture's message is tolerance. Its medium is song. And its protagonist is Frank Sinatra who has, amazingly, grown within a few short years from a lovelorn microphone-hugging crooner to become one of filmdom's leading and most vocal battlers for a democratic way of life."

The film would be awarded a special Academy Award in 1946.

That same year, Frank was called a communist by some members of the press. At that time, many prominent liberals found themselves branded as communists for nothing more than having publicly expressed a tolerance of diversity and empathy for the poor.

The "communist" charge came suddenly and surprisingly when Gerald L. K. Smith, of the conservative America First Party, testified before the House Un-American Activities Committee (HUAC) in January 1946 that Sinatra was acting "as a front" for communist organizations. Smith, a voice for racism and anti-Semitism, hosted his own radio program at the time. He didn't explain his comments about Sinatra or even qualify them. "That son of a bitch called me a commie," Frank raged privately. "How can he do that?"

Smith's accusation made no sense, yet it found traction among the paranoid anticommunists of the period.

A short time later, Gerval T. Murphy, a director of the Catholic group the Knights of Columbus, claimed that Frank had demonstrated a penchant for communism by speaking "at a Red rally of sixteen thousand left-wingers." Actually, Frank—who called Murphy "a jerk"—spoke at a rally for the Veterans Committee of the Independent Citizens Committee of the Arts, Sciences and Professions. He called for the passage of legislation that would house veterans. Therefore, he tried his best to set the record straight—"I don't like communists either, and I'm not one"—but in a climate of such fears about communism, the charge stuck. Some of the parents of his young fans began voicing their concerns about Sinatra, all of which were based on unfounded allegations.

Marilyn Maxwell

By 1946, Frank Sinatra had fully immersed himself in the Hollywood social scene and was enjoying every second of it. He was thrilled to live in California and anxious to fit in; he became friendly with many of the town's most influential and popular entertainers, such as Lauren Bacall and Humphrey Bogart, Jack Benny and Bing Crosby, all of whom were very happy to welcome him into their ranks. Restaurateurs Mike Romanoff, David Chasen, and Charlie Morrison also became close friends.

In Hollywood, Frank began attracting women of a totally different class and breed than the infamous Lips Luango of Jersey City. Actress Lana Turner was among the women interested in Frank, and she made her intentions quite clear. Frank had his pick of women, though, and was in no big rush to commit. As usual, he didn't really consider his own marriage a factor. "In the time that we were together as friends from 1945 to 1959, I never once saw him talk to her or touch Nancy, or relate to her in any way," said Phil Silvers's wife, Jo-Carroll Silvers.

Frank also met the beautiful Ava Gardner in April 1945 at the Mocambo nightclub on the Sunset Strip. Ava was then a ravishing twenty-two-year-old brunette film star, but she was married to Mickey Rooney at the time; Frank joked with her that had he met her before Rooney, he would most certainly have married her himself. Ava knew Frank's reputation with women, yet she also couldn't help but be charmed by him. Frank would keep her telephone number carefully tucked away in his wallet—"for future reference," he said to her with a wink.

In the summer of 1946, Frank pursued a contract player at MGM, twenty-four-year-old Marilyn Maxwell, an actress and singer with the Kay Kyser band. Marilyn was a stunning blonde from Iowa with an iridescent movie-star smile who bore a physical resemblance to Marilyn Monroe and embodied the sort of ribald humor of Joan Blondell or even Mae West. She was recently divorced from actor John Conte, whom she'd married in 1944. She was also well-read and had a certain depth to her, which appealed to Frank. Frank had known Marilyn for a couple of years; they appeared on *Lux Radio Theatre* the same year she married Conte. "She was gorgeous," Frank's friend Nick Sevano recalled, "and they were quickly crazy about each other."

Frank dealt with his attractions by allowing himself to become completely swept away without pausing to consider the consequences. He fell in love overnight, and he didn't care what anyone thought of it. Soon he was telling people that he and Marilyn belonged together and that he was going to—again—ask Nancy for a divorce. In the end, it wasn't Frank who actually told Nancy about Marilyn Maxwell, though. When she heard about her from mutual friends, she was a little more concerned than she'd been about the other women in her husband's life. After all, this one was a working actress, not an extra or a stripper—hardly a star, but in Nancy's eyes she was most certainly a woman to be reckoned with.

Nancy asked friends and family members for advice. Practically everyone told her that she should probably file for divorce—and not necessarily because of Marilyn, either, but rather because of Frank. Why, they all wondered, would she want to stay married to this man?

It was a good question. Frank was a serial cheater and his arrogance knew no bounds. He showed no respect for his wife or for the sanctimony of marriage. True emotional intimacy would always elude him. Nancy knew her husband well and had long ago come to terms with his limitations. She had made her choice years earlier to put up with him. But perhaps it was time to reconsider.

Just before he was scheduled to leave California for New York (where he was to film his next movie, *It Happened in Brooklyn*, with

Peter Lawford and Jimmy Durante), Frank and Nancy fought about Marilyn. "Can I be honest with you?" he asked Nancy. "All the best lies start with that sentence," she observed. This time, though, Frank wasn't going to lie—he told her he planned to meet Marilyn in New York. Nancy was devastated. "The fact that you can just tell it to me like that means you have no respect for me," she told him in a tearful argument witnessed by family members—including Dolly and Marty—who had flown to Los Angeles to visit.

According to what Dolly would later recall to relatives, Frank told Nancy, "You just take care of my folks while I'm gone. That's your job. Your job is not to worry about me and Marilyn Maxwell."

In response, Nancy picked up an ashtray and threw it at Frank. It missed him by a hair and sailed through a closed window in the kitchen, shattering it. "*And you're payin' for that,*" Frank hollered at her as he began to bolt from the room. As he was leaving, Dolly grabbed him by the back of his collar and pulled so hard, he almost tumbled backward. "Apologize to your wife," she demanded. "You apologize right now." Frank was in no mood for apologies. Breaking free of his mother, he said, "Lemme go, Ma! Mind your own business."

After Frank was gone, Nancy realized that, Hollywood actress or not, Marilyn was just another woman, like the rest of Frank's extramarital conquests, and she wasn't going to give up her marriage without a good fight. Dolly encouraged her to do something about it. Dolly had become a surprising ally to Nancy when it came to Frank's "whores," as she called them. "You have to fight to keep your family together," she told her daughter-in-law. "Don't let that son of mine ruin your family! You two got kids, Nancy!"

"Is that what you would do?" Nancy asked her, according to a later recollection. "Fight?"

"No," Dolly said, shaking her head. "I would cut his balls off, that's what I would do." Dolly said that she wouldn't put up with such behavior from Frank "for five seconds." However, she felt that Nancy was different. Maybe Nancy was stronger than she was, Dolly offered. "You're a fighter, Nancy," she told her. "You have to fight for your family."

Then, as Dolly stood with her arms folded across her chest, Nancy telephoned George Evans. "I'm afraid there's another one," she somewhat tremulously told him. "I need you to take care of Marilyn Maxwell."

Just as he had handled Dorothy Bonucelli, George Evans was more than happy to intervene on Nancy Sinatra's behalf. Dutifully, he sprang into action; he decided to use on Marilyn Maxwell the same line that seemed to work so well in getting rid of Dorothy Bonucelli.

According to Ted Hechtman, "Once again, as in the case of Dorothy, George didn't even bother talking to Frank about it. He just called Marilyn and said, 'Listen, you've got a morals clause in your studio contract that says you can't disgrace the studio by going out with a married man. You've never seen bad publicity like the kind you're gonna see if you go out on the town in New York with Frank Sinatra.' Since George was a legitimate show-business publicist, Marilyn didn't know if that was a threat, a promise, or just a warning. Therefore, she decided she didn't want to be seen with Frank in New York. Moreover, she said she needed time to reconsider her relationship with him. It was all a lot more trouble than she'd imagined it would be. Of course, Frank was upset when he found out what George had done. He called him every name in the book for messing up his New York plans."

George Evans had his hands full with Frank. "He's got more dollars than sense, let's face it," he said at this time. However, Evans had won the Marilyn Maxwell battle for Nancy—at least for the moment.

But Frank didn't waste much time lamenting the loss of Marilyn Maxwell in his life. With her out of the picture, he set his sights on bona fide star Lana Turner.

Lana Turner

*I*f Nancy Sinatra thought Marilyn Maxwell was formidable, one wonders what she might have thought of the gorgeous, twenty-six-year-old Lana Turner, a small-town girl from Wallace, Idaho, who'd been born Julia Turner to teenage parents. She and her mother moved to Los Angeles in 1931, when Julia was ten, after the murder of her father. Hollywood legend has it that she was discovered at Schwab's Pharmacy in Hollywood. Actually, it was at the Top Hat Malt Shop on Sunset Boulevard, where at sixteen she was spotted by William R. Wilkerson, publisher of the *Hollywood Reporter*. He was attracted by her beauty and personality and suggested that Zeppo Marx—one of the Marx Brothers, who also had a talent agency—sign her to a contract. In 1937, Marx got her a deal with MGM; Louis B. Mayer felt sure she could be the next big sex symbol after Jean Harlow's death six months prior to Turner's signing. By the time Frank met her, Lana had made more than twenty films and was very successful, very wealthy, and—after two marriages—very single, living in a lofty estate in Bel-Air overlooking the country club.

That Lana had a three-year-old daughter, Cheryl Crane—offspring of a brief marriage to restaurateur Steve Crane—didn't impede her celebrity lifestyle. As she once recalled of this particular time, "Ciro's was a favorite haunt. I'd walk up the steps and through the glass door and pass the velvet rope that barred the less fortunates. And the headwaiter would spring forward— 'Ah, *Miss Turner*'—and escort me in. I had a special table right by the stairs so I could watch the comings and goings. I'd head straight there, never glancing right or left.

"And then, when I was seated, I'd give the room a long casing, bowing to this one or blowing that one a kiss. Silly, I guess, but fun… Everyone would stare, and you knew you were making an *entrance*. I'd usually dress in something clingy, black or white, sometimes gold, occasionally red. I'd wear diamonds and a fur of some kind draped over one shoulder. Often white fur, my favorite. Maybe ermine or silver fox. Or sable. I had beautiful sables. I'd have jewels in my hair, or flowers, and every hair in place."

When Frank saw her film *The Postman Always Rings Twice*, he couldn't resist Lana, who appeared tanned and gorgeous in white shorts, halter top, and matching turban. "I have to have her," he said. "How can I *not*?" He obtained her phone number from a mutual friend and called her.

At the time, Lana was in love with thirty-three-year-old Tyrone Power, but the relationship was not going well. She actually had more suitors than she could count. Esther Williams, who was a close friend of Turner's, recalled, "Lana's dressing room at MGM was right next to mine. The rest of us, we just had a couch, a coffee table, and a couple of chairs in our dressing rooms. But Lana—she had a king-size bed with pink satin sheets and a roomful of mirrors. When I saw this, I thought, boy, it doesn't take an interior decorator to figure out what you like if you furnish your dressing room *this* way."

Frank would later say that he'd never been with anyone quite as carnal as Lana. She seemed uninterested in anything other than just being with Frank in the bedroom, and he didn't mind. She didn't want to talk about moviemaking or her career or his, and she definitely wasn't interested in his family life. If he tried to engage her in small talk, she was indifferent. World events? Forget it. Simply put, she just wanted to have sex with him, and as often as possible. She fascinated him. He had never known a woman so confident of her sexuality that she didn't care if a man saw her as nothing more than a sex object. In fact, she encouraged it.

It was her confidence, too, that drew him to her. When it came to women, Frank couldn't resist the strong, commanding type, like his mother, Dolly. In her own way, of course, Nancy had strength and resiliency that most of Frank's other women could never even imagine, because she had managed to stay married to the man all this time. But Frank couldn't appreciate that at this point, finding her dull compared to the likes of Lana Turner. In typical fashion, he became completely swept away by Lana with the passage of just about two weeks. This time he told Nancy he was actually moving out of the house. "I'm with Lana now," he said succinctly. "Just let me go, Nancy. Just give me a divorce."

"Hell no," Nancy told him. "*Hell no.*"

Because Frank had fallen for Lana so quickly, Nancy felt certain it was just another fling that wouldn't last. She certainly wasn't going to abandon everything she'd worked so hard to maintain just for another of his passing fancies. Therefore, as had become the status quo of late, on October 5 Nancy telephoned George Evans to tell him they had another problem, and this was a big one: Lana Turner. George didn't know how far he would get with Lana, he told Nancy, but he said he would try.

George made a few calls until he was able to find Lana's telephone number. He called her and issued to her the same warning he'd given to Marilyn Maxwell: If she dated Frank she would find herself in violation of the morals clause of her movie contract. Lana was not one to be cowed by anyone's publicist, though. She laughed. "You are so *cute* to threaten me like this," she told him, "Why, you're just *adorable*, aren't you?" She reminded him that she had thus far made a fortune exploiting her bad-girl image in the movies, and that no one at MGM would be the least bit taken aback by her having a romance with any man, married or otherwise. "In fact, they *hope* I do," she exclaimed. "More box-office dollars for them if I do!" Then she berated George, saying, "You are such a small man if that's the best you could come up with to break up me and Frank. Did his wife put you up to this? Because if she did, I feel sorry for her. This is just *so sad*! You must be so *embarrassed* right now, Mr. Evans."

By the time Lana Turner finished with George, he was sorry he'd ever thought to telephone her. He called Nancy back and told her that he could do nothing about Lana. "She's a real head case, that one," he said. "But don't worry," he hastened to add, "she and Frank will burn themselves out. We have to just give it a second."

That same night, October 5, Frank and Lana attended a party hosted by Norwegian figure skater and film star Sonja Henie. The two danced all evening and—maybe with Lana now emboldened by George's unsuccessful attempt to threaten her—it seemed clear that they were ready for their romance to become more public. After the Henie party, Frank took Lana to a new duplex apartment in Hollywood that he'd just rented two days earlier and had furnished with $30,000 worth of antiques and furniture simply for the purpose of entertaining her there. (He already had one secret apartment in Hollywood, but felt it wasn't extravagant enough for the pampered Lana.) However, Lana wasn't impressed. In fact, when she walked into Sinatra's new love nest, she took one look around and said, "Who needs this *dump*! I'm not sleeping here." Then she threw her wrap over her shoulder, raised her chin, and went for the closest exit. Lana lived her life theatrically, big entrances and big exits being her specialty. In her world, the little red light on the camera was always on, her close-up always in the offing.

"You're right, it *is* a dump," said Frank, anxious to placate her. He took her to the upscale Beverly Hills Hotel, where he rented a pricey bungalow.

On the morning of October 6, Frank told George Evans he intended to marry Lana "as soon as Nancy gives me a divorce." He was in Evans's office in Los Angeles; Ted Hechtman was present.

"You're an *idiot*," George told him, according to Hechtman's memory. George said that Nancy would never divorce Frank, and he couldn't understand why Frank didn't see it. "Then *I'll* divorce *her*," Frank said, adding that Nancy couldn't keep him in a marriage that he didn't want to be in. "Oh, I think she can," George said, "and I think she will, too. Why are you so doll dizzy?" he wanted to know. He observed that Frank had a very nice wife and two wonderful children; he didn't understand why he wasn't satisfied. "Just make the announcement," Frank told George. He reminded George that he worked for him, not for Nancy. In fact, Frank said, in thinking about it he'd decided that George and Nancy had "probably been in cahoots for months." The two then got into a war of words about George's threat to Lana. "How could you use the moral clause card on her?" Frank wanted to know.

"It's because of broads like her that the fucking moral clause card is even in the fucking deck," George Evans exclaimed.

"Frank wanted to know how many other women George had used that card with in the past," Ted Hechtman recalled. "George lied, of course, and said that Lana had been the first. 'Now you embarrassed me in front of her,' Frank said. 'She blew a fuse with me over it. She can't believe I would have a dummy like you representing me.'

" 'Oh, screw her, Frank,' George Evans said. 'You think I care what Lana Turner thinks of me? I'm trying to save your career here. Can't you see that?' "

After this argument went nowhere, George felt he had little choice but to do Frank's bidding and announce to the media that the Sinatras were indeed separating. Calling it "a family squabble," he also noted that "there's no talk of divorce." He cautioned, "This is the first public battle they've ever had, and I don't think it's serious." An irate Nancy packed a couple of Frank's suitcases and threw them out onto the front lawn. "I will never give that bum a divorce," she said, "but I also won't live in the same house with him."

Once the public release was issued, Frank felt a sense of relief. He thought maybe now he could move forward with Lana. It really wasn't about Lana, though. It was just about Frank wanting something new, something different. From a practical standpoint, did he really think Lana Turner was going to be a true partner in life for him? But his emotions were just running away with him, as usual, and he wasn't thinking about the future. This was a major character flaw that would haunt him for years to come. For Frank, it was always about the here and now. The future would handle itself. Right now, all he knew for certain was that he wanted Lana Turner.

That evening, Frank and Lana went to Palm Springs, where Lana owned a second home. They danced at the Chi Chi Club and seemed to not care about the stares and whispers. However, the next day, Lana attempted to deny the affair, calling Louella Parsons to say, "I am not in love with Frank, and he is not in love with me. I have never broken up a home. *I just can't take these accusations!*" (Lana didn't mention that she was also dating Tyrone Power at this time, who was married to French star Annabella.) Public relations were everything to Lana Turner. She was going to do anything she could to stir the pot, especially if it meant more controversy, more attention. When Parsons published Lana's statement, she and Frank had a good laugh over it. "That patsy," Frank said of the reporter. "She doesn't care what she writes, does she?"

Two weeks passed. During that time, the glow between them began to dim somewhat and they found themselves arguing about fidelity. Lana said she wasn't sure that she wanted to end it with Tyrone Power. Moreover, she had information that Frank was still seeing Marilyn Maxwell on the side. She couldn't confirm it, but her source, she said, was reliable. It would turn out that her "source" was none other than her trusted friend Ava Gardner, who was at that time married to Lana's ex-husband, musician Artie Shaw.

After a blazing row, the ever-mercurial Frank walked out on Lana, saying he was finished with her. Hot one minute, cold the next; no wonder Nancy couldn't take him seriously. "Oh, you'll be back," Lana told him. For her it was as if the curtain was just going down on act one. "You know you'll be back."

Family Intervention

*F*rank's public image had definitely taken a big hit after the Lana affair. It had been a major embarrassment for everyone concerned (except maybe Lana). Nancy's life had been turned upside down so that Frank and Lana could have sex without having to hide their relationship. According to Ted Hechtman, a meeting was called at Frank's home by George Evans. Hechtman—who was now partnered with Evans in his new Los Angeles bureau, was present—as were Dolly and Marty Sinatra, Nancy, and Frank. They all sat solemnly around the kitchen table facing Frank.

George began by saying that the situation with Lana had gone too far. Frank squirmed in his seat but didn't respond. George continued, saying that it had evolved into the kind of scandal that hurt not only the family, but also the fans. Again, no response from Frank. "*Say something,*" Dolly shouted at her son, smacking him hard on the back of the head. According to the witness—Hechtman—she was dismayed. "*Whatsa matta you?*" she demanded to know of Frank. "Nancy is a good wife to you, a good mother to your children, and this is the way you treat her?"

"At least let him talk," Marty told his wife. She gave him a look.

Frank mumbled something; it sounded like an apology.

"*Shut-uppa you mou,*" Dolly told him, punching him on the arm. At this point, Nancy said that she realized she should be finished with Frank, but that for the sake of his career and the sanctity of their marriage she was willing to give him one more chance. There were no tears from her; it was as if she was just resigned to the idea of staying with him. "Fine, Nancy, if that's what you want," Frank responded, shrugging his shoulders. He showed no remorse. At that, his mother whacked him on the back of the head again.

Frank didn't say anything else; he just stared straight ahead. Looking at him, as Ted Hechtman recalled it many years later, "You could tell that he was trying to feel something. He had his brow furrowed as if he was trying to come up with an emotion. Sorrow. Or guilt. Or regret. Or...who knows? *Something.* But looking at him in that moment, I realized the truth: He had nothing. He was just empty." Hechtman would say that it seemed that Frank was just unable to access his emotions. "He appeared to be trying to feel something," he would say, "but there just didn't seem to be anything there. I think he wanted to feel sorry, he wanted to feel remorse, but the truth was that he simply didn't feel it...and he couldn't act as if he did."

As he grew older, Frank's mood would swing from apathy, where he would feel nothing (which was where he found himself on this day); depression, where he would become morose, deeply sad, and self-destructive; anger, where he would feel enraged and act out in a reckless manner; and finally, excitement, where he would be ebullient, even ecstatic. But there were no shades of gray between them. Moreover, it was impossible to know what sort of event might trigger which mood.

In today's world, Sinatra would likely be diagnosed as bipolar. However, the only diagnosis he ever actually received from a psychiatrist would be in the 1950s when Dr. Ralph Greenson—also Marilyn Monroe's psychiatrist—would diagnose him as being manic-depressive. Beyond his sessions with Sinatra, Greenson did nothing else to treat him. He most certainly did not administer the kinds of strong medications he would later prescribe to Marilyn, drugs that many people in her life would feel led to her demise.

"George spent about thirty minutes telling him how we were going to handle the matter of Lana," said Ted Hechtman, "coming up with a strategy for what would be a public reunion with Nancy. She was on board, but wary. He was robotic, at best. His parents both struck me as being extremely agitated."

A few days later, the reunion occurred during comic Phil Silvers's engagement at Slapsie Maxie's club in Hollywood. Frank joined Silvers onstage in what looked like an impromptu moment but was actually a scripted part of Silvers's act. That night, Nancy showed up in the audience, as per George Evans's instruction. When Frank started singing the number "Going Home," he became emotional. Phil, who felt that "these two kids belong together," then walked him down to Nancy's table. She was crying. Frank put his arms around her, and as they embraced, the audience applauded their reconciliation. The next day, Frank Sinatra went home.

With the latest intrusion out of the way, Nancy said she hoped life at the Sinatra household would now continue "as if Lana Turner was never born into the world." However, the affair with Lana had caused a serious breach of trust and respect in her marriage. Maybe it was because it was so public and newsworthy, or maybe it was just one woman too many where Nancy was concerned, but for whatever reason, the Sinatras would never quite recover from Frank's affair with Lana Turner.

The Diamond Bracelet

*F*or the next two months, Frank Sinatra did his best to be repentant. In November, he bought Nancy a full-length ermine coat and muff; they went to New York together and were seen about town having a wonderful time. For Christmas he gave her an expensive three-strand pearl necklace. He was applying himself more than ever to being a good father to little Nancy and Frankie. Was he also being faithful? Nancy Sinatra didn't really want to know. She was with her husband, they were making love again, and she was just hoping for the best. She didn't want any more information than what was immediately available to her; she didn't want to ask him any questions. "In my experience," she said at the time, "cheaters are almost always liars too. So why even ask?"

One day, Nancy discovered an expensive-looking diamond bracelet in the glove compartment of the new Cadillac Frank had just purchased for her. She assumed that it was yet one more expensive gift from a husband doing his best to make amends for past indiscretions. She caught her breath in surprise. Then she gently placed the bracelet back in its box and put it back exactly where she had found it. She decided to just wait for Frank to present it to her.

On December 31, the Sinatras hosted a New Year's Eve party. It was a success, with at least two hundred people showing up. Dressed to the nines, Frank and Nancy mingled with their guests, appearing for all the world as the ideal couple. Breaking away from her husband for just a moment, Nancy was speaking to a movie studio executive when, across the room, she saw...her. It wasn't Lana Turner. Worse, it was Marilyn Maxwell. She thought George Evans had taken care of Marilyn, and in fact, she hadn't given Marilyn a second thought in months. What was *she* doing at the party, and in Nancy's home? As Nancy approached the actress, much to her great dismay she realized that Marilyn was wearing the diamond bracelet she had earlier found in Frank's glove compartment.

"Where did you get that?" Nancy demanded to know as she stood before Marilyn. She was pointing to her wrist.

"Oh, a very good friend gave it to me," Marilyn said with a frozen smile.

In a controlled but angry tone, Nancy said, "I want you out of my house. Now, go! I mean it. Right now."

"Excuse me?" Marilyn asked. "I beg your pardon?"

"No. *I beg yours*," Nancy said. She pointed to the bracelet. "That belongs to me," she proclaimed. "I've put up with a lot of crap in the last eight years of being married to that bum, and I *deserve* that bracelet."

Marilyn, her mouth agape, obediently unclasped the bracelet and handed it over.

At that moment, Frank came over to the two women, put his arm around them, and whispered something in Nancy's ear. Nancy pulled away from him. "Don't you dare say one word to me," she hissed. "You invited *her*? To our home?"

"But...I..." Frank seemed at a loss. "I'm sorry, Nancy. Jesus Christ, I'm sorry."

By this time, partygoers in the vicinity knew there was trouble and word was spreading quickly throughout the house. Nancy ran from the room, and Marilyn headed toward the coat room.

"Holy Christ," Frank exclaimed to Ted Hechtman.

"Why did you invite her?" Ted asked, according to his memory of the conversation.

"What do you think I am, an idiot?" Frank asked. "There's no way in hell I would have invited that woman to my home. Not with Nancy here. Do you think George did?" he asked, speaking of George Evans.

"Let me go get him," Ted offered. With that Ted ran to fetch George.

"What happened? *What happened?*" an alarmed George asked when he bolted out from another room. He hadn't witnessed the scene but had already heard about it. Frank asked George if he'd invited Marilyn to the party. "What? Are you crazy?" George answered. "I would never invite her here. I wouldn't do that to you, or to Nancy."

"Well, she came to start trouble, then, I guess," Frank said, trying to put the pieces together.

"But did you give her that diamond bracelet?" George asked.

"Yeah, well," Frank said, hanging his head. "I ain't gonna lie. I did."

"You're still seeing her?" George asked, now becoming angry.

"I ain't gonna lie about that either," Frank said.

George shook his head in disgust and stormed off.

A few moments later, Marilyn Maxwell returned to the living room in a white fur wrap. "It was never my intention to do anything this evening but spread good cheer," she announced grandly to the guests. "Sadly," she concluded, "that now seems impossible." She whipped around to make her exit, yanking at the brass knob of the heavy front door. It swung open. Then she turned to face her audience one last time. "And now, my friends," she declared dramatically, "I simply must go." With that, she turned again and entered the cold night air, leaving the door wide open. When a gust of wind blew into the house, one of the other guests pushed the door closed and said, "Let's keep out the chill, shall we?"

The party continued as if nothing had occurred—but without Nancy, who had also disappeared from the festivities. Even the most ardent Sinatra supporters, like Jule Styne and Sammy Davis, both of whom remembered the story, were hard-pressed to defend Sinatra's behavior.

After most of the guests had departed, Nancy returned. She had changed from her red-and-green satin evening dress to a simple white silk robe. Her eyes were red. The guests who remained were all close friends and family members, about a dozen people, and perhaps she thought that she would join them for coffee, liqueurs, and dessert. But the sight of her husband laughing with Manie Sacks and his other buddies just served to reignite her fury. She must have been wondering, why was he so happy when she was so miserable? "How can you be so cruel and unfeeling?" she asked Frank. Everyone in the dining room froze. "What have I ever done to you to make you treat me like this?" she pressed on. "I don't understand it. *What have I ever done?*"

Frank rolled his eyes. "Oh boy, here we go again, Nancy. What have I done? What have I done?" he said, mocking her tone. Clearly, he'd had too much to drink. "You, you, you. Jesus Christ, what about *me*? You think this is easy for me?"

Nancy was speechless. Frank was not. "What is it?" he continued to challenge her, his face inches from her own. "You don't have enough money? We don't live a good life? I'm not a big enough success? What is it? You tell me." It was as if he just couldn't stop himself; he was out of control.

Nancy burst into tears and left the room.

"All right," Frank announced to the stunned remaining guests. "Everybody out. Out. Out. Out! Happy fucking New Year's. Now get the hell out. Show's over."

Frank and the Mob

*O*ne of the most enduring rumors about Frank Sinatra is that he was deeply involved with the Mafia. The first stories of this nature began to circulate after his attorneys and agents extricated him from the Tommy Dorsey contract. Because it was so well known that Dorsey had been adamant about holding Sinatra to his deal, when he was free of it so suddenly, rumors had it that the singer's underworld friends had intervened on his behalf. Of course, the motley crew from Hoboken who, at Hank Sanicola's direction, actually did intervene could hardly be considered dangerous gangsters. The Dorsey business aside, the most lurid and persistent stories connecting Sinatra to the mob actually started in 1947, a few years after the contract was settled.

Frank Sinatra would always claim that the reason he was picked on by certain members of the press and accused of being a friend of the Mafia was his Italian-American heritage, because his name ended in a vowel. He and his family labeled the charges "discrimination." Their position was understandable, but why was it that other Italian Americans, such as Vic Damone, Perry Como, even Al Pacino (who actually went on to play a godfather in the series of films by that name), were not similarly persecuted because of their vowel-ending last names?

Frank and his family also suggested that many nightclubs in the 1940s and '50s were run by gangsters, and that if a person wanted to work in show business, he or she had to some extent to do business with the underworld. This appears to be true.

However, Frank was also guilty of poor judgment when it came to the people he socialized with when he wasn't working. When it came to the underworld, he couldn't seem to help himself. Going all the way back to his first exposure to *uomini rispettati* during his early days in Hoboken, he was always fascinated by colorful mobster types. These were men who, in his view anyway, were powerful enough to get away with pretty much anything. He found it an admirable way to live, and he sought to comport himself the same way—not to be bound by what might be considered normal behavior when it came to his marriage or even in how he dealt with those in his social circle. He did things his way, no matter what anyone thought of him. He expected complete loyalty, even though he often didn't demonstrate it himself. If someone crossed him, that person was banished from his life forever. "It was as if he was a mobster in his own world," is how Peter Lawford once so aptly put it. "He hero-worshipped those underworld guys, and then he treated people in his own life like he was a mob boss, like he was a don."

In January 1947, thirty-one-year-old Frank was asked by Joe Fischetti, a buddy he had known from Hoboken since 1938 (and cousin and heir of Al Capone), if he would like to meet the boss of the Cosa Nostra crime syndicate, Lucky Luciano. Thirty-nine-year-old Luciano, who had been in exile in Havana since late October 1946, was living the good life in a spacious estate in the exclusive Miramar suburb among the other properties and yacht clubs of affluent Cubans and resident Americans. At this time, he was planning the first full-scale confab of American underworld leaders since a Chicago gathering in 1932. It was to be held on the upper floors of the Hotel Nacional in Havana, a busy mecca for gamblers. There were certain decisions to be made at this meeting—one of which had to do with Luciano's determination to be, as he once put it, "the boss of bosses," *capo di tutti capi*, head of the American underworld—and each delegate would have a vote on this matter. During the convention, there would also be banquets, meetings, and parties of the Mafia and its allies, all off-limits to the other guests of the hotel.

The delegates—all known by the FBI to be members of the syndicate and recognized gangsters—began to show up in Havana for this conference. Frank Costello, Augie Pisano, Mike Miranda, Joe Adonis, Tommy "Three Fingers" Brown Lucchese, Joe Profaci, Willie Moretti, Giuseppe (Joe) "the Fat Man" Magliocco, Albert "the Executioner" Anastasia, and Joe "Bananas" Bonanno all arrived from New York and New Jersey. Santo Trafficante came from Florida, Carlos Marcello from New Orleans. Tony Accardo, the head of the Chicago underworld, came with Rocco and Charlie "Trigger Happy" Fischetti (Joe's brothers). Two other noteworthy delegates would also be present; however, they would not be able to vote on important matters because they were Jewish: "Dandy Phil" Kastel and Meyer Lansky.

As each delegate arrived, he would first go to Luciano's villa and pay homage to him. After Luciano's preeminence was acknowledged, each man would give him an envelope stuffed with cash—$150,000 in all—which Luciano would use to buy points in the casino at the Hotel Nacional. Upon the conclusion of these meetings, the delegates were dispatched to the hotel, where thirty-six opulently appointed suites had been reserved for them. Luciano would join them there later, upon the adjournment of the first general meeting of the council of the Unione Siciliana.

The plan Joe Fischetti proposed to Frank Sinatra was that Frank and Nancy meet him in Miami for a February vacation, after which Frank and Joe, Charlie, and Rocco Fischetti would go to Havana and meet Lucky Luciano. (Joe was the best-looking, most charismatic of the Fischettis, though the FBI called him "the least intelligent and least aggressive.") Frank couldn't wait to go. As earlier stated, in his old Hoboken neighborhood, thugs like Luciano were revered. He wanted to know what made a guy like Lucky Luciano tick, and he was excited about the opportunity to socialize with such a dangerous and controversial character.

On January 31, 1947, Frank made plans to go to Havana with the Fischetti brothers. He did not—at least from all available evidence—

realize that he was going to be attending any sort of underworld confab, nor apparently did he realize that he was being used as a cover for that conference in order to give it an air of legitimacy. Frank just thought he and Nancy were going to Havana to meet Luciano. But unbeknownst to him, Luciano was telling his friends all across the country that one of the perks of coming to Havana for the confab was meeting Frank Sinatra! Or as Luciano's biographer Martin A. Gosch, author of *The Last Testament of Lucky Luciano*, explained, "If anyone asked, there was an outward reason for such a gathering. It was to honor an Italian boy from New Jersey named Frank Sinatra, the crooner who had become the idol of the nation's bobby-sox set."

Nancy Makes a Decision

$\mathcal{A}$t the beginning of February 1947, Nancy Sinatra's doctor confirmed that she was pregnant again.

While Frank was elated by the news, Nancy wasn't happy. She no longer trusted Frank and wasn't even sure she still wanted to be married to him. She also wasn't sure she was ready to stop fighting for him either. She only knew that she didn't want to bring a third child into a marriage that she now viewed as fundamentally flawed. Therefore she told Frank she was thinking about terminating the pregnancy.

Frank wasn't much of a father. Yes, of course he loved his two children, Nancy and Frank. However, he wasn't exactly available to them. When he had time, he did his best. He played with them, fed them, made them laugh. They loved their daddy, there was no doubt about it. But he rarely had time for them, and when he was home he was usually preoccupied with his work. Frank was a realist about it, too. Throughout his life, he would never flatter himself by saying he'd been a great father. He knew the truth, as did his children. Nancy had accepted his limitations in this regard, but that didn't mean she was happy about them. The more she and Frank discussed it, the more Nancy was sure she didn't want to have the baby.

Frank had had strong feelings about abortion ever since his mother was convicted of performing such operations in Hoboken. He was ashamed of what she had done, and would never forget the way he was taunted by other kids in the neighborhood after her arrest. Therefore the idea of Nancy terminating her pregnancy was repellent to him. He begged her to reconsider. He suggested that their upcoming trip to Cuba might give them time to sort it all out. However, now Nancy didn't even want to go to Cuba with him. She would only agree to meet him in Acapulco afterward.

"You will *not* do *it* while I'm gone," Frank told her. It was more like an order than it was a request. However, by this time, Nancy wasn't taking orders from Frank.

She kissed him goodbye; he went his way—and she went hers, straight to a doctor. "It was hard," she later told her daughter Tina. "But I knew I was doing the right thing."

In Cuba with the Boys

On February 11, 1947, Frank Sinatra and the Fischettis flew to Havana and checked into the Hotel Nacional. It took about two days for Frank to come to the realization that he was surrounded by a bunch of known criminals, all of whom wanted his autograph.

Years later, none of Frank's friends would talk on the record about his visit to Havana that year. However, they remember it well, at least based on what Frank told them privately. Frank suggested that he took a walk on the wild side and found it maybe a little wilder than expected. But once he was there it was too late to do anything about it. Because he had too much pride to leave and believed he would look cowardly or ungracious if he did so, he decided that, what the hell, he was here and might as well have some fun. So he stayed, had a good time, gambled at the casino, went to the races and then to a party with Lucky Luciano, never giving a second thought as to how all of this merriment might appear to his public and his critics. Could he really have been so naïve? It's not likely, but that was his story... and he was sticking to it.

To Martin A. Gosch, Lucky Luciano later confided, "Frank was a good kid and we were all proud of him, the way he made it to the top...a skinny kid from around Hoboken with a terrific voice and one hundred percent Italian. He used to sing around the joints there, and all the guys liked him.

"When the time came when some dough was needed to put Frank across with the public, they put it up. He had a job working for Tommy Dorsey's band, and he was getting about a hundred and fifty bucks a week, but he needed publicity, clothes, different kinds of special music things, and they all cost quite a bit of money—I think it was about fifty or sixty grand. I okayed the money, and it come out of the fund, even though some guys put up a little extra on a personal basis. It all helped him become a big star, and he was just showing his appreciation by coming down to Havana to say hello to me."

Luciano's claim would seem to be verification of the underworld's influence on Sinatra's early career. But can he be believed? Was Lucky Luciano a credible source for information about Frank Sinatra?

Certainly, if any of the "boys" helped Frank when he was with Tommy Dorsey's band, it was news to anyone who knew Sinatra well. Ted Hechtman says, "Fifty thousand? That's what Luciano claims to be responsible for? Well, that makes no sense. Sinatra had friends with money, like Axel [Stordahl]. He would never go to the mob with a favor like that if he needed money, which he didn't at the time. He was not stupid—impulsive and unthinking, yes, but not stupid."

Hechtman adds, "And his act? It wasn't like he had this big production going on with fancy costumes and dancers. He wore one of the same three tuxedos every night.

"And publicity? Before George Evans came into his life, the only publicity Sinatra ever got was whatever Tommy would let him have and whatever Frankie would generate for himself by hounding reporters.

"Song arrangements? Those were Tommy's arrangements.

"The whole thing is a bunch of crap from a gangster trying to make himself look important."

True or not, Lucky Luciano's attempt to take credit for Frank Sinatra's career in his memoirs helped fuel the sinister stories about Sinatra over the years. But Frank had allowed himself to be in the wrong place at the wrong time with the wrong kinds of people. Of course, Frank's detractors were inclined to believe Luciano and his ilk, while his fans believed Frank. The rest of the public could only wonder.

Many years later, Frank attempted to explain his presence in Havana this way: He happened to run into Joe Fischetti when he was performing in Miami for a Damon Runyon Cancer Fund benefit. The two spoke and realized that, quite by coincidence, they were both headed for Havana for a vacation. When he got there—he didn't say with whom he went—he was having a drink and met a large group of men and women. He was invited to dinner with them, and while he was sitting at the table talking it occurred to him that one of the diners was Lucky Luciano. "It suddenly struck me," Frank said, "that I was laying myself open to criticism by remaining at the table, but I could think of no way to leave the table without creating a scene." Then, as he explained, he ran into Luciano again at the Hotel Nacional's casino, "had a quick drink, and excused myself. Those were the only times I have ever seen Luciano in my life."

A good story, but not true, at least according to all evidence.

However, even Lucky Luciano admitted that Sinatra did nothing actually illegal while in Havana. "I don't want to give the idea that he was ever asked to do something illegal, by me or by anybody else that I know about," he said. "He gave out a few presents to different guys, like a gold cigarette case, a watch, that kind of thing, but that was it. As for me, the guy was always number one okay."

Though Frank tried to ignore the fact that perhaps he had made a blunder in going to the mafioso convention, in the days ahead the media wouldn't let it go. Robert Ruark, a Scripps-Howard newspaper columnist, wrote a blistering attack on Sinatra, calling him a hypocrite for presenting himself as "the self-confessed savior of the country's small fry," yet wanting to "mob up with the likes of Lucky Luciano."

In fact, the shadow of Frank's visit to Havana would always loom large; his critics would always think the worst of him because of it. In time, gossip columnists and FBI investigators claimed that he had been carrying $2 million (in small bills!) in a briefcase that he intended to give to Luciano. One of his friends countered, "If you think Sinatra was going to give a deported drug dealer two million bucks, you're nuts. If you think he would walk around with a briefcase full of that much cash in 1947? Forget it! I know what he had in that briefcase. Clean underwear. That's what he always carried with him. Clean underwear worth about fifty bucks." (Moreover, if Sinatra ended up giving Luciano $2 million, he got taken advantage of, because all of the delegates *combined* only came up with $150,000 for their boss.)*

Regret

After leaving Havana, Frank went to Acapulco to join Nancy for their planned vacation there. He didn't know she'd terminated the pregnancy until she arrived and then told him. "It was a terrible moment for Dad," Tina Sinatra recalled.

Frank was devastated by Nancy's decision. He couldn't believe she would abort their child. He knew, though, that his bad behavior had been responsible for her decision. He would always regret it. "He had deemed his brief encounters unimportant, but now they had taken from him something dear and irreplaceable," Tina recalled. "And he told my mother, 'Don't you *ever* do that again.'"

Nancy had made her point. She didn't believe in him, nor did she have faith in their life together. He would have to win favor with her—again. If such a thing was even possible.

The FBI and the Reporter

Frank had known for some time that he was being investigated by the FBI; he'd actually had a difficult time securing a passport for his USO trip with Phil Silvers for that very reason. The FBI made a habit of investigating celebrities at this time, especially with communism a

---

* Years later, in early 1961, Lucky Luciano was planning a movie about his years in exile, with a screenplay written by Martin Gosch. Though Luciano wanted Cary Grant to play him in the film, Gosch had a better idea: Dean Martin. Gosch didn't know Dean, however, and wondered how they would go about getting the script to him. "Don't worry about that," Luciano told him. "I'll take care of it." Luciano airmailed a copy of the 175-page script to Frank Sinatra and asked him to present it to Dean. When Frank did so, Martin turned it down, explaining he didn't want to play such a shady character.

major concern. However, after Frank's Havana escapade, the Bureau began seriously looking into his association with other underworld characters.

Years later, when FBI documents regarding Sinatra were released under the Freedom of Information Act, Lee Mortimer—Frank's adversary in the press—was revealed to be a primary source of information. In fact, he was FBI associate director Clyde Tolson's main informant. For instance, Mortimer was the man responsible for the story about Sinatra bringing millions "in small bills" to Havana to lay at the throne of Luciano. This anecdote remains in the FBI records as fact, not rumor. Indeed, the persistent problem with the reams of FBI documents, often referred to in accounts of Frank Sinatra's ties to the underworld in the 1940s, is that many of them state rumor as fact. Much of it involves stories and anecdotes Mortimer hadn't even confirmed. In truth, Mortimer and Tolson were simply exchanging gossip about Sinatra.

By this time, 1947, Frank had become tired of Lee Mortimer's vitriol, especially when word leaked back to him that the reporter might be participating in the FBI's investigation of him. Therefore, through a mutual friend—a violinist named Joe Candullo—Frank sent Lee a message: "If you don't quit knocking me and my fans, I'm gonna knock your brains out."

"I'm not afraid of him," Mortimer told Candullo. "I'm not going to quit writing about him, either. Tell that to him and his cheap hoodlums."

"He's digging into my life? Fine," Sinatra told George Evans. "I'm digging into his. I think he's a queer. Find out everything you can about *that*." Actually, Mortimer—who would go on to have five wives—was not known to be gay. Still, Frank insisted he was part of what he called "the Garter Belt Mafia."

George protested, saying he wasn't a private investigator but rather a publicist. Not only that, he still had to maintain a working relationship with Mortimer; Frank wasn't his only client. Furthermore, he thought Frank's idea was mean-spirited and would just lead to more trouble.

All of this uneasiness came to a head on April 8, 1947, when Sinatra accosted Mortimer at Ciro's in Hollywood, called him a "fruit," and then decked him. As three of Frank's "hangers-on," fellows who acted as bodyguards, held down the hapless, skinny reporter, Frank punched away, calling him names and threatening him. "Next time I see you, I'll kill you, you little degenerate."

"Okay, I hit him," Frank admitted to the press later. "I'm sorry that it happened, but I was raised in a tough neighborhood where you had to fight at the drop of a hat, and I couldn't help myself." Frank also said the writer had started the fight by calling him a "little dago bastard," which Mortimer denied.

After the fracas, Mortimer had Frank Sinatra arrested and charged with assault and battery. The charge resulted in Sinatra's gun permit being revoked. Bail was set at $500. Mortimer later sued for $25,000.

During the investigation of the assault, Frank didn't come out well. The district attorney's office concluded that no slur was spoken by Mortimer and that Sinatra had attacked him without provocation. Frank claimed that he had been *told* by an acquaintance that Mortimer had made the slur, that he actually hadn't heard it himself. He now believed Mortimer hadn't called him a dago after all, or so he said. He also stated that there was "probably no reason" for him to have struck the writer. The charges were dropped.

The Mortimer lawsuit was settled on June 4, 1947, the day before it was set to go to trial. Louis B. Mayer had become so annoyed with Sinatra's histrionics that he insisted Frank settle with Mortimer by giving him $9,000, which he did. The court also ordered him to apologize.

After the Mortimer incident, George Evans did what he had become accustomed to in these sorts of imbroglios: He tried to salvage Sinatra's image. This time he had Frank apologize to columnist Louella Parsons, saying, "I know I did many things I shouldn't have, things I'm sorry for." It was too late, though. As far as the public could tell, not only did Frank socialize with murderers and drug kingpins, but he also beat up defenseless reporters in Hollywood nightclubs because they wrote about it. "Why doesn't Frankie just hang himself and get it over with?" an exasperated George Evans asked Nancy. "'Cause he's killing himself anyway." She couldn't disagree.

In the spring of 1947, as part of Evans's campaign to resurrect Frank's public image, he had his client write "An Open Letter" to his fans, which was written on MGM studio letterhead and published in many magazines and newspapers. The long letter, signed "Gratefully yours, Frank Sinatra," thanked his fans for supporting him throughout the time that he was "called a Red and the intimate chum of Lucky Luciano. Not a word of that happens to be true," he wrote. "And thousands of you, in every city and town where these cowardly attacks on my character were published, threatened to quit reading these newspapers unless they played fair with me. Thanks to you the attacks ceased."

In fact, the "attacks" would continue for years to come...

* * *

In May 1947, Frank Sinatra appeared at the Capitol Theatre in New York, where he had had his original success with Major Bowes in 1935. It was at this engagement that he had an epiphany of sorts. For years now, he had been living on the edge of rebellion, in a selfish daze, both personally and professionally. There had been so many incidents involving his volatile temper that people lost track of them. It didn't matter that he was still making excellent records. His sales were down and his image was all but ruined by bad public relations.

Back in 1945, when Frank played the Paramount Theatre, he was mobbed by so many fans he couldn't even leave the theater for dinner. "No one's ever been this hot," he boasted at the time. "This is gonna last forever." Now three years had passed, and this time he walked out to a tepid reception from an opening-night crowd at the Capitol. After the show, he found only a few fans waiting for him at the stage door.

"This isn't good," a worried Frank told George Evans the next day at a meeting with members of the entourage and his wife, Nancy. "Pay some kids. Get them in here. What's the matter with you?" he asked George.

"Frankie, let me ask you something," George said. "You think you can do anything you want to do? Think you can say anything you want to say? Think you can tell everyone to go to hell? Well, right here is where you start paying, buddy boy. 'Cause I couldn't *pay* people to cheer for you right now. So what do you say to that?"

Frank didn't know what to say. He turned to Nancy.

"Don't look at me," Nancy said abruptly. "I don't know what to tell you, Frank. What do you expect from me?"

Frank just looked at his wife blankly. "Not much, I guess," he said, his head hanging low. "I guess I got no right to expect much, do I?"

Part Four

THE AVA YEARS

Ava Gardner

By 1947, the dynamic of Frank's marriage to Nancy was more complex than ever. Though he was increasingly restless, he still loved her in his own way and enjoyed being with her and the children. "Dad made a dramatic turnaround," Tina Sinatra—who wouldn't be born until 1948—recalled. "He kept his road trips briefer and threw himself into home life. By day he was absorbed in his children. By night he was courting Mom all over again with dinner and dancing at Ciro's. He was really trying. He would make this marriage work in spite of himself." Indeed, the result of Frank's renewed interest in his marriage was that Nancy became pregnant again. This time, she decided to have the baby. She was "reasonably convinced," as she would later put it, that Frank was now as devoted to her and the family as was possible for him, given his character and temperament. All she could do was hope for the best.

Despite his renewed efforts to be a good husband and father, Frank was still living a double life. He would spend time with Nancy and the kids in Toluca Lake, but he also leased an apartment at the Sunset Tower in Hollywood, where he and Jimmy Van Heusen, Sammy Cahn, and other buddies could drink into the night and have women available to them. Nancy eventually found out about the apartment but decided not to fight about it. They both knew she wasn't going to divorce him, so Frank would do whatever he wanted and Nancy had no leverage to stop him. She found solace in her children and in the rest of her family. When Frank was present, she was happy. When he was gone, she was fine. She had learned to suppress that part of herself that longed for a committed partner. People who knew what was going on in her life began to view her as a very sad, albeit brave woman.

When Frank and his friends learned that the glamorous film star Ava Gardner lived in an apartment building across the way from the Sunset Tower, they would drunkenly call from the balcony, "Ava, can you hear us? Ava, we know you're in there. Come on out, Ava, wherever you are. Join us for a beer." Eventually she would come to the window and wave, which was pretty much all the encouragement Frank needed.

Ava was an exquisite beauty, the envy of women around the world. When she walked into a room, her green eyes flashing, everyone took notice. Ava exuded a smoldering sensuality that translated into star quality on the screen. In her private life, she was—to use a term that today describes self-involved, temperamental stars—a true diva. She knew how to conduct her professional career ("I like only reflected light on my face and a small spotlight under my chin," she once told cameraman George Folsey) and her personal life ("I like my men compliant," she once told good friend Lana Turner). Spoiled, temperamental, and a real challenge to a man's authority, she was as seductive as any woman Sinatra had ever met. Unlike Lana, though, she wasn't afraid to relax and be "offstage." While she was every bit as dramatic and theatrical as Lana in her day-to-day dealings with people, she was down-to-earth when around close friends. She enjoyed kicking off her shoes, getting comfortable on a couch, and being casual.

Frank Sinatra had been captivated by Ava Gardner as far back as the Dorsey days. The two then saw each other throughout the late 1940s at MGM and RKO, and also socially at a few Hollywood nightclubs, like the Mocambo (during the time she was married to Mickey Rooney). But after seeing her posing on the cover of the December 1944 issue of *Photoplay* (bare-shouldered and wearing an expensive-looking emerald necklace), Frank was smitten. The caption on the cover photo read, "She's sexsational!"

"Stop drooling, Frankie baby," a friend said. "You like what you see, don't you?"

Frank responded, "You bet your ass I do. And you wanna know something? I'm gonna marry that girl."

In early 1948, Frank "bumped into" Ava in the lobby of the Sunset Tower. He asked her out on a date for drinks and then dinner. Although she knew that Frank was married, she agreed to go out with him because, as she told her maid, Mearene Jordan, "he was handsome, with his thin, boyish face, the bright blue eyes, and this incredible grin. He sure was attractive. Very attractive. What else could I do?" (Mearene Jordan—an African-American woman who is today in her nineties, would be Ava Gardner's maid for forty-four years. The two were very close, almost as close as sisters. Ava and everyone else called her Rene.)

On their first date, Frank and Ava drank quite a bit, and they immediately began to confide in one another. They'd both worked hard to get where they were. They loved show business, but they resented it too, because of all of the media scrutiny of their personal lives. Even more significantly, they also felt that they always let down the people they loved the most, and were convinced that they were incapable of changing. It was as if they were laying the foundation for something serious, not frivolous. They also had fun, going to a shooting gallery at an amusement park and firing pellets at stuffed animals. At the end of the date, Sinatra took her to an apartment—she said it wasn't at the Sunset Tower, so apparently he had another secret place. They took off their clothes and almost had sex, but she suddenly vetoed the notion. She quickly got dressed and went home. "I decided I didn't want to just give it all away on the first date," she later admitted. "It's better to keep 'em wanting more."

During their evening together, though she did open up, Ava didn't talk much about her small-town background. She said something about being from North Carolina. She mentioned that her father died when she was fifteen. She was the youngest of seven children. "I had to be tough," was all she wanted to say about her childhood. "I was always a tough son of a bitch." The last thing she wanted to do was dwell on it, or even talk about it. "Who cares?" she asked Frank when he pressed about her history. Frank felt a strong magnetism toward her. He would later tell friends that he was so drawn to Ava, "it made me feel like she had put something in my drink."

"What will it take to get you into my bed?" Frank asked her.

She smiled and licked her lips. "Not much," she said. "Just a little bit more than what you've already done. But...not much."

1948–49

$\mathcal{P}$rofessionally, the last years of the decade would not be good ones for Frank Sinatra, as he continued his downward spiral.

In March 1948, he recorded "It Only Happens When I Dance with You," and "A Fella with an Umbrella," two of only ten songs he would record the entire year. March was also the month RKO released *The Miracle of the Bells*, Frank's first nonmusical film role. Remembering that his singing rival Bing Crosby had won an Academy Award playing a priest in *Going My Way* (1944), Frank hoped he would be as fortunate in this film as "Father Paul." Opposite Fred MacMurray and Lee J. Cobb, he acquitted himself nicely as an understanding man of the cloth and sang one a cappella song in the process, "Ever Homeward." When it was released, though, the movie received mostly negative reviews.

The frustration was getting to Frank. The only thing to cheer him at this time was the birth of his third child, daughter Christina (Tina) at Cedars of Lebanon Hospital on June 20, 1948. The baby was born on Father's Day, and this was the only time Frank was in town for the birth of any of his children. He drove Nancy to the hospital at two in the morning. "Mom went into labor while she and Dad were playing charades with friends," Tina recalled, "and when my father returned from the hospital in the predawn hours, he pantomimed my arrival to their anxious guests. I was definitely born into show business."

"I remember sitting with Dad on our grassy hill by the lake, listening to the radio," Nancy Sinatra would recall. "The announcer said, 'Frank Sinatra got a terrific Father's Day present—a brand-new baby girl.' We said, 'Yippee!' And I'll never forget the day Dad brought Mom and Christina home. There she was, this tiny stranger, my baby sister, all wrapped up in a yellow blanket. Mom and Dad had a new little girl, Frankie and I had a new partner in crime. Oh boy! But Tina didn't get to know life the way I had known it. She didn't get to know Daddy as I knew him. She got a bad deal."

Indeed, Frank was elated about being a father again, but, true to his nature, it wasn't an exhilaration that would last very long. It was as if he was happy *that day*, the day Tina was born, and after that it was business as usual. "He was a man who all his life looked outside for what was missing inside," is how Tina Sinatra so adeptly put it.

From July 18 to October 24, Frank worked on *Take Me Out to the Ball Game* for MGM, another musical with Gene Kelly. They played song-and-dance partners who played baseball on a team during the summer. When finally released in March 1949, the movie would fare better at the box office than his previous film, *The Kissing Bandit* (1948), but it still wasn't a solid hit.

This film was notable for Esther Williams's valiant—and successful—attempt to get through a nonswimming role. She said that she was hired for the film because "Judy Garland didn't show up for rehearsals, so they fired her. I couldn't believe they would do that to her. Then Junie [June] Allyson, their next choice, got pregnant. So they looked on the MGM list to see who wasn't working and picked me."

The late Esther Williams once recalled, "There was the little kid in Frank where he loved to stay out and party, and the producers were going to fire him because he was always late to the set. But I understood Frank. He was just living his life. At that time in Hollywood, you could be on time, you could even get there at five o'clock in the morning—like Barbara Stanwyck always did—and then sit down and talk to the crew. But you gotta figure that anyone who did that sort of thing was a really lonely person, and that sure wasn't Frank. He was such a natural actor and so well prepared, what difference did it make if he came in at noon?

"When I was introduced to him, my knees went weak," she remembered. "The way he sang was so, so real to me and so different from others. He didn't just sing a song; he owned it. Talent is attractive, very compelling. When he sang to me in the movie, I felt like his biggest fan in that moment. Here he was, singing to me! What a wonderful moment for my memory book."

Despite *Take Me Out to the Ball Game*, by the end of the year Frank would confide to friends that he felt all but washed up. His records weren't selling, his movies weren't box-office draws, and his concert appearances weren't selling out. This sort of career reversal was due in part to his scandalous personal life, which had begun to garner more attention than his work.

Sammy Davis Jr. recalled that late in 1948 he saw thirty-two-year-old Frank in New York. "Frank was walking down Broadway with no hat on and his collar up, and not a soul was paying attention to him," said Sammy. "This was the man who, only a few years before, had tied up traffic all over Times Square. Now the same man was walking down the same street, and nobody gave a damn."

Unfortunately, things would continue going downhill through 1949. When Frank learned that *Down Beat* had listed him as the number five male singer, he was devastated. It was the first time he'd not been in the top three spots since the late 1930s. The songs he released that year, such as "Some Enchanted Evening" and "Bali Ha'i," were poorly received by both the public and critics.

Still, he somehow managed to maintain the opulent lifestyle he and his family enjoyed, purchasing a three-acre estate for $250,000 at 320 Carolwood Drive in Holmby Hills during the summer of that year. Of the property, which featured a pool, a badminton court, and a citrus orchard, Frank Sinatra Jr. once recalled, "Our home on Carolwood Drive was the most wonderful of estates, situated on beautiful grounds. Nancy and I were by this time school-age. And I can still remember the smiles on my parents' faces on those mornings when the two of us would burst into their room, usually at the crack of dawn, and jump on their bed to awaken them." Sinatra truly couldn't afford the luxurious trappings, though, and the new property just added more pressure to an already stressed life.

The year ended on a somewhat hopeful note with the film *On the Town*, a fun-filled movie costarring Sinatra, with Gene Kelly (together for the third time). This film—the first musical to be shot entirely on location in New York—was a romantic comedy about what happens when sailors meet girls during shore leave, a simple premise but one that brought forth great performances by Sinatra, Kelly, Betty Garrett, Ann Miller, and Vera-Ellen. This time, Sailor Sinatra dazzled with his dancing, and the film was well received. With music by Leonard Bernstein and Roger Edens, and book and lyrics by Betty Comden and Adolph Green, this film was an adaptation of the 1944 Broadway show. (It's worth noting that the Broadway show was an adaptation of a 1944 ballet by Jerome Robbins called *Fancy Free*.) Though Bernstein, unhappy because most of the music he had written for the play was not used, in favor of songs by Edens, publicly boycotted the movie, it was still a hit with the public. It went on to win an Oscar for Best Music, Scoring of a Musical Picture.

Frank was becoming a realist, however. One good film did not a comeback make, and he knew it—especially since MGM had decided to relegate him to second billing under Gene Kelly, who had codirected the movie with Stanley Donen. (Earlier, in 1945, Sinatra had received top billing over Kelly in *Anchors Aweigh*. In 1949 he would have billing over Kelly again, in *Take Me Out to the Ball Game*.)

By the winter of 1949, Frank was more bored and restless than ever. Another man might have tried to settle into his marriage, maybe learned more about his long-suffering spouse, perhaps found some common ground upon which to build and sustain a long-term relationship, even if only for the sake of his children. But not Frank. He still wanted thrills, especially during these days when his career wasn't providing them for him.

Enter Ava Gardner. Again.

The Affair Begins

While in Palm Springs for a party in late 1949, Frank Sinatra once again ran into Ava Gardner. Immediately the sparks started flying. "I suppose we were rushing things a little the last time we met," he said, smiling.

"*You* were rushing things," she countered.

"So, let's start again," Frank offered eagerly. "What do you say?"

Ava later recalled, "That night, we drank, we laughed, we talked... and we fell in love."

This time, Ava wanted to know more about the status of Frank's marriage. He explained that it was over but that he was still committed to his three children. All she heard was the word "over," and that was enough for her. That night, they made love, and as Ava remembered it, "Oh, God, it was magic. We became lovers forever—eternally."

Ava Lavinia Gardner was born on Christmas Eve 1922 in the small farming community of Grabtown, North Carolina, located about eight miles from the town of Smithfield, in Johnston County. This sleepy, impoverished community—with no electricity and unpaved, always muddy roads—was about as far away from the life of a movie star as one could get.

Named after her dad's sister, Ava was the last of seven children born to southern sharecropper and tobacco farmer Jonas Bailey Gardner and his wife, Mary Elizabeth, who was often called Molly. William Godfrey, a friend of Ava's formerly from Grabtown, recalled, "She worked in the tobacco fields, I remember, but she couldn't wait to make her mark on the world in some way. She flailed around for a bit in the early days. She went to business school for a while after graduation, as I recall. She seemed to know, though, that whatever it was she was destined for, it was going to be big."

When Ava was growing up, young men were afraid to date her because of her wild, explosive temper. Her friends recall the time she caught a boy she was dating kissing another girl. She berated him, slapped him, and kicked him. As one friend put it, "You didn't cross Ava."

At the age of eighteen, Ava went to New York to visit her sister Beatrice ("Bappie"), now married to a photographer named Larry Tarr (who worked for the family-owned business, Tarr Photographic Studios). After he took her picture as a lark and then displayed it in his shop, it was seen by an errand boy who worked in the law department of Loew's, Inc. That errand boy wanted Ava's telephone number so that he could call her for a date. He used his tenuous connection with MGM (since MGM and Loew's were affiliated) to try to get it from Larry Tarr. He told Tarr that he believed MGM would be interested in Ava. He didn't get her phone number; Tarr refused to give it to him. However, Tarr did take the pictures to MGM himself. So struck were the MGM talent scouts by Ava's stunning looks that they suggested she do a screen test. After seeing the test, Louis B. Mayer was immediately interested. It seemed somewhat miraculous to her that without even really trying or paying her dues, she was on her way to a big career. She made the move to Hollywood at nineteen. "I didn't know anything about anything," she recalled, "but part of me had no doubt I would end up a movie queen."

Although her southern accent was so thick that many people at MGM had a difficult time understanding her, Mayer signed her to a seven-year contract and assigned her to studio voice coach Lillian

Burns. It would be four more years, though, filled with bit parts and small roles—*now* she was paying her dues—before MGM began grooming her to be a star, giving her etiquette lessons, constantly changing her hair and makeup in search of the right look, and attempting to teach her a few other things as well...like how to act.

According to all accounts, even as a major film star, Ava was insecure about her ability as an actress. She had often said that her greatest fear was that she would be "found out," that her true self would be revealed. "I'm a fraud," she'd say to intimates, "and I live in fear of being discovered." Still, between 1941, when she first arrived in Hollywood, and 1946, Ava would appear in seventeen films, many on loan to RKO and Universal, for which MGM exacted heavy fees.

"Maybe her insecurity is what made her so attractive on film," speculated her business manager from 1962 until her death in 1990, Jess Morgan. "Insecurity haunted her for her entire life and, in her personal life, made her act in ways that could be completely unreasonable. You had to learn how to handle Ava. If she saw that you were weak, she'd go after you...and run right over you."

Ava Gardner had had two brief marriages, one in 1942 to a man who was arguably the biggest star at the time, actor Mickey Rooney. It lasted fourteen months. The second was in 1945 to bandleader Artie Shaw, which lasted two years. Both were unhappy unions. She also had a turbulent relationship with Howard Hughes, whom she described as "cold and ruthless, although with me he was always gentle and concerned."

Artie Shaw treated her badly, though most of Ava's friends believe *he* was the true love of her life—not Frank Sinatra. (Ava wanted to have Shaw's child; she never wanted Sinatra's.) She moved on with her life after her second marriage ended, though she never really got over the way Shaw had treated her. Ava would charge that Shaw had been emotionally abusive, always criticizing her, making her feel worthless, and in effect validating the feelings of inadequacy that so haunted her.

On December 8, 1949, Ava and Frank ran into each other in the lobby of the Ziegfeld Theatre in New York when both attended the opening of the Broadway musical *Gentlemen Prefer Blondes*. It was during this supposedly impromptu meeting, according to Sinatra legend, that they first became attracted to one another, or as Ava's friend Ruth Rosenthal-Schechter put it, "an overpowering attraction obvious to all. The next day, their meeting was the talk of New York."

Actually, Frank and Ava had gone to the premiere together with another couple, whom they'd invited as a cover for their presence. Not only were they together at the premiere, but they were staying at the Hampshire House in New York in Manie Sacks's suite. By the end of 1949, their romance was in full bloom.

"All of my life, being a singer was the most important thing in the world," Frank told Ava at the end of the year. "Now...you're all I want."

Something about his declaration bothered her. It was too dramatic, even for her, and she loved good drama as much as the next girl. "You need more than just one person in your life," she told him. "No one should be that important."

It wasn't what he expected her to say. But there was no turning back for him now. During a time when illicit sex and extramarital affairs were strictly taboo, Ava was a bit of an anomaly. She wasn't opposed to having affairs with married men; she'd had them in the past—most notably with Robert Taylor when he was married to Barbara Stanwyck—and she now set her sights on Frank, saying that "there's no rhyme or reason to a love affair."

As they got to know each other, Ava and Frank began to feel they had a great deal more in common other than their mutual objections to the demands of show business. They both enjoyed being up all night, drinking, partying, and then sharing intimacies and secrets in a booze-induced haze. They loved Italian food and enjoyed watching televised boxing bouts.

In no time, it was impossible for Frank to imagine living his life without Ava. The feeling was not quite mutual, because Ava liked to keep her options open, just in case something better came along. Just like Frank. "Their love affair may have been meant to be," recalled Frank's daughter Tina, "but that doesn't mean it was meant to work. These were two tautly strung, ambitious, *restless* people who could never quite be satiated."

Lana's Warning to Ava

At the beginning of the affair, Frank was hopelessly romantic. For instance, Ava recalled that while he was driving her to the home she and her sister Bappie leased in Palm Springs, he pulled over to the side of the road and began to serenade her under one of the palm trees. A private concert by Sinatra? What girl would not be moved? Ava Gardner. She thought it was incredibly corny, and she never let him forget it. Still, it was a nice gesture.

The next day, Ava found herself thrilled by a different side of Frank—his reckless, dangerous side. As the two drove through Palm Springs in his Cadillac, they recklessly fired bullets from two .38 revolvers into the air like gangsters in a bad movie. Not only did they hit streetlights and store windows during their dangerous prank, but they actually nicked an innocent passerby. As a result, both were promptly arrested. It would cost nearly $20,000 for Sinatra to keep the incident out of the news: $10,000 to hide the records of the man who had been grazed by one of the bullets; $5,000 for the Indio, California, chief of police; $2,000 for the arresting officers; and another $2,000 to repair the damage to city property. (George Evans went to Palm Springs on his behalf to take care of the expensive transactions.) "Now, this is fun," Ava enthused after their shared fracas. "This is the kind of fun I like to have."

On one occasion during this period, Lana Turner spotted Ava across a crowded room at a cocktail party in Beverly Hills. Lana politely excused herself from a conversation and headed toward the powder room. Along the way, she made eye contact with Ava and, with a quick tilt of the head, summoned her to a powwow.

Ava and Lana were very good friends. Both had once been married to Artie Shaw, and both agreed Shaw was the most emotionally abusive, unkind man they had ever known. After Ava joined Lana in the ladies' room, Lana began to talk about Frank. As the two touched up their makeup, Lana left out few details while documenting the events of her own affair with Sinatra and how badly it had ended. "Not a single big female star hasn't cried on his cock," she told Ava.

According to what Ava later recalled, Lana said, "That Frank is a real son of a bitch. I'm just trying to warn you, sister. Stay away from him." She said that she thought she and Frank were on their way to the altar, when, in fact, he'd already decided that he was going back to Nancy. He didn't even have the courtesy to warn her in advance. "He will never leave that wife of his, and all those kids," Lana said. "Protect yourself."

Ava had to laugh. The idea that any woman needed "protection" from a man was so absurd to her, she didn't even know how to respond. Even when Artie Shaw was unkind toward her, she still felt she was the one in control. "Maybe *he* needs to stay away from *me*," Ava observed of Frank with an arched eyebrow.

"Sister, you don't know what you're getting yourself into," Lana continued. "The way he dumped me?" Lana explained that she didn't even know she and Frank were finished until she read in the morning paper about his very public reunion with Nancy at the Phil Silvers show. After she finished with her makeup, Lana snapped her purse shut and concluded, "To think he could do *that* to a woman like *me*."

Ava couldn't just disregard Lana's opinion. In fact, Lana had tried to warn her about Artie Shaw, but Ava didn't listen and went ahead and married him anyway. It was a disaster of a marriage, she had to admit. But Frank was different, she maintained. She said that she and Frank had something she and Artie never had—true love. According to her later recollection, she said, "Frank will most certainly leave Nancy for me if I decide he should. And if I decide I want to marry him, he'll do that, too. If I'm in love, I get married; that's my fundamentalist Protestant background. That's why I married Artie, for better or worse," she concluded.

Lana just shrugged. She wasn't so invested that it mattered to her one way or the other; she had done her best. "I just want you to be happy, sweetheart," she told Ava.

"I am happy," Ava said as she embraced her friend. "I am so very happy."

"Absolutely Not"

When Nancy Sinatra realized that Frank was now dating Ava Gardner, she didn't even want to discuss it with him. The two were living in the same house on Carolwood, but now they weren't even talking to one another.

One morning George Evans and Ted Hechtman met at the Carolwood estate to discuss the situation with Ava from a strategic public relations standpoint. Nancy's mother was also present. Sinatra was not.

"I remember that Nancy seemed exhausted. She had three little kids, one an infant, there was a nanny running around, a bunch of housekeepers... her mother in town, helping out... and Nancy looking beautiful in a floral-print dress, full makeup and hair. Gorgeous, really. I looked at her and thought, 'Why does Frank need more? This woman has it all.' She invited us in and we sat in the kitchen at the table."

"What exactly is it you want us to do about Ava Gardner?" George asked Nancy. Nancy looked at her mother, who just shook her head in the negative. She then softly said she wanted to do nothing. She reminded George that they had been unable to do anything about Lana Turner, and, at least from what she could glean, Ava Gardner was far more notorious. They then discussed whether or not they should try threatening Ava with the morals clause warning, but it was decided that if it hadn't worked on Lana, it probably wouldn't work on Ava either. Nancy's mother put forth the notion that if Frank didn't want to be married to Nancy any longer, maybe there was nothing that could be done about it. Nancy just stared straight ahead, seeming deadened to the whole subject. George then suggested that perhaps he could get Lana to reason with her. However, he didn't seem too enthusiastic about that prospect, perhaps remembering how Lana had dismissed him when he tried to talk to her about Frank. Nancy told him not to even bother. It was as if everyone had run out of options. "I'm so tired of this bullshit," Nancy finally said, becoming angry. "I don't care anymore. Screw him *and* Ava Gardner for all I care. Screw them both."

"Do you realize how many times Frank has disappointed us?" Nancy's mother asked Evans and Hechtman. She said that Frank had disappointed them so repeatedly, they no longer trusted him. She then turned to her daughter and, placing her hand over Nancy's, said that she didn't understand the world she lived in, "not one bit, dear." Mrs. Barbato well knew, though, that her husband had cheated on her throughout their marriage, and that there wasn't anything she could do about it. Nancy had always felt badly for her mom and had said she would never accept that kind of treatment from a husband of her own...yet here they all were.

"So does that mean you will give him a divorce if he asks for it?" George asked Nancy.

"Absolutely not," Nancy shot back without even having to think about it. "I won't make it easy on him. No!" Then, after a beat, she slammed both hands onto the table and rose. "*Absolutely not*," she repeated before she stormed from the room.

George, Ted, and Mrs. Barbato sat at the table for a moment, staring at one another in awkward silence. "Well, gentlemen," Mrs. Barbato finally said as she rose, "I guess you have your answer."

A Take-Charge Kind of Woman

$\mathcal{B}$y 1950, not only was Frank Sinatra's recording career in trouble, but apparently so was his voice. One Columbia recording engineer remembered, "The songs were there; the voice was not. Because he was failing vocally, he had something else to be unhappy about."

In January, Frank performed his first concert in two years, in Hartford, Connecticut. Though record sales were slow at this time and he was having trouble with his vocal cords, it was clear that the public was still somewhat interested because, unlike the scenario at most recent concerts, these dates were almost sold out. These shows generated his biggest take ever: $18,267 for two days.

Also at this time, Sinatra and George Evans—now together for nine years—tried to smooth over the many working disagreements they'd been having these past few years. Again, Evans tried to talk some sense into Frank, telling him that he would be "ruined" by the affair if the press got wind of it. "I'm already ruined," Frank said. "So what do I care?"

One morning in early January 1950, George tried to reason with Frank again in a meeting that took place in the upstairs lounge of the Copacabana in New York. Evans would later explain that he had asked the singer Lena Horne—also a client of his—to "happen by" and sit in on the meeting. With Horne perched on a barstool between the two men and sipping a coffee, they began once again to air their grievances.

During the meeting, Lena tried to convince Frank that his extracurricular activities could do irreparable damage to his image. Ironically, Lena was a very good friend of Ava's; both were MGM contract players and had often commiserated about the men in their lives. Lena believed the relationship would be damaging to both of them, and therefore she told Sinatra to "come to his senses." Why would a man with as many fans as Frank be so careless? She mentioned that his female fans in particular might take offense.

Frank didn't seem very eager to listen to advice about his private life from an outsider, even if he did admire Lena Horne as an artist. According to George Evans's later recollection, Frank told her to butt out. He threw some money down onto the bar, clinked George's glass, and took off, muttering under his breath. As he left the lounge, Lena turned to George and asked, "What does Ava see in him? Please, won't you explain it to me, because I just don't get it."

One of the reasons George hadn't contacted Ava directly was because when they met a couple of months earlier, the chill between them had been palpable. Ava knew that George was opposed to their relationship and she didn't want anyone around Frank who could exert any influence over him where she was concerned. Because he was already so vulnerable and unstable, she worried Frank might listen to negative opinions about her, especially if they came from someone he trusted. By her own later admission, Ava felt she had to employ a certain amount of strategy if she were to take him from Nancy.

Dick Moran, who worked with George Evans and Ted Hechtman as a starstruck junior publicist in 1948 and 1949, recalled, "Ava pushed Frank into getting rid of George. I overheard her one day in the office discussing it with Frank." Moran remembered that Ava had a vodka and tonic in one hand and a lit cigarette in the other. She sat on a stool with her legs crossed, her body erect, and her head tilted back in a glamorous pose. She asked Frank how it was that "this guy, a lowly publicist who works for you, tells *you* what to do, tells *you* who to see, tells *you* who to date?" She asked Sinatra to forgive her if she was being presumptuous, but she had to admit that she had never seen anything quite like it. Sinatra studied her critically. He wasn't accustomed to women taking this kind of tone with him. Making it worse, Ava had a habit of blowing little smoke rings when she had intense conversations with him, which further irritated him. ("If you're gonna smoke, just smoke," he'd tell her. "It's not art, lady. It's just a cigarette.")

"Get some backbone, Frank," Ava continued. She suggested that Frank tell George to "scram." She said she knew many publicists much more professional and talented than George Evans and that if he would allow her to, she would gladly find someone for him who would do the job: "*publicity*, and *that's it*."

Frank walked toward Ava, put his cigarette to his lips, and inhaled deeply. He shot a thick plume of smoke out of the corner of his mouth. "I'll deal with it my *own* way, sweetheart," he said, acting like a gangster.

Ava, maybe feeling that she'd lost this showdown, rose from her stool and exited the cloud of smoke—and the room. As she did, she passed Dick Moran, who had been waiting just outside the door for the tension to subside. He would remember that her perfume, as she sauntered by him, reminded him of "rose petals in an ashtray." According to what he later recalled, she turned and walked over to him. "Say, sweetie, how much sway do you have over this George Evans character?" she asked him.

"Well, not much," Moran said. "He's my boss."

"I wonder"—she began getting closer to him—"can you arrange a meeting between me and this cat?"

"Well, maybe you should ask Mr. Sinatra to do that," he suggested.

"Oh, Mr. Sinatra doesn't need to know *everything*, now does he?" she asked, stroking his arm. "For me? Please?"

"Sure, Miss Gardner," he said, swept away.

"You can call me Ava, handsome," she said with a wink as she walked away.

"She was a take-charge kind of woman," Moran recalled many years later. "My gut told me she always got her man, one way or the other. Anyway, I set up the meeting. I have no idea what happened during the meeting except that afterward, George Evans told me, 'I'm done with Frank. That crazy broad, Ava, makes Lana Turner look like a saint.' He said he planned to ditch Frank, that he'd had it with all of the drama. 'You can't fight city hall,' he said."

But then the next day Frank beat George to the punch, ending their relationship himself. "We're done," he told George. "I heard you talked to Ava about me, and that's it. No more."

"Wait! She asked to see me," George said. "She called the meeting, not me."

"That's not the way I heard it," Frank said. "Did you try using the morals clause card with her too, you bum?"

"No," George shot back. "Because that's one dame who doesn't even have morals."

Frank, according to what George later recalled, grabbed him by the collar. "You little weasel," he sneered at him. "You can't get a girl of your own so you spend all your time trying to come between me and mine? That's pretty pathetic, George," he said. He released him and then shoved him backward. "We're done," he announced. "Get lost. You don't work for me no more." And with that, it was over. Despite years of service spent trying to manage not only Frank's career but also his private life, it now appeared that George Evans was to be just another close friend of Sinatra's kicked to the curb.

Empty

*I*n early 1951, Frank Sinatra was booked at the brand-new Shamrock Hotel in Houston, which would open its doors on January 28. He traveled to the venue with his friend the songwriter Jimmy Van Heusen. While changing planes in El Paso, they learned that George Evans had died suddenly of a heart attack. He was just forty-eight.

Dick Moran said, "To be honest, I think it ate away at George that a broad got between him and Frank. He just couldn't get over it. He kept saying, 'I can't believe Frank would do that to me. I got rid of all the other dames; I just couldn't get rid of this one. *She* got rid of *me!*' The night he died, George called me and told me that he'd tried to telephone Frank but that he couldn't get through. He said, 'I don't care if I'm working for him or not. I gotta talk some sense into him.' Then he was gone."

When Frank learned of George's death, he immediately hopped on a plane for New York so that he could attend the funeral at the Parkwest Chapels on Manhattan's West Side. In subsequent years, he never let himself think much about George Evans. In fact, if someone brought up George's name in conversation, he would almost always change the subject. "Did he feel guilty?" Ted Hechtman asked. "I don't know. I have spent years wondering about Sinatra. Did he have a conscience? Did he have a moral code? I kept hoping that people who knew him better than we did knew some other side of him. But then I thought, 'Christ, if his own wife never sees it, then I don't know what to think.'"

Around the time of Evans's death, Frank found himself in another public relations imbroglio when he made some remarks about a singer and actress named Ginny Simms, with whom MGM boss Louis B. Mayer was having a romantic relationship. Mayer had recently been injured in a fall from a horse; however, Frank joked that he hadn't fallen off a horse at all. "Actually, he fell off of Ginny Simms," Frank started saying at cocktail parties. When he told the joke to Gene Kelly, Kelly said it wasn't very smart. "You stupid dago bastard," he said, according to Nancy Sinatra. "When are you going to learn to keep your mouth shut?" Kelly pointed out that if the very sensitive Mayer ever heard the gag, he would be furious.

"You're right, Shanty," Frank said, using his nickname for him. "I'm sorry. But what's the big deal?"

"First of all, Ginny Simms is married," Gene Kelly said. "She's married to the guy who owns the Hyatt hotel chain."

"No shit?" Frank said. "I sure didn't know that. Well... it's just a joke."

"Not a good one," Gene said. "You're playing with fire, Frank."

Gene Kelly was right. As head of the studio to which Frank was under contract, Mayer was the last person he could afford to alienate. "Mayer was a very difficult man who was completely devoid of a sense of humor," Sinatra later said. "Three days after I made that joke, he wanted to see me. I didn't know he had heard it. So, I'm sitting there in a meeting with him, and he's almost in tears, and he says, 'I love you like my son. I never had a son.' And I'm thinking, 'Jesus Christ, he's gonna give me the whole studio!' Then he said, 'I hear you tell a funny story about me and Ginny Simms.' My face dropped. I knew I was sunk."

Mayer told Sinatra, "I want you to leave this studio right now, and I don't want you to ever come back."*

In the end, Frank's contract with MGM was terminated a full year before it was due to expire. He was paid $85,000 to walk away, but he would much rather have had the contract.

Also complicating Frank's life and career at this time was the resignation of Manie Sacks, a staunch Sinatra ally, from Columbia Records. His replacement, Mitch Miller, would prove to be less successful in finding material for Frank, and much of the material Frank would record with Miller would not be considered suitable by fans and critics alike. In truth, Miller, who would go on to great success with singers such as Tony Bennett and Rosemary Clooney, didn't really know what to do with Frank.

With things so out of control and George Evans no longer around to do damage control, Frank began to gravitate more toward Ava than ever before. He began to view her as the only truly stabilizing force in his life. He seemed to be losing everything else, but at least he had her. While he was in New York for George Evans's funeral, he spent all of his time with her. It was more than just great sex for Frank, though. When he was with Ava, he was able to relax and forget about his flagging career and all of the disappointments of recent years. He was also able to forget about Nancy, though he felt guilty about leaving his children. "The very sight of their little faces kills

---

* In 1951, after twenty-seven years as head of MGM, Mayer was fired by the board of directors of Loew's, Inc., MGM's parent company. And Sinatra returned to MGM five years later in *Meet Me in Las Vegas*, in an unbilled guest appearance, and in *High Society*, billed third (after Bing Crosby and Grace Kelly).

me," he said at the time. Still, Ava was a distraction when he most needed it. Frank not only wanted Ava, he *needed* her. As for Ava, her long-term intentions were unclear.

At the beginning, Ava was in the throes of passion and deep infatuation. She was swept away by the sheer novelty of having Frank in her life, but was her passion for him growing into love? "She was saying what Frank needed to hear when he needed to hear it," Peter Lawford once observed. "Frank took it to heart. Very quickly, he lost himself in her," Lawford concluded. "If Ava was capable of true love, I never saw it and I dated her, too, before Frank. I knew Ava. I knew her well. She was cold as steel. But that was just my experience with her."

Maybe Dick Moran put it best: "They were hoping to fill one another. But how could they? They were both completely empty."

Ava: "Nancy Will Thank Me One Day"

*F*rank Sinatra canceled the first couple of days of his engagement at the Shamrock Hotel in order to attend George Evans's funeral. When he finally got to Houston to begin work, a surprise visitor was already there to greet him: Ava.

So far, Frank had been able to keep the affair with Ava out of the press. They tried not to be seen together in public, maybe just a fleeting appearance now and then, but not enough for the public and the media to put the pieces together. Frank knew that Ava's presence in Houston was really asking for trouble—the press would surely spot them wherever they went. He was right. Ava knew it, too. That's why she showed up. She and her maid, Rene, talked about the pros and cons, and in the end Ava did what she did best: She threw caution to the wind. It was time to move things along, she decided. How much longer were she and Frank going to act as if they weren't a couple? Also, she felt it was time for Nancy to wake up. If Nancy still thought Frank was truly hers and hers alone, perhaps, Ava decided, it was time to disabuse her of that notion.

Frank and Ava were at a dinner party at Vincento's Sorrentino Italian restaurant, hosted by the mayor of Houston, when trouble started. Spotting them, photographer Ed Schisser of the *Houston Post* asked to take their picture. Ava later said that at the sight of the lensman Frank "reacted as if he'd found a live cobra in his salad." After Sinatra told Schisser to get lost, Schisser gave him a dirty look. That was all it took to incite Frank; he plowed into the photographer, shoving him backward into a nasty fall. The next day, news of Sinatra's presence at the party with Ava and his confrontation with the photographer made all of the wire services.

In reading about it in the press, Nancy Sinatra still didn't quite know what to make of the affair with Ava. Frank always seemed to come back to her sooner or later, even if just temporarily. However, when Nancy called him in Houston, he was categorical; he wanted out of the marriage for good. He said they would discuss it when he returned to Los Angeles.

On Valentine's Day 1950—arguably not the best timing—Frank, now back home, told Nancy he was serious about Ava. He didn't want to hurt her, he said, but the fact remained that he loved another woman. Nothing in his life meant as much to him as Ava, he said. How many times had she heard *this* story? "Every time you get involved with one of these women, she's the only one for you and you want to be with her forever," she screamed at him. "Then, a month later, it's over and someone else is in the picture and the cycle starts again. Well, I'm sick of it!" Nancy was so angry, in fact, she slapped Frank hard across the face, kicked him out of the house, and had all of the locks changed. A legal separation, she speculated, might give him a little time to get Ava out of his system. She was certain of only one thing: She still wasn't going to give him a divorce.

Fundamentally, Nancy's reasons hadn't changed. As a devout Catholic, it was against her religion to divorce. She also wanted to keep her family together for the sake of her children. Moreover, Frank just couldn't be trusted; he was always "in love" with someone and she still wasn't going to end a marriage over one of his flings. Also, she knew of other women in the exact same predicament. At this same time, Dean Martin had become involved with a blonde model named Jeanne Biegger. Dean and his wife, Betty, had four kids, aged between one and seven, yet that didn't stop him from having an affair with Jeanne. Betty refused to give him a divorce until finally

Dean told her that Jeanne was pregnant, upon which she decided to grant the divorce rather than allow a child to be born out of wedlock—only to later discover that Jeanne wasn't pregnant at all. So Nancy knew that this sort of marital conflict wasn't unusual in show-business families. She wasn't alone, or at least that's what she kept telling herself.

It was at around this time that Nancy lost Dolly's support. "Give him a divorce if he wants one," Dolly told her, this according to Tina Sinatra. "It's better for you, better for the children."

Nancy was deeply disappointed in Dolly. Now was not the time for her mother-in-law to waver; Nancy needed Dolly to be on her side. "How can you say that to me?" she demanded. It's *because* I have children that I want to save the marriage. Isn't that what you once told me?"

"Yes, but that was then," Dolly said. "You can't keep a man if he doesn't want to be there."

What Nancy didn't know yet—but would learn very shortly—was that Dolly actually liked Ava very much. First, she was impressed with her celebrity; she had already been a fan. "Her birthday is December 24, and mine is December 25," Dolly liked to remind people. "How do you like *that?*" Moreover, once she got to know Ava's toughness, she respected her as a kindred spirit. And Ava knew how to make Dolly happy. When Dolly said she wanted to introduce Ava to some of her friends in Hoboken, Ava didn't blink; she made herself immediately available and then one day went from door to door with Dolly as Dolly introduced her as "the great Ava Gardner, Frankie's fiancée."

Nancy, like Frank, could hold a grudge when she wanted to, and she would against Dolly. In fact, she would never quite forgive her mother-in-law for abandoning her, encouraging the end of her marriage, and then supporting Ava. Things between them would be frosty from this time forward.

On February 15, gossip columnist Hedda Hopper reported that the Sinatras had separated. Nancy told Hedda that life with Frank had become "most unhappy and almost unbearable. We have therefore separated. I have requested my attorney to work out a property settlement, but I do not contemplate divorce proceedings in the foreseeable future." Nancy admitted that this was actually the couple's third separation. ("Really?" Ava said to a friend. "The son of a bitch never told me *that*.") "He's done it before, and I suppose he'll do it again," Nancy said of Frank's behavior. She added that the decision to separate had been her own.

The reaction of the press and the public to Nancy's news was decidedly negative for both Frank and Ava. Frank was perceived as a cheater; Ava, a home-wrecker. Movie magazines, the 1950s version of today's supermarket tabloids, trumpeted sensational details of the affair and of Nancy's heartbreak over it. "The shit really hit the fan," Ava would have to admit years later. "In the next few weeks, I received scores of letters accusing me of being a scarlet woman, and worse. The Legion of Decency threatened to ban my movies. Catholic priests found the time to write me accusatory letters. I even read that the Sisters of Mary and Joseph asked their students at St. Paul the Apostle School in Los Angeles to pray for Frank's wife. I didn't understand then, and still don't, why there should be this prurient mass hysteria about a male and a female climbing into bed and doing what comes naturally."

Ava's Metro boss, Louis B. Mayer, joined the fray in being outraged about the affair, and, citing the same morals clause in her studio contract that George Evans had decided not to try to use against her, threatened legal action against her. Indeed, as with all actresses, Ava's contract stipulated that she was to act "with due regard to public conventions and morals" and that she must not "do or commit any act or thing that will degrade her in society, or bring her into public hatred, contempt, scorn or ridicule, that will tend to shock, insult, or offend the community in general." Mayer had already gotten rid of Frank, and he said he would be happy to do the same with Ava. But Ava said she thought the morals clause was "worth a few laughs." It meant nothing to her.

Meanwhile, Ava's feelings about Frank's marriage to Nancy remained simple. "If he was happy with her, he would have stayed with her. But he wasn't, which is how I got him." She couldn't relate to Nancy Sinatra and seemed not to have much empathy for her. In fact, Ava liked to believe she would never find herself in the same situation. If a husband of hers ever wanted out of a marriage, she would say, she would be more than happy to set him free.

"Why would a woman want a man who doesn't want her in return?" she asked her friend Lucy Wellman over drinks one night at the Polo Lounge. (Wellman had been hired to be Ava's personal assistant, but the two women decided they were better off as friends; they remained so for thirty-five years.) Lucy told her that it wasn't so simple, that love was complicated and that perhaps, because there were children involved, Ava should back off. Ava strongly disagreed. "Why would Nancy Sinatra be so devastated to have a man who doesn't want her out of her life?" Ava asked. "I would say, 'Good riddance. Get out! You don't want me? Fine. *I* don't want *you.*'"

Lucy then asked Ava if she was prepared to spend the rest of her life with Frank Sinatra. She added that if the relationship was really just all about sex, "it's not right breaking up a marriage over it." However, Ava maintained that "Francis" was a "big boy," and that she most certainly wasn't forcing him to do anything he didn't want to. And as for the rest of her life? "Are you crazy?" she asked her friend. "Have you lost your mind? Who can think that far ahead?"

"Well, then maybe you should think about Nancy and those poor kids," Lucy said, still pushing.

"Jesus Christ!" Ava exclaimed. "Why are you trying to make me feel bad? I'm probably doing Nancy Sinatra a favor. She needs to move on, and she should have done so a long time ago. In fact, I bet she'll thank me one day. I'll just bet!"

Frank at the Copa

*I*n March 1950, Frank Sinatra was booked at the Copacabana in New York City. Ava accompanied him to Manhattan, sharing a suite with him at the Hampshire House. Trying to at least *act* discreet, Ava and her sister Bappie stayed in one bedroom, Frank in the other. When the popular New York journalist Earl Wilson asked for an interview with Ava to discuss the situation with Frank and Nancy, she begged off, saying that she had the flu. Instead, she issued a written statement: "The main reason I am in New York is because I am on my way to make a picture. The main reason Frankie is here is because he is scheduled to open at the Copacabana. Inasmuch as Frank is officially separated from his wife, I believe I have a right to be seen with him. However, since he is still officially married, I believe it would be in the worst possible taste to discuss future plans. One thing I am sure of is that Frank's plans to leave Nancy came into his life long before I did."

Frank approved of Ava's statement, and added, "The fact that I have had a few dates with her means nothing. Why shouldn't I have dates? I'm separated from my wife. I don't intend to sit home alone."

The Copa engagement was pivotal for Sinatra in that it was his first major nightclub appearance in about five years. However, the timing could not have been worse; the stress in his life was showing in his voice. The fact that he was usually up all night, drinking and smoking, only made matters worse. As a result, he sounded husky and hoarse, his range limited. He was on a tight schedule, committed to three shows a night at the Copa and five radio shows a week; recording sessions were also to be squeezed in. Making matters worse, toward the end of the engagement he also agreed to appear at the Capitol Theatre for matinee performances; he needed the work—and the money—so he pretty much never turned anything down. Adding to his burden was the tension he felt about facing a tough New York audience when he wasn't at his best. To get through it all, he was taking as many sedatives as his doctor would prescribe.

Jimmy Silvani, who worked as a bodyguard for Sinatra, was backstage on opening night of the Copa engagement. He recalled, "Sinatra practically collapsed before that first show. He kept saying, 'My career is over. I'm washed up, and now I have to go out and face those people—the same people who aren't buying my records, who aren't seeing my movies.'

"He was taking a lot of pills at this time—pills to get up, pills to relax, pills to go to sleep. Today, I think he would have checked into Betty Ford; that's how much trouble he was in with the pills.

"At one point that night before going on, I saw him sitting in front of his dressing room mirror, staring at himself and mumbling, 'You can do this, Frank. You can do this, pal. Just go on out there and do this.' He was trying to psych himself up. I felt badly for him. After a few moments, Ava came into the dressing room and joined him."

Silvani remembered that Ava stood behind Frank, one hand on his shoulders, the other holding her cocktail. Gazing at their image in the mirror, she announced, "Francis Albert Sinatra, you are the greatest goddamned entertainer who ever walked the face of this earth. I believe in you. I love you. And I salute you." With that, she raised her glass of champagne to their reflection. "Now, I want you to get on out there, Francis, and prove me right."

Encouraged, Frank said, "I'm gonna do it, baby. I'm gonna do it for you." Then he rose and turned to face her. Smiling at him, she melted into his arms. Frank kissed her passionately.

After Frank left the dressing room, Jimmy Silvani noticed a telegram lying on the dressing table: "Best of luck on your opening night. Love, Nancy."

When Frank Sinatra walked onto the stage that night, March 28, he appeared pale and seemed weak not only vocally but physically. From the beginning, the audience wasn't enthusiastic and seemed more interested in talking among themselves than in being entertained by him. At one point, he was forced to ask one particularly noisy group, "Am I speaking too loud for you ladies?" Then, after a few more songs fell on deaf ears, he was reduced to pleading. "This is my opening night. C'mon, give me a break."

"It was heartbreaking," Ava would later recall. "They wouldn't cut him a break. He was trying so hard. New Yorkers! They're a tough crowd."

The reviews of the Copa opening night were critical. A reporter for the *Herald Tribune* wrote, "Whether temporarily or otherwise, the music that used to hypnotize the bobby-soxers—whatever happened to them anyway?—is gone from the throat. Vocally, there isn't quite the same old black magic there used to be when Mr. Sinatra wrenched 'Night and Day' from his sapling frame and thousands swooned."

"When Frank read the reviews, he was angry with those writers," recalled Ava's social secretary, Mary LaSalle-Thomas. "Ava told me that Frank called the one reporter from the *Herald Tribune* and challenged him about his opinion of the show. She was out shopping and when she came back to the suite, she heard Frank hollering at this guy on the telephone. She heard him say something like, 'You wouldn't know a good performance if it bit you in the ass. Why do you have to get so personal, anyway? I can take the criticism, but you ruin it by getting so personal.'"

According to LaSalle-Thomas, after some more swearing, Frank slammed the telephone down, pulled the wire out of the wall, and threw the phone across the room. It smashed into a corner and produced a deep hole in the wall. Joining in the fracas, Ava picked up the telephone and hurled it out the window. The two then leaned out the window and watched in horrified enthrallment as the apparatus narrowly missed the head of a passerby below.

Gunplay

One night, during the engagement at the Copacabana, Frank and Ava had a quarrel over dinner. As always, they were surrounded by dozens of people. Frank never went anywhere without an entourage— people who worked for him, people who were friends of his...friends of friends...reporters who had snuck into the inner circle. Some were people he didn't even know. No matter how much trouble he was having in his career, he was still Frank Sinatra and would be sure to always attract a loud and raucous group of hangers-on. Everyone was always smoking and drinking or coming on to waitresses or getting into fights with one another, all with Frank presiding, an unhappy king lording over a not-so-royal court. On this evening, Ava accused Frank of flirting with a Copa Girl—one of the popular chorus line of dancers who performed before the headline act at the Copacabana. "You have me," she told him in front of many witnesses, though it was a little difficult to hear her over the din, "so why would you want to screw a Copa Girl?"

Frank said that he wasn't involved with a Copa Girl and that in fact the only thing that had happened was that she had flirted with him and he had flirted back. It wasn't a big deal. But Ava said that she didn't trust him. That was fine, Frank told her as he tossed back a drink; he said he didn't trust her either, so they were even.

It was a typical Frank-Ava spat, that is until Ava crossed the line. "I don't know what Nancy even sees in you," she said. Mentioning Nancy wasn't a good idea. Frank, according to the witnesses, almost jumped across the table at Ava. It looked like he wanted to strangle her. "Don't you ever even say her name," he told her. "That name— *Nancy*—should never come out of your mouth again, because if it does, you're gonna end up with a fat lip."

At that, Ava stormed off, going back to Hampshire House. Upon her arrival there, she telephoned her ex-husband, Artie Shaw, who happened to live in New York. The two had remained friends even though their marriage had ended badly. People in her life couldn't fathom it, actually. He had made her feel so empty-headed and stupid, a brainless pretty face, that she once took an IQ test to see if she was really as dumb as he had insisted! But after taking the test it occurred to her that if a man thinks a woman is foolish or stupid, he lowers his guard and becomes reckless. The woman then has the advantage. That was fine with Ava; she decided she didn't even need to know the results of the IQ test. She always felt she could manipulate Artie, and seeing him this evening was a bit of a manipulation, a way to make Frank jealous. She easily wrangled an invitation to Artie's apartment to share a drink with him and his then girlfriend, Ruth Cosgrove (later Mrs. Milton Berle).

Ava knew Frank thought she still had feelings for Artie and that he didn't want her socializing with him. Whenever he couldn't find her, he feared she was with Shaw and promised anyone who would listen that he would "kill the both of 'em, I swear it, if I ever find them together." Right before Ava walked out the door she left her telephone book open to the page with Artie's address on it. Upon leaving, she may have thought, "Well, this should make for an interesting night."

Ava had only been at Artie's for about twenty minutes when Frank showed up, accompanied by his friend and manager, Hank Sanicola. "They looked like gangsters out of a B-movie," Rene Jordan, Ava's maid, said. She wasn't present, but Ava told her about it. "Two hoodlums, raincoats and ark trilbies, hands deep in their pockets as if they were clutching revolvers." Frank swept the room with his eyes and found Ava sitting in a chair with a drink in her hand, looking self-satisfied. Their eyes met. Suddenly seemingly defeated, Frank didn't "kill the both of 'em," as he had threatened. Instead, he just walked right out the door without saying a word. Ava went back to her good time. About a half hour later, she departed and caught a taxicab back to the Hampshire House.

Once back at her hotel, Ava sank into the couch in the living room and, a little drunk and very sleepy, kicked off her heels and began to drift off. Suddenly she was awakened by the shrieking sound of the telephone. It was Frank, calling from the other bedroom in their suite. "I can't stand it anymore," he said, sounding quite desperate. "I'm gonna kill myself. *Right now.*" Then she heard two loud shots.

Ava screamed, dropped the phone, and ran across the living room and into Frank's bedroom. Bappie met her there. When the women burst into the room, they saw Frank lying on the floor with his eyes closed, a gun smoking in his hand. "*Oh my God.*" Ava threw herself onto Frank's body and began to cry. "My mind sort of exploded in a great wave of panic, terror, and shocked disbelief," she later recalled. Suddenly, his eyes opened. For a moment, the two lovers stared at one another. He was alive? What in the world was going on here? Actually, Frank appeared stunned, as if he couldn't believe that the gun had actually gone off.

"You son of a bitch," Ava exclaimed. Looking around the room, she noticed a gaping hole in the mattress. Thinking quickly, she picked up the telephone to call Hank Sanicola down the hall. He rushed over and got the mattress and bedding out of the room and replaced it with that from his room. Soon after, the corridor was full of police. When they knocked on Frank's door, he acted like he didn't know what they were talking about. "Gunshot? Really? I didn't hear no gunshot, did you hear a gunshot, Ava? We didn't hear nothin'."

"When the police arrived, Frank was in his robe and his innocence was very convincing," Ava would later say. "Frank's denials could have won him an Oscar. I was trembling like jelly inside..."

The next day, Dolly and Marty Sinatra heard about the fracas from a friend of theirs in the Sinatra organization; Dolly actually had a few "spies" on her son's payroll to keep an eye on things. She tried to reach Frank, but he didn't want to talk to her to explain. Finally, Ava called to tell her that everything was fine, that it was all a big misunderstanding. Dolly wasn't buying it. "Are you sure my son is okay?" she asked. Ava said she was certain, and that she would look after "Francis" herself. Dolly and Ava were both smart women; though they may have chosen not to openly discuss it with one another, certainly they could recognize a textbook cry for help from Frank, or at the very least a cry for attention. But what to do about it? Maybe it was because they didn't have an answer that they chose not to address the issue with one another.

Brink of Despair

*I*n March 1950, Ava Gardner left the United States to film the movie *Pandora and the Flying Dutchman* with James Mason, first in London and then in Spain. By this time, as she later said, she needed a breather from Frank Sinatra and the theatrics of their relationship.

While in Spain, Ava became infatuated with a dashing Spanish matador turned actor, thirty-four-year-old Mario Cabré, who was playing Juan Montalvo, her bullfighter-lover in the film. Though he had acted in just a few films, he was enormously popular, having made as much a name for himself by escorting beautiful actresses about Spain as for any ability he may have had as an actor. Ava was captivated by his charming personality, Latin good looks, and brashness. "After one of those romantic, star-filled, dance-filled, booze-filled Spanish nights, I woke up to find myself in bed with him," she would later confess.

"Well, that was typically Ava," said Mary LaSalle-Thomas. "She told me that what she had with Mario was no reflection on her feelings for Frank. It had nothing to do with him, in fact."

Like Frank, Ava rationalized her dalliances by compartmentalizing them. "Ava was very masculine in the way she looked at these things," said LaSalle-Thomas. "She would say, 'Men treat women like dirt. Well, I sometimes treat men the same way. So, go ahead, sue me.' On some level, maybe that's what Frank liked about her. She was a mirror image of him."

Of course, the fling with Mario was not a serious relationship. It was just an uncomplicated but heated little affair with a sexy actor who satisfied her lustful urges. Also, according to her own account of it, Ava hoped that her actions with Mario would make Frank jealous enough to once and for all end his marriage to Nancy and make a commitment to her.

No slouch in the art of public relations, Mario did what he could to use the affair to generate publicity in the hope of advancing his career. "I am in love with her," he said of Ava in a prepared statement. "This is pure love. The first time I saw her, I felt something that was not normal..." He hastened to add that he was using his Spanish-English dictionary to compose his statement so that it could be understood "by an international audience."

Back in the States, reading press accounts that Ava was romancing another man drove Frank to the brink of despair. He couldn't just pick up and leave New York to go to her and make sure his place in her life was secure. He was still trying to prove himself at the Copacabana and needed all of his resolve just to get through that engagement.

On April 26, 1950, he had more trouble than usual with his voice. During the dinner show, his voice gave out during "Bali Ha'i." Afterward, one of his doctors told him to cancel the third show, but he was determined to perform. He would not let his audience down. Plus, he had heard that Lee Mortimer—the Hearst reporter with whom he had a longtime feud—had made a wager that he wouldn't be able to finish the engagement, which made him all the more resolute.

The third show went on at 2:30 a.m. As Frank strolled to the microphone, he was impeccably dressed: black tuxedo with satin lapels, a floppy bow tie, shoes so highly shined that the spotlights were reflected in them. But he was also thin, gaunt, and pale. He walked on to light applause, which he acknowledged with that megawatt Sinatra smile.

The first number was "I Have But One Heart," which he dedicated to Ava. The audience responded enthusiastically. However, his voice started to falter on the second song, "It All Depends on You," and when he reached for a high note, it pretty much left him altogether. He was stunned. No matter what he had done before—

the booze, the brawls, the broads—his voice had never failed him so completely.

He clutched at the microphone. He tried to sing again. This time, he felt a trickle in the corner of his mouth. Thinking it was saliva, he wiped it away with his white handkerchief. It was blood. Later it would be diagnosed as the result of a "submucosal throat hemorrhage."

"I was never so panic-stricken in my whole life," Frank would later recall. "I remember looking at the audience. There was silence— stunning, absolute silence. Finally, I whispered to the audience, 'Good night,' and walked off the floor."

"I thought for a fleeting moment that it was a joke," said his conductor, Skitch Henderson. "The color drained out of my face as I saw the panic in Frank's. It became so quiet, so intensely quiet in the club. Like they were watching a man walk off a cliff."

Billy Eckstine took Frank's place for the rest of that ill-fated Copacabana engagement.

On May 10, 1950, Frank canceled an engagement at the Chez Paree in Chicago rather than take any more chances with his voice. As it was, the doctors said it could be as long as two months before he would sing again. Therefore, he went to Miami to bask in the sun and try to figure out what his next move should be where Ava and Nancy were concerned. Nancy kept telephoning him to express her concern. However, he refused to take her calls, saying, "If she's so worried about me, why won't she give me the divorce?" Every time he would raise his voice, however, his staff members would hover around him and plead with him not to speak. He was supposed to communicate by writing on pads of paper.

He was thirty-four years old and his career was in a shambles: the movies, the records, now the voice...all in jeopardy. Frank said he didn't know how he could take another breath if he couldn't sing. However, he felt strongly that if he had Ava in his corner, he'd be able to survive anything. While in Miami, he desperately wanted to hear her voice, her laugh. But Louis B. Mayer was having her calls blocked so that she would not be distracted by him during filming. His interference made it impossible for Frank to get through to her. Frustrated to the point of despair, Frank made arrangements to charter a plane to Spain.

Need

*B*y the time Frank Sinatra arrived in Barcelona on May 11, Mario Cabré was miles away in Gerona filming exterior scenes for the movie. Ava suspected that the director, Albert Lewin, purposely sent Cabré away on location shots after he overheard him announce that he would start trouble with Frank if they ever came face-to-face.

As soon as Frank landed in Barcelona, the press was all over him about Mario. "Is it true that Mario Cabré is having an affair with Ava?" one asked him. "Who?" Frank said. "Never heard of the guy."

He rented a car at the airport and drove sixty miles north along the Catalan coast to the Sea Gull Inn in the resort town of S'Agaró, where he and Ava rendezvoused. Frank gave her a $10,000 emerald necklace, which he'd wrapped in toilet paper and stuffed in his back pocket. He also presented her with a case of her favorite soft drink, Coca-Cola, a gesture she found amusing. The charm of that gesture wore off, though, when she realized Frank was actually taking sleeping pills with the soft drink because he'd heard it made them work faster in a person's system. He looked dreadful. Weighing less than 130 pounds, he was pale and weak.

The next day, the two drove to the La Bastida estate in Tossa de Mar, where they had adjoining haciendas, though they only stayed in his. For most of the next week Frank was sick and seemed disoriented. One morning, when they went tuna fishing, Ava found a bottle of pills in Frank's jacket and threw them overboard. She was determined to make him start sleeping unaided. However, Frank was thoroughly addicted to the pills, and he jumped in after the bottle and almost drowned. He had to be rescued by the boat's captain.

Things went from bad to worse when Ava finally got him back to the estate. There, they were greeted by a newspaper article about her and Mario Cabré, rolled up nicely on the doorstep of his hacienda. Frank had wanted a showdown with her about Cabré anyway. Now he finally had his chance. According to what Ava told Lucy Wellman, he grabbed her and shook her violently. As he throttled her, he wanted to know why she was so intent on flaunting the affair with Cabré. Didn't she know how much he cared for her? Didn't she realize what she was doing to him? "Help me," he pleaded with her. "Help *us*." Exhausted, addicted, and emotionally wiped out, Sinatra just couldn't take any more. Ava demanded that he release her. She warned him not to put his hands on her, ever. "Don't you manhandle me," she exclaimed. Sinatra let her go. With tears in his eyes, he then said, "I'm begging you, Ava. Look at me, here. Jesus, can't you see how I feel?"

It was a defining moment. Frank had just done for Ava what he never did for any other woman: made himself vulnerable and needy in front of her. Perhaps it was poetic justice, then, that she would respond with the same callous insensitivity with which *he* had treated Nancy and so many other women before her. "You're a fine one to talk," she said. "You've got me, you've got Nancy, and who knows who else you have on the side? Buzz off, buddy. Don't sing me your sad songs. I'm not falling for it." Frank defended himself by saying that the only reason he ever saw Nancy was because he wanted to visit his children. Ava insisted that she and Cabré were just friends, but Frank didn't believe her. "Don't lie to me," he told her. "What? All of a sudden we have a problem with lying?" she shot back.

One thing was made clear during the showdown in Spain: Frank needed Ava more than she needed him.

Nancy Files for Separation

*I*n June 1950, Frank Sinatra was back in Los Angeles, his voice now mostly restored as a result of rest and the strong throat medication he had been taking in Spain. Dolly and Marty were so concerned by what they were hearing in the media and from what Ava was telling them in telephone calls that they took a train to Los Angeles to talk to Frank. The three of them sat down at the kitchen table and tried to figure it all out, almost as if they were back in Hoboken as a family. Frank was too exhausted to explain himself to his parents, though. From one account, he told his mother he just wanted to be happy and that Ava was the one who made him happiest. Dolly wasn't convinced. "You sure don't look happy to me," she told him. There were no wisecracks from her this time, though. Marty suggested that Frank go back to New Jersey with them. He said that maybe they could work these problems out together, as a family. He reminded Frank that at the center of his life was his family, and that he could always turn to them in times of need. "That's what family's for," he said. But Frank felt that Nancy would be very upset with him if he went to Jersey without her and the children. "Then bring them," Marty suggested. "Maybe it will be good if we can all be together far away from all of this bullshit. Don't you think?" Dolly disagreed. She thought it made no sense to be taking family vacations with Nancy when it was Ava Frank wanted, and that leading Nancy on would be unfair. It didn't matter; Frank didn't want to go anyway. He needed a couple of weeks of bed rest, he said, and then he had to fly to England for an important engagement at the Palladium. The Sinatras went back to New Jersey disappointed that they'd been unable to make any sort of positive impact on his life.

Though the idea of engaging in a new battle with Nancy right now didn't appeal to Frank at all, he did want to see his children. Nancy agreed to let him spend the weekend at the house; he would sleep in the guest room, of course.

Frank left feeling rejuvenated, having enjoyed the time with his children, but Nancy was sadder and more depressed than ever. She wished she hadn't even made the offer. It wasn't worth the pain.

She called Frank the next day to reach out, but not to change his mind. "We love each other," she said, "and we want what's best for each other. So, I'm not going to fight this thing anymore." In fact, she was worn out; she didn't want to battle with him any longer. She said she loved him enough to let him go. "We're your family," she told him. "No matter where you go or what you do, you will always have this family." Frank so appreciated her words, he broke down and cried.

On July 10, Frank flew to London, where, by coincidence, Ava was filming "pickup" (insert) shots for *Pandora*. Frank moved into an expensive apartment in Berkeley Square, where he would stay for the next two months.

The Palladium engagement would turn out to be successful. Ava was front row center, amazed—and relieved—to find that an audience of mostly teenagers responded to Frank in much the same way the youth in the States used to back in the early days. While sipping tea onstage to soothe his throat, Frank performed a concert of classics that included "Embraceable You" and "I've Got a Crush on You." A reporter for the *Musical Express* wrote, "I watched mass hysteria. Was it wonderful? Decidedly so, for this man Sinatra is a superb performer and a great artist. He has his audience spellbound."

In September 1950, Frank and Ava returned to New York and continued their romance, now in a very open, public manner. They then attended the Joe Louis–Ezzard Charles world heavyweight championship bout at Yankee Stadium, where they were photographed, all smiles and arm in arm.

The next day, on September 28, Nancy made an appearance at Santa Monica's Superior Court in her bid for a legal separation and separate maintenance. Shaking and practically being held up by her sister Julie, Nancy pled her case to Judge Orlando Rhodes. Her marriage was over, she said. "On numerous occasions, he would go to Palm Springs for weekends without me," she said of Frank through her tears. "He also stayed several days at a time. This happened many times. When we had guests, he would go off by himself and not feel like talking. This made me terribly nervous and upset."

The proceedings had to be halted several times so that Nancy could compose herself. Nancy estimated Frank's 1949 income as having been $93,740 and assessed the value of their community property at $750,000. She was granted $2,750 a month in temporary support.

Even with all of the work he was getting, Frank couldn't possibly make the court-ordered monthly payments to Nancy. He'd even recently had to borrow money from Columbia Records just to pay back taxes. He told Ava, "I won't have enough bucks to buy you a pair of nylons once Nancy is through with me. I just have to keep working. Whatever they throw at me, I'm just going to have to take it."

"I can't believe she would do this to you," Ava said. "After all you've given her!"

Of course, Ava had no idea how much Nancy was suffering. "I would see her faint into her plate at dinner from the stress," Nancy Jr. would recall of her mother. "Sometimes it was heart palpitations, sometimes a cold, sometimes fatigue. Until then, she had never been sick. She was in pain. And, though I wasn't aware of it, her pain was exacerbated by the scandal. She was deeply in love and terribly hurt. I would hear her crying quietly at night while I was going to sleep. She would never show it in front of us, *never*, but my room was next to hers and I would sometimes tiptoe out and I'd listen at the door and she'd be crying. Sometimes I would go in to her and just put my arms around her."

In October, Ava returned to Hollywood to begin work on the MGM film version of the Hammerstein and Kern musical *Show Boat*. Meanwhile, Frank had begun working on his own television series, *The Frank Sinatra Show* on CBS, to be broadcast on Saturday nights. It was a major break for him when the show went on the air on October 7, 1950. Though the ratings were never strong—and some were astonished that the network had even given him a show considering his recent career reversals—the series would struggle along for a couple of years. At the same time, Frank would star in a weekly CBS radio program, *Meet Frank Sinatra*, on Sunday afternoons. He was doing everything he could to keep his name and talent in the public eye, and also to make a living. But his personal life was still a shambles and guilt was starting to set in where Nancy was concerned.

Frank went home to think about his future and how he should proceed. His roots were in Hoboken; it was still where he felt most grounded. Over drinks at a local bar, Marty said that he definitely was not a fan of Ava's, unlike Dolly. He said that he didn't appreciate the way she had come between his son and Nancy. However, he understood that Frank loved her. "Don't feel guilty about loving someone," he told Frank. "It's the only thing that matters. Loving someone." Marty didn't say much, but when he did speak it was always from the heart. Frank needed to hear his words; he would never forget them. "Thanks, Pop," he told him. "You're right. I'll try not to."

"But maybe don't marry her right away, son," Marty hastened to add, looking at Frank squarely. "Maybe take a minute and think this thing through. It's no good having two bad marriages, Frankie."

Frank nodded. He put his head on his father's shoulder and sighed deeply. "You're right, Pop," he whispered. "It's no good."

1951

The following year, Frank Sinatra—now thirty-five years old—was still as captivated by Ava Gardner as ever, and still conflicted about his life and career. On March 27, he gave one of his most emotional performances in the studio when he recorded "I'm a Fool to Want You," a session that marked a defining moment in the development of his interpretative skills. The anguish he felt over his relationship with Ava is clear in every note in this recording (which, incidentally, was not a hit and remains obscure, except to Sinatra aficionados). So overcome by grief was he when he first tried to record it that he left the studio in tears. He had to return later to complete the song.

"That was one of the finest recordings he ever made," observed his daughter Nancy. "It's enough to tear your heart into pieces, it's so beautiful. As a matter of fact, we played it on Thanksgiving night [1996] at his house. We were sitting at the table listening to it in the background, and he said, 'My God. That's good.'"

Sinatra cowrote "I'm a Fool to Want You" with Jack Wolf and Joel Herron. He would rerecord it for Capital Records six years later; although the remake was a stunning performance, it didn't have the same emotional intensity as the original.

At about this same time, Frank filmed a new movie, *Meet Danny Wilson*, for Universal with Shelley Winters. In the film, he portrays a shady nightclub singer who is involved with the underworld—a little too close to home, but he was just happy to work; he was paid $25,000 for the film. Though it was unsuccessful at the box office when finally released, it showcased some memorable songs, including "All of Me," "She's Funny That Way," and "I've Got a Crush on You."

His next movie, *Double Dynamite*, was a comedy costarring Jane Russell and Groucho Marx. It was a disaster. *Double Dynamite* had actually been filmed the previous year, but had been shelved temporarily. Steve Stoliar, Groucho Marx's former secretary, said, "Groucho told me Sinatra was often late to the set, stuck in his dressing room going over racing forms. Groucho went up to him finally and said,

'If you're late one more time, you're going to have to act opposite yourself, because I'm not going to show up.' Sinatra was on time after that."

On July 17, 1951, Frank and Ava attended the premiere of *Show Boat* at the Egyptian Theatre in Hollywood. Ava never looked more stunning, wearing an emerald green–and–black satin and lace evening gown courtesy of the MGM costume designer Irene. A striking diamond necklace, an expensive gift from Frank to commemorate the occasion, adorned her neck. Famed Hollywood stylist Sydney Guilaroff did her hair. From the expression on his face, Frank was proud to be with the woman described by one television reporter as "a true Hollywood vision."

"It gives me a great pleasure and pride to be able to escort Ava to a public premiere," Frank said happily. "I've cared for a long, long time. I'm very much in love with her and it's wonderful to know we can be seen together without hurting anyone. There's no ill feeling about it anywhere—with anyone." He seemed anxious.

As the glamorous couple exited a stretch limousine and walked down the red carpet to the theater, devoted fans screamed out their names in unison: "Frankie!" "Ava!" "Frankie!" "Ava!" Flashbulbs popped all about them. It was a mad scene, but exhilarating. A party was planned later at Romanoff's, but Frank and Ava bowed out because he had to be at work early the next morning, at RKO on the set of *Meet Danny Wilson*.

Shortly after the premiere, and after a quick vacation to Mexico, Frank announced that he and Ava were officially engaged to be married. On August 11, he was booked at the Riverside Inn and Casino in Reno, Nevada. While there, he decided to use the opportunity to establish a Nevada residency so that *he* could file for divorce. His filing would involve his having to stay in Nevada for at least five weeks. He rented an estate there.

"Come on up here for the Labor Day weekend," Frank told Ava on the telephone. "We can have some fun." Ava agreed. She and her maid, Rene, jumped in her Cadillac (with her Corgi dog, Rags) and sped off from Los Angeles to Reno. About halfway there, they hit a deer on the road, violently shattering the windshield. Nobody was hurt, but both women were quite shaken and the car's engine died.

"Maybe we can still drive," the plucky Ava suggested. "Without a windshield?" Rene asked. "Well, I don't see why not," Ava said as she got out of the car.

Ava lifted the hood of the vehicle and fiddled with the engine for a few minutes as if she knew exactly what she was doing. Then she got back into the driver's seat and turned the ignition. "Damn!" she exclaimed when the engine wouldn't start. "Okay, fine," she decided. "This calls for a drink." Rene reached into her purse and pulled out a bottle of brandy, uncorked it, and handed it to Ava, who took a couple of deep swigs. Then the two women got out of the vehicle and started hitchhiking along the deserted highway—Rene carrying Rags, Ava with her thumb out—before being picked up by a no doubt astonished passing driver. They were driven to Carson City, where they called Hank Sanicola. He met them there and drove them the rest of the way.

Frank thought it would be even more fun for Ava if she and Rene—along with Hank Sanicola and his wife, Paula—took a side trip with him to the Cal-Neva Lodge in Lake Tahoe.

The Cal-Neva Lodge, located exactly on the California-Nevada border, boasted a beautiful showroom (where the same performers who frequented Las Vegas—Frank's friends, for the most part—appeared), an enormous dining room, plus about twenty furnished cottages that cost about fifty dollars a day. The luxurious gambling casinos were located on the Nevada side of the compound. It was advertised as "Heaven in the High Sierras." Frank owned the largest interest in the Cal-Neva, 36.6 percent. Along with Frank were investors Dean Martin, Hank Sanicola, and Paul "Skinny" D'Amato, the charismatic owner of the 500 Club in Atlantic City.

Nancy Sinatra recalled, "Dad liked Cal-Neva because it was unpretentious but glamorous, homey but exciting. He had the final say on every employee, choosing people who were honest and hardworking and who would turn the lodge into a wonderful getaway destination. He reveled in the fun of hotel, casino, and stage ownership, throwing countless parties, even chartering planes to fly in friends, such as Lucille Ball, to share his enjoyment at ringside."

"We thought that was just a swell idea," Ava later said of their intention to visit Cal-Neva. "We were wrong."

The Suicide Attempts

On the afternoon of August 31, 1951, Frank, Ava, Rene, Hank, and Paula took a yacht out onto the water for a peaceful afternoon on the lake. After spending about two hours in the hot sun drinking copious amounts of champagne, everyone was feeling pretty drunk. As often happened when they were drinking, Frank and Ava got into a heated argument. Because Frank wasn't paying attention to his job as captain, the boat crashed into something—rocks, presumably— and suddenly the front half was on shore and the back half in water. Alarmed and too inebriated to think straight, everyone just jumped off the boat into the water and swam to shore. Everyone but Ava. "You're gonna drown, you dizzy broad," Frank hollered at her as the ship started to sink. "Jump, Ava!" Ava went into the bathroom, found a supply of toilet paper, and starting flinging the rolls at Frank. "Stop telling me what to do," she shouted back at him.

Finally, Ava got off the boat. "Later we laughed our heads off at the adventure," Rene Jordan recalled, "but the episode we were about to face was far more disturbing."

Everyone piled into a new convertible that Frank had rented, and they drove back to the Cal-Neva cabin. Then, later that night, during what had been a pleasant dinner with Hank, Paula, and Rene, Ava and Frank had yet another acrimonious exchange. Ava had drunkenly confessed that she and bullfighter Mario Cabré really *did* have an affair back in Spain. An argument grew from there about the definition of commitment, and that's when Frank's wife came up. "If you ever treat me the way you've treated Nancy," Ava said, "I'll kill you." She then went after Frank with a vengeance, detailing how he had left Nancy for another woman and had abandoned his own children in the process. Frank said that the fact that she could sit before him and make those sorts of declarations let him know that she was nothing but "a *whore*." He spit out the word. "Because no woman of class would ever say these things to me," he added.

"So you're calling me a whore now?" Ava asked, upset.

"Hey, what can I tell you, sister?" Frank said. "You the one who slept with a greaseball [Frank's name for Cabré]. And how many

The Suicide Attempts

157

times have I told you, don't ever mention Nancy's name to me," he added angrily. "How many times?"

The argument continued back at the house. At one point, Ava became very upset, opened a patio door, and took off running into the dark of night. "Wait, Miss G.," exclaimed Rene, who followed her. Ava wouldn't stop running, though, stumbling through the woods barefoot all the way down to the rocky shore. Finally, Rene reached her and managed to grab her by the waist before they both ended up in the lake. Upset and exhausted, Ava sank to her knees in the sand and started sobbing, with her maid doing what she could to comfort her. At that time, no one knew for certain how Ava's psychological pathology impacted her behavior, but it certainly seemed like she was given to the same kinds of mood swings as Frank.

"I have to tell you something, Rene," Ava said. "Frank wants me to loan him some money." How much? "Nineteen thousand dollars!" (Roughly $175,000 in today's equivalent.) Rene asked if Ava had that much money to spare. No, she didn't, she said, but maybe she could get it from her agent, Charles Feldman. Apparently, according to what he told Ava, Frank needed to give the money to Nancy, or she was going to take the Palm Springs house. "And he loves that place so much, I can't let that happen," Ava said. Discussion about whether or not—and how—he would ever be able to pay back the loan had been part of the most recent fight at the house. (Ava eventually did loan the money to Frank.) "Let's go home," Rene told Ava. "Yes, let's go home," Ava agreed, wiping the tears from her eyes.

By "home," Rene had meant their cabin at Cal-Neva, but Ava had a different idea—she wanted to go back to Los Angeles. The two made their way back through the woods to the cabin, collected Rags, got into the convertible Frank had rented, and took off in the middle of the night, headed toward California. They didn't even say good-bye to anyone. Driving at about a hundred miles per hour down the highway with the top down, it was as if Ava was determined to kill herself, her maid, and her dog. "Slow down, Miss G.," Rene yelled out. "Please!" Instead, Ava just picked up speed, all the while muttering about Frank and how it was over between them.

The sun was rising by the time Ava and Rene got back to her home in Los Angeles on Nichols Canyon Drive. They were there for maybe about fifteen minutes when the telephone rang. Rene picked it up. It was Hank Sanicola, frantic. "Frank took an overdose of sleeping pills," he told her. "The doctor is here. He doesn't think he'll make it. You two had better get back up here." Alarmed, Rene put Ava on the line. "Yes, of course," Ava said dispassionately. "We'll be there soon."

Apparently, when Frank realized that Ava had departed without saying goodbye, he popped a bunch of sleeping pills into his mouth and washed them down with liquor. When Frank's new valet, George Jacobs, found him a few hours later, he summoned physician Dr. John Wesley Field to tend to him. "Mr. S. was definitely out of it," Jacobs would recall. "If I hadn't gotten to him in time, I'm pretty sure he'd have been a goner."

Remembering what had occurred in New York with Frank's simulated suicide attempt, Ava was reluctant to run to Frank's side. Still, she and Rene caught a plane—her maid convinced her not to try to drive back—and returned to Lake Tahoe. A couple hours later, when Ava got to Frank's room, she found him lying on the bed, the doctor taking his pulse. "Oh, Ava," Frank said weakly. "I thought you had left."

"I could have killed him," Ava told Rene when she came out of the room. "He's the only one who had any sleep. You can be sure he counted how many sleeping pills he took. Hank's had no sleep, the doctor's had no sleep, you and I have had no sleep...there he is rested and fine with a good appetite. I could have kicked the crap out of him. I could have killed him. Instead I forgave him in about twenty-five seconds."

A few weeks later while in New York, Frank stayed, as he usually did, at the apartment of his close friend Manie Sacks. One evening he went out alone and, of course, had too much to drink. Afterward, he walked back to Sacks's apartment and—as he would later remember—poured himself yet another drink. He put a cigarette in his mouth, went into the bathroom for some sleeping pills, and shuffled absentmindedly into the kitchen. He popped a few of the pills and chased them down with booze. Then, turning on the gas oven, he bent over one of the burners to light the cigarette that dangled from his mouth. While in that position, he couldn't help but smell the gas as it seeped from the stove. He inhaled deeply. He must have decided in that split second that death was what he wanted, because he turned the gas up all the way. Then he ignited the other burners. As the noxious fumes coursed from the oven, he just pulled up a chair and sat in front of it. He inhaled deeply. He drifted off.

The next thing he knew, he was being jostled back to life by a frantic Manie Sacks. Had Manie arrived just a few minutes later, it would have been too late. This was no phony suicide attempt; this time, Sinatra really wanted to die.

"Damn you, Frank," Manie said, clenching his teeth. "How could you do this? What about your kids?"

"I'm sorry, I'm sorry," Frank mumbled as he came out of his stupor. "That was stupid. That was real stupid."

He was ashamed of what he'd done. He promised Manie he would never try anything like that again. He even agreed to start seeing a psychiatrist, though, as he put it, "I know what the guy's gonna say. I know what's wrong. So why pay someone to tell me what I already know?"

"Today, they would have him on medication," his son, Frank Jr., once said. "But back then, you were pretty much on your own to medicate as you will. People got help, of course, but it wasn't as prevalent, or even as accepted, as it is today."

"I only heard about this thing years after the fact," Sammy Davis would recall. "Me and Frank were having a drink at one of the bars in the Sands in 1967 when he told me about it."

"I can't believe I did that shit," Frank told Sammy, according to Sammy's later recollection of the conversation. It was all about Ava, Frank admitted. He said it was a feeling he had that he was in love with a woman who didn't love him in return, and this dilemma drove him to want to end his life. "He said he could see it in her eyes: She pitied him more than she loved him," Sammy recalled. "She thought he was weak and troubled and so he acted that way. He kept thinking things would change, he said. He kept hoping she would be the woman for him because the idea that maybe she wasn't was too much to bear, especially considering all he had given up for her."

"It was a dark enough time to lead him to deep despair," Nancy

Sinatra Sr. would observe, "even to contemplate and approach the edge of suicide. It was impossible to know whether it was the loss of this love [Ava] or the loss of all the love and luck and work that his life had known before this very 'down' hour; or what complex of motives moved him to the brink. Others may speculate on what could cause any human being to consider ending his life. We have to respect the eternal privacy, which means we can never know. Later, he would counsel me not to despair, that despair can lead to terrible things."

A couple weeks after the suicide attempt in New York, Frank was at his Palm Springs compound with Ava and Jimmy Van Heusen. He was still in a very dark mood. One night after an argument between Frank and Ava that Van Heusen had unsuccessfully attempted to referee, the three dispersed to different rooms to cool off. Frank went to the master bedroom. About a half hour later, Ava showed up in the doorway and saw Frank sitting on the edge of the bed, a gun pointed to his temple. Unwisely, she jumped at him to take the gun. The two of them tumbled off the bed and onto the floor. There was a tussle. The gun went off.

"Oh my God," Ava recalled to Rene Jordan. "It reacted like a snake...Bang! The bullet went ricocheting around the stone fireplace and whizzed out again, making a two-inch hole in a solid wood door." Jimmy Van Heusen came running down the hall after hearing the shot to make sure they were both still alive. He found them sobbing on the floor in each other's arms.

Frank certainly had his reasons for being with Ava. He thought of her as his only hope. But now Ava finally had a reason for staying: She was scared of what he would do to himself if she left.

* * *

After Frank's six-week residency in Nevada was completed, he was able to officially file for divorce there, which he did on September 19, 1950. Nancy's attorney informed him that the property settlement on which they had earlier agreed was no longer valid because Frank was about $50,000 behind in his payments. Nancy obtained a levy against an office building he owned in Beverly Hills in order to collect the payments due her. But it was out of Nancy's hands by this point. She was trying not to bear a grudge, but at the same time she wanted to protect herself and her children, and so she told her attorneys to do whatever they had to do, and to leave her out of it. Her family suggested that maybe now she would be able to find someone who would treat her well. She was only thirty-three and still quite beautiful. However, she insisted that she couldn't imagine beginning a new life with someone else. "And who wants a woman with three kids?" she asked hopelessly. Besides, she still loved Frank, she admitted, despite everything that had occurred between them.

By this time, Frank was exhausted by the legal process and told his new attorneys to give Nancy whatever she wanted. He couldn't fight her any longer, and the bottom line for him was that he was finally getting out of a marriage that hadn't worked for him for many years. He'd be free to be with Ava. Therefore, he signed an agreement to pay Nancy all of the money he owed and more, if she would just, once and for all, allow the divorce to be finalized. Nancy agreed.

Ava Comes to Dinner

The Sinatra divorce was finally granted on October 31, 1951, in Santa Monica while Frank and Ava were in New York. "Regretfully, I am putting aside religious and personal considerations and agreeing to give Frank the freedom he has so earnestly requested," said Nancy in a statement. "This is what Frank wants…"

Nancy would receive one-third of Frank's gross income on the first $150,000; 10 percent of the next $150,000; and a smaller percentage thereafter (but never less than $1,000 a month for the rest of her life). She was also awarded custody of the couple's three children, the home in Holmby Hills, part interest in the Sinatra Music Corporation, furnishings, furs, jewelry, and a 1950 Cadillac. Frank kept the home in Palm Springs, his 1949 Cadillac convertible, 1947 four-wheel-drive Jeep, bank accounts, oil interests in Austin County, Texas, and all rights to and royalties for his musical compositions and recordings. The couple agreed to sign over to Frank's parents the Hoboken home he had bought for them.

"She took her pound of flesh from him and then some," Ava bitterly observed of Nancy's settlement with Frank.

A day later, Frank and Ava obtained a marriage license.

"Whatcha gonna get each other for a wedding present?" one reporter asked the couple during one of the public outings where, as always, they were descended upon by the media. "Boxing gloves?" Even Ava had to laugh at that one. "Will it be a white wedding dress, Miss Gardner?" a photographer asked sarcastically. At that, her smile froze. Frank shoved the photographer as hard as he could. As the lensman fell backward and hit the pavement, the couple raced away, got into a limousine, and sped off into the night.

The next few days were blissful. When it worked, Frank's relationship with Ava was fueled with passion and excitement. He could lose himself in her, almost completely disappear from his unhinged world, deep into the cocoon of their relationship. As he would later explain it, "When it was good between us, it was so good that nothing else mattered. It was like it was just us two, me and Ava, in the world, and that was all I needed. Just the two of us. I felt like I could do anything if she was at my side."

A couple of days later, Frank took Ava to his parents' home to celebrate the upcoming wedding. "Hey, where's the bar?" Ava wanted to know as soon as she and Frank walked through the door. "I need a drink."

"We got no bar," Marty said icily. "But I'll get you a drink. Just hold your horses." Meanwhile, Dolly greeted her warmly, almost as if she was her daughter. It was clear that she was crazy about her.

When Marty rose to get Ava her drink, Frank noticed his jacket on the chair. He walked over and took a couple hundred-dollar bills—"C-notes," as he called them—from his money clip, stuck them in his pop's jacket, and then winked at Ava. "So he can be a big shot with his friends at the bar," Frank whispered.

"I don't even know the names of some of the things we ate that night," Ava later said of the Italian feast that Dolly had prepared. "Chicken like you've never tasted in your life, some wonderful little meat thing rolled in dough, and just about every Italian goody you can imagine."

One of Frank's cousins said, "We sat around the table eating cannolis and having coffee and the after-dinner drink, Frangelico. Everyone was having a good time, laughing and clapping, smoking at the table, which you would probably not see much of today. The booze was flowing; we were in good spirits. Framed pictures of Frank with different celebrities were hanging on the wall, all of them crooked. Dolly in her sleeveless, blue-and-white polka-dotted muumuu. Frank and Marty in their white T-shirt and dress slacks. Typical evening at Dolly's and Marty's."

According to the source, Frank and Marty began talking about Frank's first wife, Nancy. "You know, Pop, I feel badly about how it ended with Big Nancy," Frank said. (He used the nickname sometimes used in the family to distinguish her from her daughter, "Little Nancy.") "I hope she's okay. I don't know what else I coulda done."

"Guilt is the only thing that keeps us human," Marty told his son. "Animals, they don't feel guilt. So it's good that you feel guilty, kid," he continued. "It just means you're human, Frankie," he concluded. "It's good."

Frank and Ava Marry

*F*rank and Ava were to be married on November 7, 1951, at the home of Manie Sacks's brother, Lester, in West Mount Airy, an upscale neighborhood of Philadelphia. However, the night before the wedding, a handwritten letter was delivered to Ava from a woman who claimed to be a prostitute with whom Frank was having an affair. She provided details that to Ava seemed convincing. The alleged affair had been going on for months, the writer said, and right under Ava's nose. Ava had been a fool, asserted the woman, for ever having believed in Frank Sinatra. "God! I almost threw up," Ava recalled later. "I did know one thing—in the face of this evidence, there was going to be no marriage tomorrow. There was going to be no marriage, ever!"

She called off the wedding and hurled her engagement ring—a six-carat emerald stone in platinum with pear-shaped diamonds—out the window of the Hampshire House, where the couple was staying in New York. (It was never found.)

Frank swore that the writer was lying. He couldn't believe that after all they'd been through together, Ava would take as gospel the word of an anonymous accuser. Ava's sister Bappie talked to her throughout the night to convince her that she really should not place so much importance on an anonymous letter. In the end, Ava relented. "By this time, it seemed to me that the marriage was doomed even before they got within walking distance of the altar," said Rene Jordan.

It had snowed hard in the Midwest the previous day. By Wednesday, November 7, 1951, the storm had reached Philadelphia in the form of a cold, driving rain. Small-craft warnings were being posted all along the East Coast.

Adrienne Ellis, Lester Sacks's daughter, who was sixteen at the time, would recall, "Our house looked beautiful. The silver was polished and shining. There were flowers everywhere. But my mother sent me to the florist to buy even more. I hadn't said a word, but the florist said, 'We know Sinatra is getting married at your house.'"

Indeed, it wasn't long before a crowd of reporters and photographers huddled miserably outside in the rain. Frank and Ava arrived from New York in a rented chauffeured Cadillac. Frank's first reaction upon seeing the contingent of reporters was to lash out at them: "How did you creeps know we were here? I don't want a circus. I'll knock any guy on his can who tries to get in."

Adrienne Ellis remembered Ava washing her hair just before the ceremony. When she came out of the shower, she just towel-dried it, and that was it. "My mother couldn't get over that," Adrienne said, laughing.

Ava was certainly dazzling on her wedding day. Her dress was designed by Howard Greer, the Paris-trained couturier for such stars as Irene Dunne, Joan Crawford, Ginger Rogers, Rita Hayworth, and Katharine Hepburn. Greer believed in making a woman look sexy; Ava was no exception. The strapless top of her wedding dress was pink taffeta over a high-waisted mauve marquisette cocktail-length skirt. Deferring to modesty, she wore a sheer mauve marquisette bolero edged with the same pink taffeta as the top. Her jewelry consisted of a double-stranded pearl choker and pearl-and-diamond teardrop earrings.

Ava was so breathtaking, no one could take their eyes off her, certainly not Frank. Wearing a navy suit with a slim light gray tie, a white silk shirt, and a white boutonniere in his left lapel, he waited beside Judge José (Joseph) Sloane of the Common Pleas Court of Germantown, who was to perform the ceremony. Ava handed her white orchid spray to her matron of honor, June Hutton, as she approached the judge.

The ceremony began at 5 p.m. and was brief. The guests included Frank's parents; Bappie; Mr. and Mrs. Isaac Levy; Hank Sanicola; Frank's partner Ben Barton; his conductor, Axel Stordahl, and Stordahl's wife, singer June Hutton; music arranger Dick Jones; and, of course, Manie Sacks, who was now a vice president of RCA. They all watched as the couple exchanged simple, thin platinum bands. Ava, wearing stiletto-heeled shoes, was as tall as Frank. They looked into each other's eyes the entire time, mechanically repeating their vows, almost absentmindedly putting the slim, unadorned platinum bands on each other's fingers. So lost were they in the moment that when the judge pronounced them man and wife, they didn't budge.

"You may kiss your bride, Mr. Sinatra," Judge Sloane said.

It was as though he had not spoken.

"Mr. Sinatra," the judge repeated. "Your bride." He tapped Frank on the shoulder and pointed to Ava. "You may kiss her now."

With an embarrassed grin, Frank put his hands on Ava's shoulders and gently pulled her toward him. His lips brushed hers for an instant.

"I love you," he whispered.

"Of course you do," she said with a smile.

The party after the ceremony lasted until about nine. Dolly and Marty were very excited to welcome Ava into the family; Marty had accepted that she was what Frank now wanted and had decided to be supportive. As for Dolly, Ava was *"famiglia"* (family) now, and she would now make public her support. Likely Nancy bristled when she read Dolly's statement to the press: "I'd like to tell those hypocrites who send me letters without signing their names that say, 'Aren't you ashamed, Mrs. Sinatra, that your boy divorced his wife and left three children just so he could marry that actress?' I'd like to tell them that

Frank loves his three children as much as he loves anything else in the world—that I, his mother, am proud that he married a wonderful girl like Ava."

After the party, Manie Sacks, who bore a vague resemblance to Frank, was used as a decoy with the press. He and a female guest, heads down with hats on, left in a limousine with everyone saying goodbye and throwing rice at their vehicle. The car took off, and the media followed. Afterward, Frank and Ava departed quietly, headed for a private plane waiting at Wings Field in Ambler. But in her haste, Ava discovered before boarding that she had the wrong suitcase. It held the outfit she had arrived in in the morning, and her wedding dress. "My parents had to jump in a car and drive to Wings in pouring rain to give her the right suitcase," recalled Steve Sacks, who was eleven at the time.

* * *

"Well, we finally did it," Ava Gardner told Lucy Wellman a couple of days later. She was on the telephone from the Hotel Nacional in Cuba where she and Frank were honeymooning for a couple of days. "Congratulations!" exclaimed her Los Angeles friend. "Are you happy?" Ava answered by saying that Frank was "wonderful," but that what it took for the two of them to get to this point in their relationship had been "so *exhausting.*" Her friend noted that Ava's observations didn't exactly answer her question: Was she happy? Ava hesitated. "Well," she began carefully, "let's just say I'm not *un*happy." Lucy then asked how the honeymoon was going. Ava said all was well, even though "I paid for the whole goddamn thing." She then told Lucy that Frank's wedding gift to her had been a sapphire-blue mink cape stole. In turn, she presented him with an expensive gold locket with a Saint Francis medal on one side, a Saint Christopher on the other, and a photograph of her inside. But she also said that the battles between them continued to rage. "We've already had fifteen fights—and that's just today," she said. "He's under a lot of pressure. I'm just not the patient, understanding type," she admitted. "You know that. I mean, I *try* to be," she added. "But that's just not me, is it?"

"No, it really isn't," Lucy agreed.

Fifteen minutes after she hung up, Ava called her friend back. "Listen," she said, "I know I can trust you, but don't ever, *ever* mention to anyone that I paid for the honeymoon. Frank would kill me. So, you must promise me."

"I promise," her friend vowed. In fact, Lucy Wellman would keep that promise for some forty years.

Part Five

DOWNWARD SPIRAL

His Only Collateral Was a Dream

The year 1952 saw thirty-six-year-old Frank Sinatra's professional downward slide continue. Frank's film *Meet Danny Wilson* was released on February 8 to mediocre reviews; he returned to the Paramount Theatre in New York on March 26 for an engagement with Frank Fontaine, Buddy Rich, and June Hutton, but the engagement was a box-office disappointment. When he later performed at the Chez Paree in Chicago, only 150 people were in the nightclub, which seated 1,200. Then in June, Frank was dropped by Columbia Records as well as by his talent agency, MCA. It probably didn't help his ego that as his career stalled, Ava's continued to flourish. She began work on a new film for 20th Century–Fox, *The Snows of Kilimanjaro*, just as MGM was about to offer her a ten-year contract for twelve movies at $100,000 per film.

While logic dictated that Frank's time was over, he knew that all he needed was another break. But no one was handing Frank Sinatra anything at this time, so if he were to be saved, he'd have to do it himself.

"I've been up and down in my life more than a roller coaster," Frank would later observe. "At thirty-eight years old, I was a has-been," he added. "Sitting by a telephone that wouldn't ring. Wondering what happened to all the friends who grew invisible when the music stopped. Finding out fast how tough it is to borrow money when you're all washed up. My only collateral was a dream," he recalled. "A dream to end my nightmare. And what a dream it was. It began when I read an absolutely fascinating book written by a giant, James Jones. More than a book," he said, "it was a portrait of people I knew, understood, and could feel, and in it I saw myself as clearly as I see myself every morning when I shave. I was Maggio. No matter who said what, I would prove it, no matter how many tests I was asked to make, no matter what the money. I was going to become Maggio if it was the last thing I ever did."

Sinatra was referring to the character Private Angelo Maggio in James Jones's first novel, the bestselling *From Here to Eternity*, which had been published in 1951. Jones's book had been critically acclaimed, but it also was considered revolutionary because of its strong criticism of the U.S. Army.

The novel won the prestigious National Book Award for fiction and was on the top of the bestseller list for months. However, it would prove to be an enormous challenge to write a screenplay based on this work. It is over eight hundred pages long, its language strong and graphic. At a time when all films had to adhere to the Production Code, which oversaw movie morality, it would also be difficult to work around the fact that the two main female characters in the book were a prostitute and a serial adulterer.

With its brutal portrayal of the plight of enlisted men, *From Here to Eternity* presented the army in an unfavorable light at a time when most Americans did not question their government. In fact, in the 1940s and '50s it was impossible to produce a military film without help from the Pentagon. Military equipment was too expensive to duplicate; the only way to use authentic government matériel was to cooperate with the government.

Two studios had considered and turned the book down before Harry Cohn of Columbia Studios bought it in 1951. Screenwriter Daniel Taradash managed to compress the material into a 161-page working script while being true to the novel's themes. The film's producer, Buddy Adler, a former lieutenant colonel in the Signal Corps and husband of film star Anita Louise, was assigned to deal with the army's many objections. By toning down some of the brutality, Adler was able to obtain their cooperation.

When Sinatra heard that the novel was being made into a film by Columbia, he knew he was perfect for the character of Angelo Maggio, the scrappy Italian-American soldier from the streets of Brooklyn. This part would give him a dramatic break from the musicals in which he'd previously appeared, and he felt strongly that the role would revitalize his career.

"I know if I can get this part, I can hit a home run," he told Ava. "I grew up with a hundred Maggios in my neighborhood. I *am* Maggio."

Montgomery Clift had already been cast in the coveted role of army private Prewitt. Joan Crawford would have been the commanding officer's wife, Karen Holmes, had she not insisted on having her own wardrobe designers. She was replaced by Deborah Kerr, who worked hard with a voice coach to lose her British accent. Other major roles were assigned to Burt Lancaster, as Warden, the first sergeant who manages his company with saintly dedication while having an affair with Kerr's character, and Donna Reed, as Alma, Prewitt's girlfriend. (Ernest Borgnine would also appear in the film as the cruel Fatso Judson, the man who kills Maggio. Borgnine was such a fan of Sinatra's—"my idol, my everything"—that he had named his daughter Nancy after Frank's wife and daughter.) Still to be cast was Maggio.

Ava offered to use any influence she might have to persuade Harry Cohn to cast Frank in the film. However, Frank wanted her to stay out of it. If he was to get this part, he told her, it would be on his own and by his own merit. In actuality, though, he had recruited practically everyone he knew who also knew Harry Cohn to bombard Cohn with requests that he consider Sinatra for the part. He also sent telegrams to Cohn and to the film's director, Fred Zinnemann (*High Noon* and *The Member of the Wedding*), signed "Maggio."

Ava felt that if her husband had this role, perhaps it would take some strain off their marriage. So she defied Frank's orders and met with Cohn's wife, Joan, to see what she could do to secure the role for her husband. "Just have him test Frank," she asked Joan. "Please. He really needs this role."

Ava didn't know that Frank had already met with Harry Cohn over lunch about the job, and Cohn had made it clear that he was not interested—even when Frank offered to do the role for just $1,000 a week. That was a big reduction in fee, since he had previously been paid as much as $150,000 per film. "You're out of your mind," Cohn told Sinatra. As far as Cohn was concerned, Frank was a singer, not an actor. He told Frank that he didn't think he had ever made a decent movie.

Meanwhile, Ava continued campaigning for Frank. A friend of hers, Paul Clemens, lived in a guesthouse on the estate of Harry and Joan Cohn. One night, he invited Ava for dinner with the Cohns.

Over dinner, Ava started in on Harry Cohn. "You know who's right for that part of Maggio, don't you?" she said. "That son of a bitch husband of mine, that's who. Let me tell you something," she said, according to Earl Wilson. "If you don't give him this role, he'll kill himself." She wasn't kidding.

Eventually, Harry Cohn and Fred Zinnemann began to buckle under so much pressure. Cohn telephoned Sinatra and said he would screen-test him for the role. Meanwhile, he asked Frank to "call off the dogs. And Ava, too."

When the film's producer, Buddy Adler, gave Frank the script for the scenes he was to play, Frank handed it back to him. He already knew the lines. He had memorized them, having read them so many times. This was one screen test he was determined to nail, one role he intended to make his own.

Mogambo

$\mathcal{A}$s Frank and Ava campaigned for the coveted role of Maggio in *From Here to Eternity*, loose ends of Frank's recording career were being tied up. On September 17, 1952, he recorded his last side for Columbia Records in New York, "Why Try to Change Me Now?" Composed by Cy Coleman and arranged by Percy Faith, this pensive song was another that spoke to the essence of Frank's emotions at the time. Ed O'Brien and Robert Wilson said it best in their book *Sinatra 101: The 101 Best Recordings and the Stories Behind Them*: "Gone was the innocent, naive singer of the previous decade. Burned by love, the singer is able to convey the darkness, the cynicism and aching sadness that would characterize much of his work in the years to come." Like "I'm a Fool to Want You," this is another obscure Sinatra song that didn't mean much to his fans at the time but with the unfolding of the years has been recognized as a gem. (He would record the song again for Capitol in March 1959.)

Meanwhile, the "Battling Sinatras," as some members of the press had dubbed them, continued with their tumultuous marriage. The Sinatra-Ava bouts had become by 1952 the stuff of show-business legend. On November 7, they left for Africa, where Ava was scheduled to film *Mogambo* (a remake of the 1932 film *Red Dust*, which also starred Clark Gable, but with Jean Harlow).

Frank wasn't keen on the idea of his wife going to Africa with Clark Gable, her costar in the film, along with Grace Kelly, but since he had nothing else to do—he still hadn't heard whether or not he would get the role of Maggio—he decided to accompany her. "He's going with me," Ava told the press of her husband. "He's going to do some theaters around Nairobi."

The Sinatras celebrated their first wedding anniversary en route to Africa on a Stratocruiser. In Nairobi, Frank spent his time reading novels while Ava worked. "Frank was her helper," said Joseph Godfrey, who was employed on the film as a costume assistant to designer Helen Rose. "You had to feel bad for the guy. She was sort of demanding."

"Get me a drink, baby, will ya?" Ava would ask when she was done with a scene. "A Manhattan, straight up with a cherry.

"And rub my back, won't you?

"And fetch my script, will ya, sweetie?"

Frank, his face an expressionless mask, would say, "Sure, why not?"

Could he sink any lower? He was depressed and low-key. Nearly everyone present noticed that in these moments, he was hardly the tough guy the press had been writing about for so many years. Rather, he seemed quiet, defeated.

On tough days of shooting, Ava required five different kinds of sherbet—blackberry, raspberry, lime, cherry, and orange—as a special treat, a reward of sorts for getting through the day. She liked them served in pretty oval scoops on a white plate, and with tiny wild strawberries, if possible. "But if you can't get the strawberries, then I guess I'll just have to live without them," she told Frank.

"Do you know how hard it is to find *sherbet* in this goddamned jungle?" Frank asked.

"Oh, I know, Frank," she said wearily. "Just call someone in London and have it shipped in, then. And see if you can get those dainty little butter cookies too. I just love those."

"All right. All right."

"He needed a lift," recalled Bea Lowry, makeup artist Colin Garde's assistant on the film. "She was spoiled, yes, but I also know she was concerned. She called Harry Cohn from Nairobi. I heard the conversation myself. She was angry with him, and she said, 'Jesus Christ, you know Frank is right for this part. Please, I am *begging* you. Give him this role. He can't take it anymore. *I* can't take it anymore.' I believe he hung up on her, because she slammed the phone down onto the receiver."

The weather was sweltering hot, the daytime temperature as high as 130 degrees, and Ava was unhappy for most of the shoot. She hated sleeping in a tent with mosquitoes swarming everywhere and ants crawling up her legs; she was sick to her stomach most of the time and felt woefully inadequate as an actress working opposite the legendary Clark Gable. She just wanted the filming to end.

Ava's Pregnancies

It was in Africa that Ava Gardner discovered she was pregnant.

Previously, in November 1951, Ava had given an interview to Marie Torre of the *New York World-Telegram and Sun* and expressed her desire to have children. "Maybe we'll start thinking about a family," she said. "I love large families. When I was younger, I used to think about how wonderful it would be to have four sons. I'm twenty-eight now. It's too late for such a large family. So I think I can be happy with two, maybe three, kids."

However, as Frank's wife, she had changed her mind.

Frank was elated about the baby. Ava, however, was not. Frank suggested that she quit work on the film for the sake of the pregnancy, but his pleas fell on deaf ears. As Ava wrote in her autobiography, "I felt that unless you were prepared to devote practically all your time to your child in its early years, it was unfair to the baby. If a child is unwanted—and somehow they know that—it is handicapped from the time it is born." Moreover, MGM had a penalty clause in her contract that said that her salary would be cut off if she had a baby. She was the breadwinner in the Sinatra household, she reasoned. Without her income, what would they do?

There was no way Frank was going to approve of Ava terminating the pregnancy—not after what he'd already gone through with

Nancy. "These women cannot keep aborting my children," he told one of Ava's trusted attorneys who was present on the set. "What is so wrong with me that they feel that's their only option?"

"But you have three kids," the lawyer told him. "Obviously, Nancy didn't always feel that way."

"I'd have four if I wasn't such a fuckup," Frank said. "I can't let Ava do this. I have to convince her."

Frank would say that one of the major reasons he was so confounded by Ava's ambivalence about being a mother to his child was that she was so good with his daughters. Nancy Sr. would often drop Nancy Jr. and Tina off at Ava's sister Bappie's home so they could spend time there with Frank and Ava. A practical woman, Nancy never tried to keep her offspring away from Ava. If Frank was to be with Ava, she reasoned, she would have to accept Ava as a stepmother to her children. (The daughters figured more into this equation than Frank Jr., who didn't seem interested in being with either his father or his stepmother.) Ava was very solicitous to both daughters. For instance, she gave Nancy her first lipstick and taught her how to use it. She taught Tina how to sew. They spent time watching television together. They went for long walks and had fun "girls only" luncheons, and then dinners with Frank. From the start, Tina adored Ava. "She made a fundamental impression on me," Tina recalled. "She seemed to stir all my senses at once. She was gentle and accessible. She immediately knelt to come down to my level. I have never forgotten that gesture."

It took Nancy Jr. some time to warm to Ava. "One day while I was playing dress-up in Mom's dressing room, I climbed up on a chair to get a shoebox off a shelf and knocked to the floor a stack of magazines that Mom had hidden in the closet," Nancy recalled. "They were movie magazines—Modern Screen, Photoplay, and so forth— and they were filled with pictures of my dad and a pretty lady named Ava Gardner and Mom and Frankie and Baby Tina and me. I was devastated—just like Mom. He had left me too. Eventually, inevitably, I would meet this other woman. My heart just melted looking at her. I was only a kid, I didn't know about beauty—that awesome kind of beauty that takes your breath away. She was just the most beautiful creature I had ever seen in my entire life. I couldn't stop staring at her. In my pre-teenage wisdom, I had some understanding why Daddy had left us."

It's not surprising that Nancy finally "got it" where Ava was concerned. After all, she and her father had a special connection; she would say that she was always able to somehow intuit what was going on in his heart. She would be able to understand and in some way even relate to his feelings for Ava, though she knew how much those emotions were tearing apart her mother.

After Nancy came around, all she and Tina wanted was to be barefoot all the time and smell just like their stepmother, Ava—her gardenia-scented perfume fascinated them. To her credit, Nancy Sr. tolerated it. To Frank, Ava's behavior with his daughters not only demonstrated her willingness to be a part of their lives, but also suggested that she could be a fine mother to any children he might have with her. Thus for Ava to want to abort their baby was the source of great frustration for him.

What he did not know, because Ava had elected not to tell him, was that this was her second pregnancy by him. The first time, in Los Angeles, she had decided not to tell him. "I went to St. John's Hospital with her during the first pregnancy," recalled Rene Jordan. "Thing was solved very easily by what is referred to as a D and C [dilation and curettage]. In a campsite in the middle of the bush, things were not quite that easy."

Obviously, Ava was not ready to be a mother, no matter the circumstances. It's also likely that what she observed of Frank as an absentee father to his own children likely didn't encourage her in wanting to add to his brood. Before the couple was able to reach a decision, though, Frank received an exciting telegram from his new agent, Bert Allenberg, of the William Morris Agency: Harry Cohn had agreed to screen-test him for *From Here to Eternity*. Frank would have to leave on the next plane back to the States. He just hoped he and Ava would be able to work out all of this confusion between them later. Making him feel all the more dismayed, doubtless, was the fact that he didn't have enough money for a plane ticket back to the States. He was that broke! He had to ask Ava to spring for a ticket, which she did.

"Once Frank was gone and she had a chance to think about it,

Ava decided that she and Frank shouldn't bring a child into the marriage," said Lucy Wellman.

"The way we fight tells me that there is something wrong with our marriage, and I just think it's not right to bring a baby into it," Ava told Lucy in a telephone call from Africa. Lucy warned her that springing an abortion on Frank was not the best way to proceed. She suggested that Ava and Frank had to reach such an important decision together, as a couple. But Ava disagreed. She said that she knew Frank would never allow her to have an abortion. She felt she had no choice but to make the decision herself. "I have to be strong for the two of us," she maintained. Lucy reminded her of how hurt Frank would be, and Ava agreed. In fact, she said she believed Frank would be "devastated. I think he'll kill me, actually," she fretted. "But it's for the best."

"But how are *you* with all of this?" Lucy asked. "I'm very worried about you." Ava said that she just couldn't think about it any longer. In fact, she said, if she thought about it for even one more second, she wouldn't be able to do it. "I just have to block it all out of my mind and go on and do it," she said, "and then it will be done."

The film's director, John Ford, also tried to talk Ava out of it. "Ava, you are married to a Catholic, and this is going to hurt Frank tremendously when he finds out. I'll protect you if the fact that you're having a baby starts to show," he told her. "I'll arrange the scenes; I'll arrange the shots. We'll wrap your part up as quickly as we can. Nothing will show. Please go ahead and have the child."

"No, this is not the time," Ava insisted. "I'm not ready. *We're* not ready."

Ford capitulated and, along with some MGM higher-ups, arranged for his star to go to London for the procedure on November 23, 1952. Ava secretly left Africa with her publicist and the wife of cameraman Robert Surtees at her side and checked into the Savoy Hotel. From there, she went to a private nursing home, where she had the procedure. Afterward, she gave an interview to a reporter for *Look* magazine to discuss her marriage to Frank, which she painted as being very happy. That reporter only revealed to his closest friends that he did the interview with Gardner while sitting on the edge of her bed in the clinic after she had ended the pregnancy. In his story, he reported that she had dysentery.

* * *

Meanwhile, back in the United States, Frank's screen test had been very well received by the studio. During the test, Frank had improvised a saloon scene in which Maggio shakes dice and then casts them across a pool table. He used olives instead of dice. "That one scene, that one moment of ingenuity, won him the role as far as I was concerned," said director Fred Zinnemann a couple of years before his death in March 1997.

But that wasn't all there was to Frank's performance. By all accounts, it was a commanding audition in every sense: part realistic, part theatrical, and filled with as much artistry as an actor can possibly squeeze into fifteen minutes. As written, the role was dark and intense. Sinatra, a desperate actor and even more desperate man, gave it all he had.

Producer Buddy Adler recalled, "I didn't think he had a chance [of getting the role] and didn't even go down to the soundstage for the test. But I got a call from Fred Zinnemann, telling me, 'You'd better come down here; you'll see something unbelievable; I already have it in the camera. I'm not using film this time. But I want you to see it.' Frank thought he was making another take, and he was terrific. I thought to myself, 'If he's like that in the movie, it's a sure Academy Award.'"

There was nothing left to do now but to wait for a decision, but it was looking good.

* * *

As he waited for news about *From Here to Eternity*, Frank got the alarming news that Ava had collapsed on the set and had been briefly sent to a hospital in London. In a prepared statement, her publicist confirmed that she had some sort of "tropical infection" and was also suffering from anemia. Frank, concerned about the baby, tracked Ava down at the Savoy in London. Lying, she assured him that she was fine, as was the baby.

It wasn't until Frank got back to Africa around Christmas that Ava finally confessed to him that she'd terminated the pregnancy. Frank couldn't believe it. It had happened again, another life terminated by its mother and done so behind his back. He demanded to know what Ava was thinking. Staring at that familiar inscrutable expression of hers made him feel all the more helpless. She vaguely explained her reasons. However, after about fifteen minutes, she just wanted to go.

"Stay with me," he begged her. "We need to talk about this, Ava."

"No," she decided. "I really must go." However, on the way out—as Ava later remembered it—she paused for a moment. She looked at Frank and pleaded with him, "Don't hate me, Frank. Just don't hate me. I couldn't take that."

"Too late," Frank said through gritted teeth.

"I'm afraid there's no coming back from this," Ava later confessed to Lucy Wellman. She said that she just didn't see how she and Frank could ever recover. "What I've done is so monstrous," she said, sobbing. Lucy told her that she needed to take a moment and think specifically about what she wanted at this time in her life, what she now needed. She pointed out that Ava had suffered two great losses, not just the baby but maybe Frank as well. "Yes, I've ruined what was left of us," Ava said tearfully. "Maybe on purpose," she added. Then, almost as if she'd just had some sort of epiphany, she asked, "Oh my God! Do you think I did this on purpose? Do you think I ruined us on purpose?" Her friend said she didn't know, but maybe it was possible. Ava, too emotional to continue the conversation, hung up the phone.

Filming From Here to Eternity

*B*y the end of 1952, Frank Sinatra was fairly certain that another actor, his friend Eli Wallach, had gotten the role he so wanted in *From Here to Eternity*. "When I heard that Eli Wallach had tested for it, I said, 'Forget it,'" Frank remembered. "He's a seasoned actor and a fine, fine performer." But then "I got the call," he said. "They decided that I had the part [at a salary of just $1,000 a week]. "I woulda done it for nothing," he said, "because it was something I really understood."

"I'll show them," he said excitedly after he hung up with the studio. "They'll be glad they finally cast me."

Shooting for *From Here to Eternity* would begin in Hawaii on March 2, 1953. All of the exteriors were filmed at the exact locations described in the novel: Schofield Barracks, the Royal Hawaiian Hotel, Waikiki Beach, Diamond Head, and the Wailea Golf Course. Harry Cohn sent cast and crew to the islands with a strict budget regarding money and time. The chartered plane arrived at 5 a.m on March 2. By the time the plane landed, Frank and Montgomery Clift were so drunk, an annoyed Burt Lancaster said later, "They were *gone*. Deborah [Kerr] and I had to wake them up. This is the way they arrived, and Harry Cohn is down there with the press and everything."

During filming, director Fred Zinnemann was surrounded by actors with different temperaments. "It wasn't easy," he said. "But then again, it was never easy. No film is easy." Burt Lancaster was protective of Deborah Kerr in her role of the adulterous wife, a 180-degree change from her usual noble characters. But with Zinnemann, Lancaster was argumentative and difficult, trying to get the director to change his lines the way Lancaster felt they should be written. Clift made no secret of the fact he considered Lancaster "a big bag of wind."

Later, Zinnemann would say that Frank was easy to work with "90 percent of the time." When asked to elaborate, Zinnemann said, "Sinatra was really no problem at all. We had disagreements only 10 percent of the time we worked together. With other actors, you were lucky to have 40 percent cooperation. Frank was very giving, very eager. He was troubled. He had a dark side; that was definitely true. He drank much too much. He must have been an alcoholic; he simply *must* have been. Though, I have to say, he was never a falling-down drunk. He just became very, very ugly when he drank. He brooded. But I felt that whatever he was going through in his personal life somehow added dimension and depth to his performance. He imbued the role with his life experience at the time, whatever it was, and that was clear to anyone watching. He was a pleasure to work with and to watch as he worked."

The scenes between Frank and Montgomery Clift were challenging. As soon as Clift knew he was going to play Prewitt, he took boxing and trumpet lessons and also learned how to march in close-order drill so that he could appear as authentic as possible on film. He rehearsed before every scene, encouraging retakes as he discovered different nuances with each take. The intensity that Clift brought to the role had a positive effect on the other actors. They became better in their own parts because he set such high standards for himself. Frank, however, was known as "one-shot Sinatra." By the third take, he was bored, and he showed it.

"As a singer, yeah, I rehearse and plan exactly where I'm going. But as an actor, no, I can't do that," he once explained. "To me, acting is reacting. If you set it up right, you can almost go without knowing every line. But if you're not set up right, if the guy you're acting with doesn't know what he's doing, forget it, the whole thing's a mess. If I rehearse to death, I lose the spontaneity I think works for me. So, yeah, it's a problem for me sometimes working with a guy, or girl, who has to go over something fifty times before they get it right. I wanna climb the wall. I wanna say, 'Jesus Christ, just do it and let's move on.' With Montgomery, though, I had to be patient, because I knew that if I watched this guy, I'd learn something. We had a mutual-admiration thing goin' there."

Montgomery Clift had been a longtime fan of Frank Sinatra's. He felt that Frank had many personality traits that he himself lacked. It was more than Frank's superb musical ability that fascinated Clift. Inhibited and timid, Clift admired Sinatra's freewheeling ways. For Frank's part, he was just impressed by Clift's devotion to acting. So when Clift offered to help him, Frank jumped at the chance. In many ways, Clift took Sinatra to a place he had never before been as an actor. He made him look deep into the role and taught him to *experience* a part rather than just react to what the other actors were doing.

Author James Jones was usually on the set and often joined the two of them—Sinatra and Clift—after the day's work. And what a sad trio they were. Frank would try to reach Ava on the telephone, always a nearly impossible task. As Burt Lancaster put it, "In those days in Spain, if you lived next door to your friends, you couldn't get them on the telephone, let alone try to get them on the phone from Hawaii. He never got through. Not one night." James Jones was unhappy because he felt that the movie script was not being true to the book. Meanwhile, Montgomery Clift was secretly wrestling with his own demons.

The three men would break out a couple of bottles and drink away their misery, night after night, until they passed out cold. Burt Lancaster often had to gather them up, take them to their rooms, get them undressed and into bed. Frank was able to compose himself for the next day's shooting; Monty was not always so fortunate. There were times when he had to be pumped full of coffee just to do a single scene.

After forty-one days, shooting on *From Here to Eternity* was finally wrapped. All Frank could do now was wait to see if his instincts had paid off.

Frank Signs with Capitol

*W*ith the movie done, a priority for Frank Sinatra was to get his recording career back on track. While it's difficult to imagine today, back in 1953 Frank simply couldn't secure a record deal. His contract with Columbia had expired at the end of the previous year, and the company showed no interest in renewing it.

Sinatra's good friend Manie Sacks, in a top-level position at RCA at the time, attempted to sell him to that label by calling a meeting of just about every top executive and saying, "He's available. We need to sign him up. What can we do?" A few days later, Sacks got back the word: "Manie, we can't do it. There's nothing we can do with Sinatra." Frank Sinatra Jr. later remembered, "Manie said it was the hardest thing he ever had to tell my dad. 'The guys don't think they can move you,' he told him. 'I could force it and get you on the label with us. But I'd rather you went somewhere else than have you come on with these guys who think, in all honesty, they can't do it.' Pop assured Manie he understood."

Other record companies were also approached, but there was no interest. Finally, executives at Capitol Records expressed some modest curiosity about Frank and offered him a substandard one-year deal that called for no advance against royalties. All arranging, copying, and musician costs were to be incurred by Frank—the kind of contract that was offered when record-company executives felt they were taking a chance on the artist. Even then, three of Frank's supporters had to push for it: Axel Stordahl (husband of Capitol recording artist June Hutton) asked Glenn Wallachs (president of the label) for a favor in signing Sinatra, as did Dick Jones (who had played piano for Frank's wedding to Ava) and Dave Dexter, Capitol's jazz producer. Dexter was a big fan of Frank's, but Frank, ever the grudge-holder, rewarded Dexter's support for him in his hour of need by later rejecting him as a producer because he had once written some critical reviews of Sinatra's music for *Down Beat* magazine.

Frank's first recording date for Capitol was on April 30, 1953. Producer Voyle Gilmore wanted to team Frank immediately with trumpeter Billy May as arranger, but May was unavailable. So Heinie Beau substituted for him and arranged Frank's session, "Lean Baby," on April 2. Also, Axel Stordahl arranged "I'm Walking Behind You" for that same session.

For Frank's first Capitol sessions, Gilmore recruited thirty-one-year-old Nelson Riddle (former trombonist-arranger for Tommy Dorsey and arranger of the classic "Mona Lisa" for Nat King Cole) to arrange "I Love You" and "South of the Border." Other tunes were also recorded at this time, including the marvelously optimistic "I've Got the World on a String" (which Frank would often use as an opening number in his act), and the contemplative ballad "Don't Worry About Me," both arranged by Riddle. Now it seemed as if everyone was finally on to something magical; Riddle had injected new life into Sinatra's sound.

Without a doubt, Nelson Riddle was the primary architect of Sinatra's swinging sound of the 1950s at Capitol. Said Riddle of Sinatra, "There's no one like him. Frank not only encourages you to adventure, but he has such a keen appreciation of achievement that you are impelled to knock yourself out for him. It's not only that his intuitions as to tempo, phrasing, and even figuration are amazingly right, but his taste is so impeccable.

"Working with him was always a bit of a challenge, and there were times when the going got rough. Frank was never a relaxed man, as Nat Cole was, for example. He was a perfectionist who drove himself and everybody around him relentlessly. You always approached him with a feeling of uneasiness," Riddle admitted, "not only because he was demanding and unpredictable but because his reactions were so violent. But all of these tensions disappeared if you came through for him. This man is a giant. Not that there aren't other good singers around. But he has the imagination and scope of the rarest." Riddle, who collaborated with Sinatra on more than ninety recording sessions, also mentioned that Sinatra was not one to give praise to producers and arrangers after successful sessions. "He'd never give out compliments," he said. "He just isn't built to give out compliments. He expects your best."

Considering the circumstances of his signing with Capitol, the albums that resulted from Frank's next seven years at the label are among his best and most memorable. Whereas Columbia nurtured the smooth balladeer in Frank, at Capitol would be born the cool, swinging Sinatra, although he did also record some of his greatest ballads during this period. There was just something different about Frank now. At Columbia, he was a phenomenon who took the world by storm. At Capitol, where time, place, and circumstance, not to mention personal experience, all played a big part in his stunning evolution as an artist, he would become a very serious singer who carefully chose his material. During the "Capitol Years," as Sinatra devotees call the period from 1953 to 1961, he just sounded better.

"Nelson began to pump a little more power into the sound," Frank Sinatra Jr. once observed. "Instead of sounding like that silky-smooth crooner of the forties, now Pop was putting more energy into it, belting a little more. His voice lowered too, got better, lost some of its sweetness. His whole attitude was becoming a little more hip. The curly-haired, bow-tied image was gone. Now there was the long tie and the hat."

Part Six

BACK ON TOP

Success

From Here to Eternity opened at the Capitol Theatre on Broadway in New York on August 5, 1953. Harry Cohn, president of Columbia, decreed that there would be no standard grand premiere with stars, limousines, and interviews. Instead, the movie debuted with a full-page ad in the *New York Times*, signed by Cohn and urging people to see it. Incredible as it may seem, the lines were so long on opening night—advance word of mouth about the film had been so positive—that the theater management added another show at 1 a.m. to accommodate anxious ticket buyers. Shortly thereafter, the Capitol Theatre was showing *From Here to Eternity* around the clock. They closed for a short time in the early morning hours just so that the janitors could do their jobs.

Frank was astonished by the public and critical reaction to the film. "I knew it was a good movie," he said, "and I sensed that I was good in it. But the way the people reacted to it, well, I never expected all of that. I was grateful."

"He called me up, and I hadn't heard from him in a couple of years," said Joey D'Orazio, his friend from Hoboken. "And he said, 'Hey, man, you gotta go see me in this picture. I'm *great* in this picture.' I said, 'Frankie, I already seen it, and you *were* great.' 'I know it, man,' he told me. 'I know it.'

"He was just so happy. He said, 'I'm back. This is my comeback.' And I said, 'Frankie, you never left.' He laughed and said, 'You know what? There are a lot of people out there, Joey, who thought I was down. But I'm proving them wrong now, aren't I? And I'm not even *singing* in this picture!'"*

---

* Curiously, in May 1953, Sinatra recorded a song entitled "From Here to Eternity" for Capitol, obviously anticipating the success of the film that shared that title.

By September, *From Here to Eternity* was a critical and popular sensation and Frank's career was showing definite signs of revitalization. In September he appeared at the Riviera in Englewood, New Jersey, to a sold-out crowd.

Joey Bishop was Sinatra's opening act in Jersey. "Frank had seen me at the Latin Quarter in New York City," he said, "liked my act, and asked me to open for him. There were eleven hundred people in the audience opening night, and I wanted to make a good impression. I was a little nervous. So I'm saying, 'Good evening, ladies and gentlemen,' and all of a sudden the man I am looking at dead center, ringside, is suddenly on my right side. And the guy who was at my left is suddenly sitting dead center. And I'm thinking, 'What the hell is going on? The room is spinning!' Then I see Frank in the wings with his thumb to his forehead and waving the rest of his fingers at me. Turns out it was a revolving stage, and I didn't know it. Frank was back there pushing the button that made it turn. And then he said to the audience on a backstage mike, 'Place your bets, folks, 'cause I don't think he's comin' around again.' I started thinking, 'Okay, he's getting his humor back.' It made me feel like maybe things were going to be okay with him."

Eddie Fisher remembered Frank's opening at the Riviera this way: "[It was] one of the greatest performances I've ever seen. He couldn't sing a wrong note, couldn't make a wrong move. It was electrifying. There was only one empty seat on that opening night—the one reserved for Ava." Indeed, Frank and Ava had another argument and she opted out of his opening night. She was present for the second night, though. She sat with Eddie Fisher in the audience. A *Journal-American* story the next day reviewed the show: "The Voice unleashed a torrent of sound at the sultry Ava. Emotion poured from him like molten lava as he piled the decibels ceiling high. He sang twenty-four songs with scarcely a pause for breath. The customers, except those completely numbed by the moving reconciliation [with Ava], loved it. Never before in the history of nightclubs had an artist been so generous with his voice."

On October 2, Ava's *Mogambo* premiered in New York, and the Sinatras attended the festivities at Radio City Music Hall. The next day, they flew back to Hollywood.

About a week later, Ava went to the Palm Springs home to rest, while Frank was off to Las Vegas to prepare for a singing engagement at the Sands, which would commence on October 19. He was disappointed that Ava would not be joining him for opening night, but—as was par for the course by this time—apparently the two had had another fight, and everyone knew about it because it made all the papers. "I can't eat. I can't sleep. I love her," Frank told Louella Parsons from Las Vegas. She responded by saying, "You should be telling that to Ava, not to me."

The Final Straw

Marilyn Cain was a switchboard operator at the Sands Hotel at the time of Sinatra's October 1953 engagement there. "One evening, before he retired, he told me that he should not be disturbed unless his wife called. Well, she did call at about three in the morning and said, 'Connect me to Mr. Sinatra's room.' Because I had instructions not to connect anyone unless it was his wife, I politely asked, 'Who's calling, please?' And she screamed at me, 'You know damn well who this is. This is his wife. Now get him on the line.' Startled, I said, 'Yes, Mrs. Sinatra,' and she said, 'Miss Gardner. My name is *Miss Gardner*. Now get him on the line.' She was upset, to put it lightly.'"

Lucy Wellman remembered that Ava had told her that she'd heard that Frank was "shacking up in his room" at the Sands with a Copa Girl. (Much to Ava's consternation, now there were Copa Girls not only at the Copa in New York but at the Sands in Las Vegas.) "If it had been a major star, then fine," Ava reasoned. "I could deal with it. I could even compete with it if I chose to. But a showgirl?" When Ava telephoned her husband to check on the rumor, she heard a woman's voice in the background.

"That's when the fight started," Lucy Wellman said. "She was sure Frank was cheating on her. This would be, as it would happen, the proverbial straw that broke the camel's back. After all the fights, it all came down to this—again, a doggone Copa Girl! I told her that perhaps it was room service she had heard in the background.

And she said, 'At three in the morning the only room service he's getting is between his legs. Believe me. I know my son of a bitch of a husband.' She made up her mind then and there that the marriage was over. She told him on the telephone that she was filing for divorce."

A memo from Sands hotel and casino manager Jack Entratter addressed to "Front Desk Personnel" and dated October 25, 1953, seemed to sum up the status of the Sinatras' marriage at this time. The memo, found among the Sands Papers housed at the University of Nevada at Las Vegas, states, "As per Mr. Frank Sinatra's instruction, his wife, Ava Gardner Sinatra, is hereby barred from the premises of the Sands Hotel for the remainder of Mr. Sinatra's engagement here. If Mrs. Sinatra attempts to check into the hotel, she should be referred to this office. Under no circumstances is Mrs. Sinatra to have any contact with Frank Sinatra. Therefore, no telephone calls from Mrs. Sinatra should be connected to Mr. Sinatra's suite. Furthermore, as per Mr. Sinatra, all media inquiries regarding the status of the Sinatra marriage should be directed to the office of [publicity director] Al Guzman without comment."

Howard Strickling, MGM's chief publicist, issued a statement on October 27, 1953, announcing that Ava and Frank had separated and "the separation is final and Miss Gardner will seek a divorce."

The night after the divorce was announced, Sydney Guilaroff, who was Ava's personal hairstylist, was watching the evening news when he was startled by the doorbell. When he opened the door, he found Ava. Clearly shaken, she said, "I've got to talk to someone." He moved to hug her, but she backed off onto the front lawn. She started sobbing, and from her obvious tremor, Sydney recalled, he feared the worst. "Is Frank okay?" he asked. Ava took a deep breath and let out a long sigh. Her mouth hung open, and suddenly the glamour she had always worn so well seemed to vanish. She embraced him, and with her chin on his shoulder, she whispered, "I thought I could do it, but I can't talk about it." Sydney shook her free, looked into her eyes, and said firmly, "Please come inside." Ava gathered herself as best she could. "No, no. I'd just break down, and that's what I'm trying not to do," she said.

Thinking it best that she be left alone, Sydney went back into the house. For hours, he kept a vigil, peering out his front window, only to find Ava still on his lawn, pacing back and forth, awash in moonlight. Well after midnight, he turned in. Finally, a couple hours later, the roar of her car's ignition awakened him. He got up and watched as she drove off into the night.

Vegas Investment

$\mathcal{T}$wo days after the announcement concerning the status of his marriage to Ava was made, Frank appeared before the Nevada Tax Commission. As it happened, a few months earlier he had applied for the purchase of a 2 percent interest in the Sands Hotel in Las Vegas. There was a great deal of discussion among the members of the commission about the fact that Frank still owed the government $70,000 of a $160,000 levy. In fact, one commissioner argued that the $54,000 Sinatra was using to buy into the Sands should be applied to his tax debt. However, Frank had been diligent in paying his back taxes, $1,000 off the top of what he was paid for each singing engagement. He had already paid $90,000 of the debt. Because they felt he was acting in good faith, the commission would eventually vote six to one in Frank's favor, even though there was considerable concern about his connections to the Mafia.

The fact, though, was that the Sands was practically run by mobsters anyway because it was so easy to skim from the take, lie about gross receipts, and only report to the Internal Revenue Service whatever was left. Moreover, because it was not required at that time that cash transactions be reported to the IRS, Las Vegas quickly became a haven for underworld activity. Mobsters were welcome in the city as guests of the hotels and friends of many of the stars who performed there. Some of the entertainers, like Frank, always knew with whom they were dealing when they played Vegas and made "connections" there for other business opportunities. In other words, Frank was proactive in getting involved with such underworld characters. Others, like Sammy Davis Jr., just did their jobs, asked no questions, and kept their distance from unsavory types.

Frank's interest in the Sands—which in time would grow to 9 percent—would prove to be invaluable to him financially. It was a wise investment that would make him a millionaire many times over in the next couple of years. Eventually, he would become vice president of the Sands Corporation. For him, it was a combination of business and pleasure because, above all, he loved to gamble. It was one of his passions. Both of his parents were gamblers; he would say that "it's in my blood." He would be given thousands of dollars a night in credit by the Sands with which to play poker. If he won, the winnings were his. If he didn't win, he walked away without losing money. He particularly enjoyed the game of baccarat and would lose up to $50,000 a night playing.

Conflicted Christmas

There were a number of significant Frank Sinatra recording sessions for Capitol in the winter of 1953. One of the most noteworthy, on November 5, 1953, was the classic Sinatra interpretation of Rodgers and Hart's "My Funny Valentine," arranged by Nelson Riddle. Originally composed for the Broadway musical *Babes in Arms* in 1937, "My Funny Valentine" is one of the finest of the love songs by Richard Rodgers and Lorenz Hart. Frank's sentimental, graceful delivery is unforgettable, and he would go on to perform the song in nightclubs and concert halls for the next forty-some years. But "Valentine" was just one of the many classic tracks he recorded on November 5 and 6, for the ten-inch, eight-song Capitol album *Songs for Young Lovers* and Frank's *Swing Easy!*: "A Foggy Day," "They Can't Take That Away from Me," "Like Someone in Love," "I Get a Kick Out of You," and "Little Girl Blue."

On December 8 and 9, 1953, Frank was in the recording studio again. He and Ava were now separated, and though she had not filed for divorce, it seemed that they would never reconcile.

"It was all Mondays" is how Frank once remembered this time in his life. He was down to about 118 pounds. Yet he was making some extraordinary music, including the plaintive and clearly heartfelt

"Why Should I Cry Over You" and the universally beloved "Young at Heart."

Fortuitously for Frank, "Young at Heart" had been turned down by a number of artists, including Nat King Cole. But Jimmy Van Heusen convinced Sinatra to record it, and the song would take Frank to new heights of success when released a month later. Part of the magic of these recordings was their simplicity, and "Young at Heart" is a perfect example. It's a straightforward, uncluttered, lilting performance.

At Christmastime, Ava was in Italy filming *The Barefoot Contessa*. Frank telephoned her in Rome and told her that he wanted to be with her for the holidays and also to celebrate her thirty-first birthday. She didn't discourage him, but she wasn't happy about it either. During the time away from him, she had another epiphany of sorts about their marriage. "I liked myself more before Frank," she told Rene Jordan. "What I became as his wife—the way I ended the pregnancies and all of that—I don't even know who that woman is. That's not me. I need to be out of this marriage, maybe even more than Frank does. Look what it's done to me!"

Ava told people in her inner circle that she had wanted to be free of Frank for a very long time, but that she knew she couldn't do it while he was at such a low point in his life and career. "You've been my only way through all of this," he told her, a constant refrain of his. Making light of it, she would say, "The pressure of that, the *responsibility* of that, it's enough to make a girl drink." The duty of being Frank's be-all and end-all had, by her own admission, distorted her personality and character, and she had lost her self-respect. Now that his life was on the upswing again, she saw her opportunity to finally extricate herself from the marriage. She believed he was strong enough now to make it on his own.

Frank arrived in Italy armed with expensive gifts for Ava. However, Ava had already left for the Madrid home of film executive Frank Grant. Had they gotten their signals mixed up, or was she trying to evade him? It didn't matter to him; he followed her there anyway and they spent Christmas together.

Frank made it clear that he still wanted them to work on their marriage. However, by this time, Ava was in full self-preservation mode.

"We need to take some time to fix what is broken in us," she told him. "You're a good man, Frank. Let's get off of this merry-go-round while we can. It's not right." Then, perhaps to force the issue, she told Frank that she was dating someone else—a handsome Spanish bullfighter named Luis Miguel Dominguín.

"She was the prettiest and the most fierce," Dominguín said. "I had a very fierce wolf in a cage."

Ava couldn't have been surprised by Frank's reaction to the news. He proceeded to completely trash the room in which she was staying at Grant's home. First he threw the television set out the window. Then he shattered all of the crystal. He threw lamps against the walls, turned over tables, and hurled expensively framed photographs all about, sending shards of glass into the air like little missiles. Ava was terrified; she ran for cover. She later told Lucy Wellman she was scared that Frank was going to kill her. "Stop it, baby!" she demanded.

However, Frank didn't stop until the room was completely demolished. Then, before he walked out the door, he went into his suitcase and pulled from it a large envelope. It was full of hundred-dollar bills. He took the money and threw it at Ava. The cash came raining down around her. "There's the nineteen thousand dollars you lent me," he said bitterly. "And, oh, by the way, if you ever call me 'baby' again, *I'll rip your fucking tongue right out of your mouth!*" With that, he walked out the door.

On her knees and crying, Ava collected all of the money. Then, sobbing, she sat on the floor and counted it as if she didn't know what else to do.

Meanwhile, Frank took a cab to the airport, got on a plane, and went to Rome for a few days to cool off before returning to New York. "A downcast and lonely-looking Frank Sinatra sneaked out of Rome this afternoon on a New York–bound plane after a five-day attempt to win back his wife," wrote Reynolds Packard of the *New York Daily News.*

"That's it," Frank told Jimmy Van Heusen when he returned to the States. "What else can I do? I gotta move on. This broad is gonna kill me. I swear to you, no woman will ever do this to me again, because I'll never let another woman—another person—get this close to me."

Jimmy and Frank were having a drink and a smoke with Sammy Davis Jr. in Davis's home.

"Don't say that, Frank," said Jimmy.

"I mean it, Jimmy," Frank said. "This will never happen again. You will never see me like this again. You got a Bible around here somewhere, Charlie?" he asked Sammy.

"I could get one," Sammy offered.

"Get it," Frank said.

In five minutes Sammy returned with a Bible. Frank, who had a scotch in his left hand, put his right hand on the Bible. "I swear to God, this is the last time a woman will ever get to me like this," he said. "I swear on the Bible that... This. Will. Never. Happen. Again."

"Holy shit! This cat means business," Sammy exclaimed to Jimmy. "That's serious, swearing on the Bible like that. In fact, I think my man here just saved a whole lot of women a whole lot of heartache," he concluded, slapping Frank on the back.

Sammy was trying to lighten the mood, but Frank wasn't laughing.

Marilyn Monroe—Take One

During this time, another great screen star, Marilyn Monroe, was also dealing with heartbreak after her divorce from Joe DiMaggio was just being finalized. Frank and Marilyn were good friends, though it's difficult to determine when they first met. Some point to a meal at Romanoff's in 1954. It's known that a year earlier, Marilyn had rejected a script (*Pink Tights*, a remake of Betty Grable's 1943 movie *Coney Island*) that would have teamed her with Frank, causing her to be put on suspension by Fox. (She called that script "cheap, exploitive.") However, she had always been a fan of Sinatra's.

Joey Bishop recalled the time Marilyn went to see Frank at the Copacabana, "sometime in the fifties. I'm doing my act, and in the middle of it in comes Marilyn Monroe walking into the room like she owns the joint," Bishop remembered. "Of course, I lost the crowd. Who's gonna pay attention to me when Marilyn Monroe walks in? There wasn't an empty seat in the house, so they pulled a single chair up for her to sit in and stuck it ringside, about four feet away from me. I looked down at her and I said, 'Marilyn, I thought I told you to wait in the truck.'"

In 1954, Marilyn went to live with Frank for a while so that she could regain her emotional bearings. The two consoled each other over their marital woes. They were both still in love with their estranged spouses, so for a time there was nothing sexual going on between them. Frank wasn't interested in anything anymore, though it was difficult for his friends to fathom that he had one of the most beautiful and sought-after movie stars in the world living with him and there was nothing going on.

The fact that Marilyn had a habit of not wearing clothes didn't make it any easier on Frank. She simply would rather be naked. Her friends and staff were used to seeing her au naturel. Therefore, it wasn't a surprise to find her in that state, and she liked to surprise visitors by suddenly materializing in a room with nothing on but that beautiful Monroe smile. When she stayed with Frank during this time, she didn't change that behavior.

One morning—as Frank used to tell it—he awakened, went into the kitchen wearing just his boxers, and found a naked Marilyn standing in front of the open refrigerator with her little finger in her mouth, trying to decide between orange and grapefruit juice. "Oh, Frankie," she said, "I didn't know *you* got up so early." That moment marked the end of their platonic relationship.

"He told me that he took her right there in the kitchen, up against the closed refrigerator," reported one close friend of Sinatra's. It was the beginning of a long, on-again/off-again affair between them, one that lasted until she died in 1962. "Frank loved her...as much as he could love at that time, anyway."

Frank thought Marilyn was intelligent, witty, sexy, and exciting—and, most of all, unpredictable. But there were a number of reasons why he wouldn't allow himself to become more serious about her, not the least of which was that the passion he had enjoyed with Ava simply wasn't there with Marilyn. Besides that, he was still racked with pain over the breakup with Ava. When Marilyn felt strong enough to be on her own and was able to move out of the apartment, Frank was actually relieved. It certainly would not be the end of their relationship, though. In fact, in a few years' time he would find himself even more deeply immersed in her chaotic world.

After Frank?

$\mathscr{A}$va didn't apply for her divorce from Frank until 1954, the grounds she cited having to do with "desertion." Her attorney, Raul de Villafrance, claimed that "for no legal reason" Sinatra walked out of the home he and Ava shared "for more than six months." Frank didn't bother to contest it. Desertion? To him, it was all too ridiculous to even fight. The proceedings would take three years to finalize.

Ava would never marry again.

As for the other casualty of their failed relationship, Nancy had begun to rebuild her life through the love and caring of her three children. As the years passed, she regained the elegance and bearing as well as the sheer spunk that had made her so attractive to Frank in the first place. Her daughter Nancy put it best when she once said, "She has more genuine glamour in an inch of her than in all the stars and starlets put together."

"My mother, who is a little Italian girl from New Jersey, is without a doubt one of the most remarkable people I have ever had the pleasure of knowing," said Frank Jr. "She's like a real tower of strength. She's never wavered. There could have been a time when she could have made things very unpleasant for my father, but she always remained loyal to all four of us. And my father is most appreciative of this, as am I."

After their divorce, Nancy remained a respected member of Hollywood society, which is a testament to her popularity, since abandoned wives of stars are rarely heard from again. Nancy was the friend and confidante of many celebrities and so-called industry movers and shakers. "Nancy Barbato Sinatra survived the pain and the notoriety and surfaced with her dignity intact," concluded her daughter Nancy.

Like Ava, Nancy would also never marry again. When one friend asked her why she never wed, she responded, "After Sinatra?"—which could probably be taken a number of ways.*

The children would survive, as well. By 1954, Nancy was fourteen, Frank was ten, and Tina was six. Surprise visits from Daddy were the best of times. If they didn't expect him and suddenly saw him pull into the long driveway, they would feel lifted to the sky. He would take them to dinner and, for those couple of hours, be the father to them that they longed for. Then, of course, he would look at his watch and tell them it was time for him to go home. Nancy Sr. would walk him to his car, and as the kids watched, she would whisper to him. They had no idea what she was saying, but to their way of thinking as children, it always sounded loving and reassuring. Frank would listen patiently, nod his head, hug her goodbye, and then get into his car and drive away. No one knew when he would return.

Sometimes they missed their father so desperately that Nancy and Tina would sneak into the room upstairs reserved for him. Some of his freshly pressed suits were stored in a closet there, his ties...his fedoras...his colognes on a dresser. Taking in the scent of Yardley lavender soap, the girls would thumb through his shirts arranged by color on hangers, and they would wax nostalgic about the times they'd had with him. When they looked back on it as adults they both felt a sense of profound loss. Frank Jr., so disaffected at just ten, would walk by and see his sisters in Daddy's room and wonder what the fuss was all about, why they were even in there. "Daddy doesn't live here," he would tell them matter-of-factly. "I don't know why you're in here. Who cares about this room? Let's go outside and play."

---

* It bears noting that Dean Martin's wife, Jeanne, didn't remarry either after her twenty-four-year-long marriage to Dean ended in 1973. She told her stepdaughter Deana, "It's not like men were beating down my door. They were too afraid of upsetting your father. The word was, 'Dean Martin isn't someone whose wife you play around with, even if they are no longer married.' Once you've been married to Dean Martin, no one else compares, anyway. How do you follow that act?"

1954: Academy Award

March 1954 would prove to be a spectacular month for Frank Sinatra. His career was on the upswing, which undoubtedly helped him face a life without Ava. "Young at Heart" hit number one on *Your Hit Parade* and would become his first Top Five hit in eight years. He was chosen as Most Popular Vocalist of the Year by a *Down Beat* poll. Frank was also named top male vocalist by *Billboard, Down Beat*, and *Metronome*, and by the end of the year it was hard to believe that just a short time earlier no record company was even interested in him. "Only in show business can things turn around that quickly for a guy," Ava would say. "He deserved it, too. I don't know anyone who deserved it more."

Frank's return to the top was complete when he attended the Academy Awards ceremony on March 25, 1954. He was thrilled about having been nominated in the Best Supporting Actor category for his performance in *From Here to Eternity*. His competition was Eddie Albert (*Roman Holiday*), Brandon deWilde (*Shane*), Jack Palance (*Shane*), and Robert Strauss (*Stalag 17*). Although he was rumored to be the favorite, he realized that there were no guarantees. One thing was certain, though: The nomination served to validate his own judgment about the role of Maggio. He knew all along he was right for it when everyone else, except Ava, thought he was dead wrong.

On March 25, Frank sat close to the back on the left side of the Pantages Theatre, one of twenty-eight hundred people attending the ceremony. Beside him sat Nancy, and beside her, Frank Jr. That day had been Nancy Sr.'s birthday, and she had invited Frank to dinner, during which they gave him a small gold medallion. On one side was a bust of Saint Genesius, the patron saint of actors. On the other was a miniature Oscar in bas-relief. The inscription read: "Dad, all our love, from here to eternity." He couldn't have been more touched.

Of the awards presentation, Frank Jr. recalled, "I was a young boy, of course, wearing my first pair of long pants, with very little understanding of the purpose of this event. I knew that something important was going on that night because all through the previous year

I had been hearing about my father's performance in *From Here to Eternity*. As the evening progressed, I forgot the crowds of cheering people and thought only that I was getting very sleepy. But when [actress] Mercedes McCambridge announced Frank Sinatra as the winner, the audience in the theater gave a cheer and broke into spontaneous applause. The theater went crazy. Men and women cheered, tears flowed from the faces that had suddenly turned to where we were seated. My father slowly rose from his chair and began to walk to the stage, the greatest walk of his life, to receive his Oscar. On his face was a smile I will remember forever."

Frank clasped the Oscar and for a moment didn't know what to say. He was that stunned. "Ladies and gentleman," he finally began. "I'm deeply thrilled and very moved. And I really, really don't know what to say because this is a whole new kind of thing, you know? I'm a song-and-dance type." Members of the audience chuckled at the irony of his statement, for it was precisely that sentiment that nearly prevented him from getting the role in the first place. "I'd just like to say, however," he joked, "that they're doing a whole lot of songs here tonight, but nobody asked me [to sing]. I love you, though. Thank you very much. I'm absolutely thrilled."

Frank Jr. recalled, "When Dad, carrying his trophy, returned to Nancy and me in the audience, Donna Reed spoke to us in a loud whisper. 'Oh, *let me just touch it*,' she said, and she placed her hand on the gold statue. Then, just a few minutes later, *her* name was called as the winner of Best Supporting Actress for the same film. I can still see the smile on her face."

In all, the film won eight of the thirteen Academy Awards for which it had been nominated—including Best Picture—which tied the record for wins, previously set in 1939 by *Gone with the Wind*. *Variety* reported Frank's win as "the greatest comeback in theater history."

Ava had also been nominated for Best Actress for her role in *Mogambo*, but she didn't win. When she heard about Frank's victory, she cried tears of joy. As she would later admit, she felt oddly displaced knowing that he was celebrating his win with Nancy. After all, she had been at his side for the gestation of the project, and knew how much he wanted—needed—the role, and she had pushed for him to get it. Her first impulse was to call him to offer personal congratulations. However, she feared that the sound of her voice might ruin the moment for him. Instead, she sent a telegram. "He thinks I'm a monster," she told her friend Lucy Wellman. "And I suppose I shouldn't blame him. I did do some monstrous things to him, didn't I?" she asked sadly.

"Talk about being born again," Frank would later recall of the post-Oscar bash at his apartment on Wilshire Boulevard, hosted by Nancy. "I couldn't even share it with another human being. I ducked the party, lost the crowds, and took a walk. Just me and Oscar. I think I relived my entire life as I walked up and down the streets of Beverly Hills. I started the decade as 'the man least likely' and closed it out as a grateful human being given a second shot at life."

Sammy Davis's Accident

In November 1954, Sammy Davis performed with his family act, the Will Mastin Trio, at the Old Frontier Hotel in Las Vegas. During that engagement, he was involved in a terrible automobile accident. The next morning, he woke up in a hospital room in San Bernardino, California, his face covered with bandages above the nose. It all came back to him. His head had smashed into the pointed cone in the center of the steering wheel. When he woke up after the impact, he reached up to his cheek and felt his left eye hanging by a thread. He was lucky to be alive, he was told.

After a few days, when the bandages were removed, Sammy began wondering why Frank had not visited him. He became even more concerned when his father brought him a copy of the gossipy *Confidential* magazine with the headline "What Makes Ava Gardner Run for Sammy Davis Jr.?" It was a completely fabricated story about a romance between Sammy and Ava (as if Sammy would ever have taken such a chance with Sinatra's friendship). Sammy was frantic. What if Frank saw it? Even if Frank's gut told him that the story was untrue, he might still have some doubt. And what about Ava? How would she react? As if Davis didn't have enough to worry about at this time, he telephoned Ava's publicist from the hospital to find out if there'd been any repercussions. He was told that Ava had decided to ignore the story. However, there was no word from Frank's camp. For the next few days, Sammy had to sweat it out and wonder why Frank hadn't sent even a get-well telegram to the hospital.

Then, one afternoon soon after, while Sammy was being examined by a doctor, an excited nurse burst into his room. "It's Frank Sinatra," she said breathlessly. "He's on his way up." As doctors and nurses crammed the hallway to get a glimpse of the star, the buzz through the hospital was palpable. When Frank finally strutted into Sammy's room, he tossed his hat onto a chair, lit a cigarette, and then gave Sammy a big bear hug. Sammy would later say he was never so happy to see another person.

Not only was Frank not upset about the *Confidential* piece, but he arranged for Sammy to stay at his home in Palm Springs during his recuperation. "So what else is new?" he finally said of the magazine story when Sammy pushed for a reaction to it. "Forget it, Charlie," he said, using his nickname not only for Sammy but for many people for whom he had affection. "You don't even have to mention it."

During his convalescence, Sammy confessed to Frank that he feared his career was over. "Who wants a one-eyed entertainer?" he asked. Frank told him to relax. He predicted that Sammy would be bigger than ever. "Trust me," Frank said. "The public likes a good comeback story. Take it from me."

"But how am I going to dance if I can't keep my balance?" Sammy asked. He said that if he couldn't dance, he didn't even want to live. Frank hugged him tightly and kissed him on the neck. Then he held his face in his hands with more affection, as Sammy would recall it, than he'd ever seen from a man. "You're gonna be fine," Frank whispered. "Charlie, you gotta be strong. You'll come outta this thing bigger than ever. You're alive, man. *You're alive.*"

"Frank's idea of rehab was a little unusual," his valet George Jacobs recalled with a laugh. "One day he called me into Sammy's room and said, 'Your responsibility today, my good fellow, is to teach Charlie here how to light a cigarette, because he only got one good eye and his field of vision is all cocked up!' So I spent about three hours working with Sammy on how to light a cigarette. Soon he was striking up matches like nobody's business."

Four months later, Sammy Davis was back onstage, at Ciro's in Hollywood, and Frank Sinatra was the man who introduced him to an enthusiastic crowd of celebrities, including Cary Grant, Lauren Bacall, Humphrey Bogart, Edward G. Robinson, Jimmy Cagney, and Spencer Tracy. When Sammy walked out, they stood and cheered, shouting, "Bravo!"

Golden

The next two years would prove to be a creative renaissance and golden age for Frank Sinatra. In 1954 and through the end of 1955, he would make a number of successful films, including *Suddenly* (in which he played a coldhearted killer, to terrific reviews); *Not as a Stranger* (as a dedicated doctor, with Olivia de Havilland and Robert Mitchum); *The Tender Trap* (as a ladies' man and actor's agent, opposite Debbie Reynolds); and *Young at Heart* (as an out-of-work songwriter opposite Doris Day). Doris and Frank had worked well together as early as 1949 when both were Columbia recording artists, dueting on "Let's Take an Old-Fashioned Walk," from Irving Berlin's Broadway musical *Miss Liberty*. However, on *Young at Heart* they had a number of disagreements, mostly having to do with the production schedule: She liked to start early; he, late in the day. In the end, Doris's heart went out to Frank when, after a scene in which she had to cry, someone tossed a box of Kleenex at her. When it hit her in the forehead, Frank became upset and scolded the pitcher, "What's the matter with you? You don't throw things at a lady! Understand?" Even today, Doris says she often thinks of Frank whenever she reaches for a Kleenex.

Also this year, 1954, Frank would star as Nathan Detroit—proprietor of "the world's oldest established permanent floating crap game"—in the film version of the Broadway sensation *Guys and Dolls*, with its score by Frank Loesser.

Sinatra had originally wanted to play Sky Masterson, the role played by Marlon Brando. In fact, he would later say he believed the film would have been better if the two actors had switched parts (since the Masterson role was more a singing part). In the end, Sinatra and Brando feuded for most of the production; there was no love lost between those two. In fact, Sinatra said of Brando, "He's the most overrated actor in the world." And of Sinatra, Brando observed, "When he dies and goes to heaven, the first thing he'll do will be to find God and yell at him for making him bald." Of course, the film was a box-office success just the same, and in years to come, Frank would famously record the Masterson song "Luck Be a Lady Tonight."

In February 1955, Frank recorded one of his best albums, *In the Wee Small Hours*. Most albums of the time contained a hodgepodge of material—ballads and upbeat songs, with no thematic line. But many of Frank's greatest albums were "concept albums," especially at Capitol, where he did more than a dozen of them, including *In the Wee Small Hours*. This album was a collection of love-gone-bad songs, or, as some writers dubbed them, "Ava Songs." Music critic Pete Welding noted, "Ava Gardner may have left scars, but as happens so often with great artists, personal pain translated into artistic achievement."

In August 1955, Frank was featured on the cover of *Time* magazine. The report called him "just about the hottest item in show business today" and said, "Four months shy of forty, he is well away on a second career that promises to be, if anything, more brilliant than the first."

At the end of 1955, *The Man with the Golden Arm* was released. Many consider this to be Frank's finest moment as an actor. He portrays the tragic Frankie Machine, a heroin-addicted, golden-armed poker dealer and would-be drummer. He wanted the part badly after reading sixty pages of the Nelson Algren book on which the movie is based and started making phone calls. For Frank, the filming was hard work, arduous twelve-hour days.

In the climax of the movie, Frank's character endures a hair-raising drug withdrawal. Director Otto Preminger thought that the scene would be too difficult for Sinatra and suggested a great many rehearsals and the possibility of retakes. Frank had never been much for rehearsal when working on a film, and retakes were out of the question unless someone *else* flubbed a line. (*He* rarely did.) For Sinatra, a sense of immediacy was the key to his success as an actor. He knew just how he wanted to play that difficult scene. "I did some research on my part," he remembered, "and for about forty seconds, through a peephole, I was allowed to see what happens to people when they try to kick heroin cold turkey—a youngster climbing a wall. It was the most frightening thing I've ever seen. I never want to see that again. Never."

While filming that challenging scene, Frank told Preminger to keep the cameras rolling. "You'll get what you want," he said. "Trust me." Then, with no rehearsal whatsoever, the extremely grueling scene was shot in one take. Besides the scene in *From Here to Eternity* in which Maggio dies, the drug-withdrawal scene in *Golden Arm* is Sinatra at his best as an actor. When the film was finally released, ticket buyers and critics alike praised his work. Arthur Knight in the *Saturday Review* summed it up best when he wrote that Sinatra's performance was "virtuoso."

Frank's work in *The Man with the Golden Arm* would earn him an Oscar nomination for Best Actor. Though he didn't win the Oscar (Ernest Borgnine did, for *Marty*), the film remains a testament to his capabilities as an actor.

In December 1955, Frank turned forty years old, a milestone in any person's life. His work, particularly his recordings, suggested an artist who had finally matured. His voice had only gotten better, enriched and emboldened by time and experience. "If the song is a lament at the loss of love," he said at this time, "I get an ache in my gut, I feel the loss myself, and I cry out the loneliness, the hurt, and the pain that I feel. I know what the cat who wrote the song is trying to say. I've been there and back. I guess the audience feels it along with me."

* * *

Frank started 1956 back in the recording studio cutting the *Songs for Swingin' Lovers!* album with Nelson Riddle. This extremely popular album, considered his finest by some critics, contains what many Sinatra fans feel is the greatest single recording of his entire career, his rendition of Cole Porter's "I've Got You Under My Skin." It took twenty-two takes to get the orchestration right.

Ironically, "I've Got You Under My Skin" was added to *Songs for Swingin' Lovers!* at the last minute. Frank telephoned Nelson Riddle at his home in Malibu in the middle of the night to tell him that they needed a few more tunes for the album. The next day, on the way to the studio, Riddle scored "Skin" in the backseat of his car while his wife drove. The arrangement was so superb that after the musicians rehearsed it for the first time in the studio, they gave Riddle a standing ovation. (Frank and Nelson rerecorded the song for Reprise in April 1963.)

Whether working with Nelson Riddle, Billy May, or Gordon Jenkins, Sinatra—who, as earlier stated, couldn't read music—always surrounded himself with the best of everything in the studio: arrangers, producers, musicians, engineers. Not only was he talented in his own right, but he learned early on in his career something many artists of his stature never figure out: *Other* people have imagination and vision, too. What's fascinating, though, is that despite the input of various composers, lyricists, arrangers, band members, and all of the other recording personnel, Sinatra's records still come across as intensely *personal* statements.

Also in January 1956, Frank formed a film production company, Kent Productions, which would develop his own movie projects. (The Sinatra western *Johnny Concho*, in which he played the cowardly brother of a famous gunman, who of course redeems himself by the end of the film, would be the first film produced by Frank for the new company.)

Later in the year, Frank would star in MGM's musical comedy *High Society*, a successful remake of *The Philadelphia Story* (1940). Sixteen years after *The Philadelphia Story*, *High Society* arrived in Technicolor and with music. Grace Kelly, in her last movie role, is the society girl, Bing Crosby is her ex-husband, and Frank is the reporter. Louis "Satchmo" Armstrong helps out with the tunes. Cole Porter's score includes "You're Sensational," "True Love," and "Well, Did You Evah?"

At the end of April, Frank found himself in Spain for four months filming *The Pride and the Passion* with Cary Grant and Sophia Loren. The convoluted plot had something to do with the moving of a giant cannon across war-torn Spain by a band of Spanish resistance fighters.

Producer and director Stanley Kramer said of Sinatra, "He worked hard and insisted on doing a lot of things you'd normally expect a star would want a double to perform. He ran through explosions and fires. He often started scenes as though he didn't quite know what was going on. It seemed like a palpable case of lack of preparedness, but after a couple of minutes he was going like a high-precision machine."

Pack Master

*I*n 1956, the legendary Rat Pack was born when the famous actor Humphrey Bogart organized a tight-knit group of celebrity friends, which he and his wife, Betty—more famously known by her stage name, Lauren Bacall—dubbed the Rat Pack. Frank Sinatra, a close friend of Bogart's, was named "Pack Master." The rest of this contingent included Dean Martin; Peter Lawford; Sammy Davis Jr.; Judy Garland and her husband, Sid Luft; David Niven and his wife, Hjordis; and a few other stars who lived in the ritzy Holmby Hills area of Los Angeles. It was an informal social group of antiestablishment celebrities who enjoyed blowing off steam by drinking, carousing, and getting into mischief together. "We admire ourselves and we don't care for anyone else," Bogart said of the Rat Pack jokingly. He said that they hated "squares." Certainly anyone they found to be pretentious would be met with their wrath.

For instance, Irving "Swifty" Lazar—the famous literary agent and the so-called recording secretary of the Pack—once bought a Rolls-Royce and offered a ride one evening to Frank, Dean, and Judy. Proud of the automobile and its pristine state, he couldn't seem to stop bragging about it. As Swifty drove the stars about town, they busied themselves with their own little project: They built a bonfire in the backseat. It would take years for Lazar to forgive them. Another example: One time, Frank grew bored with Swifty's constant bragging about his expensive wardrobe. While Swifty was gone from his home, Frank had the door to his clothes closet bricked up and then stuccoed over and painted the same color as the rest of the walls in the room.

The members of the Rat Pack admired Frank's sense of style and his extravagant lifestyle. They marveled over his collection of one hundred suits and matching pairs of shoes. They loved the fact that he carried only hundred-dollar bills; anything smaller didn't matter in Sinatra's world. Moreover, his confounding sense of humor was the subject of fascination. For instance, a friend once wired him for money, saying he needed to "bail out an overdue hotel bill." Frank sent him a parachute and $30,000—in fake money. (But then the next day he paid the man's hotel tab.)

The way he treated reporters he detested was also the subject of great interest among his peers. For instance, after she wrote a sensational six-part exposé about him in the *Journal-American*, called "The Real Frank Sinatra Story," Frank sent the Hearst columnist and TV personality Dorothy Kilgallen a full-size marble tombstone (weighing about a ton) with her name engraved upon it. Later he saw her in a restaurant wearing a pair of sunglasses. He walked over to her table and dropped a dollar bill into her cup of coffee. "I always knew you were blind," he retorted.

For his entire life, Frank would wage battle with much of the press corps. "I feel that an entertainer has a right to his privacy that is as inviolate as any other person's," he once said, maybe somewhat naively. "Otherwise it means that a 'public figure' is a second-class citizen in that he is denied rights which others enjoy." When he felt unfairly criticized, Frank could take his obsession with payback to great lengths, as he did when he began insulting Kilgallen during his performances:

"That broad, she's got a face like a chipmunk."

"That broad, her profile looks like one of my car keys."

"That broad, she's a chinless wonder."

Frank's vendetta against Kilgallen went on for years, much to the amusement of the other Rat Packers. No matter what she wrote about him, even if it was upbeat, he would never let up. "I began to wish he had never existed on the planet," she would later say. "He was the devil incarnate. It wasn't his talent that astounded me. It was his amazing capacity for pure, unadulterated cruelty."

While he could dish it out, Frank usually couldn't take it. He had a great sense of humor, but not when it came to his alleged ties to the mob. Comics who made jokes about that were usually excised from his life, such as Shecky Greene, who said, "Frank Sinatra saved my life. His goons were beating me up and he said, 'Enough!'" It was a funny gag, but Greene was no longer a friend after he delivered it.

Lauren "Betty" Bacall

One of the men in show business for whom Frank Sinatra had the greatest admiration and respect was Humphrey Bogart. "Bogie," at fifty-six years of age, was considered by many to be the elder statesman of Hollywood actors. He and Frank had long, fascinating conversations over the years about everything from moviemaking to art to books; they had a great deal in common. Bogie considered Sinatra a close friend, and the reverse was certainly true; Frank once sent a workman to the Bogart home and had an expensive hi-fi system installed without even telling Bogart and his fourth wife, Lauren Bacall (born Betty Joan Perske and always referred to as Betty in her private life). "Frank's a hell of a guy," Bogie said. "If he could only stay away from the broads and devote some time to develop himself as an actor, he'd be one of the best in the business."

In February 1956, when Humphrey Bogart was diagnosed with cancer of the esophagus, Frank was a constant and reassuring companion. Unfortunately, Bogie would have less than a year to live.

During this dreadful time, Betty Bacall—who was thirty-one at the time—began to cry on Frank's shoulder. He would be there for her as a trusted friend and confidant during Bogie's and her darkest days. Ethel Aniston was an assistant of Lauren Bacall's at the time. She says she was hired by Sinatra to "keep an eye on Mrs. Bogart, make sure she got her rest, took certain medications." Aniston did not live in the Bogart home at 2707 Benedict Canyon Drive in Los Angeles but rather "popped in and out just to make sure Mrs. Bogart was all right and then report everything I noted back to Mr. Sinatra, who cared deeply about them both." She was paid $175 a week by Sinatra.

In fact, Betty was devastated by Bogie's illness. The radiation, the sicknesses and gradual and merciless debilitation of her once-robust husband was too much for her to take. "She would most certainly have cracked up if she had to be alone to deal with it," said Aniston. "She was unprepared for this kind of terrible thing."

"I could not think in terms of Bogie not living," Betty Bacall would later recall. "It was just totally unacceptable."

On January 14, 1957, three weeks after his fifty-seventh birthday, Humphrey Bogart passed away. Frank, who was performing at the Copacabana in New York at the time, canceled five shows, saying he was too devastated to perform. Jerry Lewis substituted for him for some performances, Sammy Davis for others. Frank did not, however, attend the funeral. That wasn't unusual for him; he often didn't attend the funerals of people for whom he had great affection, saying he preferred to remember his friends as being surrounded by laughter rather than tears.

Of course, Betty was devastated and felt she now had little to nothing to look forward to. "I wanted to wake up smiling again," she said. "I hated feeling that my life was over at thirty-two."

Now newly widowed and with two small children to raise, Betty began to view Frank as a romantic partner, attending film premieres, dinners, and other Hollywood functions with him by her side. "At all of his small dinner parties, I was his hostess," she would later remember. "People were watching with interest. It seemed to everyone that we were crazy about each other, that we were a great pair."

Bacall fell hard for Sinatra, but Frank was more tentative with his emotions. To her credit, Betty was someone who would never back off from a good fight, and—as we have seen—Frank never shied away from fireworks now and again in a relationship. Even though Betty would insist she wasn't a confrontational person, she actually loved to be challenged, especially by strong men. It excited her. Therefore, she and Frank fought about everything from the weather to her clothes, his choice of friends, and her spending habits.

They also bickered about her smoking. Frank—a chain-smoker himself—hated it when his women smoked. "Women who smoke from the moment they open their eyes until they put out the light at night—that drives me batty," he said. "It's unfeminine and dangerous—burn up the whole damn house, you know?"

And his flirting, not to mention the fact that he could walk into a room and have any woman he wanted, was a constant source of irritation to Betty. "I am a star," she told him, according to Ethel Aniston. "And let me tell you something, Frank Sinatra, if that's not good enough for you, then *screw you*." Obviously, she had a lot in common with Ava, if only in terms of the way she expressed herself, which probably only served to enhance her in Frank's eyes.

Which Is the Real Dad?

$\mathcal{B}$y January 1957, Frank's children were growing up. Nancy would be seventeen that year, Frank Jr. thirteen, and Tina nine. When he would perform in Los Angeles, they were old enough now to go and watch the show. As they would sit in the front row they'd be all but swept away by the adulation of his audience as he sang his songs and graciously accepted their applause and standing ovations. The Sinatra siblings learned at an early age that they had no choice but to share him with the world.

"We saw that people loved him as much as we did, or at least it felt that way to us," Nancy recalled. "I would stare at him, my eyes not blinking, taking it all in—the suit, the way he stood, the music, the lights—all of it just so thrilling to me in the front row. The applause behind me would be deafening and I would turn around and look at the audience and see their faces. I would think, 'That's my daddy up there.' I would burst with pride in those moments," she would say, "we all would. But still there was something a little sad about it, or maybe *unsettling* would be a better word. We didn't want to share our father with these strangers. We wanted him all to ourselves, but we knew that was never going to happen. So there was a sense of disappointment attached to the experience."

After the show, Nancy Sr. would take the children backstage to see Frank. It was always a wild scene back there, so Nancy didn't like to linger.

"For me, backstage as much as onstage made a great impression," Frank Jr. would recall. "I loved it back there, the camaraderie, the slaps on the back, the feeling of belonging. It was like the best locker room in the world, with stars all over the place. Sammy Davis might be there, or maybe Kirk Douglas or Judy Garland or Dean Martin.

You never knew who you were going to meet in that dressing room. My heart would be pounding as we walked the long hallways to my dad's dressing room wondering what I would see once I got there. As I'd get closer, I would start hearing the laughter and start smelling the cigarette smoke. Finally, we'd get to the dressing room and it would be packed with happy people. It was like the parting of the Red Sea when they would see us, everyone making a way for us to get to our dad, who would be seated on a couch in his white shirt and undone tie, his jacket hanging nearby, smoke in one hand, shot glass in the other. The way he would light up when he realized we were there would make me want to cry with joy. He'd bolt up and take us all in his arms. He'd introduce us to people and there would always be photographers back there. We would all pose for pictures with him. It was a big deal, for sure. I started to get it at an early age that my dad had a whole world going on that had virtually nothing to do with me. I would think, 'Wow, this goes on all the time, not just when I'm here to see it. He's got this whole...*life* that has absolutely nothing to do with us.'

"There was also something about seeing the response to my dad, the way people smiled when they got to meet him," Frank Jr. continued. "They admired and loved him so much, as a kid you couldn't help but be affected by it. If he signed a piece of paper for someone, you knew that person would treasure that damn slip of paper for life. I would think, 'Heck, I got about a million pieces of paper at home with his writing on them, and it don't mean a thing me. But these strangers, they would sell their souls for his signature on a friggin' napkin!'

"You sort of place your dad on a pedestal when you see others do it," he added. "I would think to myself of the times my dad might take a slice of bread and brown it in olive oil. Then he'd cut a hole in it and fry an egg in the hole. He'd slide the whole thing on a plate and hand it to me. 'Here ya go, Frankie,' he'd say with pride. I would eat it and stare at him and think, 'Wow, I sure wish this guy was around more.' But in those moments backstage I would wonder, 'Was that my real dad, the guy in the kitchen making me breakfast? Or is this guy backstage, the one being treated like a king, is this my real dad?' You start to live in this weird parallel universe when it hits you that *both* of them are your real dad."

After about twenty minutes, Nancy Sr. would gather the children and tell them it was time to go. "Every great moment seemed always to be a prelude to a great goodbye," is how Tina would put it years later. Indeed, after big hugs and kisses for Daddy, Nancy and the children would all be on their way with yet another memory, one that would mean the world to them, one they would hang on to when Frank wasn't around.

With the passing of time, if Daddy showed up, the children were thrilled to see him and would spend as much time with him as possible. If he didn't, they could adapt. They actually didn't expect much from him. They had their own friends and had created a fun-filled world in which they sometimes had a daddy present and accounted for, and sometimes didn't.

Tina, the youngest, was more sensitive to Frank's absenteeism. "I sensed that my father had a big life of his own out there," she recalled. "But I couldn't accept that whatever he did was more important than seeing me. I personally felt that Mom was being too flexible, too quick to make excuses. I'd be thinking, 'No, you get him back on the phone and tell him that he should be here.'"

In her own way, Tina would always expect more from her father than her two siblings did. Therefore, she would always feel much more let down by him as well. When Frank would visit and fall asleep in the den, she would curl up in his lap and just hope he would never awaken. As she took in his lavender soap, she knew that as long as he was asleep on that chair, he would be there for her. As soon as he awakened, she knew that he'd look at his watch and say, "Okay, kid, walk me to the door." After a hug and kiss, Tina would run up to her bedroom. She would watch sadly as Frank drove away. "These are my saddest memories," she would say. "Each of Dad's visits was an emotional parabola: the eager anticipation of his arrival; the giddy joy of his company; a swelling apprehension as his departure grew near; the dull, aching void he left in his wake."

Nancy Sr. never criticized Frank in front of the children, nor did she fight with him in their presence. Of course, his visits to the house were sometimes very difficult for her; she still loved him, after all. However, she would gladly endure the sorrow for the sake of her children. When he didn't show up as planned, she would reference her ready-made list of excuses to get him off the hook. They weren't too surprised, then, when they learned that Frank wouldn't be home for Christmas.

"He has to work in Europe," Nancy told the children over breakfast. "You know, he can't be in two places at the same time. I'll tell you what," she offered, "we'll all have Christmas together when Daddy gets back."

"Okay, sure, Mommy," the children said as they pulled away from the table and ran outside to play tag.

It was then that it hit Nancy: It meant more to her than it did them. She couldn't help but sit at the kitchen table and cry.

1957–58

*I*t's astonishing to note just how busy and productive Frank Sinatra was in the mid- to late 1950s with another barrage of memorable record albums and movies. In the 1950s, his output—four or five, sometimes more, albums a year—was not unusual. In 1957 alone, he recorded fifty-seven new songs—but likely none are more significant than "All the Way" and "Witchcraft." "All the Way," with lyrics by Sammy Cahn and written for the film *The Joker Is Wild*, would be one of Frank's bestselling singles. On the charts for thirty weeks, it went on to win the 1957 Academy Award for Best Original Song. "Witchcraft" would become a hit for Frank in 1958 and receive a Grammy nomination.

This was also the year of Frank's classic concept albums, *A Swingin' Affair* and *Come Fly with Me* (his first recording with arranger Billy May, which would soar to number one on the charts). Sinatra also issued *Where Are You?*, an album of romantic ballads in a musical collaboration with the multitalented Gordon Jenkins. Also released that year would be his premiere Christmas album, *A Jolly Christmas with Frank Sinatra*. For sheer artistry, taste, sense of pacing, and atmosphere, *A Jolly Christmas* is untouchable.

Also, in 1957, Frank made *Pal Joey*, a film with Kim Novak and Rita Hayworth. He plays the title role of the tenderhearted singer Joey Evans, who ends up in a romantic triangle with Hayworth and

Novak. The soundtrack included Rodgers and Hart songs such as "I Didn't Know What Time It Was" and "The Lady Is a Tramp."

The year 1958 is best remembered by Sinatra aficionados as the year he released *Frank Sinatra Sings Only the Lonely*, an album of torch songs that he considered his best work. Arranged by Nelson Riddle, the album contains some of Frank's finest saloon songs, such as "Angel Eyes" (the quintessential story of a loser at the game of love) and "Guess I'll Hang My Tears Out to Dry." This album, which Frank Jr. has called "the greatest blues album ever made"—remained at number one for many months.

Also noteworthy in 1958 was *Come Dance with Me*, a swing album arranged by Billy May. (It won Grammy Awards in 1959 for Album of the Year and Best Male Vocal.)

The next year, 1959, saw the release of the albums *Look to Your Heart* and *No One Cares* (arranged by Gordon Jenkins). Again, both soared to the Top Ten.

Besides *Pal Joey*, there were many other films released during this two-year period. For instance, Frank plays a crippled World War II infantry lieutenant, costarring with Tony Curtis and Natalie Wood, in *Kings Go Forth*; a disillusioned war veteran with Dean Martin and Shirley MacLaine in *Some Came Running*; a careless dreamer and widower trying to raise his ten-year-old son with Eleanor Parker and Edward G. Robinson in Frank Capra's comedy with dramatic overtones *A Hole in the Head*; and an army captain fighting the Japanese in World War II Burma with Gina Lollobrigida in *Never So Few*.

The year was capped by Frank's memorable recording of the optimistic "High Hopes" for the movie *A Hole in the Head*. The song would go on to win the Academy Award for Best Song.

Betty's Heartbreak

*B*y early 1958, Lauren Bacall, who was now thirty-three, was very much in love with Frank Sinatra and thinking about marriage. "My friends were worried I'd be hurt," she later recalled, "that he wasn't good enough, couldn't be counted on for a lifetime. But it was going so smoothly, I felt I was the center of his life, and he was the center of mine." Frank began to allow himself to bask in the warmth of her devotion and attention. Still on the rebound from Ava, he tried to convince himself that he wanted to be with Betty, that Ava no longer mattered. He was drinking heavily, as usual, and his moods at this time vacillated between being extremely elated to be with Betty and morosely sad to no longer be with Ava—typical of a manic-depressive.

He also had some apprehensions about being a father to Betty's two children. Still, despite any reservations, he wanted to move forward with his life. He knew he couldn't stay stuck in a rut, lamenting his lost love. His very good friend Manie Sacks, who had been influential in the lives of many recording artists and was very beloved in the record industry, had just died on February 9 of leukemia at the age of fifty-six.

Manie, whose most recent job had been as vice president in charge of programming at NBC, had been suffering for two years before he told Frank about it. "We gotta do something about this thing, pallie," Frank, who always felt he could handle other people's problems, if not his own, told his friend. "What I got, we can't do nothing about," Manie said. When he died, Frank was overwhelmed with grief. Manie had lived a full, wonderful life even though he'd never married. "I look around me and people are happy," Frank told Dinah Shore; Manie had also charted much of Dinah's career. "I have my career, which is fine. But I want more than just my shitty life. I want to be happy. Is there anything wrong with that?"

Dinah wasn't surprised to hear such a heartfelt observation from Frank. She and Frank weren't always very close, but as friends of Manie's they often had soulful conversations. "If you live your life like Manie, you can't lose," she told him, according to her memory. "Manie would want you to be happy. If that's to be with Betty, fine. Or if it's being alone, that's fine, too. You don't have to be with someone, Frank. You know, you can be alone."

"No," Frank said, shaking his head. "I don't think I can be alone."

"Then ask Betty to marry you," Dinah suggested. "If that will make you happy and make her happy, too, Frank, do it."

"Think that's what Manie would want?" Frank asked, his eyes misting over.

"I *know* it's what he'd want," Dinah said. (Frank and Dinah would later sing a delightful medley together on a television special dedicated to Manie Sacks for NBC, called *Some of Manie's Friends*.)

On March 11, 1958, Frank proposed marriage to Betty. She immediately accepted. The night of their engagement, they went to the Imperial Gardens restaurant on the Sunset Strip. They asked the agent Swifty Lazar to join them in their private celebration. The next day, Frank departed for Miami. Before he left, he told Betty to be absolutely sure to keep their engagement top secret. He didn't want the news to leak out until after he returned from Miami, mostly because he didn't want to have to deal with the avalanche of press attention it would generate while he was trying to work a club date.

"I was giddy with joy," Betty would recall, "and felt like laughing every time I opened my mouth. I said nothing to anyone, but now I knew my life would go on. The children would have a father, I would have a husband, we'd have a home again. It was a hard secret to keep—I was about to burst—but I kept my mouth shut."

That night, Betty went to the Huntington Hartford Theater with Swifty Lazar to see the Welsh actor Emlyn Williams perform in a Dickens play. At intermission, she went to the ladies' room, and on her way, Louella Parsons stopped her and Swifty to ask if it was true that she was going to marry Frank. "Why don't you ask him?" Betty snapped back and kept moving, lest the reporter follow up with more questions. Inside, though, she was shaking. How in the world did Parsons know?

When Betty came out of the ladies' room, she saw Swifty deep in conversation with Louella. This wasn't good.

The next morning, Betty woke up to a newspaper headline with Parsons's byline, which almost stopped her heart: "Sinatra to Marry Bacall." Parsons reported that Betty had "finally admitted that [Sinatra] had asked her to marry him. She was beaming with happiness." Of course, that wasn't true at all. Betty had told her no such thing, and when she read it she was filled with panic. She would have to explain it all to Frank, and the sooner the better.

First, she had it out with Swifty. "My God! You told her? *Are you crazy?*" she asked him later that morning, according to her memory.

"Of course I told her," said Swifty. "I didn't know she would go write about it, though."

"She's a gossip columnist," Betty exclaimed. "What did you think she would do? Keep it a secret?"

"Well, so what?" Swifty asked, not at all connecting to the gravity of what had just happened. "It's true, isn't it?"

"But it wasn't your secret to tell," Betty said, dismayed. "We have to call Frank right now. You have to tell him what you did!"

"Why are you so nervous?" Swifty asked.

"Have you met Frank Sinatra?" Betty asked sarcastically. "*Have you met him?*"

They made the call. Swifty told Frank that the news was out—"the cat's out of the bag," he said, trying to make light of it—but was a little vague about how it had happened. In other words, he didn't exactly cop to it.

Finally, Betty got on the line. "I'm so sorry about this," she told Frank. "I hope it's all okay."

Frank was noncommittal. He didn't chastise her, but he also didn't let her off the hook. She felt a little fearful about his demeanor, but hoped he was just tired. She knew he hadn't had a chance to tell Nancy about the engagement, and she figured maybe that was what bothered him the most.

Though her friends immediately started calling to congratulate her, Betty did what she could to dampen their enthusiasm. She didn't want there to be any more excitement about the engagement, not until Frank returned and she could see his face to know that everything was all right.

Frank didn't call for a few days. "So, then, the operative word was...*apprehensive*," she would recall years later.

After almost a week without word from him, Betty went from "apprehensive" to frantic. What was he thinking? How was he feeling? What was going to happen? Though she didn't know it—but later would admit that she at least suspected—Frank was having second thoughts.

It was Mickey Rudin who helped Frank make up his mind about Betty. Mickey, who was thirty-seven—born in New York City on November 16, 1920—would go on to become a pivotal person in Frank's life. Educated at UCLA, where he received his bachelor of arts degree in 1941, he went on from there to graduate from Harvard

Law. A short and stout tough guy, he was married to Elizabeth Green-schpoon, a talented cellist whose brother, Ralph, became both Marilyn Monroe's and Frank Sinatra's psychiatrist. Frank had just retained Mickey, and already the two were on their way to a great friendship and working relationship. "He was an utterly brilliant lawyer and unforgettable character," recalled Bruce Ramer, a partner in the Beverly Hills law firm of Gang, Tyre, Ramer & Brown; Mickey was a partner there from 1946 to 1966.

Frank told Mickey he had certain apprehensions about being a stepfather to Betty's two little children. He already had three children by Nancy and sometimes had a tough time doing right by them, as much as he tried. Also, he believed that what he and Betty shared was more mutual grief over losing Bogie than it was true love for one another. He explained that Manie Sacks's death had hit him hard and made him want to marry Betty.

Mickey laid it on the line, as he would do for Frank for the next thirty years. "Divorce at your level of income is a pain in the ass," he reportedly said. "If you're not sure about this thing, for God's sake, Frank, don't do it. Manie wouldn't want you to have an expensive divorce, that much I know for sure."

When he finally called her, Frank acted as if he was very angry with Betty. "Why did you do it?" he demanded to know.

"Do what?" she asked. She thought something else had happened.

"Tell that reporter about our engagement," Frank said.

"But I didn't do it, Frank," Betty said in her defense. "Swifty did it. Not me."

"Damn it, Betty, I haven't been able to leave my room for days; the press are everywhere," Frank said, really lighting into her. "Now we'll have to lay low for a while, not see each other." He lacked the courage to be honest with her and admit he'd had a change of heart.

They were to go to Chicago on March 25 to attend a Sugar Ray Robinson fight. That date would have to be canceled, Frank told Betty. They were also scheduled to go to New York on the twenty-sixth, where Betty was to be at his side when he received the Boys' Town of Italy Award. Now that trip would have to be canceled as well. On the twenty-seventh they had plans to attend a policemen's benefit in Palm Springs. "That's out too," Frank said, laying down the law.

Her heart sinking, Betty didn't quite know how to respond. "Well, what are we going to do?" she asked.

"*Jesus Christ, Betty! I just told you*," he shouted into the phone, "*we're going to lay low for a while.*"

"Okay," she said meekly. "I love you, Frank."

He hung up on her.

"From a friend, I later heard he was back in Los Angeles," Betty later recalled. "Swifty had dinner with him—*Swifty*, the *perpetrator* of it all! Frank was speaking to him, but not to me. I was so hurt, so miserable.

"I couldn't deal with it," Betty continued. "There was no way to understand it. We had been such friends for so long, how could he drop the curtain like this? I was under a permanent cloud then—trying to excuse him to others, pretending I understood—but others had seen this behavior before. No one just drops someone without discussion. It was such a shock. I spent night after night in tears."

One moment he was there, making love to Betty, confiding in her, sharing his life with her and being essential to her support system in grief. Then the next he was gone, as if he'd never existed in her life, as if they'd never even met. His feelings about her had quickly shifted from caring about her, to being angry with her, to being just plain apathetic about her. Once the relationship was breached, he no longer cared one way or the other. Apparently he could turn off his feelings, just like that. It meant little to Frank to cut someone out of his life, no matter how much he once cared about that person—or how much that person still cared about him. Would it not have been easier on all concerned if he had just leveled with Betty the way he had with Mickey Rudin about her? "That was as ruthless as I had seen Frank Sinatra at that point in our relationship," noted George Jacobs. "I was taken aback at the cold way he cut Betty completely dead. That was the first time Mr. S. showed a side that frightened me."

"He behaved like a complete shit," Betty would say years later. "He was too cowardly to tell the truth—that it was just too much for him, that he couldn't handle it. I would have understood. [I hope.]"

Soon after, Frank and Betty came face-to-face—in a manner of speaking. A month earlier when all was well between them, the two had been invited to a dinner party by Edie Goetz, daughter of Louis B. Mayer. They showed up as planned—separately, of course. Upon realizing that they were no longer together, Goetz seated someone between them.

"Frank didn't acknowledge my existence," Betty recalled. "Not a flicker of recognition. He did not speak one word to me—if he looked in my direction, he did not see me, he looked right past me, as though my chair was empty. I would have preferred him to spit in my face, at least that would have been recognition. I couldn't deal with this— there was no way to understand it. My humiliation was indescribable."

Betty Bacall pulled Edie Goetz into the kitchen to confide in her. She was sorry, she said, but she had no choice: She had to leave. Being in the same room as Frank while he ignored her so completely was nothing but pure torture. "My God. You think you know someone," Betty whispered through her tears, "and then it turns out... you don't."

Part Seven

THE RAT PACK YEARS

The Rat Pack

The date was January 26, 1960. Showtime was at 8 p.m. "Let's start the action," Frank Sinatra would say to his pals—Dean Martin, Sammy Davis, Peter Lawford, and Joey Bishop—as the orchestra played the overture and they prepared to take the Las Vegas stage. While standing in the wings, each would smoke a quick cigarette and then guzzle a final swig out of a bottle of Jack Daniel's. Then the performers would slap each other on the back as they bounded onto the stage to an enthusiastic welcome.

In 1960, few entertainers were more popular or controversial than forty-four-year-old Frank Sinatra. Despite the growing prevalence of rock and roll and British popular music, he somehow still managed to maintain his premier status in the world of show business. Though his fans were getting older, he was still the master of a particular style of entertainment. He still had his own loyal following. Of all of his touring engagements, Frank enjoyed appearing in Las Vegas more than anywhere else. He had made his Vegas debut at the Desert Inn back in September 1951, when there were only four hotels on the Strip. By 1960, though, the Strip was a mecca of colorful lights, high-rise hotels, and noisy casinos. The entertainment there was always the best in the business: Danny Thomas, Jerry Lewis, Lena Horne, Red Skelton—the list was endless, and Frank was one of the top-drawing attractions.

Since Frank's many friends and relatives would all make their way to Vegas to see him perform, the good times never really ended for anyone in his circle during an engagement in the desert. The gambling. The "dames." The audiences. For Frank, it was one big party. "He goes and goes and goes and never stops until he's completely done in," said Red Norvo, his part-time accompanist. "But to see him *really* go, you've got to see him in Vegas."

By this time, Frank Sinatra was a co-owner of the Sands, with a 6 percent share in the hotel (each point was worth close to $100,000).

He also enjoyed unlimited credit with the hotel because Jack Entratter, the corporate president, had ordered the management to tear up all his IOUs, worth anywhere from tens of thousands to hundreds of thousands of dollars, depending on Frank's gambling sprees. Just having Frank in the casino always made for big business, especially when he was joined by his pack. They were called the Rat Pack by some in the media—appropriating the name of the society that had once included Judy Garland and others—and the Clan by others. In fact, Frank preferred to refer to himself and his buddies—Martin, Davis, Lawford, and Bishop—as the Summit. Around this time, Eisenhower, Khrushchev, and de Gaulle were planning a summit conference in Paris. Frank said that he and his pals would have their own "summit conference of cool."

Frank, Dean, Sammy, Peter, and Joey were also in the midst of making the film version of *Ocean's 11* for Frank's Dorchester Productions, in association with Warner Bros. The movie, shot in Las Vegas, was the first of four they would do together. *Ocean's 11* was a comedy-drama about Danny Ocean [Sinatra] recruiting a bunch of former military buddies to rob five major Las Vegas casinos simultaneously on New Year's Eve. The filming schedule was grueling and their lifestyles made it even tougher on them. After each concert performance, which ended at two in the morning, the fellows would drink the rest of the night away, partying until the sun rose. Then, somehow, they would manage to drag themselves in front of the movie cameras at dawn for work on the film. Afterward, they'd sleep for a couple of hours and begin again.

Ironically, considering their popularity there, Las Vegas was never the place to see the Rat Pack if one wanted to actually hear them sing. In other cities, the performances were of a high caliber; each gentleman had the opportunity to sing a separate set of hits and standards before the finale, when all would gather onstage for scripted and unscripted comedy and a few jointly performed songs. In Vegas, though, it was much more impromptu. To most observers, it felt like the men were more concerned about entertaining each other than about singing for their audiences.

Shirley MacLaine, at twenty-five, was considered the Rat Pack's mascot because she was a "dame" they hung out with and, according to her, with whom they were never intimate. (MacLaine starred with Sinatra in the 1958 film *Some Came Running* and received an Academy Award nomination for her work.) In her memoir, *My Lucky Stars*, she best described the way the Rat Pack looked when she wrote about watching Frank and Dean get ready for a night on the town. "What got me were their hats. They wore wide-brimmed hats right out of the racetrack number from *Guys and Dolls*. Their shoes were uncommonly polished and I was certain their socks didn't smell. Underneath it all, I sensed their underwear was as white and fresh as soft, newly fallen snow."

They looked great, but didn't always sound it. In truth, none of the singers were in very good voice when they performed in Las Vegas. No singer's vocal cords could hold up under the pressure of the schedule they maintained, along with all the booze, the smoking, and the late hours. The fellows would spend an hour in the steam room every day, hoping to restore their vocal cords and stamina.

Most historians who have written about the Rat Pack have made note of the constant jokes relating to Sammy's race. For instance, while onstage and with the lights low, Frank would say to Sammy, "You better keep smiling, Sammy, so we can see where you are." Or when Sammy would do his Sinatra impression of "All the Way," and Frank would say, "He's just, excuse the expression, a carbon copy." While this kind of humor seems a puzzlement today, at the time it really was all in good fun.

In fact, Frank's dedication to racial and ethnic equality went back many years, all the way to his Hoboken childhood when he felt the sting of prejudice because of his Italian ethnicity. People still remember that when he first began singing "Ol' Man River" back in the 1940s, he was careful to replace the line "Darkies all work on the Mississippi" with "Here we all work on the Mississippi." (After he made that lyrical change, most other performers followed suit whenever they sang the Kern-Hammerstein song in concert.)

In the years to come, Sinatra opened up many doors for Sammy Davis, especially in Vegas, where he demanded that Sammy be allowed to perform in certain hotels and be paid what other stars were paid. Although Frank's racial humor at Sammy's expense seemed to some observers to be insensitive and condescending, Sammy shrugged it off. After all, he knew that when it really counted, Frank stood up for him against the widespread racism that had plagued him earlier in his career.

JFK

Senator John Fitzgerald Kennedy was a great admirer of the Rat Pack, especially of Frank Sinatra. As Peter Lawford's brother-in-law (Lawford married into the powerful Irish-American Kennedy dynasty in 1955 when he wed JFK's younger sister Patricia), JFK had front-row-seat entrée to the Las Vegas festivities on February 7, 1960. He was on the campaign trail and en route from Oregon to Texas on the *Caroline*, his private plane, with about a half dozen reporters when he decided to accept Sinatra's invitation and stop off in Vegas for the Rat Pack show.

Back in the summer of 1959, Frank and Peter had flown to Palm Beach, Florida, to visit with Kennedy patriarch Joe Kennedy. Kennedy had said he wanted their assistance in his son's presidential campaign, and he told Frank that he wanted him to begin outlining plans for concerts to raise money for the campaign. He also wanted Frank to network with his influential show-business friends to secure their support for his son. Moreover, he asked him to record a theme song for the campaign, and they eventually settled on a reworking of Frank's song "High Hopes." There would probably be other favors in the future, he told Frank. That was fine with Sinatra; he was eager to help JFK get elected.

For his part, JFK always looked forward to socializing with Frank. He enjoyed witnessing Frank's wild antics, sharing his exciting women, and partaking in as much show-business excess and Hollywood gossip as possible. When Peter married Pat Kennedy, the couple purchased a mansion in Santa Monica and JFK became a regular visitor, often entertaining women on the premises.

* * *

After the Summit's engagement at the Sands Hotel in Las Vegas ended on February 16, 1960, the fellows took a train to Los Angeles, where they finished *Ocean's 11*. Then it was back in the studio for Frank on March 3, 1960, to cut the *Nice 'n' Easy* album with the Nelson Riddle Orchestra. *Nice 'n' Easy* would prove to be a big album for Sinatra at Capitol, artistically and commercially. Originally it didn't even have his name on the cover, just his very recognizable face. The public was so starved for Sinatra at this time that the album shot straight to number one on the charts. It was an easygoing, relaxed project, artistically right on the nose for the moment, charming and engaging.

For the rest of 1960, Frank Sinatra and John F. Kennedy continued their friendship. JFK even spent a weekend in 1960 at Frank's home in Palm Springs after his narrow victory over Nixon. Afterward, a proud Frank had a plaque mounted on the door with the inscription "John F. Kennedy Slept Here November 6th and 7th 1960."

Frank felt that JFK was the right candidate for the White House. Not only did he respect his politics, but he was excited by the notion of having a pal in such a high place. JFK had even mentioned the possibility of Sinatra becoming ambassador to Italy, which seemed like an unlikely possibility even to Frank, but did make him smile. Always a devoted Democrat ("I've been campaigning for Democrats ever since I marched in a parade for Al Smith when I was a twelve-year-old kid," he liked to say), he would campaign tirelessly for Kennedy, raising money by performing at concerts, calling in favors, and as one associate put it, "by just being Frank."

Stark Duality

*I*n 1960, Nancy turned twenty, Frank Jr. sixteen, and Tina twelve. They were growing old enough to travel and didn't have to wait for Frank to visit them in Beverly Hills. They would go to see him in Palm Springs. Nancy Sr. would pack suitcases for them and they would spend a week in the desert during the summer with Frank on Wonder Palms Drive (soon to be redubbed Frank Sinatra Drive). Frank's place was located on the seventeenth fairway of the Tamarisk Country Club. Nancy would usually accompany the children, or sometimes Dolly and Marty if they happened to be in town from the East Coast.

It was always a big thrill not only for the kids but for Frank whenever the entire family would descend upon him in the desert. At around this time, he had expanded the property from just a small house to a virtual compound. Not only did he add rooms and bathrooms to the main house, but he also built another home on the property with its own four bedrooms, eight bathrooms, and swimming pool. The kids called it "the Christmas Tree House" because it was so traditional, with its wood-framed architecture, not at all like the main house, which was all glass and metal.

"Palm Springs Frank" was a lot more fun than "Beverly Hills Frank," and his children knew it. In the desert, their father just seemed relaxed and happier. To their delight, he would spend as much time with them as possible, playing all sorts of games in one of the two pools under the scorching sun. Sometimes he would pile them all into his jeep and take them on bumpy rides through the desert. Or he'd take them on expensive and fun shopping sprees.

Now that Nancy was a young woman, Frank enjoyed taking her to a small dress shop on Palm Canyon Drive and telling her she could have anything she liked. She would spend an hour proudly modeling different outfits for him, and Frank would wait for as long as it took until she found just the perfect ensemble. Nothing was too good for his eldest child, whom he once bought a pink Thunderbird convertible. He had it delivered, wrapped with an enormous pink bow.

Trying to also treat Frank Jr., Sinatra would take him to a local music store. There, the two would thumb through the albums and talk in depth about music, comparing their likes and dislikes. Frank Jr. would then pick out a few records by favorite artists—usually family friends, like Dean or Sammy. (Frank Jr. hated rock and roll, just like Dad.)

It didn't take much to please Tina. All she wanted was alone time with Daddy. She could curl up in his lap for hours, watch television with him, and be the happiest little girl in the world.

Getting them all together in the kitchen, Frank would make steamed rice with chocolate bits, a treat Dolly used to prepare for him when he was a youngster in Hoboken. His kids loved it.

Dinners were always a big Italian-American event when the family was together in the desert. His spaghetti sauce—which he called "gravy," the way they did back in Hoboken—would simmer with pork chops all day long, the distinctive smell wafting through the main house. If Nancy was present—and she usually was—she would be the one to make the meatballs. Spaghetti that night would be perfectly cooked by Frank, al dente.

"Let's go sit by the pool," Nancy would usually suggest to Frank after dinner. He would smile and nod. Then the two of them would pull up side-by-side lounges and watch a perfect desert sun, chatting quietly. Meanwhile, their children would watch from a safe distance. "In my mind, they just seemed absolutely perfect for each other," Nancy Jr. would recall. "I would sit and wonder why they weren't together all the time. He seemed like her best friend."

Sometimes during the week, Tina might act up and her mother would discipline her by swatting her across the butt. She would squeal and cry, and then get over it. It meant little to her, but it was something Frank hated. "You shouldn't hit her," Frank would tell Nancy. "Oh, that's not hitting her," Nancy would explain. "That's just spanking." She knew, however, that Frank was sensitive to any kind of physical parental discipline because of the way his parents had smacked him around when he was young. He would never lift his hands to his children, ever. That he seemed to take Tina's side in these kind of disputes just made her want him to be around more often.

One day, Tina just came out and asked the question foremost on her mind. "Why can't we just be together all the time, Daddy?"

Frank looked down at her and then scooped her into his arms. "Because it doesn't work like that, Pigeon," he said, using his nickname for her. "That's not the way our family works."

"But other families work like that," she protested.

"But they're not as happy as we are," Frank said. "Now, are they?"

Tina thought it over. It didn't quite seem right to her. However, he was her dad, and in her eyes he was never wrong.

Frank's relationship with Tina and Nancy was always easy and effortless. But Frank Jr., also known as Frankie, was a different story. There was just always something a little off between father and son, and no one could quite understand it. Frank could be so abrupt and short with Frankie, some in the family were reminded of the way

Marty had treated him when he was a kid. "Take time and get to know him," Nancy would tell Frank. "What for? I already know my kid," Frank would say in protest. To imply otherwise was to suggest that he wasn't a good father. Even though he knew he had his inadequacies and never fooled himself into thinking he didn't, he still didn't like it being brought to his attention.

As with many parents, Frank had an easier time being a father when his children were young. As Big Frank would stand at the mirror and shave, Little Frank would watch carefully, lather himself up with shaving cream, and do the same thing with an empty razor. Frankie wanted to be just like his father; they looked alike; they had the same mannerisms; they even had the exact same gait. When Frankie was about three and would get sick, his dad would bring a little tray into his room, set it up on the bed, and the two would slurp chicken noodle soup together and watch the puppet show *Kukla, Fran and Ollie* on a little black-and-white television. Or they would eat peanut butter and jelly sandwiches and tell each other corny jokes. "I'm about as sick as a kid can ever get," Frankie once told his father. "I'll bet you a quarter that tomorrow you feel better," Frank wagered. "How's that work, Dad?" Frankie asked. "If you feel better, I'll give you a quarter. And if you don't feel better, I'll *still* give you a quarter."

Things changed for father and son when Ava came into the picture and broke up their home. Frankie was about four when Frank left to be with her. As he got older and realized that his father was only going to be around on special occasions, Frankie seemed to take it the hardest. "He felt bewildered and abandoned and quietly traumatized," was how Tina later put it.

"For any happiness that comes from being the son of a famous father, there is an equal if not greater amount of heartache," he told the writer Fred Robbins when he was a teenager. "People are afraid of me now because they're dealing with a name rather than the individual. I'm not famous. My name is famous but I'm not. So, this makes it difficult. Being the offspring of someone who is in the public eye constantly is a lonely existence. I don't think I have to say any more than that. It's a very lonely existence. I've learned to live without a good many things which are important to people."

Unlike his sisters, Frankie refused to allow himself to feel too connected to his dad, mostly because the inevitable separation anxiety was too much for him to handle. It was such a great loss, losing Frank to Ava, that Frankie never quite reconciled it. He was a son who needed his father. Short of having him always present in his life, he would make the best of it. He was exactly the way Frank had been with Marty, the same coping mechanisms in place. The difference between the two, though, was that Marty was ever-present, even if not ever-patient.

As a youth, Frank Sr. was outgoing, gregarious, and full of personality; no doubt having Dolly as a mother helped in that regard. But conversely, Frank Jr. was withdrawn and introverted and, ironically enough, more like Marty. At any rate, with the passing of just a few years, the emotional gulf between father and son had widened to the point where by the time Frankie was in his teens they barely communicated. Very soon, Frankie would get in with the wrong crowd in school and find himself arrested for shooting out streetlamps with a pellet gun. After bailing him out, Frank and Nancy would make the decision to send him away to boarding school. His teen years would not be easy.

"Just go out and talk to him," Nancy said, motioning to their sixteen-year-old son lying by himself in the sun on one of the lounges. According to George Jacobs, who witnessed the scene, Frank shrugged and went outside. He pulled up a lounge and sat next to Frankie and tried to make awkward small talk. From the kitchen, Nancy watched sadly as father and son just lay side by side baking in the hot sun, not saying much to each other.

"Look, I tried," an exasperated Frank later told Nancy as George Jacobs brought him a shot of Jack Daniel's. "He doesn't have anything to say to me. What do you want from me? The kid hasn't smiled since he was seven!"

"Well, did you ask him about school?" Nancy asked. "He has a new girlfriend. Did you ask him about that? He's driving a truck for a sporting goods warehouse, you could talk about that! And he says he wants to be a singer like you. Did you ask him about that?" Nancy stopped herself. She could tell that Frank was feeling badly; she wanted to relieve him of his guilt. "Look, at least you tried," she said in a reassuring tone. "Frankie will come around. Don't worry."

It was when his children visited in Palm Springs that Frank Sinatra was more aware than ever of the stark duality of his life. It was as if the serene world that existed when his kids were in town had virtually nothing to do with the chaotic world in which he ordinarily moved. When the two worlds collided Frank did his best to devote himself to the one involving parenthood, not the one involving celebrity. For instance, if his publicist, Jim Mahoney, called to ask him to do an interview with a reporter, he would always decline. Not only did he not want to take time away from the kids, but he actually didn't want to be reminded of what he couldn't help but view as his "real" life. This life with his family? For him, *this* was make-believe.

Though he found it frustrating and maybe even a little painful, in his heart of hearts Sinatra always knew the truth: While he enjoyed being with his children, he was just more comfortable, more himself, when he was throwing back shots with Hank, or when he and Dean were calculating the best way to score a sexy broad in a bar, or when he was in the recording studio working out a complex arrangement with Count Basie. On those occasions when he'd lived up to his obligations as a parent, Frank Sinatra was proud of himself. But then he couldn't wait to call one of his pallies to see what kind of trouble they could get into, or maybe catch the first thing smoking out of Palm Springs and head for Las Vegas where the *real* Sinatra could once again hold court.

The Execution of Private Slovik

$\mathcal{F}$rank Sinatra's relationship with the Kennedys fell into jeopardy in March 1960 when he decided to hire Albert Maltz to write a screenplay for *The Execution of Private Slovik*, the story of the only U.S. soldier since the Civil War to be executed for desertion. Sinatra planned to produce and direct.

Maltz had been the writer of Sinatra's Oscar-winning *The House I Live In*. Since that time, he'd been imprisoned, fined, and blacklisted as one of the so-called Hollywood Ten for refusing to cooperate with the House Un-American Activities Committee. Maltz moved to Mexico in 1951, which was where Sinatra found him. He hadn't been able to work on a film since 1948. Frank, like a few other Hollywood celebrities, such as Otto Preminger and Kirk Douglas, felt strongly that not only was Maltz's blacklisting unfair but that *any* blacklisting was unconscionable. He also felt that Albert Maltz was the man to write the screenplay for *Private Slovik*.

A huge controversy resulted from Frank's decision. Newspaper editorials across the country either endorsed or decried—mostly the latter—Sinatra's bold attempt to break the blacklist. At one point, actor John Wayne said, "I wonder how Sinatra's crony, Senator John Kennedy, feels about him hiring such a man. I'd like to know his attitude because he's the one who is making plans to run the administrative government of our country."

Sinatra, angry at Wayne, bought a full-page advertisement in *Variety* defending his decision, stating, "This type of partisan politics is hitting below the belt. I make movies. I do not ask the advice of Senator Kennedy on whom I should hire. Senator Kennedy does not ask me how he should vote in the Senate...In my role as picture maker, I have—in my opinion—hired the best man to do the job."

None of this controversy made Joe Kennedy very happy, especially when religious leaders in New York and Boston warned him that Sinatra's support of Maltz could do damage to his son's career among Catholics. Joe telephoned Frank and told him he would have to choose: Maltz or the Kennedys. Begrudgingly, Frank chose the Kennedys; he paid Maltz $75,000, the entire amount he had promised to compensate him for his work. "In view of the reaction of my family, my friends, and the American public," Sinatra said, "I have instructed my attorneys to make a settlement with Albert Maltz and to inform him that he will not write the screenplay for *The Execution of Private Slovik*." (Many years later, Frank's family would say that he and JFK discussed the controversy, and that JFK told him to go ahead with the project. That's possible, too. In either event, Sinatra canceled the deal.)

Frank Sinatra never produced *The Execution of Private Slovik*. However, the story did make it onto television in 1974 as a movie starring Martin Sheen, with a script by Richard Levinson and William Link.

On the Way to the White House

With the Albert Maltz affair behind him, Frank Sinatra continued his diligent campaign for John F. Kennedy. During much of it, JFK's motorcade was preceded by a sound truck that played a recording of Sinatra's "High Hopes," with new lyrics by Sammy Cahn extolling the virtues of Kennedy. This was one of the favors that Joe Kennedy had asked for in his 1959 meeting with Frank. ("Everyone is voting for Jack / 'Cause he's got what all the rest lack / Everyone wants to back Jack / Jack is on the right track / 'Cause he's got high hopes...")

Whatever Frank could do for the campaign, he would do no matter how big or small. He unofficially renamed the Rat Pack the "Jack Pack" and started singing about "that old Jack magic." He gave concerts, made personal appearances, raised money...anything he could do.

Of a total of 1,520 delegates, JFK had 700 guaranteed by July, when the Democratic National Convention was to take place. He only needed 61 more votes to win a first-ballot nomination.

On July 10, the night before the opening ceremonies of the convention, Frank worked behind the scenes of a gala fund-raiser, a hundred-dollar-a-plate dinner at the Beverly Hilton in Beverly Hills, attended by twenty-eight hundred people. Many of Frank's celebrity friends—such as Angie Dickinson, Shirley MacLaine, Peter Lawford, and Judy Garland—sat at the head table with Kennedy. (Jackie Kennedy stayed behind in Hyannis Port; she was six months pregnant and had a history of medical problems associated with pregnancy.) Since it was so well attended, the gala actually required two ballrooms. Sinatra, Garland, Davis, and Mort Sahl performed in both. Later, Frank beamed as he sat at the table with Democratic candidates Stuart Symington, Adlai Stevenson, and Lyndon Johnson. As everyone watched, Frank would go over to Jack and whisper something in his ear, causing Jack to nod vigorously. Then Jack would whisper in Frank's ear...and Frank would laugh heartily.

The next day, the Jack Pack, along with Janet Leigh and Tony Curtis, performed "The Star-Spangled Banner" to open the Democratic convention at the Los Angeles Memorial Sports Arena.

The enthusiasm for JFK was so strong by this time that no one else stood a chance of securing the nomination. It was all but guaranteed when Wyoming gave its fifteen votes to Kennedy. As the crowd cheered and waved flags and Kennedy banners, a jubilant Frank Sinatra told Peter Lawford, "We're on our way to the White House, pallie. We're on our way..."

The Kennedys Worry About Frank and Sammy

By the fall of 1960, the Kennedys had begun to seriously reconsider the wisdom of Frank Sinatra's involvement in JFK's presidential campaign. Jack, Bobby, and even Joe Kennedy had been deluged with mail from people who felt that the family's relationship with Sinatra was unwise because of the singer's controversial reputation. There was also significant pressure from Kennedy's friends and political advisers to distance the campaign from Sinatra. Too many unanswered questions loomed where he was concerned, said the naysayers, primarily about the extent of his involvement with mobster Sam Giancana.

Sam Giancana—Chicago's Mafia boss—with his Cuban cigars, sharkskin suits, and flashy automobiles, was a dark and dangerous character. He and Frank had met a few years earlier in Miami at the Fontainebleau. Frank was with Ava at the time, and she disliked Sam immediately. It was as if she knew trouble when she saw it. However, Frank became friendly with Sam and gave him a gaudy star-sapphire pinky ring as a gift, which was just what Giancana needed to complete the stereotypical image of a gangster. "See this ring?" Sam told his younger brother, Chuck. "Frank gave me this ring. I'm his hero. The guy's got a big mouth. But he's a stand-up guy."

JFK and Bobby had begun to believe that any association at all with Sinatra might prove risky, especially considering his friendship with Giancana. In fact, now that the primary had been won, the Kennedys were inclined to distance themselves from Sinatra, from Giancana, and from any other characters they felt were unsavory—and to do so before JFK got into the White House. In October, Bobby even suggested damage control where Sinatra was concerned. JFK agreed. Bobby then had his staff check to see just how many photographs actually existed of his brother and Frank posing together with women at various parties. JFK had decided he wanted them found and destroyed. Bobby went a step further; he also wanted the negatives. To that end, a representative from RFK's office contacted Frank to request that any photographs or negatives that could prove to be embarrassing be sent to the White House immediately. Maybe insulted or maybe just not wanting to be told what to do—or maybe a little of both—Frank decided not to cooperate. Lying, he said that no such photographs existed.

Also going on around this time was the planning of Sammy Davis's wedding to May Britt, a Swedish actress (born Maybritt Wilkens) in Las Vegas. Joe Kennedy was concerned. Because interracial marriage was still illegal in thirty-one states, Joe feared that Sammy's marriage would reflect poorly on the Kennedys.

Frank was to be Sammy's best man, and he didn't care what anyone thought of it. But Frank, like a lot of broad-minded people at the time, understood that there were racists in the country who strenuously, and sometimes violently, objected to the notion of interracial dating, let alone marriage. He had to agree that it made no sense to court scandal right before the election. Still, when Bobby asked him to talk to Sammy about postponing the ceremony, Frank wasn't sure how to proceed. But Sammy offered to delay the ceremony himself; he knew the score, and he wanted to save Frank the embarrassment.

"This was when Frank was starting to get pissed at the Kennedys," said Sammy Davis in retrospect. "Now his political ambitions for Jack were beginning to interfere with his personal friendships, and that was no good. Frank was a loyal friend. They didn't come no better. You didn't mess with that. He told me, 'I'd never ask you to postpone the wedding, Sam.' And I said, 'I know that. That's why I'm doing it on my own. Because I understand.' Next thing I knew, Peter was on the line. Frank had handed him the phone, he was too broken up to continue talking. 'This was the right thing to do, Charlie,' Peter told me. 'Frank'll never forget this.'"

Still, despite these unpleasant moments, no one was happier than Frank Sinatra when JFK won a narrow victory over Richard Nixon on November 8, 1960.

On November 13, Sammy married May, with Frank as his best man. "At my bachelor party Frank cornered me and said, 'Instead of paying you a straight salary for *Sergeants 3*, I'm going to give you $75,000 plus 7 percent of the action. It should be worth a quarter of a million to you. You'll have a wife and kids to think about.' That's the kind of guy he is. It's easy for others to say that it was only right for Frank to be there, he's your friend. But it's not that simple. With all of his independence, he still knew how quickly a career can go down the drain on the whim of the public. For him to state, 'This is my friend and you can stick it in your ear if you don't like it' and putting in jeopardy everything he's worked for, lost and regained, and must fight to hold on to, it was not a minor thing for Frank to be my best man."

Matters got dicey once again when Frank and Peter Lawford were asked to produce and star in JFK's preinaugural ball. From the outset, Joe Kennedy told Frank that Sammy was not to attend the ball because of the public fervor that had, as predicted, occurred over his marriage to May. It didn't matter that Sammy had also campaigned hard for JFK. There seemed to be nothing Frank could do to convince Joe that Sammy should be allowed to perform. Then he couldn't get in touch with JFK to discuss the matter with him. Kennedy ducked his calls.

Frank called one White House aide, demanding that he find a way for him to talk to Kennedy. The aide refused, knowing that JFK didn't want to discuss the Davis matter with him. Frank said, "Jack owes me, man. He doesn't know how much he owes me. And now *this*?"

"I tried to tell him, 'No, Frank, it's not Jack. It's Bobby. *Bobby's* the one responsible,'" said the Kennedy aide.

"But Frank was adamant that it was Jack's fault. '*Shit!*' he said at me. 'I can't believe this. How can Jack do this to Sam?'" It made no sense. After all, Mahalia Jackson, Harry Belafonte, and Nat King Cole were on the bill. "Just the fact that he's a buddy of mine should be enough for Jack to call an end to this," Frank insisted. "Sam loves Jack. You can't allow this to happen."

However, Sammy's affection for JFK didn't matter at this point; he was still barred from attending the festivities. Frank was so upset, he wasn't able to make the call to Sammy himself; he had Peter Lawford do it.

No doubt Frank was beginning to see the light: He didn't have quite as much influence on "Chickie Baby" as he thought he had, and maybe even deserved. Kennedy was a politician and, as such, a pragmatist who wasn't about to allow emotion to get in the way of his political ambitions. That Sinatra didn't realize this earlier demonstrated his complete lack of understanding about how things work in the political world.

Frank and Sammy never discussed the matter of the ball. They were pals and always had an understanding about these things; it was understood between them that there was nothing that could have been done. "He told me it was one of the few times he ever felt at such a loss," recalled his daughter Nancy. "He had been able to protest and bring about change. But now he could do nothing. Yes, he could have backed out of the inaugural, but Sammy would never have allowed that."

Part Eight

AND MARILYN MONROE

Reprise

The year 1960 had been a terrific one for Frank Sinatra. He was now making about $20 million a year through his film and TV production companies (Essex, Kent, and Dorchester), four music publishing companies, his gambling interests in Las Vegas and Lake Tahoe, radio partnerships, and his many real estate holdings. He also now had his own record label, the aforementioned Reprise. The problem with Capitol had been that he felt the label was restricting the way he recorded his music. He wanted to do it his way—select his own tunes, record at the times when he wanted to do so, schedule his releases when he felt they should be in the stores, and possibly even spearhead the careers of other recording artists—and he couldn't do any of that as long as he was working for a label he didn't own. It was agreed that after he finished his term at Capitol, he could lay the groundwork for a new label of his own. Frank told the media that he was now "a new, happier, emancipated Sinatra, untrammeled, unfettered, unconfined." He was ready for 1961.

For Reprise, Frank was bursting with interesting concepts: a tribute to Tommy Dorsey; a string album; a concert album—so many ideas. Yet when he finally did get Reprise going, he started with an album indistinguishable from his Capitol work—*Ring-a-Ding-Ding!*, released in 1961.

The *Ring-a-Ding-Ding!* album is fun, but short on substance. Produced by Felix Slatkin and arranged by Johnny Mandel, it features the title track "Be Careful, It's My Heart," and "Zing Went the Strings of My Heart."

As good as the Reprise albums were, none of them quite approached the matchless quality of Sinatra's Capitol work. At the time, Frank was publicly critical of Capitol, especially after a legal battle when his former label began releasing product to compete with Reprise. But with Reprise he didn't have people around him to provide the necessary feedback. When he started doing it all himself, something was missing.

At Capitol, the reins worked *for* Frank, not against him. Left to his own devices at Reprise, he would bring forth many good ideas, but none would be burnished to the level of the Capitol work. And as for the many remakes of Capitol songs he did at Reprise, many of them just didn't equal the quality of the Capitol versions, whereas Capitol had successfully remade much of his Columbia material. And, significantly, Frank couldn't resist playing around with the material in a jokey manner, as he did by adding a hip "And don't tell your mama" to "Come Fly with Me." Such self-indulgence in the studio was new for him, and not always appealing.

Still, in 1961 and 1962, Sinatra would record a plethora of material for the new label. In May 1961 alone, he recorded twenty-four songs, to be used on two albums, *Sinatra Swings** (arranged by Billy May) and *I Remember Tommy* (arranged by Sy Oliver).

The *Tommy* album is a tribute to Tommy Dorsey, and on it can be found some of Sinatra's most evocative singing, especially "I'm Getting Sentimental Over You" and "Imagination." Obviously, the music and its legacy was more important to Frank than any bad feelings between him and his former mentor. He believed the album was one of his better ones.

Also in 1961, in November, Frank would record the unforgettable *Sinatra and Strings* album, produced by Neal Hefti and Skip Martin. Don Costa's striking arrangements of "Come Rain or Come Shine," "Stardust," and an extraordinary rerecording of Sinatra's hit "All or Nothing at All" make this album a standout. It's unique in that the sound is, by Sinatra's design, more lush and grandiose than ever, with over fifty musicians in the orchestra.

What is considered by some to be his most emotionally complex album would be recorded in January 1962, *All Alone*. In her book about her father, Nancy Sinatra writes, "If you have this album and haven't thought about it for a long time, play it now. It's one of the best."

---

* *Sinatra Swings* was originally entitled *Swing Along with Me*, but the title had to be changed after Capitol filed an injunction claiming it was too close to their own Sinatra album *Come Swing with Me*.

Sinatra's Preinaugural Gala

On January 6, 1961, John F. Kennedy sent his private plane, the *Caroline*, for Frank Sinatra and Peter Lawford so that they could spend the next two weeks in Washington planning the preinaugural gala. Drawing on a long list of his friends, Frank assembled a stellar cast for the gala, some of whom flew long distances to take part. Participants included Laurence Olivier and Ethel Merman, Leonard Bernstein, Sidney Poitier, Anthony Quinn, Joey Bishop, Louis Prima, Keely Smith, Juliet Prowse, Helen Traubel, Ella Fitzgerald, Gene Kelly, Nat King Cole, Milton Berle, and of course Sinatra. In what has to be one of the most astonishing cases of Frank doing it "his way," his daughter Nancy Sinatra recalled, "Dad wasn't fazed by the news that Olivier and Merman couldn't make the date because they were appearing on Broadway in *Becket* and *Gypsy*, respectively. He just bought all of the seats and closed the shows for that night in both theaters." Also, JFK, Lyndon Johnson, and Eleanor Roosevelt were scheduled to give speeches.

Prior to the festivities, Frank hosted a black-tie reception for the cast, the Kennedys, and the Johnsons in the Statler Hilton's South American suite. Murray Kempton, of the *New York Post*, attended the party and wrote, "All these people, the Sinatras, Nat Coles, Gene Kellys—the most inescapably valuable collection of flesh this side of the register of maharanis—sons of immigrant or second-class citizens of not so long ago. They are in their wealth, their authority, their craft, the heirs of the Roosevelt revolution."

Kempton could not have said the same thing about JFK himself. Sinatra certainly identified with Kennedy—both were liberal Democrats growing up with at least one parent deeply involved in politics, both Catholics, both womanizers, both the subjects of prejudice at one time or another, both overcoming odds to get to the top. Frank, whose loyalty to friends could sometimes border on the fanatical, had done a great deal to help Kennedy get elected. Tonight he basked in the glow of victory.

Like Frank, Jackie Kennedy also had a passion for detail when it came to organizing the event. She made specific plans to cover every aspect of the inauguration. The one thing she couldn't control, however, was the weather. On January 19, almost eight inches of snow fell on Washington, D.C. Jackie had arranged to have buses pick up people at their hotels to transport them to the preinaugural party, but those plans were ruined when the transportation didn't show up because of the storm. As a result, hotel lobbies became jammed with women in minks and men in dinner jackets, all trying, with no success, to get cabs to take them to the National Guard Armory.

The snow was so heavy that even the Kennedys were actually caught in a traffic jam. Frank was frantic that they might not show up at all. When, after ten, he heard that the Kennedys' car was pulling up to the door, he rushed into the swirling snow to personally escort them inside. Taking Jackie by her white-gloved hand, he led her into the raised presidential box. She may have had ambivalent feelings about him, but she certainly did look radiant on his arm in her white satin Oleg Cassini gown with satin elbow-length sleeves. It was stunning in its simplicity, its only decoration a rosette of the same satin at her left waist. "It was a big moment for me, walking Jackie into that joint," Frank would later say. "I'll never forget the feeling."

Sinatra's gala got off to a rousing start at 10:40 p.m. when Leonard Bernstein raised his baton for the fanfare and "The Stars and Stripes Forever." Mahalia Jackson sang the national anthem. Even though Ethel Merman had campaigned for Nixon, all was forgiven when she sang "Everything's Coming Up Roses." Frank's reworded "That Old Jack Magic" drew hearty applause from the presidential box. Although the audience may have been smaller than expected, it did not lack enthusiasm.

People were still cheering the performers when JFK took the stage. "I'm proud to be a Democrat," he intoned, "because since the time of Thomas Jefferson, the Democratic Party has been identified with the pursuit of excellence, and we saw excellence tonight. The happy relationship between the arts and politics which has characterized our long history I think reached culmination tonight.

"I know we're all indebted to a great friend, Frank Sinatra," he continued. "Long before he could sing, he used to poll a Democratic precinct back in New Jersey. That precinct has grown to cover a country. But long after he has ceased to sing, he is going to be standing up and speaking for the Democratic Party, and I thank him on behalf of all of you tonight. You cannot imagine the work he has done to make this show a success."

Frank Sinatra would say that he wanted the preinaugural gala to be "the greatest show ever." He had certainly achieved his goal. In retrospect, January 19, 1961, was likely also one of the happiest nights of his life.

Sinatra Makes a Deal with the Devil

In late 1960, President John F. Kennedy appointed his thirty-five-year-old brother Bobby as attorney general of the United States. Sam Giancana told Frank Sinatra that this was a sucker punch he hadn't expected. In Giancana's mind, the only reason JFK gave his brother such a powerful position was because he wanted Bobby to "clear away all markers." In other words, Giancana believed that JFK wanted Bobby to eradicate the very same underworld figures who had helped JFK get elected, thereby alleviating any future problems that might arise in terms of returned favors—and do it all under the guise of "a war on organized crime."

In fact, organized crime was being investigated by the Senate and RFK long before the 1960 election. Bobby's first investigations of Jimmy Hoffa had actually occurred while he served as majority counsel to the Kefauver Committee. "Would you tell us if you have opposition from anybody that you dispose of them by having them stuffed in a trunk? Is that what you do, Mr. Giancana?" Bobby asked Giancana at that time. Giancana declined to answer. "Would you tell us anything about your operations or will you just giggle every time I ask you a question?" Bobby pushed. Giancana still declined to answer. Bobby then said, "I thought only little girls giggled, Mr. Giancana." It was a moment few would forget.

It is true, though, that when Bobby became attorney general, he turned the heat way up and was more eager than ever to eradicate *all* underworld activity from the United States—not just Giancana and his cronies. To that end, he instructed J. Edgar Hoover to mobilize the FBI's resources. Bobby even recruited the Internal Revenue Service to step up its pursuit of certain syndicate figures suspected of tax evasion. Moreover, he appointed a committee to compile a comprehensive list of men to be investigated and prosecuted, some of whom were Frank Sinatra's pallies—like Giancana, Mickey Cohen, and Johnny Roselli. But some were not, like Jimmy Hoffa and Roy Cohn.

Though not directed solely at Giancana, certainly none of Bobby's pursuits were good news for him or for any of his rich and powerful underworld associates. Moreover, Sam had certain favors he had planned to ask of the Kennedys in the very near future, and he expected those wishes to be granted as a reward for his involvement in the successful West Virginia primary. Joe Kennedy had asked Frank to appeal to Sam to use his strong underworld connections to "encourage" the coal miners' unions (and anyone else on whom they had influence in West Virginia) to vote for the Kennedy ticket. Not only had Sam done as requested, but he was successful in the venture—and wasn't about to let anyone forget it.

In March 1961, Sam visited Frank at the Fontainebleau in Miami. He said he needed a big favor. "I need you to get Bobby Kennedy to back off of his investigation of me and my friends," Sam said one night while he and Frank sat at the hotel's bar. "This bullshit has to stop, Frank. You know it. And I know it."

"I got no sway with that crazy Mick," Frank said of RFK.

"Fine, then go to the old man," Sam said, referring to Joe Kennedy.

Frank hadn't been very happy when Joe Kennedy asked him to discuss the Kennedys' problem in West Virginia with Sam Giancana. Now he was just as unhappy about Giancana's request to appeal to the Kennedy patriarch. However, what was he going to do? Turn Sam down? "Don't worry about it," Frank said. "I'll take care of it for you."

"What's your plan, then?" Sam wanted to know.

"I'll start with the old man," Frank said, taking a deep drag from his cigarette. "And if I can't talk to him, I'll talk to *the* man." By *the* man, he meant the president.

Sam was delighted. "Okay, so we got a deal then, right?" he asked Frank.

Frank didn't want to go quite that far. He just smiled and tossed back his drink. But as far as Sam was concerned, they did have a deal.

The Return of Marilyn Monroe

By the summer of 1961, Frank Sinatra, who was forty-five years old, and Marilyn Monroe, thirty-four, had known each other for about seven years. At the end of the 1950s, after their marriages ended—Marilyn's to Joe DiMaggio and Frank's to Ava Gardner—the two took solace in each other's arms and ended up in bed together on a number of occasions. Marilyn continued seeing Frank from time to time, even during her marriage to Arthur Miller, from whom she officially separated at the end of 1960.

While Frank had romantic feelings for Marilyn, his relationship with her was not one to which he could ever become committed. Even after all this time, no one could take Ava's place in his heart. Moreover, Marilyn had her own problems. As it had been in the 1950s when they lived together as roommates, Frank had no patience with women he viewed as either weak or vulnerable. Marilyn's self-destructive nature and dependency on alcohol and pills bothered him now more than ever. Still, Frank was usually kind to her, and she appreciated that about him and had strong feelings for him because of it. Since she felt that she really wasn't worthy of love—especially when she was in her midthirties and agonizing about aging—she always seemed to attract men who would use her and then discard her. At least Frank didn't do that to her.

Renowned makeup artist George Masters recalled of his days working for Marilyn, "I would arrive at noon, and she'd still be in bed. Then she'd get up and start staggering around, groggy, and put on a Sinatra record. Then she would flop back in bed and tell me to keep changing the records. Always Sinatra records. Nothing else. I would stay there changing Sinatra records or talking to her, trying to bring her around."

After a brief stay at the Payne Whitney Psychiatric Clinic in New York in February 1961, Marilyn wanted to spend some time in Los Angeles; that's when Frank offered her his home in Bel-Air. However, at the last minute she changed her mind and decided against staying there, possibly in deference to Joe DiMaggio. She and Joe then enjoyed a vacation in Redington Beach, Florida, in March. Then, in June 1961, Frank invited Marilyn to Vegas. He was appearing at the Sands again and was also planning a party for Dean Martin's forty-fourth birthday on June 7.

From Sands hotel interdepartment correspondence it can be gleaned that certain tactical decisions were made, partly having to do with Frank and Marilyn. One memo, from Entratter to Guzman and Freeman, dated June 5, 1961, states, "Please be advised that under no circumstances is any backstage photographer permitted to photograph Mr. Sinatra and Miss Marilyn Monroe together at the cocktail reception to follow the performance on June 7. Any photographer who attempts to do so will be permanently barred from the hotel. Be advised that this is not only a Sands requirement, it is a requirement of Mr. Sinatra's and, as such, will be absolutely enforced. Thank you."

Another memo, to "All Concerned," dated June 6, 1961, says, "Marilyn Monroe will be Mr. Sinatra's guest. It is Mr. Frank Sinatra's intention that Miss Monroe be accorded the utmost privacy during her brief stay here at the Sands. She will be registered in Mr. Sinatra's suite. Under no circumstances is she or Mr. Sinatra to be disturbed by telephone calls or visitors before two p.m."

President Kennedy's sisters Pat Lawford and Jean Smith were also present for the Las Vegas opening night, as were Elizabeth Taylor and her then husband Eddie Fisher, as well as Dean and Jeanne Martin, with whom Marilyn sat. (Dean wasn't performing; this was a Frank Sinatra opening, not a Rat Pack engagement.) "She was beautiful, a vision with a great smile, lots of teased blonde hair, and a dress that was so low cut you couldn't take your eyes off her bosom. However, she was also quite inebriated," said a Las Vegas photojournalist who—along with a photographer for Wide World Photos—was one of the few reporters granted access to the opening-night party in Sinatra's suite.

"Oh, Frankie, c'mon, let's make out for the photographers," Marilyn said in front of the Wide World Photos lensman and the journalist. "I love you, Frankie," she added, slurring her words, "and I want the whole world to know." She was standing behind Frank and had her hands around his waist, as if she was leaning on him for support.

Frank pulled away rather than be photographed with her. When he did so, Marilyn almost lost her balance. He gave her a concerned look and told one of his bodyguards, "Keep an eye on her."

Marilyn still wanted her picture to be taken with Frank. She sidled over to him like a kitten and motioned to the photographer with her index finger, indicating that he should take the shot while Frank wasn't looking. She was being playful. Just as the photographer was about to take the picture, one of Frank's bodyguards swooped in and grabbed the camera. He handed it to Frank and whispered something in his ear. Then Frank walked up to the photographer and the writer and hissed at them, "Next time you try that, I'll crack your skull open with this camera, the both of ya."

At that moment, Marilyn walked over to Frank with very uneasy footing. "Frankie, I'm gonna throw up," she warned him. She didn't look well.

Frank appeared alarmed. "When?" he asked.

"Now. *Right now*," she exclaimed. "I mean it, Frankie!"

Frank rushed Marilyn out of the room as quickly as possible.

Sinatra Betrays Giancana

Eight months had passed since Frank Sinatra made the vague promise to Sam Giancana that he would talk to Bobby Kennedy about easing up on his investigation of him and his business associates.

In August 1961, Joe Kennedy contacted Frank once again. He wanted to reiterate his appreciation for Frank's participation in the election and for helping to swing the West Virginia primary. He also again expressed his gratitude for Frank's work on the preinaugural gala. He then extended an invitation from the president to entertain Sinatra at the White House. He also invited him to Hyannis Port, the family's compound. Of course, Frank was very happy about all of this good news.

A couple weeks later, though, Giancana took some of the air out of Frank's sails. Giancana's friend from Philadelphia Thomas DiBella remembered, "Giancana, having heard that Frank was going to be with the Kennedys, called Frank and said, 'Hey, pallie, don't forget about me.' Frank stalled and said, 'Well, I'll see what I can do. But, you know, I, uh, I can't make no promises. I mean, you know...' Sam exploded at that," said DiBella. "'You *already* promised me, Frank,' he said. 'Now deliver or you'll be sorry. *You're* the one always sayin' a deal is a deal.'"

According to DiBella, Frank didn't like being threatened by Sam. He lost his temper and said, "Don't ruin this for me. I worked hard for this honor. Now, *screw you*, Sam, if you're not gonna give me a break here. Screw you, hear me? I'm not scared of you, pal. If you think I am, well, you're an idiot. In fact, *you're* a bigger idiot than you think *I* am."

Sam hung up on him.

"This was not good," recalled Thomas DiBella. "This was not good at all. Frank must've been crazy to have said those things to Sam." In fact, Sinatra wasn't the least bit intimidated by Sam Giancana or any other underworld character. In his mind, they were tough guys—but so was he. Of course, they were also dangerous. However, because he was famous, he felt invincible. Or as he liked to say, "They're not going to take out Frank Sinatra, now are they?" So he wasn't the least bit concerned about Giancana's anger. In fact, he thoroughly enjoyed his White House visit on September 23, 1961, and never—at least not to anyone's knowledge, anyway—gave Sam a second thought. Dave Powers, a presidential aide, recalled, "I still remember how he showed the White House maître d' how to make Bloody Marys with his own fantastic special recipe. He sat on the balcony sipping his drink and looking out at the sun streaming in and the wonderful view of Washington. He turned to me and said, 'Dave, all the work I did for Jack. Sitting here like this makes it all worthwhile.'"

The next day, Frank flew to Hyannis Port with Pat Lawford and Ted Kennedy on one of the Kennedys' planes. The day after that,

Frank, JFK, and a few other friends and family members went cruising for three and a half hours off Cape Cod on the *Honey Fitz*.

Senator George Smathers recalled, "Though everyone was having a good time, JFK was just a little cold to Sinatra. It was as if he was long past the buddy-buddy phase. Sinatra didn't notice, or maybe didn't care. On that cruise, he did ask Peter Lawford to talk to Bobby about laying off of Giancana. He also said he wanted Peter to arrange for him to have a meeting with Bobby. I know for a fact that Peter did later talk to Bobby, but he was told to mind his own business; Bobby was still going after Giancana, no matter what. Bobby also said he wouldn't meet with Frank about any of it."

When Peter told Frank that he wasn't able to arrange a meeting for him with Bobby, he probably expected Frank to blow up. However, Sinatra just said, "Oh, well. Hey, pallie, you tried."

If Frank seemed relieved, that's because he *was* relieved. The last thing he wanted was to actually speak to Bobby about Sam Giancana. His entreatment to Peter was halfhearted. "I'm not gonna jeopardize my good relationship with the Kennedys for this punk mobster," he told one of his close friends. "What do I look like? Do I look like some kinda moron? I don't care if Sam's hacked off or not."

Thomas DiBella continues the story: "When Frank got back from the trip with the Kennedys, he lied and told Sam that he and Bobby *had* talked. But he never talked to Bobby on that trip. Yet Frank said, 'Yeah, Mo [sometimes he called Giancana that], I wrote your name down, and I said, 'This is my buddy boy. I just want you to know that,' and he claimed Bobby nodded in recognition that he wouldn't screw with Sam. But that was pure bullshit, and Sam somehow sensed it. His gut told him that Frank was lying.

"Then, when Sam had it checked out, he found out that Frank was confiding in certain people that, yes, it was all bullshit, that he hadn't talked to Bobby and that he had no intention of talking to Bobby.

"Now Sam was pissed at Frank—I mean, really pissed—but he didn't say nothing at that point. He just kept quiet. Sam wasn't the only one with intuition, though. Frank started suspecting that Sam was ticked off with him."

Indeed, transcripts of federal wiretaps from December 6, 1961, reflect the essence of DiBella's memory. One day, Sam and his California associate Johnny Roselli were speaking on the telephone when Johnny told Sam that Frank had "an idea that you're mad at him."

"He has a guilty conscience," Sam responded. "I never said nothing about it. But why lie to me? I haven't got that coming."

Johnny agreed. "If he can't deliver," he said, "I'd want him to tell me, 'John, the load's too heavy.' "

"That's right," Sam said. "At least then you know how to work. You won't let your guard down. When he says he's gonna do a guy a little favor, I don't give a shit how long it takes, he's got to do a guy a little favor!"

Over the years, accounts of Frank Sinatra's relationship with the Kennedys have always suggested that Frank simply had no influence over Joe, Jack, and Bobby Kennedy where Sam Giancana was concerned, no matter how hard he tried. It's true that Frank didn't have any influence over them, but it's also true that at least where Sam was concerned, *he never tried.* He may have implied that he would intervene...he may have promised he was going to do so...he may even have asked someone else, like Peter Lawford, to start a dialogue with them. However, from all available evidence, Frank backed off from truly assisting Sam Giancana with the Kennedys.

Nicholas D'Amato, a former member of the so-called Philadelphia Mafia family, observed, "Playing Sam Giancana for a sucker? If he wasn't so talented, Sinatra never would have gotten away with it. To break a promise and then lie about it? I can't think of anyone else who would've continued to breathe air after doing that to Sam."

Thomas DiBella adds, "I once asked Sam why he let Frank get away with it and Sam said, 'What can I do? Beat him up? Have him killed? He's one of the most famous men in the world and I'm gonna be the one to do him in?' So, you might say Sinatra had something on Sam and the rest of the mobsters who may have been pissed off at him. He was too famous to touch."

By the fall of 1961, word had begun to spread once again that Frank had some sort of special relationship with the underworld. But the truth is that the mob never did much for Frank Sinatra, and Frank Sinatra never did much for the mob—not that anyone has ever been able to document, anyway—except for perhaps the occasional concert.

A couple of months after Frank's betrayal of Sam, Sam's associate Johnny Formosa suggested (in another FBI wiretapped conversation) that he "take out" Sinatra. Sam, even with the passing of some time, still wasn't interested.

"Come on. Let's show 'em," Formosa pushed. "Let's show those asshole Hollywood fruitcakes that they can't get away with it as if nothing's happened. Let's hit Sinatra. Or I could whack out a couple of those other guys. [Peter] Lawford and [Dean] Martin. I could take [Sammy] Davis and put his other eye out."

"No," Giancana said. "I've got other plans for them."

It turns out that the plan Sam Giancana had in mind was to have Frank Sinatra and his "pallies" open the Villa Venice, Sam's new nightclub in Chicago.

"It was flashier than a Hollywood premiere," said George Jacobs of the Rat Pack's engagement at the Villa Venice, "with the guests here being a who's who of Illinois mob royalty. Foreshadowing the Bellagio and the Venetian by four decades, Mr. Sam had gondolas ferrying the guests to the entrance with gondoliers singing 'O Sole Mio.' There was also an adjacent den of iniquity called the Quonset Hut where huge amounts of money were won and lost at Vegas-style and -level games of chance. The Summit grossed many tax-free millions for the Giancana outfit. Shortly after the Summit, Villa Venice, for all its elaborate new trappings set up for Mr. S.'s appearance, burned mysteriously to the ground and was never rebuilt."

The Problem with Marilyn

At the end of August 1961, after Frank returned from his cruise with the Kennedys, he and Marilyn entertained guests on his own yacht. Prior to their leaving Frank's home for the boat, Frank asked Jeanne Martin to help get Marilyn dressed. Apparently she was too disoriented from her medication to do so herself. Once they were on the yacht together, Frank lost patience with her. Jeanne Martin recalled, "He couldn't wait to get her off that boat. She was giving him a hard time, taking pills and drinking. She was even talking marriage. Frank told me, 'I swear to Christ, I'm ready to throw her right off this boat right now.' When they got ashore, he called one of his assistants and had him escort Marilyn home."

"Do you think you should stop seeing her?" Jeanne asked Frank. "She seems to not be doing well."

"I don't know what to do about her," Frank said, seeming concerned, according to Jeanne's memory.

"I'm surprised you have as much patience with her as you do," Jeanne remarked.

"By now I would have cut any other dame loose," Frank told her. "But this one—I just can't do it."

By the beginning of 1962, Marilyn was in so much trouble, Frank was concerned for her well-being. Jim Whiting, a good friend of Frank's from New Jersey, related, "She refused to stop with the drugs, which, by the way, were prescribed by her doctor. It wasn't like she was scoring them in the streets. [By this time, Frank and Marilyn were sharing the same psychiatrist, Dr. Ralph Greenson.] Worried that maybe she was a lost cause, Frank threw his hands in the air and said there wasn't much he could do if she wouldn't help herself. 'She wants to kill herself,' he said. 'I've been there. I didn't know what to do about it then, and I still don't.'

"He was busy with *The Manchurian Candidate* film at the time, and that was important to him and took a lot of energy. He said it was his toughest role. I remember him saying, 'I'm too old for this shit, all this anxiety, all this memorization.' He said that all of those speeches in that film were driving him crazy. He couldn't sleep at night, he said, with all those words running through his head."

The Manchurian Candidate, directed by John Frankenheimer and based on the book by Richard Condon, with Laurence Harvey in the title role, and also Janet Leigh and Angela Lansbury, would turn out to be one of Sinatra's finest movies. He and Harvey play soldiers who are captured by the communists during the Korean War. Brainwashed and then released, they become part of an assassination plot (orchestrated by Angela Lansbury, who plays Harvey's mother). Frank's excellent performance compared favorably with those he gave in *From Here to Eternity* and *The Man with the Golden Arm*.

"The movie was tough on him," confirmed his butler, George Jacobs. "But Marilyn was taking a toll on him at the same time."

"What do you think I can do to get a break from Marilyn?" Frank asked George, whose opinion he valued. The two were packing Sinatra's suitcases for an upcoming trip.

"We can't just take a break from people we care about, Mr. S.," George said as he folded one of Frank's shirts. "Sometimes it's a full-time job."

"Yes, but Marilyn's getting worse..."

"Maybe just ditch her, then?" George suggested, according to his memory of the conversation.

"Like Ava ditched me?" Frank responded. "No. I couldn't do that to a person."

"You're too good-hearted, Mr. S.," George observed.

"I'd just like to think I can do better for Marilyn than what Ava did for me," Frank concluded. "That's all."

Publicity Stunt Engagement

*I*n February 1962, Frank Sinatra surprised many of his friends, as well as the media and public, by announcing that he was going to marry twenty-six-year-old, blue-eyed dancer, singer, and actress Juliet Prowse. The two, who had met in August 1959, had been dating off and on for the past ten months. Most people were dumbfounded by the relationship; the two had never seemed to have much in common. Because Frank was also involved with other women at this time—Marilyn included—even those in his inner circle were confused by the sudden announcement.

While promoting his third memoir, *Why Me?*, Sammy Davis hit the nail on the head when he said he thought that part of the reason for the engagement to Juliet was Frank's way of putting some distance between himself and Marilyn. "Marilyn was a sweetheart, but Frank had his hands full with her," Sammy said. "Next thing I knew, I got a call from him telling me he's involved with Juliet, and gonna marry her. And, to me, it was like my phony marriage to Loray White. I had my reasons and figured he had his. I asked him about it, and he didn't really want to discuss it with me. So, I figured, 'Hey, this isn't any of my business, anyway.' But I do think it had to do with Marilyn in some way; maybe trying to break from her a little."*

"It was a strange and brief fling," said Bea King of the Sinatra-Prowse union. King is a former Copa Girl who was a close friend of Juliet Prowse in 1962.

"What happened was, a dancer [Barrie Chase] walked out on the film *Can-Can*, which Sinatra was doing at this time with Shirley MacLaine. In came Juliet, replacing her. She was unknown at the time, originally from South Africa.

"Frank romanced her a little, got to know her. They hit it off, which was not surprising. She was beautiful. He gave her a $10,000 pearl necklace; I saw it with my own eyes, so maybe there really was something momentarily significant going on between them.

"Soon after, they were engaged. Michael Romanoff hosted an engagement party for them at his restaurant [Romanoff's]. I was there. Frank gave her a five-carat diamond. But when I asked Juliet about Frank after the engagement party, she dismissed the whole thing, telling me, 'Oh, don't be silly. We'll never marry.' When I asked why, she said, 'Frank's not serious about this thing, and neither am I. This is just for fun.' That's exactly what she told me. 'This is just for fun.'"

When Juliet invited Frank to go to South Africa to meet her parents, he decided to do it.

"He met her parents. She met his. And all for a publicity stunt?" Bea King noted years later. "But, I thought, 'Well, this *is* Hollywood, isn't it?' I happen to know that her heart really belonged to her manager, the much younger [than Frank] Eddie Goldstone. She loved him, not Frank. Since she was unable to become a United States

---

* On January 10, 1958, Sammy Davis married African-American dancer Loray White, though, as he remembered it, he was not in love with her. He was dating Kim Novak at the time and the interracial relationship had so angered egomaniacal and racist studio head Harry Cohn that, Davis said, Cohn put a contract out on his life. While Davis was appearing at the Sands in early January 1958, Sinatra warned him that he should not go back to Los Angeles until "I straightened things out with Cohn." Davis then married White just to get out of the tight jam with Cohn and the mob. The marriage lasted two months.

citizen for two more years, she became his 'ward' at about the same time she and Frank got engaged. Eddie was sponsoring her, making sure she was gainfully employed, that sort of thing."

"Frank just got swept away by the whole thing," said Dean Martin. "She was a good kid. She was young and good in the sack. It was no skin off his nose to help her out. She needed the publicity, he gave it to her. I told Frank people were thinking it wasn't a real engagement. He laughed and said, 'Oh, ye assholes of little faith.'"

"A great girl. A wonderful girl," Frank said to reporters who tracked him down after a round of golf at the Hillcrest Country Club in Los Angeles.

"You really shook us up," said one of the reporters, referring to the surprise of the engagement.

"I'm a little shook up myself," he said. "I'm forty-six now. It's time I settled down."

When asked when the wedding would take place, Frank answered, "It probably won't be for some time. Whenever she sets the day, that's okay for me. I'll let her call all the shots. That's the way it's done. I know she wants to have her parents come over from South Africa and I want to have them here, too. After all, she's their only daughter. They're wonderful people. She's got a brother who's a doctor. I know he'll want to be here for the wedding, too. A wonderful guy."

When had Frank ever been so cooperative with reporters, giving them so much detail about a relationship? It seemed a little fishy. The reporter even mentioned that Juliet was dating Eddie Goldstone, and he—Sinatra—was "linked with Marilyn Monroe." Frank didn't fly off the handle—which was also suspicious. Instead he said, "Juliet has been my one romance. Our dates have been private. Not public." He also added that Juliet was preparing a new Las Vegas nightclub act, to be written by his friends, songwriters Jimmy Van Heusen and Sammy Cahn. He was so forthcoming; it just didn't seem kosher.

Meanwhile, Juliet was just as chatty. "Frank doesn't want me to work," she told Louella Parsons. "But I do. After working this long and this hard for a career, I'd hate to give it up." Meanwhile, Eddie Goldstone began negotiating to get her out of her contract with 20th Century–Fox and set her up with her own production company, called Pirouette Productions, and all because of the sudden publicity that the association with Sinatra had thus far generated.

When asked about Juliet's comments, Frank told *another* reporter, Earl Wilson, "She's not going to do any work. I'd rather not have it." As for that deal with 20th Century–Fox? Frank said he expected her to "just walk away from it."

In fact, Juliet Prowse was anything but blasé about her career; she wasn't going to "walk away" from any opportunity or give up the spotlight. In 1962, one movie studio executive said of her, "Prowse is a cocky, arrogant kid who's been bumming around this business since she was twelve years old. Nothing is going to stand in her way."

If the purpose of the "engagement" was to encourage people to become interested in Juliet Prowse, it worked. After she and Frank were viewed as a couple, she became a major star. The engagement lasted just a short time. Supposedly, Juliet called it off. "Talk about short engagements," Johnny Carson said. "Frank has had longer engagements in Las Vegas."

JFK Snubs Sinatra

*I*n early 1962, Sam Giancana and his pals were still stewing over the way Frank Sinatra had broken his promise to intervene on their behalf with Bobby Kennedy. "Frank's got big ideas about being ambassador or something," Johnny Roselli had said in an FBI-wiretapped telephone conversation with Sam on December 4, 1961. "But Pierre Salinger [Kennedy's press secretary] and them guys, they don't want him. They treat him like a whore. You fuck her, you pay her, and she's through."

RFK's ongoing investigations of Sam Giancana and others, such as Roselli, Carlos Marcello, Mickey Cohen, Jimmy Hoffa, and by virtue of his association with them, Sinatra as well, continued unabated. For the most part, Frank hadn't been negatively impacted by his dealings with the mob. However, in March 1962 he would finally pay a steep price for his relationships with the underworld.

President Kennedy was due to stay at the Sinatra home while on the West Coast on March 24 through 26. Since Jackie had plans to be in India and Pakistan at the time, JFK was anxious to have a little downtime with his Hollywood pals. Sinatra was very excited about the visit, spending many hundreds of thousands of dollars completely renovating his compound on the grounds of the Tamarisk Country Club in Palm Springs. In the main house, he built an impressive new dining room with majestic cathedral ceilings. He also turned what had once been a small kitchen into a butler's pantry and then added an enormous new state-of-the-art kitchen. He transformed one bedroom into a library—this was the room JFK had stayed in previously; he left in place the plaque that said, "John F. Kennedy Slept Here November 6th and 7th, 1960." He also expanded the living room and bar. Outside, he relandscaped the entire pool area to shield it from the nearby golf course. He then redecorated everything else, all of the other rooms, with new wallpaper, new paint, new furnishings. The only room he didn't touch was his own bedroom, which now seemed very small compared to the rest of the house. He'd even remodeled the so-called Christmas Tree House, adding to it two bungalows that were intended to house the Secret Service.

Demonstrating his motto that excess is never enough, Frank also built a fifty-by-fifty-foot asphalt heliport for the president's helicopter. He had it built with the Federal Aviation Administration's approval. (This wasn't that unusual, apparently; Dean Martin also had a heliport at his estate in Ventura County, California.) However, later, when neighbors became upset about it, some began looking up the permits and discovered that Frank had failed to obtain one. When Frank finally applied for one, he was turned down by the Riverside County Planning Commission on the grounds that helicopter flights from his estate would endanger nearby homes.

In February 1962, Bobby Kennedy's initial investigation of the underworld was completed and a report compiled by the Justice Department. In part, it read, "Sinatra has had a long and wide association with hoodlums and racketeers which seems to be continuing. The nature of Sinatra's work may, on occasion, bring him into contact with underworld figures, but this cannot account for his friendship and/or financial involvement with people such as Joe and Rocco Fischetti, cousins of Al Capone; Paul Emilio ['Skinny'] D'Amato, John Formosa, and Sam Giancana, all of whom are on our list of racketeers. No other entertainer appears to be mentioned nearly so frequently with racketeers. Available information indicates not only that Sinatra is associated with each of the above-named racketeers, but that they apparently maintain contact with one another. This indicates a possible community of interest involving Sinatra and racketeers in Illinois, Indiana, New Jersey, Florida and Nevada."

After Bobby finished his report, JFK told him to make a decision about his visit to Frank's home, whether or not it was safe not only from a security standpoint but also as a matter of public relations. Bobby didn't have to think too long or too hard about it; he canceled the trip, reasoning that under the circumstances it made no sense for the president of the United States to stay with Sinatra.

Peter Lawford was chosen by Bobby to break the news to Frank, a task Peter dreaded.

Peter, who had known Frank since 1944, did not want to incur Sinatra's wrath. He well remembered what had happened the last time Frank was angry at him. It was back in 1954, during Frank's marriage to Ava Gardner. Peter and his friend Milt Ebbins had social drinks with Ava and her sister Bappie at a club in Beverly Hills. (Peter had once dated Ava back in the mid-1940s, years before she even knew Frank.) They were only together for about an hour, but that was enough time for the ever-pesky Louella Parsons to sniff out a story. The next day she erroneously reported that Peter and Ava had a "date" and suggested that it could be the rekindling of an old romance. When he heard about it, Frank became upset with Peter. One of his pallies fooling around with his wife. Not acceptable.

In a February 1976 interview with reporter Steve Dunleavy, Peter remembered what happened next: "I was in bed at three in the morning, and the telephone rings. Then comes a voice at the other end of the telephone, like something out of a Mario Puzo novel: 'What's this about you and Ava? Listen, you creep. You wanna stay healthy? I'll have your legs broken, ya' bum. If I hear anything more about this thing with Ava, you've had it.'"

After that call, Frank didn't speak to Peter for five years. "It was as if Frank always operated from some sort of old Italian code: Just walk away, never look back," Peter said. The two reconciled in 1959.

Now Peter had to telephone Frank to tell him that JFK would not be staying at his home. At first, Frank was hurt, then he was angry—and he chose to take it out on the messenger. "If you can't be loyal to me, then the hell with you," he told Peter.

"I'm married to 'em, Frank," Peter tried to explain. "My hands are tied."

Frank slammed down the phone and then, according to George Jacobs, who was present in the room at the time, tore it right out of the wall.

Peter had already been on shaky ground with Frank before delivering the bad news. Frank's close friend and confidant Tony Oppedisano recalled, "From what he told me, Frank had felt for a long time that the relationship with Peter had become one-sided. He felt that Peter's loyalties didn't run as deep for him as [Sinatra's] ran for Peter, and this event with Kennedy served to reinforce that in his mind. If the tables had been turned, Frank would have fought like hell for Peter, and he didn't feel that Peter had done that for him." That said, Frank would now banish Peter from his world once again. He would also cut him from the two upcoming Rat Pack films, *Robin and the 7 Hoods* and *4 for Texas*.

Again according to Jacobs, Frank's next call—from another room—was to Bobby Kennedy. "What the hell, Bobby?" he wanted to know. Sinatra reasoned to Bobby that JFK had previously stayed at the house with no problem, so what had changed? Apparently Bobby said that what had changed was that *he* was in charge now, and he wasn't going to allow it.

"They had angry words," George Jacobs recalled, "back and forth. Until Frank finally just hollered into the phone, 'Screw you, Bobby! *Screw you!*' and slammed it down. Then, again, he pulled another phone right out of the wall, and I'm thinking it's a good thing we had all those extra lines installed for the president!"

Storming to yet another room, Frank telephoned Peter for more information. That was when Peter told Frank of JFK's plans to stay elsewhere. Frank was stunned. "You'll never guess where he's staying," Frank told George. "*Bing Crosby's house!* A Republican! I can't believe this!"

"But why?" George asked.

"Peter says it's because Bing's house is up against a mountain and more secure than mine. It's all bullshit."

Then Frank went on, as George Jacobs recalled it, "a violent rampage," ransacking his home, during which he even pried the "Kennedy Slept Here" plaque off the wall. "I followed him around the house while he was searching to destroy anything that represented Peter Lawford or the Kennedys," recalled George Jacobs. "I was very scared that Mr. S. was going to have a heart attack, that's how upset he was. I didn't even try to stop him. I knew better than to get in his way."

After his tirade, Sinatra collapsed in a chair, exhausted and heaving, completely out of breath. He took a look around. "Jesus Christ almighty," he exclaimed, shaking his head in amazement. "Can you believe what just happened here?" he asked George.

"Not really," George said, studying the mess all around him.

"Well, what can I say? I guess this is why I don't have ulcers," Frank said, trying to collect himself. Then, after a moment, he got serious again. "You know, if Joe Kennedy hadn't had that stroke [in 1961, which had rendered him paralyzed and in a wheelchair], none of this would be happening. Bobby would never do this if Joe was around to stop him."

"I know that's true, Mr. S."

The two men sat silently among the ruins for a few moments. Frank chuckled. "By the way, if anyone ever asks," he said, glancing around, "you did all this shit. Not me. Got that?"

"Got it, Mr. S."

Elvis

*I*n March 1962, while Frank was making another appearance at the Fontainebleau in Miami (where he would be joined by the Summit during the last three nights), he taped a television special for ABC— his fourth and last for the sponsor, Timex—with guests Sammy Davis, Peter Lawford, Joey Bishop, daughter Nancy Sinatra, and special guest Elvis Presley, who had just returned to civilian life after two years in the army. In fact, the show was called *Frank Sinatra's Welcome Home Party for Elvis Presley.*

Despite the benevolent title of his program, Frank actually had little time for Elvis. "His kind of music is deplorable," he famously said back in 1956, "a rancid-smelling aphrodisiac. It fosters almost totally negative and destructive reactions in young people." In fact, Frank hated all rock and roll music—he said it was "sung, played, and written for the most part by cretinous goons."

"He has a right to his opinion," Elvis countered at a press conference in October 1957 when asked about Frank's comments, "but I can't see him knocking it for no good reason. I admire him as a performer and an actor but I think he's badly mistaken about this. If I remember correctly, he was also part of a trend. I don't see how he can call the youth of today immoral and delinquent. It's the greatest music ever and it will continue to be so. I like it, and I'm sure many other persons feel the same way."

Whatever Sinatra thought of Presley's style of entertainment, he was shrewd enough to realize that Elvis's return from the army was such big news that his first TV appearance would generate huge ratings. Therefore, he paid Elvis $100,000 to make a ten-minute appearance on the program. Colonel Parker, Elvis's manager—in an unintentional tip of the hat to George Evans's tricks back in the 1940s with Sinatra at the Paramount—made certain that three hundred girls from Presley's fan club were present in the audience to guarantee a strong audience response.

After Elvis, who appeared constrained wearing an ill-fitting tuxedo, did a couple of numbers ("Fame and Fortune," "Stuck on You"), Frank joined him onstage. "I'll tell ya what we'll do," Frank said, taking charge. "You do 'Witchcraft,' and I'll do one of those others…" (which meant that Elvis would sing one of Sinatra's songs and Sinatra would sing one of Presley's). Though they exhibited little chemistry together, this meeting of two pop-culture icons is still considered a classic moment by both Sinatra and Presley enthusiasts.

In retrospect, the most noteworthy part of that broadcast really had nothing to do with Elvis, and everything to do with Frank. At one point during the hourlong broadcast, Sinatra—wearing an exquisitely tailored dark suit and black bow tie—walked to center stage and casually lit a cigarette. Taking a puff, he looked at it intently as the orchestra swelled behind him. Then, tilting back his head, he began the first few notes of a lovely rendition of composer Allie Wrubel's "Gone with the Wind," from Sinatra's pensive *Only the Lonely* album. It was a natural-feeling performance, simple and elegant. During it, Frank demonstrated once again what a masterful communicator he was as he conveyed the sadness of the song ("yesterday's kisses are still on my lips") in such a direct, easy manner. At one point, he paused and casually let out a small cough. It was Sinatra at his heartbreaking, aching best. Then, at the end of the song, he took a final puff and lowered his head sadly.

"Elvis was all the rage at the time," Frank Sinatra Jr. recalled. "But I think that my father proved that when you strip away all the hysteria and mania, at the end of the day what matters is real emotion, real singing."

Frank's Plan to Marry Marilyn

*I*n the summer of 1962, Frank Sinatra embarked on a record-shattering concert tour—called the World Tour for Children—during which he visited children's hospitals and youth centers in Hong Kong (where he donated $95,000 to children's charities); Israel (where he established the Frank Sinatra International Youth Center for Arab and Jewish Children); Greece (where he was awarded the Athens Medal of Honor); Rome, Geneva, Madrid, and London (where he visited the Children's Home for the Blind); Paris (where he dedicated the Sinatra Wing of the Summer Home of the Saint Jean de Dieu for Crippled Boys at Bruyères-le-Châtel); and Monaco. In just ten weeks, Sinatra personally financed thirty concerts and raised more than a million dollars.

Frank was deeply affected by the World Tour for Children. Upon his return, he said that visiting and attempting to comfort so many ill and crippled children filled him with a deeper sense of compassion than he'd known before.

After the departure of Juliet Prowse from his life, Frank and Marilyn picked up where they left off and resumed dating. According to one of Frank's trusted attorneys, Frank actually considered marrying Marilyn in 1962. "One day he came into my office and talked it over with me, asked me for my advice," recalled the attorney. "What do you think about me and Marilyn gettin' hitched?" Frank asked. The lawyer would recall being surprised, but trying not to show it. Putting on his best poker face, he said, "You're generous to come up with this idea, Frank, but marrying Marilyn could pose a future problem."

"How's that?" Frank asked.

"She's so desperate, if you marry her and it goes sour, she'll go off the deep end and self-destruct..."

"...and I would end up feeling responsible," Frank said, finishing the attorney's thought.

"And one more thing," added the lawyer. "Do you really want history to show that Marilyn Monroe killed herself while she was married to Frank Sinatra?"

Frank mulled it over. "Maybe if she's my wife," he said, "everyone will back off, give her some space, allow her to get herself together."

"Could be," the attorney offered.

The lawyer did what he could to discourage Frank, but Frank wasn't deterred. Before he left the attorney's office, he said, "I'm gonna want to do it in Europe, not in the States. I don't want to have to deal with Joe [DiMaggio]. I want you to look into it. See how this can work, where the best place would be to do it quietly."

Astonished, the attorney asked, "Frank, what does this mean?"

"Don't go losing your head," Sinatra responded. "Let's consider it a project in development, like a picture [a film]. I'm gonna talk to her about it. And then we'll see what happens."

It's not known if Frank ever discussed wedding plans with Marilyn. The attorney said that the subject was never again raised to him. Whatever the case, the chaos involving Marilyn continued in Frank's life unabated, many of the problems having to do with her fixation over JFK. It didn't help when, after JFK cut all ties with her, he asked her to sing "Happy Birthday" to him at a Madison Square Garden birthday event. The invitation caused her to spiral out of control, thinking that there was a chance for a future with him. When she went to New York to sing for him, she was fired from the movie she was making a the time, *Something's Gotta Give*.

Memories of Marilyn

On July 26, 1962, Frank Sinatra called Pat Kennedy Lawford to say that he regretted what had happened with Peter relating to JFK's visit to Palm Springs. It wasn't an apology. It was a "regret." That said, he still didn't want to make amends with Peter. However, he wondered if Peter and Pat might consider bringing Marilyn Monroe to the Cal-Neva Lodge for a brief vacation. He felt she could probably use it. Frank told Pat he was performing in the main room and that singers Buddy Greco and Roberta Linn were working in the lounge, therefore a good time could be had by all. Pat was against the idea. If Frank wasn't going to apologize for what he'd done to Peter, she didn't want anything to do with him. However, she felt she had to at least mention the invitation to her husband. When she did, Peter couldn't wait to go. If Frank wanted to mend fences—and that's how Peter took the invitation—he was going to cooperate and hope for the best. Marilyn said she would like to go as well.

The next day, July 27, Peter, Pat, and Marilyn departed for a two-day vacation to the Cal-Neva Lodge, via a plane chartered by Sinatra. George Jacobs picked them up at the airport in Nevada in a station wagon. "She looked bad," he recalled of Marilyn. "She had on a black scarf, no makeup, just very washed-out-looking. I thought, 'Christ, when Mr. S. sees her, he ain't gonna be happy.' When he finally did see her, he looked like he'd seen a ghost. He hugged Marilyn and then asked Peter and Pat to leave him alone with her for a moment. I left the room too. Mr. S. had some time alone with Marilyn during which time he assessed the situation. Then he summoned me back and said, 'See to it that she's okay. I'm worried about her.'

"We put her in Chalet 52, one of the quarters reserved for special guests," Jacobs recalled. "Peter and Pat were next door. Mr. S. had made it his mission to ignore Peter even when they were in the same place at the same time with Marilyn. He told me, 'I don't want to make a big deal about it, I just don't want a lot to do with Lawford. For Marilyn, though, let's try to keep it civil.' So when Peter was in his presence, Mr. S. would smile and be very 'pallie'-like. But at one point I was standing next to Mr. S. and Peter came over and tried to make small talk. Frank glared at him and said, 'You're flying awful close to the sun right now. Get lost.' Peter cringed and backed away."

About three hours after Pat and Peter Lawford arrived with Marilyn, they found a surprise in the Cal-Neva lobby: Sam Giancana. Apparently Frank had sent his private jet back to Los Angeles to pick him up and bring him there. For Frank to have invited him to the resort at the same time as the president's sister and her husband seemed to make no sense. Was he deliberately trying to get the Lawfords up to Cal-Neva to force them to be in the presence of Giancana? It didn't seem likely. Still, what was one to make of it? "I can't explain it," George Jacobs recalled. "I didn't ask questions about it. I just let that one go."

Pat wasn't able to let it go, though. "That's it! We have to leave," she told Peter loud enough for Giancana to hear. Peter seemed embarrassed; he felt Giancana had heard her. He walked over to Giancana, shook his hand, and began talking to him. The two then repeatedly glanced back at Marilyn while they spoke, as if they were referring to her. Meanwhile, Marilyn told Pat she didn't feel well and that she could not possibly leave in that moment. She said she couldn't bear to fly again. She then demanded that Pat take her back to her chalet. "I don't feel well," she told her. Pat led her friend away, her hand on the actress's elbow.

Ted Stephens worked in the kitchen at the lodge: "We got this call from Peter Lawford. 'We need coffee in Chalet 52,' he screamed into the phone, then hung up. He sounded frantic. No less than two minutes passed and it was Mr. Sinatra on the phone screaming, 'Where's that goddamn coffee?' I learned later that they were in 52, walking Marilyn around, trying to get her to wake up."

Roberta Linn, who was entertaining at Cal-Neva along with Frank and Buddy Greco, recalled of Marilyn, "She wore the same green dress the entire weekend. Her hair was in disarray. She seemed out of it. She was at Sinatra's show both nights; she would sit in the back looking unhappy. I thought it was such a shame, this girl who had everything yet nothing, really. It was very hard to see her in this condition."

There was more to it than just liquor, though, for Marilyn. She had developed the alarming habit of giving herself injections of phenobarbital, Nembutal, and Seconal—which she referred to as a "vitamin shot." One day in Frank's and Pat's presence—this according to Joe Langford, who was also present—Marilyn opened her purse and pulled out a bunch of syringes while looking for something else. She was casual about it, placing all of the syringes on a table. Frank went white, stunned. "Marilyn. Jesus Christ. What are *they* for?" he asked. Marilyn said, "Oh, those are for my vitamin shots." Pat shook her head. "Oh my God, Marilyn," she said. To which Marilyn said, "It's all right, Pat. I know what I'm doing."

"[Marilyn] was still going through her purse until, finally, she found what she was looking for: a sewing pin," recalled Joe Langford. "As we all stood there with our mouths open—me, Sinatra, and Kennedy's sister—she opened a bottle of pills and picked one out. Then she put a small hole at the end of the capsule and swallowed it. 'Gets into your bloodstream faster that way,' she said cheerfully. She turned back to Pat and said, 'See, I told you I knew what I was doing.' A few hours later, Pat raided Marilyn's purse and got rid of all of the syringes."

"Mr. S. didn't know what to think about any of it," said George Jacobs. "This was pushing it. For Marilyn to maybe *die* at Cal-Neva while he was also on the premises? No. So, after he'd seen enough and realized there was nothing anyone could do for her, he said, 'Okay, that's it. Let's get her out of here, now.' As compassionate as Mr. S. may have been toward Marilyn, he had his limitations. So Pat and Peter took her back to Los Angeles. This was the last time Mr. S. would see Marilyn alive."

Less than a week later, on August 5, 1962, Marilyn Monroe was found dead at her home. In a public statement, Sinatra said he was "deeply saddened" by the news. George Jacobs remembered that "Frank was in shock for weeks, distraught."

When Frank went to Westwood Memorial Park for the funeral, he learned that Joe DiMaggio had given security guards specific instructions to keep him and most everyone else closely connected to Marilyn, including the Kennedys, away. DiMaggio blamed them all for her death, feeling *everyone* could have done a better job where Marilyn was concerned. As a man who had once beaten her, DiMaggio was hardly blameless in making Marilyn what she became.

Out of respect for her memory, Frank Sinatra quietly left Westwood Memorial Park without making a scene.

Swinging '63

$\mathcal{A}$ number of classic Frank Sinatra albums would be released in late 1962 and in 1963, but the best of the lot is doubtless the superb *Sinatra-Basie: An Historic Musical First*, the first of two albums teaming Sinatra and Count Basie. (The second was *It Might as Well Be Swing*, which would be issued in August 1964.) Basie's band swings through numbers like "Pennies from Heaven," "Nice Work If You Can Get It," and "I'm Gonna Sit Right Down and Write Myself a Letter," as Frank gives some of his best and most freewheeling performances. It all sounds improvised—which of course it isn't—lending to the entire album the buoyant feeling of a live performance.

In January, Frank flew to New Jersey to host Dolly's and Marty's fiftieth wedding anniversary party. At this time, Frank sold his parents' modest three-story home to a Hoboken truck firm owner and bought them a new one: a split-level ranch house in Fort Lee with a remote view of the Hudson River. (He purchased the home under the name O'Brien, a name that had been used by his father, who once fought in the ring as Marty O'Brien.) Dolly was proud of her son's gift to her and annoyed when one press account noted that Frank had paid $50,000 for the home. She asked friends to telephone the newspaper and make the correction: The house had actually cost $60,000.

Frank was still close to his parents. His father, Marty, had been a rock to him over the years, especially after Frank became famous and proved he wasn't a "bum." Marty was always present as a sounding board, and Dolly had never changed. She was as irascible as ever, but she loved her son and everyone knew it.

In February 1963, Frank recorded *The Concert Sinatra* in Los Angeles, a collection of Broadway classics. All eleven songs, including "Lost in the Stars" and "This Nearly Was Mine," were recorded on Stage 7 at the Samuel Goldwyn Studios, giving the album a full acoustical sound.

Also in February, *Playboy* published a fascinating in-depth interview with Frank, which raised more than a few eyebrows because of his views on politics and religion. Frank had wanted a strong and insightful piece from *Playboy* and said he wouldn't sit down with the writer unless he promised to "talk turkey, not trivia." He was interviewed on the set of *Come Blow Your Horn*; in his Dual-Ghia automobile en route home from the studio; and during breaks at a Reprise recording session during the recent Count Basie dates. In all, he spent a week with the writer.

When the journalist asked Frank a broad question about the "beliefs that move and shape your life," Frank became impatient. The question was just too vague. "Look, pal, is this going to be an ocean cruise," he wanted to know, "or a quick sail around the harbor? I believe in a thousand things, and I'm curious about a million more. Be more specific."

For starters, Frank revealed that he did not believe in organized religion. "I think I can sum up my religious feelings in a couple of paragraphs," he said. "First: I believe in you and me. I'm like Albert Schweitzer and Bertrand Russell and Albert Einstein in that I have a respect for life—in any form. I believe in nature, in the birds, the sea, the sky, in everything I can see or that there is real evidence for. If these things are what you mean by God, then I believe in God. But I don't believe in a personal God to whom I look for comfort or for a natural on the next roll of the dice. I'm not unmindful of man's seeming need for faith; I'm for anything that gets you through the night, be it prayer, tranquilizers or a bottle of Jack Daniel's. But to me religion is a deeply personal thing in which man and God go it alone together, without the witch doctor in the middle. The witch doctor tries to convince us that we have to ask God for help, to spell out to him what we need, even to bribe him with prayer or cash on the line. Well, I believe that God *knows* what each of us wants and needs. It's not necessary for us to make it to church on Sunday to reach him. You can find him anyplace. And if that sounds heretical, my source is pretty good: Matthew, Five to Seven, the Sermon on the Mount."

The topic then turned to Frank's art. "I don't know what other singers feel when they articulate lyrics, but being an 18-karat manic-depressive and having lived a life of violent emotional contradictions, I have an overacute capacity for sadness as well as elation," he said. "I know what the cat who wrote the song is trying to say. I've been there—and back. I guess the audience feels it along with me. They can't help it. Sentimentality, after all, is an emotion common to all humanity.

"Most of what has been written about me is one big blur," he said when discussing his coverage in the press, "but I do remember being described in one simple word that I agree with. It was in a piece that tore me apart for my personal behavior, but the writer said that when the music began and I started to sing, I was 'honest.' That says it as I feel it. Whatever else has been said about me personally is unimportant. When I sing, I believe. I'm honest. If you want to get an audience with you, there's only one way. You have to reach out to them with total honesty and humility. This isn't a grandstand play on my part; I've discovered—and you can see it in other entertainers—when they don't reach out to the audience, nothing happens. You can be the most artistically perfect performer in the world, but an audience is like a broad—if you're indifferent, endsville. That goes for any kind of human contact: a politician on television, an actor in the movies, or a guy and a gal. That's as true in life as it is in art."

Some feel that the *Playboy* feature was the most introspective interview Sinatra ever gave. It certainly did show him in a new, candid, and informed light.

At the end of February, as the public mulled over his *Playboy* interview, Frank finished work on the film *Come Blow Your Horn* with Lee J. Cobb and Jill St. John. He plays a womanizer in the movie; frankly, the best thing about it is the optimistic, swinging title song, which can be found on Sinatra's *Softly, as I Leave You* album. (Despite its weaknesses, the film would be released to positive reviews in June 1963.)

At this time, Frank also began a brief affair with beautiful redheaded actress Jill St. John and had his private jet fly her to and from singing engagements. Though he took her home to meet Dolly—who cooked her one of her enormous Italian meals—the Sinatra and St. John dalliance resulted in nothing much more than a lot of publicity for both of them.

In March, Frank appeared on a Bob Hope special, and then he hosted the Academy Awards.

In May, another Sinatra film went into production: *4 for Texas*, with Dean Martin as Frank's sidekick in a goofy western comedy.

When considering Frank Sinatra's film work, it's difficult to escape the conclusion that his movie career peaked with *The Manchurian Candidate* in 1961. After that, it was pretty much one silly movie after another for him, such as *4 for Texas* and later *Robin and the 7 Hoods.* Even 1965's *Von Ryan's Express*—a favorite of many Sinatra aficionados—isn't considered by critics to be a very good movie. It remains a mystery as to why after the turn of the new decade an actor as proficient at his craft as Frank Sinatra was never really offered the kinds of roles he deserved. "Maybe he was considered more a singer than an actor," Frank Jr. has opined. "Maybe he made such an imprint on our culture as a vocalist that Hollywood felt he wasn't serious about his acting, which certainly wasn't the case. It's difficult, though, to change Hollywood's perception of you, as I think my father found out."

On July 25, 1963, Frank recorded another one of those classic "swing" Sinatra numbers, "Luck Be a Lady." With words and music by Frank Loesser, this song was written in 1950 for the Broadway musical *Guys and Dolls.* (Marlon Brando sang it rather weakly in the 1955 film version.) In his recorded version, Frank's voice is full and strong, his delivery exhilarating. Clearly this is one of his favorite numbers. His singing is sensational; the orchestra sounds fantastic.

Frank Sinatra's schedule was always full, and 1963 was no exception. "I don't know how he did it," said Dean Martin, who had an incredibly busy calendar himself. "Then again, I don't know how I did it. In fact, I don't even *remember* doing it."

Frank and Ava Redux

*T*he desperate obsession Frank Sinatra felt for Ava Gardner continued to torment him six years after their divorce was finalized. While Ava most certainly loved Frank, she didn't have the same *hunger* for him that he had for her. She had never had it.

In the summer of 1963, Frank and Ava, who was now forty, started dating again, taking it slow—for about a day. Then they were once again in a full-blown relationship. After Ava moved her belongings into Frank's New York apartment, Frank excitedly told his friends,

"She's back, and I'm the happiest man in the world." George Jacobs couldn't help but ask "Mr. S." why he would return to Ava, after everything she had put him through. Frank said he realized it was crazy and that he wasn't fooling himself into thinking it could work out. "I just want to enjoy her while I have the time, while we're young and we can still...try," he said.

Frank's parents happened to be visiting him in New York, and Marty walked in on the conversation. "You fellas talking about Ava?" he asked. They told him yes, they were. "You're a grown man, Frankie," his father told him. "But can I offer you a little advice?"

"Sure, Pop."

"If you're gonna do it, don't drag it out," Marty said. "See how it goes. But if it's bad, end it, son. Don't spend years doing it. Learn from your mistakes. Don't repeat them."

"Sure, Pop."

Unfortunately, the couple's euphoria lasted only about a month. Then the battles started once again, mostly about Frank's friends.

"These creeps are going to bring you down," Ava warned him one night during their 1962 reconciliation at a gathering at Jilly's in New York. Jilly's, a bar-restaurant on West 52nd Street, was owned by Frank's good friend Ermenigildo "Jilly" Rizzo. Frank and Jilly had met a couple years earlier in Miami Beach and immediately struck up a friendship. A popular hangout for many celebrities, Jilly's was also "the" place to go in Manhattan for Chinese food. Whenever Sinatra came to New York, his fans knew that Jilly's was where they might find him.

"One of these days, you're going to end up at the bottom of some river somewhere wearing cement shoes," Ava continued that night at Jilly's, "and I'll be damned if I'm gonna end up down there with you."

"Ava was scared being around Sinatra in public," said Jess Morgan, her business manager from 1962 until her death. "She felt that at any moment there would be gunfire and she would fall dead in his arms. In fact, she told me that the only place she ever felt safe with Frank was when they were at his parents' home because she knew that no one would touch them there."

Sitting at a table at Jilly's with friends, Frank and Ava looked like the ideal couple and seemed to be having a good time over a selection of coffee and liqueurs—that is, until Sam Giancana walked in with a gaggle of his "boys." Delighted, Frank jumped to his feet. "Mooney, over here. C'mon, buddy boy," he said. "Join us. Look, Ava! It's Sam." Immediately, Ava started to seethe. Of course, Frank well knew how Ava felt about Sam. One can't help but wonder, then, why he would have invited the gangster to their table. It was as if he was purposely setting out to sabotage his relationship with Ava, squandering any hope they might have of resuming their romance.

"When Sam sat down, you could see the ice forming on the table. Ava's attitude was that chilly," said Thomas DiBella, who was present. "Sam was being Sam, you know, slapping guys on the back, buying people drinks. And Frank was grinning from ear to ear. But Ava was just staring at the two of them. She hated Frank's loyalty to those guys. 'Where was the mob when his career was all washed up and I was the one paying his rent?' she would ask. 'Where was the fucking mob *then*?' It wasn't surprising, then, that Frank and Ava ended up in an argument over pretty much nothing. As they fought, Sam kept instigating things, making statements under his breath to Frank like, 'You ain't gonna let her get away with *that*, are you?' or 'Man, now she has *really* crossed the line.'"

Suddenly, in one swift movement, Ava doused Frank with Sam's gin and tonic.

"What was *that* for?" Frank asked, astonished.

"Frank was humiliated," said Thomas DiBella. "To have this woman throw a drink in his face in front of Sam Giancana? I just remember Jilly's face in that moment. He had one glass eye and when he was mad he had a way of staring you down so that *both* eyes looked like they were made of glass. Jilly glared at Ava like he was gonna strangle her. 'You dizzy broad,' he hissed at her. 'Don't even go *dere*!'"

"Apologize to Sam, Ava," Frank said, controlling his temper. "Apologize to me, too. What's wrong with you?"

Ava turned to Sam and stared at him for a moment with narrow eyes. Then she stormed out of the room. Sam laughed. "You need to straighten that broad out," he told Frank. "She's got no respect for you. I've never seen anything like that. That was classic. You hear me? *Classic.*"

Frank didn't say much for the rest of the night. He was embarrassed and dismayed—not only with Ava, but probably with himself as well. All of the pain she had caused him was still there, just under the surface. It didn't take much for all of it to come back to him, and for him to run from it. The last thing he said to Sam before leaving was, "Don't worry. When her phone don't ring, she'll know it's me."

The next day, Ava moved out of Frank's apartment. She was out of his life again.

Sinatra Surrenders His Gaming License

By the end of 1963, Ava obviously wasn't the only one concerned about Frank's underworld connections. Since he had openly continued socializing with "the boys," his name was to be found on hundreds of FBI and police surveillance documents compiled from 1960 through the beginning of 1963. Then, in mid-1963, what started out as an inconsequential dispute between a famous pop vocalist and her road manager—one that didn't even involve Frank—ended up costing Sinatra his gaming license and severing his relationship with both Hank Sanicola and Sam Giancana.

According to FBI documents, Giancana decided to visit his girlfriend, Phyllis McGuire, while her group, the McGuire Sisters, was appearing at Cal-Neva. As one of the twelve governing chieftains of the Cosa Nostra, Giancana was persona non grata in the eyes of the Nevada gaming officials, who were attempting to ensure that no criminals were even remotely connected with the state's huge gambling industry. The FBI had issued a "Las Vegas Black Book" containing the names of the eleven known criminals not permitted in Nevada casinos. While it was not a criminal offense to permit one of the men listed in the Black Book on the premises, doing so could result in the loss of the casino's operating license. Sam was in that book—on the very top of a list. Of course, he had been to Cal-Neva on several occasions, most recently when he was there at the same time as Marilyn Monroe and Pat and Peter Lawford. Giancana's presence at Cal-Neva had actually become an issue between Frank and Dean Martin, who was one of the original investors in Cal-Neva.

According to his daughter Deana, her father warned Frank, "We could lose our gambling license." Frank told Dean, "Don't worry about it, pallie." Dean, who had a low tolerance for monkey business, said, "Fine. I want you to buy me out, then," which Frank did.

Again according to the FBI, "Giancana sojourned in Chalet Fifty at the Cal-Neva Lodge at various times between July 17 and July 28, 1963, with the knowledge and consent of the licensee [Sinatra]." It was true; Giancana was hunkered down in Cal-Neva's Chalet 50, a suite overlooking the lake—two chalets away from the last place Marilyn had stayed at Cal-Neva—that had been assigned to Phyllis McGuire. At night, he and his "boys" would drink and gamble and have fun with the ladies. During the day, he would keep a low profile.

"Frank wasn't happy about it," said Andrew Wyatt, a former Lake Tahoe police investigator who at the time was working for the Nevada gaming board. "Frank didn't send for [Giancana], as he had in the past. This time, Sam just showed up. Frank said he didn't want to take the heat for Sam's presence. But you didn't tell Giancana what to do. Sam said not to worry, he would leave in a few days. Frank just had to take his chances that nothing would happen. But this time his luck ran out."

One evening, Victor LaCroix Collins, the McGuire Sisters' road manager, got into a disagreement with Phyllis in Chalet 50. One thing led to another, and Collins inadvertently shoved Phyllis, who landed on her butt in the middle of the floor. Hearing the shrieks of the other two McGuire Sisters, Christine and Dorothy, Sam came bounding into the bedroom from the bathroom, saw what had happened, and, with a sharp left hook, decked Collins. Then Collins—either demonstrating extreme bravery or extreme foolishness, depending on how one looks at it—rose and retaliated with his own fists. Before anyone knew what was happening, he and Giancana were rolling on the floor, throwing punches at one another. "And there was Phyllis McGuire pounding on Collins's head with one of her high heels," recalled George Jacobs, who ran into the room to see what was happening. He was followed by Frank and two of Frank's bodyguards.

Somehow the fight ended up outside on the patio. Just as Victor was about to land a solid right to Sam's chin, one of Frank's body-guards hit him on the back of the head. "What the hell?" Frank asked, pulling the road manager off the gangster.

"I'm not the one who started it," Sam said as George Jacobs held Collins at bay. "Let me at 'im," he added, trying to break free of Frank. "I'll kill him. No one shoves my girl and gets away with it."

Finally, Sam stormed out of the dining room, angry at Frank and his goons for breaking up the fight.

Later, Frank and Sam went for a walk on the property surrounding Chalet 50, and as the two gazed up at a starless sky, Frank suggested that Sam leave in the morning. Sam agreed. "I caused enough trouble," he said. The two had a good laugh. "George will drive you back to Palm Springs," Frank told him.

Frank wasn't laughing a month later though when the Nevada Gaming Control Board learned that a fight had occurred at his establishment, and that Sam Giancana had been involved. This was trouble in the making.

A few weeks later, Frank was working at the Sands in Vegas when he was asked to meet with the gaming board. At that meeting, Commissioner Edward Olsen asked a great many questions; Frank didn't give many answers. He did say that he'd run into Sam Giancana at Cal-Neva but that it was a brief meeting. He also said he didn't know of any fight that had occurred. When reminded that he could lose his license if he had allowed Giancana on the premises of Cal-Neva, Frank promised that he would not see Giancana in Nevada, "but I'm gonna see him elsewhere if I want to, and I want to," he said. "This is a way of life. This is a friend of mine. I won't be told who I can see and who I can't see."

Just when Frank thought he was probably in the clear and that the Sam Giancana–Victor LaCroix Collins fight would be forgotten, it was learned by licensing officials that the entire incident had been witnessed by one of Frank's Cal-Neva employees. That employee was then called in to answer questions before Edward Olsen. However, when he didn't show, Olsen speculated in the press that perhaps he had been intimidated by Frank. When Frank read Olsen's speculation in the media, he was angry. He insisted that he did no such thing. "The guy didn't show up because he took off, scared to testify. Don't ask me why," Frank said. "I didn't have nothing to do with it. How dare he blame me?"

In the weeks to come, Frank had a few more volatile meetings with Olsen. Olsen wanted "official" meetings with Frank; Frank wanted "off the record" conversations.

During one meeting, Frank asked Olsen to put off any investigation until after the summer season was over—a few more weeks. As it happened, Cal-Neva was not doing well, and Frank wanted to get as much as he could out of the summer season, because by November, as was Cal-Neva's practice, the casino would be open only on weekends. Olsen told him he didn't care about the state of Sinatra's business.

As the discussions continued, Frank became more irate. Then, in a final telephone call, he really let him have it after Olsen threatened him with a subpoena. "You're not even in the same *class* with me," Frank hissed at him. "So don't mess with me. And you can tell that to your board and your commission, too."

Edward Olsen was the wrong man to threaten. The next day, he filed an eight-page complaint against Frank Sinatra, saying he used "vile, intemperate, base and indecent language" in their conversation. That same night, gaming control investigators showed up at Cal-Neva. Frank threw them out. Antagonized, the gaming board stepped up its investigation, filing official charges against Frank and threatening to revoke his license for having ever allowed Giancana to be at Cal-Neva. Subpoenas were served on just about everyone who knew Frank—Sam, Phyllis, and the rest. Even Christine and Dorothy McGuire got dragged into the fracas. Of course, Victor LaCroix Collins was also served.

Now questions would be asked about Giancana's financial involvement in Cal-Neva; Frank's relationship with Sam; Sam's with Phyllis; and any other relationship even remotely connected to Cal-Neva.

It all came to a head in September 1963 when the Nevada Gaming Control Board filed charges against Sinatra for having entertained Giancana—who was described in the complaint as being "fifty-four years of age, one of the twelve overlords of American crime and one of the rulers of the Cosa Nostra"—at Cal-Neva. The complaint went on to note that "Sinatra has maintained and continued social association with Giancana, well knowing his unsavory and notorious reputation, and has openly stated he intends to continue such association in defiance of Nevada gaming regulations."

Frank would now be compelled to officially address the allegations. Further complicating things, Mickey Rudin got a telephone call from Jack Warner saying that if Frank was going to continue to work for Warner Bros., the studio didn't want this kind of bad publicity associated with it. At this time, the studio was actually in the midst of a big negotiation with Frank whereby he would be a partner in its business. "I know it's all bullshit about Giancana," Warner reportedly told Mickey Rudin, according to Nancy Sinatra, "but I'm tired of the [bad] image of Las Vegas. I like having Frank as a partner, but if he's going to become involved in Warner Bros. Pictures and own a third of Warner Bros. Records, I think he should not go on with the hearings."

Therefore, on October 10, Frank announced that he would surrender his gaming license and Cal-Neva before the board had a chance to make a ruling. He knew he was beaten. Along with his license would go his 9 percent interest in the Sands casino in Las Vegas. This really hurt. Frank had purchased the 9 percent share of the Vegas resort for $50,000. In a few years, his shares' worth had swollen to a hefty $500,000, and the projected income was in the many, many millions. The total of Frank's gaming interests—Cal-Neva and the Sands—was estimated at $3.5 million. However, he knew he had no choice; he knew he had invited Giancana to Cal-Neva, and there was no getting around it.

"No useful purpose would be served by my devoting my time and energies convincing the Nevada gaming officials that I should be part of their gambling industry," Frank said in a statement. Then he added that he hoped the casinos he was abandoning would continue to thrive, "because they provide wonderful opportunities for established and new performers to present their talents to the public."

That same day, the gaming board formally revoked his license and moved to divest Frank of his $3.5 million investment in the Sands and in Cal-Neva. He was given until January 9 to sell off his interests in the two casinos.

Frank sold all of his casino holdings to Warner Studios in exchange for the lucrative deal there for his own film production company. He then issued a statement saying he was giving up the gaming business because he now had a new production deal with Warners and wanted to focus on making movies instead. He made it seem as if the new deal was totally unrelated to anything having to do with divesting his interest in the Sands and Cal-Neva. Actually, the deals were linked; it was just an expedient way for him to get out of the Cal-Neva mess and continue his relationship with Warners.

As it would happen, the incident at Cal-Neva would have a long-lasting effect on Frank's reputation as well as on his relationships with Hank Sanicola and Sam Giancana.

Where his reputation was concerned, Frank would forever more be known as the Italian-American singer who lost his gaming license because he allowed a mobster onto the premises of his casino. "There was never a finding that he would lose his license and there was never a finding that he had invited Sam Giancana to the Cal-Neva Lodge," his attorney Mickey Rudin would say. "Notwithstanding those facts, for many years afterward whenever there was a mention of the name Frank Sinatra...there would be a tag line that Frank Sinatra had invited Sam Giancana to the Cal-Neva Lodge." To clarify Rudin's comments, there may not have been a "finding" that Sinatra had invited Giancana to Cal-Neva, but in fact Frank threw in the towel before the gaming board could fully issue its findings. He knew he had invited Giancana to Cal-Neva on many occasions, and so did Mickey Rudin. He ended the investigation before anything became official.

Considering what had happened with Cal-Neva, Hank Sanicola was very unhappy about Frank's ongoing relationship with Sam Giancana. The two had worked hard over the years building the Sinatra empire—Sanicola even had $300,000 invested in Cal-Neva. They'd known each other since the 1940s when Sanicola started unofficially managing Sinatra during the Rustic Cabin days. He couldn't accept that Frank was willing to jeopardize all of their hard work for a mobster. The two had an argument about Cal-Neva and Giancana while driving through the desert from Palm Springs to Las Vegas. Frank, who was already very upset and on edge, blew up. He insisted on buying Sanicola out of all of their joint partnerships (including the one they held in Sinatra's Park Lane Films), and impulsively gave him the rights to five of his music publishing companies—Barton, Saga, Sands, Tamarisk, and Marivale—worth anywhere from $1 million to $4 million. Then he kicked him out of the car, right in the middle of the desert. Sinatra never spoke to Hank Sanicola again. Jilly Rizzo, who had been a pal for years, would now be considered Frank's best friend in place of Sanicola.

Considering the way he treated George Evans, Peter Lawford, and many others over the years, it wasn't much of a surprise to anyone in his circle that Frank had ended things so abruptly and finally with Hank Sanicola. It was well known by now that while Sinatra expected loyalty from his friends, he often didn't show much in return. "He got away with a lot because he was Frank Sinatra and people wanted to be in his world," Phyllis McGuire observed. "But really, if you looked at it realistically, why would you ever want this man for a friend?"

Meanwhile, Phyllis's boyfriend, Sam Giancana, thought Frank had been wrong for blowing up in the meeting with Edward Olsen. "Basta con questa merda!" he said in Italian ("Enough of this shit!"). "This whole thing could have been avoided if Sinatra had just kept his cool."

"Sam lost a bundle [about half a million] because he was a part owner of Cal-Neva," says Thomas DiBella. "The bigger issue, though, was that he didn't feel that Sinatra had stood up for him, had properly vouched for him. I don't know what he expected Sinatra to do, but he wasn't happy about any of it. It wasn't the same pallie relationship between Frank and Sam, not after the Cal-Neva incident."

Part Nine

THE KIDNAPPING OF FRANK SINATRA JR.

Planning a Kidnapping

Listen, I want to talk about your drinking," Frank Sinatra said, pulling Dean Martin aside.

"Whassmatter?" Dean asked, slurring his speech. "Did I miss a round?"

The small crowd laughed.

"C'mon, let's have a drink, boys," Dean suggested.

"You *are* drinking," Sammy Davis reminded him.

"What? Is that *my* hand?"

More laughter.

"Actually, I'm gonna stop drinking tomorrow," Dean offered after taking a sip.

"Well, good for you, buddy boy," Frank said, patting him on his back.

"That's right," Dean continued proudly. "Starting tomorrow, I'm just gonna freeze it and eat it like a popsicle."

It was late September 1963. The occasion was a private party in the fabled Polo Lounge of the old Mission Revival–style Beverly Hills Hotel on prestigious Sunset Boulevard in Beverly Hills. Frank, Dean, and Sammy were making a public appearance for a charity. No songs—just stage patter, audience questions, and autographs.

Among those in the small audience of about two hundred were three young men whose lives would intersect with Frank Sinatra's in a bizarre way: Barry Worthington Keenan, twenty-three; Joseph Clyde Amsler, also twenty-three; and John Irwin, thirty-two. "See, Sinatra's not so big and bad," Keenan told his pals. "That's why I brought you guys here. I wanted you to see that he's just a man, just like you and me," he said, according to his memory of the conversation. "So, do you think you guys can do it?" asked Keenan, a crew-cut blond.

"Kidnapping? Man, I don't know," Amsler said, sipping his drink. "That's a big deal."

"It's not a big deal," Keenan insisted. "I've got the whole thing worked out. We *know* the Sinatras, Joe," he reminded Amsler. "And what I don't know from going to school with Nancy, I learned at the library."

Keenan then explained that he had spent a week in the Palm Springs library researching Frank Sinatra's background and personality. He said he'd also gone to the Los Angeles library and studied the history of major kidnappings from biblical times to the present day. "Where they always go wrong," Keenan told his friends, "is that they get caught when they pick up the ransom. If we get past that point, we'll be okay. If we pull this thing off," he continued, "we'll be able to live like the movie stars who hang out here," Keenan concluded, surveying the room. "It's symbolic, us being here."

The audience laughed at another of the Rat Pack's gags, but by this time Keenan, Amsler, and Irwin weren't paying attention. Instead, Keenan continued trying to convince his friends to join him in what would go down as one of the strangest—and most bungled—capers in show-business history, the kidnapping of Frank Sinatra's son.

Frank on Frank Jr.: "I Got a Good Kid Here"

*F*rank Sinatra Jr. was always determined to forge his own way in life, never wanting to leave the impression that he was, even for a second, riding on his famous dad's coattails. "When I was twelve years old, I got a job taking care of little kids in a swimming camp," he recalled in 1963 to the writer Fred Robbins. "When I was thirteen, I sold toys in a toy store. When I was fourteen, I was a projectionist in a local movie theater. At fifteen, I went again to a summer camp where I was a counselor. When I was sixteen, I drove a truck for a sporting goods warehouse in downtown Los Angeles. When I was seventeen, I was an errand boy on a movie studio lot. When I was eighteen, I was a teller in the City National Bank in Beverly Hills. And now, in my nineteenth year," he concluded with a laugh, "I'm a lonely, old broken-down *Itralian* road singer."

Above all, Frank Jr. always had a deep love for music; he appreciated it, studied it, and understood it academically. At nineteen, he chose to follow in his dad's footsteps and be a singer. Had he been a doctor, an attorney, an accountant—*anything* but a singer—perhaps his life would have been easier. In any of those professions his name might have been a blessing, an asset. Though some critics would feel his sound was too close to his dad's for comfort, in fact Frank Jr. developed a personal style very early in his career. He actually doesn't sound at all like his father, nor has he ever set out to do so. He has his own way of turning a phrase, of connecting with a melody. However, despite his best efforts, he would always be destined for constant comparison to his legendary father.

Frank Sr. at first wanted his son to go to college. "Get your degree and then go into show business," he told him. But, frustrated with his studies, Frankie soon dropped out of the University of Southern California. At eighteen, after a stint as a bank teller, he started working part-time at Dad's Reprise Records and Essex Productions. However, he yearned to get up onstage and make a name for himself. At this same time, members of the original Tommy Dorsey band decided to tour together and found themselves in need of a lead vocalist. They asked Frank Jr. if he was interested in the job.

With the passing of the years, Frank Jr. had become even more bookish and quiet. He was intellectual and not at all "hip." His peers had long hair, wore bell-bottoms and Nehru jackets. Not Frank Jr. He came onto the scene around 1962, when Elvis was waning and before the Beatles hit. There was a small window of opportunity and he snuck in. He was a novelty. "As soon as I come out onstage for about the first three minutes of my act, there's a rather low murmur throughout the audience," he said when he was nineteen. "They compare us, and either they are very, very happy that I look like him or that I sound like my father, or they're disappointed or they feel that perhaps I'm mimicking him. Some people get up and leave. Other people are delighted and smile. Some of the ladies begin to cry. Some nights, I don't feel like being compared, but there's no getting around it. I can't fight city hall. If anyone thinks I'm trying to mimic the singing style of my father, I'm not. That's just the way I came out of the factory; it's my standard equipment."

Frank Jr. never quite understood the fascination with him just because he was a Sinatra. He often recalls the story of being in a restaurant and being approached by a fan who exclaimed, "You're Frank Sinatra's son!" She then asked, "Can I have one of your French fries?" Frank asked why. She said she wanted it as a souvenir. "I was disgusted," Frank would recall. "Is this what life is? Is this what being Frank Sinatra's son means? Giving a potato to a stranger as a keepsake. 'Look,' I told her, 'you think I'm someone special, but I'm just like you.' I shook the ketchup bottle over the French fries. 'See. The ketchup won't come out. I have trouble with ketchup bottles too.'"

On September 12, 1963, the nineteen-year-old Sinatra made his professional singing debut at the Royal Box of the Americana Hotel in New York. The audience was filled with celebrities, friends of his father's, and curious media types. It was a terrific opening, and during it Frank Jr. exuded a great deal of self-confidence and vocal proficiency. When attempts to coax him back onstage for an encore were unsuccessful, a comedian in the audience quipped, "He's just like his old man. He's already left with a broad."

Frank skipped his son's opening night because he didn't want to steal the focus during his big moment. Instead, he would attend another performance later in the week. Backstage, it was clear to any observers that the two men had great respect for one another. Privately they may have had their problems, but one thing they had in common was a love for performing. Frank couldn't have been more proud of his son. "What do you think of your kid?" a reporter from the *New York Times* asked him as he stood backstage with his arm around Frank Jr. "Well, I think he's marvelous," Frank said, his blue eyes full of sudden warmth. "I actually think he sings better than I did at his age."

"Aw, Pop, come on," Frank Jr. said with a bashful smile. "That'll be the day."

"No, I really mean it," Frank said. Frank noted that he had just seen Frank Jr. performing at the Flamingo Lounge in Las Vegas about a month earlier, "and the kid's even better now than he was then!"

"And what do you think of your old man?" the reporter asked.

"He's my hero," Frank Jr. said, without giving it a second thought. "Everything I am is because of this man," he said, beaming at his father. "I just want to be like my pop. That's pretty much all I want, you know?"

"Has he given you advice?"

"He told me not to go into the business unless you know what you're up against," Frank Jr. said as his father watched him with pride. "'Don't go into it ignorant like I had to go into it,' he told me. He had me study electronics and the use of magnetic tape, the use of speakers. He had me study instruments...to learn how to keep the horns warm...to know how to keep the reeds wet..."

"Think you guys will ever work together?" the reporter asked.

"We actually had a gig planned," Frank said. He added that it was going to be a fund-raiser for Dr. Martin Luther King Jr. in Santa Monica. It would have been the first time father and son would have shared a bill. "But it was canceled because of..." Frank shook his head; a sigh escaped his lips.

Frank Jr. picked up his dad's thought. "It was four days after President Kennedy was assassinated," he explained. "My pop couldn't sing. Me neither. It was impossible."

Frank pulled his son in closer. "He's a good kid," he concluded with a smile. "I got a good kid here."

About a month later, in early December 1963, Frank Sinatra Jr. would open at Harrah's Lake Tahoe Casino in Nevada, and it would be there that his fate and that of Barry Keenan would intersect.

Delusional Thinking

In the spring of 1997, thirty-four years after Keenan, Amsler, and Irwin planned to abduct the son of the most popular singer in the country, fifty-seven-year-old Keenan gave his first interview regarding the kidnapping and the events leading up to it. The scene of the interview was the same Polo Lounge in which the plot was concocted. At the time, Keenan was a real estate developer. He'd once been the youngest member of the Pacific Stock Exchange in Los Angeles, having received his securities license on his twenty-first birthday. His father was a prominent stockbroker with his own firm, Keenan and Company, operating from downtown Los Angeles.

Keenan's middle-class existence in West Los Angeles was rocked by a 1960 automobile accident in which he suffered debilitating back injuries. Three years later, he was depressed, in chronic pain, addicted to drugs and desperate for Percodan. Indeed, narcotics addiction and alcohol abuse were his biggest challenges. His parents were disappointed in him; he owed money to them and to close friends. At the age of twenty-three, he recalled, he was "a washed-up stockbroker." His thinking clouded by drugs, he was anxious to find a solution to his financial predicament and also to get enough money to feed his addiction. He considered robbing a bank, but decided it was too risky. Selling drugs? He didn't have the street savvy for such an undertaking. "But I knew you could get a lot of money for kidnapping somebody who was rich," he recalled.

In a mad, hazy state of mind, he compiled a list of potential victims, the wealthy youngsters with whom he had gone to school in Los Angeles. He finally settled on Tony Hope, Bob Hope's twenty-three-year-old son.

"But after thinking about Tony for a few days I discounted him because Bob Hope had done so much for our country, with the USO tours and so forth," said Keenan. "I felt it would be un-American to kidnap his son. I might have been planning a kidnapping," he recalled, a grim smile settling on his face, "but I still thought of myself as a solid citizen. I also thought of one of Bing Crosby's sons. We had palled around together for a while. But it didn't seem right to do that to Bing. Somehow, he seemed too fragile to me. I didn't think he could handle it.

"But Frank Sinatra, I thought, now *there's* a tough guy," Keenan remembered. "He could definitely take the stress of having his son kidnapped. Plus, I had seen him walk all over the parents of some of the kids at my school who were TV and film producers, so I rationalized that I didn't care too much about him because he clearly didn't care about anybody else. However, I wanted to make sure that Nancy Sr. and the girls didn't have a traumatic experience, so I planned a *short* kidnapping, just twenty-four hours."

A devout Catholic, Barry Keenan went to church weekly to pray for guidance in his endeavor. His agreement with his maker was that the caper he was planning had to be for the Sinatras' "highest good" as well as for his own; otherwise, "it would be wrong to do it. I knew that the father and son were estranged," he remembered, "that father didn't approve of Junior, they weren't close, he was away at boarding school.

"I knew all of this from having been over at Nancy's house," he explained. "She was my friend from grade school all the way to University High in West L.A. We had gone to the same schools for twelve years together, and for six of them we were in the same classroom together. We graduated together. My best friend, Dave Stephens, dated her in the sixth, seventh, and eighth grades. My mom would take Nancy and Dave places, and Nancy confided in my mom about little problems they were having."

As a friend of Nancy Jr.'s, Keenan had also met Frank Jr., but the four-year difference in age kept them from becoming friends. He also saw Frank Sr. at the home occasionally, and recognized that "he was a pretty hard-boiled guy." Sinatra took a group of youngsters, including Barry Keenan, on a school junket, all of them crammed into an Eldorado sedan, with Frank driving.

Keenan, who admitted he was "obviously delusional," recalled, "I somehow thought that a kidnapping would serve the Sinatras by bringing father and son together. Also, Senior was in a little trouble for entertaining the Mafia at Cal-Neva Lodge, and I thought, 'Well, this would take the heat off of him. Plus, it may bring him and his ex-wife, Nancy, closer together.'"

Over the course of two months, the kidnappers finalized plans for the abduction. It was decided that Frank Jr. would be abducted during an engagement at the Cocoanut Grove at the Ambassador Hotel on November 22, 1963. Keenan had a strong alibi for that day—except for the actual abduction period—because he intended to be at a UCLA football game the next day and be seen by many people there. That morning, though, the kidnapping was suddenly canceled after JFK was assassinated in Dallas. "No matter what you were doing that day, your plans were changed," said Barry Keenan.

Kidnapping Frankie

*T*he news of JFK's assassination struck Frank Sinatra, as it did the rest of the world, like a thunderbolt. Frank was in a cemetery filming *Robin and the 7 Hoods* for Warners when he heard about it. After he was finished filming cemetery location shots for the film, he went to his Palm Springs compound, where he stayed in seclusion for three days, canceling the Martin Luther King benefit concert with Frank Jr. and the Count Basie band. "My father was a private man, and never more so than when he was grieving," recalled Tina Sinatra. "He wasn't good alone, but he healed alone."

"After he disappeared, I couldn't reach him for those three dark days," Nancy Sinatra recalled. "He had gone home to Palm Springs and locked himself away in his bedroom, the only part of the house that was the same as when his friend, the president, had visited. He never stopped loving and supporting Jack Kennedy. He thought JFK was great for the country, great for the world." Frank wanted to go to the funeral. However, for some reason, he wasn't invited. He wasn't offended; it wasn't a party, after all, it was a funeral. Whatever the reasons, he accepted that he would not be present in Washington on that dark day.

Meanwhile, as Frank grieved the loss of his friend, the clock was ticking. Unbeknownst to him, his only son's safety was in jeopardy. His kidnappers had hoped to abduct him at the end of November, but the Kennedy assassination had quashed those plans. Then they hoped to nab him at a singing job at the Arizona State Fair in early December; however, the logistics for that abduction didn't work out either.

By this time, Keenan's pal Joe Amsler was beginning to have second thoughts; he wanted to back out. He had dated Nancy on several occasions and was beginning to feel guilty about the plans that were afoot. In order to keep him and John Irwin interested in the plot, Keenan began doling out fifty- and one-hundred-dollar bills to them. It would later be learned that this money was coming from Dean Torrence, of Jan and Dean, one of the top recording groups in the country. However, Torrance would insist that he didn't know what Keenan planned to do with the money, only that Keenan had promised him a big payoff in a few weeks.

Keenan knew he had to act. He learned that Frank Jr. would be appearing at Harrah's Lake Tahoe with Sam Donahue and musicians from Tommy Dorsey's band. Telling Amsler that they would both be working for a construction company in Tahoe, he managed to get his friend to Nevada before he broke the news to him: Frank Sinatra Jr. was in town and they were going to go and get him. Keenan then telephoned Reprise Records to find out where Frankie was staying during the engagement; whoever answered the phone actually divulged that young Sinatra was at Harrah's two-story South Lodge, in Room 417. The lodge was across the parking lot, about a hundred yards from the casino.

On the snowy Sunday evening of December 8, 1963, at about 9:30 p.m., Barry Keenan made his move. With Joe Amsler outside the room on the lodge's landing between the first and second stories and John Irwin in Los Angeles (where he was told to wait for further instructions), Keenan knocked on the door to Room 417.

Inside, Frank Jr. had just finished eating dinner with John Foss, a twenty-six-year-old trumpet player with the Dorsey band. Sinatra Jr., in his boxers and freshly shaved for the ten o'clock performance, was killing time before putting on his tuxedo.

"I knocked," Keenan remembered. "Someone said, 'Who is it?' I said, 'Room service. I have a package for you.' Junior, I think, said, 'Come in.' I walked into the room, and it appeared that I was delivering a liquor order to him, because I had a wine box with me. It was actually filled with pinecones. I put the box on the table.

"Then I tried to whip the gun out, a long-barreled blue steel .38 revolver. But I couldn't get it out of my pocket, I was so nervous. I actually had to struggle with it. When I did get it out, I pointed it at Frank Jr. 'Don't make any noise and nobody'll get hurt,' I told him. Then I repeated it, 'Don't make any noise and nobody'll get hurt,' like a stuck record.

"I knew Junior was a gun collector," recalled Keenan. "While he was away at boarding school, Nancy and I would go into his room just to see what was in there, snooping, I guess, and he had all kinds of guns. Gun aficionados know when they're looking at an empty or loaded weapon. So I knew that if I didn't have a loaded gun, he would have known it; therefore I made sure it was loaded.

"Joe [Amsler] walked in at that point. He was in a state of shock, as was I. This was the real thing. It was really happening. It was as if I was in a director's chair, looking down at a film as it was being made."

Frankie recently recalled, "When someone under the pretense of delivering a Christmas package screws a .38 in your ear, it gets your undivided attention and you become conscious of many things. The first thing that struck me was that I needed to change my shorts."

As Sinatra's son, Frankie was usually very aware of his surroundings; he'd had close calls in the past. Once when he was working on Long Island, a man followed him back to his motel room and confronted him, saying that his father had stolen his girlfriend back in 1941. He was very irate. Facing him in the doorway, Frank Jr. warned him, "If you take one step into this room, I'll consider it burglary and take whatever steps I have to take to protect myself." The guy charged into the room. "I picked up an ashtray and hit him right on his head and fractured his skull," Frank recalled. "The sheriff came and there was blood all over the floor and he said, 'Whose blood is that?' I said, 'His.'" Frank Jr. was asked if he wanted to press charges; he didn't. There had been other incidents as well, so Frankie was usually not caught off guard. On this night in Lake Tahoe, though, he was taken by surprise.

"'Where's some money?' I demanded," Barry Keenan recalled. "We were completely out of money, and we needed to rob Junior before we could kidnap him because we didn't have enough gas to get to the hideaway house in Los Angeles."

"But I don't have any money," Frank said, his fear rising.

"You gotta have some money," Keenan said. "Whatever you got, you better give it to me, now."

Frank started rifling through his pockets. "I've got a twenty-dollar bill," he offered, "and some change. That's it. That's all I've got."

"Fine. Hand it to me. What do you have?" Keenan asked John Foss.

"I've got nothin', sir," John Foss answered, scared out of his wits.

"Okay, well, we'd better take one of you guys with us," Keenan said. Trying to act as if he was making a random decision, he pointed to Frank Jr. "You. You're coming with us."

"But I'm in my underwear," Junior protested.

"Then get dressed, because you're coming with us."

"I taped up John Foss with adhesive tape," remembered Keenan. "Joe was freaking out by this time. So I had the gun on Joe, telling *him* what to do, to calm down, put a strip of adhesive across Foss's mouth, put a blindfold on Frank."

After taking both men's wallets, Keenan and Amsler forced Frank Jr. into the cold night at gunpoint. He was now wearing gray slacks, brown shoes without socks, and a dark blue windbreaker over a T-shirt, and was blindfolded with a sleep mask. The temperature was twenty-five degrees, and it was snowing heavily. As they left, Barry Keenan shouted at Frank's constrained companion, "Keep your trap shut for ten minutes or we'll kill your friend. *We mean business.* If we don't make Sacramento, your pal is dead." Then he turned around, went back into the room, and ripped the telephone cord from the wall.

With Joe Amsler in the passenger seat, Sinatra in the back, and Keenan at the wheel, they drove off in his 1963 Chevrolet Impala into a full-blown blizzard. Their destination: Los Angeles, 425 miles away.

"I was impressed by Junior's coolheadedness," said Keenan. "He was scared, but cool all the way. I wondered what was going on in his mind. I knew it wouldn't be long before there would be major police confusion. So I told Junior, 'Frank, somebody is likely to die tonight, and there's no need for it to have to be you. Play like you're drunk and passed out in the car if we get pulled over. If you say anything, there's gonna be gunplay.'"

"You don't have to worry about me," Frank said, frightened. "I'll play along. In fact, somebody might recognize this ring," he said, taking off his "FS" signet ring. "So, here." He wanted to demonstrate that there would be no trouble from him. Keenan was surprised by his cooperative attitude. "Okay, Frank, what I need you to do is take a couple of swigs of whiskey," he said, handing him a bottle. "And then"—he opened a plastic container—"take these sleeping pills. If we get pulled over, you'll look drunk."

Frank did what he was told. "Is this a...*kidnapping?*" he asked.

"No," Barry lied. "This is a robbery. But it's gone all wrong. So we're taking you as a hostage."

"*But to where?*"

"We'll take you to San Francisco," Keenan lied again. "Then we're going to let you loose."

Meanwhile, John Foss freed himself and ran to the front desk in the lobby, where the receptionist sat, thumbing through a magazine. "Call the police," he shouted. "Frank Sinatra Jr. has been kidnapped." The operator called Gene Evans, one of Bill Harrah's assistants, who telephoned the Douglas County sheriff's substation at Zephyr Cove, five miles away. By 10:20 p.m. the hotel was swarming with police officials and state troopers. It fell upon Frank Jr.'s manager, Tino Barzie, who was staying in the room next to Sinatra's, to call Frank Sr. Afraid of Sinatra's reaction, and knowing his reputation for taking out his temper on the bearer of bad news, Barzie called Nancy Sr. instead.

Nancy was having dinner at her home in Bel-Air with Hollywood reporter Rona Barrett when the telephone call came. "Good Lord, Rona," Nancy said, holding her hand over the telephone. "They've kidnapped Frank Jr.!"

"What?" Rona exclaimed, taking out her pad and pen.

"This isn't a *story*, Rona," Nancy said, upset. "They have my son! *They have my son!*"

"Well, my God! You have to call Frank," Rona said, putting her writing tools back into her purse.

"Oh my God," Nancy said, crumbling into a chair. "I can't do it."

"Should I?" asked Rona.

Nancy knew that Frank had ambivalent feelings about Rona. In fact, he was never sure it was a good idea having a reporter in the inner circle. She could only imagine his reaction to hearing from Rona Barrett that his only son had been kidnapped! "No, it has to be me," Nancy quickly decided. Then she went back to the telephone. "I'll call Mr. Sinatra," she said, trying to keep calm. "How can we reach you?" She jotted down a number and hung up. Then, with trembling hands, she dialed Frank's number at the compound in Palm Springs.

"Frank, they have Frankie," she said. There was a pause. "They've kidnapped him," Nancy said, now breaking down. *"They've kidnapped our son!"*

"Kidnapping My Kid?"

*F*rank Sinatra somehow always knew something like this would happen to his family; his greatest fear was that because of his fame, one of his children would be abducted. In fact, when Nancy was just two, there had been such a threat. An FBI agent named Peter Pinches posed as the Sinatras' gardener for weeks to protect her. Nothing ever happened, but still, it was frightening for the entire family. And there had been other "crackpot" threats along the way, which is not uncommon with celebrities, so Frank was always on high alert. "Be aware of everything around you," he always told his children. (On the Saint Christopher medal he gave Nancy when she first started driving were the words he had inscribed: "Be Aware.") For his son to now be kidnapped felt as if one of his worst nightmares had come to pass.

Quickly chartering a plane, Frank flew to Reno, where he met with William Raggio, Washoe County's district attorney and an old friend of Frank's. He had wanted to go straight to Lake Tahoe but was unable to because of the blizzard. Arriving in Reno after 2:15 in the morning, he was distressed to find his plane greeted by reporters and photographers. The news was out. "I got no comment to make," Frank said angrily. "Just get away from me."

Sinatra and Raggio were joined by four FBI agents, Mickey Rudin, publicist Jim Mahoney, Jilly Rizzo, Jack Entratter, and Dean Elson, special agent in charge of the FBI in Nevada.

Sinatra called John Foss in Lake Tahoe. "Did they say anything about a ransom?" he asked. "I mean, what the hell is this?"

Foss was still so shaken he could barely speak. "No, Frank, no ransom was mentioned," he said. "It coulda been me, Frank," he added.

"What are you saying?"

"I don't think they knew they were kidnapping your kid specifically," Foss said. "I think it was random. It could've been me."

"Yeah, right," Frank said, unconvinced.

The Sinatra contingent then spent the next sixteen hours waiting for a call from the kidnappers. During that time, of course, Frank made numerous telephone calls to Nancy Sr. and Tina to make sure they were all right. He was also concerned about Nancy Jr. She was in New Orleans at the time with her husband, Tommy Sands, who was appearing at the Hotel Roosevelt. Panicked, she had wanted to come home, but the FBI decided it was best to keep her out of town and guard her in New Orleans in case there was some sort of conspiracy afoot targeting Sinatra's offspring. "Just stay put, Chicken," he told her, using her pet name. Nancy was frantic, though. She could always read her father; they'd always had that kind of relationship. It was as if she knew exactly what he was going through, and it tormented her. But she decided to pay heed to the warning and stay away.

Of course, Frank also kept Dolly and Marty abreast of what was happening; both became frantic back in New Jersey when they got the call from their son. He told Dolly the whole thing was a big mix-up. Only to his father did he actually use the word "kidnap." Marty told Frank he believed all of it would work itself out. "I hope so, Pop," Frank said. "I pray to God it does." It wasn't long before Dolly heard the truth on the television news: Her grandson had been abducted. "Marty and Dolly absolutely adored their grandson," Nancy Sinatra would say. "He was their favorite. He could do no wrong. He represented immortality to them. He would carry on their name, their traditions. Grandma always called him 'my boy,' and vowed to leave him all her possessions. Now she never stopped praying for him. Her rosary beads were never out of her hands."

After speaking to his parents, Frank sat next to the phone for the rest of the night into the next day with no sleep, chain-smoking, frightened, talking nervously to the agents about his life and career... whatever he could think of to take his mind off the unfolding nightmare. "Why don't they call?" he kept asking. "*Why don't they call?* What do we do? *What do we do?*"

At one point, Bobby Kennedy called. The two spoke for about five minutes. Bobby promised to do what he could to spearhead the FBI's investigation. "We're on it," he told Frank (this according to what Frank later told his daughter Nancy). "I've got 248 men on it. There'll be more by tonight." Immediately following Bobby's call, Sam Giancana called. What could he do to help? "Nothing," Frank said. "Please. Don't do anything. Let the FBI handle it."

When Frank and Sam hung up, Sinatra said to FBI agent Dean Elson, "My God. I can't breathe. I'm dying here."

"You have to pull it together," said the agent. "We'll get him back. I promise you, we will get him back."

"Kidnapping *my* kid?" Frank asked, bewildered "Those sonofabitches have lost their minds!"

Close Call

*B*arry Keenan had problems. Roadblocks had gone up along the entire Lake Tahoe perimeter, which was under heavy police guard. A check was being made of every car entering or leaving the state. "About an hour out of town," he said, "we came around a sweeping turn to U.S. 50 and Highway 395, and there was a roadblock way down the hill, about five hundred feet away."

Keenan pulled over and got out of the car, acting as if he was about to take the snow chains off his tires, his mind racing as he tried to determine how to proceed. Meanwhile, a police car began to approach. Keenan ordered Amsler to "scram!" realizing that the authorities would be looking for three people. Amsler, at full gait, ran off into the heavy snowfall and head-on into a fencepost, knocking himself unconscious.

As Keenan began taking off the snow chains, the officer pointed a shotgun at him and demanded to know what he was doing on the road at that time of evening in a blizzard. Then he shone a flashlight in Frank Sinatra Jr.'s face, but he didn't recognize him. Sinatra, drugged but conscious, said nothing. (By this time, Keenan had removed the blindfold and the tape from his hands.) The officer then got back into his patrol car and proceeded to the roadblock. How he didn't recognize Junior and rescue him in that moment has always been one of the biggest mysteries of the case.

After Keenan got the chains off the car, he hollered out for Amsler, who was about fifty feet down the mountainside and just regaining consciousness. When Amsler climbed back up the hill, Keenan ordered him into the trunk of the car, realizing that they would have a better chance of getting past the roadblock if there were only two people visible in the automobile. Then Keenan got back into the driver's seat and began heading toward the roadblock, proceeding cautiously. He hoped the authorities would let him pass through, but they flagged him down.

Keenan rolled down the power window of the car on the driver's side; in an instant, a police officer shoved a shotgun into the opening. "But we've *already* been searched," Barry Keenan protested.

"Well, boy, we're gonna search you again."

"I knew then that it was over," Keenan remembered. "I knew that if they opened the trunk and found Joe in there, it was all over. We were so close to getting caught. Just as I was about to tell the cop that there was somebody in the trunk, the first officer who had seen us came over and said, 'Oh, just let 'em go. I've already checked them. They're okay.'"

"Okay, boy," said the other wary officer. "Next time you come to a roadblock, you'd better stop, hear me?"

"Asshole," a frustrated Frank Jr. muttered under his breath at the cop.

As he drove off, Barry Keenan breathed a sigh of relief.

"Shoot Me and See What Happens"

*B*ack at the Mapes Hotel in Reno, J. Edgar Hoover telephoned Frank Sinatra and told him, "Just keep your mouth shut. Don't talk to anyone but law officers." But Frank did what he thought was best—he issued a statement. "Sinatra is ready to make a deal with the kidnappers," his publicist announced, "and no questions asked."

"They know that I would give the world for my son," Frank added. "And it's true. But they haven't asked for money. I wish they would.

Frankie wasn't dressed too warmly, and if they have him out in the cold, what chance does he have?"

"There are fears for the life of the young Sinatra," added Sheriff Carlson to the reporters who had swarmed over the Mapes Hotel. "There always is in every kidnapping."

Meanwhile, Keenan drove along Route 395 in his 1963 Chevrolet Impala headed toward Los Angeles, his kidnapping victim in the backseat. Junior's blindfold was put back in place and his hands taped behind his back.

Nineteen hours passed.

It was now December 9, 1963. "We finally got back to Los Angeles and to the hideout house on Mason Avenue in the San Fernando Valley, recalled Keenan. "By this time, Joe wanted to call the whole thing off. I had to keep Joe medicated just to keep him from blowing the whistle. 'We're going to go to prison for the rest of our lives,' I told Joe. 'Our only chance is to get the money and get the hell out of here.'"

"Frank, I got a confession to make," Keenan told Frankie now that they were in Los Angeles. "This isn't a robbery and you're not a hostage. This is a kidnapping."

"What are you saying?" Frank asked, still blindfolded with his hands tied.

"We kidnapped you," Keenan repeated. "We're not going to San Francisco, either. We're in Los Angeles now," he said as he pushed Sinatra along a pathway into the hideout house in Canoga Park, California, about twenty miles from Beverly Hills. Once inside, he took off the blindfold and pushed Frank into a chair, his hands still tied.

"You big dummies," Frank yelled, his dark eyes now blazing, all of this according to Barry Keenan's memory. "Are you stupid? You kidnapped *Frank Sinatra's* son? *Are you crazy?*"

Keenan was not equipped to handle Sinatra's rage. It was the first time he had seen it. "It's gonna be all right, kid," he said, trying to calm him. "Don't worry. It'll be okay."

"Untie me now," Frank ordered. "I swear to God, you'd better untie me right now."

"Give me your old man's telephone number," Keenan said, ignoring the demand. "We'll call him, get some money from him, and get this thing over with."

"No. The hell with you," Frank Jr. said contemptuously. "I'm not cooperating anymore. Go ahead, shoot me. You want to kill Frank Sinatra's son? Do it then. Just shoot me and see what happens."

Instead, Keenan shoved Frankie into a back bedroom of the house and padlocked the door. Then he crumpled into a chair.

The Ransom Demand

After thinking it over, Barry Keenan remembered that Frank Sinatra Sr. wasn't even in California, so he didn't need the number after all. News reports he'd heard on the car radio indicated that Sinatra was at the Mapes Hotel in Reno. Keenan got that telephone number from directory assistance.

The next afternoon, December 10, John Irwin—who the kidnappers felt had the harshest, most adult-sounding voice—made the call. At 4:45 p.m., the phone rang in Frank Sinatra's hotel suite.

"Is this Frank Sinatra?"

"Speaking," said Frank—all of this according to FBI transcripts.

"It doesn't sound like Frank Sinatra," John Irwin said.

"Well, it is," Frank replied anxiously.

Irwin asked if Frank could be available at nine the next morning. Frank said yes. Irwin then told him that his son was in good shape, that there was no reason to worry about him. Frank then suggested that he trade places with Frank Jr. "Bring him back and take me," Frank said. "You know you don't want him. He's a kid. You want *me*."

"No," Irwin responded. "I don't think so."

"Look, you give me back my son," Frank said. "Or I'll tear you apart with my bare hands," he threatened. "*You give me back my kid.*"

Irwin hung up the telephone. Frank sank into a chair. It would be another sleepless night for him.

The following morning, the phone rang again. Now the kidnappers had decided to let Frank talk to Frank Jr. Unbeknownst to them, the FBI was again taping the conversation.

"Hello, Dad."

"Frankie?"

"Yeah."

"How are you, son?"

"I'm all right, Dad."

"Are you warm enough?"

No response.

"You okay, Frankie?"

No response.

"Are one of you guys there?" Sinatra asked, referencing the kidnappers. "Are you there?"

"Yeah," John Irwin said, taking the phone from Frank.

Frank said he wanted to make a deal. In fact, he wanted to resolve the situation as quickly as possible. What was it that the kidnappers really wanted? Irwin said that, of course, they wanted money. How much? Irwin said he wasn't sure; he needed to think about it. Now Frank was losing his patience again. "I don't understand why you can't give me an idea so we can begin to get some stuff ready for you," he pressed. Irwin said that Frank was now making him nervous. "Don't rile me," he warned. He said he would call back with further instructions.

"Wait! Can I talk to Frankie again?" Frank asked. Irwin hung up on him. "Jesus Christ," Frank exclaimed as he slammed down the receiver.

A few hours later, John Irwin called back.

"So, what do you want?" Frank asked. "Just name the amount."

Irwin said $240,000. "That's what I've decided we needed."

"What the hell?" Sinatra asked. "What kind of figure is that? You kidnapped my son for a quarter of a million dollars? I'll give you an even million, nice and clean and easy," he said.

"But we don't need that much," John Irwin said. "We're not gonna take advantage of you, Mr. Sinatra. We just need $240,000."

"You guys are nuts," Frank exclaimed. "Fine, then. I'll do it." This time it was he who hung up the phone.

Frank then telephoned his friend Al Hart, president of City National, a Beverly Hills bank, and asked him to make the necessary arrangements; each and every bill would be photographed by the FBI. Then, because the FBI sensed that Frank Jr. was now in Los Angeles, Sinatra flew back to the city and waited for another call, now at Nancy's home at 700 Nimes Road in Bel-Air. The estate was completely surrounded by reporters and photographers. Twenty-six FBI agents and over a hundred local police were assigned to the kidnapping case. This was big news—comparable in scope and attention to the notorious 1932 Lindbergh baby kidnapping—and at the center of it were three hapless young men who were just barely pulling off a Keystone Cops–like caper.

The next day, December 11, Frank and FBI agent Jerome Crowe were to deliver the money: $239,985. (Fifteen dollars of the ransom money had been used to buy a fifty-six-dollar valise in which the money was to be delivered.)

Sinatra and Crowe were then sent on a proverbial wild–goose chase: first to Los Angeles International Airport, then to a gas station, then to another gas station, where they were told they would find two parked school buses. They were told that they should leave the valise between the buses. They were promised that Frank Jr. would be released within hours after the money was dropped off. As they delivered the money, a team of FBI agents shadowed the drop-off point in a Good Humor truck and several taxicabs.

Barry Keenan picked up the money. But, typical of the daftness that had thus far characterized his caper, he lost his coconspirator, Joe Amsler, who took off when he thought he'd seen an FBI agent lurking about the site. When Keenan called John Irwin from a pay telephone to tell him that he had a black valise filled with Sinatra's money, but didn't know what had become of Joe Amsler, Irwin became suspicious. He later said he suspected that Keenan had "iced" Amsler to get rid of a witness to the kidnapping. By this time—Tuesday—there was so much confusion, it seemed as if Frank Jr. was the last thing on their minds. No one had slept in three days, and everyone except Frank Jr. was on some sort of drug. Without telling Keenan, John Irwin then decided to take matters into his own hands: He released Frank Jr. and then called his father.

Frank: "You Know You're a Dead Man, Right?"

At two in the morning on December 12, four hours after the payout, John Irwin telephoned Frank Sinatra. "Something has gone terribly wrong," Irwin said.

Frank immediately became frantic. "What do you mean, something has gone wrong?" he shouted into the phone. "We did everything you said. Now where's my son?"

"No, not with you," Irwin said. "Something has gone wrong *here*."

"Where's my kid?" Frank demanded to know.

"He's safe," Irwin assured him. "I just dropped him off at the San Diego Freeway at Mulholland."

"You know you're a dead man, right?" Frank said angrily. It wasn't a question as much as it was a statement of fact. "You know I'm gonna kill you, right?"

"I wish to hell I hadn't gotten into this thing," Irwin said, "but it's too late to get out. So...I'm sorry."

"Yeah, you're sorry, all right," Frank said. And with that he slammed down the telephone. Then he turned to Nancy, who looked as if she'd been stricken.

"What did he say?" she asked urgently. "*What did he say?*"

"I'm getting our son," Frank said as he wrapped his strong arms around his ex-wife. She collapsed in tears. "I'm bringing him home, don't worry," he said, holding her close. Tina stood next to her parents, now also crying. Frank reached out and brought her into the hug. The three stood together embracing, with Frank repeating that everything was going to be okay, that he would bring Frankie back to them. "I'm gonna get him," Frank repeatedly assured them. "Don't worry about it. I promise." He then broke away from them and, with an FBI agent in tow, left the house.

He got into his car, headlights out in order to evade reporters, and drove to what he'd been told had been the drop-off point, the overpass at Mulholland on the San Diego Freeway.

Meanwhile, Barry Keenan returned to the hideout. "When I got back to the hideout with the ransom and found that John Irwin and

Frank Jr. were both gone and I had already lost Joe, I burst into tears," he remembered. "None of this had worked out. I had the money, but I had lost the kidnap victim and *both* of my partners. I freaked out, got into my car, and started looking for Frank Jr.," recalled Keenan. "And as I'm out there looking for him, who do I pass on the road? Frank Sr. and an FBI agent, doing the same goddamn thing, *looking for Junior.* My heart almost stopped as they just passed me by."

Barry Keenan couldn't find Frank Jr.

Neither could Frank Sinatra.

Frankie Is Released

*T*he fifteen-minute drive back to Nancy's house without his son must have seemed unbearably long for Frank Sinatra. "I cried the whole way back," he later confided in one friend. "I cried, man. I was losing it. I couldn't even drive the car. *I was losing it.* I thought, 'Jesus Christ, they took the money, and they killed Frankie.' They murdered my son."

When he walked through the back door of Nancy's home without his boy, his ex-wife almost fainted from despair. Frank collapsed into a chair, tilted back his head, and stared into space.

"You don't have him?" Nancy asked, her eyes wide with horror. "*What happened?*"

"My mother and I broke down," Tina Sinatra recalled. "We just fell apart. I felt wrung out; I had nothing left."

"We've been double-crossed," Frank said, not even able to look at Nancy or Tina. He shook his head in disbelief. "How do you like that?" he said, now speaking to John Parker, one of the FBI agents. "'They got the dough, and they got Frankie. I acted in good faith.' He then told me he was going to call Sam Giancana," said Parker. "'If I have to handle it that way, then I've got no choice,' he said."

"You sure that's a good idea?" Parker asked.

"No, I'm not sure," Frank said.

"Just let us handle it, then," Parker said. "We can do this the right way."

While Sinatra and Parker discussed bringing Giancana into the situation, the doorbell rang. An FBI agent went to answer it; Nancy followed. They found a man in a uniform who appeared to be a security guard standing blank-faced in the doorway. "Mrs. Sinatra," he said, "I have your boy in the trunk of my car. And he's all right."

Nancy just stood in the doorway, her mouth wide open.

Frank came to the door. "What's going on?" he asked. "What's going on?"

"Mr. Sinatra, I have your boy in the trunk of my car."

Stunned, Frank must have thought Frankie was dead. "Get him out, get him out," he said frantically. "Get him out. *Get him out.*"

Everyone in the house raced out to the car, the trunk was opened, and Frank Jr. got out. Nancy immediately became overwhelmed at the sight of her son. "Hi, Ma," he said as they embraced. "Don't cry, Ma. It's over." Then he turned to his father. "Dad," he said, "I'm sorry."

"For what?" Frank said. "Jesus Christ. For what?"

"I'm just sorry, Dad."

A tearful Sinatra embraced his son, then backed away to let his mother hold him again. As he stood in the doorway, Frank Sinatra seemed older—much older—than his forty-eight years.

Frankie explained that when he was set free, he hadn't been told that his father was going to pick him up at the drop-off point. So he walked two miles to Roscomare Road in Bel-Air. As cars drove by, he jumped behind bushes, frightened that the kidnappers had changed their minds and had come back for him. He was finally discovered by Bel-Air patrol guard George C. Jones. Jones decided that Frankie should hide in the trunk to avoid being photographed by the media camped outside Nancy's house.

Frank Sinatra Jr. concluded, "Seeing the faces of both my parents when the ordeal was finally over, it seemed to me that they had aged ten years. I sometimes wonder if Dad has ever really recovered from the experience. I'm sure my mother hasn't."

As the happy family reunion took place, the phone wouldn't stop ringing. Someone in the house was just taking messages. But then a call came in for Frank that he was told was important. He went to the telephone; it was Bobby Kennedy. He wanted to make sure that everything was okay. Frank assured him that he had his son back, and then thanked him profusely. "I'll never forget your kindness," he told RFK. This moment marked the end of any feud with Bobby. From this point onward, Frank never had a critical thing to say about him. He would always be grateful to him for his concern about Frank Jr. and for the manpower he put behind the search for him.

Bobby wanted to speak to Frank Jr. "Are you all right, son?" he asked. Frank Jr. said he was just fine. He thanked him for his help. RFK then asked to "speak to one of my men." FBI agent Dean Elson went on the line. "Implement the ramrod," RFK said, which meant that now that Junior was safe, find the kidnappers...and waste no time doing so.

Capturing the Kidnappers

The next few days were hectic. There were phone calls to and from Dolly and Marty Sinatra to keep them apprised of how their grandson was doing. A call from Sam Giancana to express his relief. The FBI then interviewed Frank Jr., who told them, "I think they were a bunch of amateurs. The one guy looked familiar to me. They were more scared than I was. Another guy gave up the whole thing, chickened out, and got me out of there before the first guy [Keenan] came back."

When George C. Jones returned to work the day after he dropped off Frank Jr. at Nancy's home, he found a note asking him to return to the Sinatra estate. When he got there, he was greeted by one of Sinatra's aides, who handed him an envelope. "Sinatra saw me standing in the living room," recalled Jones. "He came over and shook my hand. I said, 'Mr. Sinatra, I feel I shouldn't take any kind of reward from you.' He said, 'Please take it. And have a merry Christmas.' When Jones got back to his office, he opened the envelope. In it were ten crisp one-hundred-dollar bills.

Two days later, on December 14, 1963, Frank received a telephone call from J. Edgar Hoover. The FBI had the kidnappers in custody. Joe Amsler's brother, James, had turned him in to the FBI while his brother was asleep. Amsler was arrested within the hour; Irwin followed. Barry Keenan was arrested while walking into the home owned by his girlfriend's parents in La Canada, California. Fifteen FBI agents showed up to apprehend him. "The night that we got the news that the kidnappers were in custody, we opened a magnum of champagne," Nancy Sinatra recalled. "My mother, who doesn't drink, drank most of it. She was so happy, she didn't even have a headache the next day."

Just before he was arrested, Barry Keenan had given his ex-wife several thousand dollars to buy new furniture. Later, when Sinatra found out about it, he asked the FBI not to take the furniture that had been purchased with his money. "Oh, the hell with it," he said. "Just let her keep her furniture. It's not like she did anything wrong."

The Trial

To this day, many people—reporters, fans, interested parties who remember the ordeal as it unfolded—wonder if the kidnapping of Frank Sinatra Jr. was actually just a publicity stunt orchestrated by father, son, or both. Some have even proffered the theory that Frank Jr. set the whole thing up and that his father didn't know about it—and maybe never did.

At the trial in late February 1964 in Los Angeles U.S. District Court, the kidnappers' attorneys—Charles L. Crouch (representing Barry Keenan), Gladys Towles Root (for John Irwin), and George A. Forde and Morris Lavine (for Joe Amsler)—argued that the caper had been staged by young Sinatra for the purposes of publicity, "an advertising scheme." In her opening statement, John Irwin's attorney, Root, said, "The apple doesn't fall far from the tree, and Frankie Jr. just wanted to make the ladies swoon like Papa. Frankie told my client, 'The ladies used to swoon over my father, then some wise publicity agent took that on and made my father an international star.'"

Joe Amsler's attorney George A. Forde continued, "The kidnapping headlines are doing the same thing for Frank Sinatra's son. There is a vacant seat here for a fourth defendant, a financier who financed this whole thing." It would later be learned that the lawyer was referring to Dean Torrence. When put on the witness stand, Torrence admitted giving money to Keenan to finance the kidnapping.

"How it evolved that the whole thing was supposedly a hoax was that I was in jail, lonely and desperate," remembered Barry Keenan. "I felt guilty because of the pain I had caused my parents and because of the way I had coaxed my friends to get involved in this scheme. One of the attorneys—not my own—came in one night and said to me, 'Look, if this was a publicity stunt and you are able to tell us that it was a publicity stunt, then that would be a very strong defense.' Since I was the ringleader, I was the one who had to make the statement. By that time I had sobered up and realized that we were all in a heap of trouble. I slept on it.

"The next morning, I came out with this lie about the kidnapping being a publicity stunt, and that's all my attorneys needed to hear: Frankie was in on the hoax. It became our defense. I'm not proud of it. It was a lousy thing to do to the Sinatras."

During the trial, circumstances and events were revealed that seemed suspicious to some observers and bolstered the defense's claim of an "advertising scheme." Much of Frank Jr.'s testimony seemed to actually assist the defense. According to the trial transcript, Gladys Root hammered away at Frank Jr. "Did you say to the defendants, 'You guys don't have to worry about me, I'll help you in every way possible'?" Frank Jr. said he didn't remember, but that it was possible. She then asked him if he voluntarily took a sleeping pill with liquor so that he would appear to be asleep if a police officer happened upon the vehicle? Frank said yes, he had done so, but that he was "ordered" to do it. She then demanded to know if it was true that Frank Jr. gave his signet ring to the defendants so that it would not be recognized? Frank said yes, he had done that. Had the kidnappers demanded it? No, Frank said. He did it because he was trying to act in a cooperative manner.

"Indeed," Gladys Root said suspiciously. "You were *very* helpful, weren't you? And when a police officer shone a flashlight in your eyes at the roadblock, why didn't you say something? Why didn't you say, *'Hey! It's me. It's Frank Sinatra Jr. I'm the guy you are looking for!'* Why were you being so helpful to your so-called abductors, but not to the police?"

"Because I was scared," Frank said.

"Well, this doesn't make sense, sir," she observed. "Why didn't you at least signal in some way to the police officer? Why didn't you *do something?*"

"Because Mrs. Root, the number one man [Keenan] stated that when we came to the roadblock, there was going to be some shooting," Frank said, his voice rising. "I did not want a sudden and idiotic move to cause this man, who was stupid enough to kidnap me, to voluntarily blow the brains out of an officer."

Mrs. Root shook her head in disbelief. "Indeed," she remarked sarcastically. Then she turned to the jury and shouted, "*The truth is that you would have wrecked your little kidnap plot, which you had arranged, and which would not have been successful if you were rescued by the police.*"

At that, Frank Jr. jumped from his chair and shouted at her, "*That is not true.*"

He was ordered by the judge to sit back down. Judge William G. East called for a break.

By the time Frank Jr.'s attorneys called him to the stand, he had become more emboldened. "Look, I'm not on trial here," he said. "I'm the victim. I'm not the criminal. The seeds of doubt have been sown on my integrity and on my guts and will stay with me for the rest of my life," he said angrily. His attorney asked him directly if he had anything at all to do with the kidnapping. Frank said no. His attorney then asked if the whole thing had been a hoax. Again, he said no. "No." The lawyer then asked, "Did your father have anything to do with this?" Frank's answer, again, was no.

A long letter was then produced, written by Barry Keenan prior to the kidnapping, which he had secreted away in a safe-deposit box in case of his death. Basically, it outlined the plan and totally cleared Frank Sinatra, both father and son, from any involvement.

Finally, it was time to turn the case over to the jury. In his instructions to the jury, Judge East said, "I must comment that there is no direct evidence in this case by Frank Sinatra Jr. or persons on his behalf that prearrangements were made for his abduction."

After deliberating for six hours and fifty-three minutes, the jury found all three defendants guilty. Neither of the Sinatra men were in court when the verdict was read. Frank Sr. was returning from Tokyo on business. Frank Jr. was in London, performing.

As the active kidnappers, Joe Amsler and Barry Keenan were sentenced to life in prison, plus seventy-five years, which was the maximum sentence they could have received. John Irwin got sixteen years and eight months for conspiracy. All three had psychiatric-diversion sentences and as a result were sent to the Medical Center for Federal Prisoners in Springfield, Missouri. There, they underwent four months of psychiatric evaluation.

Dean Torrence was not sentenced at all, and for a very strange reason: He had originally lied on the stand, saying he was not involved. But then he changed his story and went back onto the stand and confessed. Because he was honest (the second time), it was decided not to press charges against him. Indeed, it was another strange aspect of a very strange case. Some felt that Torrence's career suffered anyway. Among those was the inimitable Dorothy Kilgallen, who wrote, "Since singer Dean Torrence gave his sensational testimony at the Frank Sinatra Jr. kidnapping trial, he's been given 'the chill' by booking agents and producers. So obviously the word is out. Not many people in show business want to incur the wrath of Frank Sinatra Sr.—his tentacles reach into too many branches of the industry, from movies to records and you-name-it."

While he likely had nothing to do with Dean Torrence's problems, Frank did go after two of the attorneys, Gladys Towles Root and George A. Forde (leaving out Barry Keenan's lawyer, Charles L. Crouch, who had all along refused to promote the conspiracy theory).

In July 1964, Sinatra pressed to have Root and Forde charged with unethical conduct, including conspiracy, corruption, perjury, and obstruction of justice. Outside the courtroom on the day they were arraigned, the pair of lawyers charged that the indictments resulted from Frank's effort to "clear the reputation of his son for having participated in a kidnapping that was a hoax and publicity stunt." In other words, they were sticking to their story. Both attorneys said they were "shocked and bewildered" by the charges and that they had done nothing during the trial but represent their clients by presenting a defense case. "I feel sorry for anyone that vindictive," Gladys Root said of Frank. "I have always believed in the power of truth, and truth will be the winner in this case. If a person can be indicted because a plaintiff is unhappy about the way he or she has represented a defendant, then I don't know what to say about the system."

In the end, it was decided that there was no merit to any of the allegations against these attorneys. All of the charges were dismissed before they reached trial stage.

Kidnapping Postscript

As Presiding Judge William G. East reviewed case files, preparing to send them to the appellate court for Amsler's and Irwin's appeals, he discovered that someone had tampered with a key report. He found the original draft of a letter that had been sent to the court from a medical facility, which noted that Barry Keenan was legally insane at the time of the kidnapping and thus should be diverted to psychiatric counseling as opposed to being sent to prison. He also noticed what he believed was a doctored copy of the same report, which had been submitted to the court by Sinatra's attorneys.

Barry Keenan said, "The judge believed that the prosecution had manipulated the report and sent it back slightly rewritten, changing the wording to make it less favorable to me. Someone had changed it so that it wouldn't give the judge a reason to give me probation. The judge got so incensed with what had been done to the report that he censured the prosecuting attorneys and reduced my sentence to twelve years."

As a result, Barry Keenan would go on to serve only four and a half years behind bars; his two partners spent three and a half years in prison. Keenan was released in 1968. "I don't think this would ever happen today," he says. "I was unbelievably lucky. Some might say that the system failed miserably. I guess I can see that point of view too. But whatever the case, by 1969 I was ready to start my life over again and put the Sinatra kidnapping behind me."

Growing Up Sinatra

Frank Sinatra Jr. went on with his life and career after the kidnapping, but with no real change in his relationship with his father. "As for the two men in my family, and their choked and halting relationship," Tina Sinatra recalled, "our family crisis didn't forge a breakthrough, as it might have in the Hollywood version. Dad and Frankie went on as they had in the past, not quite connecting. They loved each other and knew it, but it had taken a near-death experience to bring them close and together. When the trauma was over, the connection was broken."

As a performer, Frankie may never have projected his father's charisma or magic, but he does have a certain serenity that is very self-assured. His 1971 album *Spice*, for the RCA subsidiary Daybreak Records, is an accomplished, distinctive album that still holds up.

Nancy Jr. somehow seemed to sail through her teen years, fascinated with boyfriends and school, and also music. She was about eight when Frank left with Ava, and even though she was very upset about it, at least she had eight good years with him. It was foundation enough for her to continue a good relationship with him. Like Frankie, she wanted more, of course. However, also like Frankie, she had resigned herself to reality. She signed as a recording artist with Frank's Reprise label in 1961. In 1963, Frank sold Reprise to Warner Bros.–Seven Arts, Inc., a movie company controlled by Jack Warner. This gave the company a real shot in the arm in terms of distributing its product. Reprise president Mo Ostin stayed on as head of the label, and Frank retained a 20 percent stock interest and became a vice president and consultant of Warner Bros. Picture Corp.

In 1964, Nancy was twenty-four and well on her way to becoming a success at the new Reprise Records. She had found her own identity and, because she shared her father's proclivity for concentration and focus, never let anything get in her way. The biggest problem she would face, and it would be very soon, would be the disintegration of her marriage to the young actor Tommy Sands.

Tina, who was sixteen in 1964, was the only Sinatra offspring who went through a difficult teenage rebellion. She felt, like many teens, as if nothing was right or good in her world. At this time she was attending school at the Catholic institution of Marymount, which was so restrictive in its philosophy that she seemed ready to burst with impatience and frustration by the end of every school day. The nuns didn't know what to do with her, and neither did her parents.

Frank gave Tina a powder-blue Pontiac Firebird convertible for her birthday, but it probably wasn't the best gift for a rebellious teenager. When she snuck out with her friends in the middle of the night to go dancing while visiting Frank in Palm Springs, he was very disappointed in her. For Tina, that was punishment enough; his disenchantment in her was crushing. Suggesting two totally different parenting styles, Nancy Sr. reacted differently when Tina did the same thing in Los Angeles: She hit the roof and grounded her daughter for weeks. After a couple of years watching Tina act as if she were angry with the world, Frank and Nancy sat her down at the dining room table to try to figure out what was bothering her. In their hearts, they both knew what it was, though. As the youngest, Tina had been the one most affected by Frank's leaving the family for Ava, and they suspected that she had never gotten over it. She didn't want to discuss it with them, though, so there wasn't much they could do about it.

"When he left home, I was a baby," Tina would explain, "so I wasn't accustomed to a man in the house, a father. I didn't feel the wrench; I didn't know him. Conversely, I had to deal with this very nice man coming into our lives from time to time. It was always—certainly— a special occasion. But there was a point when you realized that everything had to be just...so. You know, we had to get cleaned and washed and combed and groomed, and it wasn't comfortable. And he would come and go and come and go. And I didn't know where to *find* him. What I felt was that when he was around, I was different. I couldn't figure out why. Who is 'he' that I should change? I used to feel nervous when I was going to see him. I had anxiety."

Frank was relieved that Tina didn't want to talk about Ava. If she felt more comfortable dealing with it privately, he felt it was probably for the best. Unpacking these sorts of complex emotions was never Frank's forte. Nancy Sr. still hadn't worked through her own anger and disillusionment. Therefore, she too was less than eager to work through it with her youngest daughter.

In fact, Nancy Sr. still clung to the hope that Frank would return to her. She and Nancy Jr. often discussed it in a dreamy, romantic way. Nancy Jr. actually seemed to encourage her mother in this fantasy, and their idealizing of Frank while wishing and hoping for his return to the family only served to upset Tina. "I just felt that my dad had moved on and I couldn't understand why my mother wouldn't let this thing go," she later admitted. "Of course, I was sixteen and thought I had all the solutions to all of the problems in the world."

Prelude to the Best

*I*n January 1964, Frank Sinatra recorded the patriotic *America, I Hear You Singing* album with Bing Crosby and Fred Waring and His Pennsylvanians. Then, later that month, he recorded *Frank Sinatra Sings Days of Wine and Roses, Moon River and Other Academy Award Winners*. With this album, he kept up with the times. He quietly and seamlessly moved from concept albums into collections of covers of current hit records by other artists. While not considered by Sinatra purists to be a memorable album, *Wine and Roses* did include the lovely "The Way You Look Tonight," as arranged by Nelson Riddle.

In February, Frank and Dean appeared together on a Bing Crosby television special. By this time, Bing was also a Reprise recording artist; indeed, Frank was corralling the best in the business for his label, such as Rosemary Clooney, Jo Stafford, Keely Smith, and Dean Martin. With the exception of Martin, though, few were able to sustain a career at Reprise.

In April, the trio—Frank, Dean, and Bing—recorded the soundtrack album for *Robin and the 7 Hoods*. Then, later in the month, Frank was off to Hawaii to begin work on the film *None but the Brave* for Warner Bros., his debut as a director (Nancy's husband, Tommy Sands, also appeared in this antiwar film, along with Clint Walker and Brad Dexter). *None but the Brave* finished its principal photography by June. "It's an antiwar story that deals with a group of Americans and a group of Japanese stranded together on a Pacific island during the war," Sinatra explained. "I tried to show that when men do not have to fight, there is a community of interests."

Of Frank's work as a director, *Los Angeles Times* critic Kevin Thomas noted, "Sinatra's style is straightforward and understated. It is to his credit that he tackled a serious subject on his first try when he could have taken the easy way out with another gathering of the Clan." When released later in the year, the movie did well at the box office.

In *Frank Sinatra: An American Legend*, Nancy recalls that her dad almost drowned while in Hawaii during production of *None but the Brave*. It happened while Frank was attempting to rescue Ruth Koch (producer Howard Koch's wife) after she was swept away by an undertow. (Mrs. Koch was brought safely back to shore by a wave while Frank was on his way out to get her.) "He struggled against the surf for thirty-five minutes," Nancy wrote, until he was finally rescued by fire lieutenant George Keawe, who later said, "In another five minutes he would have been gone. His face was turning blue."

It is interesting that Nancy credits Keawe with saving Frank's life when it is well known among Sinatra's inner circle—and has been reported countless times in the media—that actor, producer, and close friend of Sinatra's Brad Dexter actually rescued him. "[When I reached him], Frankie was whispering with a sort of incredible wonder, 'I'm drowning,'" recalled Dexter. "He couldn't see anything. I've seen people drown, and they lose their eyesight and go blind—and he was completely white."

Sinatra later had a falling-out with Dexter over the film *The Naked Runner* (which he would produce), prompting him to do what he often did, banish another longtime friend from his kingdom. Later, when someone asked Frank how Brad was, Frank responded, "Brad who?" This unfortunate situation regarding Dexter may explain why Nancy decided not to give credit to him in her official Sinatra history for saving Frank's life.

(At the time, Frank and Joey Bishop were also estranged. No one, including Joey himself, seemed to remember what caused the problem between them. However, Bishop sent Sinatra a telegram after he heard of the near drowning: "You must have forgotten who you were. You could have *walked* on the water." Joey recalled, "I got a call from him the next day like nothing had happened between us.")

On June 9, 1964, Frank was back in a studio in Los Angeles recording the *It Might as Well Be Swing* album, arranged by Quincy Jones and featuring the Count Basie band. If a person can only have one Sinatra album in his collection, perhaps this should be it, because it includes one of his most memorable performances, "The Best Is Yet to Come." The remarkable Count Basie orchestra presses the music onward insistently, persistently. It's clear that all—singer, musicians, producers, and arrangers—were having the time of their lives.

On June 27, 1964, Warner Bros. released *Robin and the 7 Hoods*, the film that gave birth to the Sinatra classic "My Kind of Town," the musical tribute to Chicago that went on to become one of Frank's trademark songs. The movie was a satire on the old Robin Hood fable and starred Rat Packers Dean Martin and Sammy Davis, with Bing Crosby.

A month later, on July 13, Frank celebrated the twenty-fifth anniversary of the first time he stood in a recording studio with Harry James and sang "From the Bottom of My Heart" for the Brunswick label. It had been twenty-five years of music, performances, and images, so many of which had helped shape American culture, becoming the soundtrack to so many lives. And to paraphrase an appropriate song title, for Frank Sinatra the best *was* indeed yet to come—or at least it seemed that way when he met the woman who would become his third wife.

Part Ten

THE MIA YEARS

Mia

He met her in September 1964 when he was filming the movie *Von Ryan's Express* for 20th Century–Fox. She was a young blonde waif, one of the stars (along with Ryan O'Neal) of the new *Peyton Place* television show. She was loitering about the movie set, eyeing Frank Sinatra while wearing nothing but a sheer white nightgown from the wardrobe of her show. Reed thin, with pale skin and luminous blue eyes, she was at once childlike and seductive. At just five feet five inches and weighing only ninety-eight pounds, she had the figure of a young boy. However, she possessed something Frank would later describe as "some kind of female magic." He couldn't help but want to know her. He tapped her on the shoulder.

"How old are ya, kid?" he asked her.

"That's hardly a question to ask a lady," she responded. Then, with a flick of her long blonde mane, she answered, "I'm just nineteen."

"I was hers instantly," Frank recalled. "I loved that hair, man. I think the hair's what got me."

Born on February 9, 1945, in Beverly Hills, Maria de Lourdes Villiers Farrow—Mia—was the third of seven children of actress Maureen O'Sullivan and her husband, director John Farrow.

When she was a youngster, Mia's home life was unusual in that she and her siblings lived in a nursery with its own kitchen that was separate and apart from the main house. Maureen, who worked as a successful actress in films throughout Mia's adolescence, once explained that her husband enjoyed peace and quiet when he got home from work on the set (no easy feat with seven children) and "didn't like everything messed up." The children, therefore, were basically raised by nannies, trotted out in their expensive "Sunday best" when the rich and famous of the entertainment industry visited… and then sent back to the nursery at the end of the evening.

Farrow never criticizes her parents for her upbringing. "There was a magical element to it," she's said. "We lived in beautiful homes, our gardens were beautiful, even the nannies dressed beautifully. Beautiful birthday parties, and we had beautiful clothes. And people spoke well and thought well of each other in those days in Hollywood."

At the age of nine, Mia contracted polio. Before she left to be treated at Cedars of Lebanon Hospital in Los Angeles, the sensitive youngster wrapped all of her toys as gifts and presented them to her brothers and sisters. But after she left the house, all of the toys—and in fact the rest of her belongings—were burned by one of the maids because they were thought to be contagious. (Mia eventually recovered from the disease, with only a residual and permanent weakness in one arm.)

Mia attended a Catholic boarding school in London as well as schools in Madrid and Beverly Hills. Upon graduation from Marymount, she left Los Angeles and headed east to New York to become an actress. In short order, she found herself appearing in the off-Broadway production of *The Importance of Being Earnest*, replacing Carrie Nye (later Mrs. Dick Cavett). She signed a contract with 20th Century–Fox and appeared in a film, replacing Britt Eklund in *Guns at Batasi*.

Troubles on the home front kept Mia preoccupied in the early 1960s. Her father, John Farrow, had an unfortunate eye for the ladies and a thirst for liquor. He died in 1963 of a heart attack at the age of just fifty-three. The loss was very difficult for the family. In the midst of her grief, Maureen accepted a job on the *Today* show as cohost opposite Hugh Downs, a job she regretted having taken since broadcasting wasn't for her. Her eventual departure from the program opened the door for someone better suited for the job: Barbara Walters.

In August 1964, nineteen-year-old Mia began work on *Peyton Place*. As the pensive and brooding heroine Allison MacKenzie, she became very popular when the soap debuted in the fall of that year. She was a good actress with a raw, convincing quality, especially in big dramatic moments. The camera loved her. Still, despite the experienced ingénue she played on television, in real life she didn't have boyfriends in school; she was a wallflower. Some people thought she was kooky, what with her dreamy disposition and the fact that she ate only organic foods. After one writer interviewed her, he wrote,

"She is a fawn turned woman for an hour; a stranger from some asteroid where girls walk barefoot on the rims of flowers."

In fact, Mia was anything but simple-minded or weak-willed. She also wasn't naïve. In her own way, she could be seductive and even manipulative. She was ambitious. She was smart; she knew what she wanted out of life. She wanted to be a famous actress, there was no doubt in her mind about it.

First Blush of Romance

*W*hen Frank saw Mia looking starry-eyed around the set of *Von Ryan's Express*, he couldn't help but approach her. While she was young and innocent-seeming, she had a certain sensuality that drew him in. He walked over to her and asked her to sit down and chat.

As Mia took her seat, she dropped her purse and out of it fell all sorts of things between his feet and under his chair: a stale doughnut ("Oh my, I'm so sorry!"); a can of cat food ("Oh no, I'm so embarrassed!"); a ChapStick ("No! No! No!"); even her retainer ("Oh my God!"). He couldn't help but be amused as she repeatedly apologized while collecting her scattered things. As she stuffed everything back into her purse, he was charmed by her. Her long straight hair was definitely a turn-on for him; her doe-eyed, shy glance mesmerizing. In a 1960s world where skinny fashion models were all the rage, Mia's look definitely worked for her.

Mia and Frank talked for a few minutes while she explained why she was on the lot: "I act on a TV show called *Peyton Place*. Ever hear of it?" As she prattled on, he listened and watched. When their eyes locked, it was clear to him that something significant had just happened. Frank was certain that he'd just shared a real *moment* with a girl young enough to be his daughter.

"I thought the only thing I could do was to get out of there with any shred of dignity that might remain," Mia later remembered, laughing. "And as I stood up to leave, his eyes met mine, and my heart stopped, you know? Everything came together. I was just so alive in that moment."

"You know what?" Frank began as he walked Mia off the set. "There's a private screening tomorrow night of a movie I just directed, *None but the Brave*. "Why not go with me?"

He noticed her hesitation. Because of the obvious age difference between them, would she be frightened away? No. She nodded and smiled. "Yes, of course," she said.

The next night, Frank held Mia's hand throughout the screening. Afterward, he asked her to go to Palm Springs with him. He moved fast. He wanted her to go with him, right then and there. "We can leave from here," he told her urgently. "I have my own jet. We'll just take off and be there in an hour. What do you say, kid?"

This was a lot for Mia to digest—a famous man more than twice her age asking her to go to Palm Springs for the weekend? "I'd never been anywhere with anybody," she later recalled. "I never even had *a date* before. So, going to Palm Springs with somebody—I couldn't even wrap my mind around it. He wanted me to leave immediately! How could I possibly do that? And I just remember babbling about how I didn't have any of my stuff, my pajamas. My cat. My toothpaste!"

Frank couldn't help but laugh. "You're *marvelous*, aren't you?" he teased. "Fine, you go home and get your things in order. Tomorrow morning, I'll send a car for you. It'll take you to the Burbank airport where I have my Learjet. And my pilot will then fly you to Palm Springs. And I'll be there waiting for you. Okay?"

She just nodded.

"Oh, and don't forget your retainer," Sinatra added with a chuckle as he walked away. He winked and disappeared around a corner.

Mia and Frank in Palm Springs

The next morning, a black stretch limousine showed up at Mia Farrow's front door, as promised. It was then that she remembered she hadn't even given Sinatra her address. How had he known where she lived? As she pondered that question, she was whisked to the Burbank airport, where a jet awaited her on the tarmac. With the passing of a few moments, she had settled into a plush leather seat, a single passenger alone on a private aircraft. "Could this be true?"

she would recall wondering. A steward asked if she'd like a drink. As she sipped her Coca-Cola through a straw, the jet took off. The hour passed quickly; soon she found herself landing in Palm Springs. Then, gazing in wonder out a small round window, Mia saw him on the runway, smiling at her: Frank Sinatra in a black suit and tie with a jaunty fedora, looking like...well...looking pretty much exactly the way one might imagine Frank Sinatra would look in 1964. Cool.

Mia wasn't really a fan. Of course, she knew who he was—who didn't? But her parents never listened to Sinatra, preferring Gregorian chants. She was a fan of the pop and rock and roll music of the day. So she didn't know much about Frank other than what she'd read in gossip columns and what she'd seen on television. However, while in Palm Springs with him that weekend, she couldn't help but be captivated by him. The sharp way he dressed, the way he smelled like lavender...everything about him seemed sensual. He comported himself like a man in total control, at least that's how it appeared to her. His house was also mesmerizing. She was raised in an enormous mansion, but it was old and stuffy. Frank's place was nothing like anything she'd ever seen before—all glass and metal, sharp angles and very modern.

"The pool was too close to the house," Frank explained matter-of-factly as he took her on a tour, "so I had it moved...way back there," he said, pointing out into the distance.

He had his pool moved? "*Who does that?*" she asked herself.

"And over there, that's the helipad. That's where my helicopter lands.

"And this room right here," he said as he walked her down a long hallway, "this is where JFK once slept. See the plaque?" Mia gazed at the gold plaque with the president's name on it.

Mia would recall that her first night with Frank felt like pure magic. Dinner on the patio as the sun set, just the two of them—and an army of servants catering to their every need. At the end of the night, Sinatra swept her into his arms and took her to his bedroom. By the next morning, she was already in love with him. The more they talked, the deeper she fell.

As she wandered through the house, Mia couldn't help but notice framed pictures of a stunning brunette all over the premises. A relative? His sister, maybe? No, he told her. "That's Ava." Frank then opened up to Mia about Ava Gardner, confiding in her, as if he'd known her for years. The more he trusted her with his heartache, the more she was drawn in by him. His honesty was seductive. "I don't even know why I'm telling you this stuff," he told her with a loopy smile.

Ava. The name sounded familiar to Mia. Then it hit her. Her father had once had an affair with Ava Gardner, back in 1953 when they filmed *Ride, Vaquero* together. In fact, it was one of the many reasons her parents' marriage broke up. (Frank and Ava were still married at the time.) Should she mention it? No, Mia decided. It was all just so overwhelming; she needed time to think about it.

Getting to Know You

*H*e started calling her "Angel Face." She began calling him "Charlie Brown."

After Palm Springs, Frank and Mia began to date. She knew what she saw in him, it was obvious. In her eyes, he was everything a girl could ask for: A great lover. An amazing man. Powerful. In control. Famous. Honest. Yes, probably even a father figure. She wasn't so naïve that she wasn't able to put the pieces together: Her father was never there for her, but Frank was—at least in the moment. It made sense. She missed her father, and it felt good being with Frank.

Mia soon discovered qualities in Frank she felt were missing in herself. He was strong and defiant, whereas she often felt weak and vulnerable. He was powerful and decisive. When had she ever made a decision about which she was truly happy? Other than to date Frank, she couldn't think of one. He was supremely self-confident, a lifetime of success imbuing him with self-assurance the magnitude of which boggled her mind. She felt like a bumbling fool most of the time. To walk into a roomful of strangers and be comfortable in her own skin? For her, it had never happened. But for Frank it was a way of life.

As for Frank, the more he got to know Mia, the more he appreciated that she seemed to have no preconceived notions about him. It was as if he could reveal anything to her and she accepted and understood it. For instance, he confessed that he had a bad temper. "It's an Italian thing," he explained. "I get it from my mother. I'm like her, I can really blow up. I can be pretty mean," he admitted.

Mia said that she believed Frank's temper was actually a consequence of being pushed too hard in his career. He was overworked, she theorized, and thus short-tempered. "You're Frank Sinatra so they think you're invincible," she reasoned. "But looking at you right now, I see the truth. I see that you feel put-upon, and *that's* why you act out. I understand you better than you think," she told him.

He further told her that he was tired of his career and wanted to retire. "That's not how you *really* feel," she observed. She said she believed that because expectations of him were so great, he felt punished by his celebrity. "But I think I know you already," she said, "and I think your passion is your music and your career. Without it, you would be very unhappy." Instead of giving it up, Mia suggested he cut back on his career schedule and enjoy his private life a little more. Frank didn't even know how to respond. All he knew was that Mia was very unusual. How was it that she seemed to understand him so well at only nineteen?

In fact, as he would later come to realize, Mia Farrow saw life in simple terms: She believed that at the core of each human being was pure goodness. Since Frank had long ago become convinced that at the core of each human being was pure bullshit, her view of humanity was a twist of logic for him. Coming after Ava, Marilyn, Betty, and others who had preceded her in his life, Mia was a breath of fresh air. She was into mysticism and yoga, which he thought was eccentric. Yet he was charmed by it all just the same. She also liked to smoke pot, which he thought was unfortunate. He didn't do drugs. In fact, he was dead set against the growing drug culture in America. However, he obviously did drink a lot, so he decided not to judge her. Admittedly, the age difference was a bit disconcerting; Frank realized it would likely cause a scandal when word got out. Certainly it would appear to others that he was having a major midlife crisis. He also knew that his overprotective mother and the rest of his family would likely object. However, none of this seemed to matter. He was falling in love, or at least that's how it felt to him at the time.

"The good thing about love at first sight," he would later say, "is that it saves a lot of time."

The truth was that Frank had been discontented for so long, he felt he deserved some small measure of happiness. Therefore, he decided he was going to roll the dice with Mia. "She says she wants to get to know the real me," he told Dean Martin. "But is there such a thing?" he wondered.

"But she's young enough to be your daughter," Dean said, according to his recollection of the conversation. "You don't know what you're getting yourself into, pallie."

"God help me," Frank remarked, "but I'm tired of feeling sad, old, and washed up. We're talking marriage already, pallie."

"But this kid, she doesn't know you," Dean said.

"She sees me in a different way," Frank said. "I'm goin' after this one, pallie."

"Jesus Christ, Frank," Dean exclaimed. "I got *scotch* older than this kid!"

Red Flag

Can this really work?" Mia asked her mother, Maureen O'Sullivan, one morning over breakfast. Frank had asked George Jacobs to take the two to breakfast.

Maureen had come to the desert to visit and stay at the compound with her daughter and Frank. She hadn't been happy about the relationship. "He's having a midlife crisis, and he's using you to make him feel better about himself," she had told Mia. "This makes me mad, Mia! Why can't he just get hair plugs and a sports car like other men his age?" However, once Maureen got to know Frank better, she began to waver in her view. He was so courteous and such a gentleman, she couldn't help but be just a little swept away by him. For instance, one day the phone rang; it was a reporter. Frank let him have it—"and don't you ever call this number again, damn it!" Then, realizing that Maureen was in the room, he apologized to her for his language. That gesture impressed her. She found him to be very courtly. Still, she was worried about her daughter. Maureen, who was fifty-three, had been in show business for decades. She'd been around men like Frank before, knew they could be complex, and felt she needed more time to be sure of him.

"Well, I like him," Mia said over breakfast. "I think he's cool."

"Mr. S. *is* cool," George Jacobs said, trying to vouch for his employer.

"Well, obviously!" Maureen exclaimed with a laugh. "He's *Sinatra*, isn't he? But I'm not sure about this thing," she told her daughter. "I'm just afraid you'll get hurt."

"Well, it has to be my decision, Mother," Mia said.

"Yes, dear," Maureen said. "I'm afraid that's true."

"It didn't matter what her mom thought," George Jacobs recalled. "Mia was not going to slow down where Mr. S. was concerned. She was a very determined person, no one's pushover."

After a couple of weeks of happiness, a problem surfaced. Mia, in years to come, would always remember the day Frank came to her and said, "I was thinking. You should give up acting. Who needs it? You and I can settle down, and I'll just take care of you. So...quit."

She didn't even have to think about it. The answer was no. "My career is the only thing I have that gives me purpose," Mia said. "I'm not giving it up."

A startled expression lingered on Frank's face. He thought she'd just agree, and that would be the end of it.

"If we're going to be together, you must listen to what I say," Mia said. She added that her mother had told her that this was the way relationships were supposed to work. As George Jacobs served cocktails, he tried not to eavesdrop, but it was impossible.

"Holy shit, Mia," Frank said, exasperated. "Gimme some more gasoline," he told Jacobs, holding out his glass to him.

"Get used to me having a mind of my own," Mia said. "You are not my father and I am not your daughter. You don't get to tell me what to do."

Frank just stared at her. Mia stormed out. He then turned to George Jacobs. "And there she goes," he told his valet, "off to play with her Easy Bake Oven."

Fish out of Water

*I*n February 1965, Mia Farrow would turn twenty. She had explained to Frank that she didn't want to bring attention to the birthday. The media had already made such a big deal of the age difference, she didn't want to remind everybody that she wasn't even twenty-one. Frank didn't see it that way. He wanted to host a big celebration, and anyone who didn't approve of her age would just have to live with it. "I want to show off my best girl," he told her. "Is there anything wrong with that?"

Mia's birthday party was held at Chasen's on February 9, 1965. None of her friends were present, just Frank's—and they were all old enough to be her parents' peers. "Why couldn't you invite any of my friends?" she asked Frank. He just shrugged. "Never occurred to me, to tell you the truth," he answered before rushing off.

Mia felt out of place, a fish out of water. She couldn't hide her discomfort. It would turn out to be one of the worst nights of her young life. "Lighten up, baby," Frank said, wrapping his arms around her after finding her alone in a corner. "Why not have some fun? After all, this is your night."

It was impossible for her. "I can't," Mia said. She said that she felt as if everyone was staring at her, waiting for her to make a fool of herself. She believed they thought her nails looked bad because she bit them. "It's *my* birthday," she pouted. "Why couldn't we just celebrate the way I wanted to?"

Now Frank was annoyed. He had spent good money on the party and had invited all of his celebrity friends, only to find his new girlfriend acting like a child. He tried to calm her down, but, truth be told, he didn't have much patience for this sort of thing. Mia was definitely alone in her misery.

"Look, grow up," Frank said before leaving her side. "Have a good time, or don't. Your choice."

The Other Side of Frank

In the spring of 1964, Swifty Lazar—the noted agent—invited Frank and Mia to a holiday party at his Beverly Hills home. The two arranged to meet there because Frank had a prior television commitment and planned to go straight to Lazar's from the studio.

Mia showed up alone and, again, felt out of place. It was yet another star-studded affair—Judy Garland, Mickey Rooney, Dean Martin, Sammy Davis, and Donna Reed were present, all famous people she recognized, but none she actually knew. Again, while they may have been friends of her parents, they were not hers. As she tried to mingle, she saw a familiar face across the room, but one she couldn't place. It wasn't Ava Gardner, she knew that much, but it was definitely someone else she had seen posing with Frank in a photograph at his home. "Who's that beautiful woman over there?" Mia asked someone standing next to her. "Oh, that's Betty," came back the answer. "Betty! You know... *Lauren Bacall*." The name made Mia's heart jump; she'd heard somewhere along the way that Frank had once been engaged to Lauren Bacall, but she had no idea why it had ended between them. Watching this stunning woman saunter through the crowd, so gorgeous and self-possessed, just made Mia feel all the more inferior. *She* was a real woman. *She* was the kind of woman with whom someone like Frank Sinatra belonged. Compared to her, Mia was just a little girl, or at least that's how she recalled feeling in the moment.

Finally Frank showed up, tired and annoyed. He hated doing television shows, and was in a foul mood. He didn't even kiss Mia hello. Instead, he just nodded at her, brushed by her, and went straight to the bar. That's when he saw Betty.

Frank walked over to Betty and began talking to her. She looked profoundly unhappy to see him. Since this moment would mark the first time the two had spoken in the six years since he broke their engagement, she wasn't welcoming of it. No one knew for certain what was said between them—Betty has since described it as "superficial conversation"—but suddenly Frank pointed to Swifty Lazar and yelled out, "*It was you!* You're the reason we broke up," he said, motioning to Betty. He was acting as if this was the first time he heard that Lazar had told Louella Parsons about the engagement seven years earlier. "Damn you, Swifty. I'll send you straight to hell for this. *Straight to hell!*"

Frank was so angry, his face was flushed. He rushed over to one of the buffet tables, grabbed the corner of the white tablecloth, and in one swift motion pulled at it until everything—an entire display of iced seafood—went flying. Guests ducked as lobster tail and shrimp and crab legs rained down upon them, followed by a crash of plates and silverware.

Stunned, Mia backed herself into a corner and stared at the scene with horrified fascination. "Frank! Frank! Don't," she exclaimed, but it was too late. Partygoers were running for cover all around her. Mia huddled in the safety of her corner until suddenly she felt someone tugging at her arm. "Serves him right," Frank said as he grabbed at her. "Let's get the hell out of here." He then pulled her by the elbow—and it hurt!—through the stunned crowd, out of the house, and to their car.

The drive home was eerie. Mia's pleas to talk were met with total silence.

The Frank that Mia thought she knew would never have caused such a scene. Or maybe she didn't know him at all. Maybe her mother was right, maybe she was making a terrible mistake. The way she was raised, never was a cross word ever spoken to anyone. Of course, her parents had their share of marital problems, but they handled them with a sense of decorum that, while often strange and removed, somehow felt polite and dignified.

The next night, after work on *Peyton Place*, Mia decided to have a conversation with someone she sensed would be able to explain what had happened at the Swifty Lazar party: Frank's longtime valet, George Jacobs. The two got along quite well; it didn't take long for them to become friends. To her, he seemed like a straight shooter. "So, tell me, George, what happened between Frank and Lauren Bacall?" she asked. George said she didn't want to know; she *really* didn't want to know. However, she insisted that she did want to know, and in fact, she thought she needed to know, especially after what had transpired at Swifty's party. She was putting George in a tough spot, he said. It wasn't his place to talk about it, he explained, and if Frank ever found out that he'd discussed such a personal matter with her, he would be finished for sure. He liked his job, he said, and he didn't want to lose it. "But I won't tell him," Mia insisted. "You can trust me. I swear to God, I would never tell him."

After about fifteen minutes of working on him, Mia finally wore George down. He very reluctantly explained why Frank ended it with Betty Bacall two years earlier: He thought she had blabbed to a gossip columnist that he was going to marry her. It turned out, it hadn't been Betty who had told the reporter, it had been Swifty Lazar. "You poor kid," George added. "Must have been quite the scene."

"Do you mean to tell me that Frank ended an engagement because of *that*?" Mia asked. Now she didn't even care about the scene he had caused. She was more concerned about the way he had conducted himself in a romantic relationship with someone.

"Yep," George answered. "Betty didn't know what happened. She was blindsided."

"Why didn't he and Betty sort it all out?" she asked. "It was obviously a misunderstanding."

"Oh, little girl, that's not Mr. S.'s way," George said matter-of-factly, all of this according to his memory of the conversation. "Mr. S. doesn't wait for explanations. He just drops out of sight. One day, you're in. Next day, you're out. That's just the way Mr. S. operates. One day, you're in," he repeated. "Next day, you're out."

"Well, I have to ask him about it," Mia said.

"Hell no, don't do it," George warned. "Just forget it, Mia. If you know what's good for you, you'll just forget all about it."

Now Mia didn't know what to think. None of this made sense to her. "Well, he would never do that kind of thing to *me*," she concluded to George. But from the way George winced, now she wasn't so sure. In fact, she was beginning to fear that she really didn't know Frank Sinatra at all.

Francis Albert Sinatra in 1938, at the age of twenty-three. (mptvimages.com)

Frank Sinatra with Benny Goodman at CBS on "The Frank Sinatra Show" in 1940. (mptvimages.com)

Frank's young wife Nancy Barbato Sinatra, in 1940, pregnant with her first child, Nancy Jr. Frank and Nancy were married on February 4, 1939. (The Christaldi Collection / mptvimages.com)

Sinatra in 1943. "I think it had a lot to do with the time period," Sinatra would say of his success at the time with bobby-soxers. "It was important for people to have someone to root for during the war years. In their mind, I was one of the kids from their neighborhood who made good." (mptvimages.com)

Frank and his firstborn, Nancy Jr., circa 1944. (The Christaldi Collection / mptvimages.com)

Frank and Nancy at the Trocadero night-club in Hollywood in 1945. "If he loved you, that was it," said their daughter Nancy Jr. of Frank. "He loved you through and through. There would be no change in that." (mptvimages.com)

Frank in 1945. (mptvimages.com)

Dolly and Marty Sinatra stand proudly with their son, Frank, during the ceremonies for "Frank Sinatra Day" in Hoboken, New Jersey, October 30, 1947. (mptvimages.com)

Frank and Nancy with their daughter Tina, born in 1948. (© Mel Traxel / mptvimages.com)

Frank, from the MGM film *On the Town*, in 1949. (mptvimages.com)

Frank and Ava Gardner, on their wedding day, November 7, 1951. It was Ava's third marriage, Frank's second. Frank always loved Ava's wit: "Part of me had no doubt I would end up a movie star," she liked to say. "Deep down, I'm pretty superficial." (mptvimages.com)

The passionate—and combustible—marriage of Frank and Ava is the stuff of Hollywood legend. Here they are at the gala debut of Ernest Hemingway's drama *Snows of Kilimanjaro* on September 18, 1952, at the Rivoli Theatre in New York. Ava was one of the stars of the film. (The Christaldi Collection / mptvimages.com)

Frank stands with fellow actors Montgomery Clift (*left*) and Burt Lancaster between scenes on the set of *From Here to Eternity*. Sinatra's performance won him an Oscar as best supporting actor in 1953. (mptvimages.com)

Sinatra during a recording session at Capitol Records in 1954. "I like recording late at night," he once said. "The later the better. My voice was not meant for daytime use." (© Sid Avery / mptvimages.com)

Classic Frank, 1954. "There was a tremendous level of excitement—an air of expectation—every time he recorded," recalled his son, Frank Sinatra Jr. (© Sid Avery / mptvimages.com)

Frank and his very good Rat Pack friend Sammy Davis Jr. at Ciro's nightclub in Hollywood, August 1, 1955. Actress Lauren Bacall is visible in the background. (© David Sutton / mptvimages.com)

When Frank ended his engagement to Lauren Bacall in 1957, it broke her heart. "But Frank did me a great favor," she would say. "He saved me from the complete disaster our marriage would have been." The two are seen here at a party after the Academy Awards on March 30, 1955. (mptvimages.com)

Frank and his best friend, Dean Martin, at a 1958 recording session at Capitol Records in Hollywood for Martin's album *Sleep Warm*, which Sinatra conducted. (Photo by Ken Veeder / © Capitol Records / mptvimages.com)

Frank in 1959, during the recording of his *Come Dance with Me* album at Capitol. (© Sid Avery / mptvimages.com)

The legendary Rat Pack during filming of *Ocean's Eleven* in 1960: (*l-r*) Sinatra, Dean Martin, Peter Lawford, and Sammy Davis Jr. (mptvimages.com)

Sammy, Dean, Frank, and Joey Bishop during a playful moment in 1960. (© Sid Avery / mptvimages.com)

Frank, in the middle, taking a steam at the Sands Hotel in 1960, flanked by Peter Lawford and Al Hart (Sinatra's banker), with Sammy Davis Jr. (© Bob Willoughby / mptvimages.com)

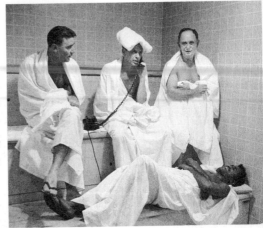

Frank and his friend President John F. Kennedy, at a Democratic Party fundraising dinner at the Beverly Hilton Hotel on July 10, 1960. Sinatra supported Kennedy's run for the presidency in 1960 and sang the campaign's theme song, "High Hopes," with refashioned lyrics touting Kennedy's candidacy. (mptvimages.com)

Frank escorting the First Lady, Jackie Kennedy, to her box at the Inaugural Celebration gala in 1961. (mptvimages.com)

A casual moment at the Santa Monica home of Peter and Pat Lawford in 1961: (l-r) Peter Lawford, Pat Kennedy Lawford, Frank Sinatra and his occasional lover Marilyn Monroe, May Britt (who was married to Sammy Davis Jr.), and Shirley MacLaine. (© Bernie Abramson / mptvimages.com)

Frank Sinatra Jr. at age seventeen, 1961. (© Gene Trindl / mptvimages.com)

Eighteen-year-old Frank Jr. performing at Disneyland in 1962. (© Ted Allan / mptvimages .com)

Frank, his daughter Nancy Jr., and first wife, Nancy, beam after Frank Jr.'s opening night at the Flamingo Hotel in 1963. (The Christaldi Collection / mptvimages.com)

Frank in his dressing room (with his friend Jilly Rizzo) at the Sands Hotel in Las Vegas, 1964. (© Ted Allan / mptvimages.com)

The Sinatras: Tina, Nancy Sr., and Nancy Jr. with Frank Jr., circa 1965. (© John Enstead / mptvimages.com)

Frank, flanked by Tina, seventeen, and Nancy Jr., twenty-five, arrive at the Beverly Hills Hotel for his fiftieth birthday in 1965. The party was hosted by Frank's first wife, Nancy, and his daughters. (The Christaldi Collection / mptvimages.com)

Frank and Mia Farrow in 1965. Frank's second wife, the much-older Ava Gardner, would tell Mia, "You, my dear, are the child Frank and I never had." (© Ted Allan / mptvimages.com)

Fifty-two-year-old Frank takes a third wife, Mia, just twenty-one, on July 19, 1966, at the Sands Hotel in Las Vegas. Their marriage would last two stormy years. (© Ted Allan / mptvimages.com)

Mia on her wedding day. She has said that the marriage was, in some ways, "more like an adoption." (© Ted Allan / mptvimages.com)

Though father and son had a difficult relationship, despite it all they had an abiding love for one another. Frank Jr. and Sr. at a taping of *The Dean Martin Show* in 1967. (© Martin Mills / mptvimages.com)

Nancy Sinatra and Frank record their hit single "Something Stupid" in March 1967. (© Ed Trasher / mptvimages.com)

Nancy could always bring a smile to Frank's face. (© Ed Trasher / mptvimages.com)

Posing for the cover of their 1968 Christmas album, *The Sinatra Family Wish You a Merry Christmas:* (l-r) Tina, Frank, Nancy, and Frank Jr. (© Ed Trasher / mptvimages.com)

Pals Frank and Dean in the late 1970s. (The Christaldi Collection / mptvimages .com)

Photo session for the *My Way* album, 1969. "I think we all see now how timeless the music is," observed Frank's daughter Nancy. "His songs, hopefully the great American songbook, will live forever." (© Ed Trasher / mptvimages.com)

Throughout his career, there was no separating the singer from the meaning of his songs. (© Martin Mills / mptvimages.com)

Frank and his fourth bride, the former Barbara Marx, on their wedding day, July 11, 1976, at the home of Walter Annenberg, former U.S. Ambassador to the Court of St. James's. (© David Sutton / mptvimages.com)

Frank and his proud mother, Dolly, on the evening Frank received the coveted Scopus Award from the Hebrew University of Israel in Los Angeles, November 14, 1976. Sadly, Dolly would die in a plane crash less than two months later, en route from Palm Springs to Las Vegas to see her son perform. (© David Sutton / mptvimages.com)

Though Barbara was always at odds with Frank's daughters, Nancy and Tina, she did seem to make Frank happy during their twenty-two years of marriage. (© David Sutton / mptvimages.com)

Frank continued to perform all the way up until February 1995; here he is at the Long Beach Arena, in California. "May you live to be one hundred," Frank would tell his audiences before leaving the stage, "and the last voice you hear be mine." (mptvimages.com)

Confronting Sinatra

Mia couldn't resist asking Frank about Betty Bacall, even though George Jacobs had specifically warned her not to do it. She had to know Frank's side of the story. "I need to know something," she began over dinner that night as Jacobs helped serve the meal. Then she laid it on the line. "I heard that you ended your engagement to Betty Bacall because you thought she told the press about the two of you. And rather than ask her about it, you just never called her back," she said, the words just spilling out, almost as if she was babbling. "And last night you found out that Swifty Lazar was the one who told the press, not Betty. And *that's* why you were so upset. Is that true, Charlie Brown?"

Frank put his fork down. He stared at her menacingly. He demanded to know who she had been talking to about him. Mia said, "No one," as she glanced nervously at George; she knew she had to protect him. Frank wasn't buying it, though. "Well, *someone* told you that," he said, his anger rising. "Who was it?" he asked, now looking at George. George looked away, avoiding Frank's steady gaze. Mia then lied and said that she thought she had read about it in Sheila Graham's gossip column. It didn't make any difference how she'd heard about it, though, she said. She just wanted to know if it was true.

"I'm not going to have this discussion with you, Mia," Frank announced.

"But..."

"Enough!" Frank shouted, raising his voice so loud that Mia became frightened. He then pounded the table with both fists. "I told you, *I am not having this discussion with you.*" And with that he rose and stormed off, leaving Mia pale and shaking at the table.

Nancy's Marriage Ends

It was 1965, the era of Motown and of the Beatles—rhythm and blues and the Liverpool sound—as well as youthful folk protest songs by artists such as Bob Dylan. The music business had changed dramatically, and by this time the youth set had little time for Elvis

Presley, let alone Frank Sinatra. However, Frank could always find an appreciative audience, especially in Vegas. In fact, the prior year had ended with him playing the Sands Hotel for a two-week engagement that was a complete sellout. With Frank sharing the bill with the Count Basie orchestra conducted by Quincy Jones, the reviews were terrific. Frank easily held on to his rightful place as an American icon with older audiences. His record buyers had grown older with him; they were still loyal and supportive of pretty much everything he did—recordings, films, and concerts. He may have been almost fifty, but as far as his audiences were concerned, he was still in his prime.

In the summer of 1965, Frank embarked on a six-city concert tour, which was promoted as "Frank Sinatra and Company with Count Basie and His Band," marking the first time Frank had toured with a band in twenty years. Mia wanted to accompany him on the road, but she became ill and had to stay behind. The tour was a huge success, breaking box-office records at each stop along the way. A couple of days after it was over, Frank's handprints, along with his signature, were immortalized in cement at Grauman's Chinese Theatre. Nancy and Tina accompanied him to the ceremony. Meanwhile, *None but the Brave* was released to critical raves. Another film, *Marriage on the Rocks* (with Deborah Kerr and Dean Martin), was also released, featuring Nancy as Frank's daughter.

Though her father seemed to be thriving professionally and personally, 1965 was not a good year for Nancy Sinatra. Ironically enough, while she was working on *Marriage on the Rocks*, her own marriage broke up. She had married former teenage idol Tommy Sands five years earlier, in September 1960. Now Sands—now an actor and pop singer—wanted out of the relationship. Nancy was stunned; she said she thought they had a good marriage. Actually, Tommy was in therapy at the time, and it was he and his therapist who decided that the marriage had to end, without asking Nancy's opinion.

Nancy recalled, "In my mother's bed, crying and feeling sorry for myself, I thought it was the end of the world. Dad came in and he said, 'I know you're sad. I know you're unhappy. And I know you're miserable. But I can only tell you that it will pass and that I'm glad you're not alone. You have me and Mom and your sister and brother.'"

"Stay away from dark thoughts, Chicken," Frank often told his daughter (using his special nickname for her), especially during this time. "Don't despair," he would tell her. She would hold fast to his words.

Dolly on Mia: "This Is Trouble. Mark My Words."

$\mathcal{B}$y August 1965, Frank Sinatra was exhausted, having just returned from Israel where he had filmed United Artists' *Cast a Giant Shadow* with Kirk Douglas. He needed some downtime. So he chartered a 170-foot-long yacht, the *Southern Breeze*, and invited Mia to sail along with him and nine other friends, including Rosalind Russell and Claudette Colbert and their husbands, Freddie Brisson and Joel Pressman.

Mia and Frank flew to New England together on Frank's private jet to begin their yachting vacation; rumors abounded that a wedding would take place either on the yacht or at one of its stopovers. The *New York Daily News* posed the question in its headline, "Sinatra and Mia Sailing to Altar?" The *Journal-American* asked in its own headline, "Are They, or Aren't They?"

"Within twenty-four hours, you couldn't see the ocean for the flotilla of paparazzi, and you couldn't hear yourself think for the helicopters," Mia remembered, "and you couldn't watch television without seeing yourself and hearing about how ancient Frank Sinatra was and how young I was."

Frank had planned occasional stops along the way for Mia to enjoy. He loved showing her new sights, sharing his success and good fortune with her. At one point, he took her to the Kennedy compound in Hyannis Port. He actually hadn't seen the Kennedys since JFK's death, and he wondered what the reception might be like. Bobby wasn't present. Jackie also wasn't there; she was in New York. However, Ted welcomed Frank with open arms, as did the Kennedy sisters, Jean, Eunice, and Pat. Rose was also very gracious, though she did pull Eunice aside to inquire as to whether Mia was a friend of Frank's or a friend of one of his children. When Eunice explained to Rose that Mia was Frank's girlfriend, the Kennedy matriarch looked a little astonished. "I can't say that I have ever quite understood that man," she declared. The entire clan then came aboard Frank's boat and played charades and drank liquor; they had a great time. Before taking her leave, Rose embraced Mia. "If you've found someone to take good care of you, then I say bully for you," she told Mia in her plucky fashion. "Just make sure you take good care of him in return." Mia said she would try her best.

Sadly, the fantasy cruise ended badly on August 10 when a twenty-three-year-old crewman, who was returning to the yacht from shore, drowned after his boat capsized. Frank and Mia were stunned, as were all of the guests.

Because news reports about the drowning focused on the fact that Frank and Mia were together on the cruise, Mia's mother, Maureen O'Sullivan, was unhappy about the publicity. She urged Mia by telephone to just come home. After the decision was made to pull the plug on the cruise and set anchor in the Hudson River, Frank's guests enjoyed a night on the town in Manhattan at the Aegean restaurant. Then it was on to Jilly's for a nightcap, and then to Frank's penthouse overlooking the East River.

"It had been the most closely observed cruise since Cleopatra floated down the Nile to meet Mark Antony," noted *Time* magazine after the cruise ended and no nuptials had taken place.

"The only reason Mia was even on that yacht was because she burned her eye while shooting *Peyton Place*," Maureen O'Sullivan told the press. "One misconception is that Mia was on the yacht un-chaperoned," she went on. "Why, all those guests were there, and they're all friends of mine; they would take care of her if she needed any taking care of—which she didn't." It seems clear that O'Sullivan either didn't know or didn't want to believe that Frank and Mia were sleeping together, and that her daughter certainly didn't need a "chaperone."

Meanwhile, Frank's mother, Dolly, had her own take on things. She insisted that Frank was only trying to help Mia launch her career. "How many times has he helped somebody to the top?" she asked one reporter. "That's what he's doing now." Dolly maintained that her son would never marry Mia. After all, two of Frank's children (Nancy and Frank) were older than Mia, she noted.

Of course, Frank wanted Dolly's approval of Mia. After the cruise, he brought Mia to Fort Lee to meet his parents over an Italian feast Dolly had spent two days preparing. Mia didn't eat a thing, a sin in Dolly's world. Though Mia politely explained that she was a vegetarian, Dolly tried to force her to at least eat one meatball—but it wasn't going to happen.

"This is the best Frank could do after Ava?" Dolly asked George Jacobs. She was perplexed. George didn't know how to respond. He and Dolly were in the kitchen. Meanwhile, Frank was cuddling with Mia on a plastic-covered sofa in the living room. Keeping his voice low so that the boss couldn't hear, George said that Mia was "a good kid, a good match." However, Dolly wasn't convinced. With all of the actresses of class and standing available to her son, she said she couldn't understand why he would end up with a girl who seemed like an innocent little waif. "What TV show is she on, again?" Dolly asked.

"*Peyton Place*," George answered.

"Never heard of it," Dolly snapped. She continued, saying that a woman had to be tough in order to survive in a relationship with her son, and Mia didn't look at all like she was up for the challenge. "Watch out for her, George," Dolly advised Frank's valet. She suggested that he "get Mia out of the picture before she gets hurt."

"Well, at least Mr. S. is happy," George said as the two continued to watch Frank and Mia on the couch. "I haven't seen him this happy in a while."

Dolly shook her head. "This is trouble," she predicted. "Mark my words."

The Walter Cronkite Interview

Right before Frank Sinatra turned fifty in December 1965, a major publicity campaign was launched with the significant birthday as its focus. At the end of the year, Reprise released the Grammy Award–winning *September of My Years* album. It was ironic that with Frank's age being such a focus due to his relationship with Mia, he would release an album with the subject of aging as its theme. It featured songs such as the "September" title track, "Last Night When

We Were Young," and "Hello, Young Lovers." Brilliantly arranged and conducted by Gordon Jenkins, each song was given a deeply personal, life-affirming performance by Sinatra. As he sang the lyrics of "How Old Am I?" ("You kiss me and I'm young"), it wasn't difficult to imagine that he was singing about his relationship with Mia.

The centerpiece of the *September* album was Frank's rendition of the hauntingly reflective, autobiographical "It Was a Very Good Year," for which he would be awarded a Grammy for Best Male Vocal Performance. In fact, the album won four Grammys, including Best Arranger (Gordon Jenkins for "It Was a Very Good Year"), Album of the Year, and Best Album Notes.

To coincide with the birthday celebration, CBS News also scheduled a program to commemorate Sinatra's twenty-fifth anniversary in show business. It was decided that Walter Cronkite would tape an interview with Frank at his Palm Springs home for the broadcast. Prior to the interview, the network was instructed by Mickey Rudin that Cronkite should not ask any questions about Mia Farrow, nor should he ask about Frank's alleged mob ties. Producer Don Hewitt, ostensibly speaking for the network, agreed that any such line of questioning would be off-limits. "Hey, if that's what Frank wants, that's what he'll get," said Hewitt. However, Walter Cronkite customarily accepted no such parameters in planning his interviews. No one ever told Cronkite what to ask or what *not* to ask during his interviews.

As the cameras rolled, Cronkite did ask about Mia. It was an innocuous question and one that Frank dodged easily. Still, Frank was annoyed by it. Then Cronkite tiptoed into more dangerous waters. As he remembered many years later, "Don [Hewitt] leaned over and whispered to me not to forget to ask him about the Mafia. So, my question was simply how did he want to respond to charges that he had Mafia connections. Sinatra's lips tightened to a tiny line. He gave me a piercing look through narrowing eyes."

"That's it," Frank announced angrily. He practically leapt out of his chair and stormed off to a bedroom with Hewitt and Jilly Rizzo following. An argument ensued that, recalled Cronkite, "featured the great voice raised to a level seldom used in a concert hall. The only coherent phrase I picked up was a charge that Hewitt had promised that the Mafia questions would not be raised."

Finally, at a loss as to how to handle things, Jilly decided to call Mia Farrow, who was back in Beverly Hills. He felt that she could reason with him. Apparently—from Frank's end of the conversation anyway—it appeared that Mia was trying to convince him to finish the interview. "Screw them," Frank said crossly at one point. "You think I care about them?" Clearly he was frustrated and lashing out, and maybe understandably so, because his desire to control his image was so thoroughly being thwarted by the reality of his life. It was obvious that the stories most people wanted to know about were precisely the ones he didn't want to talk about. After a few more moments, he said, "Okay, Mia. You're right. When you're right, you're right." After he hung up, he went back out and completed the interview. He responded to the question about the mob the way he usually did: "I do meet all kinds of people in the world because of the natural habitat from day to day; in the theatrical world, nightclub world, in concerts, in restaurants, you meet all kinds of people. So there's really not much to be said about that, and I think the less said the better, because there's no answer. When I say no, it's no, and for some reason it keeps persisting, you see, and consequently I just refuse to discuss it because you can't make a dent anywhere."

Two weeks before the show was to be broadcast, Mickey Rudin shot off an angry letter to CBS, charging the network with what can only be regarded as a novel crime: "breach of understanding." In the end, CBS deleted all references to Mia Farrow (though Frank mentioned "Miss Farrow" in the telling of an anecdote) from its broadcast of *Sinatra* on November 16, 1965. The answer about the underworld remained intact. Despite that, the program turned out to be a well-produced, evenhanded study.

Some interesting facts were revealed: Cronkite noted that Sinatra made $25 million while at Capitol and, as of the broadcast, $15 million at Reprise. He earned royalties of $60,000 a year from his recordings at Columbia. Frank Sinatra Enterprises brought in $4 million a year. "He uses his private jet like the average millionaire uses a limousine," said Cronkite. "There are no commercial airlines that would take Sinatra to the unlikely places he goes at the unlikely times he wants to go there."

Studio footage of Sinatra—tie loosened, standing before his sheet music and recording "It Was a Very Good Year"—was put to great use; it was fascinating to watch him work, tailoring the song in his unique, self-assured way. The studio was filled with people, sitting in the studio on chairs in rapt attention as if watching a concert. In fact, Frank almost always had spectators in the studio, unlike many artists who preferred to record in solitude. On the CBS broadcast, during the playback of the song when Frank heard himself sing "When I was thirty-five, it was a very good year," he turned to one of the studio personnel, flashed a boyish grin, and said, "*Those* were the swingin' years."

In the end, Frank was generally unhappy about the broadcast, even though everyone in his circle was relieved by its respectful tone. To Sinatra, a deal was a deal. It wasn't so much the benign questions about Mia and the underworld that annoyed him as it was the basic lack of principle behind them. It didn't matter to Frank that CBS couldn't control Walter Cronkite any more than it mattered that his answer regarding Mia had been excised from the broadcast. Privately, he called both Hewitt and Cronkite every name in the book.

When Frank's publicist, Jim Mahoney, suggested that as a goodwill measure, perhaps he should send a note of thanks to Don Hewitt, Frank deadpanned, "Lemme ask you something? Can you send a fist through the mail?"

What to Do About Mia?

*E*verything was going fairly well for Frank and Mia until the end of 1965. Then a serious problem arose when Nancy Sr. and her daughters, Nancy Jr. and Tina, began planning a party to celebrate Frank's fiftieth birthday. Hundreds of Frank's closest friends and associates would be in attendance—"a veritable cream of Hollywood society" is how the *Journal-American* put it, "emphatically A and not B group people." The dinner party was scheduled to be held at the Trianon Room of the Beverly Wilshire Hotel on Sunday evening, December 12.

Nancy Sr., who was forty-eight that year, didn't believe that Frank was really serious about Mia. She was so young, it just seemed hard to believe he was invested in her. Incredibly, Nancy continued to hold out hope that she would reconcile with Frank, and Nancy Jr. held on to that same dream. They were simply not going to take Mia seriously. "If my father gets serious with that girl, I will be very upset," Nancy Jr. said at the time. "I'm sorry, but how am I supposed to feel? It's no reflection on Miss Farrow, who I am sure is lovely. However, the fact remains that she is four or five years younger than I am! How am I supposed to feel about that?"

Despite her and her daughter's misgivings, Nancy Sr. still didn't want to start any trouble. Therefore, three days before the event, she suggested that Frank invite Mia. He was happy, of course, as was Mia. He took her to a Beverly Hills boutique and treated her to a shopping spree—"anything my girl wants, she can have." Among the bounty of expensive designer clothing Mia bought was a baby blue chiffon dress for the party.

"Frank's taking me to his birthday party," an elated Mia told her *Peyton Place* director, Jeffrey Hayden, the morning of the event. "It's going to be so much fun."

Hayden was immediately worried. "Mia, you are in the very first shot tomorrow morning," he told her, according to his memory. "At 8 a.m. Please, I am begging you, Mia, don't stay out too late with Sinatra. I need you here at 8 a.m. Promise me, Mia!"

That night, Mia excitedly prepared herself for the party. She had brought her change of clothes to Frank's house and decided to do her makeup and hair there as well. "How do you like my dress," she asked as she descended the staircase. She posed for Frank, twirled around, and smiled.

"I'm afraid I changed my mind, Babyface," Frank said. "I'm sorry. You can't go."

"*But why?*" Mia asked, instant tears springing to her eyes. George Jacobs ran to get a box of tissues. He knew what was coming.

"It's just not going to work," Frank explained. "My son called and he's upset and his sisters are upset. I don't know. Just do me a favor, Mia, and don't go, okay?"

"I don't understand," Mia said crying.

"Look, Mia," Frank said firmly. "You're not a little girl, you're a woman. Act like one."

Insulted, Mia angrily ran from the Sinatra mansion, got into her convertible, put it into gear, and screeched down the driveway and away as fast as her wheels could take her. Frank immediately felt badly. He knew he hadn't handled the situation well at all. "What a schmuck I am," he told George Jacobs. He asked George to jump into his car and follow her to her apartment just to make certain she got there safely.

The party celebrating Sinatra's fiftieth birthday was a glittering affair, as advertised, but Frank was distracted. He couldn't hide it. He tried to be present, but Mia rarely left his thoughts. To make things worse, Frank Jr. hadn't even shown up! Therefore, Frank Sr. had to wonder what difference it made what he or anyone else thought of Mia. He also wondered what Mia was doing all by herself back in her little apartment. Probably crying her eyes out, at least according to what he fretted to guests.

"No More Little Girl"

The day after the party, Mia was due at the set at eight in the morning. When she didn't show up, director Jeffrey Hayden was frantic and pacing. "Where the hell is she?" he asked everyone. "It's nine and she's not here. She's never late. Of all days!"

Finally, an hour later, Mia showed up. Hayden let her have it. "Mia!" he exclaimed. "We have ten pages to film here today! Get to that makeup table! Stop this little-girl stuff! You're an actress! You're a mature person! You've got a crew of seventy-five people waiting to shoot your scenes." He was tough on her.

"I'm sorry," she said, very quietly. Seeming somehow dazed, Mia then walked robotically to her dressing room. She sat down. She found a pair of scissors on the table, she gazed at her reflection in the mirror...and then she proceeded to cut off her hair. Those long locks that Frank had so loved from the moment he met her, all gone in an instant. Given the speed with which she did it, it couldn't have been done in an artful way, either. It actually looked like she just had hacked away at it. Or as Mia herself put it, "I picked up a pair of scissors and cut my hair to less than an inch in length."

"She came back a minute and a half later," Jeffrey Hayden recalls. "She walked over to me, held up her hand full of the hair from her head, and she said, 'Jeff. No more little-girl stuff.' And handed me all her hair."

Jeff was mortified. He didn't know exactly what was going through Mia's mind, but in that moment he didn't care. Whatever was going on in Mia's private life was her business. His concern was *Peyton Place*. "Mia!" he said, dismayed. "We gotta match your last scene from yesterday's shooting! What will we do?"

She shrugged. "I just wanted you to know I'm growing up," she said flatly. "No more little-girl stuff." With that, she turned and walked away.

Jeff Hayden ran to the telephone and called Paul Monash, the producer of *Peyton Place*, who also wrote for the show. "Paul, tell me what to do," Jeffrey said, panicked. "Mia, she cut off all her hair! It's not going to match yesterday's shots!"

Monash was startled, of course, but there wasn't much time to be confused. He had to solve the problem quickly. "Get two flats [blank set walls] and a bed," he said. "Get Mia into that bed and I'll be down in fifteen minutes."

Hayden did as he was told. Two walls were set up in the corner of an empty soundstage. A simple bed was placed in front of them. Mia came into the studio and Hayden told her to lie down in the bed. "Okay, she's in the bed," he said, calling Monash again. "Now what?"

"Get some bandages and wrap her head in them," Monash instructed. "I'll be down in five [minutes]."

"So we wrapped bandages around Mia's head," Jeffrey Hayden recalled. "Minutes later, in walks Paul Monash with new pages of dialogue. Turns out, Mia's character had been in an auto accident," Hayden recalls, laughing. "We shot it, boom, boom, boom—and Mia's character then stayed in that hospital bed with her head bandaged for the next several weeks."

"There were stern lectures about responsibility, and I apologized a lot," Mia Farrow would later recall. "But, privately, I couldn't see a problem."

Boots and Strangers

*I*n February 1966, Frank's daughter Nancy, now twenty-five, hit number one on the charts with the truly unforgettable song "These Boots Are Made for Walking." Nancy had actually been recording for five full years on her dad's Reprise label before finally striking gold. In fact, she had recorded about fifteen singles—such as "Cufflinks and a Tie Clip" and "Like I Do." But then she teamed up with writer-producer Lee Hazlewood, and the result was "Boots," a hard-edged, feminist song. It boasted a tough, no-nonsense lyric, and Nancy would later say that she had to dig deep to find that aspect of herself. "'Boots' was hard," she said, "and I'm as soft as they come." Hazlewood felt differently about her, though. "You're not a sweet young thing," he told her. "You're not the virgin next door. You've been married and divorced. You're a grown woman. I know there's garbage in there somewhere. Find it! Show it to me!"

"These Boots Are Made for Walking" hit the number one spot in just three weeks; it would go on to sell four million copies and garner three Grammy nominations.

Nancy had a number of hits in the 1960s other than "Boots," such as "How Does That Grab You, Darlin'?" and "Sugar Town," as well as "Summer Wine" and "Jackson," both duets with Lee Hazlewood. While she started with somewhat limited ability and a narrow range, her producers turned any limitations into an undeniable style all her own. She recorded a number of albums, many of which are today cult classics.

She was often compared to her father, which she found absurd. She became so annoyed by the constant comparison early in her career, she actually telephoned a critic. It was very much like Nancy to call a reporter with a grievance. "I have a bone to pick with you," she told the surprised writer. "Keep a sense of humor about this call, though, okay? I don't want you to get all defensive." The surprised critic agreed. "Listen, I will never be my father. I will never be Frank Sinatra. Nobody on this planet will ever be another Frank Sinatra. So critique me all you want, and in fact, I welcome it. But please promise me, no more comparing me to my father." The critic promised.

Today, Nancy still has a very loyal following. She once said that had she not chosen to become a wife and mother, she felt she could have segued into a career in adult pop or standards pop similar to that of Linda Ronstadt. Though the public mainly knew her through hit singles and her "Boots" image, she would go on to do impressive shows in Las Vegas. In her films, such as *Speedway* (1968) with Elvis Presley, she demonstrated a relaxed presence; the camera loved her.

As his daughter's career took off, Frank Sinatra began 1966 by booking another successful engagement at the Sands in Las Vegas with Count Basie and Quincy Jones. These shows were recorded and were released later in the year as a live album, *Sinatra at the Sands*.

On April 11, Frank would record one of his most classic songs, "Strangers in the Night." This tune would prove to be the third number one record for his Reprise label, following Dean Martin's "Everybody Loves Somebody" and Nancy Sinatra's "Boots."

"Strangers in the Night," with its tango rhythm, would also go on to become Sinatra's biggest worldwide hit. It even replaced the Beatles at the top of the charts on July 2, 1966, when it supplanted "Paperback Writer." One look at the *Billboard* Top Five that week and it's clear that Frank was once again relevant among a much younger pop set: the Beatles, Cyrkle ("Red Rubber Ball"), the Rolling Stones ("Paint It Black"), and Dusty Springfield ("You Don't Have to Say You Love Me").

Reprise A&R executive Jimmy Bowen was responsible for finding "Strangers" for Frank. He had first heard the melody by German composer Bert Kaempfert and promised Kaempfert that if he could write English lyrics to it, Sinatra would record the song. It took a while to set the recording date with Frank, and by the time he was ready to record the song, Bobby Darin and Jack Jones had already recorded their own versions. Three days before Jack's version was to hit the streets, Jimmy Bowen telephoned arranger Ernie Freeman to tell him that Sinatra—not Darin—had to have the hit with this one. It was just the perfect song for Sinatra, or so Bowen felt, and he wanted Freeman to come up with a classic, hitmaking arrangement.

Three days later, Bowen and an orchestra were in the studio rehearsing the new arrangement. That was at 5 p.m. By eight, Frank was behind the mike. An hour later, the session ended. Twenty-four hours after that, the record hit the streets and radio stations were playing it. "You couldn't do that today if you had a million bucks on the line," Frank later said, and he was right. (The song would later be covered by a wide array of artists, including Mel Tormé, Johnny Mathis, the Supremes, Barry Manilow, and, oddly, even James Brown.)

Frank and Nelson Riddle cut the *Strangers in the Night* album in just two days. It's an interesting collection in that it demonstrates Frank's ability to do almost any kind of album effectively. This was clearly a patched-together, hurried effort designed to capitalize on a big hit, featuring songs that have no relation to each other. Yet it is still utterly engaging and charming.

The *Strangers in the Night* album soared to number one on *Billboard*'s charts and stayed there for seventy-three weeks. Frank would go on to win a Grammy for his performance of the song, and Ernie Freeman won one for his arrangement.

While "Strangers in the Night" was the big hit, the follow-up is also an enduring classic: "Summer Wind" (with lyrics by Johnny Mercer). It is still considered by most music critics and Sinatra aficionados as one of Frank's best recordings. His laid-back vocal performance and Riddle's sultry arrangement (with jazz organ) found just the right groove, even if it didn't enjoy the commercial success of "Strangers in the Night." Though "Summer Wind" was also recorded by Perry Como and Wayne Newton, it was Frank's rendition that made the biggest impression on most listeners and disc jockeys.

Mia Meets the Family

Frank didn't know what to make of the fact that Mia had cut her hair so dramatically. Was it some sort of retaliation for the birthday party? Mia insisted that it wasn't, but he couldn't help but be suspicious. After all, she knew how much he had loved her long hairstyle. Still, there seemed no reason to belabor it. So he made light of it. "Now you can go out for Little League like the rest of the boys," he told her.

By the spring of 1966, Frank and Mia had been together for almost two years. Frank's family still hadn't even met Mia, which for her was a problem. In her mind, it stood to reason that if Frank was serious about her he would integrate her into his life, not keep her separate from it. After discussing it with her, he had to agree.

Frank realized that introducing Mia to Nancy Sr. and Nancy Jr. might be tricky. He also knew that Frank Jr. wasn't going to be a good barometer for how the family might accept Mia. Tina was different, though. She was practical, like Frank. She wasn't romantic and idealistic, she was pragmatic, or, as he liked to say, "She knows the score." He suspected that it would be Tina who would give Mia the fairest shot.

One day, Frank invited Tina over to a house he was renting in Holmby Hills. He suggested that they could play tennis, knowing full well that Mia was planning to come by. "If you stick around," he told Tina, who was eighteen by this time, "you'll get to meet Mia." Tina was excited.

When Mia finally showed up, she made a huge impression on Tina. "I thought to myself, 'She's perfect,'" Tina would recall. Mia was so disarming and fun to be around; in the weeks to come she and Tina would become fast friends. Just three years apart, they had a lot in common. Frank was right about his youngest daughter; she hadn't let him down.

Later, Tina would admit that she never believed Frank and Mia could make a real go of it as a couple, but she had no problem with them at least trying. When Frank finally introduced Mia to the two Nancys, it wasn't so bad. "I was there when he brought Mia to Big Nancy's house," George Jacobs recalled. "It was awkward, of course. But Big Nancy was very gracious and tried to make Mia feel at home, which got her a gold star in my book. Mia was so nervous, I think Big Nancy felt sorry for her. I remember her saying, 'It's all right dear. We're just an ordinary family like yours.' And Mia laughed and said, 'I sure hope not! Because my family is far from normal!' Tina seemed to get along great with her, but Nancy was very standoffish. She was not about to lose her father to a girl Mia's age. She and Mia would become friendly in time, but not in the beginning. It was tense. Meanwhile, Frankie didn't even show, which didn't surprise anyone but Mia.

"In the car on the way home, Mia said to Mr. S., 'Your son doesn't like me and he hasn't even met me.' Frank glanced at me, sighed heavily, and then looked at Mia and said, 'Well, not everything is about you, Mia.'"

Frank and Mia Marry

*B*ut my mother is going to be so upset," Mia argued. "I *have* to tell her!"

"I don't care," Frank said. "You can't."

It was July 19, 1966. The two were speaking on the phone. She was in Los Angeles. He was in London, where he was finishing up the movie *The Naked Runner* and getting ready to take a flight back to Los Angeles.

"I'm not even telling Nancy, Tina, Frank...none of 'em," Frank said. "Even my first wife, Nancy. No one can know that you and I are gettin' hitched." Maybe he realized that the impending nuptials would be a most unpopular subject among his loved ones, and he didn't want them interfering with his plans. Or perhaps he remembered the controversy that had erupted over whether or not Mia should attend his birthday party, and he didn't want any more trouble. Whatever his reasons, he decided that his loved ones should be kept in the dark about the wedding.

Mia wasn't happy about it. "But why?" she asked.

"Because I said so."

The wedding took place the next day in Las Vegas. Mia wore a white silk dress with full caftan sleeves, the kind of informal dress a woman might wear for her second wedding, not her first. Her hair was boyish, cut as close to her head as Frank's. He was dapper in a dark suit and tie. Red Skelton, the famous comedian, was one of the few witnesses. "That guy over there, Red? He just shot his wife," Frank confided to Mia right before the ceremony. She was shocked. What kind of world was she entering, where a man shoots his wife and then attends the wedding of a friend? "Don't worry. It'll be ruled an accident," Frank assured her. "She *accidentally* shot herself," he added with a wink. (Red's wife, Georgia Skelton, was in the hospital in Las

Vegas after suffering a gunshot wound to the chest on July 19, the day before the wedding. Skelton said his wife might have brushed against the loaded gun while reaching for a dressing robe. Just as Frank predicted, the shooting was ruled accidental.)

In a few hours, the newlyweds were at Frank's home in Palm Springs.

Meanwhile, back in Los Angeles, it was Dean Martin who alerted Tina. She happened to be at his home, and he asked to speak to her in his den. "I just want you to know, kiddo, your dad and Mia are getting married," he told her.

"What? *When?*" she asked.

"Right now. In this very second," he said.

"Are you kidding me?" Tina asked, shocked.

"Nope. It's happening right now," Dean said, according to Tina's memory of the conversation. "Go home and tell your mom before she hears about it on the news."*

Tina thanked Dean for the information and left his house, racing back to hers as quickly as possible. By the time she got home, her mother had already gotten the news. Dorothy Manners, who was now writing Louella Parsons's column for her, had called to get a comment after the wedding photos made the wire service. Nancy was upset. She couldn't believe Frank would marry Mia and not tell any of them about it in advance.

About an hour later, Frank finally called, but he was the last person on earth Nancy wanted to speak to. Tina took the call. Frank said he wanted to warn them; something "big" had happened. "Too late," Tina told him. "We already know." Father and daughter then had a very heated discussion.

Tina's disappointment in Frank was understandable. He had trusted her enough to allow her to meet and befriend Mia, and she had no harsh judgment about the relationship. She was on his side,

---

* Apparently it was part of the culture these men lived in to be secretive. In a few years, his daughter Deana would find out he was engaged to his third wife, Cathy Mae Hawn, when she accidentally got a bill from Bonwit Teller for $11,000 for two fur coats. When she called the store to inquire about it, she was told, "Oh, that was meant for your dad's new fiancée."

if in fact sides were to be taken. Why then would he exclude her from his plans to marry Mia? Worse yet, in her mind anyway, that her mother should have to hear about it from a gossip columnist was unacceptable.

"But I want you to be happy for me," Frank said.

"That's impossible," Tina said angrily. "I'm too busy being pissed off at you."

"That's not fair," Frank said. "I'm happy for you and Sammy, aren't I?"

At this time, Tina was dating a Realtor, Sammy Hess, who was ten years her senior; she was eighteen, he was twenty-eight. Hess would present her with an emerald cut diamond, but not before asking Frank for permission to marry her. Sinatra appreciated the gesture; he liked Hess. Even though there was a big age difference, he decided to support Tina. Now he wanted her to do the same for him. Tina actually had no problem with the age difference between him and Mia. It was his secret marriage that bothered her. "How would you like it if Sammy and I just up and eloped and didn't tell you about it?" she asked Frank. He had to admit, he would be very unhappy. (In the end, Tina decided not to marry Hess, breaking off their engagement twice just before going to the altar. Years later, Hess would end up dating Mia Farrow!)

In the end, Tina refused to give Frank her blessing, and during the ensuing argument made a few comments she would later feel badly about, and for which she would apologize. Years later, she would say, "I can't blame Dad for keeping his secret. He couldn't trust his family because he didn't want to hear what he already knew: that he was nuts."

Nancy Sr. and Nancy Jr. were just as upset at Frank as Tina. They knew they'd have to get over it, though. What were they going to do? Cut him out of their lives? Nancy, who was truly bereft, issued a statement: "Of course, none of this came as a surprise to us. Our father told us he was going to marry Miss Farrow last weekend. So we knew it was happening."

Meanwhile, Frank Jr. was performing at the KoKo Motel in Cocoa Beach, Florida, when reporter George Carpozi, hopeful of soliciting a comment from him, called him with the news of his father's marriage. "You must be kidding," Frankie gasped. "I don't believe it. When did it happen?"

After Carpozi explained the details, he asked why Sinatra Sr. had married so quickly—and quietly.

"I think you ought to confine questions like that to Frank Sinatra," Frank Jr. said.

"Is this true love?" Carpozi said, pushing.

"*How the hell am I supposed to know?*" Frank Jr. yelled into the telephone. "*You got the wrong person, I told you. Go ask Frank Sinatra.*"

Mia Meets Ava

*I*n a few days, Frank was back in London to continue work on *The Naked Runner*, a suspense drama in which he portrays an inadvertent assassin, but now with Mia at his side and the press stalking the couple at every turn. While in London, he took Mia to meet Ava one night at her new town house in Ennismore Gardens in Knightsbridge. George Jacobs recalled, "The three of us walked up to Ava's door, knocked on it, and when it opened, there stood magnificent Ava, with all of this raven hair all teased out like a big black cloud around her face. She took one look at Mia with her short, *short* haircut and her mouth dropped wide open. But she recovered quickly and welcomed us into her home."

"Francis, now why don't you and George take little Rags out for a wee-wee," Ava said, referring to her corgi. (This was the second corgi Ava had named Rags.)

"Well..." Frank hesitated. He glanced at Mia, who looked terrified.

"Oh, come now," Ava said, putting her arm around Mia. "I won't bite, I promise."

"We walked out the door with Rags on a leash," George Jacobs recalled, "and Frank said, 'Leaving Mia with Ava is like sending a lamb to the slaughter.' We tried to make it quick, but the dog wouldn't piss. 'If this little bastard doesn't go soon, I'm gonna strangle him,' Frank warned me. 'We gotta get back to Mia!' I asked him, 'Why did we even bring her to meet Ava?' And he said, 'Because Ava has been bugging me about it ever since she found out we were going to be in town. I had no choice.' He was a nervous wreck.

"Finally, when we returned, Ava and Mia were sitting on the couch, having cocktails and laughing away. Mia was just fine. Ava was very tipsy. Obviously she'd had a head start on us. We sat down and joined them.

"Francis, now why didn't you tell this child that you called me on your wedding day?" Ava asked Frank.

"Um...well..." Frank stammered, looking uncomfortable. "Did I call you, Ava?" he asked, looking like a deer in headlights.

"Why, of course you did!" Ava exclaimed. "Remember, you said, 'Tomorrow, when you read about this wedding in the papers, know that no matter how I feel about this girl, I will always have a place in my heart for you.' That was so sweet of him, wasn't it, dear?" Ava asked, turning to Mia.

Mia nodded with a frozen smile. "Well, it is interesting, I'll say that much about it," she observed. "I think what's even *more* interesting, though," she added, glancing at Frank, "is that he wouldn't let me call my own mother, yet he called *you*, his ex-wife."

"Now, that *is* interesting, isn't it, dear?" Ava agreed, nodding.

"Mr. S. looked like he wanted to dig a big hole in the floor and just jump right in," recalled George Jacobs. "After about another hour, Mr. S. decided we had to leave because he had to get up early and be on set. When we got up, Ava asked about Tina and Nancy. Frank said they were fine. Then she asked about Frank Jr. 'He's good,' Frank said quickly. 'And what does he think of this young girl?' she asked, referring to Mia. Frank stammered and turned to Mia and said, 'Have you met my son?' And Mia said, 'Um...I don't know. I don't think so. Have I?' Ava just shook her head.

"As we walked to the door, Ava took Mr. S.'s arm and I heard her say, 'I approve, Francis. I can't say that I understand. But I do approve.'

"In the cab on the way home, Mia didn't say a word," George Jacobs continued. "I think she was still a little rattled by what she found out Frank had told Ava on her wedding day. Frank didn't speak, either. I had a sense that if I hadn't been squeezed between them in the back-seat of a taxi, they probably would have had words."

The next day, Frank woke up feeling like he needed a break. Since he was a producer on the film, he felt he could take a brief hiatus if he wanted to do so. He wanted to go back to Palm Springs for a few days, maybe even film the rest of the movie there. "I'm tired and so's Mia," he told director Sidney Furie. Therefore, George Jacobs called the airline and made reservations for the three of them to depart the next morning.

Later that evening, Frank and Mia attended a party at a nightclub called Dolly's on Jermyn Street. Suddenly . . . there she was again: Ava. Frank had gone to the men's room and Mia was dancing with George on the very crowded dance floor when Ava approached. "*Daaaaarling,* I never said it," she told Mia urgently while pulling her in closely. Mia looked confused. "*The papers!*" Ava exclaimed, ignoring George. "They wrote that I said, 'I always knew Frank would end up in bed with a boy!' But I *didn't* say it, my dear," she insisted, slurring her words. "I meant to tell you this yesterday, but it completely slipped my mind. You must believe me. Tell me that you do!"

It was such a mad scene, with loud, thumping music and party-goers squeezed so tightly together, Mia could barely move, let alone think. She didn't know what to say to Ava. "Well, thank you," she finally managed over the din. "Thank you for telling me that, Miss Gardner."

And with that, someone pulled Ava Gardner back into the crowd.

Unkind

*F*or the rest of 1966 and into 1967, Mia Farrow did her best to be Frank Sinatra's dutiful wife at the desert compound. When guests would visit, she tried to be gracious, but still, she was a clumsy and inexperienced hostess. She would much rather have been at the Factory—a discotheque in Hollywood—dancing with people her own age than be stuck in Palm Springs ("Graveyard for the Dead-and-Coming," as she called it), serving cocktails to people twice—even three times—her age. "More gasoline for everyone," Frank would tell her. Always at Frank's side in Palm Springs were people like Bill and Edie Goetz—she was Louis B. Mayer's oldest daughter and a renowned socialite with an art collection worth more than $50 million; Jack Entratter, president of the Sands Hotel in Las Vegas, and his wife, Corinne; Rosalind Russell and her husband, movie producer Frederick Brisson—people who were more the peers of Mia's mother than of Mia. "All she wanted was to be Mrs. Frank Sinatra," said one of her friends. "That was all she wanted, that's all she was. So she just tried and tried."

In the spring, Mia went to Europe to make *A Dandy in Aspic*, with Laurence Harvey. Frank, not crazy about her having a movie career, decided she could make one picture a year, just to placate her. Meanwhile, he took on an engagement at the Fontainebleau in Miami while at the same time filming the movie *Tony Rome*. It was a tough schedule—before cameras by day and audiences by night. He and Mia spoke on the telephone three, sometimes four times a day, and seemed to be on good terms. It would be ten days in London for her, and three in Berlin, or so Mia promised Frank. She told him she would be home "soon."

Of course, as often happens in the movie business, there were all sorts of production delays, not the least of which was caused by the sudden death of the film's director, Michael Mann. When Mia called Frank to tell him of Mann's death, she was very distraught. He'd been such a gentleman, she said, yet when he died everyone—even his own wife—seemed more concerned about how the movie would be finished than about his demise. Mia said that they called room service instead of a coroner. And there was Michael Mann, sprawled out on the bed dead, while everyone ate and talked about how the show had to go on. Mia told Frank that based on that macabre scene alone, she didn't feel she was cut out for the movie business. Even though she was crying, none of it seemed to matter to Frank—at least not until she said, "It looks like I'll be here for at least an extra week." *Now* he was listening. "Absolutely not," he said. He didn't care about the movie's scheduling problems or even about Michael Mann's death, he just wanted his wife home. Now Mia was even more upset; she demanded to know why it was that her problems never seemed to matter. After all, she pointed out, she dealt with Frank's problems every single day of the week, yet when she had one, it meant nothing to him. He hung up on her.

When Mia finally did return to the States, things seemed different with Frank. He was more distant, aloof and even unkind. One afternoon, George Jacobs found Mia on a lounge at the pool, crying softly. He felt badly for her. He walked out to the patio, lit a joint, and handed it to her. Though the two did get high from time to time, they never did so at the house because they knew how Frank felt about drugs. Usually they'd take a drive into the canyons and fire up a joint there. But she was so sad, George felt Mia deserved a bit of a respite. Besides, Frank wasn't home; he was at a meeting. She smiled up at him, took the joint, put it to her mouth, and inhaled deeply. After he sat next to her, they finished the joint. After about twenty minutes, Mia took a final hit, closed her eyes, and exhaled a plume of smoke toward the sky. "Right now, to tell you the truth, Georgie Porgy," she said with a sigh, "I couldn't give two shits about Frank Sinatra."

"Somethin' Stupid"

On April 15, 1967, Frank Sinatra had a number one record in a duet with his daughter Nancy with the catchy song "Somethin' Stupid." The tune had been recorded back in February at the end of sessions for the critically hailed album *Francis Albert Sinatra and Antonio Carlos Jobim.*

"Somethin' Stupid" is the only father-daughter duet to ever go to the top of the charts. Lee Hazlewood found the song for Nancy— it was originally recorded in the early 1960s by folksinger Carson Parks. When Hazlewood played the Parks song for Frank, he felt it would be a perfect duet. He told Lee that if he didn't want to record it with Nancy, let him do it. The idea of Frank and Nancy on a record together was too good to resist. In the end, it was coproduced by Frank's producer, Jimmy Bowen, and Hazlewood. The single was completed in just four takes.

Some executives at Reprise were a little concerned that a father and daughter singing a love song to each other would seem...odd. One voiced that opinion to Frank, who said, "C'mon. Forget it. The song is gonna be a hit."

Mo Ostin, president of Reprise, was one of those who thought the song would bomb. He bet Frank two bucks on its quick demise. Needless to say, he lost the wager.

The song spent four weeks at number one on *Billboard*'s Hot 100 chart. It would be Frank's second gold single, and Nancy's third.

Personality Disorder

*I*n September 1967, Mia would get another strong dose of Frank's volatile temper, and it would once again place her in physical peril.

Frank was back in Las Vegas, at the Sands. Mia wasn't fond of Vegas and found herself bored whenever she went there with Frank. It annoyed her that he was usually off gambling while she—and the wives and girlfriends of his pals—dutifully watched them win or lose from the sidelines. "The women, who didn't seem to mind being referred to as 'broads,' sat up straight with their legs crossed and little expectant smiles on their carefully made-up faces," Mia later remembered. "They sipped white wine, smoked and eyed the men, and laughed at every joke. A long time would pass before any of the women dared to speak; then, under the mainly male conversation, they talked about their cats or where they bought their clothes, but more than half an ear was always on the men, just in case. As hours passed, the women, neglected in their chairs, drooped—no longer listening, no longer laughing. Often, I fell asleep with my head on my arms folded on the table."

One Friday evening, Jack Swigert, Wally Schirra, Tom Stafford, Gene Cernan, Walt Cunningham, and Ron Evans—all Apollo astronauts—came to see his show. Afterward, they joined Frank at the baccarat table. Frank asked for credit, as he did every night, but this time he was flatly rejected. He could hardly believe his ears. Eleanor Roth, who was Jack Entratter's assistant, later recalled, "He was humiliated in front of his heroes."

What Frank didn't know was that the casino's executive vice president, Carl Cohen, had just cut off his credit that very morning. An interoffice memo to the hotel's new owner, Howard Hughes, from his top aide, Robert Maheu, notes, "Carl Cohen stopped Sinatra's credit after he lost approximately fifty thousand dollars and would not cash out." Maheu also explained to Hughes that another reason Cohen cut off Sinatra's credit was because Frank had earlier been "running around the casino stating in a loud voice that [Hughes] had plenty of money and that there was no reason why [he] should not share it with him since he had made the Sands the profitable institution it is."

Frank had really prided himself on that line of Sands casino credit. He loved that he could saunter up to one of the tables with a "dame" on his arm and say, "Hey, Charlie, shoot me some credit," and always get it. But the reality of a credit line is that it's not just free money. Eventually, the tab has to be paid...but Frank never wanted to do so.

Irate about the humiliation in front of others, Sinatra found Carl Cohen. He and Cohen had a history; they hated each other. In Frank's mind, Cohen was just a hotel employee. He had no authority, he was just a chump with a high-paying job. For his part, Cohen viewed Sinatra as a blowhard, an overly indulged entertainer who, though he admittedly generated business, definitely wasn't worth all the trouble he caused.

The two had it out with one another. In the heat of the argument, Sinatra threatened to walk away from the Sands forever. In fact, he said, he wasn't even going to finish out the present engagement. That was fine with Cohen. "The sooner you leave, the better off we'll all be around here," he said. "See ya, Frank! Nice knowin' ya. *Schmuck!*"

Frank rapidly left Cohen's side and, with Mia following him and trying to calm him down, began stalking through the casino like a wild animal. He happened across the hotel's telephone department and, much to the horror of operators there, walked in and started pulling out all of the wires from the switchboard, thereby rendering service in the entire hotel inoperable. Then he came upon a golf cart in the hallway used to transport VIPs and the handicapped throughout the premises. He pushed Mia into the golf cart, then got behind the wheel and took off.

"Suddenly, without any warning, he pressed the gas pedal down as far as it would go; we were headed straight for the shiny plate-glass window," recalled Mia. "I knew it was pointless to say a word. In the final instant, we swerved and smashed sidelong into the window. By the time I realized we were both unharmed, he was already out of the cart and striding into the casino as I trotted after him, clutching my little beaded evening purse. He threw some chairs in a heap and with his golden lighter he tried to set them on fire. When he couldn't get a fire started, he took my hand, and we left the building."

"During the tantrum, no one, no guard, no clerk, dared to interfere with him," recalled George Jacobs, who witnessed the fracas. "They still treated him as if he owned the place and had the right to destroy it if he wanted to."

Just as quickly as it had erupted, Frank's anger subsided. He went from furious to apathetic in record time and no longer cared about any of it. He performed his shows that night without incident. However, Mia—still shaken from the dangerous golf cart ride—spent the evening in her room, crying about what she later called "Frank's personality disorder." The next morning, she hightailed it out of Vegas and went back to Los Angeles. That same day, Frank and Carl Cohen had another showdown, this time in the hotel's Garden Room restaurant. By this time, Frank's mood had ricocheted from apathy back to fury.

"I'm *never* playing this hotel again," Frank shouted at Cohen. "You tell Howard Hughes that, why don't you? I'm done here."

"You know what?" Cohen said. "Fuck *you*, Frank. How about *that*? *Fuck you!*"

Enraged, Frank gathered a fistful of chips and with all his might hurled them right at Cohen's face. Then he tilted the dining table, spilling food and drinks all over Cohen's lap. "You son of a bitch," he shouted at him. "How do you like that?"

Cohen very calmly rose, brushed off his suit, and then, in one quick and surprising move, let loose with a powerful right hook that landed squarely on Frank's jaw. Sinatra went down like a sack of potatoes, the caps on his two front teeth dislodging and flying clear across the room. The two men started in on each other, throwing kicks and punches and rolling around on the floor, all to the horrified astonishment of everyone else in the restaurant. At one point Frank threw a chair at Carl, but it missed him and hit a security guard on the head, which would require stitches.

After the fight, Frank went up to his room and sealed himself off in there. Now he was deeply depressed. He didn't perform that night and, as he had threatened, canceled the rest of the engagement. When he should have been onstage, he was on the phone with Mia telling her what had happened.

"His speech was unclear," Mia recalled, "but I soon made out that there had been a fight; the caps had been punched clear off his teeth, some other guy had been hurt, headlines were sure to follow, and his dentist was on the way with new teeth. It didn't much matter what started the fight; they always had to do with his powerful Sicilian sense of propriety. He sounded bewildered and upset as he said he loved and needed me, and with my whole being I loved and needed him too."

"She had so merged into him by this time, where he left off and where she began was a blur," said one of her best friends of that time. "It's not that she felt he could do no wrong, she was just too afraid to think about it at all. She was just trying to hold on to what she knew was her only identity."

The next day, as well as everyone else he blamed for the incident, Frank decided that the Sands' boss, Jack Entratter, who had been a close friend of his for many years, was also responsible for the melee. Phyllis McGuire recalled, "After Carl Cohen punched him out and Frank left the Sands, Sinatra never spoke to Jack again. Not ever. And Entratter lived right next door to him in Palm Springs!" (In fact, it would be nearly a year and a half before Frank would play Vegas again—this time at Caesars Palace, in November 1968.)

Later, when Kirk Douglas asked Frank about this incident, Frank dismissed it with a joke: "Kirk, I learned one thing. Never fight a Jew in the desert."

Rosemary's Baby

I just don't see it," Frank was saying. He was sitting at the breakfast table with Mia as George Jacobs served their meal. They were reviewing the script to a movie Mia had just been offered called *Rosemary's Baby*. "You giving birth to the devil? I don't like it," Frank said. "It's like some strange voodoo shit. My mother will flip if she sees you doing this shit."

"But it's the opportunity of a lifetime," Mia enthused. "It's Roman Polanski, and he's so hot right now. And the book [by Ira Levin] is a huge bestseller. And it's Paramount! I really want to do it."

"But what about *our* movie?" Frank said, not looking at Mia but still skimming over the script. It was true, the couple had just agreed to make a film together called The Detective for Fox, a cop thriller based on the bestseller by Roderick Thorp. It was set to begin filming on October 16, 1967.

"It's just three months," Mia said. "All of it here in L.A, except for one week in New York. Then I'll be back and we can do our film." Frank could see that she really wanted to make this "strange voodoo shit." Because it would be her first starring role, he really couldn't deny her the opportunity. "As long as you promise that this won't interfere with our movie," he said, "then...okay." With that, Mia jumped from her chair into his lap and smothered him with kisses.

Filming *Rosemary's Baby* would be tough for Mia. Roman Polanski would prove himself to be nothing if not eccentric, requiring, at one point in the filming, Mia to eat liver take after take even though she was a vegetarian. She almost threw up just from the smell of it. She weighed only ninety-eight pounds, but Roman insisted she lose more weight for the scenes when she is sickly pregnant with the devil's spawn. Twenty, thirty, forty takes was nothing for Polanski—even though it drove Mia and her costar John Cassavetes mad.

Soon after *Rosemary's Baby* started, Frank began working on The Detective in Los Angeles. But then things started to go awry in New York with *Rosemary's Baby*. The movie was four weeks behind schedule. Now Mia wouldn't be able to start work on The Detective on time, and Frank might have to replace her.

It just so happened that at this time Tina Sinatra took a vacation to New York to hang out there with Mia in her East Side apartment. Some speculated that she was on some sort of espionage mission for her father, but it wasn't true. It was just to be a fun trip for "sisters." During her few days there, Tina became even closer to Mia as they discussed their life stories and their relationships with their parents. Tina more than ever realized that Frank was a father figure in Mia's life, and this realization did little to encourage her that the marriage would last.

When Mia told Tina that she was thinking about reneging on her agreement with Frank relating to *The Detective*, Tina was quite concerned. She suspected the marriage was nearing its end, but still, she had hoped it would be civil. However, she knew her father well and recognized the trouble Mia was going to be in with him if she bailed on him and his film. She told Mia that Frank would never accept it. She added that Mia didn't know him the way she did, and that "this will not go down well."

In her defense, Mia said she didn't know what else she could do. She most certainly wasn't going to walk off the set of *Rosemary's Baby*, that much she knew. She felt it wouldn't be fair to her, the crew, the other actors...the studio. She reminded Tina that her father had been a director, her mother an actress. She said she had better manners than to leave a set in the middle of production unless it was a dire emergency. Tina sympathized with Mia, of course, but for her the bottom line was quite simple: She knew her father, and if Mia didn't show up for work on his movie, "I'm telling you, it's gonna be really bad." But, Mia asked, would Frank really want a woman as a wife who would walk off the set of a movie? Tina said, "Probably not. But he also might not want a woman as a wife who welched on a deal with him. So this is a big decision," she cautioned her friend. "I'd be very, very careful with this one."

Several days later, Mia made the telephone call that, as it happened, would change the course of her life. She told Frank that, unfortunately, she would not be able to appear in *The Detective* for a couple of more weeks.

"But you *promised*," Frank said. "I need you here. Now!"

"What can I *do*?" Mia asked.

"Quit!" Frank hollered into the phone.

"But how can I do that?" she responded, now angry herself.

Frank couldn't understand the problem; he'd walked off plenty of pictures when they went overtime. For instance, in 1956, producer-director Stanley Kramer ran behind schedule with *The Pride and the Passion* in Spain. Frank just took off, telling him, "I've had it, pallie. I'm jumping out. So, sue me." One time, he just took a stack of pages out of the middle of the script, threw them onto the floor in disgust, and told the director, "There. Now we're on time. And I'm outta here."

"Look, Mia. You need to choose," Frank said. "It's either me. Or the film. I've had enough. Choose!"

"But I can't..."

"Just ankle the fucking film," he insisted.

"No!"

He hung up on her.

Frank then telephoned the movie's producer, William Castle. "He was very pleasant about it but asked when Mia would be finished with *Rosemary's Baby*. I told him the truth, that we were behind in our schedule. Sinatra said, 'Well, I'm going to call off your picture. [He meant that he was going to force Mia to leave, thereby shutting down the production.] I said, 'Frank, that's silly.' And Frank said, 'No, that's the way I feel. I've waited long enough.'"

Frank then called Robert Evans, the new head of production at Paramount. Coincidentally, he was also the man who had held the rights to *The Detective* and who had sold the book to Sinatra to make as a film. But Paramount was also making *Rosemary's Baby*, so Evans was in a tight spot. When he talked to Frank, he said he understood the problem and he would work to solve it. As far as he was concerned, Mia should just leave *Rosemary's Baby* rather than have everyone incur the wrath of Frank Sinatra. "I wanted out," he recalled. "An actress is an actress is an actress..." However, it was just impossible. Mia had done so much work on the film, there was no way she could leave it at this late date. Sinatra didn't take the news well when Evans gave it to him, or, as Evans recalled it, "By dictate of the Chairman: 'No negotiations. Total capitulation.'"

Frank could try, but he wouldn't be successful in canceling Mia's movie, and he must have known as much. He was starting to understand that Mia was not going to capitulate.

For her part, Mia knew that she needed to stand up for herself. Frank would just have to understand that she had always wanted a career in films, and she wasn't going to sacrifice it for him. She had never been a pushover, and she wasn't going to start being one now. He had passion for his own career, she reasoned, so surely he could understand hers.

Divorce—Sinatra Style

$\mathcal{A}$ couple of days later—the day before Thanksgiving—Mia was on the set of *Rosemary's Baby* working with her costars when Frank's attorney, Mickey Rudin, showed up. "I need to see Mia," he said as he quickly walked over to her, ignoring Roman Polanski's efforts to stop him. "We've got business." Rudin pulled Mia to a corner in the kitchen of the set and presented her with a brown manila envelope. "This is for you, from Frank," he said, his expression blank. She opened it and pulled out some documents. As she read them, tears came to her eyes. They were divorce papers, all filled out in her name. *She* was filing for divorce from Frank Sinatra? "But this isn't what I want," she said. "*Who filled these out?*" Rudin seemed surprised. "Wait. You didn't know about this, kid?" he asked.

"No," she answered, bewildered. "I don't know *anything* about this..."

"Well..." Rudin was at a loss for words. "I don't know what to say." Now even he was confused. "Frank's instructions to me were to have you sign these papers," he continued. "What can I tell you? Sign them, Mia," he concluded, pulling a pen from his vest pocket and displaying the pages on the kitchen table. "It's for the best."

"But..." The words seemed caught in her throat. "He *needs* me..." she managed to say.

"Just *sign them*, Mia," Rudin repeated, now looking at her with a little more compassion. "You will be fine. Frank will be fine. It's for the best."

Mia took the pen and—not crying, not really showing any emotion—put her signature "here...and here...and here. And... here."

Frank and Mia had never once discussed divorce, and suddenly she was signing the papers. It was eerily reminiscent of the way he had treated Betty Bacall. Mia couldn't help but remember that when she'd heard about the terrible breakup with Bacall, she felt sure that Frank would never do such a thing to her. She was wrong.

Mickey Rudin quickly gathered the documents, put them back into the envelope, and made a hasty departure. "When it was time to resume shooting, there was no Mia," Roman Polanski recalled. "When I knocked on the door, she didn't respond. So I went in and I found her sobbing. She told me what had happened, that Sinatra had sent his attorney to tell her that her marriage was over. It was so cruel, it just shattered her. I felt terribly for her. But what could you do? She got caught up in Frank's world. Who could survive that, other than Frank himself?"

The very same evening Mickey Rudin served Mia with divorce papers, Frank Sinatra's publicist, Jim Mahoney, made it official, even if hedging a bit: "Frank Sinatra said today that he and Mia Farrow, his wife of little more than a year, have agreed to a separation."

Frank Fires George Jacobs

For the next seven months, as they waited for the divorce to be finalized, Frank and Mia were still off and on. Mia was heartsick. It would be almost impossible to count how many press interviews she gave at this time telling reporters how devastated she was, how she didn't want the marriage to end. "I will do anything to save this union," she told one writer in Los Angeles. "I took my vows seriously and I not only want Frank back, I want to have his children. I do! I have begged him to take me back! *Begged him!*" She was even asking reporters for advice on how to save the marriage; she seemed more than a little unhinged about things.

Meanwhile, though he had filed for divorce, Frank was delaying things. He still wasn't sure what he wanted. "He wasn't sleeping," said George Jacobs. "He was letting himself go, biting everyone's head off, impossible to be around. It was Ava all over again."

Speaking of Ava...

In July 1968, Frank got word that Ava would soon be in town. She was thinking of moving from England to the States and would be staying at the Beverly Hills Hotel for a few days. Of course, she wanted to see Frank. This wasn't a good time for him, though. He just couldn't take any more angst in his life, which usually ensued from any time he spent with Ava. "I need you to drive out to Beverly Hills and babysit Ava for a night," Frank told George Jacobs. This was fine with George. He liked Ava; they had a very good relationship and had known each other since Jacobs first went to work for Frank in 1953. It would be fun to see her.

That evening, George made the two-hour drive to Los Angeles. Ava was to attend a Count Basie concert in town with friends; she and George would meet afterward in her bungalow at the hotel. Arriving in town early enough to enjoy some nightlife beforehand, Jacobs went to a nightclub in Beverly Hills called the Candy Store, always a mad scene. While he was enjoying himself with a drink in one hand, a smoke in the other, who should he see dancing across the large floor but Mia with John Phillips of the pop group the Mamas and the Papas. As soon as Mia saw him, she motioned him over. "Come dance with us, Georgie Porgy," she said; she seemed to be in a happy place. She introduced Phillips to Jacobs, they shook hands, and then the musician disappeared into the crowd, leaving just Mia and George. They were such good friends, it meant nothing to them to be sharing one dance after another—not slow dances, of course. This was a discotheque, after all; the music was all upbeat. The lights were flashing, people were happy—many were high on drugs—and it was just a typical night on the town in Hollywood for George, who was about thirty-seven at the time. It was good to have the opportunity to blow off a little steam. After a couple of hours, he hugged Mia goodbye and was on his way to the Beverly Hills Hotel.

When he got to the Beverly Hills, he found another of Frank's wives in a very good mood. "Ava was *lit,*" he recalled later. "Very happy, having already had a few cocktails after the Basie show. She looked wonderful, though. We went down to the Polo Lounge, ordered margaritas. Ava and I ordered guacamole and Fritos at the bar, and after a couple more margaritas, I felt I had enough information to report back to Mr. S. that she was all good—no change there. I left her and then made my way back to the Beverly Hills mansion. I hit the sack, woke up the next morning, got in my car, and headed back to Palm Springs."

At noon, George drove up to the compound's gate, inserted his key into the lock, and turned it. The gate wouldn't open. He tried a few more times; still no luck. He rang the bell. In response, one of Frank's Filipino houseboys came out of the house, ran down the driveway, and stopped on the other side of the gate. "No good to come in," he told George. "Must go now before too late!"

What was going on?

"Movers pack up your belongings in big boxes," the employee told George before scampering away back up the long driveway and to the main house.

George rang the bell again. This time one of the uniformed black housekeepers came out and made her way down the driveway. Without saying a word to him, she handed George an envelope through the metal bars. Then she too ran back up to the house. George ripped open the envelope and pulled from it a typed letter. It was from Mickey Rudin, telling him that his services were no longer required. He was terminated, effective immediately. He was not to enter the premises and not to try to contact Frank in any way. Moreover, his possessions would be delivered to him in three days as soon as he contacted the Rudin office to tell him where he had relocated. Also, Mickey added, "there will be no severance pay."

It would be about a week before Jacobs would figure out what had happened. Rona Barrett had heard that George had been dancing with Mia at the Candy Store. She reported it on the early morning news. Though George had worked for him for fifteen years and the two had never had a single disagreement the entire time, Frank felt he knew what he had to do: He had the locks changed, called Mickey Rudin in Beverly Hills, had Rudin write the letter of dismissal, and then had someone drive it out to the house in the desert and deliver it...and all before noon!

Cycle of Pain

After dismissing George Jacobs, Frank Sinatra went down to Acapulco for a brief holiday. He was unhappy about the way things had worked out with George. He didn't really believe anything was going on between George and Mia, but he felt it was poor form for his valet to be dancing with his estranged wife. Why would Jacobs be careless enough to give Rona Barrett a story—a woman Jacobs knew Frank detested? Quite unreasonably, he felt let down.

While baking in the sun and trying to sort it all out, he had a bit of an epiphany about Mia. He suddenly realized that the cycle of pain that had begun with Ava years ago was repeating itself, and now, this time, he was the victimizer. He asked Mickey Rudin and an associate from Rudin's law firm, Gang, Tyre, Ramer & Brown, to fly down for a meeting with him.

In 1998, the law associate would recall that when he and Mickey showed up in Acapulco, Frank was "very despondent." He was wearing a white terrycloth robe, sitting on the deck of his suite and puffing on a cigar. "You remember what I went through with Ava?" he asked Mickey. Mickey said he remembered a great deal of it, but that he had been retained by Sinatra toward the end of the romance. "She put me through hell," Frank said. "It was unequal." When asked to elaborate, Frank said that he loved Ava "ten times more" than she loved him and that he suffered because of it. "Now," he concluded, "I'm doing the same thing to Mia." He said that Mia was "too young for this bullshit." He added that he was amazed she'd been as patient as she had been, but he suspected it wouldn't last long. He ended by telling Rudin to get rid of her.

The next morning, Mickey Rudin and his associate from the law firm knocked on the front door of the Bel-Air estate Sinatra was leasing. Mia answered, still in her robe. "Frank called me from Acapulco," the associate recalled Mickey as saying (it's not known why Mickey suggested that it had been a telephone call and not an in-person meeting), "and told me to tell you that you have to go. You can stay anywhere you want and he'll pay for it, but you can't be here when he returns." From the expression on his face, the associate said it was clear that Mickey regretted once again having to be the bearer of bad news. "I'm sorry, kid," he said. "My hands are tied."

"But can't I stay until Frank gets home," Mia pleaded, "and then he and I can talk about it?"

"No."

"But I know that if we just had a chance to *talk*," she pressed on, "he would change his mind."

"I'm sorry," Mickey said.

"But where will I go?" she asked.

"Any hotel you like," he said. "Frank will pay for it. But you just can't be here when he gets back. That's the bottom line, kid. You gotta go."

Mickey and his associate stood before Mia and waited for a response. If Sinatra wondered how much it would take before she'd finally be done with him, he might have had his answer if only he'd been present. According to the witness, Mia just glared at Mickey. She didn't need to say a single word, her face said it all. Then, as the two Sinatra emissaries waited, she whirled around, went back into the house, and gathered some of her belongings. She put as much as she could in a small red suitcase. Head held high, she angrily walked out the front door, single suitcase in hand, past Mickey Rudin and his associate without saying anything. She got into the yellow Thunderbird Frank had given her as a gift. She slammed the door closed. And she drove away.

Coda

After Frank's final decision about her destiny, Mia tried to move on with her life. She had said during her marriage that she wanted to study Transcendental Meditation (TM) with the Maharishi Mahesh Yogi; she'd been studying Zen Buddhism for years. When the Beatles began studying with the Maharishi, it lent what many might argue was an unfair air of faddishness to the concept of TM. But Mia was searching for something to fill her life and ease her pain. She was tired of feeling bewildered and helpless and determined to do something spiritual about it. Thus her trip to the Himalayas to study with the Maharishi.

When she returned to the States, she felt revitalized. She moved the rest of her belongings out of the Bel-Air house. She also said she didn't want anything from Frank, no alimony at all. She just wanted to move on with her life. Through Mickey Rudin, Frank told Mia they would always be friends.

Frank and Mia's divorce was finalized on August 19, 1968, in Juárez, Mexico. "I don't seem to be able to please him anymore," Mia told the court in her brief appearance. Mickey accompanied Mia to Mexico. Frank did not appear.

Around the time of the divorce, *Rosemary's Baby* was released, making Mia Farrow a major movie star. At about the same time, Frank's movie, *The Detective*, received a very mediocre reception at the box office.

After Mia returned from Mexico, she and her mother, Maureen O'Sullivan, had lunch at the Polo Lounge at the Beverly Hills Hotel to "celebrate" her new freedom. Later they went back to the home Mia was now renting in Beverly Hills. During their afternoon together, they tried to come to terms with what had happened to Mia's life these last turbulent four years.

Somehow, at least as much as they could figure it, Mia had been swept into a world not of her own making, a world that had nothing at all to do with her...or her career...or her friends...or her family. It had taken everything for her to find a way to fit into that world, only to discover that she never really belonged there in the first place. "Life was not easy for Frank Sinatra, or for anyone who stood beside him," she later concluded. Still, it was incredibly painful to say good-bye to him and to everything he had represented in her life. She had so idealized him at the beginning of their relationship, it was very disillusioning to finally acknowledge that he was not the man she thought he was. Eventually, she and Frank would become friends. But it would take some time.

Part Eleven

TRANSITION

Changing Times

As the 1960s came to a close, some of the more colorful personalities in Frank Sinatra's life began to vanish, starting with his longtime gangster friend, Sam Giancana. The close relationship Frank had with Sam had been irreparably damaged after the Cal-Neva incident. Then, after the Kennedy assassination in 1963, there were rumblings among some of the younger up-and-coming hoods out of Chicago that Giancana was on his way out. Sam wanted nothing to do with Frank anyway. He called Sinatra "old news," and the apathy was mutual.

On the evening of June 5, 1968, Bobby Kennedy was assassinated in Los Angeles at the Ambassador Hotel where he was celebrating the South Dakota and California primary victories. He died the next day. Frank was hit hard by the death of another Kennedy. Of course, he'd had his problems with Bobby early on, but RFK really came through for him when Frank Jr. was kidnapped, and Frank never forgot it. RFK's murder also brought forth the strong emotion Frank felt over JFK's death; his heart went out to the Kennedys.

Prior to Bobby's death, Frank had already decided that he would support Vice President Hubert Humphrey for president. Even though Humphrey had excellent liberal credentials, most liberals turned their backs on him because he was part of a Johnson administration that had sent troops to Vietnam. Frank had always been a staunch Democrat, and it would be easy to say that the older he got, the more conservative he became. In some respects, that's true. But not only were Frank's politics as complex as the times, they were also fueled by his personal feelings. For instance, he truly felt that RFK wasn't ready for the presidency and had said so publicly; it was nothing personal against Bobby.

Sinatra and Lyndon Johnson really had no interest in knowing each other. While Sinatra didn't like the president's politics, Johnson felt that Sinatra was a magnet for trouble. As far as Frank was concerned, the sooner LBJ was out of office, the better. Indeed, the war was not really a conservative-versus-liberal issue; both liberals and conservatives eventually came to oppose it. But because of Humphrey's affiliation with Johnson, most liberals were against him as well, including Sinatra's friends, such as Sammy Davis, Shirley MacLaine, Sammy Cahn, and other pals who had been in full support of JFK. In fact, Frank was one of the few stars to support Hubert Humphrey. (Diana Ross and the Supremes also came out in support of him.) Sinatra liked Humphrey and felt that, if elected, he would end the war in Vietnam.

In May 1968, Frank flew to Washington to attend a party for Humphrey hosted by columnist Drew Pearson in Georgetown. Frank was with his friend Allen Dorfman, a known associate of Jimmy Hoffa's. Afterward, Frank had dinner with Mrs. Jimmy Hoffa and Teamsters vice president Harold Gibbons. While they all may have been friends, this was precisely the kind of poor judgment call that customarily caused trouble for Frank with the media. A reporter from the *Washington Post* had already begun asking questions about the relationship among Dorfman, Sinatra, and Humphrey and whether it had to do with the possibility of Humphrey's pardoning Hoffa in exchange for Sinatra's endorsement.

In July and August 1968, Frank embarked on a stumping concert tour for Humphrey that would take him to Cleveland, Baltimore, Minneapolis, Detroit, and Philadelphia. At this same time, *Wall Street Journal* reporter Nicholas Gage wrote a scathing exposé of Sinatra that once again linked him to the Mafia—"and not just two-bit hoods, either, [but] the Mafia's elite"—using FBI contacts and certain documents from the Bureau as evidence. As could be expected, Frank was upset by the article. It was so inflammatory, in fact, that certain of Humphrey's aides suggested that he had better not align himself with the entertainer. This was exactly what had happened in the early 1960s, when RFK encouraged JFK to distance himself from Sinatra.

It got worse. Washington lawyer Joseph L. Nellis, who had been on the Kefauver Committee and had interrogated Frank in 1951 about his Mafia connections, shot off a letter to Humphrey warning him of Sinatra's mobster ties. "It's true you need support from every segment of the population," he wrote, "but surely you would agree that you don't need support from the underworld, and Frank Sinatra is unquestionably connected with the underworld." In response to this and to similar missives from concerned politicians, Humphrey said he would not disavow Sinatra completely; however, he would definitely proceed with caution.

Then Martin McNamara, former assistant U.S. attorney in Washington, contacted Henry Peterson, head of the Justice Department's organized crime division, and charged that Frank was indebted to Sam Giancana, Paul "Skinny" D'Amato, and other mobsters "for having picked him out of the entertainment doldrums a few years back."

Suddenly, Humphrey was reluctant to take Frank's telephone calls, just as JFK had been. He was usually not responsive to his letters. Frank felt as if he were on the outside, and he didn't like it. In fact, the word in Washington was that he was poison to Humphrey, and maybe even to anyone else in the political arena. Sinatra finally did get through to Humphrey on the telephone, but their relationship was strained from this point onward.

In the end, despite Frank's best efforts, Hubert Humphrey lost the presidential election in November. However, it was a close race—in fact, one of the closest in American history: Richard Nixon won by only 223,000 votes, with 43 percent of the vote, beating Humphrey and the third-party (American Party) candidate, segregationist George Wallace. Sinatra was dismayed by the loss. Meanwhile, comedic satirist Mort Sahl joked, "Once you get Sinatra on your side in politics, you're out of business."

My Way

In November 1968, Frank Sinatra recorded the *Cycles* album with Don Costa arranging. "Cycles," with its melancholy, world-weary lyrics, is one of Sinatra's best, most autobiographical songs. It tells of an aging man's recognition that life is cyclical and that, as they say, bad things happen to good people but that it is hope that remains constant. Frank's performance of this song on the television special *Francis Albert Sinatra Does His Thing*, while sitting casually on a stool, wearing a tux and smoking a cigarette, is unforgettable.

The rest of *Cycles* is less memorable, including Sinatra's renditions of contemporary songs such as "Gentle on My Mind" and "By the Time I Get to Phoenix." Frank was never at his best when tackling songs from 1960s-era writers and composers. Despite the pop success of "Somethin' Stupid" and "Strangers in the Night," he was still considered passé by much of that generation's youth, and his personalized interpretations of popular songs of the day often sounded just a little creaky and "square." He was at his best when he sang songs that really meant something to him, like "Cycles."

Frank ended 1968 by recording what is probably his best-known song, "My Way," on December 30. The song was actually a French composition, with lyrics by Gilles Thibaut and music by Claude François and Jacques Ravaux, originally entitled "Comme d'Habitude" ("As Usual"). Paul Anka, a former teen heartthrob and pop vocalist who had matured into a creditable songwriter, penned the English lyrics. In essence, the song tells of a man who at the end of his life looks back over it all and notes that he lived it the way he saw fit, regardless of who was affected by his actions. This actually *was* how Sinatra had conducted his life up to this point, and how he would continue to do so.

Paul Anka recalled, "RCA Victor, the label I was with at the time, was quite perturbed that I didn't keep the song. But my assessment was, 'Hey, I'm in my twenties [Anka was twenty-eight]. Here's a guy that's in his fifties who's got a lot more experience, and that's casting to the song the way an actor does to a play. Frank Sinatra was the right guy to do it. He did more for that song than I ever could have done."

Frank never liked "My Way." In fact, the many ways he expressed his disdain for it in concert were moments almost as popular as the song itself!

"Of course, the time comes now for the torturous moment," he said before performing it at the Los Angeles Amphitheater in 1979.

"I hate this song. *I hate this song!* I got it up to here with this goddamned song," he said that same year in Atlantic City.

It's easy to understand why Frank took issue with "My Way." Standing onstage in front of thousands of people night after night and singing about how little he cared about what people thought of him? No. Privately, yes, the song had value and meaning. However, onstage, Frank's persona was much more humble than the lyrics of "My Way" suggested. In fact, it's amazing he even recorded the song, it's so counter to what he wanted his public to think of him. Most of his fans would agree, though: Thank goodness he did!

Despite his feelings about it, "My Way" went on to become a Sinatra anthem. While the record would be a hit for him when released in 1969, it never cracked the Top Ten, peaking at number twenty-seven. (In the United Kingdom, however, it was a huge success, on the charts for 122 weeks.) What was originally considered a pleasant and interesting record became legendary. As the years progressed, Frank continually found new value in the song. The older he got, the better it seemed to fit.

Marty Sinatra—Rest in Peace

The year 1969 sounded a very sad note for Frank Sinatra when his father, Marty—now retired after twenty-four years of service with the Hoboken Fire Department—became critically ill with an aortic aneurysm. Marty's chronic asthma had developed into emphysema over the years, which made his prognosis all the more grave. Frank decided to send his father to Dr. Michael DeBakey, a celebrated cardiologist who had pioneered artificial-heart research and someone whom Sinatra greatly admired. In fact, over the years Frank had paid hundreds of thousands of dollars for certain friends of his to have heart operations performed by DeBakey at Methodist Hospital in Houston. He flew his parents to Houston to meet with the doctor on January 19 and then stayed there with his father in the hospital for the last five days of his life.

"Dr. DeBakey told me that in all the years he'd spent watching people deal with their parents' grave illnesses, he had never seen anything like my father's devotion," said Nancy Sinatra. "He was moved by such concern and especially by the unashamed displays of affection and tender love. They had always been openly affectionate, men of few words, understanding each other easily."

Frank and Marty had become close pals, particularly over the last twenty years, as Frank, in his thirties and forties, began to appreciate Marty's quiet wisdom and sensible approach to life. "He always knew the right thing to say," Frank would recall of his dad. "Without him, I felt like I had no anchor."

The funeral Mass was held at Fort Lee's Madonna Church; the burial, at Jersey City's Holy Name Cemetery. The townsfolk caused a huge traffic jam to catch a look at the hearse and procession of twenty-five limousines as it made its way from the church to the cemetery. "Frank was very unhappy with his mother," said Joey D'Orazio, his childhood friend. "She had told too many people too many things about the details of the funeral, made too many announcements, and so the scene was madness. There were cops and firemen everywhere, and it was a circus, something Frank didn't want."

Dolly, distraught and always one with a flair for the dramatic, actually attempted to throw herself onto the casket at the cemetery as she sobbed, "Oh, no. Oh, no. Oh, no. It can't be true." Frank and Jilly held her back. Frank then pleaded with the priest, Father Robert Perrella, to "hurry it up with the prayers" as his mother screamed out, "Marty, Marty, please don't leave me." The priest raced through the service as quickly as he could while everyone, strangers and friends alike, wailed, sobbed, and moaned loudly, all led by the widow's understandable outpouring of deeply felt emotion.

"It was a funeral like you've never seen before," said Diane Phipps, a fan who observed the Sinatras at the gravesite. "It was like a movie, it was so dramatic. You could tell that Frank had had it up to *here* with his mother. There were bodyguards everywhere with walkie-talkies, and people were taking pictures, and there were television cameras and people running around with microphones, and Dolly was sort of the center of attention. She was like the star of the whole thing. Obviously, she was genuinely grieving, but oh my, the show she put on! Frank and two other guys had to practically drag her away from the gravesite into a limousine."

On January 15, 1971, the Martin Anthony Sinatra Medical Education Center was dedicated in Palm Springs. Frank had personally raised the funds for the medical building and dedicated it to his father. At its dedication, Sinatra said of his beloved dad, "He's here," pointing to his head. "And here," he added, pointing to his heart.

"This splendid structure is my dad's kind of dream, just as it is yours and mine. I remember a line in a childhood prayer that said, 'Send me blessed dreams and let them all come true.'"

A $22.5 Million Deal...at Dolly's House

By 1969, Frank's Reprise Records had been sold twice, first to Warner Bros.–Seven Arts, Inc. in 1963, and then a few years later to a Canadian investor named Eliot Hyman, who helped cofound Seven Arts Productions. The way Mickey Rudin had structured the 1963 deal was that Frank retained a 20 percent ownership of the Reprise subsidiary, which Mickey felt would benefit him if Warner Bros.–Seven Arts ever changed hands. However, when Eliot Hyman purchased the company, he wasn't interested in having Frank divest his 20 percent. That was fine with Mickey and Frank; they knew that eventually Hyman would sell and Frank would then profit. That happened in 1969. Steven J. Ross, an investor who had made his money in the funeral business, wanted to invest in his first love, the entertainment world. He approached Hyman with a very good offer to buy Warner Bros.–Seven Arts. Ross also wanted Frank's 20 percent of Reprise.

At this time, New York had a very high stock transfer tax that applied not only to the transferring of stock in New York corporations but also in non–New York corporations using New York as the city in which the transfer was made. As a result, most Manhattan lawyers would move the entire transaction to Fort Lee, New Jersey. They'd find a bank that would be willing to cooperate and then use that bank to make the official transaction, thereby legally eluding the heavy taxation. Warners and Reprise were both Delaware corporations, but were represented by the top Manhattan law firm of Paul, Weiss, Rifkind, Wharton & Garrison (which represented many high-profile notables and would soon represent Spiro Agnew in his plea bargain after the Watergate scandal). Allan B. Ecker, who worked for the firm, suggested that the stock transfer not occur in the attorneys' New York office, but in Fort Lee. To that end, he leased out a conference room at a bank there. Of course, it just so happened that Frank already had a headquarters in Fort Lee: the home he had purchased for Dolly and Marty. Why not do the transfer there?

When Frank asked Dolly what she thought of the idea, of course she loved it. Her son coming to her for help? She lived for such moments!

So one day a parade of stretch limousines pulled up in front of Dolly's home, carrying Frank, Steve Ross, Mickey Rudin, and a team of attorneys from Paul, Weiss, Rifkind, Wharton & Garrison, including Allan B. Ecker. "Before the closing, Dolly insisted on showing us around," recalled Allan B. Ecker. "She was particularly proud of what she called the 'Photograph Gallery,' a series of little shrines at which Frank was pictured with each of his wives." Indeed, on the wall in her living room, Dolly had hung framed pictures of Frank with wives Nancy, Ava, and Mia, as well as pictures of him with other flames such as Betty Bacall and Juliet Prowse. The consummate tour guide, Dolly had a little anecdote to go along with each photo. Frank stood patiently by and let his mom take center stage as she told flattering stories about each of the women with whom he'd been romantically involved. "We gave Mrs. Sinatra's collection respectful and admiring attention," recalled Allan B. Ecker.

The men then all gathered around Dolly's dining room table. First, she brought out a tray of cookies that she had baked for the occasion. Then, as they sampled Dolly's cookies, the men finalized the deal. "Frank signed the assignment form on the back of the stock certificate, transferring his 20 percent interest in Reprise to Warner Communications, Inc. and then handed the certificate to Steve," said Ecker. As Dolly stood proudly behind her son, Steve Ross handed Frank a check. "How much is this check for, Ma?" Frank said, acting as if he couldn't read the type on it. "Damn eyesight," he said, acting exasperated. Dolly looked over her son's shoulder. "It says..." she began. "Holy Christ!" she then exclaimed as the men all laughed. It was for $22.5 million. Frank beamed at his mother's reaction. What a moment for him! "Do you think Pop would be proud?" he asked his mother. "He's looking down on you and smiling right now," Dolly said with tears in her eyes. "He's so proud."

After the papers were signed, all of the lawyers and Steve Ross thanked Dolly Sinatra for her hospitality, got into their individual limousines, and left, headed back to New York. Frank stayed behind. He had a gift for his mom—a check for $1 million. He would also give checks for $1 million to Nancy, Tina, and Frank Jr.

At about this time, Frank felt that Dolly should move to the West Coast so that he could care for her. She was against the idea. *"Shut-uppa you mou!"* she hollered at him when he first proposed it. Her life was in New Jersey, she said, and she didn't want that to change. She needed her close friends, especially with Marty gone.

The son of a friend of hers from Fort Lee said, "My mother and Dolly spent a lot of time talking over the pros and cons of moving to Los Angeles, and eventually there was a feeling that her life was actually over in Fort Lee. She and Marty never had the kind of relationship where they *needed* each other, but without him there, she knew it would never be the same. She was the type of woman who was always moving, always growing. She wanted a new life, and Frank gave her that opportunity. He built her a nice house right next to his estate and staffed it with servants to wait on her day and night. She loved that."

More Mob Questions

On February 17, 1970, fifty-four-year-old Frank Sinatra found himself answering questions under oath. About a year earlier, the New Jersey State Commission of Investigation had served him with a subpoena, expecting him to testify about his connections to the underworld. He received the subpoena, explained Mickey Rudin, "while on a boat that stopped in New Jersey. This seemed to be the lark of an investigator who had a subpoena with him, filled it out on the spot, added Sinatra's name, and served him with it."

Frank complained, "I'm tired of being considered an authority on organized crime." He then filed a lawsuit in federal court in hopes of not having to testify before the committee. "I do not have any knowledge of the extent to which organized crime functions in the state of New Jersey," he claimed, "or whether there is such a thing as 'organized crime.'" When Sinatra's suit was dismissed, he appealed to the U.S. Supreme Court. His appeal was rejected by a vote of four to three. Still he refused to testify, until finally the commission threatened to jail him for contempt in February 1970.

Sinatra's attorneys agreed to allow him to be questioned in a secret session in Trenton at midnight on February 17. The hope was that the veil of secrecy would prevent the media from reporting the event and turning it into a circus. Frank answered questions for a little more than an hour and repeatedly denied any association with any member of the underworld. In fact, he testified under oath that it had never been brought to his attention that Sam Giancana had ever been connected to either the Cosa Nostra, the Mafia, or the underworld. He added that he also was not familiar with Lucky Luciano's reputation as a member of the Cosa Nostra or the Mafia, and he also denied any knowledge of the backgrounds or professions of a number of other known mobsters. Finally:

Q: Do you know anyone who's a member of the mob?
A: No, sir.

Q: Do you know anyone who's a member of any organization that would come under the category of organized crime?
A: No, sir.

It's not difficult to understand why Frank felt the need to lie. Of course he knew that Giancana was a Mafia figure. However, his attorneys warned him that to admit as much would only open the door to further inquiry and that a flat "no" would just end the questioning. Nevertheless, his unbelievable testimony, when leaked to the media, only served to provide more evidence to bolster the cynics' opinion of him. His detractors thought he was protecting the Mafia; his testimony did little to disabuse anyone of that notion.

"For many years, every time some Italian names are involved in any inquiry, I get a subpoena," Sinatra angrily said afterward. "I appear. I am asked questions about scores of persons unknown to me based on rumors and events which have never happened. Then I am subjected to the type of publicity I do not desire and do not seek."

Surprising Political Support

On July 9, 1970, Frank Sinatra, an avowed Democrat, made a surprise announcement: He decided to support Republican Ronald Reagan in his bid for a second term as governor of California (even though Frank would remain a registered Democrat). Reagan had begun his political career by becoming governor of California in 1966, campaigning for law and order. Liberal-minded Sinatra had never really admired Reagan; he always thought of him as stuffy and unimaginative. However, Frank may have had an ulterior motive in supporting Reagan. Reagan's opponent was Jesse Unruh, former speaker of the California State Assembly, who had been a protégé of Bobby Kennedy's. It was thought by some pundits that Sinatra's support of Reagan was really his way of settling the score with Kennedy by getting "even" with his disciple, Unruh.

"I support the man, not the party anymore," Frank explained. "I'm not voting for a man just because he's a Democrat. If people don't like that, screw 'em." It would seem, though, that Sinatra was serious about his new policy of not voting for any specific party, because his allegiances were all over the political map in 1970: He was also supporting Democrat Edmund "Jerry" Brown Jr. for secretary of state of California, and he made it clear that he would support Nixon's opponent in the next presidential election. He put his support behind Republican John Lindsay for mayor of New York and donated thousands of dollars to Republican Nelson Rockefeller's campaign for his second bid for governor of New York.

"I got a little cold about my team [the Democratic Party] there for a while; it wasn't pleasing me," Sinatra explained to Larry King in May 1988. "And I began to move around a little bit, and it's a wonderful thing to be able to do, switch from one party to another. We have the right to do that." Of course, the fact that Frank had felt betrayed by both Kennedy and Humphrey can't be ignored as a possible factor in his sudden shift to Republican candidates. It begs the question of how deep his political convictions really were. He always publicly maintained, however, that previous slights had nothing to do with his decision to change parties.

Most perplexing, however, to many Sinatra followers was the singer's sudden friendship with and allegiance to Vice President Spiro T. Agnew. Politicians didn't come more conservative than Agnew in 1970, and Sinatra's relationship with him made him appear, at least from a public relations standpoint, about as "square" as Agnew, who was vehemently against student protesters, antiwar demonstrators, and "those damn hippies."

"It's the amorality," Frank said when asked why he felt this country was in trouble. "And so much restlessness. I guess we just got used to a way of life in my age bracket. Take the protestations, called for or uncalled for. I'm not against protestations if they're for a cause. But I don't like rebellion without a cause." This from a former Rat Packer who had once lived his life on the edge of revolt just for the hell of it? It would seem that Sinatra—not unlike a lot of his older fans—was now losing touch with the free-spirited values of his youth.

"There was instant chemistry—personally and politically— between Sinatra and Agnew," recalled Peter Malatesta, an assistant of Agnew's who also happened to be a nephew of Bob Hope's, "and because of that we started spending a lot more time with Frank in Palm Springs. He treated the vice president like royalty, even named the guesthouse he had once built for JFK after Agnew: Agnew House."

To some, it sounded as if Frank was now just replacing his former hero worship of JFK with Agnew, a politician who was the antithesis of Kennedy. To an extent, that seems true. However, it's also true that Sinatra was getting older and becoming more conservative. "He was now comfortable with Agnew's right-wing extremism," is how his daughter Tina put it, "much more than he would have been, say, ten years earlier. Some of us found it maddening. You could have a pretty good debate with Frank about these kinds of things, as I often did. But it was a good idea not to push too hard," she concluded with a laugh, "because it could get a little explosive."

Another Vegas Showdown

In September 1970, a situation occurred in Las Vegas during Frank Sinatra's engagement at Caesars Palace that would further tarnish his public image.

On September 6, one of Sinatra's employees cashed in $7,500 worth of chips so that his boss could play blackjack. The transaction caught the attention of an undercover IRS agent who at the time just happened to be investigating the entertainment industry's relationship with the underworld.

As we saw earlier when he was contracted to the Sands, Frank always had IOUs on record with the casino for large amounts of money he had lost at the tables. These amounts were rarely deducted from his salary or ever paid back from his winnings. It was an unspoken courtesy, the hotel giving him money to gamble with and rarely, if ever, getting any of it back. If Frank won, he just kept the winnings. If he lost, it was on the casino, not him. Sinatra thought this little perk was fair business, using the argument that he brought millions of dollars into the hotel and casino during his sold-out engagements. The more people who came to see him perform, the more who gambled in the casinos. In the end, everyone made more money as a result of his presence, he would argue, so why not extend him the courtesy of $10,000 or so? As earlier noted, a disagreement over this very issue was what caused a rift between Sinatra and the Sands Hotel—which was precisely why he was now contracted to Caesars.

Apparently a discussion between Sinatra and the casino manager, Sanford Waterman, about Sinatra's IOUs became ugly when Sinatra called Waterman a "kike" and Waterman retaliated by calling him a "guinea." Waterman then pulled out a gun and pointed it at Frank's head. "I hope you like that gun," Frank said calmly, "because you may have to eat it." In that moment, Jilly Rizzo—who was pretty fast for a big guy—lunged at Waterman and wrested the weapon away from him. Frank laughed in Waterman's face and said he'd never work at Caesars Palace again. Then he turned and walked away.

The press coverage that followed this melee was vociferous and very much against Frank. District Attorney George Franklin told the media that he wanted to interrogate Frank because, in a parting shot to Waterman, Sinatra supposedly said, "The mob will take care of you." He said he wanted to ask Frank "about who owned the nightclubs where he sang, the early days, who started him on his way, and his friendships with the underworld."

This DA was clearly a man who, like a lot of people, had heard a great many titillating stories about Frank over the years and was now trying to bring to the forefront once again age-old stories about Sinatra and the mob. He also claimed that Waterman "still had finger marks on his throat where Sinatra grabbed him."

Frank had no choice but to offer some kind of public explanation. "There was no such argument about credit or for how much I was going to play," he said. "As a matter of fact, I just sat down at the blackjack table and hadn't even placed a bet, since the dealer was shuffling the cards. At that point, Waterman came over and said to the dealer, 'Don't deal to this man.' I got up and said, 'Put *your* name on the marquee and I'll come to see what kind of business *you* do,' and I walked away. As for his injuries, I never touched him. And as for the remarks attributed to me relative to the mob, they're strictly out of a comic strip."

Retirement?

*A*t the age of fifty-five, how much longer could Frank create controversy? He didn't feel he had himself to blame, though. Trouble always seemed to find him, as far as he was concerned.

Frank hated getting old, and the idea of being thought of as out of touch bothered him. The year 1969 had seen the recording of two of Sinatra's lesser-known albums, *A Man Alone* (lyrics by Rod McKuen) and *Watertown* (lyrics by Bob Gaudio). To some fans, both albums seemed to be a mismatch of artist and material and added little luster to the Sinatra canon. To them, it was as if Frank was searching for a more youthful, contemporary sound but had failed.

Meanwhile, in his private life, Frank was also seeing significant change. His hair, for instance, had become a source of irritation. He despised the toupees he felt forced to wear to cover his baldness. He had gotten a hair transplant; however, it didn't "take." Also, he was gaining weight and blamed rich Italian foods, but dieting was out of the question. And he was tired more often. He could no longer drink liquor all night long and then be able to fully function the next day, as he had done for years. His voice was weakening; years of smoking Camel cigarettes had done some damage to it. Long ago, he'd been diagnosed as manic-depressive, but these days the episodes of depression were deeper, the highs fewer and farther between.

He tried to keep himself socially active and—some thought—also seemed to be trying to defy the aging process by dating two young actresses, Carol Lynley, who was twenty-nine, and Peggy Lipton (who was starring in the TV show *The Mod Squad*), twenty-five. Both were enthusiastic about dating him, and he juggled them for a while.

Of late, another problem had surfaced that just made Frank feel his age: His right hand, the one in which he usually held the microphone, was causing him great pain. At first he thought it was arthritis. However, it turned out to be Dupuytren's contracture, a shortening of muscle tissue in the hand. "It hurts like hell," Frank complained. As a result of this problem, his hand was becoming twisted; eventually he would have surgery. "Maybe I should just retire," he said at this time. "Maybe my time is up. Maybe there's nothing left to do."

At this stage of his life, Frank should have been proud of his achievements, not bored by his career. But in fact his line of show business just wasn't the same. Entertainers like Sinatra, Dean Martin, Sammy Davis, and Joey Bishop were now considered squares by the money-spending youth of America. Las Vegas was their last bastion of complete, unconditional audience approval, and, as we have seen, Frank seemed to sometimes have significant problems offstage when he played that particular city. "He says it's the end of an era, and he's right," his daughter Nancy noted. "His kind of show-business era has ended."

In March 1971, Frank surprised his public—but not so much those in his inner circle—when he suddenly announced that he was retiring from show business. In a prepared statement, he said that during the course of thirty years of touring he'd had "little room or opportunity for reflection, reading, self-examination and that need which every thinking man has for a fallow period; a long pause in which to seek a better understanding of the changes occurring in the world." Those who knew him best felt that Sinatra was just exhausted from decades of traveling and performing and that what he really needed was a break, certainly not retirement. "What I felt at the time was that he was maybe overreacting," said Frank Jr. "He wasn't ready to stop. No way was he ready to stop singing. He referred to it as a 'long pause,' didn't he? In my mind, that meant a break, not an end."

Indeed, in retrospect, it now seems injudicious to devote much attention to Frank's "retirement" concert on June 13, 1971, at the Los Angeles Music Center, considering that he would be back onstage at a fund-raiser for the Italian-American Civil Rights League just five months later. However, his "final" concert—a benefit for the Motion Picture and Television Relief Fund, which raised $800,000—was attended by many of his political and show-business friends, including Vice President and Mrs. Agnew, Governor and Mrs. Reagan, presidential adviser Henry Kissinger, Cary Grant, Jack Benny, Don Rickles, and Rosalind Russell, who introduced him to the audience.

Frank's first wife, Nancy, was present at the fund-raiser, as were his children. Frank's performances of "All or Nothing at All," "I've Got You Under My Skin," "I'll Never Smile Again," "My Way," and "That's Life" provided a well-rounded program of songs that spanned thirty years of timelessly enjoyable music. The show inspired four rousing standing ovations. In an article for *Life*, Tommy Thompson wrote, "He had built his career, he said softly, on saloon songs. He would end quietly on such a song. He slipped from his words into 'Angel Eyes,' surely a song for the short hours. He ordered the stage dressed in darkness, a pin spot picking out his profile in silhouette. He lit a cigarette in mid-sentence and its smoke enveloped him. He came to the last line, 'Excuse me while I...disappear.' And he was gone. It was the single most stunning moment I have ever witnessed on stage."

"This isn't it, Pop," Frank Jr., now twenty-seven, told him backstage in his dressing room where friends and media congregated.

"No, this is really it, Frankie," Frank said, his tone definitive. "I mean it, kid."

His son shook his head. "The world needs Frank Sinatra, Pop. The world's not gonna let Frank Sinatra just disappear like at the end of 'Angel Eyes.' It's just not gonna happen, Pop."

Frank smiled warmly at his son. Then he pulled his first wife, Nancy, into an embrace. "Our kid here, he thinks he knows it all, doesn't he?"

"He does," Nancy said, nodding her head. "And he knows exactly what he's talking about, too."

Nixon-Agnew

On November 25, 1971, Frank Sinatra played host for three days to Spiro Agnew and his family over Thanksgiving weekend. Now that he had forged a close friendship with Agnew, Sinatra was determined to see him become president in 1976. Therefore, when Nixon threatened to take him off the ticket in 1972, it was a letter-writing campaign orchestrated by Frank that—at least in part—kept him in the race. (The campaign had been financed by private contributions.)

Frank said he was a Nixon-Agnew man because of the former's stand on admitting China to the United Nations, a position Frank said he agreed with and about which he had been vocal. Though he had been extremely critical of Nixon in the past, Sinatra would now become his strongest supporter, contributing $50,000 to his campaign for reelection in 1972. "I don't happen to think you can kick eight hundred million Chinese under the rug and simply pretend they don't exist, because they do," he said. "If the UN is to be truly representative, then it must accept all the nations of the world. If it doesn't then what the hell have you got? Not democracy—and certainly not world government."

Many of Frank's friends were annoyed with him for supporting Nixon and the Republican Party. Some felt it was actually Frank's friendship with Agnew that really spurred his interest in the Republican Party. They felt that if he had been close to someone in the Democratic Party, he would have easily switched allegiances. In other words, there were those who felt that Sinatra wasn't really committed to the party's platform as much as to a friend who had political clout.

One of the most outraged of Sinatra's inner circle was Mrs. Mickey Rudin, his attorney's wife, who wrote him a letter berating him for his choice, thereby putting the job of her husband—a longtime Sinatra loyalist—in jeopardy. Sinatra didn't take it out on Mickey, but he never spoke to his wife again.

Frank's outspoken daughter Tina was another one of those dismayed by her father's support of Nixon. She and Frank had added politics to their list of common interests and often traded ideologies. She had been diligently campaigning for George McGovern and had said she would do anything in her power to help unseat Nixon. Every time she had asked Frank where he stood, he'd been evasive. However, she knew how much he had supported Nixon in the past, and also how close he was to Agnew. She just hoped he would see things her way. Then one night she was watching the television news and learned that Frank was officially endorsing Nixon. "My hair was on fire," she recalled. "I called him at the compound and vented my spleen: 'Damn it, Dad. I've been killing myself for McGovern and now you come out for Nixon?' While I'd been stationed for hours at shopping malls, registering fifty people in a day, he'd just swayed a trillion votes in a blink."

"Jesus, Tina," Frank said. "I need this right now like I need Parkinson's!" Frank realized how upset Tina was and suggested that she drive out to Palm Springs so that they could discuss it. It was midnight. She raced out to the desert, angry. She then spent a few days with her dad there; they agreed to disagree.

Richard Nixon seemed somewhat intrigued by Sinatra. He appreciated the support and seemed amused by him whenever they were together. Former Secret Service agent Marty Venker, who worked for Nixon, said, "One night the Nixons dined out in New York with Frank. As they were walking out of the restaurant, a teenage boy took their picture. Sinatra flew into a rage," Venker remembered. "He said to me, 'Take his camera.' I ignored him until he said, 'Look, you either take the kid out or *I'll* take the kid out.' I said, 'Listen, Frank. Just get in the car and settle down.' He shut up after that. In the car, Nixon later said to me, 'That Frank's got a hell of a temper, doesn't he?'"

The year ended on a triumphant note for Republicans when in November the party was victorious in forty-nine states; Nixon and Agnew were back in the White House.

Part Twelve

THE BARBARA YEARS

Barbara Marx

One of Barbara Marx's earliest memories of Frank Sinatra concerns the time she and her husband, the comic Zeppo Marx (the straight man of the famous Marx Brothers; his real name was Herbert), were invited to Sinatra's second home—Villa Maggio in Pinyon Crest—about an hour from his compound, up in the hills. It was for a late-night game of charades with other friends. At the time, the Marxes were neighbors of Frank's in Palm Springs; Frank and Zeppo had long been friends. There were two teams; each team picked someone on the opposing team to be timekeeper for the rounds. Frank, who considered Barbara more an acquaintance than a friend, picked her and handed her a large brass clock.

It was four in the morning; the game began. Though Frank did his best, his clues (having to do with tobacco packaging warnings) completely eluded his team, which included the comedian Pat Henry and baseball manager Leo Durocher. "*Time's up*," Barbara shouted triumphantly. Frank—who hated losing at anything—glared at her. "Who made *you* timekeeper?" he demanded to know. "You!" she exclaimed. Frank snatched the timepiece from Barbara's hands. For a moment, it appeared that he was going to "clock" her with it. Though she would later recall being frightened, she stood up and met his angry gaze with one of her own. Then, in typical Sinatra fashion, Frank turned and threw the clock with all his might against one of the doors. "Springs, coils, and shards of glass flew across the room," Barbara later recalled. Everyone was stunned. How does one respond to such behavior? Finally, it was the comic Pat Henry who broke the ice. "I just now got what the charade is, Francis," he deadpanned. "As Time Goes By." At that, Frank shook his head and started laughing. "To everyone's relief," Barbara recalled, "the moment of danger had passed. But already I was aware that a big part of Frank's attraction was the sense of danger he exuded," she would recall, "like an underlying, ever-present tension."

The former Barbara Ann Blakeley was born in Bosworth, Missouri, on October 16, 1927. When she was ten, her parents moved to Wichita, Kansas, where they struggled through the Great Depression. Tall and slender, she was able to find work modeling for department stores and auto shows after she graduated from high school and moved to Long Beach, California, with her parents and sister. She won several local beauty contests before marrying Robert Harrison Oliver, described in press accounts as both "an executive with the Miss Universe pageant" and "a singer," but in reality a bartender and part-time singer named Bobby Oliver, who fancied himself as sounding like Sinatra.

An enterprising young woman, at the age of twenty-one Barbara opened a beauty school—the Barbara Blakeley School of Modeling and Charm—had a child (Bobby), and then divorced Oliver. After that marriage ended, she fell in love with a singer named Joe Graydon, who also sang Sinatra standards in his act. When he accepted a job in Las Vegas, she went with him and eventually became a showgirl at the Riviera Hotel, fulfilling a "secret yearning." (She has said that she considered herself "one of the worst dancers in the history of Las Vegas.") When Joe lost his job and the romance went out of their relationship, Barbara began to notice Zeppo Marx in her audience every night. At fifty-six, he was retired from the Marx Brothers act. He now wanted to meet the "beautiful blonde who was always just slightly out of step," and they became attracted to one another and thus began their romance. Barbara was twenty-six years younger than Marx.

Though Barbara was ambitious, her long-range goals were more of a personal nature than professional. By her own admission, she intended to marry someone wealthy enough to provide for her and her son. So that Zeppo wouldn't think she was interested only in his money, she would borrow furs and jewels (from California designer Mr. Blackwell, creator of the "World's Ten Worst Dressed Women" list) to give the impression that she was well off. "No one knew better than Barbara the power of illusion in catching and keeping a man," said Mr. Blackwell of the woman who was his lead model in 1959. "Barbara bluntly stated that she was determined to marry a man of means. Zeppo Marx was her target; she'd succeed in landing the comic or die trying. Since she had no intention of dying, Zeppo didn't know what hit him." (Barbara wasn't crazy about Blackwell either: "He was mean to everyone around him, especially his boyfriend, Spencer.")

And of her skills as a model, Blackwell noted, "Barbara was a quick learner and quickly drank up the meticulous details all major models are required to master: the proper way to turn, to coo, to seduce, and still remain aloof. Her brilliant smile, sexy saunter, and golden-girl aura catapulted her into the latest flavor of the week."

Of Zeppo, Barbara recalled, "He did have charm. And he could offer me another life, far away from my punishing schedule and monthly scramble to pay the bills."

Zeppo and Barbara were married in 1959. Barbara's marriage enabled her to become a member of the Palm Springs Racquet Club and the Tamarisk Country Club, which was close to Marx's house and to Frank Sinatra's. Suddenly she had money, position, and entrée, golfing with celebrities like Dinah Shore, who became one of her closest friends. In fact, her tennis skills were so good that she was often invited to Frank's to play with Spiro Agnew when he was Sinatra's guest. Barbara and Zeppo—also a tennis enthusiast—socialized with Sinatra quite often at his home, and also at the Cal-Neva Lodge. One day, Frank called Barbara and asked, "You got a friend you can come over here and play tennis with? I need another couple for a match."

"Sure," she said. "Where will we play?"

"Here, at my place," Frank said.

"But you don't have a tennis court, do you?" she asked.

"I didn't, but I do now." Frank said. "Ava's coming, and so I built her a tennis court. She likes to play."

"You built her a tennis court?" Barbara asked, astonished. "Well, how long will she be staying?"

"Oh, just a couple of days," Frank said nonchalantly.

About a week later, Barbara showed up at Frank's with a friend. The first thing she noticed was Ava's maid, Rene Jordan, preparing Moscow Mules—vodka, ginger beer, and lime served in a copper mug—at a bar Frank had built next to the new tennis court. By this time, Ava was long past tipsy. She could barely stand up, let alone play tennis. Frank spent the entire time flirting with Barbara, trying to make Ava jealous. At one point he had Barbara pinned against a chain-link fence and was looking over his shoulder to see if Ava was watching. "She couldn't have cared less," Barbara would later recall with a laugh. Finally, Barbara left the estate, alone. The last thing she remembered seeing, looking back over her shoulder, was Ava flirting with the gentleman with whom Barbara had arrived.

"I'd always been a fan of [Frank's] singing," Barbara said in 1988. "I'd always had all of his records. But I really didn't care about knowing him because of the press I'd read. It just wasn't a pretty picture." Still, despite her perception of him, she somehow couldn't resist him. One night, she and Zeppo were being entertained by Frank. It was a large party, everyone playing gin rummy in small groups. Frank's and Barbara's eyes met; he motioned to her. He got up and went into the kitchen; she followed. "Once he turned on the charm, my defenses rolled away like tumbleweed," she recalled. "When he pulled me into his arms, I found myself returning his kiss with as much ardor."

One afternoon while Barbara was at a party hosted by another woman Frank was dating at the time, the actress Eva Gabor, he asked her to go to Monaco with him. She agreed. It was in that principality, then, that the two started their affair, unbeknownst to Zeppo. But Barbara says that when she found Zeppo with another woman on his yacht and it didn't bother her, she knew the marriage to him was over. Now she found Frank irresistible. "I think anyone who met Frank Sinatra would have to have sparks," she said at the time in trying to explain the attraction. "Because he *is* a flirt. That's just part of his makeup. And there's no way to avoid that flirtation. No *way*."

Tina Sinatra first met Barbara during that fateful trip to Monaco. She wasn't sure what to think of her. She knew that Barbara was married to Zeppo and she believed her father had more sense than to become involved with a married woman. To her it seemed as if Barbara and Frank were just friends. Though Tina ordinarily didn't trust the kind of married woman who would be in Monaco with a single rich man, she decided to give Barbara the benefit of the doubt, especially since she did have her son, Bobby, with her as a chaperone.

"I knew I was crossing a line," Barbara would later admit of the trip to Monaco. "What was I letting myself in for? Was I about to be seduced by one of the world's greatest romantics? Would it be something to fold in my memory, a story to lift out and tell my grand-children one day? Could I live with that?"

Indeed, once she got to Monaco, she decided that, yes, she could live with it just fine.

"Lucky girl, I thought to myself," Barbara recalled of her first moments in Monaco. "Remember this moment," she told herself as she gazed out at the view from Frank's penthouse in his suite at the Hôtel de Paris. "After toasting each other, we moved closer, then he enfolded me in the gentlest embrace," she remembered. "A few hours later, we watched as the dawn crept through the windows and clung to each other ever tighter. Towards the end of an uneventful next day of pretending nothing had happened, I met a group of friends and stepped into one of two waiting cars that were taking us to a dinner. Before we knew it, we were on board Frank's G2 Gulfstream jet, headed for Athens. 'I fancy Greek food tonight,' he explained, laughing."

"She was perfect for Frank," Dinah Shore said of Barbara in an interview eighteen months before her death in February 1994. "He didn't want a woman in show business, and she wasn't. She's the type of woman who would do anything to support her husband's interests. That's what I've always admired about her. She's what I call a 'team player.'"

Barbara: Trying to Fit In

*B*arbara was a woman of great charisma and few could deny the power of her personality. Whatever Frank wanted to do, she was ready for it. She would go out dancing every night if she had to; she would stay up until the early morning hours if need be; she would drink more than she usually did if he asked her to do so. In other words, she could and would keep up with Sinatra.

When she separated from Zeppo, she didn't have a place to live. She loved a small house in the desert owned by Eden Marx, Groucho's third wife, and currently for sale. She mentioned to Frank that she wasn't sure she could afford it. The next day, he bought it for her, all cash, and put her name on the deed of sale. Some observers felt she had manipulated Frank just by mentioning to him that she couldn't afford it, but it didn't matter to her what others thought. More grateful to Frank with each passing day, she happily put up with all of the stares and whispers.

Barbara knew that Dolly didn't like her, but Dolly didn't like Jilly Rizzo either—she called him "Fuck Face"—and yet Rizzo was still around, so she had to wonder how influential Dolly really was. However, taking Mia's lead, she thought it best to win over the other women in Frank's life: Nancy Sr., Nancy Jr., and Tina. Here, though, she would have her work cut out for her.

The difference between Mia and Barbara was obvious. In the Sinatras' eyes, Mia seemed to have no hidden agenda other than a quest for a father figure. They knew that, a hippie at heart, she had little interest in material possessions and wasn't after Frank's money. Even after the divorce, the daughters continued their friendship with her. However, something wasn't quite kosher with Barbara. The Sinatras had heard from multiple sources that the twice-married beauty had chosen her boyfriends and husbands based at least in part on their finances, information that immediately aroused their suspicions. When Barbara invited them to her home for cocktails so that she could break the ice, they couldn't help but be distrustful. They knew that Frank had purchased the home for her, and since she was still married to Zeppo, none of it felt right to them. They didn't really know Barbara yet, but they'd been around Frank and his women for most of their lives; they couldn't help but be suspicious of Barbara.

Barbara sued Zeppo for divorce on December 27, 1972, ending their thirteen-year marriage, shortly before she accompanied Frank to the Nixon presidential inaugural.

Dating Frank would not be easy, as Barbara would soon learn—especially when it came to dining. For instance, at a dinner party at his home, she was served a piece of undercooked veal. Because she couldn't eat it, she politely sent it back to the kitchen for further cooking. Apparently the chef took umbrage and started rattling pots and pans in annoyance. Frank sprang up and ran into the kitchen. "You have about five seconds to get your fat ass out of my house," he shouted at the cook. "Five, four, three, two..." The chef took off as fast as his feet could carry him. Barbara was a little startled, but not as much as she would be a few days later at Matteo's restaurant.

Frank liked his pasta al dente; everyone knew it, especially the staffs of every Italian restaurant he frequented. However, one night at Matteo's in Los Angeles, the pasta was served too soggy. Frank jumped up and ran into the kitchen. "Where the hell are all the Italians?" he asked as he took one look around and realized the staff was entirely of Filipino descent. He couldn't believe it, especially since the owner, Matty Jordan, was a childhood friend of his from Hoboken. "You must be kidding!" he exclaimed. He hurried back to the table. Once there, he picked up the plate of pasta and threw it against the wall, spaghetti and tomato sauce flying everywhere. "Let's go," he ordered Barbara. Alarmed, she quickly gathered her things. But just as they were walking out the door, Frank said, "Wait! Hold on!" He then went back to the wall and with his index finger carefully wrote out one word with the tomato sauce: *picasso.*

The next day, Matty Jordan put a frame around Frank's artwork, and it stayed there for years.

Cheshire Contretemps

*B*arbara Marx would get another taste of Frank Sinatra's violent temper on January 19, 1973. That was the date the two attended a party hosted by Louise Gore, the Republican national committeewoman from Maryland, at the Fairfax Hotel in Washington. One reporter covering the event, Maxine Cheshire (a society columnist for the *Washington Post*), had been critical of the Sinatra-Agnew relationship in the past. A few months earlier, she had confronted Frank at an Agnew state dinner in Washington and asked him point-blank, "Mr. Sinatra, do you think your alleged association with the Mafia will prove to be the same embarrassment to Vice President Agnew that it was to the Kennedy administration?"

Sinatra tried to act unfazed. "No," he said. "I don't worry about things like that." He was seething inside, though, irate over her temerity.

In fact, Maxine Cheshire couldn't get her mind off of what had happened between Frank and the Kennedys, often going back to the subject in her column. She seemed obsessed with the story. All of her reporting suggested that she believed the Kennedys had good reason to end their relationship with Frank due to his mob ties, and that Nixon and Agnew would be best advised to follow suit.

As Frank and Barbara were entering the Fairfax Hotel, Cheshire confronted Frank with more questions. When he was mum, she tried Barbara. "You are still married to Zeppo, aren't you *Mrs. Marx?*" she asked. Barbara immediately looked embarrassed. She wasn't used to such scrutiny, not yet, anyway. That did it. Frank instantly became furious and confrontational.

"You know what?" Frank told Maxine angrily. "You're nothing but a two-dollar..." And then he used a word that couldn't be repeated in mixed company, ever. Not only did he call Cheshire the "c" word, he actually spelled it out for her! "You know what that means, don't you, Maxine?" he continued. "You've been laying down for two dollars all your life." Pulling a couple of bucks from his pocket, he stuffed them into a plastic cup of ginger ale that Cheshire happened to be holding. "Now get away from me, you scum," he told her. "Go home and take a bath. Me? I'm getting out of here to rid myself of the stench that is Miss Cheshire."

Maxine Cheshire was so stunned and insulted, she burst into tears.

Shock waves from Frank's outburst reverberated for weeks; news reports about the incident astonished even his most devoted fans. For days later, Nixon and Agnew were both unsettled about it, as, of course, was Maxine. "If he had attacked me as a reporter, I would have taken it," she noted. "But he attacked me as a woman." She contemplated suing him, but realized that verbal abuse wasn't grounds for litigation.

Before a nightclub appearance soon after that incident, Frank's friend Peter Pitchess—former sheriff of Los Angeles County—took him to task for the Cheshire incident. He told Frank that he should have demonstrated more restraint and that he should apologize for his actions. Frank mulled it over and agreed. "You're right," he said. "I *should* apologize." That night, he went onstage, and during a break between songs, he said, "Ladies and gentlemen, I have an apology to make." Sinatra making an apology? The room fell silent. "I called

Maxine Cheshire a two-dollar whore," he said thoughtfully. "I was wrong and I apologize." Then, after a beat: "She's really just a *one-dollar* whore."

One would think that Barbara, who didn't know Frank that well yet, though she was learning about him quickly, would have gone running in the other direction rather than pursue a relationship with him. However, this was not the case. In fact, she was proud of what he'd done. "As he walked me away from Maxine," Barbara would later recall, "I thought, *Oh my God!* But I had to admit there was also something exciting about it. I'd never felt quite so defended in my life. Henry Kissinger called the next day and said, 'Frank, you overpaid Cheshire.'"

Eileen Faith was a friend of Barbara Marx's at this time. The two met when she was married to Zeppo; Faith lived in Los Angeles. "Barbara was a lot like Frank in the sense that she would never hesitate telling someone what she thought. She always believed that people should stick up for themselves. She could be sweet as pie, but when pushed she would turn on you with such anger that you'd be scared. She told me that Cheshire had been goading her, trying to embarrass her, asking questions about her relationship with Frank and inquiring, 'You *are* still married, aren't you?' So Barbara was happy that Frank came to her defense. Actually, I think that the Cheshire incident brought them closer together."

By April 1973, with the controversy over Cheshire passing, Frank performed at a White House dinner for Giulio Andreotti, prime minister of Italy. It was a wide-ranging, heartfelt concert during which he sang ten songs, including "You Make Me Feel So Young" and "The House I Live In." The question on most people's lips was: What kind of retirement is this? After that wonderful show, Nixon went up to Sinatra and said, "What are you retired for? You really should sing." Frank had to agree. He really did want to begin touring again. Barbara Marx later felt one of the reasons he wanted to go back on the road was so that she could go with him. This way, she reasoned, he would be able to get her out of Palm Springs for about a year, and away from Zeppo. "Frank would almost certainly have made a comeback sooner or later," she recounted, "but quietly and thoughtfully, my romantic lover had come up with a plan to whisk us away even earlier." The idea that Frank would plan a world tour just to keep Barbara away from Zeppo seems like a leap, in retrospect. But certainly stranger things had happened in his world.

In June 1973, Frank Sinatra was back in the recording studio with producer-arranger Don Costa and arranger Gordon Jenkins. In four sessions, he recorded eleven songs, including the lovely "You Will Be My Music" (which he would later tell Barbara was "our story, baby," since she was with him in the studio when he cut it) and the hopeful "Let Me Try Again," one of Sinatra's most enduring ballads and in many ways an appropriate title for his "comeback album," *Ol' Blue Eyes Is Back.*

Both the public and music critics joyfully welcomed *Ol' Blue Eyes Is Back.* Frank had been missed. After all, there was no one like him. The album revealed him still at full power as an artist and a man of impeccable musical taste. This was a good time in his life. His career was on track—and his personal life seemed to have new meaning now that Barbara Marx was in his world.

Spiro, Barbara, and the Aussies

*W*hile Frank was beginning to resume his career, one of his close friends was preparing to end his. On October 10, 1973, Vice President Spiro T. Agnew resigned, pleading nolo contendere to one count of income tax evasion. With the Watergate investigations occurring at the same time, the Nixon-Agnew team was clearly in trouble. Agnew had also been charged with taking cash kickbacks from a Maryland contractor, bribery, and extortion. Frank did what he could to help, even dispatching Mickey Rudin to look into the Agnew matter. In the end, Sinatra—who had felt all along that Agnew should fight back—was disappointed when he resigned.

"As a citizen who loves America and as a good friend of Mr. Agnew's, this is indeed a sad day," he said. "Certainly I offer whatever sympathy and support my friend may need. It takes great courage to pursue the route he has chosen."

In the past, Sinatra's White House friends had many high-level meetings to determine whether it was in their best interest to be associated with a man as controversial as Frank. Now the tables were turned. Sinatra, Mickey Rudin, and the rest of his staff were wondering how Agnew's troubles might affect Sinatra's comeback plans. Frank was adamant that he would not desert Agnew, however, even going so far as paying the $30,000 penalty on his tax debt and attempting to secure a publishing deal for his memoirs for $500,000 (a deal he was not able to make). He never abandoned Spiro Agnew and remained his friend long after the former vice president fell from grace.

Frank, now fifty-eight, started the new year back onstage at Caesars Palace in Las Vegas on January 25, 1974. He had vowed never to appear there again after Sanford Waterman pulled a gun on him in 1970. However, Waterman had been indicted for racketeering and Frank felt he could now go back to Caesars for one of his "comeback" performances.

Also in January, Tina, now twenty-five, married producer and writer Wes Farrell—also twenty-five—who had thus far amassed a long list of pop hits, including, most recently, many of the Partridge Family's chartbusters. It was his second marriage and Tina's first. Frank walked Tina down the aisle. By this time, Nancy had married the very successful dancer and choreographer Hugh Lambert. Four months after Tina's marriage, Nancy gave birth to her first child with Lambert, Angela Jennifer—known to all as A.J. Frank Jr. was still single and working as a singer and recording artist.

By this time, Frank and Barbara were living together in his Palm Springs estate. Wanting to be with her, Frank asked her to accompany him on a tour of the Far East in July 1974.

Frank's time in Asia with Barbara was serene and romantic. There was nothing he wouldn't do for her, no gift he wouldn't buy for her. A successful five-country tour through Europe then followed, also a memorable time. Of course, being wined and dined everywhere she went was great fun for Barbara, and Frank made sure she was treated like royalty every day. In return, she made him very happy and everyone on his crew knew it. He was in a good mood almost every day. The two would take day trips together, enjoy romantic candlelit meals, and spend as much free time together as possible between shows and traveling in his private jet.

In Frank's eyes, Barbara could do no wrong, and she felt the same way about him—even in Australia when Frank got tired of the pushy press and insulted them from the stage one night, calling the men "a bunch of fags" and the women "broads and buck-and-a-half hookers." A few Aussie reporters were even roughed up by Frank's overzealous "Dago Secret Service." It reminded some of the last time Frank had been in Australia, when he was being stalked by an aggressive fan. When the stalker found his way into Frank's suite, Jilly beat him over the head with a large standing metal ashtray. "Don't even *ax* me about the crazy bums in *dat* country," Jilly later said.

Barbara took no issue with Frank's behavior in Australia; as usual, she supported him unequivocally. Actually, she found getting caught in the maelstrom that was Frank's day-to-day thrilling and enlivening. "I loved every minute of it," she would say. "Each day was a new adventure...I had to pinch myself every time I looked across the bed to see his tousled head on the pillow next to mine."

When a press agent in Sydney insisted that Sinatra appear at a press conference and explain himself, it was Barbara who reminded him that he didn't have to do anything he didn't want to do—not that he needed reminding. The concept of "media relations" was still not one to be embraced by him. He said a lot, but never quite the right thing at the right time. The next day, one of the headlines read "Ol Big Mouth Is Back."

After Frank refused to apologize for his remarks about the media, the anger directed at him spread like a cancer, until soon the Stagehands Union refused to work for him and the Waiters Union wouldn't serve him and his crew food at his hotel. Then Transport Union workers wouldn't refuel his Gulfstream jet so that he could leave the country. Everyone wanted an apology from one of the few celebrities on the planet who pretty much never apologized for anything. "Well, good luck with that, I thought," Barbara recalled. Said Don Rickles back in the States, "Frank called me. He just declared war on Australia."

Eventually, a joint statement was issued from Sinatra and the Australian labor unions that placated everyone who had been offended by the remarks—with no direct apology from the man himself—just so that Frank and Barbara could get out of the country. Frank also agreed to tape a TV special as part of the deal. "Needless to say, we left them flapping in our exhaust fumes," Barbara concluded.

"They finally let Frank out of the country," Bob Hope joked, "right after the head of the union down there woke up one morning and saw a kangaroo's head on the next pillow."*

Finding Her Way

$\mathcal{T}$he months passed. On October 13, 1974, Frank's comeback concert at Madison Square Garden was televised to terrific reviews. The Garden concert—staged in a boxing ring and hosted by sportscaster Howard Cosell—was billed as "The Main Event." It would also be broadcast around the world, followed by an album of the same name. Frank had been nervous about the venture—he never liked doing television specials—and leaned on Barbara for emotional support. By now, she had a way of calming him like no one else in his life. But this did not mean that everything was rosy all the time for the two of them; this *was* Frank Sinatra's life, after all. He could be crude, he could be mean... and Barbara could find herself his target.

In New York, one particularly unfortunate scene unfolded, which Jilly later recounted to Tina. Apparently Frank and Barbara were in a restaurant with friends, Jilly included, and they were talking politics. Barbara said something that was—at least based on everyone's reaction—misguided. Frank, who had a few cocktails in him, laid into her. "What the hell are you talking about?" he hollered at her. "You don't got no opinion here. You just sit there. If I want to know what you think, I'll ask you. Until then, you just sit there and *keep your mouth shut.*" Barbara did what she was told. When Jilly later told Tina this story, she couldn't believe it. Yes, of course, she knew that her father could be combustible. What she couldn't fathom was why a formidable woman like Barbara would put up with it. It made no

---

* Some thirty years later, a movie, *The Night We Called It a Day*, was produced about this ill-fated Australian tour, starring Dennis Hopper as Frank and Melanie Griffith as Barbara.

sense to her. Rather than ingratiate her to Barbara, though, it actually made Tina a little more suspicious of her. In her mind, something just wasn't right about it. What she didn't realize was that Barbara was already learning to pick and choose her battles.

Laura Cruz, a former maid at the Sinatra home, recalled that Barbara also had a difficult time winning over Sinatra's cooks, butlers, groundskeepers, laundresses, and others who worked at the estate. "She still had the condo, but since she stayed with Mr. Sinatra for the most part, she was unofficially the lady of the manor," said Cruz. "She wanted fresh flowers every day; she wanted special foods; she wanted things to be nice for herself but also for Mr. Sinatra.

"For instance, Mr. Sinatra was satisfied with Italian food every night," said Cruz. "Mrs. Marx was concerned about his health and sometimes wanted foods for him that were less fatty."

One day, in the kitchen, Barbara had a discussion with the chef about his habit of putting ground beef into the spaghetti sauce. "I think Mr. Sinatra gets enough red meat in other areas of his diet, don't you?" she asked. "Why does he have to have it in his spaghetti sauce too?"

"Because he *likes* it that way, madam," said the cook, his tone surly. "With meat in it."

"Well, I don't know what to make of that," Barbara remarked.

"Well, Mrs. *Marx*, it's called Bolognese," the chef declared. "*Bo-log-nese.*"

Barbara was insulted. "I may be new around here," she said, her eyes flashing, "but if you think I'm a pushover, you are very wrong." Taking the pot of spaghetti sauce off the range, she poured it into the sink. "I hope I have made myself clear," she concluded. She then flicked on the garbage disposal to make certain all of the sauce was gone. In the process, much of it splashed on the kitchen counter. "Now, I have what I think is a very good idea," Barbara said as she grabbed a towel from a rack and threw it at the chef. "*Clean this mess up!*"

After that incident, Barbara had a meeting with the staff in the living room. According to Laura Cruz, she hosted a tea with biscuits and scones for the chef, maids, gardeners, laundresses, and others who had never before enjoyed the luxury of actually being able to sit and socialize in the Sinatra living room. "All I expect from each of you," Barbara said to the group of about twelve, "is simple respect. I promise that you will get the same treatment from me that I get from you, good or bad. Do we have an agreement?"

Everyone nodded.

"Now, please, have another cup," she said as she went around the room, pouring tea for the servants.

"After that, she had *everyone's* allegiance," Laura Cruz said. "I thought, 'This is a wonderful, smart woman.' Our boss, Vine Joubert, was an instant fan.

"Mrs. Marx really took over the house and Mr. Sinatra's life in many good ways," continued Cruz. "She made sure he got his rest, for instance. One day, Mr. Rizzo came over early in the morning and Barbara kicked him out, telling him that Mr. Sinatra needed to sleep. When Mr. Sinatra woke up at about three, he was upset and they had a row. I heard every word. I couldn't help it. They fought right in front of me in the living room."

"Listen, you crazy broad," Frank hollered at Barbara. "You don't tell me who to see and who not to see."

"I'm not trying to do that, Frank," she said in her defense. "I'm just trying to say that you need your rest, and you'll never get it with all these people hanging around here all the time. This place is like a bus station."

"These are my friends," Frank argued. "If I have to choose between you and them, I choose them!"

Barbara ran from the room, upset. "I'm only trying to help," she said as she departed in tears. Frank turned to Laura Cruz and said, "Sorry you had to see that." Then he poured himself a glass of Jack Daniel's and said of Barbara, "If she puts up with me, she's crazier than I am."

A couple hours later, Barbara found a note stuck to the refrigerator door: "To My Girl—I have reconsidered. I CHOOSE YOU." Frank signed it with a smiley face wearing a bow tie. Twenty minutes later, the two were lying out on the patio, drinking cocktails. As the sun set on the San Jacinto Mountains, they spoke softly and laughed together as if nothing had happened.

End of an Era

On the afternoon of June 20, 1975, Frank Sinatra awakened in his suite at Caesars Palace in Las Vegas. As usual, his opening-night performance had been a great success. That afternoon, over his usual omelet with basil-flavored tomato sauce, he heard the news: Sam Giancana had been murdered in Chicago.

Staff members of the Senate Select Committee on Intelligence had just arrived in the Windy City to question Giancana about his possible connection to the CIA's Castro assassination plot. It was thought that some in the Chicago underworld feared what Giancana might say. Whatever the case, sixty-seven-year-old Giancana was found dead in his basement, shot with what appeared to be a silenced .22 caliber automatic once in the back of the head, once in the mouth, and five times under the chin.

"I guess, you live by the sword, you die by the sword," Frank said of Sam's death. He was sad; they had once been pals. However, they'd had little to do with each other since the Cal-Neva incident.

"Then, after Sam died, Johnny Roselli got it," recalled Thomas DiBella. "He was butchered in Miami. They found him chopped up and crammed into an oil drum floating in a bay near Miami. Then poor Skinny D'Amato went, I believe, of a heart attack. I know Frank was broken up by Jimmy's death; he was a pallbearer at the funeral. All these guys connected to the underworld, they were dropping like flies by the end of the seventies."

"It's the end of an era, I guess," Frank said privately. "Some of these guys caused me nothing but trouble. But they were good guys. If you knew them, they were good guys."

Jackie? Or Barbara?

By the fall of 1975, Barbara and Frank found themselves in a bit of a gray area in their relationship. They had been with each other around the clock for some time, and lately there was some tension between them. Barbara was interested in marriage, but she could tell

Frank was ambivalent. She had begun to wonder what kind of future she would actually have with him. It was exciting when they were on the road together, but she knew that those were temporary highs that had to eventually subside. When they were home, off the road, what was there for them? If he wasn't ready to commit to her, she decided, then maybe she should just chalk up her time on tour with him as another wonderful memory and then walk away. She actually wasn't sure how to proceed, and neither was he. Therefore, they decided to take a break, much to the elation of Frank's mother and daughters, who still hadn't come around.

During this time, Frank had a well-publicized date with Jackie Kennedy Onassis in New York when he took her to dinner after one of his shows at the Uris Theatre in September 1975. She was working as an editor at Viking publishing company and had wanted him to write his memoir for her. He begged off, but still wanted to see her. Back in the 1960s they had been ambivalent about one another, with Jackie unsure about the influence Sinatra had on her husband, but after JFK died they stayed in touch. Talking to one another always seemed to bring forth strong feelings of bittersweet nostalgia for the Camelot years.

Later, Frank and Jackie supposedly ended up in Frank's suite at the Waldorf Towers, where they spent the night together—or at least that's what Frank suggested to his buddies.

"I was at a party at Steve Lawrence's and we were all pretty loaded," recalled Jim Whiting. "It was late and we were shooting the shit, you know? Jilly asked Frank who the biggest conquests were in his life. Sinatra said that on top of the list was Ava. Then Jackie, Lana [Turner], and Marilyn [Monroe]. Everyone said, 'Wait a second! Jackie? What are you kidding me? What was *that* like?' Sinatra got real quiet and said, 'I ain't talkin' 'bout that.'"

"The relationship with Jackie was one of his relationships that, when it came to explaining the depth of it, Frank was very tight-lipped about, even with me," said Tony Oppedisano. "He just made it clear that there were feelings there."

While Frank was in New York without Barbara, she became a little concerned. "She saw the photos of Frank and Jackie in the press and thought twice after that," said Dinah Shore. "She didn't want to lose him. By this time, she really loved him. And by the way," Dinah added, rolling her eyes, "I don't believe for a single second that Frank and Jackie Onassis were ever intimate."

When Barbara telephoned Frank in New York, they talked for many hours trying to get back on track. He was lonely and tired of feeling that way, he said. He said he knew he only had himself to blame for his loneliness, always on the lookout for the next big conquest and not focusing on creating a real bond with any one woman.

Frank agreed that Barbara should fly to New York to be with him for the rest of the Uris engagement. He was ready to clear the decks and start taking Barbara seriously, and part of that process was ending other romances that had been lingering for years without much progress, including those with the younger, blonde actresses Peggy Lipton and Carol Lynley. He ended both romances easily. However, there was still one more loose end that needed to be tied up, and it had to do with Ava. Of course.

Or Maybe Ava?

*T*hough it had been almost twenty years since his divorce from Ava Gardner, Frank still couldn't help but wonder about her. It seems odd that he would view her as the one that got away. Some in his life thought of her as the one that wouldn't go *away*. Yet at a time when he was lamenting his lost youth, something about an old love called out to him.

Frank had seen Ava in May 1975, when he was appearing at Royal Albert Hall in London. When she came backstage to say hello, he introduced her to Barbara. "She was very polite," Barbara said, "and we got along fine, but I noticed there was even more drinking going on." Someone even asked Barbara, after Ava departed, what she thought of her. Barbara paid Ava a compliment about her beauty but then said, "It could never have worked between her and Frank." Overhearing the conversation, Frank was taken aback. "Why do you say that?" he asked. "Too much hurt," Barbara explained. "That hit him hard," she later recalled, "but after thinking about what I'd said, he admitted I was right."

The fact that he and Ava had "too much hurt" between them

wasn't exactly news to Frank. It had never stopped him from thinking about her and wondering, what if? Eight months later, she was still on his mind, especially as he began to contemplate a real future without her. He began to fixate on the memory of the heart-racing passion they had together, and, as often happens with matters of the heart, he began to romanticize their relationship. Soon he was calling Ava in Rome, where she was living at the time. He was in Cherry Hill, New Jersey, appearing at the Latin Casino.

Of course, it was easy for Frank and Ava on the telephone; in person was where it always fell apart between them. Soon they were swept away by nostalgia and actually talking about marriage again. In fact, Ava, who was now fifty-four, was convinced that she was going to go through with it. She told her maid, Rene Jordan, "You know as well as I do that if I'm ever going to marry again, it will be Frank. If I don't marry Frank, I'll be alone for the rest of my life, because no one interests me." Rene asked her if matrimony was what Frank wanted as well, and Ava assured her that it was. "He has been on the phone for weeks saying he loves me," she told her, according to Rene's memory, "and asking why don't I go back and we start all over again? We're older and wiser now." Rene recalled, "I didn't think they were wiser, but it was not my business to make smart remarks. 'By starting over, you mean getting married?' I asked her. 'Yes, getting married,' she answered."

Rene well knew—as did most people by this time—that Frank was dating Barbara. She asked Ava how that situation might be handled. Ava said that Frank told her that if she came back to the States to marry him, Barbara would no longer be a factor.

In the next few days, Ava made up her mind. She was going to marry Frank again. "And you and I are going to Fontana to get them to make me a trousseau," she told Rene. The two departed for Francavilla Fontana, a municipality in Puglia, southern Italy, where they purchased a wide array of daytime and nighttime dresses and negligees for Ava. Rene would say that she had an uneasy feeling about all of it, especially when Ava told her that Frank said that if she came to America he would marry her—but if not, he would just marry Barbara in her absence. "He was giving Miss G. not so much an ultimatum, but an option," she would recall.

A few days after the excitement of purchasing the new wardrobe wore off, Ava finally came to her senses. After hanging up with Frank, she told Rene that it was over; she'd suggested to him that he go ahead and marry Barbara, that it was for the best. "From Miss G., there were no tears, recalled Rene Jordan. "There was just a depression that lifted quickly."

Perhaps one couldn't blame Frank for at least trying. After all, Ava represented something to him that apparently he didn't have with Barbara—sheer, unadulterated passion. But in fact, all he and Ava *ever* had was passion, and little else upon which to build a solid relationship. Of course, he'd realized long ago that the romance with her had been deadly for both of them. But at sixty, he couldn't resist one last chance at the woman who most characterized his reckless youth. Without her as his safety net, it now felt a little like he was jumping off a cliff.

"I guess I'm stuck with Barbara," Frank told Jilly Rizzo and Jim Whiting over drinks at the house.

"Well, you could just live together, you know?" Jilly suggested. "Yous don't gotta get married."

No, Frank told him. He said he might as well just see it through and make it legal with Barbara. "It's not the future I wanted," he added with a sigh. "But maybe it's the one I deserve." He didn't seem so much like a man in love as a man resigned to his fate.

Though Barbara Marx had acquitted herself well over the years and had proven herself in many ways, true to Frank Sinatra's restless nature, he wasn't quite satisfied. In fact, he was, as always, looking for something better.

Frank and Barbara Get Engaged

*F*rank may have continued to be ambivalent for some time where Barbara was concerned, had she not decided to apply pressure. By March 1976, she'd been with him for four years; she was tired of living in suspense. Either he was going to take the relationship to the next stage or she was going to have to end it. Frank, of course, didn't appreciate ultimatums. Therefore, Barbara left him—and thus began another "break" in their romance.

This time, Barbara was fairly sure it was over. She loved him and missed him, but she was a survivor and knew she would just have to get over it. Meanwhile, Frank defaulted to his deeply depressed state of mind and stayed close to his family, which of course delighted his daughters. Tina and Nancy wanted him to be happy; both felt sure that Barbara wasn't the woman for him, otherwise he wouldn't have such trepidation about her. They were more than happy to see him walk away from that relationship. It wasn't a break that would last, though.

In May, Frank called Barbara in Las Vegas where she'd been vacationing. He told her he wanted to resume where they'd left off. She'd heard about his calls to Ava, she said, and she was hurt. "But my heart isn't with her anymore, darling," he told her. "It was always with you." Once again swept away by him, Barbara decided to join him in Chicago. Was this to be more of the same waffling from him, though? No. When Barbara got to Chicago, Frank presented her with the biggest pear-shaped diamond—twenty-two carats—she'd ever seen. There was another gem as well, a green emerald. Frank said she could have them set any way she liked. She ran to him, embraced him, and kissed him. It still wasn't a proposal, but it was as close as she'd been to one with him.

Barbara decided to send the stones to a jeweler in Chicago and have them set in an engagement ring, hoping that this kind of commitment was really what Frank had in mind. Then, rather than pick up the ring herself—final cost: $360,000—she had it sent to Frank. She was going to make him put a ring on her finger if it was the last thing she did.

Later that week, over dinner in a Chicago restaurant, Barbara noticed something gleaming in her flute of bubbly champagne. "Is that for me?" she asked, excited. Of course, it was the ring. She fished it out, and, rather than put it on her own finger, she dabbed it on a napkin and then handed it to Frank. She held out both hands. "Just put it on whichever finger you want to put it on," she told Frank. He laughed and put the ring on her engagement finger. Still no proposal—but at least she felt they were in some sort of accord regarding their future together.

A couple weeks later, Barbara and Frank were lounging by the pool at the compound, enjoying the afternoon together. Seeming soothed and refreshed by the limitless peace of the desert, Frank turned to her and quietly said, "Darling, maybe we should set a date?" And that question was about as close to a proposal as Barbara Marx ever got from Frank Sinatra.

"He was romantic in every other way, but for some reason he just couldn't bring himself to say the words, 'Will you marry me?'" Barbara later recounted. She thought that perhaps it was because he'd had three failed marriages. Or maybe it was because he had felt somehow coerced into giving her a ring. She didn't care, though. She knew he loved her, she knew how she felt about him, and she didn't need to hear the words.

Barbara quickly told her parents and her son, Bobby, the good news. But replicating the culture of secrecy that had characterized his marriage to Mia, Frank decided not to tell his ex-wife Nancy or their three children about the engagement. It was never easy to put anything over on Tina, though. She somehow found out about it; she *always* found out about whatever was happening with her father, one way or another.

"My sister told me that Dad and his friend, Barbara Marx, were in a serious relationship, perhaps even engaged," Nancy Sinatra recalled. "I didn't believe her. Barbara wasn't Dad's type." Nancy had somehow managed to avoid the reality of her father becoming serious with Barbara. One can't imagine how she could have missed it; it had been going on for years! As far as she was concerned, though, her mother and father still had a chance. In her mind, there were still sparks between Frank and Nancy, and she believed in her heart that they were destined to be with one another. She still wasn't willing to give up her dream that her parents would reunite. Therefore, in her world, Barbara Marx didn't even exist. Until she did.

One night in June, Frank showed up with Barbara for a family party at Nancy's home. Barbara looked sensational that night, maybe even having had some work done on her face. (Tina said she "had a brand-new profile.") When the Sinatras saw the engagement ring sparkling on her finger, they figured it out. Were they happy about it? Surprised would be a better word. But why the secrecy?

With Mia, it seemed a little clearer, especially in retrospect, why Frank had been so secretive. The age difference, the debate about whether or not to invite her to his fiftieth birthday party... even though Tina had no problem with the relationship, Frank knew that everyone else did, and it just wasn't worth it to him to deal with their opposition. He didn't want them ruining the moment for him.

However, thus far no one had *openly* objected to Barbara Marx, except his own mother, and he knew she would not be satisfied with anyone. Of course, Frank wasn't living in a vacuum. He knew what the women in his life thought of Barbara from what they'd told others in his circle. He didn't want to deal with their opposition. And where Dolly was concerned, he *really* didn't want to deal with it. He dispatched poor Mickey Rudin to tell her he was going to marry Barbara. Mickey later said his ears smarted for days from the language Dolly used in response to his "good news."

Naturally, it hurt the Sinatra women that Frank had kept another major life decision a secret from them. Or was it really Barbara's doing? Actually, it wasn't her choice at all, but they didn't know that at the time. It was easier to blame her, anyway, because it didn't hurt as much.

As we have seen, no one orchestrated drama quite like Frank Sinatra, and after stunning everyone with Barbara's sparkler, he dashed away from the family party, explaining that he had a scheduled recording session. Barbara was left at the house to fend for herself with Frank's confused ex-wife and daughters. The women had no choice but to sort it out for themselves. The Sinatra women actually felt badly for Barbara; this was poor form by Frank, and they knew it. So they did their best to make her feel welcome, not uncomfortable.

Frank and Barbara soon made a public announcement that they would marry on October 10, 1976, at Kirk Douglas's home. Actually, though, they were planning a secret wedding, one that would take place much earlier, in July.

Surprise Prenup?

*T*he "secret" ceremony to join Frank and Barbara as husband and wife was to be held on July 11, 1976, at Sunnylands, the thousand-acre Palm Springs estate of publisher, philanthropist, and former ambassador to the Court of St. James's Walter Annenberg. Of course, despite Frank's best efforts, the press got wind of the impending nuptials, but the reporters were made to wait outside the gates in the 115-degree heat.

Frank's best man was to be Freeman Gosden, who played Amos on the *Amos 'n' Andy* radio program. Bea Korshak, wife of attorney Sidney Korshak, was the matron of honor. A *New York Times* reporter, noting the armed guards, considered it "security befitting an international summit conference."

On the morning of the ceremony, as Barbara was getting dressed, there was a knock on the door. It was Mickey Rudin. By this time, everyone in Frank's world knew that anytime Mickey showed up unexpectedly at your door, it probably wasn't going to be with the greatest news. There he stood before the bride-to-be, along with Sidney Korshak.

Korshak was a labor lawyer known as a "fixer" for businessmen dealing with the mob in Chicago. He'd gotten his start working for Al Capone. The FBI viewed him as one of the most powerful and influential attorneys in the world. He was also a friend of Barbara's, best friend of her ex-husband Zeppo's. By coincidence, he had dated Nancy Barbato for a short time in the late 1950s after her divorce from Frank and before he married his wife, Bea.

Barbara, still in curlers, would later recall that she welcomed the men into her room. They all sat down in front of a small table. Mickey, speaking out of the corner of his mouth because of the cigar dangling from it, took a document—many pages—out of a manila envelope, placed it on the table before her, and slid it toward her. "You have to sign this before you and Frank can get married," he said, according to her recollection of events.

"What is it?" Barbara asked.

"It's a prenup."

Barbara later recalled that she was surprised. She would maintain that she and Frank had never discussed a prenuptial agreement. She'd say that she wasn't sure if she was opposed to the idea or not, simply because she'd had no reason to consider it. "Does Frank know about this?" she asked.

"Of course," said Mickey.

Barbara thumbed through the thick stack of papers. It was legalese that would have taken some time for her to digest. She would say that the moment seemed unfair to her; it felt like a pressure tactic. "No. I'm not signing this," she decided. She slid the document back across the table to Mickey. "No way."

"Then the wedding's off," Mickey said firmly. "If you don't sign, no wedding."

"But..."

In fact, many of the 120 guests had already arrived by private planes at the Palm Springs airport, eight miles away, including the Ronald Reagans, who interrupted their presidential campaign; Spiro Agnew; Sammy Davis Jr.; the Gregory Pecks; Jimmy Van Heusen; Leo Durocher; and famed heart surgeon Dr. Michael DeBakey, who had operated on Marty. Dolly was to be present, as were Nancy and Tina. Frank Jr. wouldn't be present because of a prior commitment, an East Coast singing engagement. How would it look if the wedding was canceled so suddenly?

"Sidney, have you seen this?" Barbara recalled asking Korshak.

"Nope," he said. "But sign it. You'll be okay."

She mulled it over quickly as the two men stared at her. "I just don't think this is right," she finally said, "but, okay. I guess I have no choice." She took a black Flair pen from Mickey and signed the papers. She handed the pen back to Mickey. He gave it to Sidney, who put it in his vest pocket. Satisfied that the papers were in order, Mickey slid them into the envelope.

"Now, if that will be all," Barbara Marx said, rising. "I have to get ready for a wedding."

Interesting story. But did it really happen the way Barbara recalled it? Perhaps, but the veracity of Barbara's version of events seems somewhat compromised by a letter to Sidney Korshak from Mickey Rudin dated July 7, 1976—three days before the wedding. In the document, Rudin confirms with Korshak that a prenuptial agreement was on the table and that Rudin had advised Barbara to seek counsel relating to it, and that she had decided to be represented by Korshak. It further confirms everyone's understanding that Korshak would negotiate on Barbara's behalf, even though he was not licensed in the state of California. The document was signed by Mickey, Sidney, and Barbara. Based on this letter, it would appear that Barbara did know that a prenuptial agreement was in place. But had she not discussed it with Frank, as she claimed? That's very possible. Not only was it true that Frank often made important decisions affecting the people in his life without first consulting them, but it was also the case that his intimates were usually not confrontational with him about these important matters for fear of upsetting him and getting on his bad side.

Whatever the truth, it wouldn't be the last time the matter of Barbara's prenuptial agreement with Frank would be raised.

Frank and Barbara Marry

*A*t forty-six, Barbara Marx was a stunning bride in her Halston-designed beige chiffon wedding dress with its prominent jeweled brooch at the point of the off-center V-neck. She handled herself with enormous self-assurance as she greeted each and every guest. She would be escorted down the aisle by her father. Frank, sixty, wore a beige silk-and-linen suit with a beige silk tie and a brown-and-beige handkerchief in his breast pocket.

Nancy and Tina both looked a little stricken. In fact, Nancy later admitted that she cried for an entire week before the ceremony. Some people were confused by her reaction, but what they didn't know about her was that she and Frank had a sort of symbiotic relationship; she always seemed to know exactly what he was thinking. "We're not just father and daughter, with an easy, loving relationship; we're joined at the hip," she would say. "We *read* each other easily, even from a distance." She could sense his ambivalence about marrying Barbara from the moment she found out they were engaged, and it was impossible for her to ignore it. In fact, something in Nancy told her they were all in for big trouble with this marriage. There was just a certain imperiousness in the way Barbara held her head, in her general demeanor, that Nancy found more than a little off-putting. Call it woman's intuition; whatever it was, Nancy was on high alert. Or, as she put it at the time, "I'm lit up like a pinball machine over this thing."

Barbara didn't quite know what to make of Nancy's and Tina's obvious misgivings about her. "Is it that they're just the spoiled and pampered daughters of a very rich and powerful man?" she asked one guest. "If so, one would think they would at least try to *appear* to be happy." When told that the Sinatras weren't much for pretense, Barbara nodded. "Obviously," she said with a small, amused smile.

Barbara also knew that Tina and Nancy had once been enamored of Ava, and had also welcomed Mia into the family. That hurt a little. In fact, Frank had a lovely oil painting of Mia still hanging in a hallowed place in the master bedroom. Barbara never mentioned it to him, but it did bother her. She decided to do something about it—in her own way. She went out and had a large poster of Zeppo Marx framed, and she hung it in the same room. "What the hell is *that* doing there?" Frank asked. "Oh, I thought this room was dedicated to memories," Barbara said, motioning to the painting of Mia. Frank didn't say a word, but the next day the painting of Mia was gone—and so was the poster of Zeppo.

Immediately prior to the ceremony, with only five minutes to spare, Frank took Nancy and Tina aside for a quick private moment. "I've thought this through," he told them. "And I've really considered your mother. You know I'll always love her. It would have been great if we could have all stayed together as a family, but that's not how things worked out. This is what I want now. This marriage is what I need in my life." The Sinatra daughters had no choice but to wish their father well. In truth, they really just wanted him to be happy. What could they do? Crying, they embraced him and gave them their blessing.

Later, when Judge James H. Walsworth asked the bride if she "took" Frank for richer or poorer, Frank said with a grin, "Richer, *richer*."

After the champagne reception, the guests rode in air-conditioned buses to dinner at Frank's house, just a few blocks away. On display were his gift to Barbara, a peacock-blue Rolls-Royce, and hers to him, a gray Jaguar XJS. The newlywed Sinatras would later honeymoon with three other couples (the Morton Downeys, the Bill Greens, and the Paul Mannos).

At the reception, Nancy and Tina put on the best faces possible, but by this time they were too overwhelmed with worry to camouflage it. Nancy's toast—as Frank might have put it—"really took the cake." Raising her flute of champagne toward her father, she said, "I hope that with Barbara you'll be less vulnerable." Everyone clinked glasses, but no one was quite sure of Nancy's intended meaning. She was unable to keep the concern out of her voice, and her toast sounded ominous.

Dolly, of course, had strong feelings about Barbara. At first she just didn't like her, and that was the end of it. But then Barbara scored some points with her when she decided, about a year before the marriage, that she wanted to convert to Catholicism. She wasn't a religious woman. However, she did want to share the same religion as Frank, even though he too was far from religious. Some people were suspicious about Barbara's motivations, feeling she was just trying to work her way deeper into the Sinatra family. In fact, with some, Barbara would never be able to win favor, no matter what she did; her critics would always suspect an ulterior motive. One wonders, though, if *any* woman would have been good enough for Frank's first wife and his daughters, short of someone as completely harmless as young Mia. Realistically, an age-appropriate woman like Barbara would have to be a formidable person for Frank to even be interested in her—and that kind of woman was likely going to find opposition from his family.

When Barbara asked Dolly to be her catechism instructor and to help her with her studies, Dolly was, at first, as suspicious as everyone else—but she decided to do it. It was good that she did; it definitely brought her closer to her future daughter-in-law. She spent many hours with her during this time, and the two found common ground. Dolly was never going to be Barbara's biggest advocate, but at least she stopped speaking out against her.

For her part, Tina was also apprehensive, but slightly more practical than Nancy. She felt that if Frank decided he'd made a mistake, he'd just get out of it. He'd send Mickey Rudin over to Barbara's home one day with divorce papers and tell her to sign on the dotted line. Barbara would do so, and that would be the end of it. It certainly wouldn't be the first time. Tina did her best to console her sister throughout the wedding day. However, Nancy's worry must have been contagious, because by the end of the evening Tina was also a bit rattled. She went out onto the patio to clear her head, and while there became involved in a pleasant conversation with the actor Kirk Douglas, which took her mind off of things, at least for a moment.

"Tina, I've got something for you," came a voice from behind. It was Sidney Korshak, walking over to Tina and Kirk. He reached into his pocket. "Here's a little something for you," he said handing her a Flair pen.

"But what's this, Sidney?" Tina asked, confused.

"That's the pen Barbara used to sign the prenup this morning," Sidney said with a smile. "And believe me, this little pen just saved you guys a shitload lot of money."

Dolly Sinatra—Rest in Peace

After her husband, Marty, died, Dolly Sinatra found herself lonely and wanting to be even more involved in her son's busy life and in the lives of his offspring. "She thinks she's the big hit," Frank said in an interview at this time. "She lives next door to me in Palm Springs," he told the reporter. "If she was here with us now and she wanted to say something about me, she would refer to me as 'Frank Sinatra' while I'm sitting here. She wants to be sure that everyone knows who she's talking about." Still, sometimes she was too much for Frank. He would go days trying to avoid her, which was difficult since she lived right next door.

In August 1976, when she was seventy-nine—she would turn eighty in December—Dolly told her granddaughter Nancy that she sensed that she would not live much longer. Since her grandmother was in generally good health—though persistently swollen ankles had become a source of pain and annoyance—Nancy dismissed Dolly's morbid notion. She decided that she was simply fatigued and, as she knew Dolly was wont to do, feeling self-indulgent and self-pitying. Perhaps she just wanted more attention.

On Thursday, January 6, 1977, Frank was scheduled to open in Vegas, again at Caesars Palace. Dolly, who enjoyed Las Vegas and thrilled to the sounds and sights of gambling machines, intended to be present for her son's opening. In fact, she enjoyed gambling so much that Frank had a slot machine installed in her Palm Springs home. "When she loses, she doesn't worry about it," he said. "She just gets out the screwdriver."

At 5 p.m., Dolly and a visiting widowed friend from New Jersey, Anna Carbone, boarded a twin-engine Learjet, which Frank had hired, at the Palm Springs airport for the twenty-minute flight to Las Vegas. Dolly's intention was to go directly from the airport to Caesars. Because of a storm in the Coachella Valley, visibility was poor. Perhaps the plane should never have taken off, because once it was airborne, visibility was zero. The pilot would have to rely on radar the entire way. Two minutes into the flight, ground control lost communication. The plane had been due to land in Las Vegas at 5:20.

Nancy Sr. received a telephone call from Mickey Rudin to tell her that he'd just received a call from Jet Avia, Ltd., the company that owned the Learjet. It was feared that Dolly's plane had crashed into San Gorgonio Mountain. This seemed impossible to believe; Nancy Sr. became very upset. She quickly telephoned her daughter Nancy, who was also in Los Angeles, and the two prayed for a last-minute miracle. Then they called Frank. Of course, he was paralyzed with fear by the time he shared the bad news with Barbara. "I'm sure she will be fine," Barbara tried to tell him, before falling to her knees to pray. "Dolly and I may have had our differences in the past," Barbara later recalled. "But we'd overcome them and truly made our peace. We had spent so much time together that we'd become friends. I couldn't imagine how Frank would cope if she were to die in some unexpected horrible way."

Three hours later, Frank was onstage, somehow managing to perform for a full-house audience while a search crew was being organized to look for his missing mother. "I know he did it for his mother," Nancy said of that concert. Sinatra received a standing ovation; no one in the audience had even a hint of the nightmare unfolding in his personal life.

"It was the most terrible night of his life," said Eileen Faith, a friend of Barbara's at that time. "How he was able to go on, no one knew. There was that hope, that small ray of hope, that maybe, somehow, Dolly had escaped injury. It was impossible to comprehend her dying that way. She hardly ever flew, maybe a couple of times a year. No one could accept it. After the first show, Frank canceled the rest of the engagement and flew back to Palm Springs."

On Friday, the next morning, Nancy and Hugh and Tina (who

was by now separated from Wes Farrell) arrived in Palm Springs to support Frank and Barbara. Frankie decided to try to take a survey helicopter up to look for his grandmother, but the weather wouldn't allow it.

On Saturday, the nightmare continued. Still no word. Frank was so deep in mourning by this time, he wouldn't speak to anyone, even his wife. "I'd walk past every hour or so, catch his eye, and give him a smile, but his eyes wouldn't even flicker," she later recalled. His friends and family members told her that this was the way he grieved; it's how he had been with JFK and Marilyn, and especially with his father, they explained. Finally, he went up in a Civil Air Patrol helicopter with a pilot named Don Landells, searching the snow-swept mountainside for Dolly. They didn't find any wreckage.

By the third day, Sunday, a sense of hopelessness had enveloped the Sinatra compound as everyone—not just Frank—walked about in a daze, stunned by the sinking-in reality of what had occurred. Desperate to do something, Tina and Nancy telephoned the famed Dutch psychic Peter Hurkos. Hurkos promised the Sinatra daughters that he would do what he could and get back to them.*

Then, at 11:25 p.m., the family got the call. Wreckage from the Learjet had finally been found by Don Landells, who had again gone out in search of it. The jet was split in two, the nose destroyed. The wings and tail had been torn from the aircraft. It was later learned that the plane had crashed into the 11,502-foot mountain—the same one that would later claim Dean Martin's son Dean Paul—at full takeoff speed of 375 miles per hour as a result of a mix-up in communications from the control tower and also bad weather conditions. Of course, there were no survivors.

Heartbreaking images of poor Dolly, panicked and horror-stricken in her last moments, haunted the family when they again gathered in the Sinatra living room; Frank was devastated. "I didn't even get

---

* It's worth noting that ten years later, when Dean Martin's son Dean Paul's plane went down in the same mountain range and no one knew whether he was dead or alive, his brother, Ricci, and best friend, Scott Sandler, had a session with Hurkos to find out what he could glean. Hurkos, upon touching one of Dean Paul's flight suits, instantly announced that the young man was dead.

a chance to say goodbye," he said, crying. Mickey Rudin told everyone that Dolly was found strapped to her seat. Even though everyone suspected that this was an unlikely scenario, they tried desperately to believe it. But who would go to identify Dolly's body the next day, once it was brought back to the Palm Springs morgue? Mickey said he would do it, but then couldn't bring himself to go. It fell upon Jilly, but he couldn't go either. Eventually, it was Barbara who volunteered. It must have been terrible for her, but she summoned up her courage and did what she knew she had to do for her husband. He was very grateful.

The funeral was at St. Louis Roman Catholic Church in Cathedral City, outside Palm Springs, on January 12, 1977. Dolly was buried at Desert Memorial Park, next to Marty, whose body, at her request, had earlier been exhumed in New Jersey and moved to Palm Springs. Dean Martin, Jimmy Van Heusen, Leo Durocher, Danny Thomas, Pat Henry, and Jilly Rizzo were pallbearers. The Associated Press said that Sinatra's "eyes were unswerving from the casket covered with white lilies and pink roses."

Many of his intimates believed that Frank would never recover from his mother's sudden, tragic death.

"My father was devastated," recalled Frank Jr. "The days that followed were the worst I had ever known. He said nothing for hours at a time. All of us who were nearby felt helpless to find any way to ease his agony. Back at home after that terrible hour at the graveside, I felt it best not to leave him alone. I sat with him and watched the tears roll one by one down his face."

"Who Died and Left Barbara Boss?"

$\mathcal{F}$or the last few years, Barbara had tolerated the Sinatra daughters and their barely suppressed mistrust of her. She'd not had an actual fight with either of them, it was just a sense she got that they didn't approve of her. They were distant. Ever since they'd heard that Barbara had balked at signing the prenuptial agreement, they were suspicious. Tina Sinatra claims she heard from a mutual friend that Barbara said, "This time I married for money."

Barbara didn't know how Frank Jr. felt about her, but she suspected he was more likely to give her the benefit of the doubt, or at least that's what she gleaned based on his fractured relationship with everyone else. He was so detached, she didn't feel he was in alignment with anyone in the family about anything. As for Nancy Sr., it was never Barbara's interest to win her over. She realized after her first entreaties to Nancy that the first wife would never get along with the present wife, nor should there be any reason for her to do so if it didn't come naturally. That was fine with Barbara; she already had plenty of friends. Therefore, with the passing of the years, everyone acted quite cordially at family events and did what they could to keep smiling, and Barbara felt that was about the best she could expect from the Sinatras. Over time, the daughters' mistrust of her bothered her less. She lived in her own utopian world and had a very exciting and busy life with Frank, especially on the road. She was with Frank twenty-four hours a day, seven days a week, and if Nancy and Tina had a problem with that, it would be up to them to make the necessary adjustments, or so Barbara had long ago decided.

Barbara didn't want a family war with Nancy and Tina. However, she was also a formidable woman; she demanded respect from those around her. The Sinatra daughters were exactly the same way. So it was just a matter of time before all of the unspoken tension within the family would build to an explosive level. Ironically, it would be a disagreement having to do with Dolly that would set into motion a torrent of distrust and unhappiness for all.

The day after the funeral, Barbara went over to Dolly's house and took pretty much anything of value—diamonds, furs, mementos of her son's life and career—as well as many things that meant very little, tchotchkes such as dishes and cheap silverware, and put everything in an enormous, locked closet in her bedroom at the compound. She felt it was the safest, wisest course of action to take. After all, there was always a great deal of traffic in and out of the compound, much of it people she didn't even know. The place was filled with Frank's drinking buddies, musicians, hangers-on, and other show-business types. It wasn't exactly an environment where everyone could be closely monitored, nor should it have been; that wasn't Frank's way. Barbara felt that she owed it to Dolly to make certain that her treasured belongings were safely taken care of so that the family could have a chance to sort through them when they were emotionally able to do so. She was the newest member of the Sinatras. She'd been the one to take on the terrible job of identifying Dolly's body when no one else had the courage for it. Therefore she felt that perhaps she alone had the presence of mind at this time to think in a practical way.

Unfortunately, Nancy Jr. and Tina disagreed. Nancy went to Dolly's house to see about her possessions and discovered that they had all been removed. She was very upset. She called Tina, and the two women did their own investigation and found out from one of the household employees what Barbara had done. "But who died and left Barbara in charge?" Nancy wanted to know. "Certainly not *my* grandmother!" Tina agreed. Barbara was new to the family, so what right did she have to take and then store Dolly's belongings? For the next couple of weeks, the Sinatra women tried to keep their emotions in check. This was a delicate situation, and they knew it. But still, they were so upset it was impossible for them to just let it go.

Nancy, who was thirty-seven, was exactly like her dad; she knew what she knew and there was no talking her out of it. Like Frank, when she was angry, she was angry. She spoke her mind. This isn't to say she was completely unreasonable, but she definitely would not back down from a fight—again like Frank.

Tina, now twenty-nine, was not always as quick to come to conclusions—though she could at times beat her sister to them. Tina wasn't sure if what Barbara had done was a big deal or not. When the time was right, she figured, they would sort it all out. Nancy was not inclined to agree. She thought it *was* a big deal, and that they'd better wise up about it before these kinds of unilateral decisions became the family norm. Finally, Tina decided to telephone Frank to tell him about it.

"You're kidding me, right?" was all Frank could muster when he heard the news. Tina assured him that she wasn't joking. "Okay, I'll look into it, Pigeon," he said. "Just try to calm down."

When Frank talked to Barbara about it, she wasn't the least bit evasive. She said, "Look, you're the heir. I just did what I thought was best to protect you!" Protect him from whom, though? "This place is like a bus station, Frank," she said in her defense. "I just thought it was the right thing to do, that Grandma would have *wanted* me to. I'm so busy, you'd think you would *thank me* for taking care of this!"

Just the same, Frank told Barbara that his daughters were upset. He knew better than to take sides, though, and the fact that he didn't hurt Barbara. "I'm surprised he isn't just coming out to defend me," she told her socialite friend Eileen Faith over drinks at Don the Beachcomber restaurant in Palm Springs. She swore that her motives were innocent. Why, she asked, would anyone think she would purposely do something to alienate the Sinatra daughters? "And don't they think I don't have enough jewels and nice things from their father?" she asked. "He has already given me the world! Why would I want Grandma's few, precious treasures. It's just so ridiculous."

"Then the three of you need to sit down and hash it out, without Frank," Eileen suggested. Barbara said that she wasn't sure that was the way to handle it. She said that Frank knew his daughters better than she did, and that she should probably follow his lead. Her friend disagreed. She said that, as a woman, Barbara would best know how to deal with so delicate a situation. Also, when it came to family politics, from what Barbara had earlier suggested, perhaps Frank was not the best one to rely on to handle anything of a sensitive nature. That was certainly true.

When Barbara discussed the matter with Frank again, he told her that the best thing she could do was not to make a bigger issue of it by forcing an all-out confrontation. Maybe if she just put Dolly's possessions back where she'd found them, the storm would blow over, or at least that's what he hoped. He said Nancy and Tina could then go through everything and pick out what they wanted to keep for themselves. This arranged distribution of property was fine with Barbara. She had always figured that this was the way it would happen anyway, when the family wasn't so emotionally raw.

When Nancy and Tina finally got to Dolly's house in Palm Springs and began sorting through the valuables, they said that they found a good many things missing—jewels, furs, and other costly items. Now that the landscape was so riddled with suspicion, they couldn't help but wonder: Had Frank told Barbara she could have anything she wanted before they'd had an opportunity to make their own selections? If so, they felt it did not bode well for them. "She'd been 'protecting' Dad's interests," Tina would note of Barbara years later. "But from who? The answer was obvious and disturbing. Barbara was protecting my father from the people she perceived as her stiffest remaining competition. From his children."

Adopting a New Sinatra?

*I*n the beginning, Barbara Marx couldn't help but marvel at the fact that she was officially Mrs. Frank Sinatra. "For a long time I had to pinch myself almost daily to believe that I, Barbara Ann Blakeley, the gangly kid in pigtails from the whistle stop of Bosworth, Missouri, had somehow become the wife of Francis Albert Sinatra. Could I really be married to the singer whose voice I'd first heard at a drive-in when I was fifteen years old?" Once she got used to the idea, though, she melded into it, her identity and Frank's becoming one. She was quite happy, and she believed in her heart that Frank felt the same way. Did she also want her son, Bobby, to share in the prestige and entitlement of being a Sinatra? That's what Tina Sinatra had to wonder when in the spring of 1977 she received a telephone call from Mickey Rudin.

Something was brewing, Mickey told Tina, and he wanted to make her aware of it: Frank was about to adopt Barbara's son, Bobby. But Bobby Marx was twenty-five. Tina said she had never heard of a grown man being adopted. However, Mickey said it was definitely going to happen and that if she wanted to do something about it, she'd better hurry. Tina said she needed a moment to collect herself and try to figure out how best to handle this surprising situation.

It's not known how she learned about it—maybe also from Mickey?—but Nancy didn't need time to collect herself. She got Frank on the phone and let him have it.

Nancy, Tina, and Frankie would certainly have no financial worries after their father's death (they would still inherit all of his record royalties, while Barbara would receive most of the property), whether or not Bobby was in the picture, but that wasn't exactly the point of Nancy's contention. "My concern was that giving him the family name would be wrong, for him, for us. After all the 'Mamma Mia' jokes, what would they do with the sudden appearance of Bobby Sinatra? I couldn't help feeling that to be a Sinatra kid, you had to pay your dues, had to go through the tough times with the business and the press and the personal crises," Nancy would say. "To be a Sinatra, you needed a history that carried a mix of pain and prominence. A bit second-rate of me, perhaps. Everybody has troubles, but someone just can't step in and take over. It doesn't work."

This new family debate would be waged for many months, again with the Sinatra daughters never actually confronting Barbara or even Bobby about it. Again there was a sense, fostered by Frank, that if the three women discussed it openly, it would just make things worse. The daughters' beef, then, ended up being with Frank—not with Barbara.

Though Nancy was beyond trying to reason out this situation, Tina could actually see how Frank might decide that Bobby should be a part of the family since he was Barbara's only son. Why shouldn't he be legally embraced by the family? Ava didn't have children and neither did Mia, she maintained, so this truly was new terrain for everyone.

Tina knew her dad well. She understood the way he processed conflict. Now that there was so much contention about this issue, she suspected he was pulling his hair out trying to figure out how to make everyone happy. She also knew it wasn't possible. Someone was going to win and someone was going to lose—and she and her sister were *not* going to lose. Tina's mind was made up: She wasn't going to allow any adoption.

One major concern of both Tina's and Nancy's was how an adoption of Bobby Marx might affect Frank Jr., now thirty-three. If Frank wanted so desperately to forge a close relationship with an adult male, shouldn't it be with his own biological son? Frank Jr. wanted to stay out of the fray, though. For him it was to be business as usual. As always, he would focus on his work, his friends, and his own life. He wanted nothing to do with this present conflict.

"*Have you lost your mind?*" a very agitated Tina demanded to know of Frank on the telephone one morning. "*You can't do this!*"

Of course, trying to dictate to Frank Sinatra what he could and could not do never worked. Frank had always said his credo for others to follow was, "Don't tell. Suggest." Or as his friend David Tebbett put it, "You push Frank and you can forget all about it; there's no chance in hell of him doing what you want." Likely, Tina telling him that he was "out of his mind" didn't sit well with her dad. In fact, according to one of his associates at that time, "It came to pass that the more people said, 'No, you can't do this,' the more he became determined to do it. The more his daughters pushed it, the more pissed off he became and the more determined he became."

"Why does everything have to be such a big fucking deal?" Frank raged during one meeting with associates over the adoption matter.

"Well, look, Frank, obviously your kids weren't going to be happy about this," said one of his managers.

"But this doesn't even affect them," Frank raged. "*This hasn't got one goddamn thing to do with them!*" he shouted. "Why doesn't everyone just shut up about it! Nobody is affected here but Bobby. He gets to be a Sinatra. That's it. The will don't change. The money don't change. Nothing changes."

Of course, Frank couldn't possibly have believed that adopting a son would not eventually have some bearing on his last will and testament. He wasn't that naïve. He also wasn't thinking of the bigger picture. Of course, many in the Sinatra family assumed that the idea had been Barbara's anyway. Was this plan really her way of securing her place and that of her son in the vast Sinatra financial empire? "But I had nothing to do with it," Barbara would say in her defense. "This was all *Frank's* idea."

Barbara would later explain that she and Frank had been in his private jet, he sitting across the aisle from her, when, like a schoolboy, he passed her a note. She unfolded it. It said, "I want to adopt Bobby." It also said that he loved Bobby, wanted him to be his son, and felt that Bobby deserved to be "a part of a bigger family." She would recall that her first impulse was to believe that Frank was joking, that it seemed very odd. In discussing it with her during the flight, Frank sent for Mickey, who was in another part of the jet. Mickey came to them and tried his best to discourage the idea. However, according to Barbara, Frank's mind seemed to be made up; he told Mickey, "Just do it!"

Barbara recalled that when she got back to Los Angeles, she called Bobby and told him of Frank's plan. Bobby, too, was against the idea of a formal adoption. She says that he specifically told her, "But, Mother, I don't *want* to be adopted!" She says he told her that he thought it was very nice of Frank, but not what he wanted. "I pleaded his case to Frank," she recounted, "but my pigheaded Italian husband was determined to go ahead with it."

But maybe the idea of adopting Bobby wasn't so far-fetched to Frank. After all, Frank did enjoy Bobby's company; the two had a good relationship. They'd known each other for years before his mother had even married Frank. When the Marxes lived across the golfing green from Frank back in the early 1960s, Barbara had asked Frank to introduce Bobby to his screen idol, Marilyn Monroe. The next time Marilyn came to visit, Frank made the introduction, which thrilled the youngster. Bobby would even go on to become Frank's road manager. After the passing of some years, Frank then decided he wanted to adopt him. While it may seem like an odd decision in retrospect, it wasn't completely unusual in Sinatra's circle. For instance, about five years earlier, Dean Martin had married his third wife, Catherine Mae Hawn, and ended up adopting her daughter, Sasha. (Of course, Sasha was a child, whereas Bobby was a grown man.)

However, Barbara's versions of events loses some credibility when one considers that there were once plans afoot for her second husband, Zeppo Marx, to adopt Bobby when he was just a boy. This despite the fact that Zeppo hadn't been very solicitous toward Bobby. In fact, she had sent Bobby off to a military academy shortly after meeting Marx because he didn't want the kid around. After they got married, Zeppo built a new wing for Bobby at their Palm Springs home, just to keep him out of his hair. In the end, Bobby's biological father, Robert Oliver, refused to allow the adoption. Despite this, Bobby assumed the surname of Marx anyway.

As far as Frank was concerned, he and Barbara weren't the troublemakers in this debate. That was Mickey Rudin. The subject wouldn't even have been open for debate had Mickey not sent out a family alert.

According to a source who worked at Mickey's law firm, Rudin,

Richman & Appel, Frank had a meeting with Mickey in his office and laid into him, wanting to know what right he had to tell his family his personal intentions where Bobby Marx was concerned. Ordinarily, Mickey would never have intervened as he had with Tina and, likely, Nancy. He was always the first to know all of Frank's secrets, and he had always kept them to himself. However, he felt that this situation was different. First of all, Frank didn't tell him it was a confidential secret. If he had, Rudin might have used more discretion. But maybe not. It really wasn't that complex an issue for Mickey: If a grown man is adopted into a wealthy family, he argued, the wealthy family should at least know about it. When were they supposed to hear about it? At the reading of the will? In fact, Mickey reportedly said he had no regret about informing the Sinatra family. If Frank was angry and wanted to terminate his services, that was fine with Mickey. If Frank never wanted to speak to him again, that too was fine. Mickey did what he thought was best. By the time Frank left the meeting, he understood. He wished Mickey had kept his mouth shut, but anytime Mickey Rudin felt so strongly about something that he was willing to put his job on the line for it, Sinatra knew better than to just ignore it. He and Mickey had been in the trenches for thirty years; they were allowed to disagree.

Finally, Rudin did what he probably should have done in the first place. Apparently undaunted by his argument with Frank, he telephoned Nancy Sinatra Sr. "This thing is about to happen and there's going to be no turning back," he told Nancy. "If you're going to do something about it, you'd better do it soon."

"I will take care of it," she said.

Nancy calmly hung up with Mickey. Then she called Frank. "I'd appreciate it if you would please drop the whole idea of adopting Bobby Marx," she told him. "For me. And for the family."

That was all it took. The adoption was off. Obviously, Nancy still had great influence over Frank, and perhaps it was because she so rarely used her persuasive power over him. However, if Nancy asked Frank to do something, he usually did it. In this case, she managed to finally put an end to the controversy over Bobby Marx's adoption. However, this particular family war would leave a number of casualties in its wake. In fact, no one would ever quite get over it.

Frank's Secret Annulment

"Barbara wants a church wedding," Frank Sinatra was saying. "So, how do we make this goddamn thing happen?"

It was January 1978 and Frank was in a meeting at his home with Mickey Rudin, a priest named Father Tom Rooney, and two other officials who, because of their ongoing duties with the Catholic Church, asked to not be identified.

"It's a very nice thought, Frank," Father Rooney said. "It can't happen, though."

"Why?" Frank asked.

"Because in the eyes of the church, you're still married to Nancy," he explained.

Frank was surprised. He and Nancy had been divorced for twenty-six years, since 1951. "That's legal, isn't it? 'Cause, pardon my English, Father, but Jesus Christ! I been married three times since then."

Rooney laughed. He then explained that since Frank's marriage ceremonies to Ava and Mia had not been performed with Catholic rites, they were not recognized as valid by the church. However, the 1939 union with Nancy that had taken place at Our Lady of Sorrow Church in Jersey City was not only a legitimate marriage but, as far as the Catholic Church was concerned, still binding; the church did not recognize divorce. In fact, as far as the church was concerned, Frank and Nancy would be married until one of them died. There was one solution, though, the priest explained. Frank could have the marriage to Nancy annulled.

"Out of the question," said Mickey Rudin. He added that Nancy Sr. would never allow such a thing. "She's more Catholic than the pope," he said. "She's not going to go for it."

Frank mulled it over. "Well, I don't see why not," he said. "We can at least ask her, right?"

"Oh my God, Frank," Mickey said. "After the adoption thing? Please tell me you're joking."

"What do you think, Father?" Frank asked, ignoring Mickey's panic. The priest was noncommittal. He said that he would not make a recommendation one way or the other. He would just follow Sinatra's directive and do whatever was asked of him.

"Well, there's no harm in asking Nancy," Frank decided, a faraway look in his eyes. He added that he didn't want anything to do with the details. He just wanted the papers to be drawn up and then "let's have one of your fellows here go and get Nancy's signature on them." Frank motioned to the other two men in the room, one of whom was a priest and the other a church official not in the clergy.

Mickey just shook his head in amazement. "Unbelievable," he exclaimed.

"You got a problem with this?" Frank asked the lawyer. "What's the matter? You don't want Barbara to have a church wedding?"

"You think you got problems with your kids now?" Mickey asked, according to the witnesses. "Well, just wait until they got a load of *this*, Frank. You ain't *seen* problems yet."

Frank glared at Mickey. "Look, I got no problems with my kids," he declared. "My kids are just fine. You just let me deal with my kids, all right? *You're* the one who's gonna have problems," he concluded. The two men stared each other down until, after a few tense moments, it was Frank who relented. "Look, I'm sorry I just shot off my mouth," he told Mickey. "I know you got my family's best interest at heart. I just need you to let me handle this thing, okay?" Mickey nodded. "Okay, this here meeting is over, fellas," Frank concluded. "That'll be all. Father, would you hang around a little? I'd like to talk to you privately."

The meeting was adjourned.

Father Tom Rooney C.S.Sp. was the kind of man who, like Frank Sinatra, got things done. Nothing stood in his way, which was one of the reasons Frank so admired him. The two first met in 1975, having been introduced to each other by the singer Morton Downey. At one point when Dolly Sinatra was in the hospital, Frank called on Father Rooney to give her Communion.

Tom Rooney had actually been an oilman trying to make a fortune in the refinery business before he got the calling in 1956 at the age of thirty-two; he was ordained as a Spiritan priest, a Catholic order founded in the eighteenth century primarily to minister to sub-Saharan Africa. In 1967, Bishop Donal Murray sent him to Nigeria as a missionary, to raise funds for a hospital in Makurdi. In 1973, Father Rooney established a privately funded charity, the World Mercy Fund, that operated out of Alexandria, Virginia. Its first donation was of a million dollars from the famous hotelier Conrad Hilton. After Hilton led the way, Frank teamed up with Sammy Davis to give a concert, entire proceeds of which went to the organization. Since then, Rooney's charity had built four hospitals in Africa. By 1978 it supported 110 nurses and an equal number of volunteers in eighteen Third World countries. "He's a very calm, wise man," Frank said of Father Rooney. "Father Rooney can give solace to anyone." Barbara agreed. "He's down-to-earth, part of the real world. I feel I can talk to him about anything because he understands the other side of life, outside of the priesthood."

After Dolly Sinatra's death, Frank turned to Father Rooney for consolation. Previously, Frank and his parents, Dolly and Marty, had never been very religious.

"Back in the thirties and forties in Hoboken, you never heard the Sinatras talk much about being Catholic," said Joey D'Orazio. "Frank had his First Holy Communion, I remember, but Dolly just wanted him in on that because she liked the big ceremony behind it. Italians were God-fearing, though, even if they didn't go to church every Sunday. The one time I remember Frank really going to church was when he was nominated for an Oscar for *From Here to Eternity*. The entire month before the ceremony, he went to Good Shepherd Church in Beverly Hills to pray that he'd win—which of course he did. But for the most part, in Frank's world, *he* was God. End of story.

"You'd never catch Dolly in church either, except when she got older. I once asked Frank about that, and he said, 'Jesus! If Ma went to church, she'd try to change the whole damn thing. She'd have them doing different prayers, singing different songs. They're better off without her, trust me.' I know that Dolly became more religious in her sixties, when she actually started giving money to church charities."

Dolly's friend Doris Sevanto said, "Dolly once told me that she had a dream that she and Frankie and Marty were standing at the golden gates of heaven and couldn't get in. In her dream she was shaking and rattling the gates until finally God came over and said, 'Who the hell's out there?' And she said, 'It's us, dear Lord, it's the Sinatras of

Hoboken.' And God said, 'Who? Never heard of you. Get lost!' Then he went back to his business. After that, Dolly said, she started going to church. Over a twenty-year period, she tried to convince Frank to take his religion more seriously, but he didn't do so until after she died."

Indeed, it would seem that it was his mother's sudden death that had spurred Frank to a deeper investment in Catholicism. In searching for some logic and reason behind the senseless tragedy that had claimed Dolly, he turned to a faith he had never completely lost but had certainly ignored over the years. It would be Father Rooney who would help him come to terms with Dolly's death. Frank would continue to donate a tremendous amount of money to the World Mercy Fund. In fact, he would give a concert at Carnegie Hall as a benefit for Rooney's charity; more than four hundred patrons paid $1,000 a head for great seats to the show and then dinner with Frank and Barbara. The concert would yield $640,000 for the fund. Frank would also donate $150,000 for the building of a chapel in Dakar, Senegal. Some in his circle were a little cynical about Frank's relationship to Father Rooney, though, like his daughter Tina, who would say, "Father Rooney would play Dad like a Stradivarius."

It would be Father Rooney, then, to whom Frank would go for help in trying to find a way to make Barbara's dream to marry in the Catholic Church a reality. In fact, ever since she converted, Barbara had wanted a church wedding. Whether she understood Catholic dogma or not, she says, however, that she did not encourage the idea of an annulment. But does it make sense that a smart woman like Barbara Marx, who actually had a friend who was a priest, wasn't able to divine that an annulment of Frank's first marriage would be necessary in order for her to have her church wedding? Still, though, like the adoption of Bobby, Barbara insisted that the annulment was all Frank's idea.

"I knew the suggestion of an annulment would be controversial," Barbara later recalled, "and I had no intention of getting involved. I hadn't been with Frank all those years and learned nothing about keeping my nose out of his private affairs. In the end, he went ahead and organized it himself."

"Mr. Rudin and I had a conversation with Mrs. Sinatra about it," said one of the church officials who had been in on the original meeting where the idea of an annulment was raised. "She told Mr. Rudin, 'This is Frank's decision, not mine. I'm not getting in the middle of it. If he wants the family to know, I fully support it. If he doesn't want the family to know, I fully support that as well.' Rudin felt that Barbara might have some influence over the situation, however. 'What makes you think I have sway over Frank Sinatra if you don't?' she asked him. 'You've known the man for thirty years! Frank Sinatra does what he wants to do,' she said. 'No one tells my husband what to do, not even me.' My impression was that she felt the possible annulment and remarriage was private between her and Frank, and that she would allow him to make the decision as to when to tell others."

Barbara thought of herself as practical. She was decisive. She said that she wasn't concerned about what anyone other than her husband thought about anything. While it certainly sounds like she was intentionally setting out to hurt Frank's family members, she insists that this was not the case. She would explain that she was married to Frank, not to his ex-wife and not to his daughters. When she'd earlier come out and told Nancy Jr., "Just because we're related doesn't mean we have to be friends," Nancy couldn't help but be offended. "I suppose that's true enough," she later said of Barbara's pointed observation, "especially if it's a relationship through marriage rather than blood. Get comments like that, though, and you know where you stand. I think she's a street fighter. Fortunately, I don't have to see her very often."

It had been Frank's suggestion that one of the church officials with whom he and Father Rooney had met go to Nancy Sinatra with the annulment papers. Father Rooney decided it would be best if he handled the delicate matter himself. It's not known how his meeting with Nancy went, since neither has ever spoken of it in specific terms. However, Father Rooney returned to Frank and Mickey with the news that Nancy had adamantly refused to sign the annulment papers. Mickey, who had made it clear from the outset what he thought of the idea, was not surprised. "You don't annul a marriage that happened forty years ago and produced three grown children," he told Frank. "Yeah, you do, if you want to bad enough," was Frank's response.

Frank did a little investigating on his own and learned that Nancy was very upset about her visit from Father Rooney. As far as she was concerned there would never be an annulment. Typical of the family dynamic, she did not call Frank to ask him what he was thinking. Also typical of it, Frank didn't approach her either. He just decided to work around her. Somehow, he and Father Rooney found a way; Frank's marriage to Nancy was annulled. No one in the family seems to know how it occurred. It was just taken care of by Father Rooney at Frank's direction.

This annulment was to be another secret Frank would keep to himself. After everything that had happened regarding Bobby's possible adoption, he made sure Mickey Rudin kept this confidence. Recalled one attorney who worked with Rudin, "With the annulment, Sinatra laid it on the line. *This* was confidential. *This* was not to be shared with anybody. Mickey understood. My memory of it, though, was that Mickey didn't actually know the annulment had even happened until it was all finalized, and by that time he was just as glad to not have to tell anyone about it."

These sorts of unilateral decisions made by Frank Sinatra without much concern as to how they might affect others had begun to wear away at his long-standing relationship with Mickey Rudin. The two would have about another ten years in business together, but some of those years would be strained. Mickey had a loyalty not only to Frank but also to Frank's first wife and the children. He didn't like keeping secrets from them. However, Sinatra was his client, and therefore he would have to err on the side of ethics. "It would definitely put him in a tough spot on many occasions," said an associate.

Frank and Barbara were remarried in a secret ceremony—or as Barbara put it, they "went off quietly"—in Palm Beach, Florida, in the spring of 1978. "It was romantic and fun and felt like yet another new beginning," she would say years later. "From the day we were married, Frank had always referred to me as his 'bride,' and I suddenly felt like one again, in another lovely gown and with tropical flowers threaded through my hair."

During their romantic trip to Palm Beach, the Sinatras were invited by Ted Kennedy to play tennis at the Kennedys' summer compound there. The last time Frank took a suitor to the compound, it was Mia in 1965. While he and Teddy still weren't the best of friends, the link they shared with JFK and the Camelot years always made them feel warmly toward one another; Frank enjoyed being in Ted's company. (It's worth mentioning that Kennedy would also annul his long marriage to Joan Kennedy, which had also produced three children; however, he received her permission to do so.) Typical of the sort of unusual invitations one might receive while visiting the Kennedys, Teddy invited Frank and Barbara to attend a private Catholic Mass in the sanctuary of his mother, Rose Kennedy's, bedroom. By this time, Rose, who was seventy-three, had suffered a stroke and had lost the use of one of her eyes; she was wearing an eye patch. Barbara would recall that for the entire time she was in Rose's bedroom, Rose would not stop staring at her with that one eye. It was so disconcerting, in fact, that Teddy suggested Barbara move away from Rose and closer to him. She relocated to another seat, "but the eye followed me." It was just an odd little occurrence, but likely one the Sinatra daughters would have had a bit of a chuckle about.

A few months after their private ceremony in Florida, Barbara and Frank had an official Catholic ceremony at St. Patrick's Cathedral in New York.

For more than a year, it would be smooth sailing for Frank where the annulment and remarriage were concerned. "Don't even go dere," he would tell Mickey Rudin whenever the subject would come up between them.

Frank and Barbara continued their happy marriage, sharing what they wished and keeping to themselves what they viewed as confidential—that is, until October 9, 1979. That was the day Frank was photographed receiving the sacrament of Communion in St. Patrick's Cathedral. He was also pictured while praying after taking the host, hands clasped at his chin, eyes closed. He would not have been able to receive Communion unless his marriage to Nancy had been annulled and he'd remarried Barbara in the church. It didn't take long for his family to start putting the pieces together, and the picture that was assembled gave them pause. "Nancy and Tina were beside themselves," recalled one source. "They were pretty upset. This was really crossing a line."

Tina telephoned Frank and had it out with him. She felt the annulment had been done in a deceptive way. She believed it was very hurtful to her mother. And what did this mean in terms of his progeny? Were they now somehow illegitimate in the eyes of the law? And if so, how would it affect their inheritances? Besides the question of familial loyalty, millions of dollars were at stake, just as had been the case with the question of adopting Bobby Marx.

Now that he'd been found out, Frank had no choice but to admit that *yes*, he'd gotten an annulment from Nancy, and *yes*, he had married Barbara not once but *twice* more—in Palm Beach and then again at St. Patrick's—and *no*, his children had not been invited to either ceremony. Trying to calm Tina down, he told her that by annulling his marriage to her mother he didn't mean to suggest that it had never existed. Tina shot back with, "Pop, what part of '*an-nul-ment*' don't you understand?"

Sammy's Fall from Grace

$\mathcal{F}$rank and Sammy Davis Jr.'s friendship had been strong for many years. In fact, they hadn't had a rift since 1959. But then in the mid-1970s another conflict developed between them.

Aging was not easy for any of the Rat Pack. When Frank turned fifty, he dealt with it by keeping company with Mia Farrow. When Sammy turned the same age in 1975, he found his own way of dealing with midlife crisis: He turned to cocaine. Later, he would admit that the mid-1970s would be nothing but a blur because of all the drugs and liquor. In a 1989 interview to promote his book *Why Me?*, he remembered that he was performing in Las Vegas when he ran into Frank's good friend Jilly Rizzo backstage. "How's Francis?" Sammy asked. "What the hell's up? Why's he avoiding me?"

Jilly responded, "Well, Sam, the reason you ain't heard from Frank is because he's hacked off. He hears that you're into that coke crap. Yous been friends for years, I know. But he told me, 'If Sammy's into drugs, I don't want nuttin' to do with him.'"

Sammy was taken aback. Quickly recovering, he said, "Well, hey, screw him, then, Jilly. I'm a grown-ass man. I don't need Frank to hold my hand. It's not like the old days."

"Sure, Sam," Jilly said. "I just thought you should know, 's'all."

The two shook hands and parted company.

Sammy would recall, "I was trying to act like a big shot with Jilly, but I was dying inside. I loved Frank. To know that he was pissed off at me was tough. I also knew that he probably sent Jilly to tell me. That'd be like Frank.

"This was a hard time. Getting old in show business—it's not easy," Sammy continued. "You fall into certain traps trying to keep your youth, trying to be hip. I was doing coke, drinking, trying out Satanism, into porn. In fact, we used to rent out the Pussycat Theater in Hollywood, no shit, and go there to watch porno movies. I'd have all of Hollywood out there, had them picked up in limousines—Shirley MacLaine, Steve [Lawrence] and Eydie [Gormé], Lucille Ball—and we'd all sit in this theater and watch movies like *Deep Throat*. Can you imagine this? It was wild. But that was just good fun. I was into other shit that was destructive, like coke. Frank never did drugs," Sammy allowed. "Frank's drug was women. Safer but no less dangerous, I used to tell him."

In the next three years, Frank and Sammy only saw each other occasionally at cocktail parties, and even then it was just a curt hello and goodbye between them. "I missed my friend," said Sammy. "But I'd just go home, do some more coke, and be fine. I'd said, 'Yeah, well screw Sinatra if he can't let me live my own life. At least I got cocaine.'"

"As far as Frank was concerned," Barbara Sinatra later recalled, "Sammy might as well have been dead."

At about the three-year mark, Sammy was performing at Caesars Palace in Las Vegas, with Frank following him there with an engagement. Their wives, Altovise and Barbara, decided to arrange for a reunion dinner. "I didn't want to go," Sammy remembered. "But we were getting older. Years were going by. What a waste."

At dinner in the Caesars Palace dining room—which Frank had closed to the public for this reconciliation meal—the four slipped into a red leather booth. After pleasantries, as Sam recalled it, Frank tapped him on the shoulder and motioned him to another booth. They excused themselves for a private moment.

"Charlie, how can you do it?" Frank wanted to know as soon as they sat down again.

"Do what, Frank?" Sammy asked, trying to act innocent.

"Sam, I am so disappointed in you," Frank began, ignoring Sammy's act. "What's with this coke? Look at you. You look like shit."

"Hey..." Sammy began, protesting.

"Sam, let me finish," Frank continued, according to Sammy's later recollection. "You're breaking my heart. Can't you see that? You know how hard it's been for me not having you around? But watching you kill yourself is worse. You've always been a gasser [the best] in this business. Stop with the coke. End it now. Promise me."

"I...I..." Sammy was speechless.

"You and I, we never lied to each other," Frank said. "If you can look me in the eye right now and tell me you'll never do this drug again, I'll believe you. So look me in the eye, Sam. Tell me what I want to hear."

Sammy grabbed a cloth napkin from the table and wiped away tears. "I'll give it up, Frank," he said, looking at his friend squarely. "I'm done. No more coke. I promise."

Sammy Davis Jr. kept his promise.

Trilogy

$\mathcal{N}$ow in his sixties, Sinatra would be more active on the concert trail in the 1980s than many entertainers half his age. In January 1980 he began the year by performing at Caesars Palace. (His contract at Caesars would have him performing there throughout the coming decade, always to standing room only.) Following the Vegas engagement, he went to Brazil, where he had never before appeared. Four sold-out shows at the Rio Palace in Rio de Janeiro preceded a huge turnout of 175,000 people at the Macarena Stadium, a soccer field. When he returned to the States, Frank performed at another fund-raiser for Ronald Reagan, this one with Dean Martin at the Shrine Auditorium in Los Angeles. In March he began filming a movie, *The First Deadly Sin*, with Faye Dunaway.

Despite his advancing age, his schedule never slowed down; for Frank, it would seem there was always more to do, more to experience. Throughout the year, he performed at benefits for hospitals, research centers, the Red Cross (in Monaco, for Grace Kelly), the University of Nevada, and St. Jude's Ranch for Children. Later in the year, he would break a ninety-year record at Carnegie Hall when a two-week engagement there sold out in one day. When Liza Minnelli couldn't perform at her December 1980 engagement at the Riviera Hotel in Las Vegas, Frank happily stepped in to take her place.

At the end of 1980, Frank Sinatra turned sixty-five years old; Barbara surprised him with a country-western-styled birthday party for 250 people.

That same year, Frank had issued his first studio album release since 1973, a three-record package called *Trilogy* that took a look at his past, present, and future through music. Disc one—*Collectibles of the Early Years*—included rerecordings of some Sinatra favorites, such as "The Song Is You" and "It Had to Be You," arranged by Billy May. Disc two—*Some Very Good Years*—featured Sinatra on contemporary numbers such as Neil Diamond's "Song Sung Blue" and the Beatles' "Something." Disc three—*Reflections on the Future in Three Tenses*—featured new material arranged by Gordon Jenkins. In all, this Sonny Burke production was a monumental musical endeavor that involved five hundred musicians.

Trilogy is most noteworthy because it showed Frank still willing to do something different with his music and take chances with it. Whereas other artists his age were rerecording the same kinds of songs, Sinatra was marching ahead and trying new ideas, as he did on disc three. That third disc was critically regarded as a misfire, but a sincere one just the same—a try, at least, at something provocative and important. It was to Frank's credit that he was still on the trail of new conquests. *Trilogy* went to number one on the charts and received six Grammy Award nominations. That the album was such a sensational sales success is a plus, of course, but what remains significant is its artistic intent.

From the album came another of Frank Sinatra's signature songs, the commercial "Theme from New York, New York," arranged by Don Costa, on disc two. Originally from the Martin Scorsese box-office musical disaster *New York, New York*, starring Liza Minnelli, the song was a minor hit for Minnelli. Frank first began performing it in concert in 1978 as an opening number at Radio City Music Hall, and in months to come he would tailor the song to his own taste, transforming it into a more dramatic interpretation not only vocally but musically before finally recording it on September 19, 1979, with a superior brassy, big-band Don Costa arrangement.

"Theme from New York, New York" was a huge hit for Sinatra. Combined with the success of *Trilogy*, it marked his biggest-selling bonanza in about a decade. The song became his closing number and was a guaranteed showstopper every time.

Frank would follow *Trilogy* with another album in 1981, *She Shot Me Down*. By this time, his voice had taken on an almost completely different sound—huskier, older, sometimes richer, sometimes creaky, sometimes melodic, sometimes a tad off pitch. His impeccable phrasing and elocution shone through, however, and as a result, *She Shot Me Down* remains the definitive album—artistically and thematically—of Sinatra's maturity. Certainly one reason for the album's preeminence is that Gordon Jenkins turned out such marvelous arrangements for it. Sadly, this was "Gordy's" last work with Sinatra, or with any artist, for he had already been diagnosed with ALS (amyotrophic lateral sclerosis) and had lost the use of his tongue. Now, more than ever, the music spoke for him.

Another reason for tears was that Frank Sinatra, who many critics felt should have given up recording long before, had turned out an album as deep, moving, and revelatory as any he had produced before, with such songs as "Hey Look, No Crying," "Monday Morning Quarterback," and especially, a medley of "The Gal That Got Away" and "It Never Entered My Mind." Heard today, *She Shot Me Down* remains breathtaking in its depth of emotion. It reached number forty-two on the *Billboard* charts, which was disappointing to both Sinatra and his fans, given the album's impact on those who did listen to it.

Barbara Meets "the Boys"

At the age of sixty-five, Frank Sinatra again began taking stock of his life and career. How would he be remembered? As one of the great voices of the twentieth century? A cultural icon? Friend of presidents? Civil rights and political activist? Philanthropist who'd raised millions for charities? Certainly each of those descriptions seemed a comfortable fit. However, Frank realized that one perception of him still endured after all of these years, and it was the one that galled him the most: "friend of the mob."

Of course, it seems obvious that if Frank had exercised more caution about his relationships with mobsters over the years, there wouldn't have been anything to report in the media about them and his reputation wouldn't have involved the underworld. However, the fact of the matter was that he *did* know his fair share of gangsters. He often explained that it was just part of the business he was in as an entertainer to socialize with them, since they controlled so many of the nightclubs in which he performed. Of course, not all entertainers were mixed up with mobsters, but Frank was, and this had been the case for decades. Not only did he get a kick out of such characters, but they treated him with respect, and he did the same.

After he married Barbara, she got her own taste of the boys, albeit briefly. She and Frank were in New York and on their way to dinner when Jilly announced that some of "the fellas" wanted to meet her. Barbara wasn't interested in meeting any gangsters and said no. Frank jumped in and told her that they just wanted to meet "the new Mrs. Sinatra," telling her, "It's a show of respect. They run a lot of the clubs I play in. Come on, Barbara. Be a sport." Absolutely not, she said. The couple went to dinner, as planned. However, on the way out of the restaurant, Barbara saw Jilly at the bar with a gaggle of overweight guys, stereotypical mobster types in ill-fitting suits, some with diamond pinky rings. Frank motioned Barbara toward the bar. "For me?" he asked. "No, Frank. How many times…" But then when Frank gave her a sad look, she decided to relent. She walked over and, as Frank watched proudly, Jilly—with the biggest smile Barbara had ever seen on his round face—introduced her to his friends: "*Dis* one is…And *dat* one *ova dere* is…And *dis* one *ova* here is…"

The men treated her as if she were royalty. Still, Barbara felt she'd been forced to do something she didn't want to do. The severity of her expression didn't change as she approached her husband. "Aw, come on now. That wasn't so bad, was it?" Frank asked, kissing her on the cheek. Her demeanor softened. "Okay, just this once," she said, putting her head on his shoulder. "But you owe me one," she told him as they walked away together. "I do," Frank agreed, nodding. "I owe you one, my darling."

"Who Took That Shot?"

$\mathcal{B}$ack in April 1976, Frank had appeared at the Westchester Premier Theater in Tarrytown, New York. He was paid $800,000 for the engagement, the most money he had ever received for singing in a venue of that size. It had been rumored, though, that the Mafia had financed the establishment, namely Carlo Gambino, head of the powerful, influential Gambino crime family in New York. The rumor was that Gambino had helped bankroll the theater to the tune of $100,000 on the understanding that Sinatra would be signed to perform there. If it was true, Sinatra said, it wasn't his concern. As long as he was paid for his work, he didn't care who was behind it.

During his engagement at the Premier, a contingent of known gangsters—including Carlo Gambino, Greg DePalma, Jimmy Fratianno, Paul Castellano, Joseph Gambino, and Richard Fusco—came backstage on April 11, 1976, after a performance. True to form, Frank allowed himself to be photographed with them. His defenders might argue that he had no choice or that it would have been impolite to refuse to allow his picture to be taken with these fans, even if they were all Mafia kingpins, especially since mob chieftain Carlo Gambino was with his granddaughter, whose name was Phyllis Sinatra Gambino. But someone like Sinatra, who was surrounded by bodyguards, assistants, and others whose job it was to insulate him from the public when necessary, would most certainly be able to find a discreet way to avoid posing for a picture with a bunch of gangsters, especially given the persistent rumors about him.

Unfortunately for Frank's image, these pictures would be introduced into evidence in the summer of 1978 when certain individuals were accused of bankruptcy fraud in connection with the Westchester Premier Theater. Since the theater had generated $5.3 million during its operation, the question was, why was it bankrupt? If profits weren't going back into the theater, the thinking was that the money was probably finding its way into the coffers of the mobsters who had financed the joint. A popular rumor was that Frank had somehow been involved in skimming those funds.

Frank was not subpoenaed to testify in the matter. However, the press made much of his connection to the theater and to Gambino and the rest of the men in the photograph. Others who did testify, such as Jimmy Fratianno, insisted that Frank had indeed been involved in raising money for the mob and in skimming profits from the Westchester Premier Theater. Since Fratianno was a mobster informant who had been granted immunity by the government for his testimony, he may not have been the most reliable witness. The case ended in a mistrial, with some of the principals later being tried separately and ending up in jail, and Sinatra's image being further tarnished.

"The pictures got into the hands of the press," Mickey Rudin explained of the photos of Sinatra and the mobsters. Actually, the photos fell into the public domain as soon as they were used as evidence in the investigation. One of them would end up as a two-page spread in *Life* in January 1979. More bad publicity. "Who took that shot, anyway?" Frank asked when he saw it. "We shoulda stopped that joker from taking that picture."

Even his friend President Reagan, when asked about Frank's ties to the mob, could offer no defense, saying, "We've heard those things about Frank for years. We just hope none of them are true."

Frank knew that he had to address some of the more enduring questions about his character. His legacy had always mattered to him, which is why he had devoted so much care and attention to the music he would leave behind. That he was thought by many to be of ill repute was a perception he wanted to change once and for all.

Sinatra Sets the Record Straight—His Way

*I*n the spring of 1980, Frank Sinatra found a way to finally address his critics: He applied for a Nevada gaming license. He knew the application would open him up to heavy scrutiny, which was precisely why he did it. He had lost his original in 1963 when Sam Giancana got into a fight with Phyllis McGuire's road manager at the Cal-Neva Lodge. As the result of the subsequent investigation, Frank abandoned his license just before it was to be revoked. Now he wanted it back. However, in order to get it, he would have to submit to a full investigation of his life by the Nevada Gaming Control Board. According to the Nevada statutes regarding the approval of a gaming license, it can only be approved for "a person of good character, honesty and integrity, a person whose prior activities, criminal record, if any, reputation, habits and associations do not pose a threat to the public interest." Frank welcomed the examination, even though he was told it would cost him $500,000. "Bring it on," was how he put it at the time. This would be his opportunity to address, once and for all, in a public forum stories and rumors that had dogged him for years.

But the vetting process may not have been as thorough in Frank's case as it would have been for a less-connected individual. Most observers at the time agreed that he would be granted the gaming license regardless of the testimony offered at the hearings; he was so closely aligned to the Reagans and to other political figures and had raised so much money for charity, especially in recent years, that it seemed unlikely that the investigation would go against him. The Nevada Gaming Control Commission did not have subpoena power and therefore could not compel certain known underworld players and Sinatra associates, like Judith Campbell Exner, to testify. Sam Giancana was dead, so at least he would not be coming forward. In fact, most of the guys Frank considered friends, like Skinny D'Amato, were gone now. Instead, the committee was assisted by Mickey Rudin in locating people Frank and Mickey felt could best vouch for Sinatra's good character. Therefore this venue felt to Frank like a safe place for him to address questions and possibly reshape his image in front of a national audience. To most observers, though, it would feel like a carefully stage-managed PR effort.

Sinatra gave his testimony on February 11, 1981, in Las Vegas's city council chambers. He was accompanied by Barbara, various attorneys and publicists, and Jilly Rizzo. Earlier in the day, Frank's close friend Sheriff Peter Pitchess of Los Angeles County testified that "if Mr. Sinatra is a member of the Mafia, then I am the godfather." A Catholic priest and Sinatra family friend, Father Herbert Ward, testified that Frank "gave glory to God." While CNN cameras broadcast the proceedings live, Gregory Peck, Kirk Douglas, and Bob Hope, in sworn affidavits, testified to Frank's generosity and benevolent spirit. *Las Vegas Sun* publisher Hank Greenspun insisted that the incident that caused Sinatra's license to be revoked in 1963 was "nothing more than a shouting match" between Frank and Ed Olsen, chairman of the gaming board, now deceased. Mickey Rudin said that the FBI had always been "out to get" Sinatra and pointed out—accurately—that much of the "information" in their official files on Sinatra was rumor and innuendo masquerading as fact.

Finally, the pièce de résistance: Frank Sinatra's sworn testimony. This promised to be riveting television, and it didn't disappoint. Frank, wearing a suit and black thick-rimmed glasses and with notes, documents, and other legal records at the ready, testified that Sam Giancana never had a financial interest in the Cal-Neva Lodge and that "I never invited Mr. Giancana to come to Cal-Neva Lodge, and I never entertained him and I never saw him" on that night in 1963—"or any other night, for that matter." He further testified that Giancana had never been to Cal-Neva at any other time.

Sinatra's testimony was in direct conflict with that of Phyllis McGuire to the committee, on January 27, that Giancana was present at Cal-Neva for the first three to five days of the McGuire Sisters' engagement. She also testified that Sinatra had broken up the fight between her and her road manager, Victor LaCroix Collins (who, inexplicably, was not called to testify). Sinatra was unfazed by the contradiction. He insisted that he wasn't even in Nevada at the time, but rather in Los Angeles. However, it was pointed out that eighteen years earlier in 1963, he was on the record as having told Ed Olsen that Giancana *was* at Cal-Neva. Frank's mouth became a thin tight line as he explained, "I might have said it. I was frustrated. I was angry. I might have said anything. But if I said it, I didn't mean it." He also testified that he could not even recall how he met Sam Giancana.

Mickey Rudin then testified about the night in question in 1963: "[Sinatra] went back and forth several times [to Cal-Neva from Los Angeles]. I would have to tell you it was my recollection that he was not there when Giancana was present, and I would also have to tell you that I don't have that much confidence in my recollection. Maybe I fixed in my mind that he wasn't there and that's now the story.

"I do know [Sinatra] didn't invite [Giancana] and both of us were upset that he was there," Rudin further testified. "I don't know if [Sinatra] sent up word or I sent word to tell [Giancana] to leave or if I was even on the premises. I'm a little confused about it, but I do know that neither one of us invited him, and we were unhappy about his being there."

Frank testified that he thought he remembered Mickey telling Giancana to leave the premises, but Mickey said he didn't recall having done that. Frank also testified that he wasn't aware of any connection between Giancana and the Villa Venice nightclub in Chicago, that Giancana had never asked him to perform at the club, and that it was "just possible" that he saw Giancana while performing there.

Sinatra's final word on Sam Giancana: "I never had anything to do with him business-wise and rarely, *rarely*, socially," he said, his face darkening. "No connection whatsoever."

Sam's daughter Antoinette Giancana—who was also not called to testify—was unhappy about Sinatra's testimony, saying later that she and her father were at the Villa Venice every night Frank performed there and that her father and Frank embraced each time they saw one another. McGuire was also angry with Sinatra for disavowing his relationship with her companion, Giancana. "Frank adored the man and then, after his death, turned on him and denied their friendship just to get that license," she said later. "All the proof of Frank's friendship with Sam is in the FBI files. It's all there. Everything." In fact, even the authorized Sinatra television miniseries produced by Tina (which would not air until ten years later, in 1991) portrayed a close relationship between Sinatra and Giancana.

There was also some intriguing testimony regarding Frank's trip to Havana in 1947. Frank testified that his purpose in going was not to meet with any underworld characters, such as Lucky Luciano, but rather "to find sunshine." In response to the allegation—which seemed to have first been made by Lee Mortimer—that Sinatra brought $2 million to Havana in an attaché case, Frank said, "If you can find me an attaché case that holds two million dollars, I will *give* you the two million dollars." He further testified that he had no idea why his name and address were in Luciano's possession when the gangster was once searched by Italian officials. And as to the allegation that his early career was financed by mobsters, Sinatra had only two words: "It's ridiculous."

Regarding the photograph of Frank and the group of mobsters who visited him backstage at the Westchester Premier Theater—described by one committee member as "a who's who and what's what in the area of organized crime"—Frank explained, "I was asked by one of the members of the theater—he told me Mr. Gambino had arrived with his granddaughter, whose name happened to be Sinatra...and they'd like to take a picture. I said, 'Fine.' They came in and they took a picture of the little girl, and before I realized what happened, there were approximately eight or nine men standing around me, and several other snapshots were made. That is the whole incident that took place." Of the gentlemen in the picture, Sinatra said, "I didn't even know their names, let alone their backgrounds."

Afterward, to demonstrate the kinds of photographs that are often taken backstage, Frank displayed a scrapbook of photographs of himself with Gregory Peck and the prime minister of Israel; with his wife, Barbara, and Anwar Sadat; and with inspectors of the San Francisco Police Department, who, Sinatra said, looked like "unsavory guys. If you look at this picture without my telling you [who they are], it's frightening."

The one time Frank seemed to lose his composure came when he was asked about the volatile incident that took place in 1967 between him and Caesars Palace casino manager Carl Cohen, when Cohen cut off his credit and embarrassed him in front of the Apollo astronauts. Frank had been so upset by Cohen's actions, he took Mia on a terror ride in a golf cart and then confronted Cohen about his actions. He ended up getting punched in the face when he called Cohen a "kike." When asked about it, Frank snapped, "That was a personal incident, just between the two of us, between two fellas. I'd rather not discuss that. It was something I think has nothing to do with the Sands, Las Vegas, or anyplace." He added, "A dislike was formed between two people, and there was a scuffle." The committee members seemed stunned by Sinatra's heated response. He had so intimidated them by becoming annoyed at their bringing up Cohen that no one dared pursue the line of inquiry. When the subject was quickly changed, it appeared clear to most observers that Sinatra was in charge of the proceedings.

As to the incident at Caesars Palace in the early 1970s, when casino manager Sanford Waterman pulled a gun on Sinatra, Frank continued to testify defensively: "I came off the stage and went up to Waterman, who was in the pit. I asked for some credit, and he gave me a rough time. I thought maybe he was going senile or something because he had never spoken to me like that before. He put a gun in my rib and said, 'You're never gonna hurt me.' If we hadn't stopped the people from wanting to take his head off, he would have been hurt very badly that night. We actually saved his life and got him into an office. Because when the people saw him with a pistol in his hand...I just whacked his hand and got rid of it."

Of the Kennedys, Frank said that he had never attempted to intercede on behalf of Sam Giancana with either John or Robert Kennedy.

Before this inquiry, Mickey Rudin had turned over what he described as "fourteen pounds" of FBI files that Sinatra and Rudin had obtained under the Freedom of Information Act. Anyone who has ever seen these files, which comprise thirty years of investigation into Sinatra's life by the FBI, can attest to the fact that they are, at first glance, incomprehensible. It takes months of work to decipher them, given that so many sections and names are redacted to protect certain parties. In the end they can only be used as a road map for further inquiry. They most certainly cannot be used to draw conclusions, because so much of the material found in them is based on hearsay, gossip, and rumor.

However, perhaps because of their daunting volume, the committee apparently didn't bother to review them all. They probably reasoned that they knew everything they needed to know about Frank Sinatra—a man who has had more words published about him than probably any other figure in the history of popular entertainment—just based on his press coverage. In retrospect, it would appear that they decided to just go easy on him. There seems to be no other possible explanation as to why the committee seemed so ill-equipped to pin Frank down on any important details or to fully challenge him.

Stephen Webb, a former FBI agent, explained, "Years had passed, and Sinatra picked the right time to do this little dance with the

Las Vegas officials. Too many people were dead, and too much water had gone under the ol' bridge. No one cared as much as they might have in the 1950s, and to have to read all of those documents, well, forget it. I was one of the guys assigned to go over the paperwork before it was handed over, and I saw for myself what a complete mess it was. I didn't know what Sinatra was guilty of, and frankly I didn't care. However, reviewing the boxes of papers that were sent to the committee did nothing to illuminate anything for me. It was one big mess."

As expected, at the end of the five-and-a-half-hour testimony, Nevada Gaming Control Board chairman Richard Bunker moved that Frank Sinatra be recommended to the Nevada Gaming Control Commission for a six-month license; the other three commissioners who had interrogated Sinatra agreed. On February 19, 1981, Frank appeared before the Gaming Control Commission and answered more questions for about an hour and a half, again saying that he had never had any sort of association with members of organized crime. The commission gave Frank his gaming license, and did so even without the six-month limitation.

Frank never used the license. Actually, he didn't even want it. These 1981 hearings weren't about the license anyway. "I think I achieved what I set out to achieve," he told one of his family members after the hearings were over. "There's nothing else I can do to clear my name." In the end, he said, he realized that his critics would never truly be silenced. He was willing to let it go, though, now that he'd had his say. He finally had read into the official record exactly what he wanted history to reflect about him. In doing so, he had tried to protect his legacy in his own way, which in the end was what really mattered to him.

Frank and Nancy Tour Together

By the winter of 1982, Nancy Sinatra had been retired from the record business for some time. She had married Hugh Lambert and now had two young daughters, Angela Jennifer (A.J.) and Amanda Kate. However, she was not a scion in the sense that money was available to her whenever she needed it. That's not how the Sinatras worked as a family; everyone was responsible for earning his or her own way. If a desperate situation arose—such as when Nancy and her first husband, Tommy Sands, had separated and she had no place to live—the daughters were more apt to go to their mother for a loan. Nancy Jr. did in fact borrow from Nancy Sr. at that time, and paid her back quickly after she had her first hit, "These Boots Are Made for Walking." No one remembers Frank Jr. ever having money issues, though; he'd been working since he was a teenager and had never stopped. Tina also found a way to make ends meet. But by the winter of 1981, Nancy definitely needed financial assistance. She wanted to resume her career but, despite having sold millions of records, was not able to secure a record deal. RCA did sign her to a contract to record a duet album with Mel Tillis, entitled *Mel and Nancy*. An excellent country album, it yielded two minor hits for the duo, "Texas Cowboy Night" (which charted at number twenty-three) and "Play Me or Trade Me" (number forty-three). Today the album is much sought after by Nancy's fans because it still hasn't been released on compact disc. Back in the early 1980s, however, it wasn't enough to jump-start Nancy's career.

Not knowing how to proceed, Nancy asked Frank for advice. He suggested that they go out on the road together for about a year. Anytime an artist had the opportunity to work with Frank Sinatra it guaranteed them a tremendous amount of exposure. Plus, from a personal standpoint, the opportunity for Nancy to spend so much time with her father was priceless. She knew that Barbara would likely be on many of the dates as well, but Nancy would just keep her distance and hope for the best. This wasn't about Barbara anyway. This was an opportunity for her to work with her father, a chance to get her career back in gear, and to make money doing it. After it was agreed that she would take her daughters on the road with her as much as possible, Nancy constructed an excellent act, about thirty minutes of pure Nancy Sinatra—her chart hits as well as pop numbers such as Little Anthony and the Imperials' 1964 classic "Goin' Out of My Head."

The tour opened on March 4, 1982, at Caesars Palace, with Nancy starting the evening, the mime team of Shields and Yarnell up next (later replaced by comedian Charlie Callas), and then the headliner himself, Frank Sinatra.

One of the more interesting responsibilities Nancy shouldered opening for her father during this tour was a task most people might never even be aware of: keeping those who entered the showroom late from being embarrassed by having the spotlight shine on them while they were being seated. It actually happened quite a bit in Vegas. High rollers, especially, would show up when they felt like it—whether in the middle of Nancy's performance or during the next act's show—but never, of course, late for Frank's set.

Skilled professional that she is, Nancy, while singing, would see a group of people to her left arrive late and would immediately begin walking to her right, the spotlight following her so that the latecomers could be seated without attention. Then she would see a party arrive to her right and, still singing, would walk to her left for the same reason. Back and forth she would go throughout her set, trying her best to handle this tricky aspect of her job. It wasn't easy. In fact, it was disruptive. Vegas was not necessarily a place where good manners ruled; people would be noisy while making their way to their tables, talk rudely while being seated, and then loudly order drinks once at their tables.

Nancy had many serious conversations with the management about seating people before her show instead of during it, but to no avail. There was no way, she was told, that management could force patrons away from the gaming tables and into Circus Maximus, the Caesars Palace showroom, in time for the show. When they were ready, the customers would walk in and sit down, and there wasn't anything anyone could do about it. Nancy was frustrated, but she would deal with it.

In the end, Nancy's year with Frank on the road would be memorable in many ways; anyone who had an opportunity to see the two Sinatras perform in 1982 was fortunate. Hank Grant of the *Hollywood Reporter* noted of Nancy's set, "What struck me where the heart is, and still lingers, is Nancy Sinatra...the biggest thrill of the night. Nancy, friends, has arrived on her own."

By the end of the tour, Nancy realized that she didn't really want to be on the road after all, and that maybe a restarting of her career wasn't the best thing for her. She enjoyed being a wife and mother, and she decided she loved it more than living out of a suitcase. In fact, she couldn't imagine how Frank had done it for so many years. It was grueling. Twenty-one years would pass before she would play Las Vegas again, at the House of Blues at Mandalay Bay in July 2003.

The opportunity to have opened for her father was one Nancy would always treasure. Father and daughter would usually perform their number one hit, "Somethin' Stupid," right after Frank's rendering of "All or Nothing at All." The popular duet was sure to generate a standing ovation from the sold-out crowd.

"My girl, she ain't half bad, right?" Frank asked during his set at the new Universal Amphitheatre on July 30, 1982. "You people don't know it," he told the sold-out audience of six thousand, "but when she's onstage as she was earlier this evening, I'm standing in the wings studying her. And you'd be surprised what I learn," he said with a wink. "An old man can always learn something from his kids," he added. "You folks might want to remember that."

As If She Had a Choice

$\mathcal{M}$eanwhile, as the engagement at Caesars Palace continued, Barbara Sinatra flew up from Los Angeles to be with her husband. By this time, early 1982, there was an ongoing dispute between the Sinatras related to his drinking. Frank was used to drinking a fifth of Jack Daniel's every day. That had been his custom for many years. Once, when he told a doctor about his habit, the doctor was astonished and said, "My God, Frank! How do you feel in the morning?" Frank answered, "Hell if I know, doc. I don't get up till the afternoon."

When Frank and his friends were drinking, there was no telling what kind of trouble they might get into. During one Fourth of July celebration in Monaco, Frank, Jilly, Bobby Marx, and some others had a little too much of the bubbly and started blowing up cherry bombs on the pier adjacent to New Jimmy's open-air nightclub in

Monte Carlo. As they did so, many of the patrons ran for cover. However, Barbara sat still at her table, nursing her martini and praying for the moment to quickly pass. After all of these years, she was accustomed to these sorts of hijinks and knew that if she waited it out, it would soon be over, everyone would disperse, and she'd be able to go to bed and try to forget it had ever happened.

One of the socialites present that festive evening happened to be Hélène Rochas, the former CEO of the fashion house Rochas, which she'd turned into a multimillion-dollar fragrance business. When one of the cherry bombs rolled under her chair and exploded, poor Ms. Rochas became nearly apoplectic. Upset, her boyfriend, a French aristocrat named Kim d'Estainville, picked up a half-empty bottle of vodka and chucked it at Frank's party outside. Unfortunately, on the way out, it hit Barbara on the side of her head. She was cut and bleeding, but it wasn't that bad. Still, Bobby Marx confronted d'Estainville. The two were about to come to blows when who should swoop in but Jilly Rizzo, fists at the ready. The resulting melee saw Jilly, Frank, and anyone else who cared to join in, punching, kicking, and throwing tables and chairs all over the place. The next morning, the police came to the Sinatra suite to interrogate Jilly. "He ain't even here no more," Frank said. "I think he went back to the States, the big dope." Meanwhile, Jilly was standing behind the heavy curtains in the parlor, his size twelves peeking out from beneath it.

Another time Frank's drinking became an issue was when he and Barbara were on tour in the Far East. There was a mix-up at the hotel and they couldn't get the suite Frank had requested. Apparently the previous tenants had actually had livestock in the room, so it needed to be cleaned. The hotel put the Sinatras in another suite, which was acceptable, even if not preferable. However, Frank needed to be next to the room where his assistant, Dorothy Uhlemann, was staying, or he wouldn't be comfortable. He and Jilly had been up all night drinking, so Frank just wanted it sorted out, no questions asked. Jilly went to the room in which Frank had wanted Dorothy installed and politely asked the guest there to please move, at the Sinatras' expense, of course. The guest refused and slammed the door in Jilly's face. "But you can't stay in dere," Jilly shouted, pounding on the door. Finally, Frank told Jilly to "get a crowbar and do what you gotta do." Ten minutes later, Jilly, with crowbar in hand, began trying to pry the door open, all the while slamming his fist up against it and saying, "This ain't right. *Whatsa matta you?*" The guest, now irate, summoned the hotel manager, who called the Sinatra suite to tell Frank that he needed to accept his accommodations or check out. Frank became angry and picked up the telephone and threw it at the window. However, since the thick-paned glass wouldn't shatter, the phone ended up ricocheting back, slamming Frank right in the face. "What the hell kind of hotel is this place?" he raged to Barbara. "You can't even throw a phone through a window here?"

Of course, these events were typical of the kind of foolhardiness Barbara would find herself involved in as Frank's wife. For the most part, these capers were great fodder for cocktail-party chitchat. To say that Barbara found them offensive would be to overstate her reaction. She wouldn't have been able to exist for five seconds in Frank's world if she was that thin-skinned a woman. However, with the passing of the years, it's safe to say that frequent outbursts of this nature did tend to have a bit of a wearing effect on her.

Before this Vegas run with Nancy, Barbara had a talk with Frank and asked him to cut down on his drinking, if only for his health. He didn't take to the suggestion. When working in Vegas where there were casinos everywhere, he liked to stay up all night long, drinking and gambling. Even at his age, he didn't want to settle down; he wanted to act like a younger man. Barbara felt he was not only damaging his health, but his voice as well. Plus, the scenes of chaos that sometimes followed his heavy drinking had become, as she put it, "old hat." She had a conversation with her friend Eileen Faith, who joined her in Vegas, about it.

"The children actually think he has cut down on his drinking," Barbara said as she and Eileen watched Frank at the tables with some of his friends, Jilly Rizzo included. She said that she wasn't sure why they would believe such a thing, but added that she supposed it was easier to do so "when you're not with him twenty-four hours a day. I feel like I'm coming in during the ninth inning and trying to change the whole ball game," she added. "And it's impossible." She said that Frank's habits were set in stone. "He's Sinatra, for Christ's sake," she exclaimed. "Of course he's going to drink."

"Yes, but you're his wife," Eileen told her. "You have to put your foot down, Barbara."

Barbara said she had long ago learned to pick and choose her fights with Frank. Especially during this engagement, when Nancy was on the bill, the last thing she wanted to do was antagonize Frank and then have Nancy view them as being unhappy in their marriage. "She's just waiting to catch the smallest hint of something so she can pounce," Barbara said with a knowing smile. "Oh, she's tough, that one. She thinks I'm tough? She's ten times worse than me," Barbara added. Barbara said that perhaps she and Nancy were too much alike, and that maybe this similarity was really at the root of their problems. "She's a carbon copy of me," Barbara opined. "In fact, if I were the daughter and she were the new wife? The way she acts? That is *exactly* the way I would act," she said. Eileen suggested that perhaps Barbara should reach out to Nancy while they were both in Las Vegas, but Barbara didn't think it was a good idea. She felt that if it went poorly between them and Nancy then had any trouble at all with her performance, Frank would blame her for it. She felt that the best course of action was to stay as far away from Nancy Sinatra as possible. "An occasional meal is fine, and maybe we can nod at each other from time to time in a hallway," she said, "but that should be the extent of it, at least while she is working for Frank. I'm sure she would agree."

At this point, Jilly Rizzo joined the two women. He put his arm around Barbara; she smiled at him. "Frank's had a little too much to drink," Jilly said. Barbara looked over at her husband and asked if there was anything Jilly wanted her to do. "I don't know," he said thoughtfully, "maybe go over and see if you can get him to go up to the suite. Might not be a bad idea, Barbara." Then Jilly squeezed her hand and walked back toward Frank.

"It's not always easy," Barbara said as she gathered her things and steeled herself to face Frank Sinatra. "When he's drinking, I usually duck for cover," she said. "Especially if the gin comes out. Then I just go into my room and close the door."

The two women laughed. "Well, I supposed there are worse problems than being married to Sinatra," Eileen Faith ventured.

Barbara chuckled. "To paraphrase the song, I love him just the way he is..."

Barbara tried her best, but stubborn Frank refused to leave the blackjack table. "Leave me alone, Barbara," he said. Losing at the tables made him grouchy, and the liquor probably didn't help. Barbara tried to convince him that if they went to bed now, they could rise early and perhaps have breakfast with Nancy. Frank didn't want to hear it. He just wanted to gamble. "If I start winning, I'll quit," he told her. Meanwhile, he suggested, she should just go to bed. "Okay, I did my best," Barbara told Jilly. "I'm tired. I'm going to bed. Good luck with him." With that, she went up to her room.

About four hours later, the phone rang in her suite. It was Jilly. He told her that Frank was in a restaurant downstairs and about to get into a fight with a photographer. Even he and the rest of Frank's Dago Secret Service didn't want to intervene; it was late and everyone was just too exhausted. Jilly just wanted to go to bed, not throw punches. "I need you down here, Barbara," he pleaded. "Please?"

Barbara dressed quickly and went downstairs. Before she even walked into the restaurant, she could hear Frank's voice debating with the photographer, telling him that photos were not allowed in the casino or surrounding areas, and that he was going to have the man barred from the premises forevermore. When she walked in, Sinatra glared at her. "Now what?" he demanded to know.

"It's time for us to go upstairs," she said.

"I'm not done with this guy yet," Frank said. "If he gives me his camera, maybe then I'll leave." The photographer backed up a few steps and mumbled something about not giving up his equipment. Jilly approached the photographer and said, "In about thirty seconds, I'm gonna shove that camera right up your ass. Then we can all go to bed."

"Nobody is shoving anything anywhere," Barbara said.

"Stay out of this," Frank ordered.

"I would appreciate it very much, Frank," she said in a very even tone, "if you would now just come to bed with me."

He tossed back the last of his drink. "Okay, fine," he said. "You want to get to bed, we'll go to bed." He then threw some money onto the bar, gave the photographer one last menacing look, and dutifully followed her.

Jilly was waiting at the elevator by the time the Sinatras got there. He pushed the button and the doors opened. Barbara and Frank got into the elevator and, just as the doors closed, Jilly gave Barbara a big thumbs-up.

Part Thirteen

THAT'S LIFE

The Kitty Kelley Matter

For Frank Sinatra, 1983 would be consumed by sold-out performances in clubs and concert halls around the world, benefit shows for charities, award presentations for humanitarian efforts, and, of course, recordings. The year ended with Frank celebrating his sixty-eighth birthday, but not before being honored in December with the prestigious Kennedy Center Honors for lifetime achievement. The Sinatra family attended a dinner hosted by Secretary of State George Shultz and a White House reception hosted by President and Mrs. Reagan before the awards ceremony at the Kennedy Center. The other honorees that year were Katherine Dunham, Elia Kazan, Virgil Thomson, and Jimmy Stewart. "There's not the remotest possibility," said Gene Kelly during the taping of the presentation for a television special, "that he will have a successor."

It was during events like the Kennedy Center Honors that Frank most missed his mother. It had been six years since Dolly's sudden passing. Dolly's somewhat shady but colorful past in Hoboken had been kept secret by the Sinatra family for years out of respect not only for her but also her son. In fact, family members rarely discussed among themselves that she'd ever terminated pregnancies, preferring to forget about it and remember Dolly in a happier and more uplifting light.

It's not that the Sinatras were so opposed to abortion. Of course, Frank's first wife, Nancy, terminated a pregnancy after bearing two of Frank's children; she later went on to have a third, Tina. Also, when Nancy Jr. became pregnant at the age of nineteen, Nancy Sr. took her to have the pregnancy terminated. However, these were private matters not discussed freely over coffee and biscotti. Many of the more distant Sinatra relatives weren't even aware that Dolly had ever been arrested, which was perhaps just as it should have been.

By the summer of 1983, it appeared that all of that was about to change. It was then that Frank realized he was about to have a big problem with one of the few women in his life he would not be able to control: perky and petite but ever so dauntless and determined biographer Kitty Kelley. Kelley, who had written controversial and successful biographies about Jacqueline Onassis and Elizabeth Taylor, was in the process of researching a book about Frank. At first he didn't care. Other books had been written about him in the past. "How bad could this one be?" he asked. "They all say the same damn boring things anyway."

However, when Frank began receiving telephone calls from friends in Hoboken telling him that Kelley had been asking certain towns-folk about Dolly's illegal activities, he became concerned. He called a meeting with Mickey Rudin and some other business associates at his home in Palm Springs. He flew in his friend Joey D'Orazio from Hoboken, since Joey seemed to have knowledge of Kelley's investigation. The contingent retired to Sinatra's den and began their meeting.

"Look, this can't happen," Frank began, according to D'Orazio's memory. "What can we do?"

"Not much, Frank," said Mickey. "Not until it comes out, anyway." At that time, he said, maybe they could sue for libel or defamation of character.

Frank's spirits fell. "This kind of thing hurts me; it hurts my kids, my grandkids, not to mention my mother's memory," he said. "Maybe she won't write about Ma," he said, trying to be hopeful. "Maybe she'll do the decent thing."

No one at the meeting held out much hope in regard to Kitty Kelley's sense of propriety where Dolly Sinatra was concerned. Frank then reached into his pocket and pulled out a thick wad of what appeared to be one-hundred-dollar bills, wrapped with a rubber band. He tossed it onto the coffee table. "Throw some money at her," he told Mickey. "We'll get Joey here to do it so it's not coming directly from us."

Joey D'Orazio recalled being stunned for a second, but then jumping to attention. "Sure, I can do that," he said. "I'll track her down and I'll give her some money in an envelope. I'll tell her she'd better back off if she knows what's good for her. I'll make it clear that Frank's got friends and that if she continues with this thing, it's not gonna end well for her."

"Not gonna work," Mickey Rudin said. "First of all, it's illegal. Secondly, she'll go to the press with a threat like that to promote her book. Not only that," he said, motioning to the wad of cash on the table, "my gut tells me it's going to take a whole lot more than that to shut her up."

That particular meeting was adjourned without much progress being made. "I flew back to Hoboken after promising that I would keep my eye on things back there," said D'Orazio. "I knew all the same people Frank knew, these were childhood friends. And every couple of days I would get a call from some person saying, 'This writer called me, asking questions about Dolly.' It was upsetting."

A number of meetings were held at Sinatra's home during the next few months with Rudin and other lawyers as well as with D'Orazio, their scout from Hoboken, to determine how to proceed in what became known as "the matter of Kitty Kelley."

"How much you think she's getting paid to write this shit?" Frank asked during one meeting.

"Couple hundred thou, I heard," said Mickey.

Frank mulled it over. "You know, JFK once said, 'What makes a biography interesting is the struggle to answer one question: "What's he like?"'" [Sinatra was paraphrasing a quote from Benjamin Bradlee's book *Conversations with Kennedy*.] I guess I can understand people wanting to know about me, but my mother? That's crossing the line. That's got nothing to do with me."

"Plus, it's really bad public relations," Joey D'Orazio piped up.

Frank glared at Joey. "You know what? I oughta punch you right in the face for saying that." He leaned in and glowered at Joey. "To bring it down to that? Public relations? What's the matter with you? You think this is about me and my image? *Don't even go dere.*"

Years later, D'Orazio recalled, "I almost shit my pants. He was so mad at me. I thought he was going to reach out and strangle me."

"Fine, then. Sue her, Mickey," Frank said, changing the subject. "Sue her. That's the only answer."

Mickey wasn't sure of the wisdom of a lawsuit. Perhaps he remembered the last time he and Frank brought a lawsuit against a biographer. It had made Frank look a bit ridiculous when in 1976 he litigated against New York columnist Earl Wilson and his publisher,

Macmillan, for a million dollars over Wilson's adoring book *Sinatra*. The charge was not libel or slander. Frank had came up with another complaint: "The book is boring and uninteresting," he charged in the suit.

Sinatra also claimed that Wilson's book was unfair competition to the book he himself might one day write. Moreover, he charged that some of what Wilson wrote wasn't true. However, as to those parts he claimed were false, he said that if it was ever proved at trial that they *were* true, it would only be because he had given Wilson the information, and in that case, the statements were protected by "a common-law copyright" because Sinatra hadn't wanted the statements to be published when he made them to Wilson. Certainly this was one of the more unusual lawsuits ever brought against a writer by a public figure.

Ultimately it was decided that Mickey Rudin would file a $2 million lawsuit against Kitty Kelley and her publisher, Bantam, prior to publication of the book in the hope of preventing it from going forward. To justify the action, Sinatra would allege that he owned his own story and, moreover, that Kelley was misrepresenting herself as Sinatra's "official biographer." (She would claim that she did no such thing.)

The action was filed in Los Angeles Superior Court on September 21, 1983. Writers' groups, such as the National Writers Union, came to Kelley's defense, fearing that if Sinatra prevailed, the result would have a chilling effect on freedom of the press. Sinatra would drop the lawsuit in 1984.

Frank and Barbara Separate

$\mathcal{T}$he year 1984 would continue in the same vein of accomplishment for Frank Sinatra—concerts, benefits, award shows, telethons, trips abroad, and more. In April and May he recorded the *L.A. Is My Lady* album, produced by Quincy Jones. It was an album Frank was never fond of because he felt they didn't spend enough time choosing material for it. In the end, the public would buy it because it was a Sinatra album, but not because it was a very good one. At the end of the year Frank and Barbara had dinner at the White House with the Reagans.

By the beginning of 1985, Frank and Barbara seemed to outsiders like a couple who might want to reconsider their matrimonial bond, because they'd begun to have serious conflicts. Many of Sinatra's associates remember one particularly unpleasant scene at Bally's in Las Vegas. Frank, Jilly, and several others were drinking, gambling, and losing money when Barbara spotted them. Frank was crouched over the craps table with a cigarette hanging from his lips. He removed it for a moment as he downed the last few drops of his vodka and soda.

"Don't you think you've had enough to drink?" Barbara asked as she approached.

Frank rolled his eyes in her direction. "Listen, I'm working hard. Gimme a break. I'm relaxing."

"But you're losing all of the money you're earning while working here," she said, trying to reason with him. "Between what you lose and what you give away, you'll never be able to *stop* working."

Indeed, an ongoing quarrel between the Sinatras had to do with Frank's working hard to maintain a certain lifestyle but then spending money as quickly as he made it. Another point of contention was that Frank habitually gave Nancy, Tina, and Frank Jr. thousands of dollars' worth of gifts. Barbara said that she felt they were old enough to fend for themselves and should not accept such kinds of gifts from their father. The Sinatras, however, felt that she was really just trying to control their finances, as well as their father's. "Dad used to shower us with gifts all the time, and that stopped," recalled Nancy Sinatra. "All of his gifting was now to his new wife. This sounds selfish. It wasn't the gifts; it was what they meant. It wasn't the lack of presents; it was the lack of his presence. When you tend to show love by giving presents and they stop, well, what is there to think?"

In fact, since marrying her Frank had purchased so much expensive jewelry for Barbara—gold chains, bracelets, diamond earrings, necklaces—that they filled a steel strongbox two feet long, a foot wide, and eight inches deep. "One day she asked me and the housekeeper to carry the box out of the house so she could put her prized possessions in a safe-deposit box," said Bill Stapely, his butler at this time. "We were both grunting and groaning under the strain. That thing weighed a ton."

"And why do you *encourage* this behavior?" Barbara demanded to know of Jilly. Rizzo was a big, intimidating presence, but Barbara was never cowed by him. "You should know better," she scolded him. "You're supposed to be his friend!"

"Jilly *is* my friend," Frank shouted at his wife. Jilly didn't say a word. The throng that had gathered as the result of the commotion fell silent.

"You know what? You're outta here," Frank finally announced, glaring at Barbara. "Pack your bags, every one of 'em. I want you out of the suite before I go back up there. We're finished, Barbara. It's *ova*. You hear me. *Ova!*" Aside from his heaving chest, Frank stood motionless, his eyes darkened with rage. "Damn it!" he exclaimed as he raised both fists. "I want to punch you so bad right now, you don't *know* how bad."

Barbara wouldn't be browbeaten by him. "Oh yeah?" she asked, standing up to him. Her blue eyes were cold as steel. "Give it your best shot, then, Frank," she said, jutting out her chin at him. "Go ahead, hit me. *Hit me.*"

"And what would you do if I did?" he asked her angrily. "'Cause I could knock you right across the room right now, Barbara. I swear to Christ. Right across the room!"

"What would I do?" she repeated his question. "I'd leave you and you'd never see me again, that's what I would do. So, go ahead, do it, Frank. *I dare you!*"

Frank's hands dropped to his side.

Barbara gathered herself and moved away from the crowd and toward the elevators. She knew it was impossible to deal with Frank on any level of reason when they were both so worked up. Meanwhile, Frank went back to his gambling as if nothing had happened. Barbara returned to their suite, packed her bags—"every one of 'em"—caught a cab to the airport, and took the Sinatra private jet back to Rancho Mirage.

"Frank came home two days later," said Bill Stapely. "For the next two weeks, there was an icy chill between them. I never heard them say one word to each other. After two weeks of this, Barbara packed some bags and moved out of the house. After she left, Frank told me, 'This marriage is over. I'm glad that broad is out of my life. She was driving me crazy.'"

Frank was done with Barbara, at least in that moment; as far as he was concerned, they were separated. Some felt that the wedge his marriage had caused between him and his family members had worn him down, and had also caused him to start acting out. Certainly he was tense, upset, and irrational, but was this anything new? When he told his daughters that he and Barbara had separated, they were—in his presence, anyway—sorry to hear about it. Privately they were very happy—or, as Tina put it, "I was as gleeful as a Munchkin after the house fell on Margaret Hamilton's sister."

Working against Frank, though, in the notion of ending his marriage to Barbara was the passing of time. Previously he wouldn't have delayed ending a relationship. Ava had been his only weakness. Others, like Betty Bacall and Mia Farrow, had been quickly dispatched. But now he was seventy and much more fearful of being alone. Even though his daughters would always be there for him and he must have known as much, there had recently been so much conflict with them, he had to wonder how long it would take to repair the damage. Also, he had hurt Nancy Sr. with his annulment of their marriage. She would always be in his corner, but there was damage there, and he knew it. If Barbara was to also be gone, who would be left for him?

As well as feeling he could potentially be alone in his old age, the idea of a divorce battle with Barbara was less than appealing. She had already retained a divorce attorney, Arthur Crowley. He was a noted lawyer and he was tough; within a week of this fight, he'd already drawn up divorce papers for Barbara! She would likely not go quietly into the night, as had Mia before her. Mia hadn't even asked for alimony. Frank suspected that divorcing Barbara would be a very different experience. Still, he told Mickey to start drawing up divorce papers.

There was one other factor at work: Frank really did love Barbara. In his own way, he still loved her very much and actually couldn't imagine a life without her. At a crossroads, he asked Father Tom Rooney for his opinion. Rooney said that in his view—and of course in the view of the Church—marriage was a sacred sacrament. After all Frank had gone through to marry Barbara in the Catholic Church, the priest felt he had to fight for his union with her. It would take work, Father Rooney conceded, but it was worth it.

About a month later, Frank had changed his mind about Barbara: He now wanted to reconcile with her. She wasn't going to make it easy on him, though. He would give her all the money in the world if she asked for it, but what she wanted was a bit more of a problem for him: She wanted an apology.

As a consequence of his many turbulent fights with Ava, Frank was loath ever to offer a real apology to a woman. "He told me that he spent so many years apologizing to Ava for this and that," Joey D'Orazio said, "that when it ended with her he made up his mind that he would never tell another dame he was sorry. And I have to say, I never heard him apologize to anyone after Ava."

"Frank Sinatra never apologized to anybody," Barbara later confirmed. "Ever. Period. Not even to me. He always said, 'There are two things I never do—yawn in front of the woman I love, and apologize.' The latter was not in his psyche, for to apologize would be to admit that he might have been wrong. But I told him I'd only stay if he said sorry."

"Forgiveness and reconciliation is a very important part of the gospel," Father Tom Rooney told Frank in front of friends one night at the compound. "When a person forgives you, you are then free to forgive yourself and move on with your life. There is nothing wrong with asking for forgiveness." But Frank just didn't see it that way, and he wasn't going to change his mind about it.

"Under duress, he finally admitted, 'I didn't mean to hurt you,'" Barbara would recall. "It was a half-assed apology, but it was the only one I ever got."

"I'm a dumb guy, all right?" Frank conceded to her. "I do dumb things. That ain't news, Barbara. That ain't news at all." When he kissed her tenderly, all was well again in their world.

Sick over the Kitty Kelley Book

*I*n December 1985, Frank Sinatra turned seventy. Bob Greene said it best in a column in the *Chicago Tribune* when he wrote, "The fact that Frank Sinatra is celebrating his 70th birthday this week is something that will cause many people to stop and think for a moment. Frank Sinatra—70 years old. It has less to do with Sinatra than with the rest of us. If Sinatra is 70, what has happened to us?" Indeed, it would seem that as Frank faced his mortality, much of his public was forced to do the same. He had been a part of so many lives for so long, it was difficult, even painful, to watch him grow old, mostly because it served as a reminder that he was not alone.

When Kitty Kelley's *His Way* biography of Sinatra was finally published in October 1986, it was much worse than Frank and the Sinatra family imagined. Indeed, Kelley held back no details of Dolly's history. Dolly's secrets were now out for all to know and to scrutinize.

Of course, there was much that Frank objected to in Kelley's book. However, he would just have to accept its attendant controversies as the price of fame. The Sinatras would have their say in yet *another* book by Nancy (*Frank Sinatra: An American Legend*, with hundreds of photographs) and, later, in an authorized television miniseries produced by Tina Sinatra in 1994. Kitty Kelley's portrayal of Dolly's activities as "a mother who kills babies," though, was what most upset Frank. "He was very verbal about having Kitty Kelly whacked for what she had written about his mother," the singer Paul Anka said in 2013.

It's questionable whether Frank actually wanted Kelley "whacked," but in fact the entire family was crushed by her writings. It was as if a dark cloud had descended upon the entire fold when the book debuted at the number one position on the *New York Times* bestseller list on October 12, 1986. When Frank turned the television set on one day and saw Kelley talking about his mother's arrest, he became so agitated that his family thought he would have to be treated at a hospital for an anxiety attack.

Bill Stapely remembered the night Frank almost spoke to Kelley on a television call-in program. "I take issue with a lot of what's in it," Stapely overheard Frank saying of the book to the segment producer who was screening callers for the broadcast. "But I just want to ask one simple question: Does this dopey broad have a mother? That's all I wanna know. And if so, then how can she write that stuff about mine? That's it. That's the whole enchilada. That's all I want to know."

The producer, who must have been excited by the prospect of such an on-air confrontation, put Frank on hold. As he was waiting on the line for a commercial break to end, Barbara walked into the room. "What are you doing, Frank?" she asked with a raised eyebrow.

"I'm getting ready to talk to that broad, Kitty-Litter," he said, "and ask her how she can write those things about my mother."

"Oh my God," Barbara exclaimed.

She ran to the phone and disconnected the call. "Will you please stop it?" she asked Frank. "Don't give her the satisfaction of calling her! And on national television? Get a hold of yourself!"

"I believe that book made him ill," said Tina. "I think Kitty Kelley taxed his life," she added, "and for that I will never forgive her."

In fact, Frank was hospitalized from November 9 through 16, at Eisenhower Medical Center in Palm Springs, a month after the book was published. The diagnosis was acute diverticulitis, which is usually caused by poor diet resulting in a form of constipation that causes abscesses in the intestine. He had been performing at the Golden Nugget Casino in Atlantic City when he became ill.

His doctor, Dr. Alan Altman, said that Frank had to have a twelve-foot section of intestine removed during a delicate seven-and-a-half-hour operation. Frank was distressed by the operation and took it as yet another sign of old age. Bill Stapely remembered visiting him in the hospital. Frank had tears in his eyes. "I was surprised," he said. "I'd never seen Frank cry before."

When Frank saw his employee looking at him, he turned his head away and buried it in the pillow. Stapely reached out and took his boss's hand and squeezed it. But Frank yanked it away. "Get away from me," he hollered. "I don't need you. Just get away." Still, Bill stayed at his side and squeezed his hand a few moments longer as Frank went to sleep.

Prudent?

Naturally, Frank's children were upset about his illness, as was Nancy. Making it worse for the Sinatra women was the acrimony that seemed to exist between them and Barbara whenever they visited Frank in the hospital. By this time, Barbara was accustomed to the fact that whenever Frank's daughters were in her presence, there would be some sort of drama. However, she couldn't deal with it when Frank was so sick. Of course, they felt the same way about her. Between what had been suppressed and what had been expressed, the years of resentment had taken a toll on everyone. At the hospital, the daughters felt that Barbara was emotionally unavailable to them. In their view, they were facing their father's mortality for the first time. They felt that Barbara could have been empathetic, more supportive. Tina and Nancy approached Barbara to ask why she was being so distant toward them.

"As you both know, your father is a very private man, and he likes to keep these things private," Barbara explained, according to Tina. She was polite but firm.

"But from us?" Tina and Nancy asked her, bewildered.

"I'm not saying that," Barbara said, her manner very clipped. "I'm just saying that he would want me to be *prudent* in the way these things are handled."

That testy exchange did little to make the Sinatra daughters feel any better about things. It continued to appear to them that Barbara was acting in a territorial and controlling way. While Frank was in the hospital, however, they agreed it was best to at least try to keep the tumult from him.

"I had a lot of surgery; they had to cut up my tummy pretty badly," Frank recalled of the operation. "It was an intestinal infection that began to spread throughout my stomach and bowel and so forth. I was close to buying it. If I hadn't come back from the trip I was on, I woulda bought it. They woulda had flowers and a big band behind the casket."

After the operation, Frank would have to wear a colostomy bag for about a month and a half until his intestines healed. "Frank was destabilized by that operation," Paul Anka would recall. "When I saw him backstage after a performance, he showed me the colostomy bag that he had to wear until his insides healed. He was humiliated by this and was not happy about going in again for his third operation."

The doctors told Frank he had to deal with the colostomy bag for six weeks. Had they lost their minds? After two weeks, he was done with that phase and demanded that they go back in and do whatever they had to do to fix things so he no longer needed the bag. When he went into the hospital for a third operation, he asked Bill Stapely to accompany him into the operating room. "And if those doctors don't get this thing right," he told Stapely, "I want you to take a gun and shoot them bastards."

When Bill saw Frank later in the recovery room, Sinatra asked him, "Are the doctors still alive?" The two shared a warm smile as Frank, still under the effects of the anesthesia, drifted back to sleep. Unfortunately, he would have to have yet another operation to reverse what he'd made the doctors do, and then wait six more weeks after that before the ordeal would be over. He was miserable, and most of his friends and family couldn't help but blame it, at least partly, on the stress he felt over the Kitty Kelley book.

Many of Frank's friends and family members wanted to speak out about what they believed were inaccuracies in the book, but Frank wouldn't allow it. He now realized the book would have been less anticipated and ultimately less successful had he not drawn attention to it by filing a lawsuit against its author. "My father issued a gag order and forbade any of us to say anything public about this situation," Nancy Sinatra later said. "We nearly strangled on our pain and anger."

The book didn't make a dent in Frank's appeal. In fact, once he recovered, the rest of 1986 would be a blur of concert dates—the Golden Nugget in Atlantic City, Carnegie Hall in New York—and personal appearances. He opened at the refurbished Chicago Theatre in September to a huge reception. "This is about chicks leaving you in crummy hotel rooms where you drink whiskey for four or five days," he said while introducing the song "One for My Baby." He added, "You can ask Eddie Fisher. He'll tell you the whole goddamn thing. [Elizabeth Taylor] left him. But then she got fat, so who cares?"

"In 1986, he raised $1 million for the Desert Hospital in Palm Springs with a $1,500-a-plate benefit," Bill Stapely recalled. "Frank arranged everything, including the guest list, the food, and the entertainment. He even waited on tables. Then, after he was done serving dinner, he slipped out of his waiter's clothes and into his tux to sing for his guests."

Ironically, the success of Kitty Kelley's *His Way* demonstrated that Sinatra was still a popular figure in pop culture as he turned seventy-one. As it was, Frank worked throughout the rest of the year and throughout 1987 as well, trying not to give a second thought to the book. No doubt that's the way Dolly would have wanted it.

By this time, Frank and Barbara had bought a new home on Foothill Road in Beverly Hills. They would keep the compound in Palm Springs, but now would also have a permanent residence in Los Angeles.

Also in 1987, Frank and Mickey Rudin finally came to a parting of the ways. The split came as a surprise to many people. The two had run their course, which had been many decades of a good relationship. As often happened in Sinatra's world though, words were said—by both parties—that forever ended not only their working rapport, but their close friendship as well.

"It's difficult to explain it all," Mickey would say years later. "In fact, I would never betray Sinatra's confidence by trying to explain. Suffice it to say, Frank and I had a good working relationship until a certain time in his life when things began to change, not with his career but within the family—that's all I will say about it. Finally, at the end, we both were hotheads and the result was the end of one of the most cherished relationships in my life. It was difficult because I loved not only Frank but his kids, who I had watched grow up. So, that's all I will say about that."

It was difficult for Frank to accept that Mickey Rudin was no longer in his life, but also hard for his family members. The Sinatras knew and loved Mickey and believed he had their best interests at heart. Without him in the picture, the future seemed anything but certain.

The Sinatra Sisters Reach Out to Barbara

After Frank's hospital stay, Barbara, Tina, and Nancy Jr. decided to sit down and try to work out their differences. According to one well-placed source, it was Tina's idea. Nancy wasn't sure it would amount to much. Of course, the women had tried to do this in the past, but it never resulted in anything productive. However, Nancy agreed that it was at least worth another try. She still had hope that things could work out. Doubtless ringing in her ears were the words her father had told her repeatedly throughout her life: "Stay away from dark thoughts, Chicken. Don't despair."

The three women met for lunch in a Beverly Hills restaurant.

Considering who the Sinatras were at their emotional core, some friends of Nancy's and Tina's thought that the best course of action might have been for the sisters to just unload on Barbara with all barrels. After all, wasn't that the Sinatra way? Both daughters had learned from their parents and grandparents to assert themselves in the age-old tradition of Italian-American women, unafraid to fully express themselves and ready to face the consequences, as long as their views were heard, understood, and respected. This was most certainly the way they conducted their lives, both personally and professionally.

There weren't many people in show business who thought of either Sinatra sister as being circumspect or tactful. Like their father, they got the job done by being vocal and, when necessary, opinionated. When they've had to also go up against Frank, they did that, too. "You've got to *face* Frank Sinatra," Nancy once said. "Tell him the truth. Battle it out. Yes, he'll get mad and so will you. But you'll come to some conclusion. You can't be so in awe of him that you're awed right out of a relationship." They knew how to deal with Frank, and usually they found a way to deal with him. Dealing with Barbara? Now, that was another story.

But Nancy and Tina were both emotionally spent and now just wanted to reach out to her. They didn't want to hurt Barbara's feelings because they knew it would upset their father. As Barbara sat before them, white pearls around her neck, a fine emerald pin on her shoulder, she seemed somehow quite fragile. Was she nervous? The daughters couldn't help but notice her delicate hands with tapered fingers nervously toying with the menu. Yet there was always something a little cold and removed about her.

If they could just accomplish one thing with this luncheon, the Sinatra daughters had decided, it was to let Barbara know just how deeply they loved their father. As obvious as that should have been, they felt that she didn't fully grasp how much they cared about him, how he was everything to them. They felt that if she really understood as much, many of the slights that had taken place in the past might not have occurred. It was probably naïve of them, however, to think they could touch Barbara with such sentimentality, especially considering her previous behavior. If anything, it appears that this luncheon was just a last-ditch effort on the daughters' part.

To that end, Nancy told stories of her childhood with Frank, how he taught her to swim, to ride a two-wheeler, to paint. She talked about her teen years, her marriage to Tommy Sands, and how her father had helped her through the divorce. Tina spoke of how lucky Nancy and Frank Jr. had been to have Frank with them when they were very young, and how she had always felt that she missed out on having him present when she was a little girl. Ava had come into the picture when she was just two and her father was gone from her, she explained. She hoped that Barbara would now understand more fully why she so desperately needed her father in her life, and that if she was ever overreactive in feeling slighted where he was concerned it was because of her traumatic experience of him as a little girl. They spoke of Frank Jr.'s kidnapping, and how powerless they felt to help their father during that time, and how much they had all suffered as a family. The bond they shared as Sinatras was real and meant everything to them.

Barbara listened intently. Her steel-blue eyes, usually filled with such enormous power, brimmed over with tears several times. She said she understood. Hearing such heartwarming stories about the man she loved made her emotional and, for a moment anyway, seemed to melt her icy façade. In response, Barbara said she felt the daughters had a wrong impression of her. "I have never once tried to come between you and your father," she told the Sinatras. "I just don't know why you would think such a thing." She said that she only wanted to be a part of the deep familial bond they shared with him, and trying to fit in had always been her only intention.

Maybe one problem with the conversation the three women had on this day was a lack of specificity. While the daughters tried to outline some of their grievances, they couldn't be as open as they wanted; they still had a sense that they didn't want to make things worse. For her part, Barbara simply didn't think there was any problem—or at least not any that she wanted to acknowledge—so therefore there was nothing to address.

When the luncheon was over, neither Nancy nor Tina felt the least bit satisfied. They agreed to try to see eye-to-eye with Barbara in the future, and also to communicate with her better. Barbara promised to keep the lines of communication open as well. They all three loved Frank, they at least agreed on that much, and they said they would do whatever they needed to get along. Something was missing from this entreatment, though, at least to hear the daughters tell it years later—and maybe that was just an honest recognition and blunt summation of some of the serious problems at hand.

While Tina and Nancy left the luncheon feeling disheartened, Barbara, from all accounts, seemed just fine. She actually thought it went quite well.

Rat Pack Redux?

As performers and personalities, Frank Sinatra, Dean Martin, and Sammy Davis had been linked in the public consciousness for well over twenty-five years. By 1987, although older, they were still active as entertainers despite a myriad of physical and emotional problems that had beset all three. In October 1986, they were together doing benefit performances for the Barbara Sinatra Children's Center at the Eisenhower Medical Center in Rancho Mirage when it occurred to Sammy that the three should work together again. They still had that chemistry and had remained good friends, though there had been long stretches in the last twenty-five years when they hadn't seen each other. Why not work together?

At the end of 1986, Frank was seventy-one, Dean was sixty-nine, and Sammy was sixty-one. Sammy suggested that they perform together at Bally's in Las Vegas, where all three were presently under contract. Frank, always one to push an idea to its limits, had another suggestion: a full-fledged concert tour. Sammy, who always enjoyed performing and had a great affinity for Frank, was excited about the prospects. Dean, not so much.

By October 1987, Dean was a changed man. It had only been six months since the death of his thirty-five-year-old son Dean Paul, whose air force Phantom jet had crashed at 500 miles per hour into the same San Gorgonio Mountain near San Bernardino that had claimed Dolly Sinatra's plane in 1977. With the death of his son, it was as if the light went out of Dean's world and he began to sink into a severe depression. Even though he tried to continue working—he was onstage at Bally's in Las Vegas just eight days after the funeral— he appeared to have lost his will to live. In subsequent months, his health deteriorated and his drinking habits began to spin out of control. All of his friends were concerned about him, but none more than Frank and Sammy.

"Dean would never talk about it," Sammy once said of Dean's reaction to Dino's death. "We tried, you know? But Dean was Dean."

Two days after the first discussion about the possibility of a tour, Frank called Sammy. "Charlie, let's do it," Frank said eagerly. "It'll be hard work, but it could be exciting. And I think it would be great for Dean. Maybe get him out. For that alone, it would be worth doing."

A few weeks later, the men had another meeting at Frank's Beverly Hills home. Frank told them that he now realized that an idea he had earlier shared with them, of traveling by train, was impractical. The combined entourages, musicians, and technical crew of all three entertainers would amount to eighty-one people. Because it would take a week to travel between cities, feeding and housing that many employees would be a costly endeavor. "We'll have to fly," Frank decided. He said that he believed the three of them could sell enough tickets to fill auditoriums that seated as many as twenty thousand.

"I didn't want to do it. Hell no," Dean Martin would explain years later, sitting in La Famiglia restaurant in Beverly Hills. "I was done. My best days were behind me. I was working here, working there, just to keep myself going, somethin' to do. But this? I knew that this was gonna be a lot of work. When it was going to be by train, I thought that might be fun. But when it became airplanes and airports, I knew it wasn't going to be for me. But how could I say no? I didn't want to let Frank and Sam down. In my heart, though, I knew it would be the biggest mistake of my life."

In December 1987, Frank, Dean, and Sammy held a news conference at Chasen's restaurant in Beverly Hills to announce the tour. Wearing tuxedos, the three men met at Frank's home, talked over breakfast about what they were going to say, and were then driven to the restaurant together in a black stretch limousine. They were met at Chasen's by an unruly battery of reporters. This was big news. The Rat Pack was reuniting, and the wire services, newspapers, television networks, and foreign press were all present for the official announcement. American Express was sponsoring the tour; HBO would be televising one of the performances as a special. The three men took their places on the dais.

"Ladies and gentlemen, we thank you for coming here today," Sammy began.

Dean cut in: "Is there any way we can call the whole thing off?" Everyone laughed. ("But I wasn't kidding," Dean said later, shaking his head.)

The press conference went well. The guys heckled each other in much the same way they did in the 1960s. It was clear that they had the same irreverent sense of humor. When someone from the sea of reporters asked if the reunion would be an annual event, Sinatra quipped, "Sammy is sixty-two, and he's the kid. I'm seventy-two, and Dean is seventy. At our ages, the only annual event you hope for is your birthday."

When someone mentioned a Rat Pack reunion, Frank cut the writer off by saying that the moniker was "a stupid phrase." The tour would be billed as the "Together Again Tour."

Each of the twenty-nine city stops along the well-publicized tour sold out well in advance of the concert dates. Frank was relieved. He had wanted to remain optimistic about ticket sales, but feared the worst. Buoyed by the good news, he telephoned Sammy and said, "The accountants just told me you should come out of this thing with between six and eight million dollars." It looked good for all three men, another beginning, or maybe a glorious finish.

Rehearsals began at the Ren Mar Studios a few weeks after the press conference, where an elevated, square duplicate of the round stage they would be using was erected. The forty-piece orchestra had been organized using New York musicians under the guidance of conductor Morty Stevens.

Joseph Wilson, who worked as a sound technician at Ren Mar Studios, remembered the early rehearsals. "Frank was awesome. He sang like he was performing in front of a huge audience. I am a big

Sinatra fan, and for me this was a thrill. His presence, man, in a black satin bomber jacket with a baseball cap, lumbering along on that makeshift stage, singing 'Mack the Knife,' was incredible. This old guy looked like a champion in front of that orchestra.

"Then Sammy did some numbers, 'What Kind of Fool Am I?' 'Candy Man.' I knew Sam well. He had a new hip, he told me. They'd just operated on him shortly before this time. Still, he looked good. He sang well, like a man half his age. He was the best, vocally, of the three.

"Then Dean started singing 'Volare,' and, well, that was sad. He didn't know the words. We had a teleprompter, but he wasn't looking at it. He sat on a stool and halfheartedly sang, and as he did, you could see Frank with an expression that said, 'Oh, shit! This isn't gonna work.' Dean did a couple more things, 'That's Amore,' I think, and then he just stopped in midsong and walked offstage. He kind of crumpled into a chair, lit a cigarette, and started hacking."

Frank went over to Dean, slapped him on the back, and said, "What you just did up there? Worst goddamn thing I ever heard." Frank delivered the line like comedic sarcasm, not an all-out criticism. But Dean got the point. He grinned halfheartedly and said, "No shit."

"You know, we got teleprompters these days," Frank added. "You don't gotta know the words."

"Yeah, but you gotta know how to read," Dean said, tossing off the line as if he were in front of an audience.

Frank shook his head and walked over to Sammy. The two went into a conspiratorial huddle.

After that rehearsal, Joseph Wilson pulled Sammy aside and asked about Dean. "What's up with him, man? He looks bad." Sammy let out a long sigh. "This tragedy with his kid, it's killing him. What can we do? Why'd this have to happen to Dino? It's so damn unfair."

"You think he'll last on this tour?"

"Hell, man, I'll be amazed if he lasts through the rehearsals," Sammy said. Wilson then handed Sammy his silk jacket, which was emblazoned on the back with the words "Michael Jackson—Bad Tour." Sammy put on the coat. "But I pray to God he does," he continued.

The Trouble with Dean

The first date for Frank, Sammy, and Dean was at the Oakland Coliseum on March 13, 1988. There were early signs of divisiveness among the three Rat Packers as soon as they landed in Oakland. The plane taxied to a deserted area of the runway, where they were met by security guards. Then Frank and Sammy got into a black stretch Lincoln, while Dean went his own way in a beige stretch Caddy.

Dean remembered, "There was something cold about Frank. I didn't want to be 'round him. I felt like he thought I was a putz. Sam? He was Frank's sidekick. I was out of my league. I'd rather be playin' my own joint, doin' my own act, be my own boss. I didn't want Sinatra givin' me no orders. I was grown. This wasn't 1960." His voice trailed off. Then he clarified, "Frank just likes to have it his way, you know. His kind of food, his kind of car, his kind of living. I'm simpler. I didn't need all that crap."

With the Oakland house sold out—sixteen thousand seats—the show was a complete success. Each singer had a solo set, and then they joined together for a lengthy medley of their hits as a swinging finale. Dean held up well throughout his part of the act. His self-effacing, easygoing charm remained intact despite his uneasiness with his surroundings. He sang laid-back versions of his own special-material songs, such as "Pennies from Heaven" ("When it rains, it always rains, bourbon from heaven") and "When You're Smiling" ("When you're drinking, you get stinking...and the whole world smiles at you"), with finger-snapping ease. He had been performing these numbers for decades with little alteration.

As part of his act, Dean would often take a long drag from his ever-present cigarette, flick it onto the stage floor, and then plug his ears with his index fingers as if in anticipation of an explosion. The gag usually got laughs. During his performance in Oakland, however, he inexplicably flicked the cigarette into the audience. When he put his index fingers into his ears, the audience members laughed, as they always did, though many observers wondered if anyone had been burned. Still, the three finished the show to a standing ovation.

Backstage afterward, Frank was extremely angry at Dean. Recalled a member of the tour's road crew, "They had just gotten offstage, and Frank grabbed Dean by the arm and tugged him into the dressing room, saying, 'Come with me.' Sam followed."

"What the hell was *that* about?" Frank demanded to know.

"Huh?" Dean asked, out of breath. He seemed not to know what Frank was talking about.

"That thing with the cigarette butt into the audience?" Frank said angrily. "What, are you crazy? You don't ever do that to an audience. You don't insult an audience like that. What is wrong with you?"

"Oh, screw you, Frank," Dean said, exasperated. "Who cares? I'm tired. Gimme a break."

"Now c'mon, guys," Sammy jumped in, trying to stave off an argument. "Let's the three of us—"

"Let's nothin', Charlie," Frank said, cutting him off. "Let's just *nothin'.*"

Years later, Dean would remember the confrontation. "I was an asshole, yeah. You don't do that. Someone coulda got burned or something and they would have sued us for everything we made. Frank was right. But I was scared. I almost had to change my shorts, I was so scared that night."

After the show in Oakland, Frank wanted to go out drinking and maybe find some "broads," just like in the old days. Dean was tired, however. He wanted to stay in the hotel room and watch TV. "When'd you get so damn old?" Frank wanted to know. "C'mon, pallie. You're making *me* feel old."

"You *are* old," Dean said.

"What the hell is wrong with you?" Frank finally exploded. "Get outta here before you see my bad side," he warned Dean.

Dean bolted from the room.

There was another engagement at the Pacific Coliseum in Vancouver and then one at the Seattle Center Coliseum in Seattle. Of Dean's performance, *Seattle Times* critic Patrick MacDonald wrote, "If his drunk act is an act, it's mighty believable. He was teetering through the show. He was an embarrassment."

The fellows were then scheduled to perform at the Chicago Theatre from March 18 to 20. Despite any hard feelings between the performers, the concert was a great success. Rick Kogan of the *Chicago Tribune* called it "one of the most amazing evenings of entertainment that has ever taken place." Of Martin, Kogan noted, "He looks too fit to be the boozer of legend, still handsome around the edges, but determined to play the hooch habit to the hilt....One wished for more singing and less boozy burlesque."

After the performance, Frank complained to Mort Viner that Dean wasn't performing up to par. Viner told Dean what Frank had said, and Dean announced, "That's it. I'm quitting." Viner chartered a plane and arranged for him and Martin to fly back to Los Angeles, leaving Frank and Sammy to perform as a duet. Before they left, Dean said goodbye to Frank at the hotel.

"Frank, I gotta go," Dean said, according to his memory of the conversation.

Frank regarded him with an annoyed expression. "You son of a bitch, you," he said. "If you didn't want to do this damn thing, why didn't you just say so? Now what are we supposed to do?"

Dean didn't have an answer to the question. He just stood in place, staring at Frank.

Frank would later tell a reporter he was "disgusted." Maybe in that moment he was, but these guys went back so far, it's difficult to believe the feeling lasted very long. "Disappointed" would have been more like it. In his eyes, Dean served a sad reminder to Frank that the best was *not* yet to come, that the glory days were over...and that "you gotta love livin', baby, 'cause dyin' is a pain in the ass."

"Frank hugged me," Dean recalled. "He kissed me on the cheek. Then he said, 'Get the hell outta here, you bum. Go home.' And I left. It was as simple as that. No big deal."

After Dean left Chicago, Frank, Sammy, and Eliot Weisman, executive producer of the tour, had a meeting to determine how they would continue. Dean would have to be replaced. They thought of Shirley MacLaine or Steve Lawrence and Eydie Gormé, but ultimately settled on Liza Minnelli, if she was available. Still, Sammy hoped that Dean would return. Frank didn't. He told Sammy, "That S.O.B. better check into some hospital somewhere, because if he ruins this tour for all of us by giving us the bad rap that we couldn't get along, I'll strangle him with my own hands."

A look of astonishment crossed Sammy's face; he couldn't fathom his friend's lack of sensitivity. Noticing Sammy's reaction, Frank stopped his tirade.

"You're right, Charlie," he said, seeming to read his mind. "It was too soon after Dean Paul. I shoulda known. I get it. A man loses his son, he's never the same. We can't blame Dean."

At that, Sammy remembered, he couldn't help himself. He just burst into tears. "The stress of it, man—it was killing us all," Sammy said later. "I can't tell you how anguished I was about it, to see Dean like that. Part of me died on that tour."

When Dean returned to Los Angeles, he actually did check into Cedars-Sinai Medical Center. His publicist said he was sick with a kidney ailment. Later, his son Ricci admitted that "he...went into the hospital for the full effect."

On March 22, 1988, Frank and Sammy went onstage for the first time during the tour without Dean at the Metro Center Arena in Bloomington, Minnesota.

"We just got through talking to Cedars-Cyanide in Beverly Hills," Sammy said to the packed house before he sang his first song, "Here I'll Stay." (He had unintentionally mangled the hospital's name.) He continued, "Mr. Martin is improving. They haven't got any final word, and he's got to go through some more tests. But Frank and I wanted to come here to do this show because that's first of all the tradition of what show business is all about, the family continues. And that's what Dean would have wanted us to do in any event. This one we're dedicating to our man."

Without Dean, the whole original point of the tour was lost. Still, the show had to go on. So when Liza Minnelli joined the act, replacing Dean in April 1988, the tour was renamed "The Ultimate Event" and went on to rave reviews for the rest of the year.

On April 28, just a little more than a month after leaving Frank and Sammy, Dean Martin opened his solo act at Bally's Grand in Las Vegas. "Frank sent me a kidney," he joked, referring to the ailment that supposedly ended the Together Again Tour, "but I don't know whose it was."

The Sinatra Daughters' Revolt

*A*round the time of the so-called Rat Pack reunion, Nancy and Tina Sinatra drew a line in the sand where their stepmother, Barbara Sinatra, was concerned.

By this time—the summer of 1988—Nancy was forty-eight and Tina forty. Anytime they sat down with Barbara to work things out, the results were less than satisfying. Then their subterranean feelings about her would rise to the surface whenever they would come in contact with her, and the climate would turn cold. Moreover, they didn't feel welcome in her home. When she acted as if she was making a genuine effort to be open, they couldn't help but believe she was faking it, which frustrated them even more. Therefore, they decided the only course of action was to stay in communication with their father by telephone but no longer go to the house, even for holidays. They would have no communication with Barbara whatsoever, even though this meant their access to Frank would be severely limited. Frank Jr. was very surprised by his sisters' decision. However, he didn't try to talk them out of it. "They're old enough to make their own decisions," he said at the time. "But this one is a doozy, isn't it? Obviously, they are wanting to make a big statement."

Nancy Sr. would still be in telephone communication with Frank, but would most certainly not be visiting him as long as her daughters had taken such a position. She was heartsick about it, though, and encouraged them to reconsider, but these were Sinatra women and once they dug in their heels there was no changing their minds.

Barbara thought the Sinatra siblings were just being dramatic as usual. She knew it was very Sinatra-like to make a huge, shocking gesture and then sit back and watch as others reacted to it. But nothing really seemed to rattle Barbara. She was also aware that whenever she and Frank had any sort of problem, his daughters were hoping for a breakup. If they didn't want her in the family, that was fine with her. As Frank's wife, she knew they would lose any campaign they might wage against her. "Don't get me wrong, it's quite sad," she told one close friend, "but I have no more influence over those two girls than I have over their father. This is between them and Frank. I'm staying out of it."

At first, Frank didn't take it seriously. "Looks like da shit really hit da fan," he exclaimed when he heard that Nancy and Tina were now boycotting the household. However, when he realized they were serious, he was hurt, but felt he had to side with his wife. Perhaps ten years earlier, he might have found a way to include his daughters in his life with marriage. But now his whole world was shrinking anyway. Nothing was as it once had been. The way his daughters had abandoned his household seemed like just another consequence of his ever-dwindling life. In a way, their decision felt like a testament to the way he'd raised them. Nancy and Tina were tough and independent, like their pop. "I guess I'd do the same thing in their shoes," he told Tony Oppedisano. "I get it. I don't like it, but I get it. They *should* stand up for themselves."

One of the most disconcerting aspects of this period, which would actually last a few years, was that the Sinatra daughters would no longer be able to fully monitor their aging father's medications. He was taking a number of antidepressants and sedatives that seemed to be making him groggy and listless. He was falling into an ever-deepening emotional abyss.

Though the daughters would not go to the house, they would visit Frank on the road when Barbara wasn't around. What they found out there was upsetting. It seemed to them that he was unfocused, physically imbalanced, and suffering from memory loss. He couldn't even remember the lyrics to his songs. He had fallen deep into an apathetic state of mind, and he didn't seem to care about anything. By this time he was seventy-three. Was it his age that was causing him to fail? Or was it the medication he was on? Since they weren't around to see for themselves what was happening, Nancy and Tina began to wonder about Barbara's caregiving skills.

Meanwhile, Barbara began to assert herself more than ever. Now she wanted to take another look at the prenuptial agreement she said she was forced to sign on the morning of her wedding. She and her attorney decided to have the prenup rescinded. She had kept her divorce lawyer, Arthur Crowley, on retainer after her separation from Frank ended. It was he who drew up the new document, which was called "An Agreement to Rescind Pre-Marital Agreement."

Arthur Crowley had argued that the previous agreement, constructed by Mickey Rudin, had been unfair to Barbara because she was forced to sign under duress and hadn't had the opportunity to have an attorney review it. That prenup—the one Sidney Korshak had told Tina Sinatra saved the family "a shitload of money"—stipulated that Frank's earnings were his own and his assets prior to the marriage were separate property; Barbara was entitled to a six-figure yearly allowance. Under the *modified* agreement, however, all of the money Frank had earned during his marriage to Barbara—along with any future income—would be considered community property, with half belonging to Frank and half to her.

When they found out about this modification, the Sinatra family felt certain that Frank had not been represented by counsel when he signed the agreement. However, according to paragraph F of the contract, "Husband and wife acknowledge that each of them has been represented by independent counsel and that they fully understand and agree with the terms and conditions of this agreement."

In truth, Frank wasn't at all opposed to modifying the prenuptial agreement with Barbara. His daughters' partial exile from his life had marked a seismic shift in his psyche. As early as the Ava years, he had wondered what would happen if Nancy and Tina ever completely revolted against him and his way of life, and he always feared the possibility. Now they had actually done it, and yet he had survived. In some strange way, it was a relief.

Much the way he had done with Ava, Frank now began to feel that Barbara was the only woman—indeed, the only *person*—upon whom he could truly count. In his mind she was there for him when he felt abandoned by his family. His daughters' decision to absent themselves from his household had therefore only served to make him more emotionally dependent on the one woman in his life he knew was going nowhere. If she wanted to modify the prenuptial agreement, that was fine with him.

Ava: "I Always Thought We Would Have More Time"

On January 25, 1990, Frank received devastating news: Ava was gone. She had died a day earlier in London, at sixty-seven, of pneumonia.

Ava Gardner had not aged well. For a woman who so valued her appearance, it must have been difficult for her to deal with the loss of her beauty, but too much liquor had ravaged her face and body. Her troubled life was reflected on her face, which was now lined and puffy. By the time she was sixty, she was but a dim reflection of her former self. She claimed she didn't care, either. She felt she had been beautiful long enough.

A popular misconception about Ava in her last years is that she had fallen on financial hard times and that Frank was supporting her. Her business manager, Jess Morgan, clarified: "Frank was supportive of Ava, but he was not supporting her. She had plenty of capital, was in sound financial condition, and lived on her assets. She wasn't super-rich. However, she didn't need any money from anybody."

Morgan recalled, "Ava came down with pneumonia in January 1988. She had a doctor here [in Los Angeles] that she liked, Dr. William Smith, who was also my doctor. I arranged to get her here to see him. We had to charter a private plane because she was too ill to fly commercial. I got a telephone call from Mickey Rudin telling me that Frank wanted to help. The Italian in him, the gentleman in him, always wanted to feel that he was taking care of her. I said, 'Terrific.' I called Ava and told her he was giving her some money to use for medical expenses, and the chartering of the plane."

Jess Morgan wouldn't say how much money Frank offered (others have said it was $50,000), and his face reddened when asked Ava's reaction to this demonstration of generosity. "Let's just say that she appreciated it," he said, "but she thought it could have been a bigger gesture. She didn't think it was enough. She had given him the best years of her life, after all," Morgan said, smiling. "So, yes, she had a caustic comeback which I did not convey to Mickey. But that was just Ava."

"Ava woke up one morning, and there he was, standing at the

foot of her bed, smiling," recalled Lucy Wellman. "She said they had a nice talk. He told her that the end of their marriage had actually caused him to take a good long look at himself and that it had made him a better person. She said, 'Oh, Francis, you are so full of shit.' They had a good laugh."

It was while she was at St. John's Hospital that Ava suffered a stroke.

"After the stroke, I had a difficult time staying in touch with Ava on the phone," said Wellman. "I went to visit her maybe six months before she died. I noticed she kept a framed photo of herself and Frank kissing, on a table next to her bed. There were no other reminders of her former life in Hollywood, not a single memento, except for that picture. She was lonely; she longed for the past."

Mickey Rudin telephoned Frank, who was in New York at the time, to give him the bad news about Ava's death. The two weren't even speaking at this time, so for Mickey to make this gesture meant a lot to Frank. A member of his staff recalled, "The tears just kept coming. He just kept saying over and over, to no one in particular, 'I should have gone to see her. I should have been there for her.'"

"When I visited her before her death," recalled Lucy Wellman, "Ava said to me, 'I feel like it was just yesterday when I was giving Francis hell. Goddamn it, I really loved him, didn't I? Where did the time go?' she asked me. Then her eyes misted over and she said, 'I don't know why, but I just always thought we would have more... *time*.'"

Sammy—Rest in Peace

*F*rank Sinatra faced many challenges in the last decade of his life. He still had the ambition and drive of a younger man, but the reality was that by January 1990 he was seventy-four. Still, he refused to slow down. He was able to work; in fact, his touring schedule between 1991 and the end of 1994 was astonishing. He entertained practically every week, traveling, performing, singing for enthusiastic audiences around the world—and certainly not because he needed the money. (In 1991, *Forbes* listed his worth at $26 million, although that seems low.) The schedule couldn't have been easy for a man his age. However, for Frank it was easier than dying. It was as if he were running from death, city to city, country to country. "If I stop working," he told associates, "I know I'll be next."

The adulation and appreciation demonstrated by his audiences was like a tonic to Frank. The need for love, or perhaps vindication, now seemed to be Sinatra's guiding force. He knew he was one of the lucky ones. Dean was not well. Ava was gone. And the simple luck of the draw would make it Sammy's turn to next cash in his chips.

Sammy Davis Jr. had been having trouble with his voice throughout 1989, and during a summer tour in Europe he began experiencing pain. When he got home, he went to see his doctor. The news was bad. Throat cancer.

None of his friends wanted to accept the fact that Sammy was gravely ill, least of all Frank. It was possible to remove the tumor surgically, but that would prevent Sammy from ever singing again. He said he would rather die than not be able to sing. He chose radiation—a slow, agonizing death.

Sammy lost his eight-month-long battle with cancer on May 16, 1990, at the age of just sixty-four. His death was almost more than Frank could bear, coming so soon after Ava's. They had been such integral parts of each other's lives for more than forty years, they thought of themselves as brothers. Frank sat in the front row at the church, next to Barbara and Dean.

"It's terrible when the people closest to you start dropping," Frank told his longtime friend Joey D'Orazio. D'Orazio had come to California to visit Frank after Ava's and Sammy's deaths. The two were sitting at Matteo's bar with Jilly. "I'm tired," Frank told Joey. "This is taking the piss out of me. I'm seventy-five. Christ." Joey, who had just turned sixty-five, told Frank he had to persevere and just take things one day at a time. Jilly, who was seventy-three, agreed. "What else can we do?" he said, throwing back a scotch. "We're old men," he exclaimed. "What the hell happened? My biggest fear at this point is, tomorrow, I don't wanna wake up dead!"

"Me neither," Frank agreed.

The three men stared silently straight ahead for a long time.

"But we sure had some good times," Frank finally said, with a smile. "Remember the Palm Springs airport?" he asked. Jilly and Joey laughed. Back in the 1950s, the airport in Palm Springs didn't have a lit runway. So when Frank and Jimmy Van Heusen would land there in Jimmy's little two-seated puddle-jumper, Jilly would park at the end of the runway in his car and flash the lights on and off to guide them in. It's a wonder they never crashed! Now, almost forty years later, the memory of their youthful recklessness cheered them.

"Well, pallies, see, this is what happens if you don't die," Frank finally offered. "Your friends drop dead. Your body starts falling apart. You can't see. You can't hear. You can't piss. You can't screw." Then he raised a glass. "But you still got your memories, right?"

"That is, if you still got all your marbles," Jilly added, clinking Frank's glass.

"I gotta get back to Barbara," Frank suddenly exclaimed, looking at his watch.

"She's gonna give you hell for being out this late at night," Joey told him.

"I know," Frank agreed with a loopy grin. "Something to look forward to."

Dinner with the Sinatras

I'm not who people think I am," Frank Sinatra was telling his head butler, James Wright. "People see me onstage, they have this image of me. It's all bullshit."

"People think you're... how do they put it?" Wright asked in his clipped British accent. "*Cool.* Isn't that correct, sir?"

"Yeah, well, maybe it was thirty years ago," Frank said with a nostalgic smile.

James Wright had been hired by Frank in 1989, replacing Bill Stapely. At this time—the spring of 1990—Wright and Vine Joubert*

---

* Frank was very generous to Vine Joubert, who was at his beck and call twenty-four hours a day. Not only did he buy a house for her in Palm Springs, but he put her kids through college. For Christmas every year, he would give her at least $10,000.

were the only two employees of the Sinatras who actually lived in their home with them. Wright was helping Frank get dressed, handing him his perfectly tailored black jacket, then tying his gray tie for him.

The two were in Sinatra's bedroom, which was very plainly furnished. The carpet was burnt orange, his favorite color. There was one cushioned chair, a queen-sized bed, two antique nightstands, a big-screen TV, and two large closets. On the bureau were silver-framed photographs of Dolly, Barbara, and his children. By day, the room was darkened by blackout drapes, a heavy material so that no light would get through. At night, just a couple of soft lights glowed. A stereo sat in the corner, but no music was ever played in this space, especially not Sinatra records. Frank's bedroom and Barbara's were separated by an adjoining bathroom, which Frank used. On the other side of Barbara's room was her own private bath.

Tonight the Sinatras were expecting company for a dinner party. "You still look good, Mr. Sinatra," James Wright said, taking him in from head to toe.

Frank regarded himself critically in the mirror. "I look like an old man," he said. "Actually, come to think of it, I look like my father," he added, studying his reflection more carefully. He said he'd been thinking about Marty quite a bit lately. He was just four years younger than Marty was when he died. He said that during stormy times when his wife and daughters were at each other's throats, he sat back and wondered how Marty would handle things. "And I know what he would do," Frank said. "He'd let them crazy broads fight it out among themselves, that's what he'd do. He'd stay the fuck out of it," Frank concluded as he adjusted his toupee.

Frank usually didn't wear the toupee at home, but tonight Barbara thought it would be a good idea. "How's this thing look?" he asked James Wright, pointing to the hairpiece.

"Perfectly natural," Wright said approvingly.

"Goddamn, I hate this thing," Frank said of the toupee. Tonight—at home with friends—he didn't want to wear it at all. However, Barbara had asked him to, and he wanted to make her happy. "She don't got a lot of friends, know what I mean?" Frank joked.

Frank sat down on the bed, and James knelt before him and put his shoes on for him. He tied the laces. Then he gave them a quick shine. Frank stood back up and winced, his back hurting him. "It ain't easy being Frank Sinatra," he said, rubbing his hip. He went to the dresser and found a bottle of prescription medicine. He opened it and popped two in his mouth, swallowing them without water. "Okay, let's get this thing over with."

The Sinatra home in Palm Springs, for all its iridescent desert light and ornate furnishings, could sometimes be a sad, maudlin place. It's no wonder Frank liked to get away from it and be on the road as much as possible. He simply had more of a *life* on the road.

A typical day at home would begin with Frank rising at about 2:30 p.m. By that time, Barbara had already eaten breakfast and lunch and was off enjoying her day with her personal secretary, LaDonna Webb-Keaton. Meanwhile, Frank would venture forth from his bedroom and slowly start the day. He wouldn't get dressed right away, and if he had no specific plans for the day, he wouldn't get dressed at all, choosing to stay in his pajamas.

He would have breakfast in the living room in his pajamas and robe. He always started with half a grapefruit, then pancakes, sometimes scrambled eggs or French toast, sometimes fried eggs, always with bacon. He liked to have his two Cavalier King Charles spaniels sitting with him in the kitchen for breakfast. Afterward, he would go outside on the patio and throw a ball around and play fetch with the dogs. He would then spend the bulk of his afternoon lounging by the pool, reading newspapers or speaking on the telephone with friends. James Wright would make him a grilled cheese sandwich for lunch pretty much every day. In the early evening, he would watch the television game show *Jeopardy!* and then *Wheel of Fortune*. He never missed either program. At eight o'clock, dinner was served. Afterward, Barbara would go to her room, watch television, and then retire for the evening. Meanwhile, Frank would go to his art studio and stay there until four or five in the morning, painting in watercolors, which he'd enjoyed for quite some time.

The household only came to life when the Sinatras formally entertained, which was at least once a month. For dinner parties, the couple would hire additional help to cook and otherwise prepare the home.

The guest list—sometimes as many as forty—would usually read like a who's who of show business. Tonight, eighteen friends would be present, including Steve Lawrence and Eydie Gormé; Gregory Peck and his wife, Veronique Passani; and Merv Griffin and his companion, Eva Gabor. Even though Frank and Eva had a bit of a romantic history, it didn't seem to matter to Barbara. She wasn't threatened by her. Frank's first wife was never present for these parties; Tina and Nancy Sinatra Jr. were also rarely on the guest list. Right now, of course, the Sinatra daughters were in the midst of their household boycott. Frank Jr. was often invited; he had no real beef with Barbara, and he was present this evening.

The Sinatras' Palm Springs dining room was decorated in an Oriental motif that night, with three large round tables in the middle of the room. Six people would be seated at each table.

"The one thing I am particular about are my tables," Barbara told Vine before the party. "I like the guests to be surprised by the tables." Vine set drinking glasses, plates, knives, and forks in the right placement on the table, as well as candles and flowers—an arrangement of fresh roses perfectly centered on each table, all important details to Barbara. After everything was set with precision, Barbara went to each table and made subtle adjustments to the centerpieces. "Beautiful," she finally announced, smiling. "Just lovely."

Tonight, as with every dinner party, the guests would not see the dining room until the moment of grand presentation. After everyone had a chance to mingle over drinks and appetizers served by the waitstaff, James Wright, dressed in black trousers, white shirt, black tie, and black jacket, his normal uniform, and another identically dressed employee walked to the double doors.

"Dinner is served, madam," the butler intoned.

"Thank you, James," Barbara said, sounding equally official.

Then Wright and the other functionary opened the doors with a great flourish. As the guests filed in and saw the beautiful tables and settings, they smiled and oohed and ahhed to one another. "Always a class act," Steve Lawrence said to Barbara. She smiled.

As everyone found the setting with his place card, each person stood behind his chair, no one sitting down. Having been at the Sinatra home many times, the guests well knew the protocol. James

Wright stood behind Barbara's chair and pulled it out for her. She sat down and straightened her back, adopting her usual posture, which was contained and regal. Then he and his fellow employee went to each woman and pulled her chair away from the table. After each was seated, all of the men sat down en masse. The food served tonight wasn't as ostentatious as the environment might suggest: pasta, chicken, potatoes, broccoli, and pork.

After dinner, the guests rose from their tables and mingled for about a half hour in the living room. As the cocktails flowed, there was much laughter; everyone was having fun. The ladies then retired to the kitchen to enjoy coffee and desserts while the men proceeded to Frank's den for cigarettes and shots of Jack Daniel's. As Frank and his son, Frank Jr., spent time discussing sheet music with Steve Lawrence, Merv Griffin and Gregory Peck and some of the other male guests, such as Jilly Rizzo, sat talking quietly. Meanwhile, soft music played in the background, piped in through the entire household. However, it was Muzak—no popular vocalists.

There was only one "scene." Someone put a Kool cigarette on the bar in an ashtray and Barbara took a quick puff just as Frank happened to walk through the kitchen—unfortunate timing for her. "Put that down," he ordered her. "You know I don't want you to smoke." Of course, Frank was a chain-smoker, but that wasn't the issue. Barbara knew how he felt about her smoking; he had asked her to stop, and she had done so, for the most part, anyway. (Eventually she would give up the habit with the aid of hypnosis.) "I'm sorry, Frank," she said dutifully rather than cause a scene in front of friends. She then quickly snuffed out the cigarette in an ashtray. As Frank exited the kitchen, he seemed wobbly on his feet and a little disoriented. Eva Gabor and Eydie Gormé shared a secret look.

After about an hour, Barbara made another announcement, first to the men and then the women. "The movie is about to be shown," she gaily declared. A day prior to the festivities, her secretary had a movie reel brought in from a Hollywood film studio, a first-run feature. The entire party noisily adjourned to the home's theater.

Frank would never go into the theater with the other guests; rather, he preferred either to go to his art studio and paint or to his "train room." Tonight he chose the latter, the only difference being that he brought Steve Lawrence and Frank Jr. with him and asked James Wright to stay in case they needed anything.

Frank had always been fascinated by toy trains. "At Christmas, when I was a kid, I'd leave Hoboken and take a four-cent ferry ride and a five-cent train and head for the New York stores," he said. "I'd stand and look at the train displays for three to four hours. I wanted a train set so badly. One day, my mother pawned her fox fur piece to buy my first train set, a wind-up engine and oval track. I was old enough [age eleven] to understand the sacrifice she made."

Frank had an elaborate wood-paneled room built in his Palm Springs estate to house his enormous train collection. There were 250 expensive model train cars on an eighteen-by-thirty-foot train platform. The layout was based on the same Lionel train showrooms Frank used to visit as a youngster in New York. Along the track was a model of his Hoboken neighborhood, an Old West town, a New Orleans riverboat, and a billboard announcing a sold-out Sinatra concert. No kids' toys, these were expensive models; a locomotive bore his initials (FAS) in diamonds. He also had a crystal replica of the 1025 Chattanooga Choo Choo.

As Barbara and the other guests watched the film, Frank, Steve, and Frank Jr. smoked Camels while cleaning the tracks, oiling the engines, changing the cars, and admiring the trains—three sets this evening—as they moved along the tracks. Usually this was a hobby Frank did alone while others were in the theater. A kid all over again, he'd actually put on a bright red engineer's hat with a visor and even blow a whistle while the trains chugged along the tracks. Very often the guests would leave after the film without even having the opportunity to say goodbye to him. But tonight was different.

Anytime Frank had the opportunity for one-on-one time with Steve Lawrence, he took it. With Sammy gone and Dean no longer really in his life, Frank took Steve under his wing. A gifted vocalist in the tradition of Sinatra, Steve, who was fifty-four, and his wife, Eydie, sixty-two, had just agreed to go on the road with Frank on what would be called the "Diamond Jubilee World Tour," in honor of Frank's seventy-fifth birthday. It would be more than forty dates around the world and take almost a full year out of their lives, starting in New Jersey at the end of the year before circling the globe and then ending in New York in November 1991. It was difficult to imagine that Frank would be able to survive such a schedule, but he was determined.

Father-and-Son Detente

*T*he fact that Frank Sinatra Jr., who was now forty-six, was going to conduct the thirty-one-piece orchestra on his father's upcoming tour was an added plus, not only for the fans but also for father and son. It would be an opportunity for them to work together, and both were excited.

A couple of years earlier, Frank Jr. had been in Atlantic City getting ready to walk out onto the stage when he got the call from his father. "I want you to conduct my band," Frank told him. "Well, after my friends revived me with smelling salts," Frank Jr. liked to joke, "I said to him, 'You can't be serious!'" Sinatra was indeed serious. When Frank Jr. asked him why he wanted him, Frank said, "Because maybe a singer can understand what another singer is trying to do." What a great compliment.

Of course, as we have seen, father and son had a difficult relationship. "He has been a good father as much as it was within his power," Frank Jr. would say of his dad. Whereas Frank's relationships with his daughters changed dramatically after he married Barbara, the one with Frankie had pretty much stayed the same: just fair. It actually got slightly worse after the controversy over adopting Bobby Marx. However, that Frank Jr. did not take issue with Barbara was appreciated by Frank. Junior loved his sisters, but he did not side with them in their disagreements with Barbara. He maintained that his father knew what he was doing when he married Barbara, that none of it was his business—and that if his father needed his input he would ask for it.

As Frank grew older—and with his daughters now boycotting the Sinatra household—more than ever, he needed his son. He knew he hadn't been the best of fathers, and the gesture of entrusting Frank

Jr. with the critical job of conducting his orchestra was his way of making it up to him. He realized his son loved music more than anything—like father, like son in that respect—and that he would always treasure the moments they would have together on the road.

The timing was right; Frank just happened to be ready to enter his father's world. It was as if somewhere along the line he had decided that in order to accept his father he first had to reject him. As he got older he seemed to have a deeper understanding of his dad and had decided to finally reconcile his relationship with him.

The senior Sinatra actually had a lot more respect for him than Frank Jr. ever knew. "He has endured," Frank would say of his kid. "Through all the shit I threw at him, he has endured. He's like me that way. I think to myself, 'If my old man had been as much a shit to me as I have been to my kid, I don't know if I would have endured the same way'—and my old man was a real shit!"

The Diamond Jubilee World Tour starring Frank Sinatra with Steve Lawrence and Eydie Gormé kicked off on December 11, 1990, at the Meadowlands Arena in East Rutherford, New Jersey. As the tour wore along, the performances became more and more difficult for Frank. His memory fading, on some nights he couldn't even remember Eydie's last name. There were other nights when he couldn't remember her first.

Most Sinatra intimates agree that Frank would not have been performing at all at the end of the 1980s and into the 1990s if not for Frank Jr., who compensated for many of his father's vocal shortcomings by adeptly rearranging certain orchestrations to make the singing of them much easier. It was hard work. "It was very hard. To be his conductor was like walking on a tightrope from the top of one eighty-story building to the top of another eighty-story building. I felt some footprints on my posterior on several occasions." Indeed, the old man could be tough on Junior, but would anyone expect less? He knew he could count on him, and that's what mattered.

"Pop, there's a woman down front who's hot for you," Frank Jr. told him one night before the show.

"No kiddin'?" Frank asked. "How do you know?"

"Because she said she's gonna give you the Tom Jones treatment."

"What's that?"

"You know, the way women throw their panties at Tom, and their brassieres?" Frank Jr. explained.

"What? She's gonna do that to me?" Frank asked, wide-eyed.

"Well, she mentioned that it might be a little more age-appropriate," Frank Jr. said with a wink. "I think she said she's gonna throw a pair of support hose at you, and maybe her hearing aid too."

Father and son shared a good laugh; these were the good times they'd always needed. "That's when our relationship became really strong, during those years," Frank Jr. recalled. "It meant an awful lot to me. You know, as a boy you need your father, and that's a fact of life. But now he needed me. And that's what made it so endearing."

Indeed, Frank Jr. offered moral support when his fatigued father most needed it. He remembered, "I'd say to him, 'Listen, champ, you're too old an athlete to give up now.' Those are the exact words I said. 'You must not give up until the time comes that deep down inside yourself you know it's right. Until that time, do not be influenced by external forces; you're too old to quit. Now get in there and fight.' At night, when he'd be onstage and he'd get tired, I'd give him this," Frank Jr. said, showing a clenched fist. "*Now get in there and fight.*"

Frank Jr. was there for his father when, as one friend put it, "the chips weren't just down, they almost didn't exist." In conducting the large orchestra for the Diamond Jubilee World Tour, Frankie would attempt to focus on his massive job with the music charts and the musicians as much as possible. However, on some nights he looked visibly concerned about his dad's shaky performance, especially as Frank's troubled, smoky voice would lose power in the middle of a simple song like "Strangers in the Night."

"It's as if the kid is hoping the old man doesn't just keel over in the middle of 'My Way,' " noted one cynical critic.

"I would see him very up, then very down, and sometimes very sad," Frank Jr. would recall in 2012. "It often came to it that I simply held him, just held on to him and told him I was here for him. I owed him that."

Considered by many of his friends to be a loner, Frank Jr. would marry Cynthia McMurry in 1998 and divorce two years later. He had one son from a previous relationship, Michael, born on March 1,

1987. Other women have claimed to have had illegitimate children by Frank Jr., but McMurry's is the only child he and the family recognize as a true Sinatra. "He is twenty-five now, almost twenty-six," Frank would say in 2012 of his son. "He lives in Japan, a college professor. He gets back to the United States probably once a year and I make damn well sure that we stay in contact. Whenever he does visit, we go to dinner, just the two of us. I want him to have what I didn't."

For the last seven or so years of his father's life, Frank Sinatra Jr. had only one concern: to see to it that his father kept performing to the best of his ability. "Those seven years went by so fast, it felt like seven days," he said. "Seven of the best days of my life."

A Sad Ending for Jilly

The Diamond Jubilee World Tour had not been easy for Frank Sinatra. Among other problems, the four teleprompters at the edge of the stage, which scrolled the lyrics to all of his songs, had become more difficult for him to read because of cataracts in both his eyes. Without the teleprompters, however, he simply couldn't remember the lyrics. This memory loss was becoming concerning not only for Frank but also for his fans, who felt enormous sympathy for him. When he returned home to Palm Springs for a few days between dates, the issue of memory was even more pronounced. "At about midnight, I would go into the kitchen, and there he would be," remembered James Wright. "And I'd say, 'Can I help you, Mr. Sinatra?' And he'd be standing there in a fog and would answer, 'You know what? I don't even remember what I came in here for.' It was for the jar of pickled pigs' feet, of course, which he would eat every night. 'Make me a grilled cheese sandwich, will ya?' he'd then ask, and I would comply."

Still, once back on the road, Frank went on like a trouper and generated hysteria at each stop along the way. Sometimes he was brilliant onstage, sometimes not. But it was clear from the way he performed the songs that they still moved him. Through them—those "wonderful, wonderful songs," as he called them—he manifested not only a sensitivity that he had never been able to fully express in his personal life but also a continuing sense of identity and dignity at a time when many of his older friends were beginning to lose theirs.

Obviously seasoned professionals in their own right, Steve and Eydie could always rise to the occasion and handle any misstep that might occur. They were always concerned for Frank's dignity, and if they noticed that he was drifting, they would gently take him by the arms and move him with them, gracefully bringing him back to alertness. If he forgot his lyrics, they would softly sing them from behind, jogging his memory, filling in the lost stanzas, urging him on. Certainly he never had truer friends.

Sinatra valued his friends more than ever at this time in his life, which was why the death of his best friend was one of the greatest tragedies that could have befallen him. It happened on May 6, 1992, when Jilly Rizzo was killed in an automobile accident on the night of his seventy-fifth birthday.

Jilly's friend Jim Whiting remembers, "He was about to turn seventy-five. He wasn't even in his own car. He was in a white Jag XJ that belonged to his girlfriend, Betty Jean. He was hit by a drunk driver, and the car just exploded into flames. He couldn't get out. The doors were automatically locked. It was a horrible way to go."

Frank's very good friend and road manager, Tony Oppedisano, broke the news to Barbara. Then she and Tony told Frank. He sank to his knees in despair. He was so devastated, he locked himself in his room and stayed there for days.

"This was the toughest time for my father," Frank Jr. would recall. "To have your best and closest friend die in that way? It was so devastating."

As difficult as it was for him, Frank still went to Jilly's funeral at the St. Louis Church in Cathedral City, California. He was a pall-bearer. His face was ashen and haggard; he seemed almost stricken as he and the other pallbearers carried the mahogany casket. Betty Jean Kelly, Jilly Rizzo's girlfriend, recalled, "It broke my heart to see how much Frank was suffering. He and Jilly adored each other. There was such a look of agony in Frank's eyes, it was hard to bear."

Prodigal Daughters

*I*t had been a couple of years since Nancy and Tina Sinatra decided to stop visiting Frank and Barbara at their home. Though they stayed in touch by phone and continued seeing Frank when he was on the road without Barbara, their hearts ached knowing they couldn't see him whenever they wanted to because of their own decision. "It was killing them, actually," said one friend of the Sinatra daughters. "It was bad on Tina, but I think it was really hard on Nancy. Nancy had such a close relationship with Frank, it was as if she could feel his pain over the separation. After the deaths of Ava, Sammy, and Jilly, both women just felt life was too short to not relish every single second they could with their father. So they decided to try again to be a part of his life. Frank Jr. told them he thought it was for the best."

In their absence, a number of legal maneuverings had taken place that favored Barbara. The daughters tried to keep abreast of what was happening, but it was getting more difficult to keep track with Mickey Rudin now gone. Barbara had her own team—Arthur Crowley as her lawyer, Marshall Gelfand as her business manager, and others. She was organized and strong. Barbara's team even sought to stop Frank from paying Nancy Sr. alimony—which he had been doing the last forty years—from their community funds. Not only that, but they wanted the funds to be reimbursed for past payments!

Of course, the Sinatras had their own army of attorneys and business managers—including the savvy Eliot Weisman, who had replaced Rudin. But it seemed as if there was always a battle to be won, with poor, aging Frank Sinatra caught right in the middle of it all.

Frank was happy to have his daughters back, of course. But according to those who knew him best, he couldn't help but feel that a sacred trust had been broken by their boycott. How could he be sure it wouldn't happen again? From this point onward, he would reserve a little bit of his heart where his family members were concerned... just in case.

Tina's Miniseries

*I*n November 1992, CBS-TV aired a television miniseries based on Frank Sinatra's life entitled *Sinatra*. With his blessing, Tina, now forty-four, was executive producer.

After Kitty Kelley's 1986 biography received so much attention, Frank had wanted to write an autobiography to "set the record straight." Tina explained, "Though he knew he could fill volumes, he said, 'The biggest part of my life would be missing. My music. My songs. You couldn't hear my songs in a book.'" It was decided to produce a miniseries, which would be seven years (and three different writers) in the making.

The four-hour-long program spanned the years 1920–74, ending with Frank's return to the stage at Madison Square Garden after his "retirement." Originally the script was for a ten-hour-long miniseries. Certainly it would have had to be at least that long to do Frank's life complete justice. As it was, at four hours, it had its superficial moments, with a few sketchily drawn characters. However, it was a very good show, and the performances were first-rate, particularly Philip Casnoff's emotionally involving portrayal of Sinatra.

Much to the surprise of many critics, the miniseries didn't avoid the various controversies in Frank's life. The script even admitted to Dolly's "illegal operations" (as they were referenced in the network's press kit). In one powerful scene, Dolly (portrayed by Olympia Dukakis) and Frank (Casnoff) argue about her tarnished reputation in Hoboken after her first arrest. Sinatra's relationship with Sam Giancana (played by Rod Steiger) was also portrayed in the miniseries, as was his friendship with other gangsters. His volatile affair with Ava (Marcia Gay Harden) also received considerable attention. Tina's miniseries, the most expensive miniseries to date at $18.5 million, was definitely the truth about his life; certainly not *all* of the truth, but as much of it as she could squeeze into four hours.

Frank was scheduled to visit the set once the production was up and running, and Tina, the actors, and crew were very excited. Tina couldn't wait to show her dad off to the cast and crew, and to share with him stories about the production so far. She also desperately wanted to impress her father. But at the last minute, Frank decided not to visit the set, saying he wasn't feeling well. Tina was crushed.

He knew, of course, that his appearance on the set was vitally important to her. The truth, though, was that he was just too nervous to go through with it. He felt that expectations of him were just too high. Could he live up to them? After all, his whole life had been on display for this cast and crew for months. They knew about the suicide attempt, for instance, when Manie Sacks saved him at the last possible moment. It was in the script. They knew about his vulnerable passion for Ava and about at least one of her abortions. They knew about his battles with the media over his mob ties. All of it was in the script. Now he was expected to be the physical embodiment of all of this legend, and it was just too heavy a load for him to shoulder at this time in his life. No longer the cocky guy of his youth, the aging Sinatra was more and more riddled with insecurities about the way he was perceived by his adoring public. He knew he had changed—he was older, more feeble, less invincible—but he also knew the public still viewed him the same way: as an icon.

When Frank confessed his fears to Barbara, she told him, quite simply, that he shouldn't have to do anything he truly didn't want to do, not at this stage of his life, anyway. "You have been keeping commitments for fifty years," she said. "Now is the time to start begging off." She also told him to be very open to Tina about his reasons, because she didn't want Tina blaming her for the decision. Of course, Frank didn't do that, he just said he was not well and that was the end of it. The date wasn't even rescheduled. Tina did her best to get over it and move on, but she was deeply hurt.

In the fall, with the miniseries done, CBS was determined to give it the launch it deserved. The network intended to host a splashy reception at the Rainbow Room for the cast, crew, and press. Afterward, the plan was for everyone to then attend a concert by Frank Sinatra and Shirley MacLaine at Radio City Music Hall. It promised to be a grand event, befitting the premiere of a miniseries about an American legend, produced by his own daughter.

On the day of the concert, Tina got an urgent call from Eliot Weisman. Frank wasn't well. Tina didn't know it at the time but, again, her father was filled with anxiety. The idea of the miniseries had become such a hot-button issue for him, just the mere thought of it made him apprehensive. Yes, of course, he had authorized the project. Now he just wanted the entire business to go away.

Tina raced to his apartment at the Waldorf, and, sure enough, there he was in bed, feigning illness. "You're not performing tonight?" she asked, fearful of the answer. No, he wasn't. It was devastating. It felt to Tina as if Frank didn't care enough about her to overcome his anxiety and support her hard work. Then, with either the worst timing ever (or maybe the most deliberate?), Barbara came into the bedroom and offered a small box to Tina. "This is for you from your dad," she explained. "It's for all the hard work you did on the show." When Tina opened the box, she found a gold cigarette lighter from Cartier. It looked like something Frank might have given an employee for a few years of dedicated service. Of course, it wasn't the value of the gift that hurt Tina; it was that it seemed so dismissive of the work she'd put into her labor of love for her dad.

When it was broadcast, the Sinatra miniseries was not only a ratings success, but it also garnered many Emmy nominations and eventually won a Golden Globe for best miniseries. Tina, always the pragmatist, felt, when she finally saw the completed product, that it could have been even better, but on the whole she was very happy with it. The professional achievement—her biggest to date—was all well and good, but what really mattered to her was Frank's approval of it.

Tina sent a tape of the show to the Palm Springs compound for Frank to watch. A few days later, she called to see how he liked it. Barbara answered the telephone; she made it clear that she didn't much care for the miniseries. Who knows, but maybe she resented the fact that she wasn't portrayed in it? The time line ended in the early 1970s before Frank met her, which, if one considered the dramatic possibilities given that the program was produced by Tina, was probably in Barbara's best interest. When Frank came on the line, he seemed blasé and uninterested. Was his medication off? Was he just not feeling well? Or did he really not care?

According to someone in the Sinatra household with knowledge of the situation, Frank actually did begin watching the miniseries, with

Barbara at his side. He knew it would be difficult, but he wanted to do his best to get through it for Tina. By the time the program began to depict Marilyn Maxwell wearing the bracelet Nancy thought had been intended for her, he knew where the plot line was headed—after all, he had lived it. How could he now watch it all unfold on television as entertainment? For him, this was gut-wrenching stuff. "I can't do it," he told Barbara. "I'm sorry, but this is just too much for me." She understood. She got up and turned off the television.

Frank's Secret Daughter?

The Sinatra miniseries may have ended up being more trouble than it was worth for the family. It was while watching the program on television that Julie Lyma in California began to suspect that her mother, Dorothy Bonucelli, might have had an affair with Frank—and that she, Julie, might actually be Frank's daughter.

In fact, Dorothy did have a long romance with Frank. She was the woman known by the stage name Alora Gooding, with whom Frank was romantically involved for a time. Dorothy's daughter, Julie, started putting the pieces of her life together after watching Tina's miniseries, even though the affair was not depicted. However, a scene in which Alora Gooding was portrayed as swooning over Frank on the set of *Las Vegas Nights* started her thinking.

The day after the broadcast, Julie telephoned Dorothy—from whom she had been long estranged—to ask if in fact Frank Sinatra was her biological father. Her mother confirmed it, almost fifty years after the fact. Dorothy said she had her reasons for keeping the secret. She explained that Frank's press agent, George Evans, had threatened her with the morals clause of her contract—which he was wont to do to Frank's girls at that time. Also, he promised to represent her if she kept her mouth shut about the pregnancy. She says she decided at that time not to tell anyone. She says that even Frank didn't know she was pregnant.

Dorothy had the baby on February 10, 1943, and claimed that the father was her husband, a traveling salesman named Tom Lyma. However, her career foundered, and when George Evans dropped her as a client, she plunged into a spiral of alcohol abuse. She became moody and unhappy, and according to Julie was abusive to her. In the end, Dorothy lived a difficult, tragic life.

When Julie learned the truth, she contacted the Sinatras with her revelation.

"Tina Sinatra fired the first shot with a 'cease and desist' order, essentially telling me to buzz off," Julie recalled. This seems understandable. One can only imagine what went through Tina's mind when a woman claiming to be Frank's illegitimate child suddenly surfaced, given all of the Sturm und Drang of recent times. She wasn't eager to welcome a stranger into the fold, someone who had no idea what it truly meant to be a Sinatra daughter, especially after what they had gone through with Bobby Marx's possible adoption. Moreover, how could she even be sure Julie wasn't a fraud? "That left me with no other option," Julie said, "but to go to court."

A lengthy and very contentious legal battle would ensue after Frank's eventual death. Though the Sinatras steadfastly refused to allow any DNA testing, there must have been enough evidence to convince them that Julie was telling the truth, because they agreed that Julie had the legal right to use the name Julie Sinatra, and they also provided her with a six-figure settlement.

Today, Julie Sinatra believes that Frank Sinatra never knew he was her father.

Duets

In 1993, Frank Sinatra would find himself back on top of the charts with his first studio album in ten years, *Duets*. With Phil Ramone producing and Hank Cattaneo coproducing, thirteen of Sinatra's better-known songs were recorded as duets with popular singers of the day. The repertoire included "I've Got the World on a String" (with Liza Minnelli), "New York, New York" (with Tony Bennett), "Witchcraft" (with Anita Baker), and "I've Got a Crush on You" (with Barbra Streisand).

"There were a lot of people who didn't believe it could be done and that he would change his mind or walk away from it," said producer

Phil Ramone. "I mean, right until the minute before he actually sang, he said to me, 'This better work.' And I said, 'It's gonna work.' And he said 'It'd *better* work.' I thought to myself, 'Oh, okay. I got it. The pressure's here. We'd better make it work.'"

During the sessions at Capitol in Hollywood, Sinatra sounded surprisingly strong and compelling for a man his age. As one music journalist asked, "Is Sinatra half the singer he was in 1942 or 1956? Actually, he's about three-fifths the singer he was—but that still makes him about twice the singer anyone else is."

Although the album appealed to a wide audience—and as a result of its success, some of Sinatra's most enthusiastic supporters were now under thirty—longtime Sinatra aficionados were divided in their opinions of the *Duets* recording. Was this really a Frank Sinatra album? Or was this just studio wizardry? One might have been able to overlook the fact that Frank was never in the studio with any of his duet partners had it not been so well publicized that the singers never had any real contact with him. Either they recorded their parts later in the same studio or actually phoned in their parts using a digital system that had been developed by George Lucas's Skywalker Sound. This fact did not enhance the listening experience for many fans and critics. For instance, it sounded odd to hear artists like Aretha Franklin and Barbra Streisand mention Frank's name in the middle of their songs ("What Now My Love" and "I've Got a Crush on You," respectively), knowing that they were standing alone at a microphone in a darkened recording studio just listening to his vocal stylings on their headphones.

However it was constructed, though, the album was still a big success, selling millions of copies and soaring to the number one spot on the *Billboard* chart. It was Sinatra's most successful album *ever*. Teaming Sinatra with more contemporary artists had been an inspired idea, because it gave the project a broad commercial appeal.

A follow-up album, *Duets II*, was issued a year later, using the same technology, with duets on songs such as "Embraceable You" (Lena Horne), "Where or When" (Steve Lawrence and Eydie Gormé), and "Luck Be a Lady" (Chrissie Hynde). For many, this was a much less engaging package than its predecessor. The only reason to purchase

Duets II was to hear the duet with Frank Jr. on "My Kind of Town." It's a great and memorable performance by the Sinatra men, especially if the listener is aware of their tortured history.

As with the first album, *Duets II* received generally favorable reviews and sold millions of copies.

One More for the Road

*I*n 1994, Frank Sinatra was awarded a Legend Award for Lifetime Achievement at the Grammy Awards presentation at Radio City Music Hall in New York City. Pop group U2's leader, Bono (who had appeared on the *Duets* album on "I've Got You Under My Skin" and in a video with Frank for the song), presented the award after introducing Frank.

As Frank appeared onstage to a standing ovation, he paused for a long moment, taking in the young faces looking back at him. He then spoke thoughtfully and introspectively about New Yorkers, his love for Barbara, the backstage booze, about not being asked to perform. In truth, he was rambling. But this was his special night; he was overwhelmed by his own strong emotions at being so honored. After about three minutes, someone—widely rumored to be Sinatra's press agent, Susan Reynolds—decided to pull the plug on him.

Pierre Cossette, executive producer of the broadcast, later said, "Sinatra's people were saying, 'Get him off, get him off now. He can't remember what he was going to say.'"

Thus, without warning, the band began to play and Frank was simply forced to stop speaking. Understandably, his PR woman was trying to protect his image. No one wanted him to appear old and confused. To the viewing audience, however, what happened was insulting and disrespectful.

Cut off in midsentence? Frank Sinatra?

There was a time in the not so distant past when no one—let alone someone on his own payroll—would have dared cut off "the Chairman of the Board." But according to a longtime associate, Frank was ready to retire after the Grammy incident. "He's too smart. He knew that he wasn't 100 percent that night. He knew that he couldn't do it anymore. He said, 'I'm gettin' out while the gettin' is good.'" He would call it quits when the tour ended.

Tina had already made the tough decision to stop going to her father's performances. She simply couldn't take it. She didn't want to hurt him, but watching him at half—sometimes a quarter—of his former glory was just too emotionally draining. It would take her days to get over each show.

A week after the Grammys, on March 6, a frightening moment occurred onstage. It happened when he was at the Mosque in Richmond, Virginia. Halfway through an uncertain delivery of "My Way," he began to feel dizzy. During the song, he turned to Frank Jr. to ask for a chair. Then he noticed a stool behind him and began to sit down. He touched the corner of the stool before slowly sinking to the floor, hitting the stage with a thud. The microphone fell from his hand and made a loud noise when it hit the floor. An audible gasp came from the stunned audience of thirty-seven hundred. His handlers were about to carry him out when he came to after maybe ten minutes. Someone brought out a wheelchair, and he got in it. As he was being wheeled offstage, Frank waved to the audience and blew them a kiss to let his fans know he was all right.

After a three-hour stay at the hospital, his doctors wanted to keep him for observation, but he vetoed that notion. Instead, he flew back to Palm Springs in a private plane. Doctors diagnosed that the collapse was probably the result of "overheating," and he may also have been slightly dehydrated after perspiring heavily throughout the performance. Barbara was upset with herself; she felt that she should have taken the initiative to go out on the road with him, just in case there was a problem.

In just a couple of weeks, though, Frank was back onstage. However, from this point on, nothing would ever be quite the same. There was an almost palpable sense of fear among the musicians onstage and his audiences that what had happened in Virginia might happen again, and with more serious consequences.

He had a great many more contracted dates, almost a year's worth, but after they were fulfilled, it would all be over.

"This may be the last time we will be together," Frank told an audience of more than five thousand at Radio City Music Hall in April 1994. Indeed, he would continue to perform throughout the rest of 1994, fulfilling commitments all the way up to his seventy-ninth birthday in December. Then, on Saturday, February 25, 1995, he gave what would turn out to be his final performance at Marriott's Desert Springs Resort and Spa for a private party of about twelve hundred on the last day of the Frank Sinatra Desert Classic golf tournament.

For five songs, Frank was young again. First, he did "I've Got the World on a String," "Fly Me to the Moon," and then "Where or When," which writer Jonathan Schwartz reported was "performed by a forty-five-year-old man. It is everything Sinatra wishes to convey. It is a ballad with tempo that gathers rhythmic steam and explodes at its conclusion. Its last long line, the 'where or when' is sustained to the last drop of the high E-flat, not repeated for lack of breath." Then "My Kind of Town"—his voice young and agile—and a standing ovation.

"You mean it's time to go home," Frank said, laughing, as the applause died down.

Ironically, the encore he chose was "The Best Is Yet to Come." His road manager, Tony Oppedisano, said, "It was a jubilant evening, reaching for notes and holding them. It was a phenomenal, phenomenal show. He was fantastic and made mincemeat out of the critics."

"When are you going to learn to swing?" Barbara jokingly asked him as they entered the limousine that whisked them from the Marriott back to the Palm Springs compound.

After that show, Sinatra was elated. That youthful part of him that had always wanted more, more, *more*, now wanted…even more. He felt that the audience's reaction to his performance was so enthusiastic and that he was in such excellent voice for a man his age that surely he had another couple of years left in him. "I ain't quittin'," he announced. "Just takin' some time off, that's all."

The Sinatra family humored him. Frank Jr. agreed that, following a short rest, he and the old man would go back out again "and kick some ass." However, everyone knew that this was not meant to be.

It was over.

Sinatra: Eighty Years—Her Way?

$\mathcal{M}$ay you live to be one hundred and the last voice you hear be mine," Frank Sinatra used to say at the end of some of his performances. On December 12, 1995, he turned eighty. He had finally reconciled himself to the fact that he would no longer be performing. "I'll never sing again in public," he told Larry King, "because those days are just gone. But I'm very, very happy."

About a month prior to his birthday, a television special was taped at the Shrine Auditorium to celebrate the event. Called *Sinatra: 80 Years My Way*, it had been Barbara Sinatra's and producer and longtime family friend George Schlatter's idea, the proceeds of which would go to AIDS Project Los Angeles and the Barbara Sinatra Children's Center. Frank wanted nothing to do with it. In fact, when he had attended a similar tribute to Sammy Davis, he was said to have told Eliot Weisman, "Don't you ever do this kind of bullshit tribute thing for me."

Barbara was determined that her husband should participate in the affair, even though what he really wanted was to go off with his pallies on his eightieth birthday and get drunk. Nancy, Tina, and Frank Jr. also wanted nothing to do with the show and refused to participate in it. According to Tina, Frank even telephoned her and instructed her to get him out of the commitment. She said she would try, but in the end she faced too much opposition.

A maid who worked in Sinatra's home from time to time remembered, "Mr. and Mrs. Sinatra had many arguments about the TV show. He didn't want to go; he thought it would be an embarrassment. During one battle about it, he took a plate and smashed it against a wall. He said, 'Goddamn it, Barbara. I'm not going. Come on! You know I hate this kind of thing. *You* go. *You* have a good time. Tell everyone I said, 'Thanks,' but I was too sick to show up.' Then he asked the cook to open a can of pork and beans for him."

The night before the taping, Barbara encouraged Frank to have dinner with Bruce Springsteen and Bob Dylan, who were scheduled to participate in the event; they came to the house and stayed about two hours. Barbara had reasoned that if Frank saw how excited younger entertainers would be in his presence, he would become enthused about the show. Steve and Eydie were also present for what had to have been a most interesting dinner party. It was a great success. Frank, Bruce, and Bob got wasted on Jack Daniel's. Frank had a wonderful time with his new friends. After a dessert of cheesecake with raspberries, the singers gathered around the piano and sang such songs as "All or Nothing at All" and "It Had to Be You" while Sinatra watched, amused and bleary-eyed. "What great guys," Frank said of Springsteen and Dylan. "We should have those two over more often."

Unfortunately, Frank's instincts about the television special *Sinatra: 80 Years My Way*, which aired on December 14, 1995, were astute. If not for Steve and Eydie, Vic Damone, and Tony Bennett, the evening would have been a total loss. At the end of the show, during the finale, Frank went up onto the stage from the audience to sing the last two notes of "Theme from New York, New York" with a disparate array of performers, some of them colleagues, others pop stars and rock and rollers.

Part Fourteen

AND NOW THE END IS NEAR . . .

Eightieth Birthday Family Showdown

Another family battle between the Sinatra daughters and their stepmother, Barbara, would be waged in mid-December 1995. It was then that Barbara agreed to a dinner at the Beverly Hills home television producer George Schlatter shared with his wife, Jolene, on Frank's birthday, December 12. The Schlatters would be present, as would the Kirk Douglases and the Gregory Pecks. Frank told Barbara that he didn't want to celebrate the birthday in a big way. So when the Schlatters extended the invitation to a small gathering, Barbara accepted.

The problem was that Nancy and Tina had expected the family to celebrate the milestone birthday with a quiet family dinner either at Frank and Barbara's home, at Nancy's home, or at a restaurant. It would be attended by the Sinatra daughters, Frank Jr., Nancy Sr., and Nancy's two daughters. (Tina has no children. Frank Jr. has a son.) In fact, Tina recalled that she and Barbara had agreed to this arrangement many months earlier in July, and that the only detail left to work out was the specific location. Therefore, when she found out that Barbara had accepted the Schlatters' invitation, Tina was quite upset.

Perhaps Barbara was disappointed in the Sinatra daughters for not being fully supportive of the birthday television broadcast and accepted the invitation as retaliation. However, there was also a disagreement at the time concerning the rerelease of certain Sinatra songs.

As it happened, Nancy and Tina were primarily responsible for decisions on the reissuing of their father's music on Columbia, Capitol, and Reprise. Sometimes they reluctantly agreed to allow previously unreleased material to be issued, but both were adamantly opposed to the release of alternate takes of Sinatra sessions. Earlier in 1995, Capitol released *Live in Concert*, a collection of performances by Frank of standards such as "My Way," and "New York, New York," which sold around three hundred thousand copies. The Sinatra children held the rights to the original recordings; their father had signed those over to them and had promised not to rerecord them. The siblings felt it was a conflict for Frank to then allow a release of their *live* versions—in which, ostensibly, they would not participate financially. (It probably didn't help that Frank dedicated the album to Barbara, "the love of my life.") Frank's offspring—though it's not clear that Frank Jr. was involved—discussed with their longtime lawyer, Robert Finkelstein, the notion of taking legal action not only against Capitol but against Frank, too. "It was in our best interest then, as always, to protect the catalog," Tina later confirmed. "Yes, it put Dad on notice; he was the artist who signed the agreements."

It's unlikely, given everything that was already going on at this time, that the Sinatra children would have actually litigated against their own father. Due to the situation of late, some speculated that perhaps they were actually targeting Barbara since she too would be profiting from royalties generated by these rerecordings. However, the fact that they even sought to put Frank "on notice" speaks volumes about the tension in the air.

As for the birthday celebration, Tina learned of Barbara's intentions from Frank's secretary, Dorothy Uhlemann. Dorothy said that Barbara told her that since she hadn't heard back from Tina or Nancy, she had accepted the Schlatters' invitation for December 12. The daughters were free, then, to celebrate with their father the next day. "So, they'll see you on the thirteenth," a very cheery Dorothy said, probably trying to get off the line as quickly as possible.

This didn't make sense. Besides the fact that Tina thought she and Barbara had an agreement, George and Jolene Schlatter were longtime friends of hers, Nancy's, and Frank Jr.'s. It made no sense that they would not include them on the guest list for any dinner celebrating Frank's eightieth—unless they were asked not to. The fact that attorney Eliot Weisman and his wife, Maria, were also invited just made things worse.

George and his elegant wife, the former actress Jolene Brand Schlatter, were very familiar with the way people trafficked in Sinatra's world, and they both knew it was best to stay out of the line of fire. They'd been married since the mid-1950s and had been friends of Frank's for decades. "First of all, you can't take sides when it comes to Frank," George Schlatter said in 1999. "There are a lot of people in his life, and all of them are not only vying for his attention but also to be in his favor. Sometimes people get shoved out of the way by accident, and sometimes not so accidentally. Oftentimes people crash into each other and force each other out of the picture, and Frank doesn't even know it's happened until it's too late. Other times he pushes them out himself, and that, of course, has been his prerogative. My philosophy has been to just be fair and loyal to Sinatra, and to then let everyone else find their own way. In other words, I stay out of it. Especially the family interaction, I stay out of."

At a loss as to how to proceed, a distraught Tina telephoned Frank and laid it on the line. She'd been trying very hard for a very long time, she told him, to navigate the rocky shores of his marriage, but "enough is enough." The fact that he would turn eighty and that she and her siblings and their mother would not be present to celebrate with him was more than she could bear. "I've had it, Dad," she said angrily. "This is it for me. I'm done. I'm serious. *I'm done.*" It was as if the last almost twenty years of family turmoil had finally worn her down, and she had nothing left to give to the fight.

"What do you mean you're not invited?" Frank asked. He seemed not to have a clue about any of it.

Tina told him that Barbara had made other plans and that other people had been invited, even their attorney Eliot Weisman and his wife—but not the Sinatra siblings. Frank said he would handle it. However, he sounded so detached, Tina knew from past experience that his efforts would amount to nothing but more disappointment. No, when she said she was done, she meant it. No telephone calls, no visits, nothing.

This birthday celebration was the catalyst for the reemergence of great sadness; it felt to Tina as if her childhood was playing itself out again with Barbara now cast in the Ava role. It was as if Barbara had finally been successful in taking her father from her, and she had to protect herself. She had to withdraw.

By the time Tina hung up the telephone, she was in tears, but also, to hear her tell it later, she felt a wave of relief wash over her. If she had learned anything from Frank, it was that no one was going to look out for her the way she must look out for herself. She was tired of being at the mercy of his marriage, and she wanted a "divorce." When she told Nancy about her startling decision, she spoke about it with renewed confidence. It was the right choice for her, and she knew it.

Though she knew Frank would be hurt by Tina's choice, Barbara wasn't going to do anything to change her mind. "To be honest with you," she told one very close friend of hers, "I don't have the strength to deal with Tina right now. I don't think she gets it," Barbara said, exasperated. When asked what she meant, she said, "Being Frank's rock? It takes everything out of you." She elaborated by saying she was so bone tired, the last thing she had time to do was to "deal with Frank's daughters and their hurt feelings about this, that, and every other little thing under the sun." She said she had to keep her priorities straight. On top of her list was Frank's health," she clarified, adding, "Every day, it's about his different medicines, his doctor's appointments, his many sadnesses, and my many worries. I'm sorry," she concluded, "but I don't have anything left to give to his daughters." Of course, it could be said that Barbara's legitimate concerns about Frank's medical condition don't seem sufficient grounds for her not inviting his daughters to such an important milestone birthday party. Was she really so blind to the turmoil such decisions would likely cause in the family? Or did she just not care?

For his part, Frank fairly quickly made peace with Tina's decision. This wasn't new terrain, after all. Tina's and Nancy's previous boycott of the household had already set the stage for the present turmoil. After they rescinded their boycott, Frank hadn't allowed himself to fully commit to his relationship with them for fear of something similar happening one day in the future. He understood that Tina felt the need to protect herself, because he too was protecting himself.

Not surprisingly, Tina's pronouncement instigated a debate between Frank and Barbara over the dinner party. Barbara held her ground. By this time, she was just fed up with the whole thing. "The kids could have planned something and they didn't," she said, according to one of the household employees who witnessed the debate. "So I told George and Jolene that we would go to their house for a nice dinner. The kids can celebrate the *next* night. And there's always next year. I just don't see what the problem is."

"No," Frank bellowed. "If my kids aren't going to be there, I'm not going. I'm too old and tired for this shit."

"Why does everything have to be such a big deal?" Barbara asked, frustrated. "I'm sick of it, Frank," she said. "I'm old too. I'm tired too. You're not the only one around here who is old and tired." Barbara was sixty-eight at this time.

"What kind of birthday party is it supposed to be without my kids?" he demanded to know.

"It is *not* a birthday party," Barbara sternly reminded him. "It is a *dinner* party. And I am not the hostess. Therefore, I am not responsible for the guest list. Jolene is. And *yes*, you are going."

And yes, he did go.

"Goodbye, Dag"

On Christmas morning 1995, Dean Martin died at the age of seventy-eight. The reported cause of death was acute respiratory failure brought on by emphysema. With many of the key players in his life being toppled one by one—Ava Gardner, Sammy Davis Jr., Jilly Rizzo, and Sammy Cahn—after Dean's death, Frank fell into another deep depression. "I'm next," he told friends at Matteo's restaurant in Beverly Hills. "I'm not scared, either. How can I be? Everybody I ever knew is already over dere."

Though the two had drifted apart since that last tour together ended, they had seen each other on the occasion of Dean's birthday, in June, then once again for dinner just weeks before Dean died.

Earlier in the year, Frank and Barbara had sold the Palm Springs compound, which Frank had owned since 1954. It sold for $4.9 million. They'd decided that they wanted a "simpler" life and would stay exclusively in their $5.2-million, four-bedroom, six-bathroom Beverly Hills mansion. They also still had their $6 million beachfront Malibu home.

For Frank, leaving the desert compound after almost fifty years was incredibly difficult, but everyone felt he should be in the Beverly Hills estate exclusively, closer to the doctors and hospitals there. His family had campaigned for the move, also, so that he could be closer to them. It took a lot out of Frank, though, and once he was in the new home, everyone could tell that he was a little less himself.

Barbara decided that they should also sell many of their prized possessions in an auction at Christie's rather than try to squeeze everything from the desert estate into the other two homes. Therefore, the 1976 Jaguar XJS Barbara gave to Frank as a wedding present went to a retired real estate developer in Delaware for $79,500. Frank's black lacquer Bösendorfer grand piano went for $51,750. His glass-and-brass mailbox sold for $13,800. A white-and-blue golf cart—with the driver's side bearing the inscription "Ol' Blue Eyes" and the passenger side reading "Lady Blue Eyes," and featuring a built-in stereo system, went for $20,700. A statue of John Wayne, a gift from the Duke, went for $7,475. It was sad; Nancy and Tina grew more discouraged as much of their father's life was sold off, piece by piece. Every now and then, Frank would pull Tony Oppedisano aside and squeeze a pair of gold cuff links in his hand and say, "Make sure Tina gets these," or a lighter and say, "This should go to Frankie." Tony would just say, "Consider it done, pal." In all, Frank and Barbara earned $2 million from the auction.

With his life shrinking more and more with each passing day, Frank was nostalgic for the old days. "He calls me up," Dean said while sitting at his table at La Famiglia restaurant six months before his death, "and we shoot the shit, you know. Two old guys. Frank wants to talk over old times. Only problem is, I don't remember the old times. I can't even remember the *new* times."

Dean's daughter Deana says Tony Oppedisano made the arrangements for dinner at Da Vinci's Italian restaurant; it would be Frank, Dean, Tony, and Mort Viner. Frank seemed at least almost partially deaf at this point, wearing a hearing aid. During the evening, he attempted to tell Dean a story about Don Rickles. However, Dean couldn't hear him because Frank was sitting on his left side and Dean was almost deaf in that ear. Frustrated, Frank pulled his hearing aid out of his ear and handed it to Tony. "Shove this in Dean's ear so he can hear me," Frank suggested. Tony did as he was told. Then Frank repeated his story. "Why are you talking so loudly, pallie?" Dean asked. "I can hear every word you're saying." At that, Frank looked at Dean and said, "Huh? What'd you say? Speak up, I can't hear you." They were still funny, even when they didn't intend it.

Frank would speak to Dean one more time, on Christmas Eve, the day before he died. Tony would say that Frank signed off as he always did with Dean: "Goodbye, Dag."

Frank tried to attend Dean's funeral at Westwood Village Memorial Park, but he broke down while getting dressed. "I'm sorry," he said, "I want to do this, but I don't know if I have the strength." The family felt it would be better for his health if he didn't attend. "He stayed in bed for two days after the funeral," Barbara later recalled. Barbara attended the services, as did Nancy—the Sinatra women sat on opposite sides of the chapel. Tina, who had removed herself, was not at the funeral and didn't speak to her father personally about Dean's death. Crying—she loved her Uncle Dean as much as everyone else—she listened in on her sister Nancy's telephone conversation with Frank.

In a prepared statement, Frank Sinatra said, "Too many times I've been asked to say something about friends who are gone. This is one of the hardest. Dean was my brother—not through blood but through choice. Our friendship has traveled down many roads over the years, and there will always be a special place in my heart and soul for Dean. He has been like the air I breathe—always there, always close by."

A Fourth Wedding Ceremony

Six months later, Frank and Barbara renewed their wedding vows on their twentieth anniversary, July 11, 1996, at Our Lady of Malibu Church. Frank was eighty-one, Barbara sixty-nine.

This event would actually be Frank and Barbara's fourth wedding ceremony, the first having been in Palm Springs and the second and third, in Palm Beach and then New York, after Frank's marriage to Nancy was annulled.

Not only did Frank love Barbara, but he appreciated the way she had taken care of him through recent years of illnesses—the sleepless nights, the tears, the anguish she'd gone through where he was concerned. He'd been touched by all of it. Loyalty was always a paramount consideration in his life, and Barbara had more than proved hers over the last twenty years. But he had to at least wonder, at what cost? Tina wasn't speaking to him at all. Nancy was very cautious. In fact, she was speaking to her father only occasionally at this point. Frank Jr. was, though slightly more accessible, never going to be completely available to Frank; of course this strained dynamic preceded Barbara by years.

"Twenty-four years after we'd first started dating, we were still together, still in love," Barbara would recall. "We had defied all the critics; we'd lost money for those foolish enough to gamble on us not staying together more than a few months. We'd risen above all the attempts of those who tried to break us up. Ours was a deep and lasting love, full of trust and loyalty... Was it easy? Not always. Was it calm? Rarely. But was it fun? Oh yes; a thousand times, yes."

Tina and Nancy chose not to attend the ceremony. Frank Jr., however, was present, as was Bobby Marx. "I just want to congratulate you, Pop," Frank Jr., who was now fifty-two, said to his dad as they stood at the bar together with some of the guests. The two men shook hands. "You sure know how to shake up the ol' henhouse, don't you?" Frank Jr. said with a smile. Laughing, Frank slapped his son on the back and said, "Yeah, well, I always been pretty good at that, haven't I?"

Surrounded by Love

$\mathcal{A}$t the end of 1996, Francis Albert Sinatra was about to turn eighty-one years old.

Dolly and Marty were gone.

Sammy, Dean, and Peter, gone.

The Kennedys—JFK and Bobby and even Jackie—gone.

Sam Giancana, gone.

Lana, Ava, Marilyn, gone.

Jilly, gone.

And everyone who was left was getting on in years.

"With each passing, I think my father loses a tiny piece of his spirit," observed Tina Sinatra.

"I haven't spoken to my father much lately, because he has really been withdrawn since Dean died," admitted Frank Jr. "And then there's the other thing. The inner, the deeper-set problem that goes beyond poignancy. There's the actual state of depression; the fact of knowing that we're just getting old now," he added. "Emotionally, he's down. He's a little bit heartsick. He sees a lot of his friends are getting old and dying, and it hurts him."

Like many people when they near the end of their lives, Frank couldn't help but reflect upon and take stock of his long, eventful personal history. He vacillated between emotions about it. Sometimes he felt that people knew exactly what they were getting into by being in his life, it was a privilege and an honor for them because he was who he was—and too bad for them if they got hurt. Other times, he was regretful. For instance, he deeply regretted the impact his leaving Nancy for Ava had on his children—but he had lamented that for years. He also never seemed to completely reconcile the matter of Peter Lawford. "I shouldn't have done that to Peter," he told Joey D'Orazio on the telephone at this time. Joey was calling from Hoboken to congratulate him on the renewal of his vows to Barbara. Joey told him, "We were young and stupid. We can't kick ourselves about it now." But Frank said he wished he could "go back," that he "probably could have been *nicer* to some people."

"Then you wouldn't have been Frank Sinatra," Joey observed.

"Yeah," he agreed. "I wouldn't have been Frank Sinatra."

Tina had said back in 1993, "As much as we would like to see Dad not work so hard, we also know that singing is his life force. For him to stop before he's ready might kill him." Frank had felt the same way. Now it was as if everyone's greatest fear was coming to pass. Without his songs, his soul had begun to wither. He seemed to have lost the will to go on; his body began to break down. While he was once a young man trapped in an old man's body, by the end of 1996 he was simply...an old man. Still, he would not give up. When his daughter Nancy asked him what he might want for his upcoming eighty-first birthday on December 12, Frank put it succinctly: "Another birthday." He was also tired of the family melodrama, he said. Therefore, everyone wondered if maybe they should make a concerted effort to get along. But could such a thing even happen?

Before the family members had a chance to reevaluate their rapport with one another, something occurred that transformed the family dynamic. In November 1996, Frank had a heart attack. He was rushed to Cedars-Sinai hospital. Once they got him stabilized, they realized he was also suffering pneumonia in the lining of his left lung.

When Tina got the call, her boycott was instantly over; she had to be with her dad. She rushed to the hospital, and with just a few words that were barely audible, the slate was wiped completely clean and Tina was once again her daddy's "Pigeon."

Doctors said that Frank was lucky to have survived the attack. However, this sobering event shook the entire family to its core. All of the bad blood between them these last twenty years no longer mattered. The fact that Frank seemed to be approaching the end of his days caused his family members to reconsider their priorities. Everyone knew without even having to acknowledge it that they needed to be present for not only him, but for each other.

Frank stayed in the hospital for eight days. On the afternoon of his release, Barbara called Tina, Nancy, and Frankie out into the hallway. She extended her hands to Tina. Tina took them into her own. "I just want all three of you to know that anytime you want to visit your father, you are more than welcome to come by the house," Barbara said. She would be seventy next year and, at least on this day, she looked her age, which for her was rare. Usually meticulously put together, she now seemed a little less elegant, slightly more bedraggled. But it had been an awful week. Actually, it had been an awful year.

In January 1996, Barbara had suffered a terrible accident when she fell down a flight of stairs. She says she broke her T12 thoracic vertebra, as well as almost every bone in one of her feet. Few people knew about it, though; she says she kept it to herself rather than worry Frank. She was fitted with a cast up to her knee and a steep brace around her torso. Somehow she managed to function that way for three long months wearing housecoats and very loose clothing with high-necked blouses; she says that Frank never suspected a thing, though that somehow seems unlikely.

"Day or night," she continued while talking to Frank's daughters in the hospital. "You are more than welcome." She seemed sincere.

"Oh my God, Barbara," Tina said. "I have waited so long to hear you say that."

"We've all been on a wrong path," Barbara told the Sinatra girls. They agreed. Barbara then embraced Tina and Nancy.

Even though it appeared to most observers that Frank was on his deathbed—magazines and newspapers prepared his obituaries and waited for the sad announcement—he rebounded, was checked out of the hospital, and, as soon as he got home, enjoyed a smoke and a glass of Jack Daniel's, loving every last sip.

During his life, it had always been "all or nothing at all" for Frank. Unfortunately, it would seem that particular credo would also characterize the many ailments subsequent to the heart attack. Cancer. Kidney problems. Bladder ailments. "Mini-strokes." A touch of dementia, even. He would have them all; of course, Frank could never die in any way other than dramatically. He steadfastly refused to allow information about his failing condition to be released to the public. He insisted upon being remembered as he was in his heyday, not as he was at the end. While his life had been unique in many ways, his slow, painful decline wasn't. "You gotta love livin'," he'd always said. "Dyin' is a pain in the ass." Now, more than ever, he must have believed those words to be true.

There was always so much preparation whenever he had to be rushed to the hospital; Frank didn't want the media to know what was going on, and Barbara made sure his wishes were honored. She would have sheets raised in front of him to protect him from the paparazzi lurking about the property. She would tape aluminum foil to the windows of the ambulance before he was wheeled into it. She would ask that the emergency workers not use their sirens, at Frank's insistence, meaning they would have to actually stop at red lights, which only added to her stress. She would also make sure he was checked in as "Charlie Neat" or "Albert Francis" to protect his anonymity. "He was fighting for his life," she would recall. "I was fighting for his privacy."

For the next year and a half, the family would call a truce. Tina, Nancy, and Frankie would spend more time than ever at the Beverly Hills mansion as Frank convalesced, and Barbara would welcome them with open arms. Of course, there would always be problems, but this was not the time to dwell on them. Everyone wanted to get as much out of these precious family moments as possible.

The doctors had told the family that it was possible Frank could live another two years, and the thought of that lifted their spirits. However, they also knew that they could wake up tomorrow and he could be gone. There was simply no way to predict it. All they could do was hold fast together and create as many new memories as possible.

On December 12, 1996, Frank celebrated his eighty-first birthday. This time, there was no familial conflict about the celebration. The entire family was at his side for the celebration.

In January 1997, Sinatra would find himself back in the hospital with erratic blood pressure and arrhythmia. Again, he survived. Things weren't the same, though. Everything seemed darker, a sense of foreboding informing each moment at the manse.

At the end of April, Congress voted to give Frank a Congressional Gold Medal, which had been sponsored by New York Democratic representative José E. Serrano (with a push by Republican senator Alfonse D'Amato), who first heard English listening to Sinatra as a two-year-old in Mayaguez, Puerto Rico. The first Congressional Gold Medal was issued to George Washington by the Continental Congress in 1787. One of the oldest awards in the country, it predates even the Constitution; the 320 past honorees include Robert Frost, Bob Hope, Thomas Edison, John Wayne, Louis L'Amour, H. Norman Schwarzkopf, and Colin Powell.

"It's more than just an honor from his country as far as I'm concerned," said Frank's daughter Nancy. "It's like the country saying, 'Okay, Frank, we know the truth, and we love you.'" Certainly, as Nancy suggested, the timing was right for such an honor in that there was a prevailing national nostalgia for a cultural icon who seemed to be nearing the end of his life.

Whether Frank would be able to personally accept the honor from President Bill Clinton remained to be seen; he was extremely sick during the summer of 1997. "I think he's wishing he were about twenty years younger," Nancy said. "But then, so am I. Aren't we all? I don't know if he'd sell his soul to the devil, but he would certainly try to make a deal to get more time," she concluded. "He ain't goin' easily." (In the end, he would not attend.)

On Thursday, November 27, the entire family enjoyed Thanksgiving dinner together: Barbara; Nancy Sr.; Nancy Jr. and her daughters, Amanda and A.J.; Tina; Frank Jr.; and Bobby Marx were all present, just as it should have been. They had all been through a lot. Just before the meal was to be dished out by a uniformed servant, a nurse wheeled Frank into the room. Still, no one was used to seeing this once-vital man sitting in a wheelchair, a colorful blanket draped across his knees; there was something incongruous about it. The nurse pushed him up to the table and then applied the brakes to the chair. "Hello, family," Frank said as he surveyed the room. Never had he looked more frail, his body ravaged by the recent years of debilitation. Yet there was still something about those blue eyes and the way they danced when he looked at those he loved.

As Nancy Sr. gazed across the table at Frank, she beamed. What a turbulent history she had shared with him, almost fifty years of their lives, some good, some bad, but all of it memorable. Somehow she had persevered, and today, at the age of eighty, Nancy seemed serene and content. She had none of the infirmities of the aged; she was vital and totally in command.

Frank Jr. stood up. "Let's have a toast," he declared. "To Pop," he announced, raising his glass of wine. "We love you very much, Dad. But I think you know that by now."

"And I love you back," Frank said with a weak smile. "Each and every one of you." When he raised his glass of wine, there was a noticeable tremor.

Everyone smiled and clinked glasses all around the table. It was a moment they would always remember. Frank wasn't what he used to be. Nothing about him, in fact, was what it used to be. But for now, it was enough.

Frank took just a sip of wine, swished it around in his mouth, and then put the glass down before him. "Italian Barbera," he said, a gleam of satisfaction in his eyes. "Now that right there?" he remarked, nodding his head with approval. "That's one fine wine."

Fine

*I*t happened quickly. On May 14, 1998, Frank was taken to Cedars-Sinai hospital in Los Angeles. He died shortly thereafter.

Frank's doctor, Rex Kennamer, called Tina at home a little after 11 p.m. "We lost him." Just three words. But they changed everything for the entire Sinatra family, indeed the entire world.

Tina had many questions, but once she learned that Frank was at Cedars, she threw on some clothes, got into her car, and raced over there. She called Nancy on the way, and then picked up her tearful sister. When they got to the hospital, there was Frank, on a gurney. He was gone, eyes closed, hands over his chest. Barbara was sitting stoically on a chair in a corner, as if in shock.

Barbara had been at dinner at Morton's restaurant in Beverly Hills after a very uneventful day at home with Frank. He was convalescing as usual, adjusting to new heart medication, and for the most part spent the day in a very groggy state. Barbara planned to check with his doctor the next day to make sure the medicine was at the proper dosage. Frank was lying in bed in his pajamas when she went in to say good night to him. The television was on very loudly; his hearing had been seriously compromised in the last year or so. She turned down the volume and then kissed him on the forehead. "Good night, darling," she said. "Sleep warm." She nodded at the nurse at his bedside. "I'll be back in a few hours," she told her. "Vine has the number to the restaurant in case you need me. Be sure to call me the second anything unusual happens," she said.

Barbara had only been at Morton's for a short time when a waiter approached. "There's a telephone call for you, madam," he told her. Instantly anxious, she rose and went to the front desk. It was Vine. "You'd better come right away," she told her. "The paramedics are here. They're going to take Mr. S. to the hospital." Less than an hour had passed since Barbara left the house; she couldn't believe things had taken such a bad turn in such a short time. "They can't find a pulse," Vine said.

One of the household staff drove Barbara to the hospital at record speed. After making her way through a maddening maze of hallways, she finally found her husband surrounded by doctors working on him. She raced to him and held his hand in hers. He looked weak, very close to death. "You must fight, my darling," she told him. "You have beaten greater odds than this. Please fight." He looked up at her, his blue eyes still somehow shining through his pain and suffering, and he began to move his lips. "I can't," he whispered. And then he died.

AFTERWORD:
A FINAL CONSIDERATION

I crashed Frank Sinatra's funeral.

Allow me to explain...

Frank Sinatra's death occurred just about six months after the first edition of this book was published. In fact, since I was still promoting the work when the entertainer passed away, I covered his funeral for MSNBC, reporting on the events live as they took place on Wednesday, May 20, 1998, at the Good Shepherd Catholic Church in Beverly Hills. However, I had no intention of actually attending the church service. I knew I wouldn't be granted access since it was reserved strictly for close friends and family members.

Wearing my press credentials, I was standing at the bottom of the steps of the church, speaking to the always vibrant Debbie Reynolds, who was wearing a black pillbox hat and diamond earrings. "You're coming in for the service, aren't you?" she asked me. I told her I wasn't invited. She laughed. "Oh please," she exclaimed. "You wrote a whole book about Frank. Do you think not being invited ever stopped him from attending *anything*? Now, march in there," she told me, "and if one of those Sinatras kicks you out, so be it! At least you will have tried. This is *history*," she told me, "and you are an historian. So... don't miss out." I told her no, I wasn't willing to risk news reports about Frank's biographer getting tossed out of his funeral by his grieving family members. "Fine, suit yourself!" Debbie said, a flicker of annoyance crossing her face. "You big chicken!" As she left my side, she winked at me conspiratorially and slipped something into my hand. I looked at it. It was a glossy white ticket. Printed in purple on it were the words "Francis Albert Sinatra Funeral Mass," along with the date, the time, and the address of the church. "But how will you get in?" I asked Debbie. As she walked away from me, she laughed and said, "Oh please!"

Dare I? I couldn't imagine doing it, but I did it anyway. I gathered my courage and walked up to the top of the stairs where security guards were taking the tickets, and I handed one of them mine. Then I quickly glided into the church behind someone else before anyone had a chance to ask me any questions. It all happened so fast, I actually couldn't believe it. Now that I was in the church, I knew I had no choice but to follow through and commit myself to my pretense.

As I looked around the church, I saw so many of Sinatra's famous friends, such as Paul Anka; Sophia Loren; Robert Wagner; Jack Lemmon; Kirk Douglas; Vic Damone; Larry King; Ed McMahon; Sidney Poitier; Jack Nicholson; Tony Curtis; Joey Bishop; Liza Minnelli; Steve Lawrence and Eydie Gormé; Anthony Quinn; and Nancy Reagan. At the altar, Frank's closed coffin was covered with a blanket of white gardenias. Next to it was a large portrait of the man himself, on an easel. Up front in the first row sat his grieving children—Nancy, fifty-seven; Frank Jr., fifty-four; and Tina, forty-nine—along with Frank's widow, Barbara, seventy-one. Behind them was Frank's wife, Nancy, eighty-one. I listened as "Ave Maria" was sung by a choir, followed by remembrances by Kirk Douglas (who speculated that "heaven will never be the same" once Frank showed up at its gates); Gregory Peck, Robert Wagner, and, most emotionally, Frank. Jr.

"My father's whole life was an anomaly," Frank Jr. said in his eulogy. "His birth was so difficult that the fact that he lived at all was an anomaly. That he even became a singer, that he became a great singer, and that he made such wonderful movies, all this was an anomaly...And how did he live to such a ripe old age? Which was certainly not because he took care of himself. That's the greatest anomaly." He finished with the same words his father had spoken at bandleader Harry James's 1983 funeral. "Thanks for everything," said Frank Jr. "So long, buddy, and take care of yourself."

Toward the end of the ceremony, Frank's velvety voice wafted in through the sound system singing, "Put your dreams away for another day / and I will take their place in your heart." While listening, it was difficult for me to contain my emotion. If anything, it reminded me that even though he was gone, the Voice would most certainly live on.

After the ceremony, I watched as the pallbearers—Don Rickles, Steve Lawrence, Tony Oppedisano, Bobby Marx, and Frank Jr.— carried Frank's casket down the middle aisle and out of the church. A regal Barbara, her head bowed, followed with the cardinal at her side. She looked bone tired, her grief seeming to have exhausted her. In her hand were a few crucifixes she'd had made to give out to friends at the service. Following her were Frank's first wife, Nancy, and the rest of the family, including Frank's three children, all struggling to control their emotions. I noticed that Frank Jr. in particular appeared to be drained, an empty expression in his sad, dark eyes. Before getting into their limousine, Nancy and Tina—both still somehow beautiful and elegant even in their aching sadness—seemed to have the same instinct at the same time; they turned and embraced their bereft brother and held him close. "Poor kid," Vic Damone said to no one in particular as he walked by me. "Losing the old man like that. At least he's got his sisters, though." Later, the limousines carrying Sinatra's casket and his family members would be en route to Desert Memorial Park in Cathedral City, where Frank's parents, Dolly and Marty, are also interred.

As the heartbreaking scene unfolded, I looked for some moment of closeness between Nancy, Tina, and Barbara, but there really wasn't one, at least not one for public consumption. A photographer shouted out at them, asking if they would pose together for a photo. Understandably, Tina threw him a scathing look; this was obviously not a moment for posed photos.

The day after Frank's funeral, attorneys for the Sinatra estate filed a copy of his thirty-page 1991 will for probate in Los Angeles. There had been some confusion about the will. First, the family was presented with a will dated October 31, 1991. It was pretty much what everyone expected in terms of bequeathments. But then one of the lawyers told the Sinatra children that "there seems to be a second will." One was produced that had been revised and signed four days later on November 3. The wills were mostly identical, except for a provision in the second in which Sinatra gave Barbara an additional $3.5 million. "It was something that had to be done," said Eliot Weisman, who was privy to the negotiations relating to the will. However, by this time the Sinatra family was so emotionally spent and grief-stricken no one cared to even pursue a line of questioning about the additional clause in the second will.

In the end, according to Frank's final wishes, Barbara also ended up with all of the Sinatra residences, one each in Beverly Hills and Malibu, two in Rancho Mirage, and another in Cathedral City. She also received the rights to his *Trilogy* recordings as well as most of his material possessions, including all the silverware, books, and paintings in the homes, as well as a Mercedes-Benz and a Rolls-Royce. She would also control most of his name and likeness rights. Barbara also got 25 percent royalties from Sheffield Enterprises, the company Frank set up to license his name and likeness. Daughter Nancy was said to be chief executive of the firm.

Frank Jr., Nancy, and Tina each got $200,000 in cash, as well as some stock. Their mother and Sinatra's first wife, Nancy Barbato, received $250,000. Frank Jr. got the rights to his dad's sheet music. Robert Marx, Barbara's son from a previous marriage, got $100,000. In addition, the children received rights to most of their dad's lucrative music catalog.

It may seem to some observers that Frank's children were short-changed in the will, but the bulk of Sinatra's net worth—between $200 million and $600 million—was set aside in a living trust enacted before his death. Unlike the will, which is subject to a review in probate court and is therefore a public document, the contents of the trust are confidential. It is known that each child had a trust, but what is not known is how much was in it. Therefore it would be unfair to assume that their father didn't see to it that his children were well taken care of. Sinatra's attorney Harvey Silbert said, "There are very substantial assets in the trust." (One little-known fact about Frank Sinatra, according to his official website, www.Sinatra.com, is that during his life he donated more than a billion dollars to various charities around the world.)

With royalties of his music catalog going mostly to his children, the cumulative amount would have to be staggering considering the scores of posthumous compilations of Sinatra's music that found their way to release after his death—some very good, some redundant of what had already been released.

In October 2013, Frank Sinatra Entertainment—which is run by the Sinatra family alongside Warner Music Group—made an official announcement about a deal it struck with the Universal Music Group to have Frank's classic 1950s Capitol and 1960s Reprise recordings combined for future compilations. The packages are being released on Capitol Records under the new "Signature Sinatra" imprint. "We today approach the Sinatra Centennial [December 12, 2015] with an opportunity to showcase our father's prodigious body of work to a world of new and loyal fans," stated Nancy, Frank, and Tina Sinatra. The first release under the new deal, *Sinatra: Best of the Best*, featured such Capitol classics as "I've Got the World on a String" and "Love and Marriage" alongside Reprise hits like "Strangers in the Night" and "That's Life." For the Sinatra loyalist, these sort of compilations amount to more of the same material just being reissued with new artwork, but for the more casual fan this sort of collection provided a novel way to hear a wide breadth of Frank's material on a single CD.

* * *

In 2013, Frank's daughter Nancy, then seventy-three years old, issued an album of previously unreleased material on her own Boots Enterprises Inc. label, which features her renditions of many popular songs from the 1970s, such as Neil Diamond's "Holly Holy" and Jimmy Webb's "MacArthur Park," mixed in with show tunes like Rodgers and Hammerstein's "A Cockeyed Optimist" from *South Pacific* (with its beautifully lush arrangement by Billy May). It's an understated, artfully produced collection, well worth hearing.

Still in the public eye after all of these years, Nancy doesn't shy away from controversy. As it happens, it can sometimes inadvertently pit her against Barbara, whom she hasn't seen much of—if at all—since her father's death. For instance, in November 2013, Mia Farrow, who was sixty-eight at the time, gave an interview to *Vanity Fair* and revealed that "possibly" her son, Ronan, could be Frank's biological child. Nancy immediately came forth with the magnanimous statement that "Ronan is a big part of us, and we are blessed to have him in our lives." But for her part, Barbara, who was eighty-six, said of the possibility, "I can hardly believe that. It's just a bunch of junk. There's always junk written—lies that aren't true." She was also quick to note that Frank left nothing to Ronan in his will. (For that matter, Mia wasn't mentioned in the will either, though she insists she and Frank "never really split up.")

In fact, Ronan was born in 1987, during Frank's marriage to Barbara. Frank was seventy-one. Mia was forty-two. At the time, Mia was involved with Woody Allen (long presumed Ronan's biological father). It seems unlikely that Frank and Mia would have secretly reunited nineteen years after their marriage to have a child together. But then again...who knows? In Frank's baffling world where no relationship could be painted with a wide brushstroke, pretty much anything was possible. It's more likely, though, that Mia was just teasing the *Vanity Fair* writer, Maureen Orth, with a provocative comment, and that the whole business just got blown out of proportion.

To his credit, Ronan Farrow had the last word on Twitter: "Listen, we're all 'possibly' Frank Sinatra's son."

It's been seventeen years since the day I crashed Frank Sinatra's funeral, and today I'm glad I mustered up the courage to do it. Debbie Reynolds was right; some moments in history should not be missed. Certainly Frank never missed out on any of the big ones of his life. He seized each and every one and made the most of it. As he sang in his trademark song, "My Way," he had his regrets, sure—"but then again, too few to mention."

After the ceremony, I walked out of the darkened Good Shepherd Church into the blinding glare of daylight. Before me, I saw what had to be more than a thousand onlookers standing behind endless yards of yellow police tape, representing Frank's adoring public, many holding up colorful signs and banners with sentiments such as "We'll Miss You, Ol' Blue Eyes," and "R.I.P.—The Chairman." They were peaceful, orderly...respectful. Of course, there was also the mad crush of reporters and cameras, which reminded me that I too was supposed to be working, and that I had been derailed for more than two hours!

Behind a long line of sleek limousines parked and waiting for celebrity passengers, I noticed some fans pointing upward and smiling. When I raised my head, I saw a small plane streaking across a vast, unblemished sky, skywriting Frank's initials in sleek white contrails—an F and an S both elegantly written, beautifully succinct. One of Frank's more pragmatic quotes popped into my head. "I'm not one of those complicated, mixed-up cats," he had said. "I'm not looking for the secret to life. I just go from day to day, taking what comes."

As I watched the skywriters' handiwork slowly fade into a vaporous haze, I was more than ever aware of the fleeting nature of life and the urgency of living it to the fullest, like Sinatra did, with all his flaws and foibles and mistakes and misjudgments just as much a part of his life's story as his joys, his passions, and his music. In fact, there will never be another man quite like him. Frank was one of a kind, an extraordinary man cut from a special kind of cloth, a character never to be duplicated. Not in this lifetime, anyway. Which, one might imagine, is exactly as he would have wanted it.

—J. Randy Taraborrelli

SOURCE NOTES AND ACKNOWLEDGMENTS

ORIGINAL 1998 SOURCES AND NOTES

While the following notes are by no means comprehensive, they are intended to at least give the reader a general overview of my research.

Over a five-year period between 1991 and 1996, 425 people were interviewed for this work, either by myself or by my researcher, Cathy Griffin. Whenever practical, I have provided sources within the body of the text. Some who were not quoted directly in the text provided observations that helped me better understand Sinatra and his life and career.

Some of the books and newspaper and magazine articles that I consulted are included below; however, there are simply too many to be listed in their entirety.

Obviously, I viewed innumerable hours of Sinatra's television programs, television specials, concerts, press conferences, and documentaries (as well as those relating to Dean Martin, Sammy Davis Jr., Peter Lawford, and other principal players in this story), and also hundreds of hours of radio interviews and other broadcasts in which Sinatra took part or of which he was the subject. It would be impractical to list them all here.

Frank Sinatra has many fan clubs, but two in particular are amazingly well organized and informative: the Sinatra Society of America (headed by Charles Pignone, a longtime trusted friend of the Sinatras) and the International Sinatra Society (directed by thorough

Sinatra historians Mary and Dustin Doctor in memory of the late Gary L. Doctor, who compiled Citadel Press's excellent *Sinatra Scrapbook*). Through their newsletters and other forums, including invaluable Internet resources, I was able to confirm important details and add color to certain sections of this book. I also obtained historically important videotapes and recordings from the International Sinatra Society. Mr. Sinatra is fortunate to have these two fan clubs so devoted to preserving his legend and reputation.

In writing about a person as powerful and influential as Frank Sinatra and about the Sinatra family, a biographer is bound to find that many sources with valuable information prefer not to be named in the text. This is understandable. Throughout my career, I have maintained that for a person to jeopardize a long-standing, important relationship for the sake of a book is a purely personal choice. Because I so appreciate the assistance of many people close to Sinatra over the years who gave of their time and energy for this project, I will respect their wishes for anonymity. Those who could be named are named in these notes. Also, some sources are named in the text but asked specifically not to be named in the book's acknowledgments so as not to have their contributions singled out and held up to scrutiny by the Sinatra family. Of course, I've respected their wishes as well.

1915–39

"Unbelievable! I don't believe that there's [yet] another person writing a book about Sinatra," said Nancy Sinatra Sr. to my researcher, Cathy Griffin, on May 30, 1997. "Nobody ever gets it right, and it's just exhausting to me," she said. "However, I wish the author well with it anyway. Maybe this one will make some sense." Laughing, she added, "I just hope he does a good job, for *his* sake."

I would like to thank Mrs. Sinatra for her limited participation, for clarifying certain points of which I was uncertain, and for shedding light on other areas. A dignified, positive-thinking woman, she is not anxious to discuss the past, which is why I appreciate her time even more.

"I refuse to say anything bad about anybody, any way or anyhow," she said when pushed about one particularly painful memory, "because I have been hurt too many times through the years. Recently I was asked something about Ava Gardner and I said, 'Look. It's just too late. It doesn't matter to me anymore, and it shouldn't matter to anyone else. I'm eighty years old, and I'm just not going to get into that anymore, *ever*.' And if people want to know how I feel, then tell them that, because that's how I feel. I don't mean to be rude, but this is my life, and I have a right to feel as I do about it. Don't you agree?"

I feel that Mrs. Sinatra's candid comments speak volumes for the way she has decided to deal with her life's history, and I admire her point of view.

Over the last five years, I spent many hours in Hoboken, New Jersey, where a number of people opened their homes—and their scrapbooks—to me as they remembered young Frank. I am indebted to so many people who lived in Hoboken when the Sinatras did—many of whom live elsewhere today—and also to the sons, daughters, grandsons, and granddaughters of people who were friendly with Dolly and Marty Sinatra and whose memories of them, as relayed to them by their ancestors, remain intact. I was impressed by their affection for the Sinatras and appreciate their trust.

I utilized the Park Avenue library in Hoboken to glean details of Hoboken's history as well as the Sinatra family's. My appreciation to all of its staff for their assistance. Regarding Hoboken's history, I also utilized *The Hoboken of Yesterday* by George Long; *The Italians* by Luigi Barzini; *Gritty Cities* by Mary Procter and Bill Matuszeski; *Beyond the Melting Pot* by Nathan Glazer and Daniel P. Moynihan; *Halo over Hoboken* by John Perkins Field; and *The Changing Nature of Irish-Italian Relations* by Joseph A. Varacalli.

My thanks to Tina Donato for her insights and for taking me to all of the pertinent Sinatra sites in Hoboken, allowing me to enjoy the atmosphere and ambience and to get a sense of what it must have been like for Sinatra and his family in the 1930s and '40s. Doris Sevanto, who no longer lives in Hoboken but took the time (and incurred the expense) of returning there after twenty-five years to assist me, was invaluable to my research. I am grateful for her amazing memory, good cheer, and hospitality. Thanks are due those who submitted to interviews, including Tony Martin, Tom Gianetti, Rocco Gianetti, Thomas LaGreca, Debra Stradella, Delilah Lawford, Tom

Raskin, and Salvatore Donato. Thanks also to Lisa's Italian Deli on Park Avenue in Hoboken.

My special thanks to Joseph D'Orazio, a friend who was close not only to Sinatra but to Hank Sanicola and Emmanuel "Manie" Sacks. He and I became pals during the course of my five years of research, and I thank him for so many hours of interviews. "Joey Boy" is one of a kind.

I was deeply saddened by the recent death of Nancy Venturi, who, even though she was quite ill, spent hours sharing vivid memories of young Frank. I will miss her.

Thanks to the staff of the Hudson County Courthouse for its assistance in locating certain arrest records and other court documents relating to Sinatra's arrest on morals charges vital to my research. My thanks also to the staff of the Hudson County Records Bureau. I also reviewed editions of the *Hudson Dispatch* to confirm other details.

Throughout this book, I culled quotes from many published and televised interviews with Mr. Sinatra as well as from radio broadcasts. Most helpful to the early years was "He Can't Read a Note but He's Dethroning Bing" (*Newsweek*, March 22, 1943); "Sweet Dreams and Dynamite" by Jack Long (*American Magazine*, September 1943); "The Voice" (*Newsweek*, December 20, 1943); "Phenomenon, Parts I and II" by E. J. Kahn Jr. (*New Yorker*, 1946); "Star Spangled Octopus" by David G. Wittels (*Saturday Evening Post*, 1946); "The Nine Lives of Frank Sinatra" by Adela Rogers St. John (*Cosmopolitan*, 1956); "When Ol' Blue Eyes Was Red" by Jon Wiener (*New Republic*, 1986); "Here's Why Sinatra Is a Camp" by David Hinckley (*Daily News*, March 13, 1994); "Frank Sinatra Had a Cold" by Gay Talese (*Esquire*, April 1966); "Lauren Bacall—'Be Open to Whatever Happens'" by Dotson Rader (*Parade*, May 18, 1997); and *Dark Victory: Ronald Reagan, MCA, and the Mob* by Dan E. Moldea.

Frank Sinatra gave a lecture at Yale Law School in May 1986 for the Zion Lecture Series. The transcript of this lecture proved an excellent source of information.

I also referred to "The Un-American Activities in California— the (California) Senate Fact-Finding Committee on Un-American Activities, Third, Fourth and Fifth Reports" (Sacramento, 1947), which is on file at the Margaret Herrick Library of the Academy of Motion Picture Arts and Sciences in Beverly Hills.

I reviewed the personal papers and files of columnist Sidney Skolsky and the files of the Production Code Administration, also on file at the Margaret Herrick Library.

Nancy Sinatra's two books, *Frank Sinatra: My Father* and *Frank Sinatra: An American Legend*, were both helpful in forming a time line. I was careful to independently verify her material, however, and found that her work is accurate. Where points of view differ as to the Sinatra family's opinion on certain issues and the views of others, I attempted to present both sides. I also studied the authorized television miniseries *Sinatra*, produced by Frank's daughter Tina, to glean details of the official family viewpoint, and studied the narration by Frank Jr. of his oral history and musical study of his father, *As I Remember It*.

I also made judicious use of Kitty Kelley's Sinatra biography, *His Way*, in order to establish a framework of Sinatra's life, but was certain to independently verify information from her research before incorporating any of it into my own.

I also referred to *Sinatra! The Song Is You: A Singer's Art* by Will Friedwald and *Sinatra 101: The 101 Best Recordings and the Stories Behind Them* by Ed O'Brien and Robert Wilson, as well as *Sinatra: The Man and His Music; The Recording Artistry of Francis Albert Sinatra, 1939–1992* by Ed O'Brien and Scott P. Sayers. These three books are the best of the lot where Sinatra's music is concerned and should most certainly be included in the library of any Sinatra enthusiast. Since any complete Sinatra discography would take a book in itself to publish, I recommend that anyone interested in such a listing refer to these three titles for an intelligent examination of the music, if not a discography. I also made use of *Legend: Frank Sinatra and the American Dream*, an excellent compilation of articles about Sinatra edited by Ethlie Ann Vare.

At the Library of Congress, I reviewed tapes of the *Major Bowes and His Original Amateur Hour* programs with the Hoboken Four, including Sinatra's first appearance (September 8, 1935); the *Fred Allen Show* (May 2, 1937); and Sinatra's farewell appearance with

Tommy Dorsey (September 9, 1942). Vital to my research was a booklet called *The Music of Frank Sinatra*, written by respected and thorough Sinatra historian Charles Granata. This booklet includes "Frank Sinatra: An A to Z Discography," a listing of every song Sinatra has released commercially, in alphabetical order, with writers, producers, arrangers, and recording dates. This partial discography is not credited, but I suspect it was compiled by Granata in association with Nancy Sinatra Jr. I also utilized *The Sinatrafile (Parts 1, 2 and 3;* 1977, 1978, 1980) by John Ridgway.

1940–59

My thanks to Jess Morgan, Ava Gardner's business manager for nearly thirty years, for his assistance and memories of Miss Gardner, which were invaluable to me. My interview with Morgan was most appreciated.

My appreciation to Esther Williams (Sinatra's costar in *Take Me Out to the Ball Game*) for her time, astute observations about Ava Gardner and Lana Turner as they related to Sinatra, and for so many years of entertainment.

My appreciation to Joey Bishop for allowing himself to be interviewed three times and for his boundless energy and memories interspersed throughout this book, particularly in the sections about the Rat Pack.

As the former editor in chief of *Soul* magazine, I had the opportunity to interview Sammy Davis Jr. on several occasions over the years, notably in 1976, 1980, 1984, and 1989. I utilized many of Davis's memories about Sinatra in this work. I have recreated certain conversations between Davis and Sinatra, based on the former's excellent memory, particularly from my interview with him on February 1, 1989. Mr. Davis was a kind and generous man who is deeply missed. I also referred to his autobiographies *Yes I Can!, Hollywood in a Suitcase,* and *Why Me?*

I had the good fortune of interviewing the late Jule Styne at the Mayflower Hotel in New York in 1988 for a new edition of my book *Carol Burnett: Laughing Till It Hurts,* and I utilized many of his comments about Sinatra from that interview. The talented production director Joe Layton introduced me to Styne when Layton and Gary

Halvorson directed *A Tribute to Jule Styne* at the St. James Theatre that year. Layton is also much missed.

My thanks to Patti Demarest for the interviews she granted me regarding her early memories of Nancy Sinatra Sr. in Jersey City. Thanks also to Ted Hechtman for his assistance and his invaluable recollections and for the many hours we spent poring over his old appointment and date books.

Thanks to certain friends and family members of Lee Mortimer, who requested anonymity because of what they feared might be reprisals against them from the Sinatras. After so many years, it is true that the Sinatras are still—and perhaps justifiably so—angry about much of what Lee Mortimer wrote about Frank in the 1950s and '60s and whatever participation he had in the FBI's ongoing investigation of Sinatra. It says a great deal about the public's perception of the Sinatra family's influence, though, that anyone would ever think they would retaliate against people who were or are associated with the Mortimers, even after all of these decades. It's simply not true; however, I respect their concerns.

Thanks to Betty Wilkin and Josephine Barbone for allowing me to go through photo scrapbooks and for making themselves available to answer my endless questions.

I also had access to an oral history taped by Dick Moran, which he still one day hopes to have published. Mr. Moran allowed me to utilize many work-related papers and original drafts of press releases, which are fascinating and enlightening as to Sinatra's relationship with George Evans in the 1940s and '50s.

Of all of the Sinatra biographies published over the years, two were particularly helpful to my research and are recommended for their insightful approach: *Sinatra* by Earl Wilson (1967) and *Sinatra: Twentieth-Century Romantic* by Arnold Shaw (1969).

Many of Earl Wilson's notes, memos, and correspondence can be found at the New York Public Library for the Performing Arts at Lincoln Center. I utilized a great many of them throughout my book, and I thank the staff of the library for all of their assistance throughout the years of research on this project.

Dorothy Kilgallen's husband, Richard Kollmar, donated seventy of his wife's scrapbooks to the New York Library for the Performing

Arts. They are filled with her articles, columns, unpublished notes, and other material that she personally accumulated over her lifetime, including her rough drafts of her exposé "The Frank Sinatra Story." Much about Sinatra and her relationship with him can be found in her papers, and I reviewed them all thoroughly as part of my research.

Thanks also to the staffs of the New York Public Library, the Beverly Hills Library, the Glendale Central Public Library, and the Brand Library Art and Music Center.

I viewed every film Sinatra ever made to determine which were important to my needs and which were not. I also reviewed all of the press clippings, press kits, and other studio-related material, biographies, and other releases for each of Sinatra's films, all of which are on file at the Margaret Herrick Library. I also viewed and culled certain quotes from *Frank Sinatra: Relive the Magic*, a video history of Sinatra, and viewed many episodes of *The Frank Sinatra Show* for background purposes, as well as episodes from other Sinatra series, television specials, and miscellaneous appearances.

I reviewed hundreds of FBI documents that were released under the Freedom of Information Act. My thanks to Thomas DiBella for helping to make them available to me.

Thanks to William Godfrey, Dick Moran, Ida Banks, Mack Millar, Beatrice Lowry, William Merriman, Marilyn Lewis, Shirley Jones, Terrence Gibb, Ethel Aniston, and Jeanne Carmen for interviews.

Lucille Wellman and Mary LaSalle-Thomas are two gracious, generous women who were both friends of Ava Gardner's. They spent hours with me, individually and together, and helped me recreate moments in the Sinatra-Gardner relationship based on what Gardner told them. They also shared with me much correspondence from Ava, sent by her when she was married to Sinatra, which practically acted as a diary of their relationship and helped to finally clear up inaccuracies that had been published in other books. I am so grateful for their help and trust, as I am for the assistance of Gardner's friend Nancy LaPierre.

I also referred to Ava Gardner's autobiography, *Ava: My Story*, as well as Lana Turner's *The Lady, the Legend, the Truth*; Lauren Bacall's *By Myself*; Sammy Cahn's *I Should Care*; and Tony Curtis's

Tony Curtis: The Autobiography. Also, *Ava* by Charles Higham; *Ava Gardner* by John Daniell; *Kim Novak: Reluctant Goddess* by Peter Harry Brown; *Lana: The Public and Private Lives of Miss Turner* by Joe Morella and Edward Z. Epstein; *The Private Diary of My Life with Lana* by Eric Root; *Always, Lana* by Taylor Pero and Jeff Rovin; *Sinatra and His Rat Pack* by Richard Gehman; *Frank Sinatra: Is This Man Mafia?* by George Carpozi; *Frankie: The Life and Loves of Frank Sinatra* by Don Dwiggins; *Sinatra* by Tony Sciacca; *The Big Bands* by George T. Simon; and *For Once in My Life* by Connie Haines. *The Frank Sinatra Reader*, edited by Steven Petkov and Leonard Mustazza, is an excellent compendium of Sinatra features, which I also utilized. I also referred to *The Sinatra Celebrity Cookbook* by Barbara, Frank, and Friends; *Sinatra* by Robin Douglas Home; *B.S., I Love You* by Milton Berle; *The Great American Popular Singers* by Henry Pleasants; *The Frank Sinatra Scrapbook* by Richard Peters; *The Revised Compleat Sinatra* by Albert I. Lonstein; *Sinatra: An Exhaustive Treatise* by Albert I. Lonstein; *Frank Sinatra* by John Howlett; *Yesterdays: Popular Song in America* by Charles Hamm; *Music in the New World* by Charles Hamm; *Sinatra* by Frank Alan; *Tommy and Jimmy: The Dorsey Years* by Herb Sanford; *Dr. Burns's Prescription for Happiness* by George Burns; *Kilgallen* by Lee Israel; *Rainbow: The Stormy Life of Judy Garland* by Christopher Finch; *The Other Side of the Rainbow: With Judy Garland on the Dawn Patrol* by Mel Tormé; *Judy* by Gerold Frank; *Weep No More My Lady* by Mickey Deans and Ann Pinchot; *Brando for Breakfast* by Abba Kashfi Brando and E. P. Stein; *Sammy Davis Jr.: The Candyman; His Life and Times* (L.F.P., Inc., 1990); "Tips on Popular Singing" by Frank Sinatra and John Quinlan (Embassy Music Corporation, 1941); and "So Long Sammy" by Marjorie Rosen (*People*, May 28, 1990).

Hedda Hopper's personal notes and unpublished material are housed in the Margaret Herrick Library of the Academy of Motion Picture Arts and Sciences. I utilized many of her papers throughout this book, especially those having to do with Sinatra's suicide attempts. Most helpful were her unpublished notes relating to her story in *Photoplay*, "What's Wrong with Frankie?" (May 1947). I also reviewed her copious notes from over thirty interviews she conducted with Sinatra through the years. Any biographer would be grateful for such a find, and I must thank the Margaret Herrick Library for making all of this material available to me and the estate of Hedda Hopper for having the vision to donate it. I also referred to *Hedda and Louella* by George Eells.

Access to a complete library of *Photoplay* and *Look* magazines from the 1950s, granted by a generous person who wishes to remain anonymous, was beneficial to my research, particularly the three-part series on Sinatra that *Look* published in the summer of 1957. Thanks also to that same benefactor, who gave me access to hundreds of notes and transcripts from Louella Parsons concerning Sinatra, Dean Martin, Sammy Davis, and Joey Bishop.

I consulted the transcript of Joseph Nellis's questioning of Frank Sinatra on March 1, 1951. I also reviewed numerous court documents related to the separation, and the October 1951 divorce, of Frank Sinatra and Nancy Sinatra.

I interviewed the late Fred Zinnemann (who died on March 14, 1997) on the telephone in June 1995. He was gracious enough to respond in his own hand to a list of questions I sent to him regarding *From Here to Eternity* and his observations on Sinatra. At his direction, I also utilized his private papers in the Fred Zinnemann Collection at the Margaret Herrick Library. Of course, I also referred to *The Godfather* by Mario Puzo, and also his memoirs, *The Godfather Papers*, as well as *Monty: A Biography of Montgomery Clift* by Robert LaGuardia; *Montgomery Clift* by Patricia Bosworth; *Adventures in the Screen Trade* by William Goldman; and *Uncle Frank: The Biography of Frank Costello* by Leonard Katz.

I utilized tapes of Cathy Griffin's many hours of interviews with the late famed hairstylist Sydney Guilaroff for his memories of Ava Gardner and Frank Sinatra. Miss Griffin was the author of Guilaroff's memoirs, *Crowning Glory*.

I also had access to Cathy Griffin's taped interviews with the late private investigator Fred Otash for background material regarding the Wrong Door Raid as well as the *Confidential* magazine report in February 1957 and many court documents related to that particular case. I also reviewed notes and other unpublished material from the *Los Angeles Examiner*'s file on the raid and on subsequent hearings.

I examined the Stanley Kramer Collection in the Special Collections Department of the UCLA Library, from which were culled Kramer's comments.

Maryanne Reed allowed me access to her complete collection of Sinatra memorabilia, most of which was culled from the files of the newspaper the *Hollywood Citizen News* and the *Woman's Home Companion*, both of which are now defunct. This material was invaluable to me in that it provided many leads and also included the unpublished notes and interviews of reporters who were covering Sinatra for the *News* and *Companion* in the 1950s. I listened to and utilized in this work thirty-five previously unpublished taped interviews and conversations with Sinatra intimates, including George Evans, Hank Sanicola, Jimmy Van Heusen, Sammy Cahn, Jule Styne, Jack Entratter, Edie Goetz, Axel Stordahl, Sammy Davis, and Marilyn Maxwell, as well as employees of Lana Turner's and Ava Gardner's, all of which Ms. Reed generously had transferred from reel-to-reel format to cassette for my convenience. I am very grateful to her for her assistance. I am also grateful to Isabella Taves for her diligence in keeping such excellent notes for her stories on Sinatra in 1956.

1960–79

I interviewed Dean Martin at La Famiglia restaurant in Beverly Hills on June 24, 1994. His comments about Sinatra are found throughout this book.

"Frank's an okay guy," Dean told me. "No one understands him because they try to figure him out. You can't figure out Frank, so don't bother trying to do that in your book. You just gotta accept him. He never thought about a thing he ever did. He just did it. He just lived his life, like me, like all of us. Singin', workin', havin' a good time, taking our raps. He coulda been nicer, though," Dean added thoughtfully. "We all coulda been nicer, especially to each other, and to the dames, too. Especially to the dames."

When in doubt, because Mr. Martin's memory was sometimes cloudy, I independently confirmed what he told me during our two-hour conversation.

"Don't be so quick to jump to conclusions," he warned me when I brought up the subject of Frank and his underworld ties. "Nothing about Frank Sinatra is what you think it is. Remember that, kid."

My thanks to Barry Keenan, who gave me his first interviews about the Frank Sinatra kidnapping. Mr. Keenan demonstrated by his experience that a man can turn his life around and be a success in this world no matter what crazy thing he did in his youth. His vivid memory was invaluable in reconstructing the events that led up to his kidnapping of Sinatra Jr.

No one could write about the Rat Pack without reviewing their films *Ocean's 11, 4 for Texas, Robin and the 7 Hoods,* and *Sergeants 3.* Again, Joey Bishop's memories were helpful, as were Sammy Davis's. I also listened to a number of unreleased Rat Pack concerts on audiotape and viewed and studied an unreleased videotape of a concert by Sinatra, Davis, and Martin at the Sands Hotel in 1963.

My thanks to Bud Gundaker, a longtime family friend who made available to me a taped interview with Paul "Skinny" D'Amato, which proved invaluable to my research. Mr. Gundaker made available a number of Sinatra interviews as well. I so appreciate his assistance.

My thanks to Mike Santoni for allowing me to listen to his tape-recorded observations of Sam Giancana and other characters from that period. Mr. Santoni is working on a book about Giancana, and I appreciate his assistance.

Thanks to Thomas DiBella, whom I interviewed on seventeen different occasions. His insight into Sam Giancana's relationship with Frank Sinatra proved invaluable. He also made available to me a transcript of the federal wiretap from December 6, 1961, referred to in the text, as well as a number of transcripts involving Johnny Formosa and also many taped conversations among himself, Sam Giancana, and Johnny Roselli (which he is hoping to one day publish in book form).

Thanks also to Nicholas D'Amato for providing information I was able to use for background purposes throughout this work concerning Lucky Luciano, Carlos Marcello, and Jimmy Hoffa.

I interviewed two former members of the Secret Service who requested anonymity. I also interviewed four FBI agents who requested the same, one of whom kept a comprehensive scrapbook about the relationships among Sinatra, Giancana, and the Kennedys that was most helpful.

My time at the John F. Kennedy Library in Boston was well spent, and I thank its gracious staff.

I consulted Sam Giancana's Justice Department file, obtained through the Freedom of Information Act, as well as transcripts of federal wiretaps and Justice Department files on John F. Kennedy.

Thomas Calabrino made available to me the Justice Department's February 1962 report on organized crime, and other important documents relating to the department's investigation of organized crime and how it related to Frank Sinatra, including documents dated September 27, 1962, and October 1962 having to do with Giancana and Phyllis McGuire. Calabrino also allowed me to peruse Joe Fischetti's FBI files.

Calabrino made available to me a copy of the Justice Department's FBI report, "Francis Albert Sinatra a/k/a Frank Sinatra," which I examined.

I also referred to *The Luciano Story* by Sid Feder and Joachim Joeston; *The Green Felt Jungle* by Ovid Demaris; *The Lucky Luciano Inheritance* by David Hannah; *Lucky Luciano: His Amazing Trial and Wild Witnesses* by Hickman Powell; *The Last Testament of Lucky Luciano* by Martin A. Gosch and Richard Hammer; and *Meyer Lansky: Mogul of the Mob* by Dan Eisenberg and Meyer Lansky Landau; also, "The Last Act of Judith Exner" by Gerri Hirshey (*Vanity Fair*, April 1990) and "The Private Lives of Mia Farrow" by Betsy Israel (*Mirabella*, March 1997).

My appreciation to Don Dandero, an AP photographer working at the Cal-Neva Lodge during the Sinatra-Monroe years, who also covered the Sinatra Jr. kidnapping in Reno. Mr. Dondero was most helpful in giving me leads and ideas; also, one of his photos appears in this book.

My appreciation also to Darlene Hammond, who took many wonderful photos of Sinatra in the 1940s and '50s and shared her memories (and pictures) with me. Some of her work appears in this book.

My thanks to Charles Casillo, who helped me understand Marilyn Monroe's psychology, and also my deep appreciation to Marilyn

Monroe historian James Haspiel and to Marilyn Monroe fan club president Greg Shriner.

I owe a debt of gratitude to Donald Spoto, the bestselling author of *Marilyn Monroe: The Biography* for having donated his interview tapes for that project to the Margaret Herrick Library of the Academy of Motion Picture Arts and Sciences. His donation made it possible for me to obtain previously unpublished quotes from Sinatra's attorney, Milton "Mickey" Rudin; Marilyn Monroe's publicist, Patricia Newcomb; Peter Lawford's close business associate Milt Ebbins; and Lawford's longtime friend Joseph Naar.

I also consulted the following books: *Marilyn* by Donald Spoto; *Goddess: The Secret Lives of Marilyn Monroe* by Anthony Summers; *Marilyn Monroe* by Maurice Zolotow; *Conversations with Marilyn* by W. J. Weatherby; *The Masters Way to Beauty* by George Masters; *The Decline and Fall of the Love Goddess* by Patrick Agan; *The Agony of Marilyn Monroe* by George Carpozi; *Marilyn Monroe* by Norman Mailer; *My Story* by Marilyn Monroe; *Monroe: Her Life in Pictures* by James Spada with George Zeno; *Marilyn: The Tragic Venus* by Edwin P. Hoyt; *The Marilyn Monroe Story* by Joe Franklin and Laurie Palmer; *Marilyn: The Last Take* by Peter Harry Brown and Patte B. Barnham; *The Secret Happiness of Marilyn Monroe* by James E. Dougherty; *The Mysterious Death of Marilyn Monroe* by James A. Hudson; *The Marilyn Conspiracy* by Milo Speriglio; *The Curious Death of Marilyn Monroe* by Robert F. Slatzer; *Marilyn Monroe: An Uncensored Biography* by Maurice Zolotow; and *Norma Jean* by Fred Lawrence Guiles. I also used with caution *Marilyn Monroe Confidential* by Lena Pepitone and William Stadiem, and I reviewed tapes of her appearances on *The Mike Douglas Show* and *The Joan Rivers Show*.

I utilized *The Encyclopedia of Hollywood* by Scott Siegel and Barbara Siegel; *My Lucky Stars* by Shirley MacLaine; *Dino: Living High in the Dirty Business of Dreams* by Nick Tosches; and *Peter Lawford: The Man Who Kept the Secrets* by James Spada (the latter two being important works for anyone who ever appreciated Mr. Martin and Mr. Lawford). I also referred to *Jackie Oh!* by Kitty Kelley; *The Making of the President* by Theodore S. White; *The Kennedys: Dynasty and Disaster, 1848–1984* by John H. Davis; *The Other Mrs. Kennedy* by Jerry Oppenheimer; *With Kennedy* by Pierre Salinger; *Jacqueline*

Kennedy Onassis: A Portrait of Her Private Years by David Lester; *The Joan Kennedy Story: Living with the Kennedys* by Marcia Chellis; *The Kennedys: An American Drama* by Peter Collier and David Horowitz; *JFK: The Man and the Myth* by Victor Lasky; *Jacqueline Kennedy Onassis* by Lester David; *My Life with Jacqueline Kennedy* by Mary Barelli Gallagher; *The Kennedy Women* by Pearl S. Buck; *A Woman Named Jackie* by C. David Heymann; *My Story* by Judith Exner, as told to Ovid Demaris; "The Exner Files" by Liz Smith (*Vanity Fair*, January 1997); *Double Cross: The Explosive Inside Story of the Mobster Who Controlled America* by Sam and Chuck Giancana; *The Boardwalk Jungle* by Paul "Skinny" D'Amato, as told to Ovid Demaris; *Mafia Princess* by Antoinette Giancana and Thomas C. Renner; *Vinnie Teresa's Mafia* by Vincent Teresa with Thomas Renner; *Wall Street Swindler* by Michael Hillman and Thomas Renner; *Johnny, We Hardly Knew Ye* by Kenneth O'Donnell and David E. Powers; *Crime in America* by Estes Kefauver; *Mickey Cohen: Mobster* by Ed Reid; *Bugsy* by George Carpozi; and *The Don: The Life and Death of Sam Giancana* by William Brashler.

Also, *Debbie: My Life* by Debbie Reynolds; *Richard Burton: A Life* by Melvyn Bragg; *Eddie Fisher: My Life, My Loves* by Eddie Fisher; *Las Vegas Is My Beat* by Ralph Pearl; *The Fifty-Year Decline and Fall of Hollywood* by Ezra Goodman; *Revelations from the Memphis Mafia* by Alanna Nash; *Bogie and Me* by Verita Thompson and Donald Shepherd; and "We Might Call This the Politics of Fantasy" by Frank Sinatra (*New York Times*, July 24, 1972).

Sid Mark has been hosting the preeminent radio show about Sinatra, *Sounds of Sinatra*, for forty-two years, and I utilized transcripts of many of his interviews over the years with the Sinatra family as well as with Sinatra's producers and arrangers.

I also reviewed the television program *Turning Point*'s profile on Sinatra ("The Man Behind the Legend," December 12, 1996), as well as *20/20*'s interview with Judith Campbell Exner.

And I thank Liz Smith for certain tips and advice to my researcher, Cathy Griffin.

Hundreds of articles were made reference to, but most helpful were "Is This Really His Life?" by Claudia Puig (*Los Angeles Times*, July 26, 1992); and Sinatra's "Me and My Music" (*Life*, April 23, 1965).

My thanks to Jimmy Whiting for ten hours of interviews regarding Jilly Rizzo, Frank Sinatra, and Marilyn Monroe. I so appreciate his help and access to his personal notes and records. Please note that the name "Jimmy Whiting" is a pseudonym that he chose to protect his identity. It is the only pseudonym in this book.

Thanks also to Bea King for her insights into Sinatra's relationship with Juliet Prowse. Jim McClintick, Marty Lacker, Lamar Fike, Joe Langford, Paula DeLeon, Andrew Wyatt, Mickey Song, and Evelyn Moriarity were also all interviewed.

I referred to *Peter Lawford: The Man Who Kept the Secrets* by James Spada and *The Peter Lawford Story* by Patricia Seaton Lawford. Also, I utilized the *Playboy* interview with Sinatra (February 1963).

I reviewed Edward A. Olsen's oral history, on file at the University of Nevada in Reno, which was helpful as concerns the Cal-Neva incident.

I also referred to numerous Los Angeles District Court documents—in particular, Frank Sinatra Jr.'s testimony in court during his February 1964 kidnapping trial—and newspaper and magazine accounts. Also, some of Frank Sinatra Jr.'s comments are from the popular Sid Mark weekly radio program devoted to his father, Frank Sinatra. I also utilized the book *Miss Rona* by Rona Barrett.

I referred to FBI transcripts of conversations between Sinatra and the kidnappers; thanks also to former FBI agent John Parker for his time and patience.

I also referred to court documents and newspaper accounts regarding legal action taken by Sinatra against Charles Kraft, Morris Levine, and Gladys Root. George Carpozi's book *Is This Man Mafia?* was also helpful. And I utilized my interview with James Wright, Sinatra's valet, and with Sammy Davis. Nancy Sinatra's book *Frank Sinatra: An American Legend* was also referenced.

I also referred to Ava Gardner's memoir, *Ava: My Story* and Sydney Guilaroff's memoir, *Crowning Glory.* John Huston's and Nunnally Johnson's comments are culled from Charles Higham's *Ava.* I also reviewed *An Open Book* by John Huston.

My thanks to Theresa Lomax for all of the hours of interviews relating to the Frank-Mia years.

I also referred to, and used quotes from, transcripts of Mia Farrow's television appearances on *20/20*, *Today*, and the *Oprah Winfrey*

Show in 1997 to promote her memoir *What Falls Away* (which I also consulted).

I consulted *The Life of Mia* by Edward Epstein and Joe Morella. I utilized the files of Sheila Graham from the Academy of Motion Picture Arts and Sciences.

I referred to and am grateful for my interviews with Deidra Evans-Jackson, Doris Sevanto, and Monica Hallstead.

Comments from Sidney Furie are also from my interview with him regarding, primarily, *Call Her Miss Ross* in 1985.

I viewed the November 16, 1965, CBS-TV Walter Cronkite interview with Sinatra (and I thank Maryanne Mastrodanto for providing me with same) and referred to Jack O'Brien's comments about it in the *Journal-American*. I referred to numerous published accounts of Sinatra's conflict with Frederick R. Weisman and consulted police reports about the incident.

I referred to published reports regarding the fracas between Sinatra and Carl Cohen at the Sands, to the Howard Hughes files at the Academy of Motion Picture Arts and Sciences, and also to Nancy Sinatra's two books as well as Mia Farrow's memoirs. I also consulted *Confessions of a Hollywood Columnist* by Sheila Graham and my interviews with Marjorie Nassatier, Florene LaRue, and Diane Phipps.

Other important books and miscellaneous material consulted include *Sinatra: His Life and Times* by Fred Dellar; *Frank Sinatra: A Photobiography* by George Bishop; *The Films of Frank Sinatra* by Gene Ringgold and Clifford McCarty; *Frank Sinatra* by Anthony Scaduto; *The Sinatra Scrapbook* by Gary L. Doctor; *Sinatra: The Entertainer* by Arnold Shaw; *Sinatra: A Celebration* by Stan Britt; *Sinatra* by Ray Coleman; *Sinatra* by Robin Douglas-Home; *Sinatra: The Pictorial Biography* by Lew Irwin; Sinatra's monologues from *Sinatra: A Man and His Music* (Reprise Records); "So Frank Is Seventy-Five" by William Kennedy (from *Frank Sinatra: The Reprise Collection*); "The Legacy" by Nancy Sinatra and "The Capitol Years" by Pete Kline (from *Frank Sinatra: The Capitol Years*); *The Industry* by Saul David; *Report on Blacklisting* by John Cogley; *American Entertainment* by Joseph Csida and June Bundy Csida; *The Encyclopedia of Jazz* by Leonard Feather; *Elizabeth Taylor: The Last Star* by Kitty Kelley; *Miss Peggy Lee: An Autobiography* by Peggy Lee; *Shelley: Also Known as Shirley* by Shelley

Winters; *Marilyn Beck's Hollywood* by Marilyn Beck; *Grace* by James Spada; *Grace* by Robert Lacey; *The Billboard Book of Number-One Hits* by Fred Bronson; *If I Knew Then* by Debbie Reynolds with Bob Thomas; *The Complete Directory to Prime Time Network and Cable TV Shows, 1946–Present* by Tim Brooks and Earle Marsh; *The Last Mafioso* by Ovid Demaris; *Natalie Wood: A Biography in Pictures* by Christopher Nickens; *Brando: A Biography in Photographs* by Christopher Nickens; *Brando* by Peter Manso; and *Iacocca* by Lee Iacocca with William Novak.

Probably the best article about Ava Gardner was written by Rex Reed and published in his book *Do You Sleep in the Nude?* In it Ava is quoted as saying, "Ha! I always knew that Frank would end up in bed with a boy." She denied having made the statement later, but most of her close friends believe that she did say it.

Thanks also to Mary Jenkins for her time and patience and for the interview she gave me in memory of her mother, Choral.

I consulted copious court documents relating to the New Jersey State Commission of Investigation and Sinatra's testimony on February 17, 1970, and also conducted three interviews with one of the investigators, who asked for anonymity.

I reviewed documents and transcripts relating to the House of Representatives Select Committee on Crime Hearings on July 18, 1972, and I also reviewed the *Congressional Record*.

I reviewed copious documents and legal paperwork relating to the Westchester Premier Theater case, including transcripts of depositions and wiretaps. I interviewed three attorneys connected with the case, all of whom asked for anonymity.

Throughout the book, I relied on Larry King's television interview with Sinatra (May 1988) for certain quotes.

I also consulted news reports of the conflict between Sinatra and Sanford Waterman and spoke to a number of people involved with Waterman at the time about the fracas, none of whom wished to be named in this book but all of whom provided details not only about this specific incident but also about Sinatra's general relationship with Caesars.

Of course, there were many hundreds of published articles reviewed about Sinatra's "retirement," some of which were incorporated into the text. The best, of course, is the feature by Tommy Thompson for *Life*. I also had access to Robert L. Rose's drafts and transcripts relating to his articles about Sinatra for the *Chicago Daily News* in 1976.

I also made reference to "Protecting Sinatra Against the Big Beef Story" by Christopher Buckley (*New York*, 1971); "My Father, Frank Sinatra" by Tina Sinatra as told to Jane Ardmore (*McCall's*, December 1973); "Frank Sinatra: He Still Does It His Way" by Mark Sufrin (*Saga*, November 1974); "Sinatra: Still Got the World on a String" by Michael Watts (*Melody Maker*, November 9, 1974); "Kennedy Never Cut Sinatra Ties" by Jack Nelson (*Los Angeles Times*, January 19, 1976); and "The New Mrs. Sinatra" by Ron Home (*Ladies' Home Journal*, October 1976).

I referred to *Once in a Lifetime* by Zsa Zsa Gabor with Wendy Leigh; *Rags to Bitches* by Mr. Blackwell; *The Show Business Nobody Knows* by Earl Wilson; *Sammy Davis: My Father* by Tracey Davis; and *Life with Jackie* by Irving Mansfield and Jean Libman Block.

I utilized Paul Compton's radio interviews with Sinatra on KGIL in San Fransisco on June 5, 1970, and December 30, 1973. I also viewed *Suzy Visits the Sinatras* (May 25, 1977).

During the five years I lived in Palm Springs (1989–94) I had the pleasure of Dinah Shore's company on several occasions. She was an extraordinary, giving person, and I interviewed her three times. Comments included in this book are from an interview she gave me in the spring of 1992 during the Dinah Shore Golf Classic.

Thanks also to Eileen Faith, Nancy Wood-Furnell, Laura Cruz, and Carol Lynley for their insights during interviews for this work.

I obtained a bootleg copy of Sinatra's performance at the White House dinner for Giulio Andreotti and consulted it for this work for quotes from that evening.

My researcher Jim Mitteager interviewed Sinatra's valet of eighteen years, Bill Stapely, on May 28, 1997.

1980–97

My thanks to Mort Viner, Dean Martin's friend and manager of over thirty years, for his assistance in clearing up certain inaccuracies about Martin, Sinatra, and others.

Again, Ava Gardner's business manager of thirty years, Jess Morgan, was tremendously helpful in providing insights into Sinatra's continued relationship with Miss Gardner. And thanks again to Lucille Wellman, Esther Williams, and James Wright.

I reviewed a videotape of the press conference Sinatra, Martin, and Davis held in December 1987 at Chasen's. I personally attended the first date of the "Together Again Tour" with Frank, Dean, and Sammy at the Oakland Coliseum on March 13, 1988. I also obtained a bootleg copy of the Sinatra-Davis concert on March 22, 1988, their first without Martin.

I am also indebted to the staff of the Department of Special Collections of the University of Southern California, which provided me with much material, including Lew Irwin's excellent 1981 *Earth News* radio interview with Sinatra.

I reviewed videotapes of testimony at the Nevada Gaming Control Board's hearings regarding Sinatra's application for a gaming license in February 1981 as well as copious FBI notes, documents, and transcripts relating to the hearings. Thanks also to Stephen Webb and Clarence Newton.

I had access to the *News of the World* files on Frank Sinatra in London, which I used judiciously. More than anything, they provided me with leads and the names of sources to verify information.

Thanks go to Philip Casnoff for his memories of portraying Sinatra in the family's authorized miniseries, which I studied—and enjoyed.

I interviewed a number of former White House staff members who requested anonymity.

Many published accounts were consulted, but most helpful were "The Majestic Artistry of Frank Sinatra" by Mikal Gilmore (*Rolling Stone*, September 18, 1980); "Doing It Her Way" by Nikki Finke (*Los Angeles Times*, February 28, 1988); "Under My Skin" by William Kennedy (*New York Times Magazine*, October 7, 1990); "Frankly, My Dear" by Michael Roberts (*Westword*, December 5–11, 1990); "Are You Ready, Boots? Start Talkin'" by Jeff Tamarkin (*Goldmine*, March 22, 1991); "Sinatra's Doubleplay" by David McClintick (*Vanity Fair*, December 1993); "Secrets of Sinatra—Inside Tales of His Life and Career" by Budd Schulberg (*New Choice for Retirement Living*, 1993);

"Frank Sinatra Jr. Is Worth Six Buddy Grecos" by Tom Junod (*GQ*, January 1994); "Frank and the Fox Pack" by Julie Baumgold (*Esquire*, March 1994); "Sinatra's Last Audition" by Jonathan Schwartz (*Esquire*, May 1995); "The Voice of America" by Will Friedwald and Jennifer Kaylin (*Remember*, November 1994); "The Boots Are Back" by Steve Pond (*Playboy*, May 1995); "A Gold Medal for Ol' Blue Eyes" by Kitty Kelley (*Newsweek*, October 2, 1995); and "Frank Analysis" by Gregory Cerios (*People*, December 18, 1995).

Thanks to Debra Stradella, Joseph Wilson, Marjorie Hyde, Larry Culler (maître d' at Matteo's), and my anonymous friend in the Sinatra camp who provided me with a copy of Frank's performance contract. Thanks to Steve Stoliar, Groucho Marx's secretary and archivist and the author of *Raised Eyebrows: My Years Inside Groucho's House*. I also reviewed Sinatra's radio interviews with Sid Mark (April 28, 1984) and Jonathan Schwartz (on WNEW, 1988).

Again, thanks to Maryann Mastodonato for providing me with a copy of Bill Boggs's WNYW interview with Sinatra.

Thanks to Amanda Bridges, Tina Roth, Felicia Sands, and Betty Monroe for all of their notes, personal papers, and other documents relating to Frank Sinatra's later years.

Thanks also to George Carpozi, whose unusual—but useful—book *Kitty Kelley: The Unauthorized Biography* proved helpful. I also referred to court documents relating to *Sinatra v. Kelley et al*. I reviewed *Reagan* by Lou Cannon; *The Crime Confederation* by Ralph Salerno and John Tompkins; and *Sinatra: An American Classic* by John Rockwell.

I must mention Ed Shirak Jr.'s book, *Our Way: In Honor of Frank Sinatra*, which is an account of Shirak's three-year journey to meet Mr. Sinatra. Shirak, who is from Hoboken, wrote passionately of his experiences related to Sinatra and to the people who knew him in the early days of his life. I found his work fascinating and invaluable to my own research.

Finally, I made extensive use of the Sands Hotel Papers throughout *Sinatra: Behind the Legend*. These papers include many interoffice memos (some of which were utilized in this work) as well as newspaper clippings, photographs, negatives, brochures, press releases, audiotapes, news clips, interview transcriptions, and correspondence, all of it stored in forty-nine boxes. The papers were donated to the James R. Dickinson Library of the University of Nevada, Las Vegas, in December 1980 by the Sands Hotel through the office of Al Guzman, director of publicity and advertising. The collection comprises essentially the files of Al Freeman, director of advertising and promotion for the Sands Hotel from 1952 until his death at the age of forty-eight in 1972. My thanks to Peter Michel, head of special collections of the Dickinson Library, for his assistance with this material.

2015 SOURCES AND NOTES

Since the original publication of this volume, all sides of the stormy saga of Nancy and Tina Sinatra versus Barbara Sinatra got a full airing in books authored by the principal players. As well as independent interviews, I utilized these books in researching the new material found in this volume regarding those relationships.

First, in 1985, Nancy would write *Frank Sinatra: My Father*. Frank was still alive at the time, so she was discreet about Barbara, and even generous toward her. (This book was referenced in the original edition of *Sinatra: A Complete Life*.) Then in 1998 she published *Sinatra: An American Legend*. This volume, more a scrapbook chronology than a strict narrative, is about as comprehensive a look at Frank's career as anyone will ever find. It's stunning in its detail. Nancy cannot be accused of sanitizing her father's story, either. Her books about him are candid; she has always preferred to present him with warts and all rather than in an unrealistic, sycophantic way. "This is a love letter but not a whitewash," she wrote in her first book. "My Dad doesn't need—and wouldn't want—that."

After Frank's death in 1998, Tina would publish *My Father's Daughter: A Memoir*. Like her sister, Tina has also made it her mission to be as honest as possible. Anyone expecting a superficial work by her would likely be surprised by Tina's unflinching account of her family's battles with Barbara. Slowly and methodically, she built a case against Barbara as a woman who only married Frank for his money and lifestyle, and then did anything she could think of to drive a wedge between him and his children—and anyone else he held dear. Tina even claimed that Barbara had small video cameras surreptitiously placed in Frank's den and bedroom so that she could secretly monitor his conversations. "I thought about the talks I'd had with Dad, the private moments between father and daughter," Tina wrote. "Now I realized that they may not have been so private after all." It felt authentic, fair-minded, and convincing, especially coming from Tina, who was known previously to default to diplomacy where Barbara was concerned. It was only when she felt pushed up against a wall that Tina would retaliate.

In 2012, twelve years after Tina's book, Barbara Sinatra would offer her own memoir, *Lady Blue Eyes*. Her account of her life with Frank is very different from Tina's, filled with lovely reminiscences of fun times and glamorous excess. She glosses over any sort of family feud.

In reading some of the same stories previously told by Tina but now from Barbara's viewpoint—with the Sinatra children carefully excised from each memory—one was reminded of Tina's recollection that framed photos of her and her siblings that once had an honored place on the grand piano in Sinatra's home disappeared soon after he married Barbara. "It was as though Dad had no children," Tina wrote. "*Out of sight...*"

While about half of Tina Sinatra's book was devoted to Frank's marriage to Barbara and the trouble it caused her and her family, Barbara took a very different approach to the story. In a stunning statement all her own, she didn't mention that Frank even *had* daughters: Tina's and Nancy's names are nowhere to be found in Barbara's four-hundred-page book.

In fact, Barbara and the Sinatras would have very little, if any, contact with each other after his funeral. "Peace will never happen with my stepmother," Tina would later say. "There's no point. There was nothing untruthful in the book [that she would later publish], so there's not much she can do. I don't harbor any animosity or resentment," she clarifies, "it's really gone now, and that all comes through the cathartic experience of writing the book. It's like I vomited it up, spewed it up," she says. "But I can tell you a very brief funny story. I went to some of the bookstores in Beverly Hills for signings that the publisher had set up, and one store said: 'This is our fifteenth shipment of your book; everybody you know has bought it.' And I said: 'Oh, really? Like who?' And they said, 'Predominantly, your stepmother's friends.'"

For years, Barbara worked for her husband's causes, and she was—and still is—active in the Barbara Sinatra Children's Center at the Eisenhower Medical Center in Rancho Mirage, which treats young victims of child abuse. Frank was never allowed to spend time at the center, however, despite his contributions to it in excess of a million dollars. Molesting fathers often came in for treatment, and Barbara was afraid of her husband's reaction to them. "My husband's from a totally different school," she admitted in 1988. "He wants to break their legs. He wants to round up all the men and break their legs. He said, 'You can talk to them all you want, but let *me* teach them and they'll never do it again. If you put them in a hospital for a year, when they come out, they're not going to do that.' So he's not allowed in there."

* * *

As earlier stated in this book's author's note, I returned to many of the original tapes of interviews conducted for the first edition of this book to mine new material, which has been threaded throughout this text. I also referenced research involving Frank Sinatra for books I wrote since the original edition of this one was published in 1997, and those include *Jackie, Ethel, Joan; Once upon a Time; Elizabeth*; and *After Camelot*.

Moreover, I interviewed Frank Sinatra's valet George Jacobs on three separate occasions in January 1999. Since those interviews took place after the original publication of this book, material from them is now published for the first time in this edition. I also referenced Mr. Jacobs's book, *Mr. S: My Life with Frank Sinatra*, which was published in 2009. Sadly, George Jacobs died at the age of eighty-six in December 2013. He was a true gentleman's gentleman. I also reinterviewed Ted Hechtman, Thomas DiBella, Jimmy Silvani, Dick Moran, and Lucy Wellman for the paperback edition of this book, which was never published. Their additional stories appear in this edition for the first time. I also interviewed Jeffrey Hayden and Allan B. Ecker for the unreleased paperback edition of this work, their stories regarding Mia Farrow and Frank Sinatra, respectively, told here for the first time. I also interviewed George Schlatter for that unreleased edition.

The comments by Lester Sacks's daughter, Adrienne Ellis, about the wedding of Ava Gardner and Frank Sinatra were culled from the feature "Frank & Ava: An Unforgettable Day" by Rose DeWolf (*Philadelphia Daily News*, May 18, 1998).

After Barry Keenan was interviewed for the first edition of this book—his first interview ever about the kidnapping of Frank Sinatra Jr.—there was great national interest in his story. Six months after the book was released, Keenan gave an interview to reporter Peter Gilstrap for an article called "Snatching Sinatra," which was published in *New Times Los Angeles* magazine. His story was then offered to Hollywood as a movie and eventually sold to Showtime. The movie, *Stealing Sinatra*, aired on Showtime in 2003, starring David Arquette as Barry Keenan, with James Russo as Frank Sinatra and Thomas Ian Nicholas as Frank Sinatra Jr. William H. Macy, who portrayed John Irwin, was nominated for an Emmy.

For this volume, I also reinterviewed Tom Gianetti (January 30, 2014); Eileen Faith (March 14 and March 16, 2014); Doris Sevanto (March 17, 2014); and Tina Donato (March 18, 2014). My source Joey D'Orazio—quoted liberally in the first edition of this book and now in this edition based on new material gleaned from his original interviews—died in 2006. I interviewed his son, Tony D'Orazio (March 18, 2014), to corroborate some of his father's earlier stories. I also spoke to Nancy Venturi's daughter, Angela (June 12, 2014), to corroborate some of her mother's memories found in the first edition.

I referenced the following books: *Under My Skin* by Julie Sinatra; *Ava Gardner: The Secret Conversations* by Peter Evans and Ava Gardner; *Living with Miss G* by Mearene Jordan; *Memories Are Made of This* by Deana Martin with Wendy Holden; *That's Amore* by Christopher Smith and Ricci Martin; *My Way* by Paul Anka and David Dalton; and *By Myself and Then Some* by Lauren Bacall.

2015 ACKNOWLEDGMENTS

I am so happy to have had the opportunity to revisit Sinatra, a favorite subject of mine, with the rerelease of this now revised book. I would like to thank my publisher, Jamie Raab, for shepherding this project, and also my editor, Gretchen Young, for another terrific job. *The Hiltons: A Family Dynasty* was a collaborative effort on many levels, from inception to publication. Here I would like to acknowledge those who assisted me in this endeavor. I would like to also thank Jamie's capable assistant, Deb Withey.

It's been my great honor for the last sixteen years to call Grand Central Publishing my home, and I am deeply indebted to Jamie Raab for creating such a nurturing environment. As always, I would like to thank my managing editor, Bob Castillo, for his invaluable contributions. Special thanks to Anne Twomey for her excellent cover design. I would also like to thank Claire Brown in art, Sara Weiss in editorial, and Tom Whatley and Giraud Lorber in production. A special thanks to my copy editor, Roland Ottewell.

I would like to thank John Pelosi and the staff of Pelosi Wolf Effron & Spates for their legal review of this work, which, as always, was thorough and much appreciated.

I would like to acknowledge my domestic agent, Mitch Douglas, for sixteen years of excellent representation.

I would also like to acknowledge my foreign agent, Dorie Simmonds of the Dorie Simmonds Agency in London, who has been with me for almost twenty years.

I am fortunate to have been associated with the same private investigator and chief researcher for more than twenty years, and that is Cathy Griffin. I owe her a great debt of gratitude for her work on this book. Thanks also to my personal copy editor, James Pinkston, who spent many hours with *Sinatra* back in the 1990s.

I would also like to thank Maryanne Reed for helping me organize all of the tape-recorded interviews and transcripts that were pivotal to the research behind this book.

My thanks also to Jonathan Hahn, my personal publicist and good friend.

Thanks also to all of those from "Team JRT": attorney James M. Leonard; CPA Michael Horowitz, of Horowitz, McMahon and Zarem in Southern California, Inc.; and also Felinda deYoung, of Horowitz et al.

Thanks to Andy Steinlen; George Solomon; Jeff Hare; Andy Hirsch; Samuel Munoz; Bruce Rheins and Dawn Westlake; Richard

Tyler Jordan; and all of my good friends, too many to list here but they know who they are.

I have always been so blessed to have a family as supportive as mine. My thanks and love go out to Roslyn and Bill Barnett and Jessica and Zachary, Rocco and Rosemaria Taraborrelli and Rocco and Vincent, and Arnold Taraborrelli. Special thanks to my father, Rocco. A big smile, also, for Spencer.

INDEX

ABC-TV Sinatra Timex specials, 263
Academy Awards, 76, 87, 200–202, 215,
    216, 273
Accardo, Tony, 104
Adler, Buddy, 171, 173, 179
Adonis, Joe, 104
Agnew, Spiro T., 378, 383, 387, 388, 394,
    398, 399, 401, 416
AIDS Project Los Angeles, 512
Algren, Nelson, 205
All Alone (album), 243
Allen, Woody, 536
Allenberg, Burt, 177
"All of Me," 153
"All or Nothing at All," 46, 48, 73, 243,
    387, 455, 513
"All the Way," 215
Allyson, June, 120
Altman, Alan, 471
America I Hear You Singing (album), 315
Americana Hotel, NY, 287
American Federation of Radio Artists, 74
American Mercury magazine, 75
Amsler, James, 307
Amsler, Joseph Clyde, 284–85, 288, 291,
    292–99, 303, 307–8, 311
Anastasia, Albert, 104
Anchors Aweigh (film), 78–79
Andreotti, Giulio, 400
"Angel Eyes," 216, 387, 388
Aniston, Ethel, 210, 211
Anka, Paul, 375, 470, 479, 532

Annenberg, Walter, 414
Arden, Harold, 29, 30
Armstrong, Louis, 207
Astaire, Fred, 77
"As Time Goes By," 80

Babes in Arms (Broadway musical), 193
Bacall, Lauren, 88, 204, 210–12, 216–22,
    330–31, 332, 363, 468
Baker, Anita, 507
"Bali Ha'i," 121, 146
Ball, Lucille, 155, 440
Bantam Books, 465
Barbato, Mike, 25
Barefoot Contessa, The (film), 194
Barrett, Rona, 295, 366
Barton, Ben, 165
Barton, Eileen, 71
Barzie, Tino, 295
Basie, Count, 233, 270, 271, 291,
    345, 365
Beatles, 442
Beau, Heinie, 184
"Be Careful, It's My Heart," 242
Bennett, Tony, 25, 134, 507, 513
Benny, Jack, 63–64, 88, 387
Berle, Milton, 244
Berlin, Irving, 85, 204
Bernstein, Leonard, 244, 245
Berrigan, Bunny, 49
"Best Is Yet to Come, The," 317, 511
Billboard, 50, 59, 200, 443, 508

Bishop, Joey, 189, 196–97, 224, 225, 244, 263, 316, 532

Blackwell, Richard, 393–94

"Blue Skies," 61

Bobby Tucker Singers, 72

Bogart, Humphrey, 88, 204, 208, 210–11

Bonanno, Joe "Bananas," 104

Bono, 509

Bonucelli, Dorothy (Alora Gooding), 58–59, 91, 506

Boots Enterprises Inc., 535

Borgnine, Ernest, 172, 206

Bowen, Jimmy, 345, 355

Bowes, Major, 27, 28

Boys' Town of Italy, 220

Bradlee, Benjamin, 464

Brando, Marlon, 204–5, 273

Brazil, Rio Palace shows, 441

Brisson, Frederick "Freddie," 335, 354

Britt, Mai, 237–38

Brown, Edmund "Jerry," Jr., 382

Brunswick record label, 46, 317

Bunker, Richard, 452

Burke, Sonny, 442

Burns, Lillian, 123–24

Bushkin, Joey, 49

"By the Time I Get to Phoenix," 375

Cabré, Mario, 145–46, 148–49, 156

Caesars Palace, Las Vegas, 359, 402, 440, 441; Sinatra and daughter act, 453–54; Waterman incident, 384–85, 451

Cagney, Jimmy, 204

Cahn, Sammy, 54, 60, 72, 78, 84, 116, 215, 235, 258, 373, 530

Cain, Marilyn, 190

Callas, Charlie, 454

Cal-Neva Lodge, Lake Tahoe, 155, 267, 394; Marilyn Monroe and Sinatra at, 267–69; Sam Giancana incident, 276–79, 372, 446, 448–49; Sinatra investment in, 155; Sinatra sells share of, 280–81; Sinatra's suicide attempt and, 156–57

Can-Can (film), 257

Candullo, Joe, 110

Candy Store, Beverly Hills, 365, 366

Capiello, Steve, 11–12, 17

Capitol Records, 60n, 153, 173, 183–85, 188n, 228, 242, 516, 535; 1953 recording sessions, 184, 193–94; 1993 recording sessions, 507–8; "I'll Never Smile Again" recorded, 50n; Sinatra's earnings and, 339

Capitol Theater, NYC, 112, 140

Capone, Al, 260

Capra, Frank, 216

Carbone, Anna, 421

Carnegie Hall, NYC, 442

Carousel (Broadway Musical), 84

Carpozi, George, 350–51

Carson, Johnny, 259

Casnoff, Philip, 503

Cassavetes, John, 360

Cast a Giant Shadow (film), 335

Castellano, Paul, 445

Castle, William, 362

"Castle Rock," 47

Cattaneo, Hank, 507

CBS-TV, 152, 338, 340

Chase, Barrie, 257

Chasen, David, 88

Chasen's Restaurant, 478–79

Cheshire, Maxine, 398–400

Chester, Bob, 44

Chez Paree, Chicago, 147, 170

Chicago Theatre, 482–83

"Ciribiribin," 46

Ciro's, Hollywood, 110–11

Clemens, Paul, 172

Clift, Montgomery, 172, 181–83

Clinton, Bill, 527

Clooney, Rosemary, 134, 315

Cobb, Lee J., 119, 272

"Cockeyed Optimist, A," 535

Cohen, Carl, 356–57, 358, 450

Cohen, Mickey, 259

Cohn, Harry, 172–73, 175, 177, 181, 188, 257n

Cohn, Joan, 172–73

Cohn, Mickey, 247

Cohn, Roy, 247

Colbert, Claudette, 335

Cole, Nat King, 184, 194, 238, 244
Coleman, Cy, 173
Collins, Victor LeCroix, 277–79, 448
Colombo, Russ, 17
Columbia Pictures, 71, 171
Columbia Records, 47, 60, 60n, 62, 74, 134, 151, 185, 516; drops Sinatra, 170, 183; Sinatra records "Why Try to Change Me Now," 173; Sinatra's earnings and, 339
Come Blow Your Horn (film), 271
Come Dance With Me (album), 216
"Come Fly with Me," 243
Come Fly With Me (album), 215
"Come Rain or Come Shine," 243
Come Swing With Me (album), 243n
Como, Perry, 24, 25, 102
Concert Sinatra, The (album), 270
Condon, Richard, 255
Confidential magazine, 202–3
Congressional Gold Medal, 527
Conte, John, 89
Conversations with Kennedy (Bradlee), 464
Copacabana, NYC, 72, 130, 142; 1950 engagement at, 139–42, 146, 147; 1957 engagement at, 211; Monroe sees Sinatra at, 196–97
Corrado, Doris, 12
Cosell, Howard, 404
Cosgrove, Ruth, 143
Cossette, Pierre, 509
Costa, Don, 85, 243, 374, 401, 442, 443
Costello, Frank, 104
Costra Nostra (Mafia or "the Mob"): cancellation of JFK's visit to Sinatra's home and, 259–63; Cronkite interview and, 338–39; end of an era, 407; Havana, Cuba meeting, 103–9; in Hoboken, 9–10, 103; Justice Department report, 260; Kennedy's war on, 246–48; New Jersey investigation of, 380–81; Sinatra and, 74–75, 102–9, 109n, 250–54, 275–82, 373–74, 385, 398, 407, 444–46; Sinatra's gambling license and, 276–82, 446–50
Count Basie Band, 317, 334

Crane, Cheryl, 92
Crane, Steve, 92
Crawford, Joan, 172
Cronkite, Walter, xix, 338–40
Crosby, Bing, 17, 19, 24, 49, 59, 73, 88, 119, 134n, 207, 262, 263, 289, 315
Crosby, Chris, 289
Crouch, Charles L., 308, 311
Crowe, Jerome, 303
Crowley, Arthur, 468, 486–87, 501
Cruz, Laura, 405–6
"Cufflinks and a Tie Clip," 344
Curtis, Tony, 216, 235, 532
"Cycles," 374
Cycles (album), 374–75

D'Amato, Alfonse, 527
D'Amato, Nicholas, 253
D'Amato, Paul "Skinny," 155, 260, 374, 407, 447
Damone, Vic, 25, 102, 513, 532, 533
Dandy in Aspic, A (film), 354
Dane, Pat, 75
Darin, Bobby, 345
Davis, Beryl, 71
Davis, Sammy, Jr., 101, 120–21, 159, 192, 208, 212, 254, 263, 284, 512; accident, 202–4; charity concert with Sinatra, 434; cocaine and, 439–41; death of, 490; Kennedy inaugural and, 237–39; magazine article about Ava Gardner and, 184–86, 202–3; marriage to Loray White, 256, 257n; marriage to Mai Britt, 237–38; politics and, 373; Rat Pack films, 225, 317; Sinatra-Marx wedding and, 416; Sinatra rifts with, 440; Sinatra's friendship, 203–4, 211, 237–39, 257n; Sinatra's racial humor and, 226–27; Sinatra's stand against racism and, 226–27; Sinatra swears on Bible and, 196; Together Again Tour, 477–84
Day, Doris, 204
DeBakey, Michael, 376, 416
"Deep Night," 47
de Havilland, Olivia, 204
Demarest, Patti, 55, 57, 71

DePalma, Greg, 445
Desert Hospital, Palm Springs, 473
Desert Inn, Las Vegas, 224
Desert Memorial Park, Cathedral City, 533
d'Estainville, Kim, 456
Detective, The (film), 360, 361, 369
de Villafrance, Raul, 198
DeWitt, Allan, 48
Dexter, Brad, 315–16
Dexter, Dave, 184
Diamond, Neil, 442, 535
DiBella, Tommy, 251–53, 275, 282, 407
Dickinson, Angie, 235
DiMaggio, Joe, 196, 248, 249, 266, 269
Dominguin, Luis Miguel, 194, 195
Donato, Salvatore, 39–40
Donato, Tina, 5, 23
"Don't Worry About Me," 184
D'Orazio, Joey, 14, 30, 35, 39, 40, 55–56,
    60, 66, 67, 68, 74, 75, 188, 377, 434,
    463, 464, 469, 490, 524
Dorchester Productions, 225, 242
Dorfman, Allen, 373
Dorsey, Tommy, 46, 51–53, 57, 60–61, 75,
    76, 184; Sinatra contract with, 46, 48,
    57, 61, 62, 73–76, 102, 107; Sinatra's
    solo recordings and, 59; Sinatra tribute
    album, 242, 243
Double Dynamite (film), 153
Douglas, Kirk, 212, 234, 335, 359, 414,
    419, 447, 516, 532
Down Beat, 59, 121, 200
Downey, Robert, Sr. and wife, 418
Duets and *Duets II* (albums), 508–9
Dukakis, Olympia, 503
Dunaway, Faye, 441
Dunham, Katherine, 462
Dunleavy, Steve, 261
Durgom, George H. "Bullets," 51, 62
Durocher, Leo, 392, 416
Dylan, Bob, 333, 512, 513

Earle Theatre, Philadelpha, 73
East, William G., 310, 312
Ebbins, Milt, 261
Eberle, Ray, 62

Eberly, Bob, 24
Ecker, Allan B., 378–79
Eckstine, Billy, 147
Egan, Jack, 49
Eisenhower Medical Center, 471, 477,
    562; Barbara Sinatra Children's
    Center at, 477, 512
Ellington, Duke, 65
Ellis, Adrienne, 164
Elman, Ziggy, 49
Elson, Dean, 296, 307
"Embraceable You," 151, 508
Entratter, Corinne, 354
Entratter, Jack, 191, 225, 249, 296, 354,
    356, 359
Evans, Gene, 295
Evans, George (press agent), 65–72,
    73, 78, 80, 107, 111–12, 129–30, 264,
    506–7; death of, 133; Lana affair
    and, 97–98; nicknaming Sinatra
    "The Voice," 66n; Sinatra and Ava
    Gardner, 128–29, 132–33; Sinatra and
    Lee Mortimer, 110; Sinatra drops,
    130–32, 282; Sinatra-Gardner arrest
    in shooting prank and, 126; Sinatra's
    affairs and, 91, 93–95, 100–101
Evans, Robert, 362
"Ever Homeward," 119
"Everybody Loves Somebody," 345
"Every Day of My Life," 46
"Everything's Coming Up Roses," 245
Execution of Private Slovik, The (film),
    233–34
Exner, Judith Campbell, 447

Faith, Eileen, 400, 421, 426, 457–58
Faith, Percy, 173
"Farewell, Farewell to Love," 47
Farrell, Wes, 402, 422
Farrow, John, 320, 321, 325
Farrow, Mia, 320–33, 341–43, 346–55,
    363–64, 468; Ava Gardner and,
    351–53; career of, 321–22, 328, 354, 369;
    character and personality, 322, 326,
    328, 362, 397, 468; childhood, 320–21;
    cuts off her hair, 342–43, 346; Dolly

Sinatra and, 336–37; Himalayan trip, 368; meets Sinatra's family, 346–48; *Rosemary's Baby* and, 359–62, 369; Sinatra and, 320, 322–29, 335–36, 337, 353–68; Sinatra and, after divorce, 369; Sinatra and Bacall and, 333; Sinatra divorces, 363–64, 368, 468; Sinatra's Cronkite interview and, 339; Sinatra's fiftieth birthday party and, 340–43; Sinatra's violent side and, 330–31, 333, 357–60; Sinatra throws her out, 367–68; Sinatra wedding, 348–49; son, Ronan, as Sinatra's child, 535–36

FBI, 109–10, 306, 373, 448, 449, 451; Frank, Jr. kidnapping, 296–98, 301–3, 307–8; "Las Vegas Black Book," 276

"Fella With an Umbrella," 119

Field, Dr. John Wesley, 158

Finkelstein, Robert, 517

First Deadly Sin, The (film), 441

Fischetti, Charlie, 104

Fischetti, Joe, 104, 106, 108

Fischetti, Rocco "Rocky," 104, 106

Fisher, Eddie, 189, 249, 473

Fitzgerald, Ella, 244

Flamingo Lounge, Las Vegas, 287

"Fly Me to the Moon," 511

"Foggy Day, A," 193

Folsey, George, 117

Fontaine, Frank, 170

Fontainebleau Hotel, Miami, 236, 247, 263, 354

Ford, John, 178

Forde, George A., 308–9, 311

Formosa, John, 254, 260

Foss, John, 292–95, 296–97

4 for Texas (film), 262, 272–73

Francis Albert Sinatra & Antonio Carlos Jobim (album), 355

Francis Albert Sinatra Does His Thing (TV special), 374

Francke, Toni, 38–40

Frankenheimer, John, 255

Franklin, Aretha, 508

Franklin, George, 384–85

Frank Sinatra—An American Legend (Nancy Sinatra), 470; Sinatra's near drowning recounted in, 316

Frank Sinatra Desert Classic, 511

Frank Sinatra Entertainment, 535

Frank Sinatra International Youth Center for Arab and Jewish Children, 265

Frank Sinatra Show, The (TV series), 152

Frank Sinatra Sings Days of Wine and Roses, Moon River and Other Academy Award Winners (album), 315

Frank Sinatra Sings Only the Lonely (album), 216, 265

Frank Sinatra's Welcome Home Party for Elvis Presley (TV special), 263–65

Fratianno, Jimmy, 445, 446

Freeman, Al, 249

Freeman, Ernie, 345, 346

From Here to Eternity (film), 173, 177, 179, 180–83, 188–89, 200–201, 434; Ava Gardner and, 171–73, 175, 201–2

From Here to Eternity (Jones), 170, 171

"From the Bottom of My Heart," 46, 317

Furie, Sidney, 353

Fusco, Richard, 445

Gable, Clark, 77, 174

Gabor, Eva, 395, 494, 495

Gage, Nicholas, 373–74

"Gal That Got Away, The," 443

Gambino, Carlo, 445

Gambino, Joseph, 445

Gambino, Phyllis Sinatra, 445

Garavante, Rosa (grandmother), 12

Garde, Colin, 174

Gardner, Ava, 116–18, 135, 145, 408, 503; affair with Gominguín, 195; affair with John Farrow, 325; affair with Mario Cabré, 145–46, 148–49, 156; in Africa, filming *Mogambo*, 173–75; alcohol and mood swings, 156–57; background, 122–24; Corgi dog, Rags, 154, 155, 157, 351; death of, 488; Dolly Sinatra and, 152, 165–66, 274; in Europe (1950), 145–49; film career, 123–24, 152, 170, 174, 189, 194, 201; firing of George

Evans and, 130–32; George Jacobs and, 364–65; *From Here to Eternity* and, 171–73, 175, 201–2; Lana Turner's advice to, 126–27; Lawford's date with, 261; magazine article about Sammy Davis and, 202–3; marriage to Artie Shaw, 123, 143; marriage to Mickey Rooney, 80, 117, 124; Nevada escapade (1951), 154–55; pregnancies and abortions, 175–80, 504; separation and divorce from Sinatra, 191, 193, 194–96, 198; Sinatra affair, 124–63; Sinatra and, after divorce, 394–95, 489; Sinatra reunion attempts, 273–76, 409–11; Sinatra engagement, 154, 163–64; Sinatra gives money to, 488; Sinatra keeps photos of, 324–25; Sinatra loaned money by, 157; Sinatra marriage, 173–80, 182, 189; Sinatra meets, 88–89; Sinatra-Mia Farrow and, 351–53; Sinatra's career problems, 141–42, 170; Sinatra's comeback and Academy Award, 200, 201–2; Sinatra's family and, 162–63, 176–77; Sinatra's gifts to, 148, 154, 194; Sinatra shooting incident and arrest, 126; Sinatra's mob connections and, 274; Sinatra's suicide attempts and, 144–45, 156–60l Sinatra's wife Nancy and, 128–29, 135–36, 138–39, 151; Sinatra wedding and honeymoon, 163–67

Garland, Judy, 120, 208, 212, 225, 235
Garrick, Frank, 8
Garydon, Joe, 393
Gatto, Anna, 8
Gaudio, Bob, 385
Gelfand, Marshall, 501
"Gentle on My Mind," 375
Giancana, Antoinette, 449
Giancana, Chuck, 236
Giancana, Sam, 236, 259, 372, 374, 381, 446–50, 503; Ava Gardner-Sinatra fight and, 275–76; Cal-Neva Lodge incident, 276–79, 372, 446, 448–49; Kennedy's visit to Sinatra's home cancelled and, 260–61; kidnapping

of Frank, Jr., and, 305–6, 307; murder of, 407; requests Sinatra's intercession with the Kennedys, 246–48, 251–53, 451; Sinatra betrays, 250–54; Sinatra invites to Cal-Neva Lodge, 268; Villa Venice and, 254, 449; West Virginia primary and (1960), 247

Gianetti, Rocky, 15, 16
Gianetti, Tom, 15, 16
Gibbons, Harold, 373
Gibson, Andy, 46
Gilmore, Voyle, 184
Godfrey, Joseph, 174
Goetz, Bill, 353
Goetz, Edie, 222, 353
"Going Home," 98
"Goin' Out of My Head," 453
Golden Nugget Casino, Atlantic City, 471
Goldtone, Eddie, 257–58
"Gone With the Wind," 265
Goodman, Benny, 44, 63, 64, 72
Gordon, Waxey, 10
Gore, Louise, 398
Gormé, Eydie, 440, 483, 494, 495, 496, 498, 501, 508, 513, 532
Gosch, Martin A., 104, 105, 106, 109n
Gosden, Freeman, 414
Graham, Sheila, 333
Grammy Awards, 215, 216, 337, 338, 344, 346, 442; Legend Award for Lifetime Achievement (1994), 509
Grant, Cary, 109n, 204, 207, 387
Grant, Frank, 194–95
Grant, Hank, 454
Greco, Buddy, 267
Green, Bill and wife, 418
Greene, Bob, 469
Greene, Shecky, 210
Greenschpoon, Elizabeth, 220
Greenson, Ralph, 98, 220, 255
Greenspun, Hank, 448
Greer, Howard, 164
Griffin, Merv, 494, 495
Griffith, Melanie, 404n
"Guess I'll Hang My Tears Out to Dry," 216
Guilaroff, Sydney, 154, 191–92

Guys and Dolls (film), 204–5, 226, 273
Guzman, Al, 191, 249

Haines, Connie, 49, 50
Haley, Jack, 76
Hall, Fred, 47
Harden, Marcia Gay, 503
Harrah's Lake Tahoe Casino, 288, 292
Hart, Al, 302
Hart, Lorenz, 193
Hartford, Connecticut, concert (1950), 129
Harvey, Laurence, 255, 354
Havana, Cuba, 103–5, 106–7, 108, 110, 449
Hayden, Jeffrey, 341, 342–43
Haymes, Dick, 47, 61, 62
Hayworth, Rita, 215
Hazlewood, Lee, 344, 355
Hechtman, Ted, 29, 69, 70, 91, 95, 97, 98, 100, 107, 133
Hefti, Neal, 85, 243
"Hello, Young Lovers," 338
Henderson, Skitch, 147
Henie, Sonja, 94
Henry, Pat, 392, 423
"Here I'll Stay," 484
Herfurt, Arthur "Skeets," 45
Herron, Joel, 153
Hewitt, Don, 338, 340
"Hey Look, No Crying," 443
Higher and Higher (film), 73, 76
"High Hopes," 216; JFK campaign and, 227, 235
High Society (film), 31, 134n, 207
Hilton, Conrad, 434
His Way (Kelley), 470, 473, 503
Hoboken, NJ, 2–5, 10, 11, 15; gangsters in, 9–10, 103; Sinatra family's saloon, 10, 11; Sinatra homes in, 7, 8, 17, 20; Sinatra singing in, 24; World War I and, 9–10
Hoboken Four, 27–28
Hoffa, Jimmy, 246, 247, 259, 373
Hoffa, Mrs. Jimmy, 373
Hole in the Head, A (film), 216
"Holly Holy," 535
Hollywood Bowl concerts (1943), 73
Hollywood Reporter, 92

Hollywood Ten, 233
Hoover, J. Edgar, 247, 299, 307
Hope, Bob, 273, 289, 404, 447
Hope, Tony, 289
Hopper, Dennis, 404n
Hopper, Hedda, 137
Horne, Lena, 65, 130, 224, 508
Hotel Sherman, Chicago, 46
"House I Live In, The," 400
House I Live In, The (film), 86–87, 233
House of Blues at Mandalay Bay, Las Vegas, 455
"How Does That Grab You, Darlin'?," 344
"How Old I Am," 338
Hughes, Howard, 124, 356
Humphrey, Hubert, 372–74
Hurkos, Peter, 422, 422n
Hutton, June, 165, 170, 184
Hyman, Eliot, 378
Hynde, Chrissie, 508

"I Couldn't Sleep a Wink Last Night," 76
"I Didn't Know What Time It Was," 216
"If I Loved You," 84
"I Get a Kick Out of You," 193
"I Have But One Heart," 84, 145
"I'll Never Smile Again," 50, 50n, 55, 58, 387
"I Love You," 184
"I'm a Fool to Want You," 153, 173
"Imagination," 243
"I'm Getting Sentimental Over You," 49, 243
"I'm Gonna Sit Right Down and Write Myself a Letter," 270
"I'm Walking Behind You," 184
Independent Citizens Committee of the Arts, Sciences, and Professions, 88
In the Wee Small Hours (album), 205
I Remember Tommy (album), 76, 243
Irwin, John, 284–85, 288, 301, 302, 303–5, 308, 311
"I Should Care," 84
"It All Depends on You," 146
"It Had to Be You," 442, 513

It Happened in Brooklyn (film), 89–90
It Might as Well Be Swing (album), 270, 317
"It Never Entered My Mind," 443
"It Only Happens When I Dance With You," 119
"It Was a Very Good Year," 338, 340
"I've Got a Crush on You," 151, 153, 507, 508
"I've Got the World on a String," 184, 507, 511, 535
"I've Got You Under My Skin," 206–7, 387, 509

"Jackson," 344
Jackson, Mahalia, 245
Jacobs, George (valet), 203; Ava Gardner and, 274, 364–65; on Cal-Neva Lodge, Monroe, and Giancana, 267–69; on Cal-Neva Lodge incident, 277–78; on *From Here to Eternity*, 255–56; on Rat Pack at the Villa Venice, 254; on Sinatra and Bacall, 221; on Sinatra and Frank, Jr., 232; on Sinatra and JFK, 262–63; on Sinatra and Mia Farrow, 327–28, 331–33, 337, 351–53, 355, 359; Sinatra fires, 364–66; Sinatra's suicide attempt and, 158; on Sinatra's temper, 358
Jaffe, Henry, 74
Jahn, E. J., Jr., 80
James, Harry, 44–48, 532
Jenkins, Gordon, 85, 215, 216, 338, 401, 442, 443
Jilly's, NYC, 274, 336; Sinatra-Ava Gardner fight at, 275–76
John, Elton, 85
Johnny Concho (film), 207
Johnson, Lyndon, 235, 244, 372–73
Joker Is Wild, The (film), 215
Jolly Christmas with Frank Sinatra, A (album), 215
Jones, Dick, 165, 184
Jones, George C., 306, 307
Jones, Jack, 345
Jones, James, 170, 182–83
Jones, Quincy, 317, 334, 345, 465
Jordan, Matty, 398

Jordan, Mearene "Rene," 117–18, 135, 143, 154–58, 160, 177, 194, 394, 410–11
Joubert, Vine, 406, 491–92, 491n, 494, 529

Kaempfert, Bert, 345
Kastel, "Dandy Phil," 104
Kazan, Elia, 462
Keaton, LaDonna Webb, 493
Keawe, George, 316
Keenan, Barry Worthington, 284–85, 288–95, 299–312
Keller, Jack, 78, 80
Kelley, Kitty, 462–65, 470–71, 473, 503; Sinatra's lawsuit against, 465
Kelly, Betty Jean, 501
Kelly, Gene, 77, 78, 79, 120, 121, 133, 244
Kelly, Grace, 134n, 174, 207, 441
Kempton, Murray, 244
Kennamer, Rex, 528
Kennedy, Edward "Ted," 251, 335, 437–38
Kennedy, Jacqueline. *See* Onassis, Jacqueline Kennedy
Kennedy, John F. "JFK", 227–28, 233–39, 464; assassination, 287, 290, 291; "High Hopes" as campaign theme song, 227; Marilyn Monroe and, 266; photographs and, 237; Sammy Davis and, 237–38; Sinatra and, 227–28, 235–39, 250–54; Sinatra and pre-inaugural gala, 237–39, 244–46; Sinatra snub, 259–63; West Virginia primary, 247; womanizing of, 227
Kennedy, Joseph P., 227, 234, 236, 247, 250–51, 263
Kennedy, Robert F., 247, 259, 260, 372, 382, 451; assassination, 372; cancellation of JFK's visit to Sinatra's home and, 259–63; Frank, Jr. kidnapping and, 298, 306–7; mob investigation by, 246–48, 252, 253; Sinatra and, 236–37, 238
Kennedy, Rose, 335–36, 438
Kennedy Center Honors for Lifetime Achievement, 462
Kerr, Deborah, 172, 181, 334
Kilby, Harry, 66n

Kilgallen, Dorothy, 209, 311
King, Bea, 257
King, Larry, 382, 512, 532
King, Martin Luther, Jr., 288, 291
Kings Go Forth (film), 216
Kissinger, Henry, 387, 400
Knight, Arthur, 206
Koch, Howard, 316
Koch, Ruth, 316
Kogan, Rick, 483
Korshak, Bea, 415
Korshak, Sidney, 415–17, 420, 487
Kovak, Kim, 215
Kramer, Stanley, 207–8, 361

"Lady Is a Tramp, The," 216
Laine, Frankie, 25
L.A. Is My Lady (album), 465
Lambert, Hugh (son-in-law), 402, 421, 452; children of, 402, 453
"Lamplighter's Serenade, The," 60
Lancaster, Burt, 172, 181, 182–83
Landells, Don, 422
Landis, Charles K., 2
Langford, Joe, 269
Lansbury, Angela, 255
Lansky, Meyer, 104
LaSalle-Thomas, Mary, 141–42, 145
"Last Night When We Were Young," 337–38
Last Testament of Lucky Luciano, The (Gosch), 105
Las Vegas, 386; barring of mobsters from casinos, 276; growth of, 224; mobsters in, 192; Rat Pack and, 224–25, 233; Sinatra as top draw, 224, 334; Sinatra debut, 224; Sinatra gaming license, 276–82; Sinatra-Waterman incident, 384–85. *See also specific hotels*
Las Vegas Nights (film), 54–55, 58
Latin Casino, Cherry Hill, NJ, 410
Lavine, Morris, 308
Lawford, Patricia Kennedy, 227, 249, 251, 267, 268–69
Lawford, Peter, 208, 224, 227, 235, 236, 254; on Ava Gardner, 135; JFK,

Sinatra, and, 252, 261, 262–63; JFK pre-inaugural gala and, 234–35, 244; Monroe's death and, 267–69; Rat Pack and, 225; Rat Pack films, 225; Sinatra rift, 261–63, 267–68, 524
Lawrence, Steve, 408, 440, 483, 495, 496, 500, 501, 508, 513, 532, 533
Lazar, Irving "Swifty," 208, 218–19, 221, 330–31, 332
"Lean Baby," 184
Leigh, Janet, 235, 255
Lemmon, Jack, 532
Leonard, Jack, 46, 62
LeRoy, Mervyn, 87
"Let Me Try Again," 401
"Let's Get Away From It All," 50
"Let's Take an Old-Fashioned Walk," 204
Levinson, Richard, 234
Levy, Mr. and Mrs. Isaac, 165
Lewin, Albert, 148
Lewis, Jerry, 65, 211, 224
Life magazine, 387, 446
"Like I Do," 344
"Like Someone in Love," 193
Lindsay, John, 382
Link, William, 234
Linn, Roberta, 267, 268
Lipton, Peggy, 386, 409
Lisella, Richie, 64
"Little Girl Blue," 193
Live in Concert (album), 516–17
Loesser, Frank, 204, 273
Lollobrigida, Gina, 216
London Palladium (1950), 150–51
Long, Johnny, 71
Look to Your Heart (album), 216
Loren, Sophia, 207, 532
"Lost in the Stars," 270
"Love and Marriage," 535
Lowry, Bea, 174
Luango, Laura Lee "Lips," 70–71
Lucchese, Tommy, 104
Luciano, Lucky, 103–5, 109n, 110, 112, 381, 449–50
"Luck Be a Lady Tonight," 205, 273, 508
Luft, Sid, 208

Lux Radio Theatre, 89
Lyma, Tom, 506
Lynley, Carol, 386, 409

Macagnano, Tony, 10
"MacArthur Park," 535
MacDonald, Patrick, 482
"Mack the Knife," 480
MacLaine, Shirley, 235, 373, 440, 504; Rat Pack and, 225–26
Macmillan publishers, 464–65
MacMurray, Fred, 119
Magliocco, Giuseppe, 104
Maharishi Mahesh Yogi, 368
Mahoney, Jim, 233, 296, 340, 364
Malatesta, Peter, 383
Maltz, Albert, 87, 233–34
Man Alone, A (album), 385
Man and His Music, A (album), 50n
Manchurian Candidate, The (film), 255, 273
Mandel, Johnny, 85, 242
Mann, Michael, 354
Manno, Paul and wife, 418
Man With the Golden Arm, The (film), 205–6
Marcello, Carlos, 104, 259
"Marie," 49
Marriage on the Rocks (album), 334
Marriott's Desert Spring Resort and Spa, 1995 performance, 511
Martin, Cathy Mae Hawn, 349n, 430
Martin, Dean, 24, 25, 65, 109n, 208, 212, 226, 249, 254, 260, 273, 478, 521; acting roles, 334; adoption of Sasha Hawn, 430; aging of, 477, 482; alcohol and, 478, 482, 483; Cal-Neva Lodge and, 155, 276–77; death of, 520; divorces, 136–37, 199n; Dolly Sinatra's death and, 423; drinking skits, 284; film with Sinatra, 216; marriage to Catherine Mae Hawn, 430; number one hit, 345; Rat Pack and, 224; Rat Pack films, 225, 272–73, 317; Reprise Records, 315; secretiveness, 349n; Sinatra and, last conversations, 521–22; Sinatra and Mia Farrow and, 327, 349; son's death

and, 422, 477–78, 480; special material songs, 481; Together Again Tour, 477–84; TV special with Sinatra, 315
Martin, Deana, 199n, 277, 349n, 521
Martin, Dean Paul "Dino," 422, 422n, 477–78, 484
Martin, Jeanne Biegger, 136–37, 199n, 249, 254
Martin, Ricci, 484
Martin, Skip, 243
Martin, Tony, 23
Martin Anthony Sinatra Medical Education Center, Palm Springs, 377–78
Marx, Barbara. *See* Sinatra, Barbara Marx
Marx, Bobby, 393, 395, 413, 427–31, 455, 523, 527–28, 533, 534
Marx, Eden, 395
Marx, Groucho, 153–54
Marx, Zeppo, 92, 392, 393–94, 395, 396, 397, 400, 430
Mason, James, 145
Masters, George, 248, 249–50
Matteo's restaurant, Los Angeles, 398
Maxwell, Marilyn, 80, 89–91, 96, 506; diamond bracelet incident and, 99–101
May, Billy (arranger), 45, 85, 207, 215, 216, 243, 442, 535
Mayer, Louis B., 77, 92, 111, 123, 133–34, 134n, 138, 147, 222
MCA: drops Sinatra, 170; Sinatra's Dorsey contract and, 74
McCambridge, Mecedes, 201
McCartney, Paul, 85
McGovern, George, 389
McGuire, Christine, 277, 279
McGuire, Dotty, 277, 279
McGuire, Phyllis, 276–79, 282, 359, 446, 449
McKuen, Rod, 385
McMahon, Ed, 532
McMurray, Cynthia, 499–500
McNamara, Martin, 374
Meadowbrook Ballroom, NJ, 51
Meadowlands Arena, NJ, 498
Meet Danny Wilson (film), 153, 154, 170
Meet Frank Sinatra (album), 152
Meet Me in Las Vegas (film), 134n

Meheu, Robert, 356–57
"Melancholy Mood," 46
Mel and Nancy (album), 453
Mercer, Johnny, 346
Merman, Ethel, 244, 245
Metronome magazine, 200
MGM studios, 71, 77, , 88 134, 134n, 154; Ava Gardner and, 170, 175, 178; Sinatra contract with, 77, 78; Sinatra films *High Society* with, 207
Miller, Ann, 71
Miller, Arthur, 248
Miller, Mitch, 134
Mince, Jonny, 49
Minnelli, Liza, 442, 483, 484, 507, 532
Miracle of the Bells, The (film), 119
Miranda, Mike, 104
Mitchum, Robert, 204
Mocambo (club), Hollywood, 118
Mogambo (film), 173–75, 189–90, 201
Monaco, Josephine Garavente (aunt), 26
Monash, Paul, 343
"Monday Morning Quarterback," 443
Monroe, Marilyn, 98, 220, 408, 430; at Cal-Neva Lodge, 267–69; drug use and death, 255, 266, 267–69; JFK and, 266; Sands Hotel and, 249–50; Sinatra and, 196–98, 248–50, 254–56, 265–66
Monteforte, Helen Fiore, 11, 13, 30
Moran, Dick, 130–31, 132, 135
Moretti, Willie, 74, 104
Morgan, Jess, 124, 274, 488
Morgan, Michèle, 76
Morrison, Charlie, 88
Mortimer, Lee, 86, 110–11, 146, 449
Mosque Theatre, Newark, NJ, 63
Motion Picture and Television Relief Fund, 387
Murphy, Gerval T., 87
Murray, Bishop Donal, 433–34
"Music Stopped, The," 73
"My Funny Valentine," 193
"My Kind of Town," 317, 509, 511
"My Love for You," 45
My Lucky Stars (MacLaine), 226
"My Way," 375–76, 387, 499, 516, 536

Naked Runner, The (film), 316, 348, 351
NBC radio: *Major Bowes and His Original Amateur Hour,* 27–28; Sinatra working at, 31; Tommy Dorsey Orchestra and Sinatra on, 52
Nellis, Joseph I., 373
Nelson Riddle Orchestra, 228
Nevada Gaming Control Board, 279–80, 446–52
Nevada Gaming Control Commission, 452
Nevada Tax Commission, 192
Never So Few (film), 216
New Jersey State Commission on Investigation, 380–81
"New York, New York," 442–43, 507, 513, 516
Nice 'n Easy (album), 228
"Nice Work If You Can Get It," 270
Nicholson, Jack, 532
"Night and Day," 31, 60, 60n, 71, 72
"Night We Called It a Day, The," 59
Night We Called It a Day, The (film), 404n
Niven, David, 208
Nixon, Richard M., 374, 388–89, 397, 399, 400
None But the Brave (film), 315–16, 323, 334
No One Cares (album), 50n, 216
Norvo, Red, 224
Not as a Stranger (film), 204
Novak, Kim, 257n

Oakland Coliseum, 481
O'Brien, Ed, 173
Ocean's 11 (film), 225, 228
"Oh, Look at Me Now," 50, 61
Ol' Blue Eyes Is Back (album), 401
Old Frontier Hotel, Las Vegas, 202
Oliver, Robert Harrison, 393
Oliver, Sy, 49, 243
Olivier, Laurence, 244
"Ol' Man River," 77, 226
Olsen, Edward, 278–79, 282, 448
Onassis, Jacqueline Kennedy, 235, 244–45, 259–60, 407–9, 463
O'Neal, Ryan, 320

"One for My Baby," 473
On the Town (film), 121
"Open Letter, An" (Sinatra), 111–12
Oppedisano, Tony (road manager), 408, 486, 501, 511, 521–22, 533
Orth, Maureen, 536
Ostin, Mo, 313, 355–56
O'Sullivan, Maureen, 320, 321, 327–28, 336, 369

Pacino, Al, 102–3
"Pale Moon," 61
Pal Joey (film), 215–16
Pandora and the Flying Dutchman (film), 145, 150
Paramount Studios, 362
Paramount Theater, NYC, 170; 1942–43 engagements at, 63–64, 71; 1944 engagement and riot, 79–80; Dorsey and Sinatra at, 50, 55, 76
Parker, Colonel, 264
Parker, Eleanor, 216
Parker, John, 305
Park Lane Films, 281
Parks, Carson, 355
Parsons, Louella, 96, 111, 190, 218–19, 258, 261
Passani, Veronique, 494
Pasternak, Joe, 78–79
Paul, Weiss, Rifkind, Wharton & Garrison law firm, 378–79
Pavarotti, Luciano, 85
Pearson, Drew, 373
Peck, Gregory, 416, 447, 450, 494, 495, 516
"Pennies from Heaven," 270
"People Will Say We're in Love," 73
Perrella, Father Robert, 377
Peterson, Henry, 374
Petrillo, James "Little Caesar," 30
Petrozelli, James "Skelly," 27
Peyton Place (TV show), 321–22, 341, 343
Philadelphia Story, The (film), 207
Phillips, John, 365
Phipps, Diane, 377
Pied Pipers, 49, 50
Pink Tights (film), 196

Pisano, Angie, 104
Pitchess, Peter, 399, 447
Playboy, Sinatra interview in, 270–71, 273
"Play Me or Trade Me," 453
Podell, Jules, 72
Poitier, Sidney, 244, 532
Polanski, Roman, 360, 363, 364
Polo Lounge, Beverly Hills Hotel, 139, 284, 288, 365
Porter, Cole, 30–31, 206, 207
Postman Always Rings Twice, The (film), 92
Power, Tyrone, 92–93, 96
Powers, Dave, 251
Preminger, Otto, 205–6, 234
Presley, Elvis, 263–64, 345
Pressman, Joel, 335
Pride and the Passion, The (film), 207–8, 361
Prima, Louis, 244
Principe, Pat "Patty Prince," 27
Profaci, Joe, 104
Prowse, Juliet, 244, 256–59, 265
"Put Your Dreams Away," 84

Quinlan, John, 61
Quinn, Anthony, 244, 532
Quonset Hut, 254

Raggio, William, 296
Ramer, Bruce, 220
Ramone, Phil, 507–8
Rat Pack, 208, 224–25, 477; films, 225, 262, 272–73, 317; as the Jack Pack, 235; opening the Villa Venice, 254; other names for, 225; Together Again Tour, 477–84
Ravaux, Claude Francois and Jacques, 375
RCA, 183, 453; Bluebird label, 59, 62; Daybreak Records, 313; Victor, 375
Reagan, Nancy, 387, 416, 462, 465, 532
Reagan, Ronald, 382, 387, 416, 441, 446, 447, 462, 465
Reed, Donna, 172, 201
Reprise Records, 50n, 242–43, 271, 286, 313, 315, 337, 516, 535; Dean Martin and, 345; Nancy Sinatra and, 344, 345; sale of, 378–80; Sinatra's earnings and,

339; Sinatra's hits for, 345; "Somethin' Stupid" and, 355–56

Reveille with Beverly (film), 71

Reynolds, Debbie, 531–32, 536

Reynolds, Susan, 509

Rich, Buddy, 48, 49, 51, 170

Richman, Danny, 72

Rickles, Don, 387, 403, 521, 533

Riddle, Nelson (arranger), 85, 184–85, 193, 206–7, 216, 315, 346

Ride, Vaquero (film), 325

Ring-a-Ding-Ding! (album), 242

Riobamba nightclub, NYC, 72

Riviera, Englewood, NJ (1953), 189

Rizzo, Ermenigildo "Jilly," 274, 296, 338–39, 403, 404, 406, 408, 411, 449, 490, 495; Caesar's Palace dust-up and, 384; Dolly Sinatra and, 397; Dolly Sinatra's death and, 423; fatal auto accident, 501; fight in Monaco, 455–56; Sammy Davis coke addiction and, 439–40; Sinatra and, drinking in the Far East, 457–58; Sinatra-Ava Gardner fight in front of Giancana and, 275; as Sinatra's best friend, 282; Sinatra's drinking and, 457–60

RKO Pictures, 76, 77

Robbins, Fred, 231

Robin and the 7 Hoods (film), 262, 273, 291, 317; soundtrack, 315

Robinson, Earl, 87

Robinson, Edward G., 204, 216

Rochas, Hélène, 456

Rockefeller, Nelson, 382

Rockwell-O'Keefe agency, 74

Rodgers, Richard, 193

Romanoff, Michael, 88, 257

Rooney, Father Tom, 432–34, 435, 436–37, 468, 469

Rooney, Mickey, 80, 117, 124

Roosevelt, Eleanor, 244

Roosevelt, Franklin D., 76

Root, Gladys Towles, 308, 310, 311

Rose, Helen, 174

Roselli, Johnny, 247, 253, 259, 407

Rosemary's Baby (film), 359–62, 363, 369

Rosenthal-Schechter, Ruth, 125

Ross, Diana, 373

Ross, Frank, 87

Ross, Steven J., 378–79

Roth, Eleanor, 356

Ruark, Robert, 108

Rudin, Milton "Mickey" (attorney); adoption of Bobby Marx and, 427, 429, 430–31; Agnew investigation, 401–2; background, 219–20; Barbara Marx separation and, 468; Cronkite interview and, 338, 339; Dolly Sinatra's death and, 421, 423; firing of George Jacobs and, 366; Frank, Jr. kidnapping and, 296; Kitty Kelley book and, 463–65; Reprise Records deal and, 378–79; Sinatra dumps Bacall and, 220, 221; Sinatra dumps Mia and, 363–64, 367, 368; Sinatra gives money to Ava Gardner and, 488; Sinatra-Marx marriage and, 419; Sinatra-Marx prenuptial and, 415–17, 487; Sinatra's mob connections and, 280, 281, 380, 446, 451; Sinatra's relationship with, 437; Sinatra's annulment and, 432, 433, 435–37, 438; split with Sinatra, 474, 489

Rudin, Mrs. Mickey, 389

Rudin, Richman & Appel law firm, 430–31

Russell, Jane, 153

Russell, Rosalind, 335, 354, 387

Rustic Cabin, Englewood Cliffs, NJ, 29, 30–31, 35; Harry James sees Sinatra at, 44; Sinatra arrested at, 38, 40

Sacks, Emmanuel "Manie," 62, 74, 76, 101, 125, 134, 183; death of, 217–18, 220; Sinatra-Gardner wedding and, 165, 166; Sinatra suicide attempt and, 158–59, 504

Sacks, Lester, 163

Sahl, Mort, 235, 374

Salinger, Pierre, 259

Samuel Goldwyn Studios, 270

Sands, Tommy, 297, 313, 315, 334, 453

Sands Hotel, Las Vegas: 1953 engagement at, 190; 1961 engagement at, 249–50; 1964 engagement at, 334;

1966 engagement at, 345; Monroe and Sinatra at, 249–50; Rat Pack and, 224–25; Sinatra fight at, 358–59, 450; Sinatra financial interest in, 191–93, 224, 280–81; Sinatra gambling at, 225, 356–57; Sinatra's cancellation, 359; Sinatra's infidelity and Gardner's discovery, 190–91

Sanicola, Hank (manager), 29, 60, 68, 72–75, 102, 143, 144, 156, 158, 165; Cal-Neva Lodge and, 155, 281; mob and, 74–75; Sinatra drops, 281–82

Sanicola, Paula, 155, 156

Schisser, Ed, 136

Schlatter, George, 512, 516, 517–18

Schlatter, Jolene, 516, 517–18

Schrieber, Marion Brush, 34–35

Schuchman, Harry, 35

Schwartz, Jonathan, 511

"September," 337

September of My Years (album), 337–38

Sergeants 3 (film), 238

Serrano, José E., 527

Sevano, Nick, 58, 65, 89

Sevanto, Doris, 23, 59, 434

Shamrock Hotel, Houston, 132, 135

Shaw, Artie, 96, 124, 143

Shea Theatre, Buffalo, 47

Sheen, Martin, 234

Sheffield Enterprises, 534

"She's Funny That Way," 72, 163

She Shot Me Down (album), 443

Shields and Yarnell (mime team), 453

"Shine," 27

Shore, Dinah, 217–18, 394, 396, 408–9

Show Boat (film), 152, 154

Shultz, George, 462

Silbert, Harvey, 534

Silvani, Jimmy, 140–41

Silvers, Jo-Carroll, 80

Silvers, Phil, 98, 109

Simms, Ginny, 62, 133–34

Sinatra (TV miniseries, 1995), 503–6

Sinatra (Wilson), 464–65

Sinatra, Anthony Martin "Marty" (father), 3, 5, 6, 10, 18–23, 420, 533;

Ava Gardner and, 149–50, 152, 162–63, 274; character and personality, 10, 14; death of, 376–77; response to son's success, 67–68; Sinatra-Gardner wedding and, 165; Sinatra's Lana Turner affair and, 97; son's relationship with, 14, 21–24, 28–29, 67–68, 68n, 149–50, 152, 162–63, 228, 270, 376–77, 494

Sinatra, Barbara Marx (wife), 392–409; accident, 525; affair with Sinatra, 395–411; Asia/Australia tour with Sinatra, 402–4; auctioning of Sinatra's possessions, 521; background, 393; Catholic wedding ceremony, 438; character and personality, 397, 405–6, 457, 485, 494; death of Sinatra and, 528–29; Dolly Sinatra's death and, 421; financial maneuverings by, 501; Jackie Kennedy and, 408; Kitty Kelley book and, 471; Kool cigarette incident, 495; marriage to Robert Harrison Oliver, 393; marriage to Sinatra, 427–39, 455–60, 485–90, 491–96, 512, 522–23; marriage to Zeppo Marx, 392, 394–95, 397, 400–401, 430; prenuptial agreement, 415–17, 486–87; renewal of vows with Sinatra, 522–23; separation from Sinatra, 465–69; Sinatra and the Mob and, 443–44; Sinatra engagement, 411–14; as Sinatra heir, 533–34; Sinatra's annulment and, 432–39; Sinatra's children and, 423–27, 436, 438–39, 466, 468, 471–72, 474–77, 485–87, 501, 505, 516–20, 523, 525, 526; Sinatra's drinking and, 455–59; Sinatra's eightieth birthday and, 516–20; Sinatra's funeral, 533; Sinatra's gifts to, 402, 412, 418, 466; Sinatra's health and, 471, 510, 521, 525–26; Sinatra's temper, violence, and, 397–400, 404–5; son of, Sinatra's adoption plan, 427–31 (see also Marx, Bobby); TV special on Sinatra and, 512–13; wedding to Sinatra, 414–19

Sinatra, Christina "Tina" (daughter), 106, 109, 305, 313–14, 434, 516; adoption of Bobby Marx issue, 427, 428–29; auctioning of father's possessions and, 521; Ava Gardner and, 125, 176–77; Barbara Marx and, 397, 405, 412, 413, 417–18, 468, 471–72, 474–77, 485–87, 501, 516–20, 523, 525, 526; birth of, 119–20; death of Sinatra and, 528–29; Dolly Sinatra's death and, 421–22; father's relationship with, 198, 212–15, 228–30, 314–15, 334, 485–86, 501, 504–5, 516–20, 525; final estrangement from her father, 518–20, 521; on her father's grief for JFK, 291; on her father's infidelity, 56–57; kidnapping of Frank, Jr., and, 313; Kitty Kelley book and, 471; marriage to Wes Farrell, 402, 422; Mia Farrow and, 347, 360–61, 397; politics and, 389; rights to Sinatra's recordings held by, 427, 516–17, 534–35; Sinatra-Gardner wedding and, 350; Sinatra-Marx wedding and, 417–19; *Sinatra* produced by, 449, 503–6; Sinatra's bequests and, 534–35; Sinatra's eightieth birthday and, 516–20; Sinatra's fiftieth birthday and, 340; Sinatra's final Thanksgiving and, 527–28; Sinatra's funeral and, 532, 533; Sinatra's gifts to, 466; Sinatra's performances, final years and, 510

Sinatra, Dolly (Natalie Catherine Garavente, mother), 5–23, 307, 533; Ava Gardner and, 137, 149–50, 152, 162, 274; Barbara Marx and, 397, 414, 416, 419; character and personality, 11, 16–17, 29, 33, 34; death of, 420–23, 462; death of husband and, 377; Democratic Party politics and, 11, 24, 30, 33, 33n, 34; fiftieth wedding anniversary, 270; Jill St. John and, 273; Kitty Kelley book and, 463, 464, 470; Mia Farrow and, 336–37, 419; as midwife/abortionist, 32–35, 33n, 105–6, 462, 463, 470, 503; mob connections and, 10–11; move to West Coast, 380; Nancy Sinatra and, 40, 42, 137, 165, 421; property of, after death, 425–27; religion and, 32, 419, 434–35; Reprise Records deal at home of, 379; saloon owned by, 10–11, 20; Sinatra born, 8; Sinatra-Gardner wedding and, 165; Sinatra-Lana Turner affair and, 97; Sinatra purchases homes for, 270, 378–79, 380; Sinatra's relationship with, 12, 14, 21–25, 29, 30, 32, 35, 42, 228, 379–80; Sinatra's success and, 67; Sinatra's suicide attempt and, 144–45; Sinatra's womanizing and, 40, 90; Toni Francke and, 38, 40

Sinatra, Frank: alcohol and, 118, 142, 156, 181, 183, 224, 225, 326, 455–59, 495, 526; appearance, 13, 35, 45, 51, 57, 72, 117–18, 146, 185, 193, 324; as bipolar, 98; character and personality, 13, 14, 15, 16, 69, 78–79, 89, 97–98, 116, 126, 133, 182, 184–85, 209, 232, 233, 237–38, 271, 332, 333, 413, 428–29, 521, 526, 537; cleanliness obsession, 49; "communist charge," 87–88; cutting people from his life, 16–17, 132, 210, 221, 261, 268–69, 282, 316, 359, 474, 524; Democratic Party and, 228, 234, 235–36, 244, 245–46, 372–74 (*see also* Kennedy, John F.); drug use, 140–41, 148, 149; finances, wealth, and lifestyle, 66, 72, 77, 81, 129, 151, 153, 177, 180, 193, 224, 242, 260, 280, 313, 324, 335–36, 339, 395–97, 445, 457, 479, 487, 489–90, 492, 493–96; gambling and, 192, 193, 225, 356, 384–85, 466; generosity of, 51, 66, 81, 99, 380, 434, 435, 441–42, 443, 447, 466, 473, 488, 534; hearing loss of, 67, 521; Hollywood friends and hangouts, 88, 101, 117, 118 (*see also* Jilly's); home, beachfront Malibu, 520, 534; home, Villa Maggio in Pinyon Crest, 392; home in Beverly Hills, 473, 478, 520, 534; home in Palm Springs, 151, 157, 160, 161, 190, 203, 228, 229,

260, 324, 338, 353, 402, 463, 474, 493, 494, 520; humor and practical jokes, 189, 208–9; insomnia, 69; media and, 40, 86, 87, 110–11, 112, 129–30, 136, 138, 151, 162, 209, 272, 335 (*see also* Kilgallen, Dorothy; Mortimer, Lee); mob connections, 10, 74–76, 102–9, 109n, 209–10, 236, 246–48, 250–54, 259–61, 275–82, 339, 373–74, 380–81, 385, 399, 407, 444, 445–46; nicknaming friends "Dag," 29; as parent/relationship with his children, 76–77, 105–6, 116, 119, 134–35, 198, 212–15, 228–32, 287–88, 314, 485–86, 494, 497–98, 501, 519, 521, 523, 524; as reader and favorite books, 69; refusal to apologize, 267, 399–400, 403, 469; religion and, 32–33, 270–71, 435, 438–39; Republican Party and, 382–83, 388–89, 441 (*see also* Reagan, Ronald); sex and, 15, 35–38, 41, 70; as smoker, 211, 224, 495, 526; stand against racism, 86–87, 226–27; suicide attempts, 144–45, 156–60, 255, 504; taxes and, 192; temper and violence, 13–14, 15, 35, 71, 98, 110–11, 142, 149, 162, 195, 262–63, 279, 326, 330–31, 357–60, 389, 392, 397–400, 467; train collection, 496; women and, 15, 16, 35–38, 40, 41, 45, 54–59, 88, 99–102, 149, 211–12, 224; website, 534

—1915–1947 (Hoboken years and first success), 2–113; arrest for assault on Mortimer, 111; Ava Gardner and, first meeting, 88–89; birth, baptism and naming, 8–9; birth of daughter, Nancy, 52; birth of son, Frank, Jr., 76; brief move to New York City, 22; career slide and bad press (1947), 112–13; childhood, 12–20; clothes of, 13, 18, 66; diction classes, 61; Dorothy Bonucelli affair and child with, 58–59; early sexual behavior, 15; family intervention on Lana affair, 97–99; finances and earnings, 54, 59; Harry James and, 44–48; Havana,

Cuba trip (1947), 104–5, 106–9, 449; high school, 17, 18–19; Hollywood secret apartment, 94; homes, first, 72, 77, 116; junior high, 13; Lana Turner and, 91–99; manual labor, early jobs, 22; Marilyn Maxwell and, 89–91, 96; Marilyn Maxwell diamond bracelet incident, 99–102; move to West Coast and movie-making, 77–79; Nancy Barbato and marriage, 26–27, 31, 41–42, 44, 45, 54–59, 76–77, 88, 105–6, 109, 116; Nancy Venturi and, 36–38; prejudice against Italians and, 13–14; self-invention of, 52–54; singing, early days, 17, 19, 26, 27–32; singing career takes off, 63–81; success, effect of, 80–81; summers at the Jersey shore, 26; Tommy Dorsey and, 48–52, 59–62; Toni Francke and morals charges, 38–40

—1947–1958 (from Ava Gardner to Lauren Bacall), 116–222; Academy Awards, 200–202; Africa, trip to (1952), 173–75; arrest in shooting prank, 126; Ava Gardner affair and marriage, 116–46, 148–63, 173–80, 194; Ava Gardner and, press and public reaction, 129–30, 138; Ava Gardner's abortion and, 175–80; Ava Gardner divorce, 191, 193, 194–96, 198; in Barcelona, 148–49; birth of daughter, Tina, 119–20; Cal-Neva Lodge, Lake Tahoe ownership, 155; career comeback, 171–73, 180–85, 200–201; career problems, 119, 140–42, 147, 170, 183; Carolwood estate of, 121, 128; death of Manie Sacks and, 217–18, 229; distancing of feelings and, 195–96; Lauren Bacall and, 210–12, 216–22; Marilyn Monroe and, 196–98; Sunset Tower, Los Angeles apartment, 116; voice injured, 146–47, 149; wife Nancy, divorce, 135–36, 154, 160–61, 163; wife Nancy, relationship after divorce, 200, 202, 212–15

—1960–1968 (Rat Pack to Mia Farrow), 224–369; albums and films (1963), 270–73; Ava Gardner

and, 273–76, 324–25, 351–53, 367;
Cal-Neva Lodge incident (1963),
276–79, 372, 446, 448–49; Cronkite
interview, 338–40; Democratic
National Convention and, 235–36;
duality of life, 228–32; fiftieth birthday
celebrations, 338; handprints at
Grauman's Chinese, 334; home in
Palm Springs expansion, 229; JFK and,
227–28, 234, 235–39, 244–46, 250–54,
259–63; JFK assassination and, 291;
Jill St. John affair, 273; kidnapping of
Frank, Jr., and, 288–307; Las Vegas
performances, 334; Marilyn Monroe
and, 248–50, 254–56, 265–69; Mia
Farrow and, 320–33, 346–68; mob
connections and losing Cal-Neva
and interest in the Sands, 276–82;
near-drowning in Hawaii, 316; Prowse
engagement, 256–59; Rat Pack, 208,
225, 262, 224–27, 254, 317
—1968–1998 (Barbara Marx and final
years), 372–537; adoption of Bobby
Marx attempt, 427–31, 484; aging and,
385–86, 441–42, 486, 490–93, 498,
500, 521, 524, 526–28; annulment
of marriage to Nancy, 432–39, 468;
auctioning of possessions, 521; Ava
Gardner and, 409–11; Barbara Marx
and final marriage, 392–409, 427–39,
455–60, 465–69, 485–87, 491–96, 512,
522–23; Barbara Marx prenuptial
agreement, 415–17, 486–87; Barbara
Marx renewal of wedding vows, 521;
Barbara Marx wedding, 414–19; career
and popularity, 401, 402, 404, 441–43,
445, 453–54, 462, 465, 473–74, 489–90,
500–501, 510, 536–37; Congressional
Gold Medal, 527; dating younger
women, 386; daughter with Dorothy
Bonucelli surfaces, 506–7; death of,
528–29; death of Ava Gardner, 488,
489; death of Dean Martin, 520, 522;
death of Dolly Sinatra and, 421–23;
death of Jilly Rizzo, 501; death of
Sammy Davis Jr., 490; depression

and, 386, 520, 523–24; dinner parties,
493–96; eightieth birthday, 512–13,
516–20; final performance, 511; final
Thanksgiving, 527–28; final words,
529; funeral, 531–33, 536–37; health
issues, 386, 471–73, 510, 524–25; Jackie
Kennedy Onassis and, 407–9; Kennedy
family and, 437–38; Kitty Kelley book
and, 462–65, 470, 473; Legend Award
for Lifetime Achievement, 509; money
for Ava Gardner, 488; Nixon and, 397,
400; Reprise Records sale, 378–80;
retirement in 1971), 386–88; retirement
comeback in 1973–1974, 400, 404;
Ronald Reagan and, 382, 416, 441, 446,
447, 462, 465–66; seventieth birthday,
469–70; *Sinatra* TV mini-series and,
503–6; sixty-fifth birthday party, 442;
Steve Lawrence and, 496; touring with
daughter, 453–55; typical day, 493; will
and bequests, 533–34
—acting and film production: Academy
Awards, 200–202, 206; *Anchors Aweigh*
and stardom, 79; behavior during
production, 78–79, 120, 153–54, 181,
182; directing debut, 315–16; director
Kramer on, 207–8; *The Execution of
Private Slovik* and 233–34; film and
TV production companies, 207, 225,
242, 280–82, 286; films of 1951, 153;
films of mid- to late 1950s, 204–6,
215–16; films of 1963, 272–73; first
acting role, 73, 76; first film, 54–55;
first film with Tommy Dorsey, 71; first
nonmusical role, 119; *Guys and Dolls*
and Brando, 204–5; *From Here to
Eternity* and career comeback, 171–73,
180–83; *The Manchurian Candidate*
and, 255, 273; *The Man with the Golden
Arm* and, 205–6; MGM contract, 77,
134; Montgomery Clift's influence,
182; poor box office (1948), 120; Rat
Pack films, 225, 262, 272–73, 317; RKO
contract, 76; talent of, 120, 179, 205–6;
Warner Bros. Studios and production
company, 280. *See also specific films*

—singing career: Academy Awards, 76, 215, 216; aging and, 507–8; album he considered his best, 216; albums, song choice and, 84; "All or Nothing at All" as major hit, 73; Asia/Australia tour, 402–4; audiences and fans, 57, 63–66, 72, 73, 79–80, 85–86, 112, 130, 150–51, 154, 224; Australia, 1974 tour in, 403–4; "Ava Songs," 205; biggest world-wide hit, 345; as *Billboard* top band vocalist, 59; bobbysoxers and, 64, 64n; Capitol Records and "Capitol Years," 183–85, 242–43, 535; Carnegie Hall record-breaking performance, 442; classic albums, 270; classic songs, 50, 84, 151, 317, 345, 346, 535; classic songs, new releases (2015), 535; cockiness and, 44–45, 49, 51; collecting orchestrations, 24; comeback (1953–1954), 189, 194, 200; concept albums, 84, 205, 215, 315; Crosby's influence, 17, 19; Diamond Jubilee Tour, 496–501; Dorsey contract, getting out of, 74–75; Dorsey influence, 60–61, 76; downward career spiral (1947–1952), 112–13, 119, 140–42, 147, 170; *Duets* and *Duets II* albums, 507–8; final performance, 511; first break, 27–28; first hit, 50; first manager, 29, 73; first recordings, 45, 50; first singing jobs, 24, 26–27, 29, 30–31, 35, 38, 44; first tour, 28; Grammy's, 215, 216, 334, 337, 338, 346, 442; greatest single, 206; Harry James Band and, 44–47; highest paid performance, 445; "I'm a Fool to Want You" recording, 153; invention of his persona, 54, 67; London, Palladium engagement, 150–51; mature voice of, 206, 443; MCA represents, 74; most successful album, 508; Motion Picture and Television Relief Fund concert, 387–88; music in the 60s and, 333–34, 345; music publishing companies, 282; must-have album of, 317; "My Funny Valentine" as standard for, 193; "My Kind of Town" and "New York, New York" as trademarks of, 317, 443; "My Way" as anthem for, 375–76; name change considered, 32; named Top Male Vocalist in 1954, 200; NBC radio jobs, 31, 52; Nelson Riddle's influence, 184–85; *Nice 'n Easy* album and popularity, 228; parental disapproval, 19; parental support of, 23–25; press agent, 65–66, 132–33 (*see also* Evans, George); recording sessions, 84–85, 193, 340, 345–46, 507–8; recordings for RCA Bluebird Label, 59; recordings of 1950s, 215–16; recordings with Harry James, 47–48; recordings with Tommy Dorsey, 55, 61; remakes of early songs, 60n; Reprise Records and, 242–43, 313, 315, 535; retirement comeback of 1973, 400–402; rock and roll and, 264; Rockwell-O'Keefe agency, 74; Sinatramania, 63–66; six-city concert tour, 334; solo career begins, 28–29, 60; *Songs for Swingin' Lovers* recorded, 206–7; star quality, 30, 44–45; style and technique, 24–25, 44, 49, 52–54, 60–61, 62, 64, 153, 264–65, 271–72, 442–43; "Summer Wind" as exceptional, 346; talent of, 49, 72–73, 85–86; as teenager, 17, 19; Together Again Tour, 477–84; Tommy Dorsey Orchestra and, 46–54, 61–62; *Trilogy* recordings, 442–43; unable to read music, 85; USO tours, 86, 109; as "the Voice," 66, 66n, 84–86, 189; voice problems, 29, 129, 141, 146–47, 151, 215, 386; voice register, 24; wardrobe, 66; "Why Should I Cry Over You" recorded, 193–94; World Tour for Children, 265; "Young at Heart" as number one hit, 194, 200; as *Your Hit Parade* regular, 71. See also *specific albums*; *specific songs*

Sinatra, Frank, Jr. (son), 285–88, 512; adoption of Bobby Marx issue and, 428; Barbara Marx and, 416, 424, 485, 494, 523, 525, 526; birth, 76; character and personality, 499; childhood, 121; Diamond Jubilee Tour and, 497–501; Dolly Sinatra's death and, 423; duet in "My Kind of Town," 509; father's relationship with, 77, 212–15, 228, 229, 230–32, 287–88, 313, 495, 496, 497–501, 511, 523; as heir to Sinatra's record royalties, 427; on his mother, Nancy, 25, 198; kidnapping, 284–85, 288–307, 309–12; marriage of, 499; naming of, 76; parents' divorce and, 198; Sinatra-Mia Farrow and, 341, 350–51; Sinatra's Academy Award and, 200–201; on Sinatra's acting, 273; Sinatra's bequests and, 534–35; Sinatra's fame and, 231, 286–87; Sinatra's final Thanksgiving and, 527–28; Sinatra's funeral and eulogy, 532–33; Sinatra's gifts to, 466; on Sinatra's retirement, 387–88; on Sinatra's singing, 216, 265; on Sinatra's suicide attempt, 159; on Sinatra's voice, 185; singing career, 285–88, 313, 402, 453; son, 499–500, 516

Sinatra, John (grandfather), 3

Sinatra, Julie Lyma (daughter), 506–7

Sinatra, Nancy Barbato (wife), 25, 26: at Academy Award ceremony, 200, 201–2; adoption of Bobby Marx issue and, 431; annulment of marriage, 432–33, 437, 468; Barbara Marx and, 397, 424, 471–72, 485; birth of daughter, Christina, 119–20; birth of daughter, Nancy, 52; birth of son, Frank, Jr., 76; Catholicism of, 136; death of Dean Martin and, 522; divorced by Sinatra, 147, 160–62; Dolly Sinatra and, 40, 42, 137, 165, 421; fantasy of Sinatra returning, 315, 341; finances and, 81; first apartment, 42; on Harry James Band tour, 45–46; kidnapping of Frank, Jr., and, 295–96, 304, 305, 306; life after Sinatra, 198–99; Marilyn Maxwell diamond bracelet incident, 99–102; marriage to Sinatra, 42, 55, 56, 57–58, 71, 76–77,

80, 88, 89, 97, 105–6, 116; meets Sinatra and courtship, 26–27, 31, 38; Mia Farrow and, 347, 349, 350; move to West Coast, 77; parenting style, 314; pregnancies, 47, 70; pregnancy terminated by, 105–6, 109, 462; secretarial job, 42; separations from Sinatra, 95, 136–38, 151–52; Sinatra and, after divorce, 212–15, 228, 230–31, 387, 388, 431; Sinatra and Ava Gardner, 128–29, 136–37, 165; Sinatra and Toni Francke, 38–40; Sinatra's affair with Lana Turner and, 93–99; Sinatra's affair with Marilyn Maxwell and, 89–91; Sinatra's bequests and, 534; Sinatra's career problems and, 113; Sinatra's eightieth birthday and, 516; Sinatra's fiftieth birthday and, 340–41; Sinatra's final Thanksgiving and, 527–28; Sinatra's funeral, 532, 533; Sinatra's infidelity and, 35, 40–41, 54–59, 71, 89, 94–102; on Sinatra's suicide attempts, 159–60; Sinatra visiting his children and, 149, 176, 177, 198, 212–15, 228–32; supportive of Sinatra's career, 27, 31, 44, 66; support payments for, 151; wedding, 41–42

Sinatra, Nancy (daughter), 263, 290; acting roles, 334, 345; adoption of Bobby Marx issue and, 427–31; album of 2013, 535; annulment of parents' marriage and, 438; auctioning of father's possessions and, 521; Ava Gardner and, 176–77; Barbara Marx and, 397, 412, 413, 417–18, 424–31, 436, 453, 458, 471–72, 474–77, 485–87, 501, 521, 523, 525, 526; birth, 52; birth of sister, 110; on Cal-Neva Lodge, 155; character and personality, 424; daughters, 402, 452, 453, 516, 527; death of Sinatra and, 528–29; divorce from Tommy Sands, 313, 334–35; Dolly Sinatra's death and, 421–22; duet hit with Sinatra, 355–56; on ending of show-business era, 386; fantasy of Sinatra returning to family, 315, 341,

413; father's relationship with, 77, 177, 198, 200, 212–15, 228–30, 313, 334–35, 453, 485–86, 501, 512, 521; financial problems, 453; "I'm a Fool to Want You" recording and, 153; kidnapping of Frank, Jr., and, 290, 291, 292, 297; marriage to Hugh Lambert, 402, 421; marriage to Tommy Sands, 297, 453; Mia Farrow and, 347, 350, 397; on mother, Nancy, 151–52, 198; number one hit, 344; pregnancy terminated by, 462; rights to Sinatra's recordings held by, 427, 516–17, 534–35; *Sinatra: 80 Years My Way* (TV special) and, 512; on Sinatra and JFK, 239; on Sinatra joining Dorsey, 49; Sinatra-Marx wedding and, 417–19; Sinatra's bequests and, 534–35; on Sinatra's care for his parents, 377; Sinatra's eightieth birthday and, 516–20; at Sinatra's farewell concert, 387; Sinatra's fiftieth birthday and, 340; Sinatra's final Thanksgiving and, 527–28; Sinatra's funeral, 532, 533; Sinatra's gifts to, 466; on Sinatra's grand gestures, 244; on Sinatra's quitting high school, 18–19; on Sinatra's recordings, 243; singing career, 313, 344–45, 452–55, 535; "These Boots Are Made for Walking" and other hit songs, 344–45; touring with Sinatra, 453–55

Sinatra, Rosa (grandmother), 3

Sinatra: 80 Years My Way (TV special), 512–13

Sinatra 101—The 101 Best Recordings and the Stories Behind Them (album), 173

Sinatra and Strings (album), 243

Sinatra at the Sands (album), 345

Sinatra-Basie: An Historic Musical First (album), 270

Sinatra: Best of the Best (album), 535

Sinatra Christmas Album, The (album), 215

Sinatra Swings (album), 243, 243n

Siravo, George, 85

Skelton, Georgia, 348–49

Skelton, Red, 224, 348

"Sky Fell Down, The," 50

Slatkin, Felix, 242

Smith, Gerald L. K., 87

Smith, Jean, 249

Smith, Keely, 244, 315

Smith, Dr. William, 488

Snows of Kilimanjaro, The (film), 170

Softly, As I Leave You (album), 272

Some Came Running (film), 216, 226

"Some Enchanted Evening," 121

Some of Manie's Friends (TV special), 218

"Something," 442

Something's Gotta Give (film), 266

"Somethin' Stupid," 355, 375, 455

"Song Is You, The," 60, 442

Songs for Swingin' Lovers (album), 206–7

Songs for Young Lovers (album), 193

"Song Sung Blue," 442

"South of the Border," 50, 184

South Pacific (Broadway musical), 535

Speedway (film), 345

Spice (album), 313

Springsteen, Bruce, 512, 513

Stafford, Jo, 49, 315

Stanwyck, Barbara, 120, 125

Stapely, Bill (butler), 466, 467, 470, 471, 473, 491

"Stardust," 243

Steeper, Harry, 30

Steiger, Rod, 503

Stephens, Dave, 290

Stephens, Ted, 268

Step Lively (film), 76

Stevens, Morty, 479

Stevenson, Adlai, 235

Stewart, Jimmy, 462

St. John, Jill, 272

Stoliar, Steve, 153

Stordahl, Axel (arranger), 49, 59, 73, 85, 107, 165, 184

Stradella, Debra, 33

"Strangers in the Night," 345–46, 346, 375, 499, 535

Strangers in the Night (album), 346

Streisand, Barbra, 507, 508

Strickling, Howard, 191
Styne, Jule, 78, 101
Suddenly (film), 204
"Sugar Town," 344
"Summer Wind," 346
"Summer Wine," 344
Surtees, Robert, 178
Swing Along With Me (album), 243n
Swing Easy! (album), 193
Swingin' Affair, A (album), 215
Symington, Stuart, 235

Take Me Out to the Ball Game (film), 120
Tamburro, Fred "Tamby," 27, 36
Taradash, Daniel, 171
Tarr, Beatrice "Bappie," 123, 126, 139, 144, 164, 165, 176, 261
Tarr, Larry, 123
Taylor, Elizabeth, 249, 463, 473
Taylor, Robert, 125
Tebbett, David, 429
Tender Trap, The (film), 204
"Texas Cowboy Night," 453
"That Old Jack Magic," 245
"That's Life," 387, 535
"Theme From New York, New York." *See* "New York, New York"
"These Boots Are Made for Walking," 344, 345, 453
"They Can't Take That Away From Me," 193
Thibaut, Gilles, 375
"This Nearly Was Mine," 270
Thomas, Danny, 224, 423
Thomas, Kevin, 316
Thompson, Tommy, 387
Thomson, Virgil, 462
Thorp, Roderick, 360
Tillis, Mel, 453
Time magazine, Sinatra cover, 205
Tolson, Clyde, 110
Tommy Dorsey Orchestra, 46–54, 59, 62, 107
Tony Rome, 354
"Too Romantic," 50
Torre, Marie, 175

Torrence, Dean, 291–92, 311
Tracy, Spencer, 204
Trafficante, Santo, 104
Traubel, Helen, 244
Tredy, John, 32
Tredy, John (cousin), 13
Trilogy (album), 442–43, 534
"True Love," 207
Turner, Lana, 92–93, 117, 408; warns Ava about Sinatra, 126–27
20th Century-Fox, 170, 258–59; Marilyn Monroe and, 196; Mia Farrow and, 321, 360

Uhlemann, Dorothy, 456, 517
United Artists, 335
Universal Amphitheatre, 455
Universal Music Group, 535
Unruh, Jesse, 382
Uris Theatre, NYC, 408
U. S. Congress, House Un-American Activities Committee (HUAC), 87

Vallée, Rudy, 80
Van Heusen, Jimmy (songwriter/friend), 84, 116, 132, 160, 194, 195–96, 258, 416, 423, 491
Vanity Fair, 535, 536
Venker, Marty, 389
Venturi, Nancy, 36–38
Victor Hugo's, Beverly Hills, 46
Villa Venice, Chicago, 254, 449
Viner, Mort, 483, 521
Voice, The (album), 84
Von Ryan's Express (film), 273, 320, 322

Wagner, Robert, 532
Walker, Clint, 315
Wallach, Eli, 180
Wallachs, Glenn, 184
Walsworth, James H., 418
Ward, Father Herbert, 447
Waring, Fred, 315
Warner, Jack, 313
Warner Bros. and Warner Bros.-Seven Arts, 225, 313, 378; buys out Sinatra's

interest in the Sands and Cal-Neva, 280–81; Sinatra as a vice president with, 313; Sinatra films, 317
Warner Music Group, 535
Waterman, Sanford, 384–85, 402, 451
Watertown (album), 385
Wayne, John, 234
"Way You Look Tonight, The," 315
Webb, Jimmy, 535
Webb, Stephen, 451–52
Weisman, Eliot, 483, 501, 512, 517, 518
Weitman, Bob, 63
Welding, Pete, 205
"Well, Did You Evah?," 207
Wellman, Lucy, 139, 148, 166–67, 178, 180, 190, 195, 489
Westchester Premier Theater, Tarrytown, NY, 445, 446, 450
Weston, Paul, 49
"What Now My Love," 508
Where Are You? (album), 215
"Where or When," 508, 511
White, Loray, 256, 257n
Whiting, Jim, 255, 408, 411, 501
Why Me? (Davis), 256
"Why Should I Cry Over You," 193–94
"Why Try to Change Me Now?," 173
Wilken, Bea, 75
Wilken, Betty, 75
Wilkerson, William R., 92
Williams, Emlyn, 218
Williams, Esther, 77, 92–93, 120
Will Mastin Trio, 202

Wilson, Earl, 51, 72, 139, 173, 259; book and Sinatra's lawsuit, 464–65
Wilson, Joseph, 479–80
Wilson, Robert, 173
Wilson, Woodrow, 9
Winchell, Walter, 86
Winters, Shelley, 153
"Wishing," 44, 45
"Witchcraft," 215, 507
"Without a Song," 55
WNEW radio, 29
Wolf, Jack, 153
Wood, Natalie, 216
World Mercy Fund, 434, 435
World Tour for Children, 265
World War II: film industry and, 63; "I'll Never Smile Again" and, 50; Sinatra rejected for service in, 67
Wright, James (butler), 491, 492–95, 496, 500
Wrubel, Allie, 265
Wyatt, Andrew, 277

"You'll Never Know," 73
"You Make Me Feel So Young," 400
"Young at Heart," 194, 200
Young at Heart (film), 204
"You're Sensational," 207
Your Hit Parade (radio show), 71
"You Will Be My Music," 401

"Zing Went the Strings of My Heart," 242
Zinnemann, Fred, 172, 173, 179, 181